Kinesiology and Applied Anatomy

Health Education, Physical Education,
and Recreational Series

RUTH ABERNATHY, Ph.D., EDITORIAL ADVISER

Director, School of Physical and Health Education,
University of Washington, Seattle, Washington 98105

Kinesiology and Applied Anatomy

The Science of Human Movement

PHILIP J. RASCH, Ph.D., F.A.C.S.M.

*Chief, Physiology Division, Naval Medical
Field Research Laboratory,
Camp Lejeune, North Carolina.*

ROGER K. BURKE, Ph.D., F.A.C.S.M.

*Professor of Physical Education,
Occidental College, Los Angeles, California.*

Fourth Edition, 240 Illustrations, 18 in Color

Lea & Febiger

PHILADELPHIA

NUDE DESCENDING A STAIRCASE, Number 2—1912, by Marcel Duchamp, is reproduced on the cover of this book with the permission of the Philadelphia Museum of Art. The painting belongs to the Louise and Walter Arensberg Collection.

First Edition, 1959—Reprinted, 1960

Second Edition, 1963—Reprinted, 1964, 1965, 1966

Third Edition, 1967—Reprinted, 1968, 1969

Fourth Edition, 1971—Reprinted, 1972

First Spanish Edition, 1961

Second Spanish Edition, 1967

ISBN 0-8121-0342-4

Library of Congress Catalog Card Number: 76-146027

Published in Great Britain by Henry Kimpton, London

Printed in the United States of America

Preface

In 1917, Lea & Febiger published *Applied Anatomy and Kinesiology—The Mechanism of Human Movement*, by Wilbur Pardon Bowen, under the editorship of R. Tait McKenzie. Its pioneering excellence generated seven editions, including revisions by other authors after Bowen's death.

World War II was followed by an explosive production of pure and applied kinesiological research, especially in electromyography, physical medicine, and clinical therapy for the victims of war and epidemic poliomyelitis. As we prepared for a 1959 revision of Bowen's classic work, both the quantity and the integrated implications of this voluminous research seemed to call for a new book instead of a revision. We changed the title to *Kinesiology and Applied Anatomy* to reflect a subtle change in the nature of the subject matter. Perhaps the sub-title, *The Science of Human Movement*, was at that time a bit pretentious, but subsequent history has enabled us to claim that it was prophetic.

Research production did not level off but continued to increase exponentially. The exploration of space and other exotic environments placed a priority on knowledge about man's adaptability. Computer technology and information theory suggested conceptual models for the mechanisms of human function. Factual discoveries emerged from electron microscopy, from the study of cell physiology at the molecular level, and from the ability to monitor and stimulate single neurons. When antibiotics liberated medicine from its traditional preoccupation with pathogenic organisms, interest shifted to the problems of aging, growth, endocrinology, and chronic diseases. Specializations developed in human factors, engineering, sports medicine, gerontology, physical fitness, and environmental physiology. "Witch doctors" were replaced by professional athletic trainers, some holding credentials as registered physical therapists or corrective therapists. Successful intercollegiate coaches found it increasingly necessary and possible to consult with mathematicians, physicists, physiologists, psychologists, and sociologists. Physical educators have been busy defining their "body of knowledge." In all of this, there is a common focus on *man in motion*—motion that is sometimes productive, sometimes sportive, sometimes artistic, sometimes therapeutic, sometimes developmental, sometimes symbolically communicative. Human needs generate new disciplines, and so it was inevitable that descriptive human anatomy would evolve into a unified discipline of kinesiology—the study of human movement.

Since the day of publication of the previous edition, a short four years ago, we have been selecting fresh material for this fourth edition. Sixty-nine per cent of the pages in the third edition have been altered; references have been up-dated; and much has been added, including two entirely new chapters (on Analysis of Human Movement and on Principles of Kinesiology).

But the approach has not been changed. The hundreds of practical examples and applications have been included for the purpose of clarifying factual material and conceptual generalizations, and not with the idea of writing a "how-to-do-it manual," for we believe that the purpose of a textbook is to present basic information and general principles with which the reader may solve his own problems in his own way in professional practice. Nor do we suggest that the chapter headings will necessarily make an appropriate course outline. To many instructors, the chapters devoted primarily to detailed study of individual muscles will best be used as reference material rather than as a learning unit; to others, these sections will be the focus of a course. The elementary material on human anatomy, physiology, and mechanics will be no more than a convenient review for students with a background in these sciences, but it will enable inquiring students from other disciplines to explore kinesiology without collegiate prerequisites. Advanced students and those with special interests will appreciate the careful attention devoted to the citation of pertinent references and related readings. These constitute in effect a selected bibliography of classic and recent kinesiological literature. We have been pleased to find that previous editions have been adopted for courses at every educational level from high school to graduate school, and in fields ranging from general education to orthopedics.

Each of the 240 illustrations has been selected specifically to clarify or expand some particular point discussed in the text, and only incidentally for decoration, although we find beauty in every representation of the human body in motion. Figure 23–3 is reproduced on the cover, for we consider it to be at once the most meaningful and beautiful of all.

Because we have tried to achieve authenticity and recency by depending primarily on original sources, our own contribution has been the amalgamation and integration of the widely dispersed and highly specialized work of people who are recognized in the bibliographic citations. Beyond this, we are tremendously indebted to our personal associates and professional colleagues who have been unstinting in their criticisms and assistance. We appreciate also the voluminous correspondence from anatomists, physical educators, physicians, physical therapists, electromyographers, and undergraduate students in India, Australia, England, Canada, and South America. Every comment has influenced us in some way. Finally, we appreciate the permission given by publishers and individuals to reproduce photographs and other materials, the sources of which are credited as they appear in the text.

Camp Lejeune, North Carolina   PHILIP J. RASCH
Los Angeles, California   ROGER K. BURKE

Contents

Chapter 1

The History of Kinesiology*

The term kinesiology is a combination of two Greek verbs, "kinein," meaning "to move," and "logos," "to discourse." Kinesiologists—those who discourse on movement—in effect combine anatomy, the science of structure of the body, with physiology, the science of function of the body, to produce kinesiology, the science of movement of the body.

The title "Father of Kinesiology" is usually given to Aristotle (384–322 B.C.), whose treatises, *Parts of Animals*, *Movement of Animals*, and *Progression of Animals*, described for the first time the actions of the muscles and subjected them to geometrical analysis. He recorded such practical observations as the following:

> . . . the animal that moves makes its change of position by pressing against that which is beneath it. . . . Hence athletes jump farther if they have weights in their hands than if they have not, and runners run faster if they swing their arms, for in the extension of the arms there is a kind of leaning upon the hands and wrists.[1]

Aristotle was the first to analyze and describe the complex process of walking, in which rotatory motion is transformed into translatory motion. His discussion of the problems of pushing a boat under various conditions was, in essence, a precursor of Newton's three laws of motion. For his time, Aristotle demonstrated a remarkable understanding of the role of the center of gravity, the laws of motion, and of leverage.

Another Greek, Archimedes (287–212 B.C.), is credited with having determined hydrostatic principles governing floating bodies which are still accepted as valid in the kinesiology of swimming. Some of

---

* Where possible, citations are usually to an edition which the student may readily secure rather than to the original edition. In the cases of prolific authors, only the item most important or most typical of their work is cited.

them are now being used to develop means of space travel. The broad scope of his inquiries included the laws of leverage and problems related to determining the center of gravity. His treatises on the latter have been described as "the foundation of theoretical mechanics."[2]

Claudius Galen (131–201 A.D.), a Roman citizen who tended the gladiators owned by the ruler of Pergamum, in Asia Minor, and who is considered to have been the first team physician in history, had a substantial knowledge of human motion. In his essay *De Motu Musculorum* he distinguished between motor and sensory nerves, and between agonist and antagonist muscles, described tonus, and introduced terms such as diarthrosis and synarthrosis which even today are of major importance in the terminology of arthrology. The idea that muscles were contractile seems to have originated with Galen. He taught that muscular contraction resulted from the passage of "animal spirits" from the brain through the nerves to the muscles.

Following Galen's myological studies, kinesiology remained almost static for over a thousand years. It was not until the time of one of the most brilliant men in history, Leonardo da Vinci (1452–1519), that the science of kinesiology was advanced another step. Artist, engineer and scientist, da Vinci was particularly interested in the structure of the human body as related to performance, and the relationship between the center of gravity and the balance and center of resistance. He described the mechanics of the body in standing, walking up- and down-hill, in rising from a sitting position and in jumping. Da Vinci was probably the first to record scientific data on human gait. To demonstrate the progressive action and interaction of various muscles* during movement, he suggested that cords be attached to a skeleton at the points of origin and insertion of the muscles.[3] Although he was a prolific writer, da Vinci's notebooks were designed to be unintelligible to the unauthorized reader. As a result, most of his writings were not published until two or three hundred years after his death; and his influence during his life was restricted principally to a small circle of acquaintances.

After studying medicine at the University of Pisa for three years, Galileo Galilei (1564–1643) became convinced that "nature is written in mathematical symbols"; whereupon he turned to mathematics in search of the laws underlying physical phenomena. His demonstrations that the acceleration of a falling body is not proportional to its weight and that the relationship of space, time and velocity is the most important factor in the study of motion inaugu-

---

* Before the 18th Century few muscles had names. Galen used numbers and da Vinci used letters in their illustrations.

rated classical mechanics and have been acclaimed as the introduction of experimental methodology into science.[4] His work gave impetus to the study of mechanical events in mathematical terms, which in turn provided a basis for the emergence of kinesiology as a science.

Alfonso Borelli (1608–1679), who studied under one of Galileo's pupils, endeavored to apply the master's mathematical formulae to the problems of muscular movement. In his treatise *De Motu Animalium,* published in 1630 or 1631, Borelli sought to demonstrate that animals are machines. The amount of force produced by various muscles and the loss of force as a result of unfavorable mechanical action, air resistance, and water resistance were among the aspects of muscular movement which he explored. It was Borelli's theory that bones serve as levers and that muscles function according to mathematical principles. Although realizing that the contraction of muscles involved complex chemical processes, Borelli's explanation of these processes was fanciful in the extreme: he suggested that the nerves are canals filled with a spongy material through which flow animal spirits (*succus nerveus,* sometimes translated "nerve gas"); that agitation of these spirits from the periphery to the brain produces sensation; and that agitation from the brain produces filling and enlargement of the porosities of the muscles, with resultant turgescence. Reaction of these spirits with a substance in the muscles themselves, said Borelli, initiated a process resembling fermentation, with subsequent contraction.[5] He distinguished between tonic and voluntary contractions and perhaps even vaguely perceived the principle of reciprocal innervation of antagonistic muscles. Steindler has praised him as "the real founder of modern kinetics" and as "the father of modern biomechanics of the locomotor system."[6] Singer credited him with having effectively founded and developed that branch of physiology which relates muscular movement to mechanical principles.[7]

Borelli is also regarded as the founder of the iatrophysical school of medicine, which affirmed that the phenomena of life and death are based on the laws of physics. The tenets of this school were supported by Giorgio Baglivi (1668–1706), who, in 1700, published *De Motu Musculorum,* which differentiated for the first time between smooth muscles, designed for long sustained efforts, and striated muscles, designed for quick movements. Eventually, however, the iatrophysicists' neglect of the rapidly advancing science of chemistry caused their school to fall into disrepute and to disappear.

Borelli's theory of muscular contraction was attacked almost immediately. Among his critics was Francis Glisson (1597–1677), who contended that the muscle fibers contract, rather than expand, during flexion, as demonstrated by plethysmographic experiments. He suggested also that all viable tissue possesses the capacity to react to stimuli. This capacity he referred to as "irritability." Glisson's concept was later elaborated by Albrecht von Haller (1708–1777), the outstanding physiologist of the Eighteenth Century, into the theory that contractility is an innate property of muscle which exists independently of nervous influence.

Although the circulation of the blood through the body was first demonstrated by William Harvey (1578–1657), he erroneously attributed to the heart the function of recharging the blood with heat and "vital spirit."[8] Subsequently, Niels Stensen (1648–1686) made the then-sensational declaration that the heart was merely a muscle, not the seat of "natural warmth," nor of "vital spirit." This has been acclaimed as the greatest advance in our knowledge of the circulatory system since Harvey's discovery.[9] Three years later, Stensen, who has been credited with laying the foundation of muscular mechanics, wrote *Elementorum Myologiae Specimen,* an "epoch-making" book on muscular function. In this he asserted that a muscle is essentially a collection of motor fibers; that in composition the center of a muscle differs from the ends (tendons) and is the only part which contracts. Contraction of a muscle, wrote Stensen, is merely the shortening of its individual fibers and is not produced by an increase or loss of substance.[10]

The word "orthopedics" was coined by Nicolas Andry (1658–1742) from the Greek roots "orthos," meaning "straight," and "pais," meaning "child." It was the opinion of this author that skeletal deformities result from muscular imbalances during childhood. In his treatise, *Orthopedics or the Art of Preventing and Correcting in Infants Deformities of the Body,* originally published in 1741, he defined the term "orthopedist" as a physician who prescribes corrective exercise.[11] Although this is not the modern usage, Andry is recognized as the creator of both the word and the science. His theories were directly antecedent to the development of the Swedish system of gymnastics by Per Henrik Ling (1776–1839).

In *Principia Mathematica Philosophiae Naturalis,* which is "perhaps the most powerful and original piece of scientific reasoning ever published,"[12] Isaac Newton (1642–1727) laid the foundation of modern dynamics. Particularly important to the future of kinesiology was his formulation of the three laws of rest and movement, which express the relationships between forces (interactions) and their effects:

I. Every body continues in its state of rest, or of uniform motion, in a right line, unless it is compelled to change that state by forces impressed upon it. (This is sometimes known as the Law of Inertia, and was originally proposed by Galileo in 1638.)

II. The change of motion is proportional to the motive force impressed and made in the direction of the right line in which that force is impressed (Law of Momentum).

III. To every action there is always opposed an equal reaction; or, the mutual actions of two bodies upon each other are always equal and directed to the contrary parts (Law of Interaction).[13]

The application of these laws to muscular function may be demonstrated by the following analogy: While he is pivoting, a discus thrower must grasp the discus firmly (exert centripetal force) to prevent it from flying out of his hand. In accordance with the Third Law, the missile exerts an equal and opposite reaction (centrifugal force). When his grip is released and centripetal force no longer interacts with the discus, the implement flies off in a straight line tangential to its former circular path. The distance covered by the missile is proportional to the motive force imparted to it, in accordance with the Second Law. The trajectory of the missile is affected by gravity, wind velocity and other forces tending to alter its state of uniform motion, as predicted by the First Law.

According to the Newtonian world-view, changes of motion are considered as a measure of the force which produces them. From this theory originated the idea of measuring force by the product of mass and acceleration, a concept which plays a fundamental role in kinetics. The greater the speed with which the discus thrower whirls, the greater the acceleration applied to the mass of the discus, the farther it will fly before gravity returns it to earth, and the greater the force said to have been applied to the discus.

Newton is also credited with the first correct general statement of the parallelogram of force, based on his observation that a moving body affected by two independent forces acting simultaneously moved along a diagonal equal to the vector sum of the forces acting independently. By further analysis of the laws of movement as applied by the discus thrower, it can be demonstrated mathematically that the horizontal and vertical forces acting on the flying discus are equal. The diagonal, which is equal to the vector sum of the horizontal and vertical forces, is, therefore, 45 degrees and the missile should traverse the greatest distance when it travels at this angle. In actual practice, of course, other factors of lift, drag, shape, gyroscopic rotation, and so forth enter the situation and it is possible that the most effective angle of release may not always be the one which is the theoretical optimum. However, since two or more muscles may pull on a common point of insertion, each at a different angle and with a different force, the resolution of vectors of this type is a matter of considerable importance in the solution of academic problems in kinesiology.

Within the past few years physicists have demonstrated that Newton's theories are valid only within the frame of reference in which they were conceived; they do not apply to relationships between forces in the Einsteinian world-view. This discovery has little significance for the kinesiologist, however, since he deals primarily with the forces of gross muscular movement and these are governed by the laws of motion set forth by Newton.

In his studies of muscular contraction, James Keill (1674–1719) calculated the number of fibers in certain muscles, assumed that on contraction each fiber became spherical and thus shortened, and from this deduced the amount of tension developed by each fiber to lift a given weight. In *An Account of Animal Secretion, the Amount of Blood in the Human Body, and Muscular Motion* (1708), Keill drew the erroneous conclusion that a muscle could not contract to less than two-thirds of its greatest length.[10]

In *An Essay on the Vital and Other Involuntary Motions of Animals,* published in 1751, Robert Whytt (1714–1766) rejected Baglivi's theory of muscular action and contended that movement originates from an unconscious sentient stimulus. This brought him into disagreement with von Haller. Possibly Whytt may not have comprehended the principle that movement may originate as reflex reaction to external stimuli; however, it appears that he was cognizant of the stretch reflex and the fact that a given stimulus may be adequate to excite one nerve ending but not another. Their differences of opinion arose from the fact that von Haller thought in terms of isolated muscle; Whytt in terms of the reflex control of the movements of an organism.[10]

The subject of anatomy, as taught prior to the time of Marie Françoise Xavier Bichat (1771–1802), consisted of little more than dogmatic statements handed down through the ages. Through his efforts anatomy became a science solidly founded on the systematic observation of an experimentation with the various systems into which he divided the living organism. Bichat observed that the organs of the body are composed of individual tissues with distinctive characteristics and was the first to describe the synovial membranes.[14] He is regarded as the author of the modern concept of structure as the basis of function, which led to the development of rational physiology and pathology.

The six Croonian Lectures on Muscle Motion* delivered by John

---

* William Croone (1633–1684), a professor at Gresham College, England, and author of *De Ratione Motus Musculorum* (1664), an important early work on muscle, left a will providing for annual lectures on the physiology of muscular motion. Fulton commented, "It is literally true that the history of muscle physiology in the Eighteenth, Nineteenth and Twentieth Centuries has been largely developed at these annual lectures." (*Muscular Contraction and the Reflex Control of Movement,* pp. 15–16.)

Hunter (1728–1793) in 1776, 1777, 1779, 1780, 1781, and 1782,[15] brought together all of this great anatomist's observations concerning the structure and power of muscles and the stimuli by which they are excited. Muscle, he declared, while it is endowed with life, is fitted for self-motion, and is the only part of the body so fitted. He emphasized that muscular function could be studied only by observations of living persons, not cadavers. In his lecture series Hunter described muscular function in considerable detail, including the origin, insertion, and shape of muscles, the mechanical arrangement of their fibers, the two-joint problem, contraction and relaxation, strength, hypertrophy, and many other aspects of the subject. His lectures may be regarded as summarizing all that was known about kinesiology at the end of the Eighteenth Century, when, unwittingly, kinesiologists stood at the threshold of a discovery which was to revolutionize their methods of investigation.

About 1740 physiologists became excited over the phenomena produced by electrical stimulation of muscles. Haller summarized many of the early experiments in his treatise on muscle irritability, and Whytt reported clinical observations on a patient treated by electrotherapy. "Animal electricity" was proposed as a substitute for the "animal spirits" which earlier investigators had believed to be the activating force in muscular movement. During the summer of 1786, Luigi Galvani (1737–1798) studied the effects of atmospheric electricity upon dissected frog muscles. He observed that the muscles of a frog sometimes contracted when touched by a scalpel, which led him to the conclusion that there was "indwelling electricity" in animals and that the movement of a muscle was the result of its exterior negative charge uniting with the positive electricity which proceeded along the nerve.[16] His *Commentary on the Effects of Electricity on Muscular Motion* (1791) is probably the earliest explicit statement of the presence of electrical potentials in nerve and muscle.

The study of animal electricity at once became the absorbing interest of the physiological world. The greatest name among the early students of the subject was that of Emil DuBois-Reymond (1818–1896), who laid the foundations of modern electrophysiology.

Fascinated by the prospect of investigating muscular response produced by electrical stimulation, Guillaume Benjamin Amand Duchenne (1806–1875) set out to classify the functions of individual muscles in relation to body movements, although he recognized that isolated muscular action does not exist in nature[17] (Fig. 1–1). His masterwork, *Physiologie des mouvements*, appeared in 1865, and has been acclaimed "one of the greatest books of all times."[18] Unfortunately, translations of this classic into English have appeared only in small editions, and it is not always available to the student for reference.

The modern concept of locomotion originated with the studies of Borelli; however, very little was accomplished in this field prior to the publication of *Die Mechanik der menschlichen Gerverkzeuge* by the Webers in 1836. Their treatise, which still stands as the classical work accomplished by purely observational methods, firmly established the mechanism of muscular action on a scientific basis. The Weber brothers, Ernst Heinrich (1795–1878), Wilhelm Eduard (1804–1891), and Eduard Friedrick Wilhelm (1806–1871), believed that the body was maintained in the erect position primarily by tension of the ligaments, with little or no muscular exertion; that in walking or running the forward motion of the limb is a pendulum-

Fɪɢ. 1–1.   Guillaume Benjamin Amand Duchenne de Boulogne investigating the effect of electrical stimulation of the left frontalis muscle. (Jokl and Reich, courtesy J. Ass. Phys. & Ment. Rehabil.)

swing due to gravity; and that walking is a movement of falling forward, arrested by the weight of the body thrown on the limb as it is advanced forward. The Webers were the first to investigate the reduction in the length of an individual muscle during contraction and devoted much study to the role of bones as mechanical levers. They were also the first to describe in chronological detail the movements of the center of gravity.[19]

The study of animal mechanics was expanded by the talented and versatile Samuel Haughton (1821–1897) in numerous papers bearing such titles as *Outlines of a New Theory of Muscular Action* (1863), *The Muscular Mechanism of the Leg of the Ostrich* (1865), *On Hanging, Considered from a Mechanical and Physiological Point of View* (1868), and *Notes on Animal Mechanics* (1861–1865). However, advancement of knowledge concerning body mechanics was greatly impeded by lack of a satisfactory method of chronological reproduction of movement. This advance was made when Janssen, an astronomer who had utilized serial pictures in 1878 to study the transit of Venus, suggested kinematographic pictures to study human motion. Eadweard Muybridge (1831–1904) produced his book *The Horse in Motion* in 1882, and his monumental *Animal Locomotion*, in eleven volumes, in 1887, an abridgment of which was reissued in 1955 under the title of *The Human Figure in Motion*.[20] Étienne Jules Marey (1830–1904), who was convinced that movement is the most important of human functions and that all other functions are concerned with its accomplishment, described graphic and photographic methods for biological research in *Du mouvement dans les functions de la vie* (1892) and *Le mouvement* (1894).

These photographic techniques opened the way for the experimental studies of Christian Wilhelm Braune (1831–1892) and Otto Fischer (1861–1917), which are still considered of major importance in the study of human gait. Even more famous than these investigations was their report of an experimental method of determining the center of gravity, published in 1889. An abridgment of this is readily available in an Air Force Technical Documentary Report.[21] Their major premise was that a knowledge of the position of the center of gravity of the human body and its component parts was fundamental to an understanding of the resistive forces which the muscles must overcome during movement. Their observations were made on four cadavers, which, after having been preserved by freezing, were nailed to a wall by means of long steel spits. The planes of the centers of gravity of the longitudinal, sagittal and frontal axes were thus determined. By dissecting the bodies by means of a saw and locating the points of intersection of the three planes, they were able to establish the center of gravity of the body.

The center of gravity of the component parts was determined in the same manner. Because one cadaver began to decompose and the investigators were not permitted to dissect a second cadaver, complete observations were made on only two of the four bodies. When the centers of gravity were plotted on a life-size drawing of one of the cadavers and compared photographically with those of a soldier having similar body measurements, the investigators observed a remarkable similarity. Braune and Fischer concluded that the original position of their frozen cadavers could be considered a normal one and referred to it as "normalstellung," which was intended to indicate only that it was the standard position in which their measurements were taken. Unfortunately, this term came to be understood as the ideal position, and generations of students were exhorted to imitate it. Their work with cadavers has recently been carried on and extended by Wilfrid Taylor Dempster.[22]

On the basis of subsequent studies, Rudolf A. Fick (1866–1939) concluded that the theory of "normalstellung" was not entirely valid, as the recumbent position of a cadaver could not be transferred to the vertical stance. The degree of lumbar lordosis is much less when the body is recumbent than when vertical; in the latter position the center of gravity shifts forward considerably more than Braune and Fischer assumed. Fick contended that when peoples of different races and cultures are considered, there is no one posture that is normal for all. Recent anthropological investigations have confirmed his opinion.[23] Fick's work on the mechanics of articular and muscular movement is an indispensable guide for students of kinetics. Unfortunately, his masterworks, *Handbuch d. Anatomie und Mechanik der Gelenke* and *Spezielle Gelenk und Muskelmechanik*, each of which comprises several volumes, have not been translated into English and remain largely inaccessible to those who do not read German. This is also true of the works of Hans Strasser (1852–1927), whose four volume *Lehrbuch der Muskel und Gelenkmechanik* remains untranslated.

The late Nineteenth and early Twentieth Centuries were most productive of physiological studies closely related to kinesiology. Adolf Eugen Fick (1829–1901) made important contributions to our knowledge of the mechanics of muscular movement and energetics and introduced the terms "isometric" and "isotonic." The study of developmental mechanics was introduced by Wilhelm Roux (1850–1924), who stated that muscular hypertrophy develops only after a muscle is forced to work intensively, a point of view which was later demonstrated experimentally by Werner W. Siebert.[24] B. Morpurgo showed that increased strength and hypertrophy are a result of an increase in the diameter of the individual fibers of a muscle, not a result of an increase in the number of fibers. The theory of progressive resistance exercise is based principally on the studies of Morpurgo and Siebert.[25]

John Hughlings Jackson (1834–1911), "the father of modern neurology," made definite contributions to knowledge pertaining to the control of muscular movement by the brain. His conclusions* are summed up in these words:

> . . . The motor centres of every level represent movements of muscles, not muscles in their individual character . . . the distinction between muscles and movements of muscles is exceedingly important all over the field of neurology. . . . The occurrence of convulsion of a muscular region which is already imperfectly and yet permanently paralyzed is unintelligible without that distinction. And without it we shall not understand how it can happen that there is loss of some movements of a muscular region without obvious disability in that region.[26]

Jackson mentioned post-epileptiform asphasia and hemiplegia as practical examples of his dictum. His ideas were cited approvingly by Charles Edward Beevor (1854–1908) in his 1903 Croonian Lecture on Muscular Movements.[27] The aphorism "nervous centers know nothing of muscles, they only know of movements," which has frequently been attributed to Beevor, should be credited to Jackson.

Beevor himself pointed out that the technique of utilizing electrical stimulation employed by Duchenne demonstrated what a muscle *may* do, not what it *does* do; and since only the stimulated muscle responds, this method fails to show the action of associated muscles, which may often or always contract simultaneously in the natural situation, and this may modify the resultant movement. He referred to James Benignus Winslow's† previous objection to the use of cadavers to demonstrate muscular action and the fallacious conclusions which had been based on these observations. After careful study of the muscular actions involved in the movements of certain joints, Beevor proposed that the muscles be classified as prime movers, synergic muscles, fixators, or antagonists. He was of the opinion that the antagonistic muscles always relaxed in strong resistive movements.

In this respect Beevor was influenced by the work of Charles Sherrington (1857–1952), who advanced the theory of "the reciprocal innervation of antagonistic muscles" in a number of papers published near the end of the Nineteenth Century and later incorporated into his book *The Integrative Action of the Nervous System* (1906), a monumental work in the history of kinesiology which has since been

---

* Quoted by permission.
† Winslow (1669–1760) was the author of *An Anatomical Exposition of the Structure of the Human Body.* Originally published in 1749, it was translated into several languages.

republished many times. Contemporaneously, Henry Pickering Bowditch (1814–1911) demonstrated the treppe phenomenon (1871), the "all or none" principle of contraction (1871), and the indefatigability of the nerves (1890). The Sherrington theory and the "all or none" principle are considered "fundamental for an understanding of kinetic events in the human body."[28] Of inestimable morale value to kinesiologists, who at that time were insecure in their profession and depressed by the jibes of critics who contended that the study of the body was unworthy of man, was Sherrington's insistence that "the importance of muscular contraction to us can be stated by saying that all man can do is to move things, and his muscular contraction is his sole means thereto."[29] Actually much the same thing had been said in 1863 by the famous Russian physiologist Ivan Mikhaflovich Sechenov (1829–1905) when he declared, "All the endless diversity of the external manifestations of the activity of the brain can be finally regarded as one phenomenon—that of muscular movement."[30]

Karl Culmann (1821–1881), a German engineer, reviewed in *Die Graphische Statik* all that had been accomplished up to 1865 in the solution of static problems by graphic methods. Speaking at a meeting of scientists in 1866, he called attention to the fact that when the calcium phosphate was dissolved from the upper end of the femur, the internal architecture of this bone coincided with graphostatic determinations of the lines of maximum internal stress in a Fairbairn crane, which he assumed resembled the femur in shape and loading. Although his basic assumption has been severely criticized, his analysis forms the basis of the trajectorial theory of the architecture of bones (see p. 28).

The trajectorial theory was supported by Roux and became the basis for his interpretation of the trajectory system of other bones. In 1892 this theory was classically expressed by Julius Wolff (1836–1902) in the famous Wolff's Law: "Every change in the form and function of a bone or of their function alone is followed by certain definite changes in their internal architecture, and equally definite secondary alteration in their external conformation, in accordance with mathematical laws." He believed that the formation of bone results both from the force of muscular tensions and from resultant static stresses of maintaining the body in the erect position, and that these forces always intersect at right angles.

In his paper on the "Laws of Bone Architecture,"[31] which has been proclaimed "the most thorough study of stress and strain in a bone by mathematical analysis of cross sections,"[32] John C. Koch concluded that the compact and spongy materials of bone are so composed as to produce maximum strength with a minimum of material;

and that in form and structure bones are designed to resist in the most economical manner the maximum compressive stresses normally produced by the body weight. Because the stresses from body weight are so much greater than the tensions which are normally produced by the muscles, reasoned Koch, the effect of muscular action is of relatively little importance in determining the architecture of the bones, and, therefore, could be ignored in his analysis. In endeavoring to draw practical applications from his theoretical studies, Koch commented that alterations in posture increase the stress in certain regions and decrease it in others, and that if postural alterations are maintained, the inner structure of the affected bones is altered. The proper mechanical means of counteracting these alterations, said Koch, was to impose new mechanical conditions by the use of braces, jackets, or other suitable devices to reverse the transformative process and restore the original structure.

Murk Jansen's monograph *On Bone Formation* (1920) disagreed with many of Wolff's premises, including the "dualistic" doctrine that bone formation is dependent on both tension and pressure. Wolff's hypothesis that these forces intersect at right angles in the trabeculae of cancellous bone constituted a fatal flaw in the theory, contended Jansen, since the major trabecular systems do not always cross at right angles. Jansen reputedly insisted that the jerking action of a contracting muscle, combined with gravity, is the chief mechanical stimulus for the formation of bone and, moreover, is a determinative factor in the structure of cancellous bone.[32,33]

Eben J. Carey[34] also criticized Koch's denial of the role of muscular tension in the formation of bone, and asserted that the powerful back pressure vectors produced by the forces of muscular contraction are the dominant factors affecting the growth and structure of bone. He rejected Koch's emphasis on static pressure. The body, he said, is sustained in the upright posture by mutual interaction between the skeleton and the muscles, and he expressed the opinion that the dynamic action of the muscles may exceed the static pressure of body weight. He contended that the normal growth and structure of mature bone is the result of this dynamic muscular activity and the intrinsic capacity of skeletal cells to proliferate centrifugally against extrinsic centripetal resistances.

F. Pauwels endeavored to demonstrate that muscles and ligaments act as traction braces to reduce the magnitude of stress in the bones. His work was criticized by F. Gaynor Evans on the grounds that it was concerned only with the stresses produced by loads placed on solid models shaped like bones. Discussing the validity of the various theories, Evans concluded that a decision must await experimental evidence. It is possible that Wolff and Roux overemphasized the importance of mechanical stresses without proper consideration for biological factors which sometimes exceed mechanical influences. Nevertheless, the theory of functional adaptation to static stress remains a major hypothesis in the study of skeletal development. J. H. Scott[35] has reviewed the material in the field in an effort to construct a working hypothesis of the developmental and functional relationships which exist between the skeletal system and the neuromuscular system.

Prior even to the time when the development of bone became a subject of neated debate, yet more highly controversial hypotheses were introduced into the scientific world. Charles Darwin (1809–1882) published two books, *The Origin of the Species* (1859) and *The Descent of Man* (1871), which have since become classics and have revolutionized man's ideas concerning the human body.[36] His conception of man as a "modified descendant of some pre-existing form" whose framework is constructed on the same model as that of other mammals, and whose body contains both rudimentary muscles which serve useful functions in the lower mammals and modified structures which resulted from a gradual change from quadrupedal to bipedal posture was at first bitterly opposed. Now generally accepted, his concepts have clarified many questions pertaining to kinesiology which might otherwise have remained obscure, and have attracted to the study of kinesiology many physical anthropologists whose contributions have been of great value.

Yet another scientist of the Nineteenth Century, Angelo Mosso (1848–1910) made an important contribution to the study of kinesiology, the invention of the ergograph in 1884. This instrument, now available in an endless array of specialized forms, has become a nearly indispensable tool for the study of muscular function in the human body.

The first extensive compendium on body mechanics, *The Human Motor*, by Jules Amar, was published in 1914. Inspired largely by the increase in work productivity achieved by Frederick Winslow Taylor's[37] application of scientific principles of body mechanics to industry, Amar (1879–?) sought to bring together "in one volume all the physical and physiological elements of industrial work." The book was translated into English in 1920.[38] It is now out of print but the text is readily available on Micro-cards, and, in an abridgment, in an Air Force Technical Documentary Report.[21] Since its publication, countless industrial studies based on Amar's principles have been published, perhaps the best known of which are the numerous reports of the British Industrial Fatigue Research Board and of Frank B. (1868–1924) and Lillian M. (1878–1972) Gilbreth. This type of kinesiological research initiated studies in the unexplored areas of time and motion. Investigations in this field have been greatly accelerated as a result of rapid advances in engineering and the development of machines so complex that the physical abilities of the human operator become a limiting factor in their use. Scientists have brought together massive collections of data pertaining to the application of scientific principles of body mechanics to industry, now known as human engineering,[39–42] or the science of ergonomics—"the customs, habits or laws of work." Attempts to solve the problems of space flight have provided further impetus to studies of this nature.

Kinesiology of the Human Body Under Normal and Pathological Conditions, by Arthur Steindler (1878–1959), seems destined to become the classic kinesiological text in the medical field. Knowledge of this subject is still limited, as is reflected in Hooton's dictum that "an adequate comprehension of bodily mechanics has not been achieved as yet."[43] Nevertheless, information is accumulating, and some of the facts and theories which have been presented are both curious and instructive. As an example, it has been observed that men frequently sustain femoral fractures as a result of automobile accidents, whereas women are more likely to incur dislocations of the hip. This difference is attributed to the social conditioning of women to sit with their knees or legs crossed, whereas men sit with their legs spread apart. An impact on a person sitting with the knees or legs crossed tends to drive the head of the femur out of the acetabulum, but a similar impact on an individual sitting with his legs apart tends to drive the head of the femur further into the acetabulum until the femur buckles and breaks.[44]

As early as 1880, Wedenski demonstrated the existence of action currents in human muscles, although practical use of this discovery had to await the invention of a more sensitive instrument. This became available when W. Einthoven developed the string galvanometer in 1906. The physiological aspects of electromyography were first discussed in a paper by H. Piper, of Germany, in 1910–1912; however, interest in the subject did not become widespread in the English speaking countries until publication of a report by E. D. Adrian in 1925.[45] By utilizing electromyographic techniques, Adrian demonstrated for the first time that it was possible to determine the amount of activity in the human muscles at any stage of a movement. The development of the electromyograph represents one of the greatest advances in kinesiology. By means of this instrument many generally accepted concepts of muscle action have been proved erroneous and new theories have been brought forth.

In the study of the physiologic aspects of striated muscular activity, however, one name stands preeminent. The brilliant studies of

Archibald V. Hill[46] unquestionably distinguish him as the world's leading authority in this field.

Interest in the subject of posture has declined among kinesiologists in the United States during the last few years. In part, this may have resulted from general acceptance of the dictum that "the physiological benefits obtained from correction of common postural defects are mostly imaginary";[47] in part, it may reflect the growing realization that individual differences almost preclude valid generalizations. Perhaps much of the effort which in earlier times was devoted to the study of static posture is now directed to research concerning dynamic locomotion. Wallace Fenn, Plato Schwartz, Verne Inman, Herbert Elftman, Dudley Morton[48-52] and Steindler[6] should be listed among the scientists who have made important contributions to knowledge concerning this phase of kinesiology.

The use of cinematography for kinesiological studies of athletes and industrial workers has become commonplace. An important recent development in the study of human motion is the use of cineradiographic techniques. In time, advances in technique may make it possible to record the complete sequence of musculoskeletal movements rather than only a fraction of them. A fascinating new parameter was opened up with the invention of the electronic stroboscope by Harold Edgerton. This instrument, which is capable of exposures as short as one-millionth of a second, can record in a series of instantaneous photographs an entire sequence of movement (Fig. 22-20). This apparatus seems particularly promising for analysis of the various sequences of skilled movement. In a somewhat related field, the new science of aerodynamics has greatly increased our knowledge of the movement of objects in space through investigations involving the use of wind tunnels and other specialized research tools and artificially produced environments.

Psychologists, psychoanalysts, psychiatrists and other social scientists have become interested in investigating the psychosomatic aspects of kinesiology. The studies of J. H. Van Den Berg,[53] Edwin Straus,[54] and Temple Fay[55] may be cited as representative analyses which have contributed significantly to our knowledge concerning the "why" of human movement.

According to the old psychological stimulus → response theory, the individual is merely a communication channel between the input and the output. This view fails to consider the contribution which the individual makes to the circuit. In information theory it is recognized that through experience man accumulates certain knowledge about his external environment, as, for example, how an object travels through space, and that the signals he received from his kinesthetic proprioceptors reveal to him how his body is responding to the external presentation. The individual is viewed as a limited capacity channel, receiving and responding to signals originating from internal sources as well as from the external display. The relative importance of these two types of stimuli in determining individual response appears to vary with practice and with the ease or difficulty of the required response. One of the chief difficulties confronting a performer is to separate one signal from another when they are presented in rapid succession. Perception of essential data is usually obscured by competing signals which create "noise" on the input circuits. A distinguishing characteristic of a skilled performer is his ability to select, integrate, and respond only to those signals which are germane to the situation; that is, in effect, to filter out signals which are mere noise. The fact that stimuli may be correlated with each other may enhance the difficulty for the performer.

Engineering theory treats communications systems as organisms. Since the two are operationally equivalent (Table 1–1), the insights of the cyberneticians (scientists who postulate that the processes of control are similar in the animal, the machine, and an organizational structure) and the psychologists are also equivalent and may be used interchangeably. (Fig. 1–2.)

The modifications which a man makes in his environment cause a change of input from that environment into his organism. Feedback from these functional alterations affects his structure. Alterations of structure affect the relationship between the various components and result in changes in function. Thus man to some extent is his own architect.[56]

Since the appearance of the first edition of this book the physiologically motivated researchers have largely concerned themselves with the wave-forms of electrical activity in the nerves or brain, or in the transmission properties of nerve tissue. Psychologically oriented investigators have tended to search for regular descriptions of the input-output of the human organism. For example, the

TABLE 1–1. Operational Relationships of Communications Systems and Biological Organisms

Communications Systems	Biological Organisms
Source of Input	Environment
Transmitter	Sensory organs
Communications Network	Peripheral nervous system
Receiver	Central nervous system
Communication controls	Kinesthetic processes
Feedback	Learning

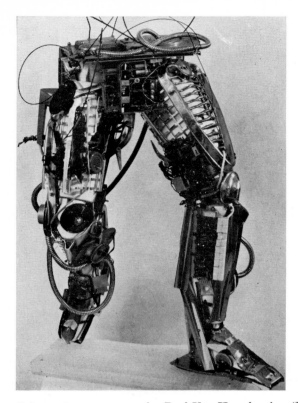

FIG. 1–2.   Cybernetic man, as seen by Paul Van Hoeydonck.   (Reproduced by special permission of the artist and the Museum of Contemporary Art, Chicago.)

neurogeometric theory holds that the receptor and the motor systems are linked by space-time organized feedback mechanisms. These are multidimensional. Motion is made up of posture, transport, manipulation, and tremor movements, each controlled by its own sensory feedback. The brain coordinates and regulates these feedbacks. Learning is thus based upon the brain's integration of the anatomical and physiological relations between the efferent and the afferent systems.

Such new insights have rich import for kinesiology, but also introduce new complications. The advanced student must now become accustomed to such explanations as the suggestion that a smooth landing after a drop is due to the release of a "complete preprogrammed open-loop sequence of neuromuscular activity virtually unaided by myotatic feedback.[57]

In spite of its long and honorable history, kinesiology has yet to achieve recognition as a major course of study in colleges and universities. The organization of a National Kinesiology Council within the American Association for Health, Physical Education and Recreation in 1965 marks a long step forward in its emergence as a discipline in its own right. The kinesiologist can no longer limit his scope to the mere mechanical analysis of movement; he must consider increasingly the meaning and significance of musculoskeletal movements. The human is a plastic being, and the study of mechanical principles alone will reveal only a fraction of the entire spectrum of his movements—perhaps the fraction of the least importance.

A vivid example is seen in the work of Kortlandt and Van Zon, whose study of chimpanzees led them to conclude that living in the forest encourages a pacific way of life and walking on all fours while living in the open grasslands favors aggressive hunting and the use of weapons, which demand walking on two limbs in order to free the other two. One of the major concepts of biology holds that "ontogeny recapitulates phylogeny," and it is intriguing to interpret Kortlandt and Van Zon's observations from both the ontogenetic and phylogenetic viewpoints.

It is becoming increasingly evident that kinesiologists are no longer satisfied to deal merely with the mechanical analysis of human movement. There are portents which suggest that the student of the future may be required to distinguish five subdivisions within the discipline: (1) Structural and Functional Kinesiology, dealing with the interrelations between the form and function of the body; (2) Physiologic Kinesiology, or the correlation between kinesiology and basic sciences such as physiology and biochemistry; (3) Mechanical Kinesiology, the investigation of human movement by means of the concepts of classical physics and their derivatives in the practical arts of engineering; (4) Developmental Kinesiology, i. e. the relation of kinesiology to growth, physical development, nutrition, aging, and similar topics, and (5) Symbolic Kinesiology, the study of the mutualities of movement and meaning, as implied in such topics as body image, self image, esthetic expression, cultural communication, personality, and motivation.

References

1. Aristotle: *Progression of Animals*. English translation by E. S. Forster. Cambridge: Harvard University Press, p. 489.

2. Heath, Thomas Little: Archimedes. *Encyclopaedia Britannica*, II, 297–298, 1965.

3. O'Malley, Charles D. and Saunders, J. B. DeC.: *Leonardo da Vinci on the Human Body*. New York: Henry Schuman, Inc., 1952.

4. Castiglioni, Arturo, *et al.*: A Symposium on Galileo in Commemoration of the Three Hundredth Anniversary of His Death. Bull. Hist. Med., *12*, 226–273, 1942.

5. Foster, Michael: *Lectures on the History of Physiology.* Cambridge: The University Press, 1941, pp. 71–72 and 279–281.

6. Steindler, Arthur: *Mechanics of Normal and Pathological Locomotion in Man.* Springfield: Charles C Thomas, 1935, pp. 1–9.

7. Singer, Charles: *A Short History of Medicine.* New York: Oxford University Press, 1928, p. 129.

8. Harvey, William: An Anatomical Disquisition on the Motion of the Heart and Blood in Animals. In *Classics of Medicine and Surgery,* collected by C. N. B. Camac. New York: Dover Publications, 1959, pp. 24–113.

9. Miller, William Snow: Niels Stensen. Bull. Johns Hopkins Hosp., *25,* 44–51, 1914.

10. Fulton, J. F.: *Muscular Contraction and the Reflex Control of Movement.* Baltimore: The Williams and Wilkins Co., 1926, pp. 3–55.

11. Andry, Nicolas: *Orthopaedia.* Facsimile Reproduction. Philadelphia: J. B. Lippincott Co., 1961.

12. Taylor, F. Sherwood: *A Short History of Science and Scientific Thought.* New York: W. W. Norton & Company, Inc., 1949, p. 118.

13. *Sir Isaac Newton's Mathematical Principles of Natural Philosophy and His System of the World,* July 5, 1668. English translation by Andrew Motte, 1729; revision by Florian Cajori. Berkeley: University of California Press, 1946.

14. Thayer, William Sydney: Bichat. Bull. Johns Hopkins Hosp., *14,* 197–201, 1903.

15. *The Works of John Hunter,* edited by James F. Palmer. London: Longman, Rees, Orme, Brown, Green, and Longman, 1837, *4,* 195–273.

16. Galvani, Luigi: *Commentary on the Effects of Electricity on Muscular Motion.* Translated by Margaret Glover Foley. Norwalk, Conn.: Burnaby Library, 1953.

17. Duchenne, G. B.: *Physiology of Motion,* translated and edited by Emanuel B. Kaplan. Philadelphia: W. B. Saunders Co., 1959.

18. Jokl, Ernst and Reich, Joseph: Guillaume Benjamin Amand Duchenne de Boulogne. J. Ass. Phys. & Men. Rehabil., *10,* 154–159, 1956.

19. Haycraft, J. B.: Animal Mechanics. *Textbook of Physiology,* edited by E. A. Schafer. Vol. 2, New York: The Macmillan Co., 1900, pp. 228–273.

20. Muybridge, Eadweard: *The Human Figure in Motion.* New York: Dover Publications, 1955.

21. *Human Mechanics.* AMRL-TDR-63-123. Wright-Patterson Air Force Base: Aerospace Medical Research Laboratories, 1963.

22. Dempster, Wilfrid Taylor: *Space Requirements of the Seated Operator.* Washington, D.C.: U.S. Department of Commerce, 1955.

23. Hewes, Gordon W.: The Anthropology of Posture. Scient. Amer., *196,* 122–132, 1957.

24. Siebert, Werner W.: Investigation of Hypertrophy of the Skeletal Muscle. Translated by Robert Kramer. J. Ass. Phys. Men. Rehabil., *14,* 153–157, 1960.

25. Steinhaus, Arthur H.: Strength from Morpurgo to Muller—A Half Century of Research. J. Ass. Phys. & Men. Rehabil., *9,* 147–150, 1955.

26. *Selected Writings of John Hughlings Jackson,* edited by James Taylor. Vol. 1. London: Hodder & Stoughton, 1931, pp. 420–421.

27. Beevor, Charles: *The Croonian Lectures on Muscular Movements Delivered Before the Royal College of Physicians of London, June, 1903.* London: Macmillan and Co., Ltd., n. d.

28. Steindler, Arthur: *Kinesiology of the Human Body Under Normal and Pathological Conditions.* Springfield: Charles C Thomas, 1955, p. 7.

29. Sherrington, Charles: *Man on His Nature,* 2nd Ed. Garden City: Doubleday & Co., Inc., 1953, p. 110.

30. Cited in Ruch, Theodore C. and Patton, Harry D.: *Physiology and Biophysics*, 19th Ed. Philadelphia: W. B. Saunders Co., 1965, p. 114.

31. Koch, John C.: The Laws of Bone Architecture. Amer. J. Anat., *21*, 177–298, 1917.

32. Evans, F. Gaynor: *Stress and Strain in Bones.* Springfield: Charles C Thomas, 1957.

33. Tobin, William J.: The Internal Architecture of the Femur and Its Clinical Significance. J. Bone Joint Surg., *37-A*, 57–72, 1955.

34. Carey, Eben J.: Studies in the Dynamics of Histogenesis. Experimental, Surgical and Roentgenographic Studies in the Architecture of Human Cancellous Bone, the Resultant of Back Pressure Vectors of Muscle Action. Radiology, *13*, 127–168, 1929.

35. Scott, J. H.: Muscle Growth and Function in Relation to Skeletal Morphology. Am. J. Phys. Anthrop., *15* (NS), 197–234, 1957.

36. Darwin, Charles: *The Origin of Species* and *The Descent of Man.* New York: The Modern Library, n. d.

37. Taylor, Frederick W.: *Principles of Scientific Management.* New York: Harper & Brothers, 1915.

38. Amar, Jules: *The Human Motor.* New York: E. P. Dutton & Co., 1920.

39. Damon, Albert, *et al.*: *The Human Body in Equipment Design.* Cambridge, Mass.: Harvard University Press, 1966.

40. Woodson, Wesley E. and Conover, Donald W.: *Human Engineering Guide for Equipment Designers*, 2nd Ed. (Revised). Berkeley: University of California, 1964.

41. Murrell, K. F. H.: *Ergonomics: Man in his Working Environment.* London: Chapman & Hall, 1965.

42. Morgan, Clifford T., *et al.*: *Human Engineering Guide to Equipment Design.* New York: McGraw-Hill Book Co., Inc., 1963.

43. Hooton, E. A.: An Anthropologist Looks at Medicine. Science, *83*, 271–276, 1936.

44. Ritchey, Sterling J., *et al.*: The Dashboard Femoral Fracture. J. Bone Joint Surg., *40-A*, 1347–1358, 1958.

45. Adrian E. D.: Interpretation of the Electromyogram. Lancet, *2*, 1229–1233, 1925; *2*, 1283–1286, 1925.

46. Hill, A. V.: *First and Last Experiments in Muscle Mechanics.* London: Cambridge University Press, 1970.

47. Karpovich, Peter V.: *Physiology of Muscular Activity*, 6th Ed. Philadelphia: W. B. Saunders Co., 1965, p. 253.

48. Fenn, W. O.: Frictional and Kinetic Factors in the Work of Sprint Running. Amer. J. Physiol., *92*, 583–611, 1930.

49. Schwartz, Plato and Heath, Arthur L.: The Definition of Human Locomotion on the Basis of Measurement. J. Bone Joint Surg., *29*, 203–214, 1947.

50. Inman, Verne T.: Human Locomotion. Canad. Med. Ass. J., *94*, 1047–1054, 1966.

51. Elftman, H.: The Basic Pattern of Human Locomotion. Ann. New York Acad. Sci., *51*, 1207–1212, 1951.

52. Morton, Dudley J. and Fuller, Dudley Dean: *Human Locomotion and Body Form.* Baltimore: The Williams & Wilkins Co., 1952.

53. Van Den Berg, J. H.: The Human Body and the Significance of Human Movement. Philosophy and Phenomenological Res., *13*, 159–183, 1952.

54. Straus, Edwin: The Upright Posture. Psychiat., *26*, 529–561, 1953.

55. Fay, Temple: The Origin of Human Movement. Amer. J. Psychiat., *111*, 644–652, 1955.

56. Du Brul, E. Lloyd: A Neuroanatomical Basis for the Evolution of Behavior. Proc. Inst. Med. Chicago, *25*, 99–101, 1964.

57. Watt, D. and Jones, G. Melville: On the Functional Role of the Myotatic Reflex in Man. Proc. Canad. Fed. Biol. Soc., *9*, 13, 1966.

Recommended Reading

58. Clein, Marvin J.: The Early Historical Roots of Therapeutic Exercise. JOHPER, *41*, 89–91, 1970.

59. Jokl, Ernst: Motor Functions of the Human Brain. A Historical Review. Medicine and Sport, Vol. 6. Biomechanics II, 1–27. Basel: Karger, 1971.

Chapter 2

The Framework and Joints of the Body

There are approximately 206 bones in the adult skeleton. The use of dried bones as skeletal demonstration materials frequently generates the impression that the skeleton is a hard, rigid, static structure comparable to steel girders in a skyscraper. One purpose of this chapter is to show that skeletal structures are dynamic, living, developing, growing tissues whose metabolism influences function and is influenced by function.

THE COMPOSITION AND STRUCTURE OF BONES

Constituents of Bone Tissue. About 25 to 30 per cent of bone is water. The remainder is what engineers describe as a "two-phase" material. Approximately 60 to 70 per cent is composed of mineral (calcium phosphate and calcium carbonate), which gives bone the ability to resist compression; the balance is made up of collagen (a protein) which provides its ability to resist tension. Generally speaking, a bone can withstand about six times the stresses to which it is subject in ordinary activities.[1] If all organic material and water are removed, the remaining structure crumbles easily. On the other hand, if all inorganic salts are extracted from a long bone, the remaining structure, when fresh and moist, can be bent easily and tied into an overhand knot. After maturity, the proportions of fluid and of organic material gradually decrease with age. For these and other reasons, the bones of aged people are brittle and healing becomes more difficult.

The organic portion of bones can be divided into (1) *cells*, which constitute only a minute fraction of the total weight of bone, (2) *fibrous matrix*, formed largely of fibrils of *collagen*, which can be extracted as glue or gelatin, and (3) *ground substance*, consisting mostly of protein polysaccharides (protein-sugar compounds). The relationship of the ground substance to the tissue fluid is poorly understood,[2] but along with the tissue fluid it is interspersed among the collagenous fibers. All this organic matter is impregnated with the inorganic bone salts.

Organization of Bone Tissue. Bone tissue is sparsely permeated with blood vessels, lymph channels, and nerve branches. The microscopic *Haversian system* is the structural basis of compact bone. Most conspicuous are the cylindrical tunnels about 0.05 mm. in diameter, called the *Haversian canals* or *central canals*, which are usually aligned with the long axis of the bone. They branch irregularly, and contain small blood vessels, lymph vessels, and nerve fibers. Bone tissue is laid down around each Haversian canal in very thin cylindrical concentric layers known as *lamellae*. Between the lamellae are found many small cavities, called *lacunae*, each of which contains an *osteocyte*, or bone cell. A lacuna is roughly cigar-shaped, but is made irregular by the exit of numerous minute chan-

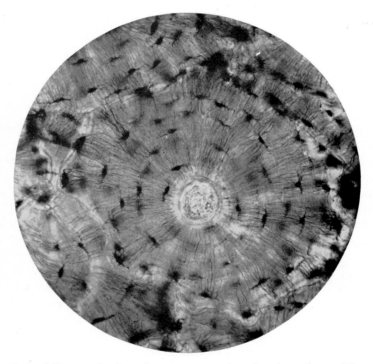

Fig. 2–1.   Microscopic view of transverse section of compact bone. The roughly circular light area near the center is an Haversian canal. The black spots are lacunae. They are connected to the Haversian canal and to each other by radiating lines called canaliculi. The concentric rings of bone surrounding an Haversian canal make up an Haversian system. Portions of adjacent systems are visible near the edges of the photograph. (Courtesy General Biological Supply House, Inc., Chicago.)

nels known as *canaliculi,* which communicate with other lacunae and with the Haversian canals. These passageways are filled with tissue fluid (Figs. 2–1 and 2–2).

Kinds of Bones. *Long bones,* such as the humerus and tibia, are found in the limbs. *Short bones* are roughly cubical, and are represented only by the carpal and tarsal bones. *Flat bones,* represented by the sternum, ribs, some of the skull bones, ilium, and scapula, have outer layers of compact bone with an interior of spongy bone and marrow. They are designed to serve as extensive flat areas for the attachment of muscles and ligaments, and, except for the scapula, to enclose cavities. They are usually curved, thick where tendons and fascia sheets attach, and thin to the point of translucence where the fleshy muscle fibers attach directly to the bone. *Irregular bones,* such as the ischium, pubis, maxilla, and vertebrae, are adapted to special purposes.

Structure and Functions of the Long Bones. Evolutionally, the long bones are adapted for weight-bearing and for sweeping, speedy excursions. They serve these purposes admirably because of their tubular form, their broad and specialized articular surfaces and shapes at their ends, and their great length.

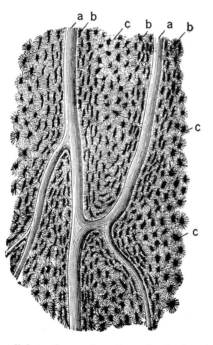

Fig. 2–2. Section parallel to the surface from the body of the femur × 100. *a,* Haversian canals; *b,* lacunae seen from the side; *c,* others seen from the surface in lamellae, which are cut horizontally. (*Gray's Anatomy.*)

The long central tubular part of a long bone is called the *shaft, body,* or *diaphysis.* It contains the hollow *medullary cavity,* filled with marrow and surrounded with compact bone. After maturity, the compact bone of the shaft blends gradually into the compact bone of the two *ends.* The proximal end is usually called the *head.* Both the proximal and distal ends typically display protrusions called *condyles, tubercles,* or *tuberosities,* which serve as attachments or "pulleys" for tendons and ligaments. The shapes of the articular surfaces are commonly specialized to enable the bone to fit securely into the conformations of its neighbors, and to determine or limit the kind of action possible at the joint. Each articular surface has a cap of hyaline cartilage. This articular hyaline cartilage functions to increase the smoothness of fit, prevent excess wear, absorb shocks, and prevent dislocations of the joints.

Toward the ends of long bones, the medullary cavity gives way to *spongy* or *cancellous bone* within the external layers of compact bone. Spongy bone is as hard as compact bone, but is arranged in a complex grillwork. These bars of latticework are called *cancelli* or *trabeculae* (from Latin, meaning lattice bars or little beams). The basic tubular structure of long bones conserves weight, at the same time providing great resistance to stress and strain (Figs. 2–3*A* and 2–3*B*). The tensile strength of compact bone is 230 times greater than that for muscle of a similar cross-section.[3]

Membranes of Bone. The *periosteum* is a connective tissue which covers the outside surface of bones, except at articular surfaces, where it is replaced by the articular hyaline cartilage. It has two layers, an outside layer of collagenous fibers, and a deep layer which is osteogenic (that is, capable of producing *osteoblasts,* which in turn may develop into osteocytes). Periosteum is supplied with blood vessels and nerve branches. It is extremely sensitive to injury, and from it originates most of the pain of fractures, bone bruises, and "shin splints." It adheres to the outer surface of compact bone by sending tiny processes, similar to small roots, into the bone. Muscles are attached to periosteum, not directly to the bone.

The *endosteum* is a similar connective tissue which lines the medullary cavity and Haversian canals, and covers trabeculae of spongy bone. It, too, is osteogenic.

Bone Marrow. The primary function of red bone marrow is to manufacture red blood cells, although it also has osteogenic properties. At birth, red marrow fills both the medullary cavities and the intra-trabecular spaces of all long bones. As spongy bone increases in amount with age, the red marrow retreats to the intra-trabecular spaces, leaving the medullary cavity filled with fatty yellow marrow. By the time of puberty, almost all of the marrow in limb bones is

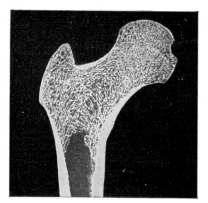

FIG. 2–3*A*. Frontal longitudinal midsection of the upper portion of a femur (from Koch). The construction of this bone has been discussed in a paper by William J. Tobin. The Internal Architecture of the Femur and Its Clinical Significance. J. Bone Joint Surg., *37-A*, 52–72, 1955.

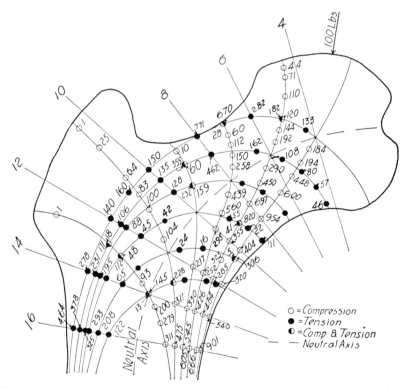

FIG. 2–3*B*. Paths of maximum tensile and compressive stress (in pounds per sq. in.) for a load of 100 lbs. on the femur head. These figures should be multiplied by 1.6 for walking and by 3.2 for running. The femur head will fail at approximately 2,000 lbs. load. (From Fig. 19*A*, Koch, Amer. J. Anat., *21*, 249.)

yellow, and red marrow is normally found only in parts of the ribs, skull, sternum, and vertebrae.

Effects of Bone Function upon Bone Structure. Pages 12 to 14 in Chapter 1 have presented an historical account of the hypothesis that the trabeculae are formed in response to the stresses and strains of weight-bearing and other functions of bone. The *trajectorial theory* of bone structure, as developed by Culmann, Wolff, and Roux, postulated that the trabeculae were laid down along lines of compressive or tensile force. Mathematical analyses were made in an attempt to show that the trabeculae did indeed follow the lines of force, and that they originated at right angles to the surface of the bone and crossed each other at right angles, as was demanded by the engineering theories and methods which were employed. Wolff's classic statement was that "Every change in the form and function of bones, or of their function alone, is followed by certain definite changes in their internal architecture and equally definite secondary alteration in their external conformation, in accordance with mathematical laws." The theory has been attacked continuously since its proposal. An exhaustive critical review of the evidence has been made by Evans,[4] from whose book the following conclusions are adapted: *First,* the mathematical analyses which tended to support the trajectorial theory were of doubtful validity. *Second,* functional stresses undoubtedly influence bone formation and growth, but the extent and nature of this mechanism is the subject of much disagreement. *Third,* other factors, including hereditary tendencies, nutrition, biochemical influences, and vascular conditions, may have an influence equal to or greater than functional stresses.

Wolff's Law of Bone Transformation seems to have been an overstatement, especially with regard to its phrase "in accordance with mathematical laws." Yet it cannot be discarded entirely. Normal bone repair after fractures is found to be suited to the stresses received; bones atrophy or cease to develop after muscular forces are removed by paralysis; constant pressures on bone may cause atrophy, but intermittent pressures seem to result in bone growth; bone growing in tissue culture, separated from any organism, has been known to adapt itself to the artificial forces present; and inactivity, resulting from encasement in plaster casts and from other causes, is often followed by atrophy or cessation of growth.

GROWTH AND DEVELOPMENT OF BONES

Ossification of Bones. *Ossification* means the depositing of bone salts in an organic matrix. It must be preceded by the differentiation and proliferation of cells which will lay down the collagenous matrix, and this may occur either in an existing connective tissue membrane, producing *intramembranous ossification*, or in hyaline cartilage, producing *endochondral or intracartilaginous ossification*. The clavicle and most skull bones ossify intramembranously, the short bones intracartilaginously, and the long bones by both methods.

Ossification of Long Bones. In the embryo, hyaline cartilage models of the bones appear. Well before birth, a primary center of ossification, known as a *diaphysis*, arises near the center of the future shaft of long bones. Ossification progresses in all directions from these primary centers. At the same time, a *bone collar* ossifies intramembranously in the periosteum around the shaft, defining its outside diameter. One or more secondary centers of ossification, called *bony epiphyses*, develop at the ends of the long bones. The time of such development is specific for each center, some appearing before birth and some as late as adolescence. This epiphyseal (pronounced epi-FISS-ē-al) ossification also progresses circumferentially, and finally all the original cartilage has been replaced except for a comparatively thin *epiphyseal cartilage*, *epiphyseal plate*, or *epiphyseal disk* which separates the shaft or diaphysis from the end or epiphysis. The most recently formed bone at the end of the diaphysis is called the *metaphysis*.

Growth of Long Bones. Growth in diameter occurs most rapidly before maturity, but can continue during nearly all of the life of the individual. The periosteum produces concentric layers of bone on the outside, while a more or less proportional resorption of bones takes place in the medullary cavity, enlarging its diameter.

Growth in length is a continuation of ossification of the diaphysis toward the epiphysis. However, the epiphyseal cartilage continues to proliferate and keep the diaphysis and epiphysis separated. At an age that is specific for each epiphysis, varying from middle childhood to adulthood, the epiphyseal cartilage ceases to proliferate, and bony union *(closure)* takes place between diaphysis and epiphysis, usually leaving an elevated ridge called the *epiphyseal line* on the surface of the matured bone.

Trained physical educators often pay attention to the size of the bones, as seen at the wrist, ankles, and hips, in order to get a better estimate of an individual's capacity for bearing weights and stresses. In general, the bones of the negro skeleton are denser than those of the white skeleton, and those of the male are denser than those of the female.

Growth of Short Bones. A short bone usually grows as if it were an epiphysis, except that it maintains its independent identity.

Influence of Trauma. Numerous factors affecting bone growth were mentioned earlier in this chapter, in the discussion of Wolff's Law. In addition, bone growth may be affected adversely by trauma. Either a single catastrophic force or repeated severe insults can stop bone growth or dislocate the growing parts at the epiphyseal cartilage. Interrupted growth is often considered to be more serious than a clean fracture in a fully ossified area of the same bone, partly because pain and deformity are less obvious at the time of injury, resulting in the delay of corrective measure until an irremediable defect has resulted. The strength of the fibrous capsule and ligaments surrounding a joint is two to five times greater than the strength of the metaphyseal-epiphyseal junction. Consequently "sprains" in children must be carefully evaluated to rule out possible injury to the epiphyses[5] (Fig. 2–4).

Most of the major epiphyses do not close until seventeen to nine-

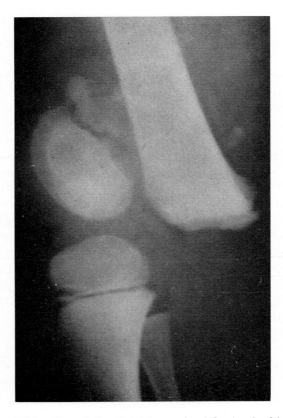

Fig. 2–4. Dislocation of the distal femoral epiphysis of a high school football player. The patient suffered considerable shortening of this leg as a result of premature closure of the epiphysis and subsequently required a shortening of the good leg. (Courtesy Leonard F. Bush, M.D.)

teen years of age. Therefore, many orthopedists regard football, wrestling, pyramid building, and other stressful contact sports as undesirable during the period of bone immaturity. From the kinesiological point of view, the following questions are pertinent:

How serious is the danger of anatomical injury?

Is it greater in the organized sports programs than in the unsupervised sand-lot activities which it replaces?

Can the rules be modified to minimize the danger of trauma?

Is adequate protective equipment available and used?

Is there adequate medical supervision of injuries?

Are medical examinations required of participants?

Are the managers, teachers, coaches, and officials aware of anatomical-physiological factors in growth and development, and do they use their prestige and authority in such a manner as to protect the safety of the participants?

In particular the obese child and the uncoordinated, lanky type with poor muscular development and relaxed ligaments are susceptible to epiphyseal injury and should avoid contact sports until they become mature.

Ossification Dates. The statement that the age at which epiphyseal fusion takes place is specific for each epiphysis should not be interpreted too literally. It is true that the fusion ages at various centers provide an amazingly accurate physiological time clock, but the clock can run slow or fast according to state of endocrine secretion, health, and nutrition of the individual. Undoubtedly there are racial, geographical, and hereditary differences, although these have not as yet been adequately determined. On the average, a given epiphysis will ossify and growth in the length of the bone will cease from one to three years earlier in a female than in a male. Trauma or overstrain may cause premature closure, but ill-health and malnutrition are likely to delay the date. None of the epiphyses of the limbs fuse before puberty, but all of the epiphyses will normally be fused before age twenty-one. Average times of epiphyseal closure of typical long bones are given in Table 2–1.

A youngster who is larger than average, or who is obese, is often subjected to unwarranted epiphyseal stresses. His bulk may give a false impression of the degree of his bony maturity. For this reason, age should be a factor in athletic classification indices, and sports leaders should not (for example) always put the biggest boy on the bottom of a pyramid in gymnastic lessons. X-ray pictures of the degree of ossification of carpal bones provide a precise estimation of skeletal and physiological maturity of pre-adolescents, but are seldom used because of the expense.

TABLE 2–1.   Ossification Dates for Typical Long Bones

Center of Ossification	Appearance Date	Epiphysis	Closure Date
HUMERUS			
Body	8th fetal week	Head with tubercles	6th year
Head	1st year	Distal end with body	16th–17th year
Capitulum	2nd year	Head with body	20th year
Greater Tubercle	3rd year		
Lesser Tubercle	5th year		
Medial Epicondyle	5th year		
Trochlea	12th year		
Lateral Epicondyle	13th–14th year		
ULNA			
Body	8th fetal week	Olecranon with body	16th year
Head	4th year	Distal end with body	20th year
Olecranon	10th year		
RADIUS			
Body	8th fetal week	Proximal end with body	17th–18th year
Distal end	2nd year	Distal end with body	20th year
Proximal end	5th year		
FEMUR			
Body	7th fetal week	Lesser trochanter	
Distal end	9th fetal month	with body	Puberty
Head	1st year	Greater trochanter	
Greater Trochanter	4th year	with body	Puberty
Lesser Trochanter	13th–14th year	Head with body	Puberty
		Distal end with body	20th year
TIBIA			
Body	7th fetal week	Distal end with body	18th year
Proximal end	Birth	Proximal end with body	20th year
Distal end	2nd year		

THE ARCHITECTURE OF JOINTS

Types of Joints.   The junction of two bones is called a *joint* or *articulation.* There are three classes of joints, the *synarthrodial* or immovable, the *amphiarthrodial* or slightly movable, and the *diarthrodial* or freely movable. The first two classes have no true joint cavity; the third class has a joint cavity and is subdivided into seven types. The classification and terminology of joints are presented differently by various authors. A reasonably complete listing of types and terms is presented in Table 2–2, with descriptive explanations, but students are cautioned to be alert for small differences in classification when consulting other source books. Each specific joint of the body has its own peculiarities.

Diarthrodial Joints. The diarthrodial, freely movable, or synovial joints are of greatest interest to students of human motion. The typical structural aspects are shown in Figures 2–5 and 2–6. The weight-bearing or articular surfaces of the bones are covered with a layer of hyaline cartilage known as *articular cartilage*. Being resilient, but not especially brittle, this cartilage absorbs shocks, prevents direct wear on the bones, and modifies the shapes of the bones to insure a better fit. It has no nerve or blood supply of its own. In some joints, the articular cartilages show specialized modifications and are given distinct names, as is the case with *glenoid labrum* of the shoulder joint and the *semilunar cartilages* or *menisci* of the knee. The joints must not be thought of as a hard surface. They should be considered resilient bearings, with the articular cartilage having characteristics somewhere between those of a solid and of a liquid. Under pressure the cartilage appears to exude lubricant in advance of the point of pressure, but the mechanics involved are only poorly understood.[6]

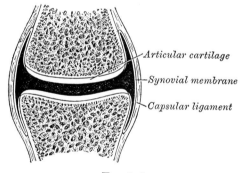

Fig. 2–5

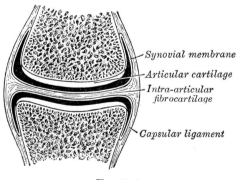

Fig. 2–6

Figs. 2–5 and 2–6.   Typical diarthrodial joints, with and without intra-articular fibrocartilage. (*Gray's Anatomy.*)

A ligamentous sleeve called the *capsule* or *capsular ligament* is attached firmly to both bones of the joint, enclosing it completely. This capsule is lined internally by a thin vascular *synovial membrane*, which secretes *synovial fluid* or *synovia* into the *joint cavity*. The synovial fluid provides nourishment to the articular cartilages, and serves to lubricate the joint. Normally, only a tiny bit of synovial fluid is present, and there is a slight negative pressure (suction) in the joint cavity. Thus, the "cavity" is difficult to find and explore in dissection, unless it has previously been injected so as to expand it. Injury or irritation, however, causes profuse secretion of synovial fluid, sometimes causing evident swelling.

Some diarthrodial joints have an intra-articular *fibrocartilage disk* which partitions the joint cavity into two parts. This makes it resemble a synchondrosis or cartilaginous articulation (Table 2–2), except that the latter has no cavity or synovial membrane. The sternoclavicular and distal radio-ulnar joints are diarthrodial joints having fibrocartilage disks. The attachments of these disks have peculiarities which enable them to assist in holding the bones together.

The ligamentous capsules sometimes have definite thickenings on one or more aspects, and these are sometimes named as separate ligaments. In addition, there are typically several other ligaments which join the two bones and which are discrete from the capsule. Ligaments are tough and practically non-elastic. Their function is to bind bones together, to prevent dislocation, and to limit the possible kinds and ranges of movement. Tensile stresses, if constantly applied, may result in their gradual lengthening—even to the point of destroying their function of maintaining the integrity of the joint.

Every synovial joint contains at least one male and one female articular surface. There is only a single position in which they are fully congruent. In this position the two surfaces fit point for point and gravity and/or muscular force cause the principal ligaments of the joint to become so taut that they screw the articular surfaces together in such a way that the two bones function as a single unit. This is known as the *close packed* position. Here the ligaments, especially in hinge joints, tend to be taut. In all other positions the male and female surfaces are not fully congruent. The ligaments tend to be slack and the joint is said to be in the *loose packed* position.[7]

Numerous factors contribute to the stability and integrity of synovial joints. Suction in the joint cavity can be a powerful inhibitor of traction-dislocation. Depth of fit of the male and female surfaces may (as in the acetabulum) or may not (as in the shoulder joint) provide stability. Ligaments bind adjacent bones tightly together when the joint is close packed or at the extreme of its range of

TABLE 2–2. Classification of Joints by Structure and Action

KIND	CLASS	TYPE Common Name	Technical Name	EXPLANATION AND EXAMPLES
Without a joint cavity	I. Synarthrosis (immovable)	A. Fibrous	Suture*	Two bones grow together, with only a thin layer of fibrous periosteum between. *E.g.*, sutures of the skull.
	II. Amphiarthrosis (slightly movable)	B. Ligamentous	Syndesmosis*	Slight movement permitted by meager elasticity of a ligament joining two bones, which may be distinctly separated. *E.g.*, coraco-acromial "joint"; mid radio-ulnar joint; mid tibio-fibular joint; inferior tibio-fibular joint.
		C. Cartilaginous	Synchondrosis or symphysis	Bones are coated with hyaline cartilage, separated by a fibrocartilage disk, and joined by ligaments. Motion is allowed only by deformation of the disk. *E.g.*, between bodies of vertebrae; symphysis pubis; between manubrium and body of sternum.
Having a joint cavity	III. Diarthrosis (freely movable)	D. Synovial 1. Gliding joint	Arthrosis or plane joint	Non-axial. Allows gliding or twisting. *E.g.*, intercarpal and intertarsal joints.
		2. Hinge joint	Ginglymus	Uni-axial. A concave surface glides around a convex surface, allowing flexion and extension. *E.g.*, elbow joint.
		3. Pivot joint	Trochoid joint	Uni-axial. A rotation around a vertical or long axis is allowed. *E.g.*, atlanto-axial joint; proximal radio-ulnar joint.
		4. Ellipsoid joint	Ellipsoid joint	Bi-axial. An "oval" ball-and-socket joint, allowing flexion, extension, abduction, adduction, and circumduction, but not rotation. *E.g.*, carpo-metacarpal (wrist) joint.
		5. Condyloid joint	Condyloid joint	Bi-axial. A spheroidal ball-and-socket joint with no muscles suitably located to perform rotation, which otherwise could take place. *E.g.*, interphalangeal joints; 2nd to 5th meta-carpophalangeal joints (but not of the thumb).
		6. Ball-and-socket joint	Spheroid, or enarthrosis	Tri-axial. Spheroidal ball-and-socket allows flexion, extension, abduction, adduction, circumduction, and rotation on the long axis. *E.g.*, shoulder and hip joints.
		7. Saddle joint	Saddle joint	Tri-axial. Both bones have a saddle-shaped surface fitted into each other. Allows flexion, extension, abduction, adduction, circumduction, and slight rotation. *E.g.*, carpo-metacarpal joint of the thumb.

* Some classification systems include both sutures and syndesmoses under the heading of fibrous joints. Both sutures and syndesmoses tend to ossify completely in later life, in which case the union is known as a *synostosis*.

motion. Contracting muscles can exert tremendous stabilizing forces. Injuries and habitually sagging postures can permanently overstretch the ligaments; when coupled with weak muscles, this predisposes a joint to easy dislocation.

Tendons and sheets of fascia cross most joints. Although their function is usually considered to be the transference of muscle tension, so as to cause movement, the fact that they hold bones together should never be overlooked. Because most muscles insert at very small angles, a large component of muscular force is usually directed along the bone toward the joint, tending to reinforce the joint by pulling the bones together.

Bursae and Tendon Sheaths. Wherever soft structures are frequently submitted to frictional rubbing on a bony protuberance, the friction is reduced by the appearance of tough connective tissue and some form of synovial sac. Even tendons cannot withstand constant friction on a bone without further protection. Therefore, they are surrounded by a cylindrical sac consisting of two layers of synovial membrane enclosing a cavity into which synovial fluid is secreted—this is called a *tendon sheath,* and its function is lubrication. Non-tendinous soft structures are similarly protected. Thus, the fascia and skin at the back of the elbow are separated from the olecranon process by a simple synovial sac called a *bursa.* Bursae occur in many other places. For example, as the supraspinatus muscle passes under the acromion process, it is separated from that hard structure by the *subacrominal bursa;* similarly the patellar ligament is protected from the head of the tibia by the *deep infrapatellar bursa.* Bursae and tendon sheaths are not parts of joints in a technical sense, but may be regarded as associated structures.

ACTIONS OF JOINTS

Kinesiologists require precise terminology to describe joint movements and muscle actions. For the purpose of defining joint movements, it is always assumed that the body is in *anatomical position;* that is, elongated as if suspended by its skull from a hook, with arms and legs dangling and palms of the hands facing forward. The skeleton in Figure 8–1 is in anatomical position except that its right hand has been turned in toward the thigh.

Flexion at any joint takes place when any body segment is moved in an antero-posterior plane so that its anterior or posterior surface approaches the anterior or posterior surface, respectively, of an adjacent body segment. Thus, moving the left limb from anatomical position to scratch the back of the left shoulder blade involves flexion of the arm at the shoulder joint, of the forearm at the elbow, of the hand at the wrist, and of the fingers at the metacarpophalangeal and interphalangeal joints. Bringing the front surface of the thigh toward the abdomen is hip flexion. Bringing the calf of the leg toward the back of the thigh is knee flexion. Raising the foot toward the tibia is ankle flexion. Curling the toes is toe flexion. *Extension* is the reverse—the moving from a flexed position back toward the anatomical position.

Abduction means moving a segment away from the center line of the body. Once started, the movement is called abduction throughout it entire range, even though, as in the case of abducting the arm at the shoulder joint, the part seems to be coming back toward the center line of the body during the second 90 degrees of its excursion. *Adduction* is the reverse of abduction—the moving from a position of abduction back toward the anatomical position. There is no abduction or adduction at the elbow or knee joints. At the wrist, abduction is also called *radial flexion,* and adduction is also called *ulnar flexion.*

Rotation around the long axis of a bone can take place, for example, at the shoulder, hip, and knee joints. *Inward rotation* occurs when the anterior surface turns inward; *outward rotation* is the reverse of this, when the anterior surface turns outward. With regard to rotation, the anatomical position is often regarded as the *neutral position;* thus, from a position of inward rotation, the thigh may be rotated outward to the neutral position and then further rotated outward.

Circumduction is a movement in which a body part describes a cone, with the apex at the joint and the base at the distal end of the part. There is no term to distinguish circumduction around a base of small radius from that around a base of large radius. Circumduction does not involve rotation; therefore, it may occur in biaxial joints like the metacarpophalangeal joints by a combination of flexion, abduction, extension, and adduction.

Hyperextension means a continuation of extension past anatomical position, usually. Thus, from the normally extended anatomical position of the elbow, slight further extension is possible in some people. This is characteristically seen in gymnasts. In no case does the prefix "hyper" indicate a different motion, but only an exceptional continuation of the movement involved.

Certain movements of some articulations require special consideration. Descriptions and terminology for such movements of the radio-ulnar joint, first carpometacarpal joint and thumb, foot and ankle, and the spine or trunk are given in detail in Chapters 11, 12, 13, and 17 of this text.

In the tremendously varied activities of athletics, aquatics, combatives, gymnastics, dance, and recreational and vocational pursuits, the joint actions can become complex indeed. Confusion in terminology must be carefully minimized. For this reason, it is perhaps better to describe a joint action as (for example) "hip flexion" or "shoulder joint abduction" rather than "thigh flexion" or "arm abduction," although both usages are correct. If the term "thigh flexion" is employed, beginning students are sometimes confused when it is used to refer to a motion of the pelvis forward onto the thigh, as in doing situps. The word "thigh" seems to indicate to some that the thigh must be the moving part, whereas there is no such connotation if "hip flexion" is used because attention is centered upon the joint rather than on the body part. The preference is strictly pedagogical.

MOBILITY OF JOINTS

Range of motion may be limited by ligaments (including the joint capsule), length and extensibility of muscles and fascia, tendons, occlusion of soft tissue masses, or impingement of bone against bone. The transient state of voluntary muscular contraction, as well as the autogenic stretch reflex regulated by muscle spindle mechanisms, may also influence range of motion.

Flexibility (the common synonym for range of joint motion) is a consideration in physical fitness, sports ability, posture, surgery, and physical medicine. Although in many instances lack of flexibility obviously limits performance and the voluntary correction of postural defects, experimental evidence indicates that improvements in performance and posture do not result from increased flexibility nearly as often as has generally been supposed. In fact, excessive flexibility sometimes sacrifices desirable stability and support, and may predispose a joint to injury. Determination of the optimal amount of flexibility in a particular joint for a particular purpose is a matter for careful professional judgment, and is not subject to standardization.

Contrary to popular belief, flexibility is not a general factor, but is highly specific to each joint.[8] Even the two joints of a bilateral pair in the same individual may vary markedly, although comparison is useful in making surgical decisions and in evaluating the nature and extent of injuries. In general, flexibility decreases gradually from birth to old age. Girls and women, on the average, are more flexible than males at the same age. Leighton[9] has shown that swimmers, baseball players, basketball players, field event performers, and champions in wrestling, weight-lifting, and gymnastics demonstrate flexibility patterns typical for each sport. These patterns are significantly different from those of non-athletes, at least with respect to 16-year-old boys. An overview of experimental evidence supports the conclusion that flexibility correlates with habitual movement patterns for each person and each joint, and that age and sex differences are secondary rather than innate. Linear measurements of flexibility, such as the sit-and-reach test, are crude and unsatisfactory for comparison of individuals.

Habitual postures and chronic heavy work through restricted ranges of motion lead to adaptive shortening of muscles. Over a period of years, inflexibility tends to become permanent and irreversible, especially as the usual development of osteoarthritis invokes calcification of tissues near the joints. Thus, the foot of a baby shows remarkable flexibility, while the foot of an adult tends to be rigid after years of encasement in shoes. A rounded program of progressive resistance exercise is likely to increase flexibility beyond normal ranges,[10] when the movements are carried through a complete range of motion and when exercises are selected to include both members of antagonistic muscle groups (Fig. 2–7). Lack of normal flexibility may be responsible for bad posture, compression of peripheral nerves, dysmenorrhea, and other ailments.[11,12]

Tables of normal ranges of motion are available, but are remark-

Fig. 2–7. Walt Baptiste demonstrating that muscular strength and hypertrophy resulting from the practice of progressive resistance exercises are compatible with flexibility. (Courtesy Strength and Health.) Relationships between static tests of strength and ranges of flexion and extension of the lumbar spine are generally not statistically significant.[13]

able for their lack of agreement. Discrepancies arise from unreliable instruments, lack of standardized measurement procedures, the shifting axis of rotation during movement in some joints, and a startlingly wide range of individual differences. Furthermore, average flexibility is not necessarily synonymous with optimum flexibility. Excellent reviews and bibliographies by Harris[14] and Holland[15] provide a starting point for a more detailed knowledge of flexibility.

References

1. Hamilton, W. J., editor: *Textbook of Human Anatomy*. New York: St. Martin's Press, 1956, p. 39.

2. McLean, Franklin C. and Urist, Marshal R.: *Bone*. 3rd Ed. Chicago: The University of Chicago Press, 1968, pp. 45–49.

3. Koch, J. D., cited in Martz, Carl D.: Studies on Stress and Strain in Treatment of Fractures. J. Bone Joint Surg., *46-A*, 409–415, 1964.

4. Evans, F. Gaynor: *Stress and Strain in Bones*. Springfield: Charles C Thomas, 1957.

5. Larson, Robert L. and McMahan, Robert O.: The Epiphyses and the Childhood Athlete. JAMA, *196*, 607–612, 1966.

6. Editorial: Lubrication of Joints. Brit. Med. J., *1*, 384–385, 15 February 1964.

7. MacConaill, M. A. and Basmajian, J. V.: *Muscles and Movements*. Baltimore: Williams & Wilkins Co., 1967, pp. 25–56.

8. Leighton, Jack R.: On the Significance of Flexibility for Physical Educators. J. Health, Phys. Ed., Rec., *31*, 27 *et seq.*, 1960.

9. Leighton, Jack R.: A Study of the Effect of Progressive Weight Training on Flexibility. J. Ass. Phys. & Ment. Rehabil., *18*, 101–110, 1964.

10. Harris, Margaret L.: A Factor Analytic Study of Flexibility. Res. Quart., *40*, 62–70, 1969.

11. Billig, Harvey E. and Loewendahl, Evelyn: *Mobilization of the Human Body*. Stanford: Stanford Press, 1949.

12. Golub, Leib J. and Christaldi, Josephine: Reducing Dysmenorrhea in Young Adolescents. J. Health, Phys. Ed., Rec., *28*, 24 *et seq.*, 1957.

13. Troup, J. D. G. and Chapman, A. E.: The Strength of the Flexor and Extensor Muscles of the Trunk. J. Biomech., *2*, 49–62, 1969.

14. Harris, Margaret L.: Flexibility. Phys. Ther., *49*, 591–601, 1969.

15. Holland, George J.: The Physiology of Flexibility: A Review of the Literature. *Kinesiology Review, 1968*, Washington, D.C.: AAHPER, 1968, pp. 49–62.

Recommended Reading

16. Vaughan, Janet M.: *Physiology of Bone*. Oxford: Oxford University Press, 1970.

17. Adrian, Marlene J.: An Introduction to Electrogoniometry. *Kinesiology Review, 1968*, Washington, D.C.: AAHPER, 1968, pp. 12–18.

Laboratory Exercises

1. Which bones are the most useful to physical anthropologists and detectives in determining stature from skeletal material? (Suggestion: See Mildred Trotter and

Goddine C. Gleser: A Re-Evaluation of Estimation of Stature Based on Measurements of Stature Taken During Life and Long Bones After Death. Am. J. Phys. Anthropol., *16* N.S., 79–123, 1958.)

2. Karate students practice striking a board called a *makiwara* in order to toughen their fists. In the December 1968 issue of Black Belt a practitioner of the art explained: "Pounding a makiwara gradually powders and slowly crushes the knuckle, rounding it off and depositing a calcium mold into a solid mass." Evaluate this statement from the standpoint of the kinesiology of bones and joints.

Chapter 3

The Structure and Action of Striated Muscle

TYPES OF VERTEBRATE MUSCLE

The muscles of the body are the machines by which chemically stored energy is converted into mechanical work. The correlate of this is that the amount of mechanical work done controls the amount of chemically stored energy which is converted. Three different types of contractile tissue are found in the body. In certain characteristics all are quite similar. They are affected by the same kind of stimuli, they produce an action potential soon after stimulation, they possess the ability to contract, the force of the contraction (within physiological limits) is dependent upon their initial length, they have the ability to maintain muscle tone, they will atrophy from inadequate circulation and will hypertrophy in response to increased work. In certain other respects they may show marked differences.

Smooth Muscle. Smooth, or involuntary, muscle forms the walls of the hollow viscera, such as the stomach and bladder, and of various systems of tubes, such as are found in the circulatory system, the alimentary tract, the respiratory system, and the reproductive organs. These muscle cells possess myofibrils, but they do not have cross striations and have only one nucleus. Probably smooth muscle contains pain endings but no proprioceptors. Compared with skeletal muscle, they display more sluggish contraction, greater extensibility, the power of more sustained contraction and of rhythmic contraction, greater sensitivity to thermal and chemical stimuli, and a longer chronaxie. The minimum amount of electrical current required to produce a response in a muscle is termed the *threshold stimulus*. The *time* required for a current of twice this strength to produce a response is called the *chronaxie*. The chronaxie of the muscles varies; those of nerves innervating pale muscles are shorter than those of nerves innervating red muscles; the chronaxies of smooth muscle are longer than those of skeletal muscle. The general rule seems to be that a short chronaxie is related to quick contraction; a long chronaxie to slow contraction. Charts have been prepared in which the muscles are classified into groups according to their chronaxies. Since changes in chronaxie are correlated with changes in physiologic function, these have considerable value in determining degenerative and regenerative changes in nerves and muscles. Contraction of smooth muscle forming a hollow organ will cause that organ to empty. In the case of the digestive tract waves of contraction propel its contents onward. If contraction occurs in the circulatory system, however, the flow is impeded and the blood pressure rises. Smooth muscle is innervated by both the sympathetic and parasympathetic nervous systems. Its action is usually involuntary and it can function in the absence of its extrinsic nerves.

Cardiac muscle displays structural and functional resemblances to both skeletal and smooth muscle. Its contractile elements are transversely striated and the A, I, and Z bands (see below) can be observed in the myofibrils, but the sarcoplasm is more abundant, the sarcolemma is much finer, and the striations are less distinct. The most characteristic features of the fibers are that they give off branches which furnish a means of communication between adjacent fibers for the conduction of the impulse for contraction. This led to the belief that cardiac muscle was an anatomical syncytium, that is, that the cells themselves were connected, but recent electron microscope studies have shown that they are actually separated. However, they can be considered a *functional* syncytium, as the whole tissue acts electrically as though it were a single cell.

Striated Muscle. Striated muscles are composed of thread-like fibers displaying alternating dark and light bands. Each fiber is actually a greatly elongated, multinucleated cell. It may be over 30 cm. in length and have a diameter of 0.01 to 0.1 mm. Each cell is separate. According to one estimate there are about 270 million striated muscle fibers in the body.[1] They are innervated by the cranial or the spinal nerves and are under voluntary control. This type of muscle contains both pain endings and proprioceptors. Its principal functions are body movement and the maintenance of posture. This is the type of muscle with which kinesiologists are primarily concerned, and the following discussion of muscle structure and function will deal only with striated muscle.

GROSS STRUCTURE OF STRIATED MUSCLE

Numbers and Shapes of Muscles. The muscles make up approximately 40 to 45 per cent of adult body weight. The voluntary muscular system includes approximately 434 muscles, but only about 75 pairs are involved in the general posture and movement of the body and will be considered in this text. The others are smaller and are concerned with such minute mechanisms as those controlling the voice, facial expression, and the act of swallowing. Some muscles are in flat sheets, like the trapezius and the transversalis; some are long and slender like the sartorius and the peroneus longus; some are spindle-shaped, like the biceps and the pronator teres; some are fan shaped, like the pectoralis major. Most of them are of such irregular shape that a classification based on form is not practicable. Each is named, some of the names indicating their form, as in the case of the rhomboid and teres major; some indicating their action, as the levator and the supinator; some indicating their location, as the intercostal and supraspinatus; some indicating the bones which they join, as the brachioradialis and the sternomastoid.

Attachments of Muscle. Units of 100 to 150 muscle cells or fibers are bound together with a connective tissue called *perimysium* to form a bundle termed a *fasciculus*. Several fasciculi are in turn bound together by a sheath of perimysium to form a larger unit. These units are enclosed in a covering of *epimysium* to form a muscle. The soft, fleshy, central part of a muscle, where the contractile cells predominate, is called the *belly*. Towards the ends of the muscle, the contractile cells disappear, but their investment of connective tissue (the perimysium and epimysium) continue in order to attach the muscles to bones. If the site of the bony attachment is distant from the belly of the muscle, these extensions of the connective tissue sheaths merge to form either a cord-like *tendon* or a flat *aponeurosis*. The fibers of the tendon or aponeurosis are plaited or braided with one another, so that tension in any part of a muscle is usually distributed more or less equally to all parts of the attachment to the bone. The tensile strength of adult tendons is about 4169 psi.[2] Since a tendon collects and transmits forces from many different muscle cells onto a small area of bone, the site of the tendinous attachment is normally marked by a rough tubercle on the bone. Likewise, an aponeurosis gives rise to a skeletal line or ridge at its attachment.

The thickness and strength of the external sheath will vary greatly, depending upon the location of the muscle. It is usually very heavy if the muscle is situated near the distal end of a limb where the muscle might be exposed to blows and abrasions. Ordinarily there is additional fascia covering the muscle to give further protection. On the other hand, a muscle situated deep within the body and consequently well protected, such as the psoas, has a minimum of connective tissue in the various sheaths.

These sheaths form a sort of structural framework for the muscle. This structure is tough and somewhat elastic and will return to its original length even after having been stretched as much as 40 per cent. The fact that the relative amounts of connective and contractile tissue vary greatly from muscle to muscle has at times been disregarded and has led to great discrepancies when experimental physiologists have reported the physical properties of muscle.

The fleshy fibers of some muscles do not give way to tendons at their attachments, but continue almost to the bone, where the individual sheaths of the contractile tissues make the attachment over an area as large as the cross section of the muscle belly. In these cases, the skeleton will be smooth, as on the surface of the scapula, because tensile forces are widely distributed.

Origin and Insertion. When a muscle contracts strongly it tends to move both of the bones to which it is attached, but to simplify the problem it is usually assumed that the bone moving least is stationary. The point where the muscle joins the stationary bone is called the *origin* of the muscle, and its point of attachment to the moving bone is called its *insertion.* By this definition the insertion is the place where the force is applied to the moving lever, and the distance from the insertion to the joint which serves as the axis of movement is the force arm of the lever. It frequently happens that the bone that acts as the lever in one movement is stationary in another; for example, when one lies on his back and then lifts his feet the trunk is stationary and the lower limbs are levers, but when from the same starting position he rises to a sitting posture the limbs are stationary and the trunk is the lever. The same muscles are involved in both cases, and it is evident that the origins and insertions are reversed when the movement is changed. The question as to which end of a muscle is origin and what is insertion depends therefore on the movement made. Although the matter is of importance for kinesiologists, for the sake of clearness of description the custom of the anatomists will be followed and the end nearer the center of the body will be referred to as the origin. The true origin and insertion can be told with ease when any mechanical problem is involved.

Longitudinal and Penniform Muscles. The musculoskeletal machine is basically an arrangement providing relatively large forces for the rapid manipulation of long lever arms. This mechanical system possesses only low mechanical advantages, with the result that the high speeds of motion are made possible only at the price of great exertion. While the human body may be said to be specialized more for speed than for strength, the forces required for various movements are relatively enormous. It may, for example, require 300 pounds of tension in the deltoid to enable it to raise an arm and hand holding a 10 pound weight to 80 degrees of elevation.

The internal structure of muscles, that is, the arrangement of their fibers, bears an important relation to the force and distance of their contraction. There are two main types of muscle structure: the longitudinal, or *fusiform*, and the *penniform*, but there are many variations from each basic type. The longitudinal is the simpler of the two forms; it consists of parallel fibers running the length of the muscle. In general, muscle which is long and slender is weak but can shorten through a relatively large distance, while muscle which is short and broad has much strength of contraction but can exert it through a proportionately short distance. The sartorius, for example, is a narrow band of extremely long fibers, well suited to contract with little force through a relative great distance, whereas the intercostals, consisting of a great number of very short fibers, are constructed to contract with considerable force through a very short distance. Fusiform muscles are very common in the extremities.

Fully three-fourths of all the muscles in the human body are so situated that they need to exert more strength than a longitudinal muscle would afford, while the latter's greater extent of contraction would be wasted. As a consequence the longitudinal muscles are replaced by the penniform. Penniform muscles are shaped like a feather, with the tendon in place of the shaft and the muscle fibers in place of the barbs. Since the muscle fibers are arranged diagonally to the direction of pull, more fibers can be brought into play, but the range of motion is reduced.

Penniform muscles come in several different arrangements:

Unipennate—Muscle to one side of the tendon, as in the semimembranosus.

Bipennate—Muscle converges to both sides of a tendon, as in the rectus femoris.

Multipennate—Muscle converges to several tendons, giving a herringbone effect, as in the deltoid.

Some of these arrangements are depicted in Figure 3–1.

Red and Pale Fibers. Muscle fibers may be divided into two general types: red (*tonic*) and pale (*phasic*). The relatively large amounts of *myoglobin* and granular material in the red fibers give them a much darker and redder appearance than is true of the pale fibers, which have few granules and very little myoglobin. Dark fibers have a smaller diameter and contain more sarcoplasm and mitochondria per unit area than do the white ones. The pigment in tonic fibers may serve as a means of storage of oxygen. These fibers depend primarily on oxidative metabolism and are adapted to sustained contraction, such as is required in maintaining posture. Phasic fibers depend primarily on glycolytic metabolism, fatigue

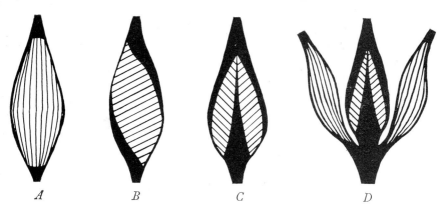

A B C D

FIG. 3–1. Diagrams showing kinds of arrangements of fibers of skeletal muscles. *A*, Fusiform. *B*, Unipennate. *C*, Bipennate. *D*, Multipennate. (Douglas.)

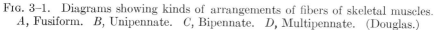

more easily, and are better adapted to perform fast contractions. The tonic fibers are innervated by thresholds which are lower than those innervating phasic muscles. Consequently they are usually more active. Hence the amount of electrical activity in a muscle is in part determined by its proportion of red fibers. Similarly, the amount of protein catabolism and synthesis is greater in tonic muscles. This suggests a direct correlation between the physiological activity of a muscle and the amount of protein metabolism.[3]

It has been postulated that the motor pool supplying a muscle is composed of small and large motor-neurones. The small ones supply small motor units of the predominantly slow, red fibers; the large ones supply large motor units of the predominantly fast, white muscle fibers. Since the former have a low threshold for stimulation and the latter a high one, the former are used under ordinary conditions and are active at all intensities of functioning; the latter are involved when stronger contractions are required and become active at higher levels of training.

The red fibers have an extensive supply of mitochondria and respiratory enzymes, but are relatively poor in glycogen; the white fibers are especially rich in both glycolytic enzymes and phosphagens. Since the energy for anaerobic work may be obtained from the breakdown of high energy phosphate bonds in ATP and creatin-phosphate or may result from glycolytic processes, it is possible that these two types of muscle may be selectively trained and that different aspects of muscular function may be separate parameters.[4]

In the domestic fowl the legs, which are in continuous use, are largely composed of red fibers, whereas the wings and breast, which

3

are little used, are largely composed of pale fibers. In contrast wild fowl which engage in long flights have red fibers in both the wings and breast. In mammals, including man, the common type of muscle is a mixed one, containing varying amounts of tonic and phasic fibers, depending on its task. Typical examples are the soleus and medial gastrocnemius, which are predominantly dark, the tibialis anterior and flexor digitorum longus, which are intermediate, and the extensor digitorum longus and semitendinosus, which are predominantly pale. Cross re-innervation of motor neurones following denervation causes white muscles to assume the characteristics of red, and vice versa.[5]

NUTRITION AND BLOOD SUPPLY

Each muscle receives its supply of oxygen, sugar and other foodstuffs from the circulatory system, and is therefore necessarily supplied with one or several arteries. Each artery divides into smaller arterioles and they, in turn, finally divide into an incredible number of small capillaries which lie in the endomysium. The walls of the capillaries are extremely thin and provide for an easy transfer of needed substances from the blood to the fiber itself. There is an intermittent ebb and flow of blood through the capillary network, due to the opening and closing of capillaries and arterioles in response to local tissue changes. If the fiber is inactive its metabolic needs are slight and little or no blood flows through its capillaries. Upon commencing exercise the acid metabolites resulting from muscular contraction cause the capillaries to dilate, thus permitting an influx of needed blood.

Faster vasomotor changes are probably due to the sympathetic vasoconstriction and vasodilation. These independent unsynchronized contractility changes are believed responsible for the basal vasomotor tone and are probably more important in the vasodilatation accompanying muscular exercise than are the local metabolites. The principal regulation of the blood vessels for homeostatic purposes is probably through the sympathetic innervation, although humoral factors also play a role. The working of the nervous system is clearly seen in the physiological changes which accompany the anticipation of exercise.

There is considerable experimental evidence indicating that the body responds to meet the need for a greater blood supply in the heavily exercised muscle by the development of additional new capillaries within the muscle. One experimental study reported this increase was about 45 per cent.[6]

During a strong, sustained muscular contraction the circulation is temporarily arrested. Within a short time, however, the limb volume begins to rise, indicating that while strong muscular contraction does compress the vessels, this compression is insufficient to prevent them from dilating to a certain extent under the influence of dilator substances released from the muscle fibers. Static contractions, such as standing at attention, weight training and gymnastics may thus hinder the venous return to the heart. During dynamic exercise the rhythmic contractions of the skeletal muscle exert a strong pumping action on the blood flow. During the periods of relaxation the veins of the muscle become filled with blood. During contraction the blood is squeezed out of the muscle. The presence of valves in the veins permits it to move only toward the heart. Immediate relaxation after strenuous exercise results in a removal of this pumping action and the venous return to the heart may become insufficient to maintain the cardiac output. If an athlete, after an exhausting race, relaxes and is carried in a vertical position by his teammates, the sudden stoppage of this pumping action may reduce the venous return.

MICROSTRUCTURE OF VERTEBRATE STRIATED MUSCLE

Organization of Muscle Fibers. A muscle fiber is an elongated cell enclosed in *sarcolemma,* a thin, structureless, selectively permeable membrane which adheres to an outer network of reticular fibers termed *endomysium.* The sarcolemma keeps adjacent fibers from merging into a single jelly-like mass, isolates them so that they can act as separate units, and mediates the passage of ions and molecules, admitting some and excluding others. Each muscle fiber may run for the entire length of the fleshy part of a muscle, and its endomysium becomes continuous with the other connective tissue sheaths. Within each muscle cell is a specialized but undifferentiated protoplasm termed *sarcoplasm.* This is a protein *sol* (a liquid solution of colloids) of relatively low viscosity.

Embedded within the sarcoplasm are *myofibrils,* semi-crystalline *gels* (firm solutions of colloids) in which the actual contractile activity takes place. It is here that metabolic energy is transformed into mechanical energy and potentially into work. Their basic unit is the *sarcomere.* These appear to be compartments lying between two Z (zeischenscheibe, or intervening) discs (Fig. 3–2) in which certain processes are believed to occur during contraction.[7] The Z discs themselves adhere to the sarcolemma, stabilize the structure and localize damage. When an electrode is applied to a Z disc, a contraction of the two adjacent half-sarcomeres results.[8]

Myofibrils run parallel to each other and to the long axis of the

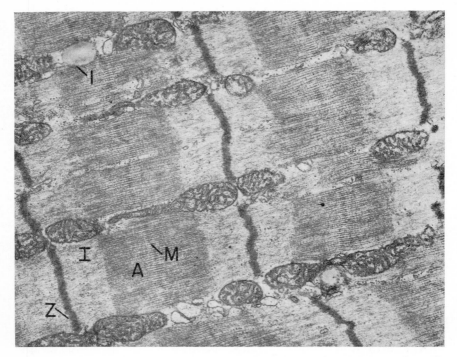

Fig. 3–2. Longitudinal section of a red fiber from a human vastus lateralis muscle as seen under the electron microscope at a magnification of 25,000 ×. The *A*, *I*, *Z*, and *M* bands are indicated. The mitochondria are mostly in pairs on either side of the *Z* discs. *l* is a lipid droplet. (From Shafiq, S. A., *et al.*, Anat. Rec., *156*:289, 1966.)

muscle fiber, merging into the sarcolemma at each end of the cell. Seen under polarized light, they consist of alternating anisotropic (light) and isotropic (dark) striations termed A bands and I bands (Fig. 3–2).   Under plain light or with different settings of the microscope this coloring is reversed.

The A bands contain thick, rough filaments composed primarily of myosin, each surrounded by six thin, smooth filaments composed primarily of actin. The H (after Hansen, who discovered them, or heller, meaning clear) zones, located in the center of the A bands, contain only thick filaments. The I bands contain only thin filaments, which extend into the A bands as far as the H zones (Figs. 3–3 and 3–4). When a muscle actively shortens, the Z discs are drawn in towards the A bands. No change occurs in the width of the A bands, but the I bands narrow. As a result the A bands come closer together. The H zone is obliterated in full contraction, but reappears as an area of lesser density when the length of the muscle

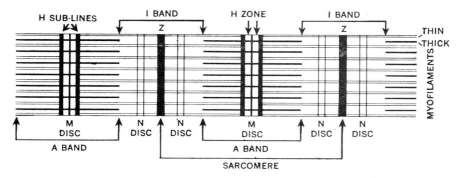

FIG. 3–3. Schematic representation of the myofibril from skeletal muscle.

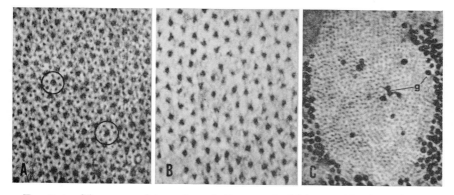

FIG. 3–4. Human quadriceps femoris tissue under high magnification. *A*, Cross section through an A band, showing both thick and thin myofilaments. It will be observed that six thin filaments appear to surround each thick filament. ($\times$ 130,000.) *B*, Cross section of an H zone. Only thick filaments are present. ($\times$ 130,000.) *C*, Cross section of an I band. Only thin filaments are present. ($\times$ 80,500.) g, Glycogen granules. (Prince, courtesy Amer. J. Med.)

increases. If the muscle goes into a state of rigor, forcible attempts to stretch it will result in a tearing of the filaments, usually in the I bands.[9]

There are projections on the myosin filaments termed *cross bridges* which are believed to furnish a mechanical linkage between the actin and myosin filaments. The sliding force required for muscle contraction is developed by direct physical contact between these cross bridges and the actin. When a muscle shortens the length of the filaments remains essentially constant, but the thin filaments, which extend from each end of a sarcomere, slide towards each other.

The M (mittelscheibe, or intermediate) disc is so-called to indicate its position in the middle of the sarcomere. Its function and that of the N (nebenscheibe, or next to) discs, is not understood. Perhaps this is because certain of these are seen only at a given stage in the contraction cycle.

Within the cell are units known as *mitochondria* (Fig. 3–5), often located opposite the I and Z bands. About 95 per cent of the *adenosine triphosphate* (ATP) which furnishes the energy necessary for contraction is produced in them and their main function is to provide this substance to the myofibril. For this reason they have been described as the "power plants" of the cells.

Surrounding the myofibrils is a complex network of two different types of tubules: The *T (transverse) system* and the *sarcoplasmic reticulum*. In most mammalian muscles the former are located near the end of the A bands. Apparently an excitation wave proceeds from the surface membrane into the center of the fiber along these tubules. The sarcoplasmic reticulum tubules are arranged parallel to the fibers and surround each fibril. Near the end of each sarcomere there is a terminal sac, each pair flanking a T system tubule. This tripartite structure is called a *triad*. These terminal sacs are thought to contain calcium ions. Depolarization releases these ions, initiating a contraction. Relaxation occurs when they are reaccumulated. Since the two systems do not appear to have direct connec-

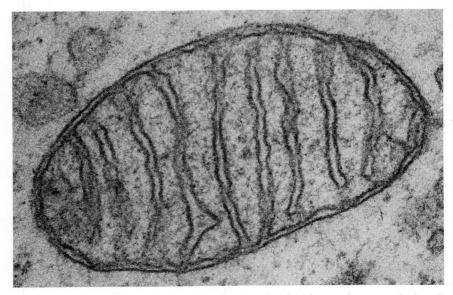

Fig. 3–5. Typical mitochondrion, showing the double membrane enclosing it and the septa which partially divide it into a series of compartments. (× 71,000.) (J. André, courtesy M. Steinert, Université Libre de Bruxelles.) The fact that mitochondria and bacteria have certain features in common suggests that they may have had common ancestors.

tions, it remains to be learned how depolarization of the T system produces the release of calcium ions from the sarcoplasmic reticulum.[10]

These constituents are summarized in Table 3–1. Physiologically and anatomically there is a great deal more to be learned about muscle contraction. In the words of Peachey, it seems that the concepts presently formulated at best "can be taken as a first approximation to the real mechanism."[11] Here the effort has been to give no more than an extremely brief description of the constituents most intimately concerned with the processes of muscular contraction.

Since the investigations of Morpurgo it has been believed that increases in hypertrophy resulted from increases in the cross-section of the muscle fibers and not from an increase in the number of muscle fibers. Recent studies[12] suggest that exercise may produce an increase in the number of myofibrils within the fibers and that disuse atrophy is associated with a loss of myofibrils, but confirmation of this claim will have to await further experimental evidence.

Components of Muscle. If muscle were a relatively simple mechanism like a spring, there would be a direct relationship between the tension it could develop at different lengths and the amount of work it could accomplish. Actually it appears to be composed of three independent elements: a *contractile component,* a *series elastic component,* and a *parallel elastic component.* The contractile component actively develops tension and shortening. This is transmitted to the muscle tendon through the series elastic component. In part this may lie in the tendinous filaments into which the

TABLE 3–1. Constituents and Function of Some Major Muscle Cellular Compartments

Compartment	*Pertinent Biochemical Constituents*	*Function*
Sarcoplasm	Enzymes	Glycolysis
Mitochondria	Enzymes of oxidation and phosphorylation	Steady-state aerobic activity or recovery from oxygen debt
Fibrils	Actin and myosin	Contraction
Sarcotubular system	Concentration and release of calcium ions	On-and-off control of active state
Membrane	Lipoprotein structure with variable selective permeability for ions	Excitation and impulse conduction

(After Pearson *et al.,* Ann. Int. Med., *67*:615, 1967.)

muscle fibers insert; in part it may lie in the Z discs. Its function appears to be to protect the muscle against possibly injurious consequences of too rapid changes in tension. The parallel elastic component is believed to come into action only when the muscle is stretched. It is thought to be largely connective tissue and to bear the resting tension of a muscle. At the present time this structure is poorly understood. Because of these elastic components and the elasticity inherent in mechanical ergometer systems, the work measured externally in careful laboratory experiments may not be exactly the same as the work done in the muscle by the contractile component.

Comparative Sizes of Structures. Whole muscle fibers are from 10 to 100 microns in diameter (1 micron equals 1/1000 of a millimeter). Myofibrils range from .5 to 2 microns in diameter. The diameter of the thick myosin filament is about .01 micron; that of the thin actin filament is about .005 micron.

INNERVATION OF MUSCLE

Not only are the muscles penetrated and served by the vessels of the circulatory system, but they are also well supplied with nerves. One or more nerves containing both motor and sensory fibers enter each muscle from the central nervous system. Such nerves contain a large number of motor axons, each of which is thought to serve a single fasciculus. At the fasciculus the nerve divides into a number of twigs (Fig. 3–6) each of which has its *end-plate* embedded into a single muscle fiber, providing it with direct communication with the central nervous system. The number of muscle fibers innervated by a single motor nerve fiber varies from three to several hundred. Under normal conditions the group of muscle fibers innervated by a single nerve fiber contracts as a single *muscle unit.*

A nerve cell, its axon with its various branches, and the muscle fibers served, are known as a *motor unit.* The motor unit may be considered the fundamental functional unit of neuromuscular contraction. The sarcolemma serves as a container for the muscle fiber and aids in preventing the stimulating effect of a nerve impulse from spreading from one muscle fiber to its neighbors, although there is evidence that when there is a massive stimulation of one muscle it may irradiate other muscles.[13] Estimates have been made of the number of muscle fibers and motor units in human muscles.[14] Some typical examples are given in Table 3–2.

Not only does the number of motor units in different muscles vary greatly, but the average tension in tetanic contraction developed by the motor units of one muscle may differ greatly from that of an-

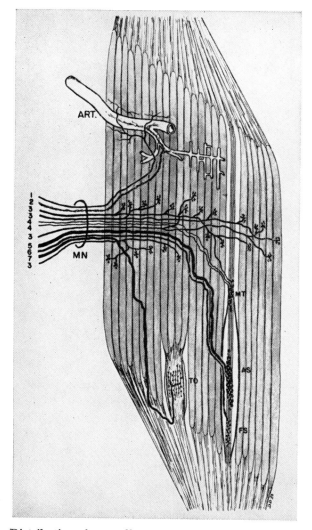

Fig. 3–6. Distribution of nerve fibers to a striated muscle. The muscular nerve (MN) contains approximately 50 per cent of fibers derived from the anterior roots. Of these the medium-sized fibers (3,3,3) are distributed to motor end-plates, and the small fibers (4,4) to the end-plates of muscle spindles. Of fibers derived from the sensory nerve roots the largest (5,6,7) are distributed to muscle spindles (to the annulo-spiral ending, AS, and the flower-spray ending, FS) and to tendon organs (TO). Small sensory fibers (1), often non-medullated in their peripheral part, are distributed in the connective tissue surrounding blood vessels. Fibers derived from the sympathetic nervous system (2) are distributed to the muscular coats of arterioles and the smaller arteries. (Adams, Denny-Brown and Pearson, *Diseases of Muscle,* courtesy of Paul B. Hoeber, Inc., 1954.)

TABLE 3–2.   Estimated Number of Muscle Fibers and
Motor Units in Human Muscles

Muscle	Mean Diameter of Muscle Fibers (Microns)	No. of Muscle Fibers	No. of Large Nerve Fibers	Calculated No. of Motor Units	No. of Fibers per Motor Unit
Platysma	19.8 ± 0.3	27,100	1,826	1,096	25
Brachioradialis	34.0 ± 0.8	129,200	525	315	410
Tibialis anterior	56.7 ± 0.2	250,000	742	445	657
Gastrocnemius, medial head	54.1 ± 1.2	1,120,000	965	579	1,934

TABLE 3–3   Motor Units and Muscular Tension in the Cat

Muscle	Number of Motor Units (Estimated)	Average Tension (in Grams)
Soleus	250	9.9
Extensor digitorum	330	8.6
Gastrocnemius—medial head . . .	430	30.1
Semitendinosus	630	5.5

other. A study has been made of the number of motor units and the tension which may be exerted by the muscles of the cat.[15] Some typical examples are shown in Table 3–3. Since about 30 per cent of the nerve fibers are gamma (γ) efferents which do not add to the tension of muscular contraction, it has been argued that the values for motor unit tension should be increased accordingly.[16] The gamma system, proprioception, and other sensorimotor phenomena are discussed in more detail in Chapter 5.

In the case of the thumb, where not only strength but the ability to do delicate and accurate work is required, each motor unit is composed of relatively few muscle fibers. Because of this structure, forces exerted by the thumb can be changed by relatively small increments as compared with the heavy postural muscles. The smallest motor units are to be found in the muscles which control movements of the eye, where great precision is required.

ROLES IN WHICH MUSCLES MAY ACT

A muscle can do only two things: develop tension within itself or relax. The size, shape, and number of fibers of a muscle, the type of joint traversed, the nature of the tendinous or fleshy origin and insertion, the angle and place of insertion, the mechanical advantage of the bone-muscle levers, and other factors may affect its actions. In addition, muscles may function singly or as members of a team in various combinations and patterns of movement. The various roles which a muscle may play are designated by technical terms, some of which will be defined in the following section. Unfortunately, these terms have been given varying connotations in different fields, and in some cases the usage has changed with the passage of time. Any teacher or author is forced to employ these definitions with a certain amount of arbitrariness, and students who consult a variety of textbooks must determine carefully which definitions are accepted by particular authors.

The Role of MOVER or AGONIST. If a muscle contracts concentrically it is said to be a *mover* or *agonist* for the joint actions which result. For example, the movers for elbow extension are the triceps brachii. Some muscles are movers for more than one action in a given joint; many may have single or multiple actions on each of two or more joints which they happen to traverse. The biceps brachii, for instance, is a mover for both elbow flexion and radioulnar supination, and in addition it is a mover for several shoulder joint actions, because of its two-headed origin on the scapula. It is an axiom that a muscle, when it contracts, tends to perform all the actions for which it is a mover, although some or all of these actions may be prevented from occurring, in specific situations, by contraction of other muscles, or by some external force, such as gravity.

The Role of PRIME MOVER and of ASSISTANT MOVER. Movers are often subclassified as *prime movers* or as *assistant* or *secondary movers* for a given joint action. A *prime mover* is a muscle primarily responsible for causing a specified joint action. An *assistant mover* is a muscle which aids the prime mover to effect joint action. In borderline cases, writers often disagree in distinguishing between prime and assistant movers. In this text, an attempt has been made to conform to the most general usage, but it has sometimes been necessary to be arbitrary.

The term *emergency muscle* may be used to designate an assistant mover which is called into action only when an exceptional amount of total force is needed. The long head of the biceps brachii, for example, is not often called into action when performing shoulder joint abduction, but it may assist that action in times of great need, and some therapists claim to have taught patients to abduct the shoulder joint by contraction of the long head after polio has paralyzed the deltoid and supraspinatus.[17]

Some writers have stated that every muscle must have at least one prime mover function. This rule appeals to one's sense of orderliness, but does not appear to have a clear biological basis. The subclavius, for example, does not appear to be able to do any joint action very well, and it is usually listed only as an assistant mover for shoulder girdle depression. (See discussion of subclavius on pp. 196–197.)

Most two-joint and multijoint muscles are listed as prime movers for action at their most distal joints, but this is not a hard-and-fast law. The actions of the biceps brachii, the flexor digitorum profundus, and the gastrocnemius, for instance, conform to this rule, but the actions of the hamstring muscles do not.

The Role of ANTAGONIST. An antagonist is a muscle whose contraction tends to produce a joint action exactly opposite to some given joint action of another specified muscle. An extensor muscle is antagonistic, potentially, to a flexor muscle. Thus, the biceps brachii is an antagonist of the triceps brachii with respect to elbow extension, and to the pronator teres with respect to radio-ulnar pronation. The biceps is not an antagonist of the brachialis, because it cannot oppose any motion for which the brachialis is a mover.

The Role of FIXATOR or STABILIZER. A *fixator* or *stabilizer* is a muscle which anchors, steadies, or supports a bone or body part in order that another active muscle may have a firm base upon which to pull. If a person reaches forward to pull open a resistant door, he must stabilize his body parts if he is to overcome the resistance. To open the door, elbow flexion may be needed, and if the scapula (for example) is not stabilized, the contraction of the biceps may cause a pulling forward of the shoulder girdle rather than an opening of the door. When a muscle contracts, it tends to pull both of its ends toward its center, with equal force. Typically a person is desirous of causing motion only at one end of the muscle. Therefore, he attempts to stabilize the bone to which the opposite end of the muscle is attached.

In the ideal case, a fixator or stabilizer muscle will be in static contraction. In practice, these terms are extended to include instances in which there is a slight motion in the "stabilized" part, so as to continuously adjust the stabilization to the requirements of the desired motion—this condition may be called "moving fixation" or a "guiding action."

A good example of fixation or stabilization occurs in the floor pushup exercise. The abdominal muscles contract statically during pushups, so as to prevent an undesirable sagging of the body in the hip and trunk region. In this example, the fixation is necessary not so much to provide a firm base for the action of other muscles as to counteract the action of gravity upon the hip and spine joints.

Turning to another example, the static contraction of the neck extensors may be cited as a fixation of the cervical spine in order to provide a firm base for the action of the sternocleidomastoid muscles on the anterior surface of the neck, so that the latter can assist in lifting the rib cage during forced breathing after running a race. Without such fixation, the head may curl forward on the chest, interfering with deep breathing.

The Role of SYNERGIST. The term *synergist* has been used with so many different connotations, both historically and in contemporary works, that its meaning has become very generalized, if not actually ambiguous. Some writers define *synergist* as a muscle which acts along with some other muscle or muscles as a part of a team; others use the term in a more restricted sense, but there is little agreement among these viewpoints.

Wright[18] identified two specific kinds of synergy: *helping synergy* and *true synergy*. In this usage, synergy in general is defined as a counteracting of undesired side action, or secondary action, on the part of active muscles. *Helping synergy* occurs during the action of two muscles, both of which have a common joint action and each of which have a second action which is antagonistic to that of the other. As both of these muscles contract simultaneously, they act together to produce the desired common action, and they act as helping synergists to each other as they counteract or neutralize each other's undesired secondary action. An example occurs in the sit-up exercise from supine lying position. Several abdominal muscles cooperate in producing spine flexion in this exercise, but we may for the moment consider only the right and left external oblique abdominal muscles. Both of these muscles cooperate in flexing the spine, since each is a prime mover for this action. But the right external oblique is also a prime mover for right lateral spine flexion and for left spine rotation, while the left external oblique is a prime mover for left lateral spine flexion and for right spine rotation. The lateral flexion and the rotation tendencies, in opposite directions, are mutually counteracted, ruled out, or neutralized, and the resultant motion is pure spine flexion.

True synergy occurs when one muscle contracts statically to prevent any action in one of the joints traversed by a contracting two-joint or multi-joint muscle. According to the axiom that a muscle tends to perform all of its possible actions when it contracts, a two-joint muscle will tend to cause movement at every joint which it crosses. Sometimes, however, a two-joint muscle must contract for the purpose of performing its actions at only one of the joints, and in this instance another muscle must contract in order to prevent an undesired action from occurring at the other joint. For example, when the fist is clenched, the extensors of the wrist act as true synergists. If the wrist were not held extended, then the long flexors of the fingers would produce wrist flexion as well as finger flexion. Now, flexion of the wrist added to flexion of the fingers stretches the tendons of the long finger extensors until they can yield no more, at which point continued wrist flexion causes the fingers to open out and the grip to slacken. This is the explanation of the success of the trick of compelling an opponent to drop a weapon from his hand by forcibly flexing his wirst.

The Role of NEUTRALIZER. A *neutralizer* is a muscle which contracts in order to counteract, "rule out," or neutralize an undesired action of another contracting muscle. Thus, the term "neutralizer" is a synonym for describing the role played by a helping synergist or a true synergist as defined in the preceding section. As a technical term, it has the distinct advantage of avoiding the several different meanings which have been attached to the general term "synergist" by various authors and teachers.

Tonus and Relaxation. The term "relaxation" may refer to the *process* of relaxing (the stage during which the force of contraction is diminishing) or to the *state* of inactivity or the absence of any contraction. But even a relaxed muscle has a residual low-level turgor or feeling of firmness. At the lowest levels, this is known as *tonus* or *muscle tone*. It has been suggested that muscular tone is a function of the natural fullness (turgor) of the muscular and fibrous tissue and of the response of the nervous system to stimuli.[19,20]

Muscles that are much used are apt to have more tone than those used less. When the tone in two antagonists is different, the segments upon which they act may deviate from their normal position. This is the cause of one type of postural defect.

The fact that muscle groups can be made to develop increased tonus and certain muscles can be shortened by exercise within a limited range of movement is used in some phases of corrective physical education. Through such procedure certain muscles of the dorsal aspect of the shoulder girdle may be shortened and their tonus increased, adducting the scapula, with resultant stretching and temporary change of tone of certain antagonistic muscles of the ventral aspect. This will result in a shifting of the relative position of the shoulders, causing them to be pulled back more than heretofore. Still another factor to be considered in this connection is that when a muscle is habitually held in a shortened position and is used, in time the muscle will shorten and accommodate itself to the new length with the restoration of normal tonus; the joint affected will then have a new resting position. This implies, of course, that the antagonistic muscle group will be correspondingly stretched, and that it will also accommodate itself to the new length and re-establish its normal tone. This readjustment is a common experience of children who wear shoes in winter, go barefoot in the summer months and then revert to the wearing of shoes upon the advent of cold weather. When footwear is discarded, the soleus and gastrocnemius are stretched and the antagonistic muscles shorten. When shoes are again worn, the reverse process occurs.

Residual Tension. Since the term tonus is usually reserved for minimal contractile states which can be reduced only by severing the motor nerves, any persistent involuntary contraction above this level may be called *residual tension*. Residual tension varies with the degree of general or local alertness generated under conditions of attention, interest, alarm, fear, excitement, or worry.

SPURT AND SHUNT MUSCLES

Mathematical analysis led MacConaill to conclude that skeletal muscles act as "spurt" or "shunt" muscles. Spurt muscles have their origin at a distance from the joints on which they act and are inserted near them. They direct the greater part of their force across the bone rather than along it and provide the force which acts along the tangent to the curve transversed by the bone during movement. Shunt muscles have their origin near the joints on which they act and their insertions at a distance from them, so that the greater part of their contractile force is directed along the bones. This tends to pull the joints together, so that these muscles are largely stabilizers, but they provide the increase in centripetal force required in rapid or resisted movements. The pronator quadratus, for example, a spurt muscle, is the prime mover in pronation of the forearm; when rapid or resisted action is involved the pronator teres, a shunt muscle, is called in to assist.

When a muscle acts on two joints, it is chiefly a shunt muscle to one and a spurt to the other. Thus the biceps is a shunt muscle for the shoulder joint and a spurt muscle for the elbow joint. In some cases the role of the muscle may be interchanged when the direction of contraction is reversed. Some muscles may combine both types; for instance, the posterior fibers of the adductor magnus are shunt muscles and the anterior fibers are spurt muscles.[21]

KINDS OF MUSCULAR CONTRACTION

To the kinesiologist the term *contraction* refers to the development of tension within a muscle. It does not necessarily imply that any visible shortening of the muscle takes place.

Static or Isometric Contraction.   When a muscle develops tension which is insufficient to move a body part against a given resistance, and the length of the muscle remains unchanged, the contraction is said to be *static* or *isometric*.   (See p. 85.)

Concentric Contraction.   When a muscle develops tension sufficient to overcome a resistance, so that the muscle visibly shortens and moves a body part in spite of a given resistance, it is said to be in *concentric* contraction.   For example, the biceps brachii muscle contracts concentrically when a glass of water is lifted from a table toward the mouth.   In this case, the resistance is the combined weight of the forearm, the glass, and the water, and the source of resistance is the force of gravity.

Eccentric Contraction.   When a given resistance overcomes the muscle tension so that the muscle actually lengthens, the muscle is said to be in *eccentric* contraction.   Although developing tension (contracting), the muscle is overpowered by the resistance.   For example, when a glass of water is returned from the mouth to the table, the biceps brachii muscle contracts eccentrically.   Actually, of course, muscular contraction is not essential in this instance.   If the muscles were simply relaxed, gravity would extend the elbow joint and lower the glass, albeit with unwanted and disastrous consequences.   Still another way of getting the glass to the table would be to contract the triceps brachii muscle concentrically, thus adding to gravitational force and extending the elbow with great vigor.   Such an action might be appropriate in driving nails with a hammer, but not in the example cited.

Both concentric and eccentric contraction are known to physiologists as *isotonic* contraction.

The identification of eccentric contraction is a persistent and crucial problem in exercise analysis.   In performing floor pushups, it is clear that the up-phase involves elbow extension and shoulder girdle abduction.   The resistance is gravitational force: the weight of the body, which tends to flex the elbow and adduct the shoulder girdle.   Therefore, the elbow extensors and the shoulder girdle abductors must contract concentrically, overcoming the force of gravity, to perform the movement.   When analyzing the down-phase of pushups, beginning students do not always find the problem so simple.   It is easy to see that elbow flexion and shoulder girdle adduction takes place, and it is tempting to believe that the elbow flexors and shoulder girdle adductors are contracting concentrically.   Such is not the case.   Gravity is quite sufficient to energize the movement; if muscle force were added to it, the body would hit the floor hard enough to cause injury.   Instead, the elbow extensors and the shoulder girdle abductors must develop enough tension to modify the gravitational force and lower the body to the floor at a reasonable speed. In doing pushups, the same muscles act throughout the exercise, contracting concentrically on the up-phase, statically during momentary held position between phases, and eccentrically during the down-phase.

During World War II, a writer not professionally trained in physical education advocated the following exercise for conditioning the abdominal muscles: From a position of standing with arms raised overhead, bend forward downward and touch the toes on count 1; return to starting position on count 2. The abdominal muscles may receive some passive squeezing during this exercise, but it is obvious that the spinal extensors are the active muscles, contracting eccentrically on the way down and concentrically on the way up. The abdominal muscles remain relaxed during both motions.

In exercise analysis it is always necessary to consider the external forces which may be operative. The most important of these is gravity, but it is by no means the only one. In sports and work, there are countless other forces acting in various directions, which must be considered. Muscular forces exerted by opponents in such contact sports as football and wrestling; the force of moving objects such as balls and other sports implements; the force of waves, tides, and currents in swimming—all these must be carefully evaluated in the analysis of muscular action of bodily movement.

KINDS OF GROSS BODY MOVEMENT

Preceding sections on Roles in Which Muscles May Act, and on Kinds of Muscular Contraction, may now be generalized further by means of a classification of Kinds of Gross Body Movement. This classification provides a necessary starting point for any formal analysis of coordinated movement (see Chapter 18), since the categories typify unitary movements such as lifting, batting, holding a "scale" on the balance beam, performing elemental dance movements, etc. More complex sequential movements, such as serving a tennis ball or fielding a bounding ball and throwing to first base, must be broken down into phases before an orderly analysis can be delineated.

1. **Sustained Force Movement** (SF). Sustained force movements may be fast or slow, strong or weak. Sustained force is applied against a resistance by contracting mover muscles, or agonists, while their antagonists are relaxed (reciprocal relaxation). If a weight is to be lifted, for example, the agonists contract concentrically and overcome the resistance (SF+). If a weight is to be lowered, the resistance overcomes the force of the agonists as they

contract eccentrically (SF—). Holding a weight stationary requires that the sustaining force be equal to the resistance (SFO). Other examples of SF movement are: an armstroke in swimming; initial leg thrust in a sprint start; forcing a wrestling hold; pressing up to a handstand; sustaining a slow body extension in contemporary dance.

2. **Passive Movement** (**PAS**). Any body movement, however originated, that takes place without continuing muscle contraction can be categorized as passive. Three major subdivisions of passive movement may be identified.

2A. *Manipulation* (*MAN*). The motive force for manipulation is another person, or an outside force other than gravity. Examples: being lifted or swung, while relaxing, by a partner in ballet dancing or skating; unresisted limb movements performed by a therapist on a completely relaxed patient; body movement resulting from unresisted collision. Therapists distinguish passive or manipulative exercise from *assistive* and *resistive exercise,* in which the patient is active and the therapist either assists or resists the movement.

2B. *Inertial Movement* (*INER*), *or "Coasting."* Inertial movement is a continuation of a pre-established movement, with no concurrent motive muscular contraction. For convenience and practicality, inertial movement is considered to include frictional influences—air resistance, tissue viscosity, residual tension in ligaments and stretched muscles, and other deceleratory elements. Examples: the glide phase of the elementary breaststroke in swimming; sliding into a base; the horizontal component of the free flight of a jump or racing dive. Although a football fullback, plunging through the line, attempts to use sustained force by continuing to drive with his legs, he also depends strongly upon the inertial movement resulting from his previously established momentum.

2C. *Gravitational Movement* (*GRAV*), *or Falling.* Actually, this is a special case of manipulative movement, but it is given special consideration because it results from acceleratory force which is constant in direction and magnitude, in all practical terrestrial problems. Examples: free fall; the vertical component of the free flight of a jump; relaxed pendulum movements of limbs in contemporary dance or of the whole body in gymnastic stunts.

3. **Ballistic Movement** (**BAL**). Ballistic movement is a compound movement. The first phase is a sustained force movement (SF+), with body parts accelerated by concentric contraction of agonists, unhindered by contraction of antagonists. The second phase is an inertial, or coasting, movement (INER), without muscular contraction. The final phase is a deceleration resulting from eccentric contraction of antagonists (SF—) and/or from passive resistance

offered by ligaments and stretched muscles. The three phases overlap only at the transition stages, where one kind of movement blends smoothly into the next. Examples: batting a baseball; smashing a badminton bird; stroking a tennis ball; many typical movements of vigorous sports.

4. **Guided Movement (GUI) or "Tracking."** Where great accuracy and steadiness but not force or speed are required, the muscles antagonistic to the movement as well as the principal movers are active. In attempting to hold some instrument as steady as possible, both members of a pair of antagonistic muscle groups contract together. Exact balance is difficult to achieve. When errors appear as alternate domination of antagonistic pairs, *tremor* occurs. The absence of these errors is a measure of *steadiness*. Steadiness may be required in guided movement, as well as in stationary holding. The dominance of one muscle group, the mover, then exceeds the force of the other, the antagonist—the difference being roughly proportional to the speed and force of the total movement. Examples of guided movement are writing; repairing a watch; threading a needle; lifting a very full cup of hot coffee; and even such skills as dart throwing for accuracy over a short distance. In addition to the guiding, dragging, controlling contraction of antagonists in these movements, a number of other muscles may act in graded contraction, constantly or intermittently, for the sole purpose of preventing deviations of the movement from the desired path. Probably these guiding muscles also act sometimes simultaneously in antagonistic pairs, and sometimes in alternation. The existence or timing of these contractions is almost impossible to predict, for they result primarily as feedback from error signals.

5. **Dynamic Balance Movement (DB).** Muscle spindles detect deviations from a desired position of balance, and initiate a servo-control system to make corrections. The result is a series of irregular oscillations, precisely mediated by reflex contraction of appropriate muscle groups, in order to maintain the balanced position. Example: erect "stationary" standing. Chapter 5 details the sensori-motor systems involved.

6. **Oscillating Movement (OSC).** The movement is rapidly reversed at the end of each short excursion, with co-contracting antagonistic muscle groups alternating in dominance. Examples: tapping; shaking an object. The maximum possible speed of such alternating movement is highly subject to motor learning, and is also dependent upon the weight or inertia of the moving parts and upon the strength of the active muscles.

The following "maximum rhythms" have been established for movements of the various segments of the upper extremity:

Shoulder	5–6	Movements per second
Elbow	8–9	Movements per second
Forearm	3–4	Flexions per second
Wrist	10–11	Movements per second
Fingers	8–9	Strokes per second[22]

Flexions are said to be faster than extensions.[23] There appears to be little correlation between power and velocity of movement and various anthropometric measurements.[24,25] The validity of the hypothesis that speed of muscular contraction is conditioned by a general factor has not been clearly demonstrated, but recent studies[26] have tended to support it. The maximum rate of high speed movement may depend upon some intrinsic physiological property of the reflex circuit. Maximum velocity is presumably limited not by the properties of muscle itself but by the necessity that the agonists relax in order to permit the antagonists to halt the movement. The limiting factor may be the speed with which excitation and inhibition can be made to alternate in the central nervous system.

References

1. Ruch, Theodore C. and Patton, Harry D.: *Physiology and Biophysics.* 19th edition. Philadelphia: W. B. Saunders Co., 1965, p. 125.

2. Blanton, Patricia L. and Biggs, Norman L.: Ultimate Tensile Strength of Fetal and Adult Human Tendons. J. Biomech., *3*,181–189, 1970.

3. Goldberg, Alfred L.: Protein Synthesis in Tonic and Phasic Skeletal Muscle. Nature, *216*, 1219–1220, 1968.

4. Asmussen, Erling: Some Physiological Aspects of Work and Sport. Proc. Roy. Soc. Med., Symposium 11, The Meaning of Physical Fitness, *62*, 1160–1163, 1969.

5. Guth, Lloyd: "Trophic" Influences of Nerve on Muscle. Physiol. Rev., *48*, 645–687, 1968.

6. Jokl, E.: Petren on the Effect of Growth and Training on the Capillarisation of the Central Nervous System. Res. Quart., *17*, 127–131, 1946.

7. Garamvölgyi, N., *et al.*: The Z- and M-Formations of Striated Muscle. Acta Physiol. Acad. Sci. Hung., XXII, 223–233, 1962.

8. Johns, Richard J.: The Electrical and Mechanical Events of Neuromuscular Transmission. Amer. J. Med., *35*, 611–621, 1963.

9. Bendall, J. R.: *Muscles, Molecules and Movement.* New York: American Elsevier Publishing Co., 1969, p. 20.

10. Page, Sally: Structure of the Sarcoplasmic Reticulum in Vertebrate Muscles. Brit. Med. Bul., *24*, 170–173, 1968.

11. Peachey, Lee D.: Muscle. In Hall, Victor E., Editor: *Annual Review of Physiology, 30*:401. Palo Alto: Annual Reviews, Inc., 1968.

12. Van Linge, B.: The Response of Muscle to Strenuous Exercise. J. Bone Joint Surg., *44-B*, 711–721, 1962; Holmes, Richard and Rasch, Philip J.: Effect of Exercise on Number of Myofibrils per Fiber in Sartorius Muscle of the Rat. Amer. J. Physiol., *195*, 50–52, 1958.

13. Panin, Nicholas, *et al.*: An Electromyographic Evaluation of the "Cross Exercise" Effect. Arch. Phys. Med., *42*, 47–52, 1961.

14. Feinstein, Bertram, *et. al.*: Morphologic Studies of Motor Units in Normal Muscles. Acta Anat., *23*, 127–142, 1955.

15. Eccles, J. C. and Sherrington, Charles S.: Numbers and Contraction Values of Individual Motor-Units Examined in Some Muscles of the Limb. Proc. Roy. Soc. Med. B., *106*, 326–356, 1950.

16. Ruch and Patton: *op. cit.*, p. 132.

17. Brunnstrom, Signe: Comparative Strengths of Muscles with Similar Functions. Phys. Ther. Rev., *26*, 59–65, 1946.

18. Wright, Wilhelmine G.: *Muscle Function.* New York: Hafner Publishing Co., Reprinted 1962, pp. 6–7.

19. Ralston, H. J. and Libet, B.: The Question of Tonus in Skeletal Muscle. Amer. J. Phys. Med., *32*, 85–92, 1953.

20. Basmajian, J. V.: *Muscles Alive. Their Functions Revealed by Electromyography*, 2nd Ed. Baltimore: The Williams & Wilkins Co., 1967, pp. 71–74.

21. MacConaill, M. A.: Spurt and Shunt Muscles. Some Minimal Principles Applicable in Myomechanics. Bio-Med. Engr., *1*, 498–503, 1966.

22. Amar, Jules: *The Human Motor.* New York: E. P. Dutton & Company, 1920, pp. 129–131.

23. Glanville, A. D. and Kreezer, G.: The Maximum Amplitude and Velocity of Joint Movements in Normal Male Adults. Human Biol., *9*, 197–211, 1937.

24. Rasch, Philip J.: Relationship of Arm Strength, Weight, and Length to Speed of Arm Movement. Res. Quart., *25*, 328–332, 1954.

25. Henry, F. M. and Whitley, J. D.: Relationships between Individual Differences in Strength, Speed, and Mass in Arm Movement. Res. Quart., *31*, 24–33, 1960.

26. Pierson, William R. and Rasch, Philip J.: The Generality of a Speed Factor in Simple Reaction and Movement Time. Percept. Mot. Skills, *11*, 123–128, 1960.

Recommended Reading

27. Rodahl, Kaare and Horvath, Steven M., editors: *Muscle as a Tissue.* New York: McGraw-Hill Book Co., Inc., 1962.

28. Huxley, H. E.: The Structural Basis of Muscular Contraction. Proc. Roy. Soc. Lond., B178, 131–149, 1971.

29. Bourne, G. H., editor: *The Structure and Function of Muscle*, Vols. I and II. New York: Academic Press, Inc., reprinted 1965.

30. Rasch, Philip J.: Some Aspects of Muscular Movement: A Review. Amer. Correct. Ther. J., *23*, 151–153, 1969.

31. Stern, Jack T., Jr.: Investigations Concerning the Theory of 'Spurt' and 'Shunt' Muscles. J. Biomech., *4*, 437–453, 1971.

32. Huxley, A. H. and Simmons, R. M.: Proposed Mechanism of Force Generation in Striated Muscle. Science, *233*, 533–538, 1971.

Chapter 4

The Physiology of Muscular Contraction

The only function of nerve fibers is to conduct impulses. Any analysis of how they do this involves both chemical and electrical considerations.

Propagation of Neural Impulses. The membranes of all living cells have one characteristic in common: the ability to separate charged ions. Under resting conditions the concentration of sodium (Na) ions in the fluid outside of the living cell is 10 to 20 times as high as that in the fluid on the inside. The opposite is true for potassium (K). The electrical potential outside the cell is positive and that inside the cell is negative. Nachmansohn and his co-workers[1] have hypothesized that acetylcholine (ACh) is stored in the nerve fibers in an inactive form. When released by an environmental change (stimulus), it triggers a transient local change in the ionic permeability of the cellular membrane. Na ions flow inward; K ions slightly later and more slowly flow outward. This is known as *depolarization*. For a brief period the interior of the cell becomes positively and the exterior of the cell negatively charged. These changes in the ionic concentration gradients generate small bio-electric currents called *action potentials* (Fig. 4–1). It is thought that the influx of sodium is responsible for the rising action, and that the efflux of potassium takes place during the descending limb of the *spike*, which lasts approximately 0.5 second and attains an amplitude of approximately 130 mv. The spike is followed by the *negative after-potential*, which lasts 12 to 80 milliseconds, and the *positive after-potential*, which may last from 40 milliseconds to 1 second. The origin of these after-potentials is not clear, but they appear to reflect the metabolic process associated with recovery. An action potential stimulates the adjacent area in the neuron into the same process. In this way the length of the membrane is successively activated and the electrical impulse is propagated along the axon,

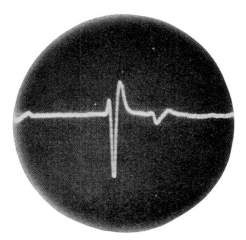

FIG. 4–1. Normal Motor Unit wave, showing large characteristic negative phase both preceded and followed by smaller positive phases. (Meditron Co.)

its velocity and duration being determined by the properties of the type of nerve fiber involved.

Within a millisecond or less the ACh is inactivated by hydrolysis and the permeability barrier is restored. During rest the initial electrolytic distribution is restored and the nerve becomes ready to respond to the next stimulus.

Neuromuscular Transmission. At rest there is a continual discharge of minute *end plate potentials* (e.p.p.) at the motor nerve ending, believed due to a spontaneous random discharge of quanta of ACh from globular bodies called *vesicles*. Depolarization of chemosensitive areas of the nerve terminal by a neural impulse appears to release relatively large quantities of ACh. This produces a prolonged negative discharge perhaps a hundred times the size of the resting e.p.p. This in turn propagates the muscle action potential. The excitatory event is believed to be transferred from the cell membrane to the fibrils by means of the *sacrotubular* structures found on either side of the Z lines. The link between depolarization of the membrane by the action potential and the contraction of the I bands may be the release of calcium ions at the level of the Z lines.[2] This may establish the active state by offsetting the Marsh-Bendall factor (see p. 76) and by activating the actomyosin.[3,4] Direct spread of electrical impulses from the nerve to the muscles has yet to be demonstrated experimentally. Dun,[5] in fact, has reported obtaining perfect neuromuscular transmission without the fiber action of ACh. Discussions of these problems are highly technical and fall outside the scope of this text.

Muscle Fiber Action Potential. Activity in a nerve fiber may set off an action potential in a muscle fiber. Starting at a neuromuscular junction, this passes over and depolarizes a muscle fiber, thus causing it to contract. In mammalian muscle conduction velocity is about 5 m. per sec. The duration of action potentials in persons twenty to forty years of age shows no significant differences between individuals or sexes, but becomes prolonged with age or low muscle temperature, thus leading to an increased reflex time.

Contraction passes down the muscle fiber like a wave emanating from the point of stimulation. From the arrival of the electrical stimulation at the muscle until the start of the development of tension in the fibers there is a *latency-relaxation period* of about 3.0 msec. During this time the muscle actually relaxes. This delay between stimulus and contraction may be due to molecular rearrangements required for the release of chemical energy necessary for contraction, although recent studies have indicated that the chemical reactions may be well advanced before any detectable shortening begins.[6] The loss of tension at higher speeds is believed to be related to the rate at which chemical energy is made available, and not the viscous resistance of the muscle.

Oxidation and Muscular Work. Ultimately, all of the energy for muscular work is derived from the oxidation of foodstuffs, in particular carbohydrate and fat. During work oxygen intake increases proportionately to the severity of exercise, and may continue at a raised level long after the work ceases. When the energy expenditure is sufficiently low that the circulorespiratory system can immediately supply the muscle cells with all the oxygen they need, the work is said to be *aerobic*. When the demands for oxidation exceed the immediate capabilities of these systems, the work is termed *anaerobic*. In anaerobic work, the additional energy is derived from the breakdown of various energy-rich substances stored in the body, as long as these last. Eventually these substances must be resynthesized and replaced by means of oxidative reactions; therefore, their temporary use creates an *oxygen deficit* or *oxygen debt* which must be repaid after exercise. Quantitatively, oxygen debt is the difference between the total energy expenditure of the work and the amount of that energy supplied during the work by oxidative reactions on a "pay-as-you-go basis."

Metabolic Energy and Muscular Work. When exercise begins, there is a time lag before the major oxidative and anaerobic reactions can become established. Although the exact sequence of events in muscular contraction is still under investigation, probably actin and myosin, the two proteins of the filaments of the myofibrils, combine to form actomyosin as tension develops. This requires an immediate source of anaerobic energy. The only direct source of energy for contraction comes from local stores of *adenosine triphosphate* (ATP) as it is hydrolyzed by breaking one of its high-energy bonds to yield *adenosine diphosphate* (ADP) and phosphoric acid:

$$ATP + H_2O \rightarrow ADP + H_3PO_4 + \text{energy for contraction.}$$

Actomyosin is the enzyme required to catalyze this reaction; thus, the contractile protein catalyzes its own energy-supply reaction.

Only a small amount of ATP is stored in muscle, and it must be continually regenerated and re-used if exercise is to continue. Energy from elsewhere is required. In vertebrates, a secondary energy supply in larger quantity is available from local stores of *creatine phosphate* (CP), which yields its high-energy phosphate radical in order to regenerate ATP from ADP, leaving creatine (C):

$$CP + ADP \rightarrow ATP + C.$$

If these simultaneous reactions are listed and "summed," the supply of ATP remains virtually constant, although ATP is being used continuously to provide energy for contraction:

$$ATP + H_2O \rightarrow ADP + H_3PO_4 + \text{energy for contraction}$$
$$\underline{CP + ADP \rightarrow ATP + C}$$
$$\text{Net result: } CP + H_2O \rightarrow C + H_3PO_4 + \text{energy for contraction.}$$

Muscle contains an amount of CP sufficient to recharge the ATP Cycle for a minute or two, more or less, depending on the intensity of the work. The CP breakdown reaction is called upon largely at the beginning stages of light, moderate, or heavy work, and perhaps at the end of exhaustive work. The CP reaction is readily reversible when ATP is abundantly available, so we look next for other sources of energy to resynthesize ATP.

In sustained work, two other major chemical sources of energy are usually available for the regeneration of ATP. Anaerobically, the major energy source is *glycolysis*, the degradation of glycogen to pyruvate or lactic acid. Aerobically, energy emerges from the complex oxidative reactions of the *Krebs Cycle* or *Citric Acid Cycle*. Neither source yields direct energy for contraction, but both serve to recharge the ATP-CP Cycles. Figure 4–2 presents a simplified summary of these energy pathways, which are explained below.

Anaerobic Energy from Glycolysis.   Carbohydrate foods are digested and absorbed into the blood as glucose or some closely related simple sugar.   An excess of glucose is converted to glycogen and stored in the liver and, to a lesser extent, in the muscles.   Well-trained muscles contain significantly greater amounts of glycogen

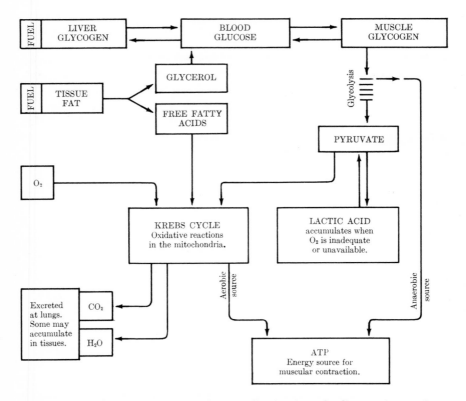

Fig. 4–2.   Schematic summary of metabolic chemistry leading to the synthesis of ATP through aerobic and anaerobic channels.   Many intermediate steps have been omitted.

than do untrained muscles, when the body is at rest.   During exercise, liver glycogen is mobilized and transported as blood glucose to the muscles, where it replaces the muscle glycogen that is degraded to pyruvate through the process of glycolysis.   Without detailing the several intermediate reactions of glycolysis, Figure 4–2 indicates the extraction of some of the energy of glycogen for the purpose of reversing the ATP reaction.   The end product is pyruvate, but in the absence of oxygen pyruvate "spills over" and accumulates in the tissues as lactic acid, a virtual poison. If lactic acid accumulates to more than 0.4 per cent, it causes severe local acidosis, pain, and spasm or contracture of the muscles. Eventually, most of the lactic acid must be removed by oxidation, and its accumulation accounts for a large proportion of the oxygen debt which must be repaid during recovery from work. Temporarily, the acute local effects of lactic acid may be mitigated by several mechanisms: (1) a very small amount may be excreted in the urine; (2) it may be dispersed evenly throughout the blood and tissue fluid remote from the site of its formation in active muscles; and (3) much of it may be temporarily neutralized by *blood buffers* (substances capable of changing strong acids to weak acids). The sum of the blood buffers is known as the *alkaline reserve*, and is greater in trained than in untrained individuals. When these temporary mechanisms for dealing with lactic acid are overwhelmed or exhausted, fatigue symptoms become acute and work must cease.

How much work can be supported anaerobically? This is another way of asking how much oxygen debt can be incurred. Bypassing a quantitative answer, suffice it to say that the stored energy of the ATP-CP Cycles will support the start and acceleration phases of a 100-yard dash, whereas the anaerobic energy of glycolysis additionally will support an all-out sprint of about 200 yards. An all-out race longer than 200 yards will utilize completely the ability to incur oxygen debt, and also will require some aerobic energy during the performance. Longer races depend more and more predominantly on the ability to supply and utilize oxygen during the task, but the performer's capacity to incur oxygen debt will energize the initial acceleration and the final sprint, and therefore may become a crucial factor in competition.

Aerobic Energy. Glycolysis also occurs in aerobic work, but lactic acid does not accumulate because pyruvate is readily oxidized in the multiple reactions of the Krebs Cycle. *Free fatty acids* (FFA) also can enter the Krebs Cycle as an alternative or additional fuel for oxidative reactions. The site of these oxidative reactions is within the mitochondria of the muscle cells. They require copious circulation and respiration in order to supply oxygen and to remove the resulting carbon dioxide and water. The oxidations extract a large amount of energy for the resynthesis of ATP from ADP and phosphate. During recovery, and probably also during aerobic work of submaximal intensity, the energy emerging from the Krebs Cycle is used to rebuild the stores of ATP, CP, and other intermediate compounds—or, in other words, to repay the oxygen debt.

Fuel for Muscular Work. Glycogen and fat are the important fuel substances for muscular work. When they are in short supply, as in starvation or in deficient diets, protein foods or body tissue proteins can be utilized as fuel, after being converted to glycogen or fat, but the processes are extremely inefficient since more oxygen is required per unit of external work produced. Although athletes and heavy workers do require more protein than sedentary persons for the purpose of building and replacing tissue, the almost exclusive protein diets advocated by some faddists are costly in performance ability as well as in dollars.

The role of glycogen in energy production has been elucidated. During moderate and severe aerobic work, the body seems to prefer to burn fat. Stored tissue fat is mobilized into the blood after being broken down into *glycerol* (a carbohydrate) and *free fatty acids* (FFA). Glycerol is easily converted to glucose and glycogen, whereupon it contributes to glycolysis in the usual manner. FFA enters the Krebs Cycle directly, where it is oxidized in a manner similar to pyruvate oxidation.

Because the body tends to utilize glycogen for short bursts of strenuous activity (anaerobic work), and FFA for steady state activity (aerobic work), it might seem that steady state work is preferable for persons who exercise in order to reduce fat deposits. This has not yet been clearly established. When tissue fat is burned, it may be replenished by conversion of carbohydrate or protein. For weight reduction, the more important factors are the total food intake and the total amount of exercise.

Vitamins and minerals are absolutely essential for energy production, since most enzymes and many intermediate reagents in metabolism require them as components. They are not, however, regarded as fuels. Since they are not consumed in significantly greater quantity when additional amounts of work are performed, but may be re-used in catalyzing metabolic reactions, the idea of gaining benefits by supercharging the body with vitamins and minerals is merely wishful thinking. The best diet for athletes and workers is the standard balanced diet that has been advocated for years, with caloric intake balanced to caloric expenditure.[7] More attention should be given to eliminating undernutrition and malnutrition, and less to the fallacious attempts to supercharge the organism with vitamins or to seek some magic ergogenic aid.

Chemical Limitations of Muscular Performance. If ATP and CP were entirely exhausted, muscular contraction would no longer be possible. But this seldom occurs, because glycolysis recharges the ATP-CP Cycles, creating lactic acid in anaerobic work. Ordinarily, then, it is the concentration of lactic acid that limits anaerobic performance. In aerobic work, lactic acid is removed by oxidation of pyruvate, and the ability of the heart and circulation to supply oxygen to the muscles becomes the most common limiting factor. In exceptional kinds of prolonged work, like marathon running, it is possible that the stores of glycogen in the liver may be exhausted and it is only in events of this kind that "quick energy foods," like glucose tablets or sweetened tea, are likely to be helpful. Supplies of glycogen are unlikely to be entirely used up in the course of ordinary sports, and the feeding of candy bars, soft drinks, or glucose tablets may even have deleterious effects because of their tendency to dehydrate the body, or, by raising blood sugar levels, to interrupt the reactions tending to mobilize liver glycogen.[7] Further, foods other than monosaccharides require at least some digestion before being absorbed into the blood. Some athletes become nauseated when food supplements are given during activity. On the other hand, some psychological benefit may be derived from administration of foods or liquids during activity, if the performer is accustomed to them and can tolerate them.

Muscular activity is probably never purely anaerobic or purely aerobic, although one or the other condition may predominate. Even when hand muscles are exercised while circulation is completely occluded by a blood pressure cuff, a small part of the work is aerobic, because a small quantity of oxygen is stored in the form of oxymyoglobin in the muscles. Trained muscles have a larger supply than untrained muscles.

Oxidation is the most important mechanism for preventing the kind of fatigue due to accumulation of lactic acid. Its efficiency depends upon (1) the development of cardio-respiratory endurance through training, (2) avoidance of tight clothing, bandages, and work or sports implements, (3) avoidance of continuously-held static positions, by frequent changes of position and other means, (4) avoidance of breath-holding, which may result from hypertension in chest and arm musculature (related to "tying-up" in running), from extreme exertion, or from abnormal breathing habits, (5) use of oxygen masks, self-contained underwater breathing apparatus (SCUBA), or other devices when working under water, in the thin air of high altitudes, or in oxygen-depleted air, and (6) deliberately adjusting the exercise so that it involves a rhythmical alternate contraction and relaxation of large muscle groups, so as to stimulate circulation and the return of venous blood to the heart.

Eventually, lactic acid must be oxidized, but it may be dealt with temporarily in some other ways. The *buffers* of the blood, which are substances capable of neutralizing acids, can neutralize great quantities of lactic acid during exercise. After exercise, when further oxygen is available, the chemical reactions of buffering may be reversed and the re-freeing of lactic acid can be met by the oxidative process during post-exercise recovery. Training over a period of weeks or months will greatly increase the amount of blood buffers (collectively referred to as the alkaline reserve of the body), but the ingestion of alkaline substances in attempts to build up the alkaline reserve beyond the regular physiological capacity has proven fruitless.

If only one part of the body is active, the locally produced lactic acid may be diffused by the blood into inactive parts of the body, thus preventing the build-up of acidity in any one area. This explains why fatigue may be felt in the arms following vigorous exercise of the legs. Also, small amounts of lactic acid can be excreted in the urine, and the heart muscle is unique in being able to utilize lactic acid as a fuel.

In single muscle fibers fatigue may result from an inadequate functioning of the mechanism coupling excitation to contraction. The fatigue which follows repeated intense muscular contraction is now believed to result largely from chemical changes in the muscle, although the neuromuscular junction may be involved when maximal contractions are exerted.[8] Long-continued, less intense activity may produce fatigue in various parts of the nervous system from the myoneural junction back up to the higher levels of the cerebral cortex.

Chemistry of Muscular Relaxation. The question of what keeps a muscle from contracting all of the time cannot be satisfactorily answered. One theory holds that in the relaxed state the membrane potential of the muscle fiber is high, magnesium (Mg) ions are bound to a relaxing agent termed the *Marsh-Bendall factor*, and calcium (Ca) ions are bound to the actomyosin. When the muscle is stimulated the resting potential is disturbed, Mg transfers to the actomyosin, and Ca transfers to the Marsh-Bendall factor. This shift simultaneously inhibits the relaxing factor and releases actomyosin to catalyze hydrolysis of ATP, thus liberating energy for contraction. When the resting potential is restored the Marsh-Bendall factor again inhibits the breakdown of ATP by actomyosin and the muscle relaxes. The chemical changes involved are extremely complex and much research will have to be done before they are understood.

Muscle Chemistry During Recovery. Athletes train by alternating periods of strenuous activity with rest pauses, the latter being fully as important as the former. Among the chemical changes in the muscles during rest are the following:

(1) ATP and Phosphocreatine are completely resynthesized,

effectively reconstituting the energy-rich substances at the site of contraction.

(2) All residual lactic acid, including that which has diffused into inactive parts of the body, is oxidized or resynthesized. While some lactic acid continues to be oxidized in the Krebs Cycle in the mitochondria, much of it is carried to the liver, where one-sixth of it may be oxidized to supply energy for reversing the glycolysis reactions so that the remaining five-sixths of lactic acid can be resynthesized to glycogen.

(3) Muscle glycogen stores are replenished and, under the stimulus of a training regimen, may be increased.

(4) Liver glycogen stores are replenished and increased, provided that adequate carbohydrate food is ingested and digested.

(5) The end products of the neutralizing activity of the body buffers undergo reverse chemical reactions, freeing lactic acid and other acids for oxidation or elimination.

(6) Muscle protein and other tissue proteins which were destroyed during the activity are replaced. Moderate to severe activity usually results not only in repair of damaged tissues, but also in further growth, strengthening, or toughening of the protein structures.

Mechanics of Muscular Contraction. The physical rearrangements which take place during muscle contraction are as controversial as are the chemical processes involved. The most popular current interpretation is that when changes occur in the length of a muscle, the actin filaments in the I band slide past the myosin filaments in the A band,[9] *i.e.* the muscle shortens but its filaments do not. While there is a great deal of evidence in support of this theory, it has not received universal acceptance. It has been objected that such a system does not provide for more than 50 per cent of the amount of shortening which may actually take place, that it is difficult to reconcile it with the kinetics of muscular contraction, that the actual structure of the muscle filament does not correspond to that required by this theory, and that the filaments may develop tension even when stretched so that they cannot interdigitate. Some researchers believe that in addition to sliding, spiraling or folding of the filaments must also be involved.[10,11]

Twitch. When studying muscular contraction, physiologists use what is known as a muscle-nerve preparation. This usually consists of a freshly excised gastrocnemius of a frog or the tibialis anticus of a dog, cat, or rabbit, together with its motor nerve. When an electrical stimulus of sufficient size is applied to the motor nerve, the muscle responds with a spasmodic contraction known as a *muscle twitch* (Fig. 4–3).

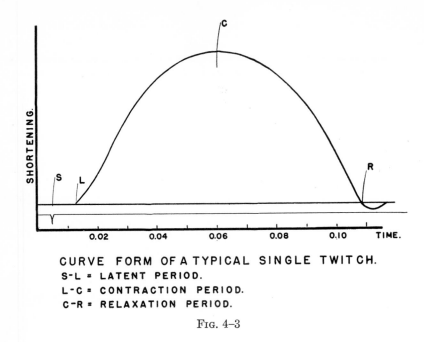

CURVE FORM OF A TYPICAL SINGLE TWITCH.
S-L = LATENT PERIOD.
L-C = CONTRACTION PERIOD.
C-R = RELAXATION PERIOD.

FIG. 4–3

When recorded under standardized conditions, the shape of the twitch curve is similar for all striated muscle, but the time factors involved show great variations in different muscles and species, and at different temperatures.

The action potential constitutes an *absolute refractory period*. During its existence a stimulus in the area cannot initiate a fresh potential, nor can an impulse generated elsewhere pass through the area. The next few milliseconds comprise a *relative refractory period*. A very strong stimulus can excite the fiber, but a subnormal spike is evoked and conduction velocity is below normal. These changes reflect alterations in the inward flow of sodium ions and the outward flow of potassium ions as a result of depolarization of the membrane during the impulse.

Treppe. When a muscle is stimulated in such a way that complete single twitches rapidly follow each other, the first few contractions progressively increase in height. This is known as *treppe*, or the "staircase effect." This successive increase in the extent of the contraction has led some authors to cite it as the mechanism responsible for the benefits of warm-up in sports. The fallacy in this reasoning is that treppe occurs (1) only in well-rested muscle and (2) only as the result of spaced single nerve impulses.[12] In the intact muscle, even the briefest stimulation consists of a volley of closely spaced nerve impulses. Treppe would take place in a fraction of a second the first time the muscle is used, whereas the asserted warm-up benefits presumably require a prolonged preliminary activity (Fig. 4–4).

Wave Summation. An adequate stimulus produces a muscle contraction which lasts for a definite period. If a second stimulus is received while the muscle is still contracted, its shortening and tension is increased. The force finally exerted may be 4 times as great as that afforded by a series of single twitches. The phenomenon of summation has been demonstrated with single fibers as well as with whole muscles.

Tetanus. If successive stimuli are administered very rapidly, no time is allowed for the muscle to relax. This fusion of superimposed twitches is known as tetanus or tetanic contraction. It is the normal type of voluntary muscular contraction and may be maintained until fatigue intervenes. Tetanic contraction in voluntary muscle is maintained by a series of nerve impulses which range from 5 to 50 or more a second in each nerve fiber. From Table 4–1 it is seen that pale fibers display a short latent period but require a high rate of discharge to maintain tetanus, whereas the opposite is true of red muscles.

The refractory period of cardiac muscle is so long that the muscle becomes almost completely relaxed before a second stimulus can become effective. For this reason tetanus cannot develop in normal cardiac muscle and the heart does not display fatigue in the same manner that skeletal muscle does.

All-or-None Law. In the past the All-or-None Law has been

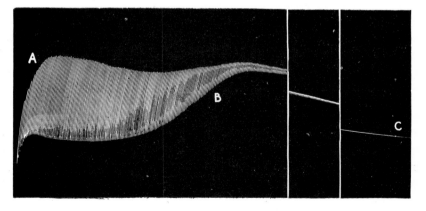

Fig. 4–4. Effects of repeated stimulation of frog muscle. *A*, Treppe; *B*, Contracture; *C*, Fatigue. (From Francis, Knowlton, and Tuttle, *Textbook of Anatomy and Physiology*, courtesy of The C. V. Mosby Co.)

TABLE 4–1.   Contraction Time and Stimulation Requirements in Mammalian Muscle[13]

Muscle	Contraction Time	Rate of Stimulus for Twitches	Rate of Stimulus for Tetanus
	In Seconds	Per Second	Per Second
Internal rectus	.0075	133	350
Gastrocnemius	.025	25.6	100
Soleus	.049–.120	8.3–10.6	31–33

stated as follows: If a muscle fiber contracts at all, it contracts to the maximum extent of which it is capable. It is much more accurate to say that the amount of contraction of a muscle fiber is independent of the strength of the stimulus, but even this concept is subject to severe, if not disqualifying, limitations. Under laboratory conditions, in which it is possible to stimulate a muscle fiber by special direct methods (rather than through the usual action potential), the amount of contraction is shown to be proportional to the strength of the stimulus over a wide range. Even under normal conditions of stimulation through an action potential in the innervating neuron, the law is at best an over-simplification.

It is helpful to distinguish sharply between the conductile mechanism and the contractile mechanism of a muscle fiber. The conductile processes, like those of nerve fibers, do indeed follow the All-or-None Law. That is, the magnitude of the response is independent of the magnitude of the stimulus, provided that the stimulus achieves at least a certain threshold value. This in turn depends upon many factors, such as temperature, chemical state, elapsed time from a previous stimulus (whether adequate or sub-threshold), and others. The contractile processes, on the other hand, do not follow strictly the All-or-None Law. For example, summation may occur if successive stimuli are sufficiently rapid.

Gradation of Contraction. Obviously, whole muscles do not follow the All-or-None Law. Whole muscles have the ability to contract very weakly or very strongly, or at any of a large number of finely graded intermediate levels. The strength of contraction, or *gradation*, results mainly from the interaction of three factors—the number of motor units stimulated (recruitment); the frequency of the stimuli (summation), and the timing of stimuli to various motor units (synchronization).

The major mechanism of gradation is the ability of the central nervous system to send stimuli to a greater or lesser number of motor units. When greater tension is needed, more motor units are stimulated. This is known as *recruitment.*

Summation is a function of the frequency of stimulation. Impulses spaced at intervals greater than the time required for a single twitch will result in minimal contractions, which may produce (in a single muscle fiber) only one-fourth the tension that would be produced in tetanus. A somewhat smaller interval between stimuli will result in partial summation, or incomplete tetanus. Even when successive stimuli are equal in strength, very rapid volleys of impulses will cause maximum response (tetanus). These phenomena have been identified as properties of single muscle fibers, of motor units, and of whole muscles.

Ordinarily, the impulses reaching different motor units are out-of-phase (asynchronous). When a sudden great effort is required, impulses to many or all of the motor units may occur simultaneously *(synchronization).* The extra strength resulting from synchronization cannot be employed for a sustained contraction. Undesired or uncontrolled synchronization is the basis of certain chronic neuromotor diseases. The frequency of response increases quite evenly with gradually increasing effort, whereas the addition of each new motor unit represents a discrete step. It appears that the change in frequency is the more delicate method of grading the strength of a contraction, while the accession of units is probably a quicker and more potent factor. Under experimental conditions the strongest voluntary effort does not drive motor units at frequencies above 50 per second. It is possible that under the stimulus of an emergency or athletic competition this rate becomes increased.[13]

To complicate matters further, there are two separate nerve-muscle systems, innervated by the large neurons and the gamma neurons, respectively (see page 114). Reflex contractions and inhibitions initiated by proprioceptors and the gamma neurons are responsible for feedback, which exerts critical control over the activity of the larger motor neurons; indeed, this is the basis for the mechanisms of posture regulation and of other delicate reflexive controls.

Although a single neuron cannot activate more than the total number of muscle fibers it innervates, it is not necessarily true that it must activate all the muscle fibers it innervates. A stimulus may be inadequate to activate some of the least irritable muscle fibers (that is, those whose thresholds are at the moment relatively high) in a motor unit, because the various fibers may differ from each other in temperature, accumulation of fatigue products, or adequacy of circulation. It has been postulated that one of the benefits of training with near-maximal weights in progressive resistance exercise is that this brings some of the high-threshold neurons within the orbit of voluntary activity.[14]   Such factors as those mentioned in this and the preceding paragraph can modify the three major gradation mechanisms considerably.

Rhythmic and Arhythmic Contraction.   Under certain conditions of disease or injury either cardiac muscle or skeletal muscle may display *fibrillation,* a rapid, uncoordinated, rhythmical twitching of individual muscle fibers that accompanies atrophy of muscle following denervation or certain other injury.   *Fasciculation* is a spontaneous twitching of bundles of muscle fiber resulting from single impulses in motor units.   It may be produced by irritations of the cell bodies of the motor neurons, as in poliomyelitis.

The contraction of a muscle as a whole is smooth because the jerky responses of the motor units are out of phase with each other and there is a continuous alternation of units.   If the activity of the units becomes synchronous and the contractions alternately and rhythmically appear in muscle groups and their antagonists, *tremor* results.   If they appear simultaneously in both a muscle group and its antagonists, *rigidity* is seen.   Both are characteristic of paralysis agitans.   Coordinated grouping of the discharge of muscle units results in the gross tremor of *shivering.*

Training produces a reduction in the electrical activity required for a muscle to produce a given degree of tension, indicating that the process of muscle stimulation by the central nervous system becomes more economical.[15]

Contracture.   Any state of prolonged resistance to passive stretch in a muscle may be called *contracture. Physiological contracture* results from mechanical, chemical, or other agents acting directly on the contractile mechanism without involving an action potential.   Figure 4-4 shows the result of one kind of physiological contracture in which complete relaxation fails to occur between stimuli.   This sort of physiological contracture occurs when a working muscle has become fatigued, as in a runner who "ties up," but its mechanisms are not well understood.   *Myostatic contracture* is a fibrotic condition of the supporting connective tissues of a muscle or joint, resulting from immobilization of the muscle in the short position while the innervation remains intact.   Myostatic contracture occurs after a limb has been immobilized in a cast, after a tendon has been severed or detached, or after antagonistic muscles have been paralyzed.

Cramps.   During vigorous exercise or during sleep healthy persons may experience an involuntary, sustained, painful contraction of skeletal muscle termed a cramp.   It is uncertain whether these have their origin in muscle, peripheral nerve, or the spinal cord.   For experimental purposes they can be voluntarily induced by a maximum voluntary effort while the muscle is in a shortened position. The pattern of the action potentials recorded electromyographically indicates that they are due to excitation of most of the muscle fibers in a given motor unit, suggesting that the cramp must be explained in terms of motor unit activity originating in the central nervous system. The pain seems to be proportional to the total number of active units.

There is evidence that the onset of cramps during vigorous physical activities results from a loss of sodium and chloride in the serum, due to sweating, but the actual change in the muscle or nerve is unknown. Hypertrophied muscles appear more liable to cramping than are normal muscles, but physiologically hypertrophy is not associated with any known change in excitability or EMG pattern and no relief is afforded by the ingestion of sodium chloride.

Spasticity. The central nervous system receives information about changes in the length of muscles by means of proprioceptive impulses arising from the muscle spindles (see p. 109) and other end organs. Normally when the muscle surrounding a spindle contracts, the discharge from the spindle ceases. A disturbance in the gamma efferent control over the spindle may result in its continued discharge. As a result the muscles may display an exaggerated stretch reflex (*hypertonus*).[16] Electromyographic activity of the motor units of the affected limb at rest does not differ from that of a normal limb, but if an attempt is made to move the limb an exaggerated motor unit activity is observed. The limb is then said to be *spastic*. In man such hypertonus occurs only in the antigravity muscles. Attempts to flex a leg joint which result in a stretch of spastic extensor muscles of the hip, knee, or ankle encounter marked resistance, but the same joints may be extended freely. In the arm it is the flexors which normally counteract the force of gravity, and a spastic arm resists attempts at extension.

Reciprocal Innervation and Co-Contraction. Sherrington observed that in decerebrate or anesthetized animals, in whom voluntary control is abolished, afferent neural impulses which stimulate the motorneurones of a given muscle reflexly inhibit the motorneurones of the antagonistic muscles. This is known as the *principle of reciprocal innervation*, and the mechanism by which it functions is termed *reciprocal inhibition of antagonistic muscles*. If the excitation of the agonist is not accompanied by this corresponding reflex inhibition of the antagonist, uncoordinated movement results. He also noted that antagonistic muscles may contract simultaneously with the agonists, which he attributed to *double reciprocal innervation*.[17] Recent studies of the role of the muscle spindles in the production of the stretch reflex suggest that this theory is no longer tenable.[16]   Sherrington further observed that after being subjected to reflex inhibition, the activity of the motor center of a skeletal muscle tends to increase (*rebound discharge*).   As a result, application of a stimulus which causes flexion (extension) of a limb tends to be followed by active extension (flexion) of the same limb (*successive induction*) when the inhibitory effect is withdrawn.   Theoretically, then, when the discus thrower swings his arm backwards (Fig. 22–14), the horizontal extensors of the shoulder joint are activated and the horizontal flexors are inhibited.   The resulting rebound and successive induction of the horizontal flexors reflexly give greater force to the subsequent swing forward.   However, these phenomena are but poorly understood.

As early as 1925 Tilney and Pike found that under normal conditions they were unable to observe Sherrington's phenomena, and concluded that "muscular coordination depends primarily on the synchronous co-contractive relationship in the antagonist muscle groups."[18]   They suggest that if this co-contractive relationship is disturbed, one possible result is overextension by the agonists, followed by overcorrection by the antagonists.   An irregular series of oscillations would result, and this might explain the clinical symptoms of ataxia.

Only muscles acting on a single joint can be assumed to be true antagonists.   Muscles acting on more than one joint may at times act as antagonists and at other times as synergists.   The rectus femoris normally acts as an antagonist to the hamstrings, but if the hip and knee are flexed simultaneously, the rectus femoris acts synergistically with them.   In some muscles one part may act as an antagonist and another part as a synergist.

As an agonist goes into the final range of contraction, it begins to cause proprioceptive stimulation through stretch reflexes of the antagonist muscle.   The resulting contraction of the antagonist then offers resistance to the final phase of movement of the agonist.   The angle at which this occurs varies with the joint and the muscles involved.

It has been possible to demonstrate reciprocal innervation in the human in unresisted voluntary movement, in reflex movements, such as the knee jerk, and in cases of spasticity, a condition which leads to a structural shortening of the muscles involved.   Electrical stimulation of muscles antagonistic to those in spasm has been found to result in relaxation of the spastic muscles.   Some investigators[19] believe that in normal voluntary movement co-contraction seems to be the rule rather than the exception and satisfactory evidence that reciprocal innervation plays the part usually assigned to it by kinesiologists is lacking; others[20] contend that during movement the antagonist relaxes completely, with a single exception—the finish of a whip-like motion of a hinge joint.

Barnett and Harding[21] suggest that antagonistic muscles behave in at least three distinct ways:

1. When external resistance is so great that the joint cannot move, the antagonists relax.

2. When the muscles are acting against moderate resistance, the antagonists become active to decelerate the movement and their electrical activity is proportional to the rate at which the joint is moving.

3. When there is no external resistance to be overcome and the limb must move with great precision, tension tends to be maintained in both the agonist group and the antagonist group, with the former predominating.

Isometric Tension. When force is exerted by a muscle against an object which it cannot move, the muscle remains at the same length and technically accomplishes no work. The energy which would normally be displayed as mechanical work is dissipated as heat. In such a case the muscle is said to develop *isometric tension* and the length of the A bands and the I bands remains unchanged. However, there is some internal shortening of the contractile components with a corresponding extension of the elastic components. Actually, no muscle action is perfectly isometric. Even under the most rigid conditions the contractile elements shorten by about 3 per cent of their length by stretching the elastic components.[22] There is good evidence that the muscle fibers are not of uniform strength; some of the heat produced may result from the extending of the weaker fibers by the stronger ones. Posture is largely maintained by isometric contractions of certain muscles of the back and legs, where muscular tension is required to offset the effects of gravity upon the body. Isometric exercise is also employed for "muscle setting" exercises in physical medicine.

Isotonic Contraction. When a muscle is able to move a load, work is accomplished and the muscle is said to have performed an *isotonic contraction.* With a given stimulus a muscle develops more energy when doing isotonic work than when developing isometric tension. This is known as the *Fenn effect* and is typical of most active movements of the limbs in work or sport. During the process of contraction a muscle "gains" energy, but this is offset by the fact that its antagonist "loses" energy. At a constant velocity of shortening, the electrical activity has been found to be directly proportional to the tension; at a constant tension, the electrical activity increases linearly with the velocity of the shortening.[23]

The A bands remain at a constant length during normal muscular contraction, the I bands shorten, and the H bands close up, creating a dark line in place of the H zone. This has been interpreted as a crumpling of the ends of the actin filaments, and may constitute the M band. In spite of these observed differences, the amount of tension which may be developed by a single isometric contraction of the elbow flexors and the amount of weight which may be moved in a single isotonic flexion do not appear to be appreciably different.[24]

As a rule the tendon is stronger than the muscle, and does not rupture when a limb is subjected to severe strain. Loads great enough to produce lesions usually pull the tendon insertion away, rupture the muscle belly, separate the muscle-tendinous junction, cause the muscle origin to pull out, or fracture the bones.

Stretching. If a muscle is stretched during contraction, as when the extensor muscles of the hip act to halt the forward swing of the leg during walking, the total energy liberated is approximately equal to the total mechanical work done. Although physical work is done, the energy thus developed cannot be used by the muscle and is degraded as heat. When a muscle is stretched the A bands remain at a constant length, the I bands increase in length, the actin filaments are pulled out of the A bands, and the H bands become longer by a amount equal to the increase in the length of the I bands. A muscle can resist a stretch with a greater amount of force than it can develop in an isometric contraction.

The three types of muscular contraction and the characteristics of each are conveniently summarized in Table 4–2.

Work Done by Muscular Contraction. The amount of work done by a contracting muscle is a combination of two elements of equal importance: the amount of force used and the distance of the movement. Stated mathematically, the amount of work done is

TABLE 4–2. Types of Muscle Contraction*

Type Tension	Type of Contraction	Function	External Force Opposing Muscle	External Work by Muscle	Energy Supply
Isotonic (shortening)	Concentric	Acceleration	Less	Positive	Increases
Isometric (constant length)	Static	Fixation	Equal	None	
Lengthening	Eccentric	Deceleration	Greater	Negative	Decreases

* After Fenn, W. O.: Contractility. In Hober, Rudolph, editor, *Physical Chemistry of Cells and Tissues.* Philadelphia: Blakiston, 1945, p. 176.

the product of the force multiplied by the distance ($W = F \times d$). One unit of work is the amount involved in exerting one unit of force through one unit of distance, regardless of what these units are, so that work may be expressed in gram-centimeters, foot-pounds, kilogram-meters, foot-tons, or any other appropriate combinations, according to the units of force and distance employed.

The force that a muscle can exert depends on the number and size of its fibers; the distance through which it can contract depends on the length of its fibers. It follows from the first that the strength of skeletal muscles is proportional to their muscular cross section. Since the tension developed by a muscle decreases as the muscle shortens, the force per unit of cross section also decreases. Hence abolute muscle force varies with the length of the muscle at the time of the test. Further, when making measurements of muscle strength *per se*, allowance must be made for the angle of insertion. Unless each of these factors is equated, data from different studies may not be comparable. As a result the literature contains widely varying estimates of muscle strength. Muscle force varies from muscle to muscle, but approximately 3.3 kg. of isometric force per cm.[2] of cross section is generally accepted.[25] It is probable that normal muscle can contract up to about 25 per cent of its relaxed state. Thus a longitudinal muscle that has 2 square centimeters of cross section and fibers normally 8 centimeters long could do 13.2 kilogram-centimeters of work in a single contraction ($3.3 \times 2 \times 2 = 13.2$).

In order to illustrate how muscular structure is related to muscular work, assume that a muscle has 800 fibers, each 4 cm. long and each able to exert a force of 1 gm. (Fig. 4–5).

Under this supposition the muscle can exert a force of 800 gm. cm. of work at one contraction. Now suppose the muscle split lengthwise and the halves placed end to end, making a muscle of exactly the same total bulk, with half as many fibers twice as long; it can now pull with a force of 400 gm. through 2 cm. of distance, doing the same amount of work as before. If the above process is repeated, the muscle can now pull with a force of 200 gm. through 4 cm. of distance. The number of variations in the arrangement can be multiplied indefinitely, with the same amount of work being done in each case.

Negative Work. In the case of an eccentric, or lengthening, contraction, as occurs when lowering a heavy weight slowly or when walking down stairs, no external work is being done, according to the above definition. In such cases instead of work being done by the muscles on the weight, it is done by the weight on the muscles, and is referred to as negative work. Its numerical value is calculated

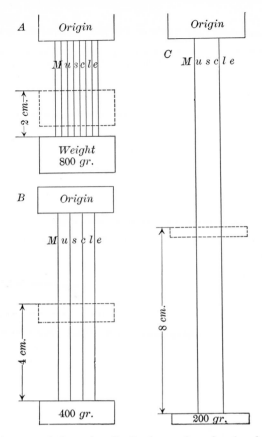

Fig. 4–5. Diagram of three longitudinal muscles, showing how number and length of fibers affect power and extent of movement. *A* has 800 fibers 4 cm. long, *B* has 400 fibers 8 cm. long, and *C* has 200 fibers 16 cm. long. Arrows indicate extent of contraction.

exactly as in the above formula; if a 100 pound weight is lowered slowly through 3 feet the work done is —300 foot-pounds.

Static Work. Muscles which are in a state of tonic contraction to overcome the force of gravity are obviously expending energy, but since the load is not being moved through space, technically no work is being accomplished. The student must keep the definition of work clearly in mind if confusion is to be avoided.

Work Load. The ability of a muscle to perform useful work varies greatly with the load applied. A very light load does not make full use of a muscle's potentialities and uses an excessive amount of its potential energy in simply overcoming the frictional resistance of the muscle itself. As the weight of the load is increased, the speed of lifting becomes slower. A typical relationship between load and maximum velocity is shown in Figure 4–6.

Two-Joint Muscles. The fact that some muscles pass over two joints of the skeleton affects their work efficiency. For example, when the leg is moved forward, the tensing of the rectus femoris simultaneously contributes to the flexing of the hip joint and the extending of the knee joint; when the leg is moved backward, the tensing of the hamstrings simultaneously contributes to the extending of the hip joint and the flexing of the knee joint. When the sartorius functions efficiently, it tends to flex simultaneously the hip and knee joints. Thus while one muscle is accomplishing positive work at one end, it is simultaneously accomplishing negative work at the other end. If this work had to be accomplished by two separate muscles, each would have to do positive work. Since the total work done is the algebraic sum of the positive and negative work, a considerable saving in energy expenditure is achieved by the two-joint muscles. This subject is further discussed in Chapter 16.

METHODS OF STUDYING MUSCULAR ACTION

There are at least five ways of studying a muscle to determine its action.

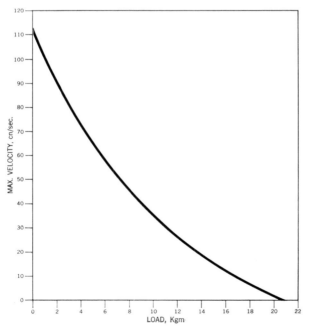

FIG. 4–6. Smoothed curve showing relationship between load and maximal velocity of contraction in human pectoralis major muscle. Based on data of Ralston *et al.*[26]

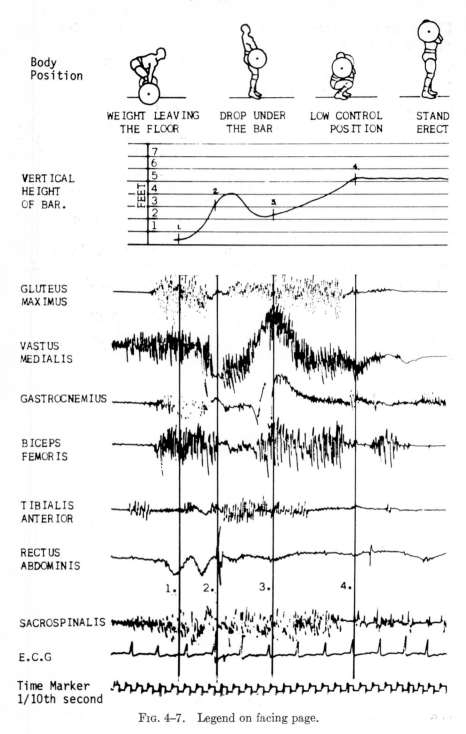

Body Position

WEIGHT LEAVING THE FLOOR

DROP UNDER THE BAR

LOW CONTROL POSITION

STAND ERECT

VERTICAL HEIGHT OF BAR.

FEET

GLUTEUS MAXIMUS

VASTUS MEDIALIS

GASTROCNEMIUS

BICEPS FEMORIS

TIBIALIS ANTERIOR

RECTUS ABDOMINIS

SACROSPINALIS

E.C.G

Time Marker 1/10th second

Fig. 4–7. Legend on facing page.

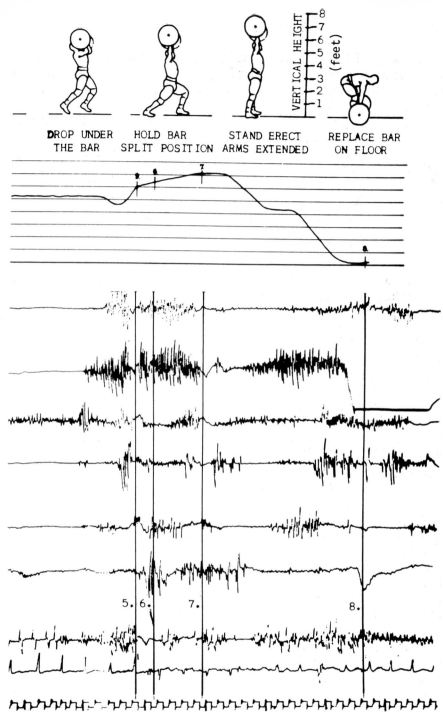

FIG. 4–7. Recording of electromyograms and other data during a two hands clean and jerk. (Courtesy V. Thomas, "Sportsmen Under Stress," New Scientist, 1969. Copyright Corser, Saville & Thomas.)

1. Study of the conditions under which a muscle acts by the use of a mounted skeleton, noticing its points of attachment, direction of pull, leverage, and any other points bearing upon the problem that can be discovered.

2. Pulling upon the partly dissected muscles of a cadaver and noticing the resulting movements.

Both of these methods have their uses, but it does not necessarily follow that the muscle action *in vivo* can be deduced from either one of them. Synergistic actions cannot be determined by such methods. Muscular movements usually involve groups of muscles and a muscle may work with different groups in different movements.

3. Stimulation of individual muscles by electric current and noticing the resulting movements. This was the method of the classic researches of Duchenne. It has served greatly to increase our knowledge, but may be applied only to the superficial muscles and is largely subject to the objections made to the use of the first two methods.

4. The study of subjects who have lost the use of certain muscles, to determine what loss of power and movement has resulted and whether any abnormal postures have been produced. Studies of this kind have added materially to our knowledge of muscular action, but it is difficult to obtain a sufficient variety of subjects to study the muscles in a systematic way.

5. Study of the normal living body, to find what muscles contract in certain exercises and what movements call certain muscles into action. This is perhaps the most practical approach to kinesiological problems. Normal subjects are always available. Whatever we may deduce from other methods, this one must provide the final decision, for neither observations made on a cadaver or a skeleton nor data provided by electrical stimulation experiments can tell what a muscle *will* do, although they may tell what a muscle *can* do. We need to learn not only what action a muscle is able to perform because of its position and opportunity, but also what, in an actual case, the nervous system calls upon it to do and when it permits it to lie idle. Some of Duchenne's most brilliant discoveries by means of electrical stimulation have been found to be misleading, because observation of the living body shows that certain muscles which might help greatly in a movement actually never do so. An example is the gluteus maximus, which could participate in leg extension in walking but does not.

Observations on normal subjects may be made by two quite different techniques. The first and best suited to beginners is to determine the action of muscles in a given exercise by seeing or actually feeling the muscle contract. This method is limited by the fact that many muscles are so situated that they cannot be observed directly and dependable results cannot be obtained by it.

The student with some technical background may make use of an electromyograph. With this apparatus small metal disks are placed on the skin over the muscle or tiny needles are inserted directly into it. These pick up the action potentials every time a muscle moves. These may be amplified and shown on an oscilloscope, where they may be photographed if desired. A more general technique is to record the potentials on moving paper so that a permanent record of the action of the muscle throughout a given movement is made. In isometric contraction the electrical activity in a contracting muscle is roughly proportional to the tension in the muscle. In isotonic contractions, however, the EMG output is affected by the load, velocity, acceleration, and length of the muscle. It is lower for an eccentric contraction than for a concentric one. By this means the action of a number of muscles may be observed simultaneously, and the student can tell at exactly which point each one comes into play and when its action ceases (Fig. 4–7). Even with this method it is difficult to study the action of the deeper muscles, such as the iliopsoas, and it cannot be used when the muscle changes drastically in length. Some investigators have overcome these difficulties by inserting fine insulated wire directly into the muscles via a hypodermic needle or by implanting it during surgery.

Further, the electromyogram is affected by age. Studies of older persons show a decreased amplitude for motor unit potentials, believed to result from a decrease in muscle fiber size and number, a high incidence of polyphasic motor unit potentials, suggesting a delay in end-plate transmission or muscle fiber response, and a decay in amplitude on sustained contractions, which presumably reflects an inability of the fibers to maintain sustained tension.[27]

References

1. Nachmansohn, David: *Chemical and Molecular Basis of Nerve Activity.* New York: Academic Press, Inc., 1959.

2. Podolsky, R. J. and Costantin, L. L.: Regulation by Calcium of the Contraction and Relaxation of Muscle Fibers. Fed. Proc., *23*, 933–939, 1963.

3. Johns, Richard J.: The Electrical and Mechanical Events of Neuromuscular Transmission. Amer. J. Med., *35*, 611–621, 1963.

4. Mommaerts, Wilfried, F. H. M.: The Muscle Cell and Its Functional Architecture. Amer. J. Med., *35*, 606–610, 1963.

5. Dun, F. T.: Neuromuscular Transmission and Acetylcholine. J. Amer. Osteopath. Ass., *58*, 600–601, 1959.

6. Hill, A. V.: The Priority of Heat Production in a Muscle Twitch. Proc. Roy. Soc. Med., *148-B*, 397–402, 1958.

7. Anonymous: *Nutrition for Athletes.* Washington, D.C.: AAHPER, 1971.

8. Lind, A. R.: Muscle Fatigue and Recovery from Fatigue Induced by Sustained Contractions. J. Physiol., *147*, 162–171, 1959.

9. Huxley, A. F.: Muscle. In Hall, Victor E., editor: *Annual Review of Physiology*. Palo Alto: Annual Reviews, Inc., *26*, 131–152, 1964.

10. Podolsky, Richard J.: Muscle Physiology and Contraction Theories. Circulation, *24*, 399–409, 1961.

11. Frank, G. M.: Some Problems of the Physical and Physiochemical Bases of Muscular Contraction. Proc. Roy. Soc. Med., *160-B*, 473–476, 1964.

12. Karpovich, Peter V.: *The Physiology of Muscular Activity*, 6th Ed. Philadelphia: W. B. Saunders Co., 1965, p. 13.

13. Cooper, Sybil and Eccles, J. C.: The Isometric Response in Mammalian Muscle. J. Physiol., *69*, 377–385, 1930.

14. Knowlton, G. Clinton: Physiological Background for Neuromuscular Reeducation and Coordination. Arch. Phys. Med., *35*, 635–636, 1954.

15. Stepanov, A. S.: Electromyogram Changes Produced by Training in Weight Lifting. Sechenov Physiol. J. USSR, *45*, 115–121, 1959.

16. Herman, Richard: The Physiologic Basis of Tone, Spasticity and Rigidity. Arch. Phys. Med., *43*, 108–114, 1962.

17. Denny-Brown, D., editor: *Selected Writings of Sir Charles Sherrington*. New York: Paul N. Hoeber, Inc., 1940, pp. 237–313.

18. Tilney, Frederick and Pike, Frank H.: Muscular Coordination Experimentally Studied in its Relation to the Cerebellum. Arch. Neurol. Psychiat., *13*, 289–334, 1925.

19. Levine, Milton G. and Kabat, Herman: Cocontraction and Reciprocal Innervation in Voluntary Movement in Man. Science, *116*, 115–118, 1952.

20. Basmajian, J. V.: *Muscles Alive. Their Functions Revealed by Electromyography*, 2nd Ed. Baltimore: Williams & Wilkins Co., 1967, p. 86.

21. Barnett, C. H. and Harding, D.: The Activity of Antagonist Muscles During Voluntary Movement. Ann. Phys. Med., *3*, 290–293, 1955.

22. Davson, Hugh and Eggleton, M. Grace, editors: *Starling and Evans' Principles of Human Physiology*, 14th Ed. Philadelphia: Lea & Febiger, 1968, p. 825.

23. Bigland, Brenda and Lippold, O. C. J.: The Relation Between Force, Velocity and Integrated Electrical Activity in Human Muscles. J. Physiol., *123*, 214–224, 1954.

24. Rasch, Philip J.: Relation Between Maximum Isometric Tension and Maximum Elbow Flexion. Res. Quart., *28*, 85, 1957.

25. Elftman, Herbert: Biomechanics of Muscle. J. Bone Joint Surg., *48-A*, 363–377, 1966.

26. Ralston, H. J., *et al.*: Dynamic Features of Human Isolated Voluntary Muscle in Isometric and Free Contractions. J. Appl. Physiol., *1*, 526–533, 1949.

27. Carlson, Karl E.: Electromyographic Study of Aging in Skeletal Muscle. Amer. J. Phys. Med., *43*, 141–145, 1964.

Recommended Reading

28. O'Connell, A. L. and Gardner, E. B.: The Use of Electromyography in Kinesiological Research. Res. Quart., *34*, 166–184, 1963.

29. Hall, Elizabeth A.: Electromyographic Techniques: A Review. Phys. Ther., *50*, 651–659, 1970.

30. Rasch, Philip J.: Isometric Exercise and Gains of Muscle Strength. In Shephard, Roy J., editor: *Frontiers of Fitness:* Springfield, Illinois, Charles C Thomas, 1971, pp. 98–111.

Chapter 5

Neurology, Kinesthesia, and Servomotor Control

THE NEURON AND ITS FUNCTIONS

The nerves can transmit only electric pulses, whose sizes are constant but whose frequency may be varied; the greater the stimulus, the greater the frequency. Consequently muscle action potentials and neural action potentials are identical; the discharge of a motor cell nerve can hardly be told from that of a sensory organ, and reflex response to electrical stimulation gives an identical electromyogram to those obtained by mechanical percussion of a tendon. The only way the brain can distinguish between the inputs from the various sensory organs is for it to be aware of which nerves have been stimulated. It follows that for the brain to be really sure of what is happening to the body several sources of sensory input are highly desirable. Most of this chapter will be devoted to a consideration of the brain's sources of sensory information.

The Neuron. The structural and functional unit of the nervous system is the single nerve cell, or *neuron* (Fig. 5–1). It consists of a nucleated *cell body* and two or more processes called *nerve fibers*. The processes may be divided into *axons* (*axis cylinders*) and *dendrites*. Usually there are several dendrites, which may traverse either a very long or a very short distance between the cell body and the multiple branching at their terminal *arborizations*. Dendrites serve a receptive function; they normally conduct impulses toward the cell body. Generally, a neuron has but one axon, which may be up to 3 feet long, serving to carry impulses away from the cell body and to pass the impulse along to the dendrites of other neurons. The cell bodies are located in the gray matter of the spinal cord and brain or in ganglia (collections or bunches of cell bodies) located outside of, but relatively close to, the spinal cord. Nerve fibers may be found intermingled with the cell bodies of the gray matter, or they may be arranged longitudinally in white bundles. White bundles within the spinal cord and brain are known as *tracts, columns, commissures,* and so forth; those outside the spinal cord and brain are known as *nerves.* Neurons should not be confused with nerves. The former are individual nerve cells; the latter are bundles of fibers.

The nerve fiber is essentially a protoplasmic extension (*axis cylinder*) from the body of the cell. This axis cylinder is sometimes clothed with a fatty *myelin* or *medullary sheath.* In some areas, a thinner nucleated membrane, the *neurilemma,* invests the axis cylinder, and if a myelin sheath is also present, it lies between the neurilemma and the axis cylinder. Both of these coverings, when

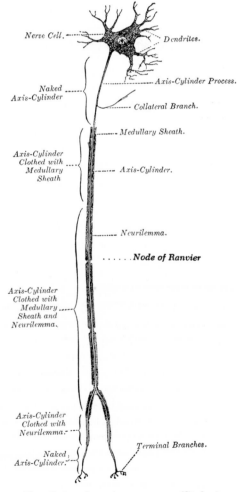

Fig. 5-1. A motor neuron. (Stohr.)

present, probably serve as insulation to prevent irradiation of impulses, and the neurilemma is an essential factor in the regeneration of nerve fibers.

Axons and dendrites may or may not have specialized *end organs*. Motor axons have *motor end-plates* (Fig. 5–2) that lie upon individual muscle fibers and are necessary for transmission of an impulse across the *myoneural junction*. Sensory fibers sometimes have specialized receptor end organs, such as the proprioceptor end organs discussed later in this chapter.

If a cell body is sufficiently damaged, the entire neuron will degenerate irreversibly. But if a process is severed or damaged, usually only the portion peripheral to the cell body will degenerate, and if the cell body and the neurilemma of the degenerated portion remain intact, the central end of the process may grow out (regenerate) along its former course by following the path provided by the neurilemma. In the case of a cut nerve, the suturing together of the severed nerve ends may enhance the possibility of regeneration by approximately restoring the continuity of the neurilemma pathway. Unfortunately, no regeneration is possible if the cell bodies of motor nerves lying in the spinal cord are destroyed, as is the case in poliomyelitis. When a muscle atrophies, both the muscle fibers and the motor endings diminish in size,[1] as is shown in Figures 5–3 and 5–4.

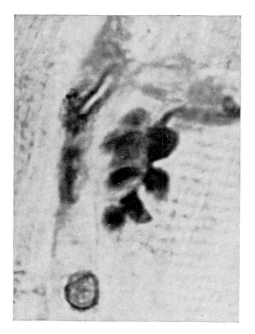

Fig. 5–2. The terminal arborization of the motor end-plate in man. (Coërs.)

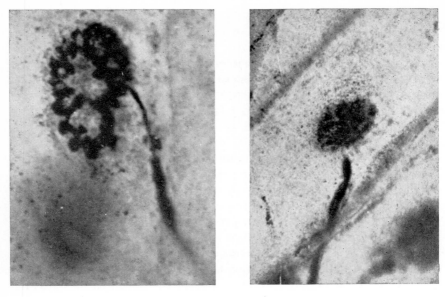

<table>
<tr><td align="center">Fig. 5–3</td><td align="center">Fig. 5–4</td></tr>
</table>

Fig. 5–3. Motor ending (myoneural junction) in gastrocnemius of normal male rat.
(× 450.) (Cole.)

Fig. 5–4. Motor ending (myoneural junction) in gastrocnemius of a male rat whose
femur has been immobilized for fourteen days. (× 450.) (Cole.)

Peripheral neurons (those extending outside the brain and spinal
cord) may be divided into *afferent* or sensory neurons, and *efferent* or
motor neurons. Most nerves are *mixed nerves*—that is, they contain
both afferent and efferent fibers. Neurons within the spinal cord
and brain are known as *internuncial* or *intercalated neurons*, serving
as connectors, collators, integrators, analyzers, and organizers of
sensory and motor impulses.

Neural Conduction. A neuron is potentially capable of responding
to electrical, mechanical, chemical, or thermal stimuli, although a
receptor end organ may make it especially susceptible to a certain
kind of stimulation. In any event, an adequate stimulus causes a
physicochemical change known as a *local excitatory state* (*l.e.s.*). If
the stimulus has sufficient strength, duration, and rate of change of
intensity the l.e.s. triggers the propagation of a wave of excitation
(nerve *impulse*) along the fiber—this is known as *conduction*. The
nerve impulse is self-propagating, like a spark "traveling" along a
string of gunpowder. It is carried from the point of stimulation to
all parts of the neuron, at speeds up to 120 meters per second,

depending upon the diameter of the fiber and its physiological state at that moment. A neuron obeys the All-or-None Law—that is, conduction depends on a stimulus whose intensity reaches a certain *threshold* value. A stimulus of greater than threshold value has no extra effect on the quality of the impulse, although it may irradiate at its point of application and cause conduction in adjacent neurons as well.

After conduction, there is an *absolute refractory period* (about 0.0004 second in mammals) during which no stimulus will arouse a response from the neuron. This is followed by a *relative refractory period* (about 0.01 to 0.02 second) during which excitability gradually returns to normal, and only an intense stimulus will arouse a response from the neuron.

The Synapse. The junction between two nerve fibers is called a synapse. Here the ends of the axons are in very close contact with the brush-like endings of the dendrites and other neurons. Because each neuron is a discrete anatomical unit, the synapse becomes the point of communication between one neuron and another. The nervous impulse travels along an axon and across the synapse to the dendrites of the other neuron; never in the reverse direction. The synapse offers some resistance to the passage of the nervous impulse, which may vary from one synapse to another. It also causes a slight delay, about 0.002 second, in the transmission of the nervous impulse.

The synapse acts as a one-way valve or gate which permits the passage of the nervous impulse from one neuron to another. Because of their variable resistance, synapses may tend to be selective and to direct the pathway of the nervous impulse, nervous impulses resulting from feeble stimuli being conducted across only the synapses with low resistance, but nervous impulses resulting from powerful stimuli crossing those with high resistance as well.

Inhibition. The foregoing material on synaptic transmission pertains to neurons whose function is excitatory. In the brain and spinal cord there are many presynaptic neurons whose function is inhibitory rather than excitatory. Inhibitory neurons have only one major difference from excitatory neurons: instead of depolarizing the post-synaptic neuron, they increase the resting polarity. Like local excitatory states, local inhibitory states are additive when several occur simultaneously. The post-synaptic neuron will "fire" only when the algebraic sum of inhibitory and excitatory states balances out on the excitatory side, at or above threshold level. An inhibitory neuron *receives* its neural stimulation by a preponderance of excitatory influence, just like any other neuron, even though its *influence* across its terminal synapse is inhibitory.

Some of the reasons for the complexity of neural functioning should now be clear. Although we can define two-neuron reflex arcs, and even isolate them functionally under sophisticated laboratory circumstances, *in vivo* a nerve cell body is subject to the modulating influence of several, or even hundreds, of impinging excitatory and inhibitory neurons. Thus, the net effect on the motoneuron is determined by a myriad of modulations, feed-backs, and filtering from both peripheral and central sources, including some from higher brain centers.

Examples of graded inhibition are seen in most voluntary movements. The concept of co-contraction (pp. 83–85) specifies that movement usually involves the simultaneous contraction of antagonistic muscle groups, although there may be a distinct difference in the forces exerted by the members of the pair. When the external resistance to the agonists is great, the co-contraction of the antagonists is minimal. Apparently there is a central inhibitory effect upon the antagonists, the purpose being to reduce the resistance to the movement. This inhibition occurs as an involuntary, though perhaps learned, reflex. It is controlled in the spinal cord and lower levels of the brain, and is roughly proportional to the amount of force required in the agonists to perform the movement.

A therapist, first aider, or athlete can sometimes make practical use of the phenomenon of inhibition of antagonists. Muscle cramps and spasms, especially those of an acute nature, can sometimes be relieved by a strong voluntary or electrical stimulation of the muscle's antagonist.

Like other reflexes, the inhibition of antagonists may be overridden or modified under certain conditions. For example, at the extreme range of motion the inhibited antagonist may be stretched sufficiently to initiate a myotatic contraction.

Excessive general tension, associated with emotional stress, can also modify the reflex inhibition of antagonists. In the early stages of motor learning, such factors as fear, embarrassment, and intense motivation can result in indiscriminate contractions of muscle groups, thus interfering with smooth and effective performance. Expert performers have learned coordinated patterns of contraction and inhibition. These have been so strongly conditioned that only intense stresses are capable of interfering. In any performer, the removal of excess general tension minimizes the output of irrelevant motor impulses, allowing the conditioned reflexes for contraction and inhibition to occur. Coaches, teachers, and therapists who stress general relaxation, minimize fear, and use care in applying motivational stresses during the learning process are acting upon sound physiological and psychological principles.

ORGANIZATION OF THE NERVOUS SYSTEM

Divisions of the Nervous System. The nervous system may be divided into (1) the *central nervous system,* consisting of the brain and spinal cord and (2) the *peripheral nervous system,* consisting of all ganglia and nerves outside of the brain and spinal cord (Fig. 5–5). From another aspect, the nervous system may be divided into the *autonomic* nervous system, which involves responses of the endo-

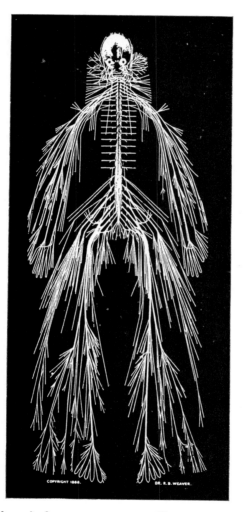

FIG. 5–5. Cerebrospinal nervous system. Harriet Cole, a scrubwoman at Hahnemann Medical College, willed her body to Anatomy Professor Rufus B. Weaver. The doctor used it for what is probably the only preserved dissection of the human nervous system. The brain was removed, but the spinal cord and the peripheral nervous system are shown. (Hahnemann Medical College and Hospital.)

crine glands receiving a nervous supply, the heart, intestines, urogenital tract, and blood vessels, and the *somatic* system, which deals with sensory impulses and motor responses of the skeletal musculature.

Cranial Nerves. The peripheral nerves arising from the brain innervate skeletal muscles, such as the muscles of the eyeball, face, and tongue, but they are mainly concerned with olfaction, vision, taste, balance, audition, and other sensory functions, and with involuntary control of the heart, lungs, stomach and other viscera. The spinal part of the *accessory nerve* (11th cranial nerve) is the only cranial nerve which innervates important postural muscles. It arises by several roots from the cervical area of the spinal cord and is joined by branches of the spinal nerves from the cervical plexus before sending motor fibers to the sternocleidomastoid and trapezius muscles.

Spinal Nerves. There are usually 31 pairs of spinal nerves, arising from the spinal cord and leaving the vertebral canal through the intervertebral foramina. Each of the 8 pairs of cervical nerves is named for the vertebra just below it (except the 8th, which arises between the 7th cervical and the 1st thoracic vertebrae), and each of the 12 thoracic, 5 lumbar, 5 sacral, and 1 coccygeal pairs is named for the vertebra just above it. Spinal nerves are called *mixed nerves* because they are made up of both sensory and motor fibers along most of their length. They are mixed in another sense, too, for most of them carry fibers of both the autonomic and somatic nervous systems.

The Spinal Cord. The spinal cord is a fluted column about 18 inches long and about one-half inch in diameter, although its diameter differs considerably at various levels. Its features are best identified in cross section (Fig. 5–6). At its center is the vertical *central canal*, surrounded by an H-shaped mass of gray (nonmedullated) matter. The two dorsal extensions of the H are called *posterior horns*; the ventral extensions are called *anterior horns*. Surrounding the gray matter is the medullated *white matter* of the cord, and this is marked off into right and left halves by a *posterior median septum* and by an *anterior median fissure*. The horns, septum, and fissure block off the white matter roughly into 6 parts; *anterior*, *lateral*, and *posterior* white columns on each side.

Microscopic study of the white columns shows them to be composed of medullated nerve fibers, the medullary sheaths being responsible for the white appearance. Most of these white fibers are arranged vertically, appearing in microscopic cross section as circles with dots in the center; a smaller number pass horizontally. The vertical fibers of the white columns have been functionally subdi-

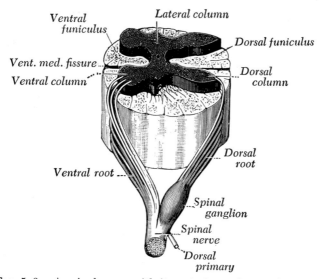

Fig. 5–6.   A spinal nerve with its anterior and posterior roots.
(*Gray's Anatomy*.)

vided into numerous *tracts*, each of which has been specifically
named.   Their function is to connect different levels of the spinal
cord with one another and with various higher centers of the brain.

Microscopic study of the gray part of the cord shows it to consist
mainly of cell bodies and non-medullated nerve fibers of various
sizes, having no uniformity of direction.   Some of the fibers seen are
the dendrites of the cell bodies; some are the axons of these cells;
some are the terminals of axons from nerve cells situated in distant
parts of the nervous system.   A large number of synapses occur in
this area.

Pathways of the Spinal Nerves.   The peripheral course of a
typical spinal nerve is shown in Figure 5–7.   As the spinal nerve root
approaches the spine, it bifurcates into an afferent root carrying
impulses of proprioception, touch, pain, heat, cold, and so forth, and
an efferent root.   The former enters the spinal cord in the region of
the posterior horn of the gray matter and is, therefore, termed the
dorsal or *posterior* root; the latter enters the spinal cord in the region
of the ventral horn of the gray matter and is termed the *ventral* or
anterior root (Fig. 5–6).   After entering the cord, the afferent fibers
take various courses, some ending in the gray matter at the same
level, some taking a vertical course in the white columns and sending
terminal endings into the gray matter at higher or lower levels, and
some traversing the white columns as far as the base of the brain.
They make synaptic contact in an exceptionally versatile manner,

either joining dendrites of motor neurons directly or joining dendrites of internuncial neurons. The internuncial neurons serve as middlemen in transferring impulses to motor neurons at the same or different spinal levels or to higher centers in the brain.

The dendrites and cell bodies of efferent (motor) neurons are located in the gray matter of the spinal cord. They collect impulses from fibers descending from the brain, from internuncial neurons, or directly from afferent spinal neurons of the same or different levels of the cord.

The basic plan of distribution of spinal nerves is clearly an evolutionary holdover from that seen in limbless segmented lower forms. At the cervical and upper thoracic spinal regions, and in the lumbar and sacral spinal regions, the adjacent spinal nerves interconnect with each other in complex patterns. These interconnections are called plexuses, of which there are five: the cervical plexus, the brachial plexus, the lumbar plexus, the sacral plexus, and the coccygeal plexus. Walshe suggests that the acroparesthesia sometimes seen in women engaged in manual work results when the supporting musculature becomes atonic and permits the shoulder girdle to sag. Pressure by the first rib and traction and compression of the lower components of the brachial plexus follows.[2] Contrariwise, elevating the arms overhead is restful, because it relieves the pull on the brachial plexus. The details of arrangements of these plexuses and of the resulting peripheral nerves are important to students of medicine, corrective therapy, physical therapy, and occupational therapy, and are shown in Appendix B. Physical educators generally require a less detailed knowledge of peripheral neurology, but it is necessary for them to understand that athletic injuries may involve nerve trauma.

SPINAL REFLEXES

A *reflex* is an involuntary muscular contraction or glandular secretion resulting from a sensory stimulation. Reflexes may be very complex, and may involve the higher brain centers. The simplest reflex is the *spinal reflex*, requiring a minimum of two neurons. An afferent neuron receives a stimulus at its peripheral end and carries the resulting impulse along a spinal nerve to the gray matter of the spinal cord by way of the dorsal root. The impulse crosses a synapse in the spinal cord to a motor neuron which transmits the impulse along the ventral horn, along a spinal nerve, and to a muscle or gland. More frequently, a third neuron (an *internuncial neuron*) lying in the gray matter of the spinal cord mediates the impulse between the sensory and the motor neurons.

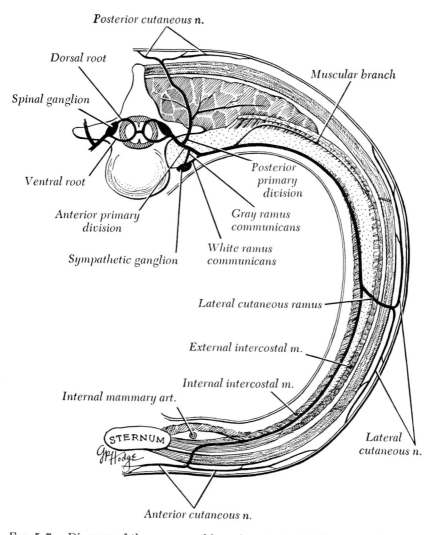

Posterior cutaneous n.

Dorsal root

Muscular branch

Spinal ganglion

Ventral root

Posterior primary division

Anterior primary division

Gray ramus communicans

White ramus communicans

Sympathetic ganglion

Lateral cutaneous ramus

External intercostal m.

Internal intercostal m.

Internal mammary art.

STERNUM

Lateral cutaneous n.

Anterior cutaneous n.

Fig. 5–7.   Diagram of the course and branches of a typical intercostal nerve.
(*Gray's Anatomy.*)

Simple spinal reflex arcs involving only two or three neurons exist.
but are hardly typical even of the most elemental reflex activity
At the synapse in the spinal cord, the impulse from the sensory
neuron is likely to trigger not only the motor neuron which com-
pletes the reflex arc, but also a number of others which carry sensory
or motor impulses along parallel pathways, to the contralateral side
of the body, to higher or lower spinal levels, to the lower brain centers,
and even to the higher levels of consciousness.   The original sensory

neuron itself may send branches to adjacent spinal levels. Internuncial neurons generally connect not with one but with numerous motor neurons at several spinal levels, as shown in Figure 5–8 by a diagram based on the unlikely assumption that only one sensory neuron was stimulated to initiate the reflex.

The oversimplified notion of a simple reflex arc is made more realistic by noting that each involved neuron has a threshold of sensitivity governed at any given moment by the algebraic sum of various inhibitory and excitatory influences supplied through many other existing synaptic connections. Some of these additionally impinging influences arise locally; others originate from distant sources, perhaps including voluntary cortical emanations. The most elementary activity usually involves countless thousands of neural elements, giving a picture of reverberating circuits and a multitude of continuous modulations from positive and negative feedback mechanisms.

A great proportion of our actions are reflexive in nature. Even a simple pinprick on the hand, causing withdrawal of a limb without

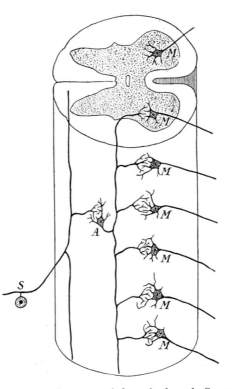

Fig. 5–8.   An internuncial neuron of the spinal cord; S, sensory neuron, A, internuncial neuron; M, M, M, motor neurons.

waking a sleeping person, irradiates to the lower brain centers. It is difficult to conceive such reflex actions as being either "simple" or "spinal" in any limiting sense of the words.

Corrective and physical therapists make use of some of the more complex reflexes in the treatment of certain types of patients. Thus the spastic hand may be "unlocked" by placing it palm up over the buttocks of the prone patient and turning his head away from the involved side. The evolutionary mechanisms underlying such phenomena and the ways in which reflexes of this type may be utilized have been summarized by Fay.[3]

KINESTHETIC AND SERVOMOTOR CONTROL

Kinesthesis or *kinesthesia* is the perception of the position and movement of one's body parts in space. It also includes perception of the internal and external tensions and forces tending to move or stabilize the joints. Various kinds of receptors contribute to kinesthesis, including (1) free, unencapsulated nerve endings sensitive to pain, (2) Meissner's corpuscles, sensitive to touch, (3) joint receptors resembling flower spray endings and giving a steady discharge proportional to changes in joint capsule tension resulting from its position (Fig. 5–9), (4) joint receptors resembling elongated Pacinian corpuscles, giving a discharge proportional to changes in capsule tension during movement[4] (Fig. 5–10), (5) Pacinian corpuscles (Fig. 5–11) sensitive to deep pressure resulting from deformation of body tissues, (6) labyrinthine receptors, (7) visual receptors, (8) auditory receptors, (9) Golgi tendon organs, and (10) muscle spindles.

Kinesthetic perceptions generally are relayed to cortical centers of consciousness, although the process of motor learning may allow them to exert their influence automatically or subconsciously. However, two of the above listed receptors operate essentially at a peripheral level, although they are markedly susceptible to central control. The Golgi tendon organs and the muscle spindles, in association with skeletal muscle fibers, form a basic servomotor system, knowledge of which is essential to an understanding of terminal muscle function. Consequently the structure and function of these organs must be considered in some detail.

Golgi Tendon Organs. The Golgi tendon organs (Fig. 5–12) consist of fusiform fibrous capsules enclosing myelinated nerve fibers. Since most of them are located at the junction of muscle fibers and their tendinous attachments at both ends of the muscle, they are said to be "in series" with the muscle. They are sensitive to both muscle stretch and muscle contraction, but cannot distinguish be-

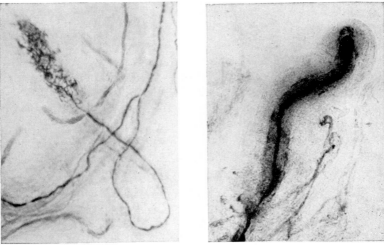

FIG. 5–9   FIG. 5–10

FIGS. 5–9 and 5–10.   Sensory endings in human synovial joint capsule.

FIG. 5–9.   Spray type ending.   Slowly adapting.   Believed to signal joint position in the steady state.

FIG. 5–10.   Lamellated or paciniform ending.   Rapidly adapting.   Believed to respond to movement and pressure.   (McCarry, with permission J. Physiol., November 1965.)

FIG. 5–11.   Phase-contrast photomicrograph of a living (unstained) Pacinian corpuscle of a cat's mesentery.   Magnification about 150 ×.   (Werner R. Loewenstein, Columbia University, College of Physicians and Surgeons.)

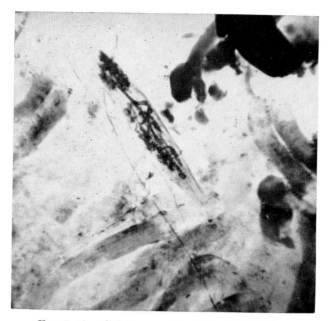

FIG. 5–12.   Golgi organ of rat. (× 100.) (Cole.)

tween the two.   In other words, they discharge as the result of tension in the tendon.   Such tension must be fairly great, since they have relatively high thresholds.   At one time they were thought to be the source of stretch reflexes, but now it is known that their discharge causes inhibition of their own muscle and facilitation of its antagonist.   This "safety valve" action prevents damage from excessive contraction on the part of the muscle in which they occur.

Muscle Spindles.   A *muscle spindle* (Fig. 5–13) consists of a connective tissue capsule about one millimeter long, six or more *intrafusal* ("within the spindle") *muscle fibers*, and some specialized motor and sensory nerve endings.   Spindles are located between the *extrafusal muscle fibers* of the whole muscle, oriented parallel to them.   The ends of the capsule extend into and merge with the connective tissue of the whole muscle.   The important point is that the spindles lie "in parallel" with the muscle, in contrast to the "in series" arrangement of the Golgi tendon organs.   Like the latter, the receptors of the muscle spindles are sensitive to stretch (Fig. 5–18*A,B,C*).   Stretching the muscle will accelerate the discharge of both Golgi receptors and spindle receptors, but contraction of the muscle will stimulate only the Golgi receptors, since as the muscle shortens it tends to slacken the tension on the muscle spindles, with a consequent decrease in the discharge rate of its receptors.   Combi-

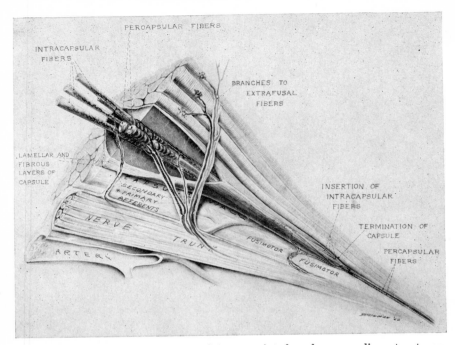

Fig. 5–13. A muscle spindle and its associated and surrounding structures. (From Eldred, Earl: The Dual Sensory Role of Muscle Spindles. J. Amer. Phys. Ther. Ass., *45*, 290–313, 1965. Courtesy of Dr. Earl Eldred and Dr. Charles F. Bridgman.)

nations of sensory information received from the various receptors render an accurate report of the situation in the muscle to the spinal level, and thence to higher centers. It is the superior recognition of and response to clues of this nature which enable the skilled performer to accomplish movements requiring a remarkable degree of neuromuscular coordination (Fig. 5–14).

Two types of intrafusal fibers occur within the same spindle. *Nuclear bag* or *percapsular fibers* perforate the capsule at both ends and extend beyond them. These large fibers are striated at their polar ends, but have a non-striated, non-contractile central equatorial region with cell nuclei clustered in a "nuclear bag." *Nuclear chain* or *intracapsular fibers* terminate within the capsule, are smaller in diameter, and have their nuclei dispersed along their length in a "nuclear chain." Muscle spindles have two kinds of sensory receptors. *Primary (annulospiral, A2, or nuclear bag) endings* wrap around the larger intrafusal nuclear bag muscle fibers at the equatorial regions (Fig. 5–15). The afferent nerve fibers leading from them are relatively large Group I fibers (8 to 12 μ in diameter), indi-

Fig. 5–14.   Muriel Davis Grossfeld, member of the 1956, 1960 and 1964 United States Olympic Teams, holding a difficult version of the "yogi stand."   Note that the position of the head makes it impossible to utilize visual clues to assist in maintaining the balance, and the performer must depend almost entirely upon proprioceptive impulses from the hands for knowledge of the adjustments which must be made.   The ability to thus sacrifice certain input channels and still function perfectly is a sign of unusually fine kinesthetic proficiency.

cating fast conduction rates. Some, but not all, muscle spindles have *secondary (flower spray, A1, or nuclear chain) endings* on the smaller intrafusal nuclear chain muscle fibers and/or on the larger intrafusal nuclear bag muscle fibers at the polar regions (Fig. 5–16). The afferent nerve fibers in this case are relatively small Group II fibers (6 to 9 μ in diameter), indicating slower conduction rates. These secondary endings are usually believed to be responsible for a flexor reflex, with inhibition of the extensors.

5

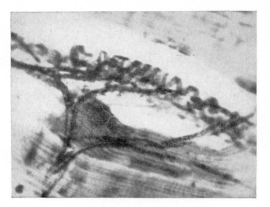

FIG. 5–15. Primary (annulospiral) endings around the intrafusal fibers in the mouse (× 450.) (Cole.)

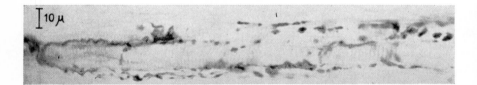

FIG. 5–16.   Secondary (flower spray) endings of the cat's muscle spindle. (Coërs.)

The primary endings have a lower threshold than do the secondary endings. They are sensitive to stretch and their discharge produces a reflex contraction known as the *stretch reflex*. This causes the muscle to contract to a degree roughly proportional to the amount of the applied stretch, thus restoring the muscle to its original length. The familiar *knee jerk* or *patellar tendon reflex* is an example.   The athlete attempts to take advantage of this phenomenon by a quick stretch in the preliminary back swing preparatory to throwing and other similar movements.   The afferent impulse from the primary endings also connects, through inhibitory internuncial neurons in the spinal cord, with the muscle's antagonist. Their output is responsible for reciprocal innervation, which reduces the "drag" of the antagonist on the agonist. If the stretch reflex is too extensive, however, it will stretch the antagonist as well, whose own primary endings will be stimulated, thereby initiating a stretch reflex in the opposite direction and causing double reciprocal inhibition.

Not as much is known about the effects of discharge from the secondary endings. Eldred[5] presents evidence that the discharge of secondary endings in flexor muscles facilitates the flexors and inhibits the extensors (like a stretch reflex), but discharge of secondary endings in extensor muscles also facilitates the flexors and inhibits the extensors (unlike a stretch reflex). Therefore, the arrangement is not doubly reciprocal (Fig. 5–17). Recent work suggests that the stretch reflex depends upon the excitation of both the primary and sensory endings of the spindle.

While these findings have cast doubt on Sherrington's explanation of some of his observations, the fact remains that the interplay of these reflexes serves to correct each other and to provide a means of fine adjustment and control over body position and movement.

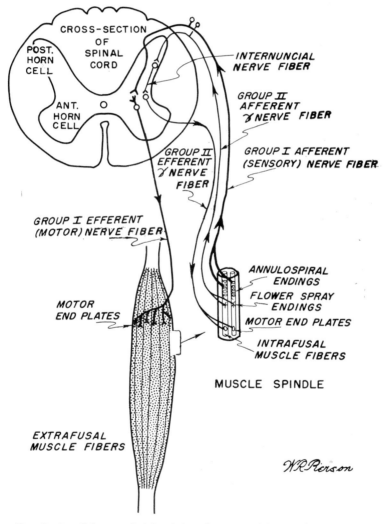

FIG. 5–17. Schema of alpha (α) and gamma (γ) neural systems.

However, attempts to exploit these phenomena to augment the development of muscular strength have proved disappointing.[6]

The Fusimotor or Gamma System. The muscle spindle has recently been the subject of a comprehensive review by Matthews,[7] to which the student is referred for a detailed discussion of the subject. A number of the body's sensory systems are subject to central control by which their sensitivity can be set at various levels, somewhat like a thermostat. These sensitivity settings can be predictive— that is, the sensitivity level may be set at one moment in order to serve an anticipated sensory need which will occur several moments later. Were it not for such settings, body reactions would always be a little bit late, for there is an inevitable time delay in the working of any system employing negative feedback controls.

In the muscle spindle, the mechanism for selective sensitivity settings depends upon its *gamma motor neurons*, which are functionally independent from the *alpha motor neurons* that initiate contraction in the extrafusal fibers of the whole muscle (Fig. 5–17). The gamma neurons end on the intrafusal fibers, and their impulses result in contractile shortening of the spindle without any detectable influence on the strength or shortening of the whole muscle. When a whole muscle contracts under the influence of the alpha motoneurons, the muscle spindles are slackened (Fig. 5–18*D*). The result is a cessation of discharges from the primary and secondary endings within the spindles, and abolition of the stretch reflex. As the spindles become slack, however, gamma motor discharge can be increased, restoring tension within the spindles and re-setting the sensitivity of the sensory mechanism (Fig. 5–18*E*). The same thing may happen when the whole muscle slackens as the result of muscular relaxation. The gamma neurons and the intrafusal muscle fibers thus appear to be a servo-mechanism for controlling afferent discharge. In the spinal cord, the gamma motoneurons are under the integrated control of several efferent tracts originating in both the subconscious and the volitional centers of the brain. These higher centers can "decide" in advance what level of reflex sensitivity will be required, and set the tension within the spindle accordingly. Technically, this might be called a "follow-up length servo."

CONDITIONED REFLEXES

Although some reflexes are developed prenatally, most are learned. It is a mistake to think of all reflexes as inherited reactions, or as a limited number of very primitive reactions. The usual goal in motor learning is to reduce the new movement patterns to subconscious automaticity, dependent merely upon a push-button sort of stimulus

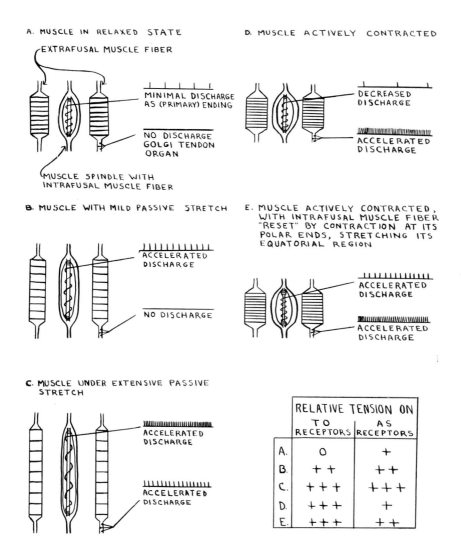

Fig. 5–18. Simplified scheme of possible variations in afferent discharge from Golgi tendon organs (*TO*) and from muscle spindle primary or annulospiral receptors (*AS*), under various conditions of extrafusal relaxation, stretch, and contraction. Both *TO* and *AS* receptors are sensitive to passive stretching, although *TO* receptors have a higher threshold (*A, B,* and *C*). The *TO* receptors respond indiscriminately to extensive stretch (*C*) and to active extrafusal contraction (*D* and *E*). Active contraction relieves the tension on *AS* receptors (*D*), unless gamma efferent activity "resets" the tension within the intrafusal fiber (*E*). Intrafusal secondary or flower-spray receptors have been omitted here, although in actuality they add still another variable factor to the array of afferent information.

at either conscious or unconscious levels. Highly complex motor activities, such as those involved in sports situations, may at first thought seem to be predominantly under conscious modification according to the changing environmental situation. If the performer is an expert, this supposed emphasis on conscious direction may be false. It is true that there must be attention to cues, but the performance is likely to be a complex learned reflexive response. The many re-directions which occur during the performance are also reflexive, arising directly in response to the stimuli of the changing situation, rather than being deliberately and rationally inaugurated by the highest levels of the brain. The conscious mind of a star shortstop, while making a sensational pick-up of a hard-driven bounding ball, is likely to be concerned more with the possible wisdom of starting a double play than with specific direction of his bodily actions.

MOTOR LEARNING

It has been suggested that the properties of bone and muscle and the way in which they are constructed may account for many psychomotor abilities.[8] However, the field of motor learning is so broad, so complicated, and so poorly understood that it would be absurd to attempt even an overview of principles within the scope of a text in kinesiology. The following discussion, therefore, is fragmentary, and is limited to a few elementary applications of anatomic and kinesiological principles to the problem of learning to perform neuromuscular skills. Extensive discussions of this topic are available in texts such as the one by Cratty.[9]

Maturation and Motor Learning. Maturation means growing accompanied by changes in functional ability; the emphasis is on "ripening" rather than on changes in size, shape, and volume. Every teacher of motor skills should be familiar with the crucial relationship between physical or physiological maturation and motor learning. For example, motor learning during the first two years of life is limited by the degree of myelination of nerve fibers, which is incomplete during this period. Certain coordinations such as creeping and walking must await the development of myelin sheaths in the appropriate nerves and spinal tracts, perhaps to prevent a chaotic "short-circuiting" of the necessary impulses. Because maturation is correlated highly with age, parents and teachers should become familiar with descriptions, of average abilities at various age levels, so as to adjust teaching processes to the known periods of readiness of the child. But because maturation is not perfectly correlated with age, an intelligent person should guard against a blind application of such norms. Norms are guides, and should never substitute for observation and testing of the individual child.

Rathbone and Hunt[10] have emphasized the progressive sequence in the development of motor skills, dependent partly upon maturation. Although a particular kind of skill cannot be mastered prior to the necessary physical maturation, attainment of the skill can be by-passed, perhaps irretrievably, if the environment does not allow it to be mastered in the normal sequence, soon after maturation produces the potentiality. Rathbone and Hunt contend that crawling, for example, is a vital activity in the development of trunk musculature, and that children who for some reason omit the crawling stage before learning to walk have missed a valuable neuromuscular experience which can never be replaced. The relationship of such omissions to posture, visceral function, and physical development in later life needs to be investigated experimentally. It is well known among physical education teachers that basic attainments in sports and aquatic skills are most easily achieved before or during adolescence, although the proportional influence of physical factors and social or psychological factors remains obscure.

Progression. It is a matter of common observation that a child stands before he walks and walks before he runs. Complex motor learning, even more than other types of learning, such as problem solving and rote memorizing, requires an order of prerequisites, a background of specific attainments. Complex coordinations cannot be mastered until certain basic movement patterns have been reduced to the automaticity of conditioned reflexes. In general, fine movements are distilled out of gross movements; new skills are based upon recombinations of the elements of old skills. It is a principle of physical education that early motor training should be broad, varied, and general to provide a basis for later learning which is more refined, specialized, and complex. This principle rests upon a sound neuromuscular basis.

This concept has implications for therapy as well. Rood emphasizes that general functional activities, muscle groups, and patterns of movement pass through developmental sequences. In her system the therapeutic approach is essentially designed to reproduce the normal developmental sequences which are missing from the abnormal motor sequences of the patient.[11]

Individual Differences in Structure. Structure influences performance. The relationship may be either permissive or restrictive, and is variable according to the nature of each separate activity. Each of the following factors, many of which are discussed extensively elsewhere in this text, contributes to the individual differences which affect motor performance: (1) Somatotype or body type; (2) height of the body and length of bony levers; (3) proportions of bone, muscle, and fat; (4) specific gravity or buoyancy of the body; (5) adequacy of nutrition; (6) acuity of vision, audition, proprioception, and other sensations; (7) mobility of various joints; (8) hereditary or congenital structural abnormalities; and (9) residual defects from disease or trauma. The trained kinesiologist views a performer or a would-be performer with an analytic eye, assessing his individual abilities and capabilities for particular activities.

Standard Form. Much kinesiology has implications for determining the mechanical technique or "form" to be employed by the learner. Class teaching methods often imply that there is a best way to perform in a given situation, whether it be postural adjustment, crutch-walking, or participation in a sport. But teachers should not insist upon too rigid a "form." In the first place, better "forms" are still being discovered for most activities, as the history of championship performance clearly demonstrates. In the second place, individual differences can never be completely understood. There is a wisdom of the body which supersedes academic knowledge or analysis, and a little trial-and-error learning frequently produces a more effective performance technique than could rigid direction.

The seemingly authoritative descriptions of technique by champion athletes are sometimes at variance with the form they actually employ. Motion picture analysis and electromyographic studies have frequently uncovered discrepancies between what a performer thinks he does and what he really does. (See Fig. 22-2.) The expert performer functions so largely on the reflex level that he does not find it necessary to analyze routine movements and is therefore often unconscious of precisely how he executes them. For this reason experts are sometimes poor teachers, whereas less accomplished individuals may be forced to develop the ability to analyze performance effectively.

Practicing for Speed and Accuracy. If a finished skill requires both high speed and great accuracy, as does a tennis serve, practice should emphasize both of the qualities from the beginning, as much as possible. If accuracy is emphasized to the neglect of speed, much relearning must take place in the final stages of practice when a faster speed is employed. A target-directed skill like pitching a baseball involves one kinesiological pattern when performed slowly and an entirely different pattern when performed rapidly. The difference consists largely of variation in the degree of contraction of muscles antagonistic to the prime movers. This difference between slow controlled movements, rapid controlled movements, and ballistic movements has been discussed in Chapter 3.

Speed of movement should not be confused with haste in performance. In most gross skills, speed implies the application of great force, and the verbal admonition to the performer might well be "harder" or "more forceful" performance rather than "faster" performance. General haste, on the other hand, is likely to cause a central irradiation of neural impulses to muscles whose contraction would be unnecessary or disadvantageous. This is one reason why a performer "ties up."

NEUROMOTOR COMPLEXITY AND CONTROL: A SUMMARY

The varieties and qualities of human motion are infinite in number. Yet at the level of terminal action, the effector mechanism basically is very simple. The operational structure is the motor unit—a group of skeletal muscle fibers innervated by a motor neuron arising in the spinal cord. This motor unit either can act, with contraction of its muscle fibers, or not act. There are no other possibilities. All the versatility of human motion depends upon the selective activation of individual motor units in various combinations.

But the functioning of motor units is only superficially simple. Variety, versatility, and complexity are inherent in the very nature of this effector system. The first variable is the great number of individual motor units, and their independence of action. None, some, or many motor units may be activated, in all sorts of combinations, at any given moment. The second variable is the possibility of graded contraction of the motor units, dependent largely upon the frequency with which motor impulses arrive at the muscle fibers. The third variable is the organization of groups of muscle fibers into separate muscles, with tendons arranged variously so as to produce different joint actions. The fourth variable is the variety of combinations in which different muscles can be activated synergistically; for example, a flexor and an abductor can work together to produce an intermediate diagonal movement, or a flexor and an extensor can cooperate to attain rigid stability. A fifth variable is the physiological condition of the tissues, involving relative states of nutrition, fatigue, training, oxygen availability, and other factors. And as yet virtually nothing has been said about the control system.

Spinal reflexes are the basis for control of human movement. Certain sensory and motor neurons are morphologically located so as to provide for reflex action. Functionally, some of these reflexes appear to be innate; others are acquired or learned through complex processes, after which they become relatively simple and peripherally automatic. Some reflexes are opposite or antagonistic to each other;

for example, an extensor thrust and a flexor withdrawal. Obviously, there must be control mechanisms to account for the selection, in terms of activation or inhibition, of reflexes in various combinations or patterns at different times.

An interesting example of the functioning of the proprioceptors is seen in the knockdown in boxing. The blow causes a violent rotational movement of the head. The subsequent synchronous discharge of the proprioceptors results in an intense reflex counterrotation, with the result that the boxer falls in the direction from which the blow came.[12]

One major determinant for the selection of reflex patterns is sensory input. Here variety is evident not only with respect to kinds of inputs, but also with respect to numbers of individual units available and the intensity of their stimulations. Light pressure might elicit a mild extensor thrust reflex; obnoxious pressure might result in a more vigorous thrust; a pinprick might generate a withdrawal reflex.

Numerous as they are, the different kinds of sensations are inadequate to provide effective versatility of response. The possible responses are tremendously increased by combinations of sensations. For example, three of the more important sensory detectors are Golgi tendon organs, spindle primary endings, and spindle secondary endings. These can act separately or in various combinations and permutations, multiplying the possible effects. Further, there are built-in feedback circuits. Some are complex and indirect; others are simple and direct. In the Renshaw loop a motoneuron gives off side branches before leaving the spinal cord, so that whenever it activates a muscle it simultaneously activates an internuncial inhibitory neuron which is functionally connected to the cell body of the original motoneuron. This results in a self-inhibiting or "start-stop" circuit. An example of a more indirect servo control is double reciprocal inhibition, whereby two similar stretch reflexes in antagonistic muscles limit and modulate each other, producing a postural position which is stable except for minute oscillations.

Although the foregoing discussion of peripheral neuromotor mechanisms is schematic and simplified, it does indicate the complexity and versatility of this system. Obviously, the peripheral neuromotor pathways must be capable of producing *all* possible human motion. Supraspinal mechanisms do not increase the repertoire of possible responses; rather, they provide control and coordination by facilitating or inhibiting the peripheral neurons. Ritchie[13] has classified the descending nerve tracts from the various brain centers into (1) the voluntary system, from the cerebral cortex, (2) the antigravity system, from the vestibular nucleus, and (3) the suppressor system, from the red nucleus and the reticular formation. Each of these may have both excitatory and inhibitory elements, and each transmits the selected and filtered output of various processing stations of the brain. As Ritchie pointed out, one of the more important centers of motor coordination is the cerebellum, which has no direct communication with the spinal motoneurons but which directs its output to other centers of integration. Man's nervous system is not capable of detailed rational understanding of its own complexity!

Plasticity—the ability of the nervous system to fashion and modify itself functionally through functioning—constitutes the highest level of neural complexity. Conditioning, learning, remembering, forgetting, relearning, and other sophisticated psychophysical aspects of man's behavior give evidence of the plasticity of his nervous system. At the limits of human understanding are the qualities of personality, motivation, body image, consciousness, meaning, and significance. All of these are crucial considerations in even the least complex human body motions, including "simple spinal reflexes.'

References

1. Cole, W. V.: The Effect of Immobilization on Striated Muscle and the Myoneural Junction. J. Comp. Neur., 115, 9–13, 1960.

2. Walshe, F. M. R.: On "Acroparaesthesia" and So-Called "Neuritis" of the Hand and Arm in Women. Brit. Med. J., 4426, 596–597, 1945.

3. Fay, Temple: The Origin of Human Movement. Amer. J. Psychiat., 111, 644–652, 1952.

4. Gardner, Ernest D.: Physiology of Joints. J. Bone Joint Surg., 45-A, 1061–1966, 1963.

5. Eldred, Earl: The Dual Sensory Role of Muscle Spindles. J. Am. Phys. Ther. Ass., 45, 290–313, 1965.

6. Awad, Essam A. and Kottke, Frederic J.: Effectiveness of Myotatic Reflex Facilitation in Augmenting Rate of Increase of Muscular Strength due to Brief Maximal Exercise. Arch. Phys. Med., 45, 23–29, 1964.

7. Matthews, P. B. C.: Muscle Spindles and Their Motor Control. Physiol. Rev., 44, 219–288, 1964.

8. Guilford, J. P.: A System of Psychomotor Abilities. Amer. J. Psychol., 71, 164–174, 1958.

9. Cratty, Bryant J.: Movement Behavior and Motor Learning, 2nd Ed. Philadelphia: Lea & Febiger, 1967.

10. Rathbone, Josephine L. and Hunt, Valerie: Corrective Physical Education, 7th Ed. Philadelphia: W. B. Saunders Co., 1965, pp. 75–76.

11. Stockmeyer, Shirley Ann: An Interpretation of the Approach of Rood to the Treatment of Neuromuscular Dysfunction. Amer. J. Phys. Med., 46, 900–956, 1967.

12. Govons, S. R.: Brain Concussion and Posture: The Knockdown Blow of the Boxing Ring. Confin. Psychiat., 30, 77–84, 1968.

13. Ritchie, A. E.: Physiological Control of Muscle. Physiotherapy, 49, 16–19, 10 January, 1963.

Recommended Reading

14. Barker, D.: The Innervation of the Musclespindle. Quart. J. Mic. Sci., *89*, 143–186, 1948.

15. Granit, R., editor: *Muscular Afferents and Motor Control*. New York: John Wiley and Sons, 1966.

Chapter 6

Center of Gravity and Equilibrium

The center of gravity of the body is the point at which the weight of the body may be considered to be concentrated. An understanding of the concept is essential to the solution of nearly every problem in the analysis of human motion. "The displacement pattern of the center of gravity," say Saunders, *et al.*, "may be regarded as constituting the summation or end result of all forces and motions acting upon and concerned with the translation of the body from one point to another."[1]

Gravitational force may be considered as having three unique characteristics: (1) it is applied constantly, without interruptions; (2) it is applied in one direction only, toward the center of the earth; and (3) it acts upon each mass-particle of the body and of other implements and objects. As thus stated, these characteristics are somewhat oversimplified. Expressed more technically, gravitational force constitutes the attraction which each mass-particle in the universe has for every other mass-particle. In the case of any two particles, each attracts the other with a magnitude porportional to its mass and inversely proportional to the distance between the two particles. However, the total mass of the earth is so great and its proximity to the individual so close that no significant error is produced in the solution of practical problems by assuming that the force acts only toward the center of the earth and only on the object attracted by the earth. Since the force of gravity acts on every particle of an object and since all these forces are directed toward the center of the earth, it is mathematically demonstrable that the total gravitational force on the object is the same as if all of the object's mass were concentrated at a single central locus—the center of gravity of the object. It is a purely mathematical construct having no physical reality, and one which merely provides a generalization that greatly simplifies computation and understanding.

The center of gravity of a rigid symmetrical body of uniform density coincides with its geometrical center. Other rigid bodies, such as a tennis racket, may be suspended from any one point and a vertical line dropped from the point of support through the object. This can then be repeated using any other point of support, and the intersection of the two lines will locate the center of gravity. The determination of the center of gravity of a non-rigid, asymmetrical object of heterogeneous density such as the human body is more difficult. Usually it is most convenient to balance the body on a

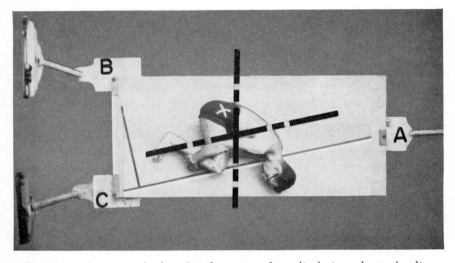

Fig. 6–1. Apparatus for locating the center of gravity in two planes simultaneously, photographed from directly overhead. The rectangular balance board rests on three weighing scales by means of pointed bolts (A,B,C). Theoretically, only two scales are needed; the third permits an accuracy check. The center of gravity of the subject will be located (as shown by the intersecting dashed lines on the photograph) directly above a point which is G_A distant from line BC and G_B distant from line AC, as calculated by the formulas

$$G_A = \frac{(a_2 - a_1)\,(D_A)}{W}, \text{ and } G_B = \frac{(b_2 - b_1)\,(D_B)}{W},$$

where

G_A = perpendicular distance of center of gravity from line BC.
G_B = perpendicular distance of center of gravity from line AC.
a_1 = scale reading for board alone at Scale A.
a_2 = scale reading for board and subject at Scale A.
b_1 = scale reading for board alone at Scale B.
b_2 = scale reading for board and subject at Scale B.
D_A = perpendicular distance from line BC to point A.
D_B = perpendicular distance from line AC to point B.
W = weight of the subject.

knife edge and erect vertical lines. Sometimes the body can be frozen, as was done by Braune and Fischer (p. 9) or placed on a solid platform for measuring purposes (Fig. 6–1). There are, of course, complex mathematical methods for locating centers of gravity under research conditions, but for practical studies in sports and medicine it is seldom necessary to know the location of the center of gravity with such precision.

In the normal erect standing position with the arms hanging at the sides, the center of gravity of adult males is approximately 56 to 57 per cent of their total height from the floor. The center of gravity of adult females is somewhat lower, being about 55 per cent of their standing height. There are relatively large deviations between individuals due to differences in physique. The center of gravity of small children and adolescents is higher than in adults because of the disproportionate size of the head and thorax and the relatively small legs. In general, the younger the child the higher the center of gravity and hence the lower its stability. The center of gravity of the segments of the body is about 4/7 of the distance above their distal ends.[2] It is seldom necessary to calculate this in the type of problem encountered by the student.

Through repeated experiences in maintaining balance a performer's own kinesthetic and proprioceptive mechanisms teach him to locate his center of gravity and that of his equipment and implements with remarkable accuracy, and this information may be passed along to others in the form of coaching advice. However, such knowledge is deepened if the underlying theory is understood. For instance, many students who are unschooled in physics are surprised to learn that the center of gravity of an object may fall outside of its physical dimensions. In a plain wedding ring it lies at the center of the space within the ring. If the body is in effect curled to form a ring and the individual dives over a bar instead of jumping over it, the center of gravity passes just *beneath* the bar instead of crossing over it. The rules governing high jumping forbid diving, and thus debar jumpers from taking advantage of this phenomenon.

The Gravitational Constant, Mass, and Weight. Due to the fact that the earth is flattened at the poles and bulges at the equator, the force of gravity varies from place to place on its surface. It is slightly greater at the poles than at the equator, partly because the distance to the center of the earth is less at the poles and partly because the centrifugal force of the earth's rotation exerts a counter-gravitational force (Coriolis effect) which is greater at the equator. It has been calculated that a javelin thrower would hurl the spear 6 inches farther at Melbourne than he would at Helsinki, and a long jumper would jump 1.5 inches farther. Tables have been computed to determine the correction factors necessary to equalize performances at various latitudes and to show their effect on various field events.[3,4] Similarly, a football passer facing east throws slightly farther than he does when facing west.[5] For ordinary purposes not requiring research precision g is taken to be 32.2 ft./sec./sec., (or 32.2 ft./sec.[2], which is read 32.2 feet per second per second). This is the *gravitational constant* (g)* expressing the acceleration which gravity imparts to a freely falling object in the absence of air resistance or friction. The speed of a falling object increases by 32.2 ft./sec. each second; its *acceleration* is 32.2 ft./sec.[2] As a result it travels 16.1 feet in the first second, 48.3 feet in the next second, 80.5 feet in the third second, and so on until it reaches a terminal velocity of 120 m.p.h. after a fall of about 482 ft. at sea level. As indicated in the preceding footnote, the actual figures will vary with the location. The weight of the object has no influence on g. Thus, if the distance an object falls is known, the time taken in the fall can be calculated by the formula

$$t = \sqrt{\frac{S}{1/2g}} \text{ or } S = 1/2gt^2$$

where S = distance, g = gravitational constant, and t = time. Suppose a gymnast loses his grip and falls to the floor of the gymnasium from a height of nine feet. What will be the time taken in the fall? Substituting in the above formula:

$$t = \sqrt{\frac{9}{16.1}} \qquad 9' = 16.1 \times t^2$$

$$t = \sqrt{.5990} \text{ or } t^2 = \frac{9}{16.1}$$

$$t = .75 \text{ sec.} \qquad t = \sqrt{.56} = .75 \text{ sec.}$$

It will be observed that the time taken in the fall is independent of the weight of the gymnast. Similarly, if the time of the fall is known, the distance of the fall can be computed. In either case no reference to the weight of the object is necessary. However, the position of the body, the clothing worn, body surface area, and similar factors alter the air resistance and thus affect the speed of the fall.

* Technically this is expressed as 981.274 gal. (galileos), that is 981.274 centimeters per second as measured at Helmert Tower, in Potsdam, Germany. Gravity measurements elsewhere are calibrated with those at Potsdam, either directly or indirectly.

Mass is a true constant, representing the amount of matter in an object. In the human being, one-half of the mass is within one inch of the surface.[6] The weight of a given mass will vary from place to place in the universe and on earth, depending on the gravitational constant at that particular place. Mass may be defined as the quotient of weight, measured in a given place, divided by the gravitational constant at that place, or

$$m = \frac{W}{g}.$$

Mass appears as an element in some of the mechanical formulae used in subsequent chapters. Wherever the term m appears, its equivalent, $\frac{W}{g}$, which is more directly obtainable, may be substituted.

Weight is the product of the mass of an object and the gravitational constant, or $W = mg$. In practical problems, weight is determined directly from a set of scales. The constant g, for any particular latitude on earth, may be found in tables in physics books, or it may be taken roughly to be 32.2 ft./sec.[2] anywhere on earth in the solution of most practical problems.

Anatomical Reference Planes. Kinesiologists make use of an orientation system which defines three cardinal orientation planes placed at right angles to one another with a common intersection at the center of gravity of the body while it is in the anatomical position. The various resulting halves are conventionally labelled as shown in Figures 6–2, 6–3, and 6–4. By use of these coordinates any position of the body may be described mathematically. The distance of a point from the line of gravity (see below) gives the lever arm upon which gravitational stresses act and enable us to compute the rotatory moment which gravity develops about the joint.

Planes other than the cardinal planes which pass through the center of gravity are often referred to, in which case the word "cardinal" is omitted and some other landmark, such as the shoulder joint, is designated or inferred in order to locate the plane.

The Gravital Line. The vertical intersection of the cardinal antero-posterior and frontal planes defines the *gravital line (line of gravity,* or *line of weight).* This locates the center of gravity, which is a point, in two planes, but leaves its height unspecified. In a balanced position, the line of gravity passes approximately through the geometrical center of the base of support, *i.e.,* the area in which the body is in contact with the ground. In the erect position this line normally falls approximately 5 cm. in front of the ankle joint.

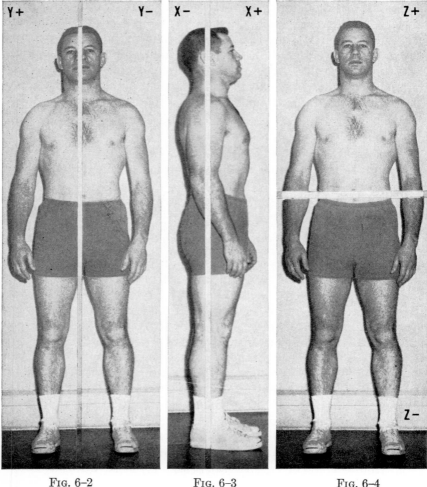

FIG. 6–2   FIG. 6–3   FIG. 6–4

FIG. 6–2. Sagittal plane.

FIG. 6–3. Frontal or coronal plane.

FIG. 6–4. Horizontal or transverse plane. (Photos by Pierson.)

As long as the line of gravity remains inside the base of support the body is stable; if it falls outside of the base, the balance is lost. This has been termed the first principle of body mechanics.[7] A skater, runner, or other athlete may, of course, deliberately assume an unstable position while rounding a curve or changing direction in order to offset the centrifugal forces which he develops. Contrariwise, the sprint start (Fig. 6–5) and similar movements involve an extreme displacement of the center of gravity outside of the base of

| The Lunge | The Crouch | Stand-Up Crouch | The Dab |

FIG. 6-5. This historically valuable photograph depicts the evolution of starting style in the sprints. What are the kinesiological reasons for the superiority of the Crouch over the Stand-Up Crouch and of the Stand-Up Crouch over the Dab? What mechanical principle was involved in the lunge? Why would you expect this to be unsatisfactory in practice? (Photograph courtesy Thomas K. Cureton.)

support in order to render the runner's equilibrium unstable in the direction of the desired movement. Conversely, the defensive wrestler increases his stability as much as is feasible by lowering his center of gravity and increasing his base of support.

Variations in the Center of Gravity. The anatomical position and the cardinal planes are used for purposes of standard reference, but the body is seldom in this position and it must not be assumed that the location of the center of gravity so defined is constant. Any change in position, even those resulting from respiration and the circulation of the blood, causes the center of gravity to move. Raising an arm, bending, wearing high heels, pregnancy, and similar circumstances cause the center of gravity to shift in proportion to the percentage of the body's mass which is moved. The rhythmic upward and downward motion of the body during walking (see Fig. 21-4) was described by Aristotle[8] hundreds of years ago, and in our own time has been studied with highly sophisticated cinematographic techniques. In the normal male adult the center of gravity of the body is displaced about 1.8 inches during the cycle from one striking of the heel to the subsequent striking of the same heel. The center of gravity thus describes a smooth undulating curve of low amplitude, which requires less energy than would be true in other possible bipedal gaits. This illustrates another important principle of body mechanics: the individual tends to function in the way which affords the greatest conservation of energy.[1] Even breathing takes place at frequencies which are close to those which are the most economical in terms of average muscle force.[9] Plato identified this principle with beauty by observing, "The most beautiful motion is that which accomplishes the greatest results with the least effort."[10] In sprinting, in which all efforts to conserve energy are discarded, the displacement of the center of gravity is approximately 11 cm.

One aim of postural integration in man is to keep the line of gravity within ±7 per cent of the geometric center of the base of support.[11] If a person carries a load, but remains on balance, the body weight is shifted so that the center of gravity of the combined body and load is more or less directly over the supporting base. If the load is carried to one side, the body leans toward the opposite side; if the load is carried in front, the body leans backward. Much practical work in kinesiology has been sponsored by the armies of the world in order to determine the effect of various types and positions of army packs on the line of gravity, and many studies have been undertaken in efforts to determine where this line should fall ideally, but differences in human physique have made it difficult to generalize from the findings.

When an outside force is directed on the body, the resulting movement depends upon the direction of the force with reference to the center of gravity. An unopposed force from any direction which is directed at the center of gravity causes the whole body to move in the direction of the force, with no rotational effect. An impinging outside force aimed anywhere except in the center of gravity tends to cause both movements of the whole body in that direction and also a rotation of the body around its center of gravity. The "secret" of judo is simply that it is a highly developed technique of applying the above laws. The judoka applies force, or utilizes the force developed by an opponent, to cause the latter first to move and then to fall in a desired direction (Fig. 8–7). More familiar examples may be found in football, where it will be observed that a horizontal charge aimed at the level of the center of gravity of opponent tends to move him to another place; a higher charge tends to tip him over while moving him, and a lower charge tends to topple him forward over the charge while moving him. By observing the way in which the blocks are applied by the offensive team, the kinesiologist should be able to anticipate the type of play that is developing.

Equilibrium. An object is in a state of stable equilibrium or rest when the resultant of all forces acting upon it is zero. Unless a force from any direction is exactly balanced by an equal force from the opposite direction, either rectilinear or rotary motion, or both, will result.

Someone has defined walking as "a series of catastrophes narrowly averted." This is the story of dynamic equilibrium. Dynamic equilibrium differs from stable equilibrium in that the situation is constantly changing and there are relatively few, if any, momentary positions in which the conditions of stable equilibrium, as defined above, are met. Such sports activities as dribbling a basketball, broken field running, holding a one-arm handstand on the parallel bars, walking a tight wire, skiing a slalom course, or pirouetting on ice skates are but intensified versions of the same equilibrium problems which confront the individual who is walking. In all of these situations, the area of the base of support is relatively very small, the center of gravity is relatively high, and the forces acting on the body are diverse, with constant changes in both magnitude and direction (Fig. 6–6). Even so-called "static standing" has been

FIG. 6–6. Carol Caverly in a superb exhibition of dynamic equilibrium. It would, of course, be impossible for any performer to maintain this posture as a rigid position. (Courtesy of Miss Caverly, formerly with Shipstads and Johnson Ice Follies.)

found to be impossible; there is always a swaying which gives evidence of a dynamic situation requiring unremitting adjustments and counteradjustments of position in order to maintain balance.

On page 505 and following is a discussion of the principles of stability applied to starting positions in sports. In that section, rules for increasing the stability of positions are outlined. All of them apply equally to the problems of dynamic balance; in addition, there are other rules which apply specifically to the unstable conditions of dynamic balance.

Since oscillations are characteristic of efforts to maintain balance under unstable dynamic conditions, some attention must be given to the nature of the sensory mechanisms which provide information necessary for gauging the timing and amplitude of the movements designed to maintain the balance. Many performers tend to rely too heavily upon the visual reflexes which detect unbalancing movements of the body. However, vision may become blurred by perspiration, violent effort, or lack of steady environmental reference points. A skilled performer also becomes very sensitive to proprioceptive sensations in the tendons and joints, and information from the semicircular canals of the inner ear. Since too much dependence upon visual information may inhibit a development of the proprioceptive and labyrinthine mechanisms, coaching advice which centers attention upon non-visual mechanisms may be helpful. A few coaches have even tried blindfold practice sessions as a training device. In any event, a highly-developed awareness of the occurrence of unbalancing movements is essential to expert performance.

After the unbalancing movement is perceived, some motion is initiated to counterbalance it and move the center of gravity of the body back over the supporting base. Typically, this countermovement is too great, producing an unbalancing movement in the opposite direction. This calls again for detection and countermovement. As the process is repeated, oscillation occurs. The beginner, whose detection and compensation mechanisms are both poorly trained, usually finds that the oscillations progressively increase in amplitude, until he finally loses his balance. In the skilled performer, the sensory mechanisms detect the imbalance at a very early stage, and the compensatory movements are made precisely and with controlled magnitude, so that the oscillations diminish (or at least do not increase) in amplitude. Thus, the skilled performer doing a handstand appears to be stationary; the skilled bicycle rider appears to remain upright, moving forward only. Actually, continuous fine fluctuations and oscillations are characteristic of all such skilled activities. A rigid position is impossible for dynamic balance skills, and the performer or coach who emphasizes rigidity is predestined to failure. A fluid, relaxed, smoothly controlled pattern of movement is essential for successful performance.

In many sports, dynamic balance problems are intensified by the presence of outside forces which impinge upon the performer irregularly during the activity. The fast-moving basketball player must accurately estimate the direction and magnitude of forces about to be thrust upon him by a moving ball passed to him, or by another player who hits him. In such situations, his own compensatory movements and position adjustments must frequently be initiated before the actual impingement of the force upon him. Since forces of this nature are irregular and unpredictable before their occurrence, they cannot be relegated to the performer's repertoire of unconscious skill habits, but require his conscious attention in scanning, anticipating, and compensating as they occur during the activity.

McCabe[12] reported a study of Ronnie Robertson, star skater of the Ice Capades, who spins at his maximum speed of 420 r.p.m. for a full 12 seconds without evidence of vertigo or nystagmus either during or after his performance. Collins[13] found no instances of complete suppression of nystagmus, and observed that the marked reduction of vestibularly induced ocular movements did not occur when skaters spun in the dark or with eyes closed. When deprived of visual fixation after rotation, skaters were disoriented in much the same manner that unpracticed subjects would be. Dancers, who pirouette at a much lower angular velocity, can obtain visual fixation by using a "spotting" technique for most of the duration of their rotation. The experiments with skaters suggest that expert performance requires not the ignoring of sensory input but the development of a remarkable ability to interpret and selectively integrate various sensory inputs.

Tight rope walkers and similar performers may employ artificial aids to assist in maintaining their equilibrium. One such device is a limber pole weighted at both ends to lower the acrobat's center of gravity. The so-called "rolling gait" of the small boat sailor results from his habit of spreading his legs to increase his base of support and of slightly flexing his knees to lower his center of gravity. Industrial workers seldom stand with the weight equally distributed on the two feet. Those working with one hand tend to place the greater portion of the weight on the opposite foot, as the most stable equilibrium under such circumstances is secured by a crossed, diagonal adjustment of forces.

References

1. Saunders, J. R. DeC., *et al.*: The Major Determinants in Normal and Pathological Gait. J. Bone Joint Surg., *35*, A, 543–558, 1953.

2. Dempster, Wilfrid Taylor: The Anthropology of Body Action. Ann. New York Acad. Sc., *63*, 574, 1955.

3. Rapp, Richard H.: Ohio State University News and Information Service Release, January 4, 1968.

4. Grombach, John V.: The Gravity Factor in World Athletics. Amateur Athlete, *31*, 24–25, 1960.

5. Parkinson, William J.: Unitas Can't Pass as far in One Direction as in Another. Baltimore Evening Sun, September 28, 1959.

6. Carlson, L. D.: *Maintaining the Thermal Balance in Man.* Fort Wainwright, Alaska: Arctic Command Laboratory, 1963.

7. Metheny, Eleanor: *Body Dynamics.* New York: McGraw-Hill Book Co., Inc., 1952, p. 101–102.

8. Aristotle: *Progression of Animals,* IX. Translated by E. S. Forster. Cambridge: Harvard University Press, 1945, p. 511.

9. Mead, Jere: Control of Respiratory Function. J. Appl. Physiol., *15*, 325–336, 1960.

10. Plato, cited in Metheny, *op cit.,* p. 3.

11. Hellebrandt, F. A., *et al.*: The Influence of the Army Pack on Postural Stability and Stance Mechanics. Amer. J. Physiol., *140*, 645–655, 1944.

12. McCabe, Brian F.: Vestibular Suppression in Figure Skaters. Trans. Amer. Acad. Ophthal. Otolaryng., *64*, 264–268, 1960.

13. Collins, William E.: Problems in Spatial Orientation: Vestibular Studies of Figure Skaters. Trans. Amer. Acad. Ophthal. Otolar-inlogy, *70*, 575–578, 1966.

Recommended Reading

14. Broer, Marion R.: *Efficiency of Human Movement,* 2nd Ed., Philadelphia: W. B. Saunders Co., 1966.

15. Williams, Marian, and Lissner, Herbert R.: *Biomechanics of Human Motion.* Philadelphia: W. B. Saunders Co., 1962.

16. Logan, Gene A. and McKinney, Wayne C.: *Kinesiology.* Dubuque: Wm. C. Brown Company, 1970.

17. Clauser, Charles E., *et al.*: Weight, Volume, and Center of Mass of Segments of the Human Body. Aerospace Medical Research Laboratory Report AMRL-TR-69-70, 1969.

Chapter 7

Mechanics

Mechanics is that branch of the science of physics which encompasses the action of force on material bodies. It deals with motion, and includes the physical principles and laws which make possible the applied sciences of *biomechanics*, the study of the motion of living organisms, and *kinesiology*, the study of the motion of animal bodies, especially human, in conjunction with a consideration of their structural and physiological as well as mechanical aspects.

The field of mechanics may be divided into *statics*, which considers particles and rigid bodies in a state of static equilibrium, and *dynamics*, which studies objects in motion. Dynamics may be further subdivided into *kinematics*, the geometry of motion, which includes displacement, velocity, and acceleration without regard for the forces acting on a body, and *kinetics*, which incorporates the concepts of mass, force, and energy as they affect motion.

The human body may be considered as a machine, every movement of which must be in accordance with the laws of mechanics. Classical or Newtonian mechanics is probably the most thoroughly explored and developed subdivision of science. Although relativity, quantum mechanics, and other theories of modern physics have produced laws which are more fundamental and pervasive than those of classical mechanics, the latter remain valid and useful for the solution of practical problems in the realm of sports, work, and voluntary human motion.

The application of mechanics to human motion is a particularly practical endeavor, and is widely employed. Even a rudimentary knowledge of mechanics enables the track coach to estimate the trajectory of the center of gravity of a long jumper and subsequently to make pointed coaching suggestions in order to improve performance through alteration of takeoff velocity, angle of takeoff, and control of body position for absorbing landing forces effectively.

The modern coach need not depend upon hunches, traditions, super-stitions, or sketchy memories of his own past performances (which, alas, often were inferior to the performance of the person he is coaching!).

In Chapter 6, some of the concepts of statics were applied to human problems. In Chapter 8, the workings of simple machines whose counterparts are found in human motion, will be presented. This chapter provides a brief review of mechanical principles, with their applications to kinesiological problems.

DYNAMIC MECHANICS

There are three general types of motion. In *rectilinear* or *transla-tory motion*, every particle of a body moves the same distance along a straight line which is parallel to the path of every other particle. Motion of the whole human body seldom fulfills these conditions. Even when a person jumps feet-first off a diving board with body perpendicular and rigid, there is some slight rotation of the body around its center of gravity and the path of the center of gravity fol-lows a slight curve. Perhaps some point on the fist of a boxer executing a straight left jab exhibits rectilinear motion, but most parts of his arm will move neither in a straight line nor parallel to the first point. In practical problems, small discrepancies from strictly rectilinear motion are ignored; thus, the approximate horizontal distance traversed by the center of gravity of a walking person is sometimes viewed as the "translatory motion of the person," even though it is known that the center of gravity actually oscillated laterally, forward and backward, and up and down slightly during the "straight" walking, and that other body points deviated even more radically from a rectilinear path.

In *angular* or *rotary motion*, each particle of a rigid body moves in a circle or along the arc of a circle. The center of rotation, or "axle" of the rotation, may either be within the volume of the body, as in the case of a pirouetting dancer, or outside of the body, as in the case of a gymnast swinging on the flying rings. The various points in the rotating body tend to form concentric circles, with radii proportional to their distances from the center of rotation.

In *curvilinear motion*, the particles of the body follow a curve other than a circle. Depending upon the circumstances, such a curve may be variable and irregular, or it may take the form of one of the defined curves, such as a parabola. Neglecting such forces as air resistance, the center of gravity of a body always follows a parabolic path when it is a projectile, as in diving, high jumping, long jumping, and tumbling (Fig. 7–1).

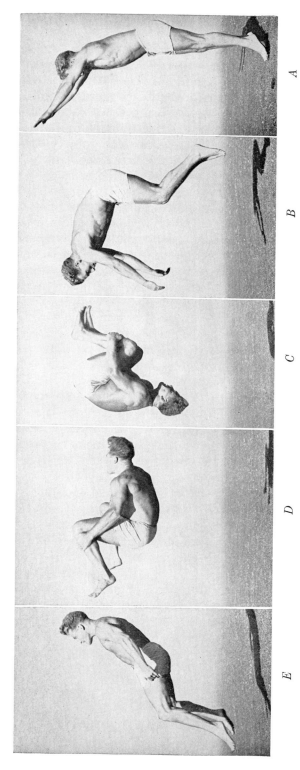

E   D   C   B   A

FIG. 7–1. From right to left, former National Tumbling Champion Charles Thompson performs the forward somersault. *A,* The force and the angle of takeoff determined the parabolic path of the center of gravity. *B, C,* The tightness of tuck regulates the speed of rotation of the body around its center of gravity. *D, E,* Proper timing of emergence from the tuck decelerates the rotation and places the body in a position for landing. (Photograph by Thomas McDonald.)

Actual motion of the human body seldom fits one of these types of motion to the exclusion of the others. The case of a tumbler performing a front somersault exemplifies this. After the takeoff, his center of gravity follows an almost perfect parabola, although no other point of his body does so. During the tucked phase of the somersault, the tumbler's body exhibits angular or rotary motion around his center of gravity. If the parabolic motion be temporarily ignored, and if the center of gravity be considered at all times a fixed point, a fairly pure case of rotary motion is seen. From this point of view, and with a knowledge of the principles of rotary motion, even a coach who had no knowledge of tumbling but who understood elementary mechanics could suggest modification in the tightness and duration of tuck in order to make the somersault more successful. In the last part of the movement, when the performer has emerged from tuck position into a rigid extended position before landing, the motion is roughly an example of rectilinear motion. By analyzing the motion into its components, the complex performance becomes easier to understand. In daily practice, the coach and the performer make the mechanical analysis by mental consideration; but students and research personnel may utilize high speed cinematography, stop-action projectors, and quantitative measurements in order to make a complete and precise analysis.

For all practical purposes the joints of the body permit only angular or curvilinear motion. The gliding motions of some joints are slight, and they usually occur along a curved surface. Any translatory movement of a part of the body must be produced by multiple angular movements at two or more joints, or by some force originating outside the body.

The mathematical treatment of curvilinear motion is far too complex for discussion in this text except in a brief and superficial manner. Aside from the movements of the body, perhaps the most common examples of such motion observed by kinesiologists are the paths of such missiles as the ball, shuttlecock, shot, javelin, and discus.

Ignoring for the moment the effect of air resistance, the horizontal distance which a missile will be propelled from the ground can be computed by the formula

$$R = \frac{V^2 \sin 2\theta}{g}$$

where R = horizontal range; V = initial velocity of object, θ = angle of projection, and g = acceleration of gravity.* If it is assumed

* A summary of simple trigonometric relationships, together with a table of sines, is located in Appendix C.

that a shot is released at a height of eight feet, the horizontal range
will be the distance to the point at which the shot returns to a
height of eight feet above the ground. To determine the additional
distance gained from this point to the place where the shot strikes
the ground requires the use of a more complicated formula than is
within the scope of this text. It will be noted in Figure 7–2 that the
greatest range is achieved when the angle of projection is 45°. This
results from the fact that sin 2θ is at a maximum when θ = 45°.
Modifications of this same formula will give the maximum height
attained by the object and the time the projectile is in the air.
Height may be computed by the equation

$$\text{Height} = \frac{(V \sin \theta)^2}{2g}.$$

Since θ reaches its maximum at 90°, the maximum height will also be
reached at this angle. The time the projectile is in the air can be
calculated by use of the formula

$$\text{Time} = \frac{2V \sin \theta}{g}.$$

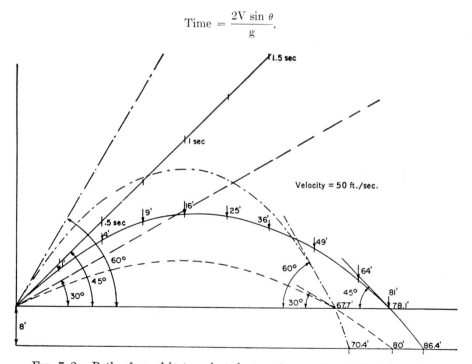

FIG. 7–2. Path of an object projected at various angles at 50 ft./sec. from a
height of eight feet (air resistance neglected). (From Broer, *Efficiency of Human
Movement*, courtesy W. B. Saunders Co.)

While the uses of such formulae are largely theoretical, the physical laws which they describe may have definite practical applications. In football, for instance, it may be more important to gain height and time on a punt to enable the ends to cover a dangerous receiver than it is to achieve maximum distance on the kick. The kicker must vary the θ of the ball accordingly. For an "onside" or "squib" kick an appropriate reduction of V may be essential. Again, if a baseball player desires to "pick off" a base runner, the time during which the ball is in the air becomes more important than the maximum distance which it can be thrown. By use of the above formula it can be demonstrated that the ball travels faster (horizontally) when thrown at an angle of 30° than when thrown at an angle of 45°.

In Figure 7–2 the path of the missile is shown as a true parabola, and it will be observed that the object returns to the horizontal at approximately the same angle at which it was projected. In actuality the velocity and horizontal distance travelled will be reduced by air resistance, so that the path of the object will not be a true parabola. As air resistance varies with square of the velocity, the resistance is four times as great for an object traveling twice as fast as another similar missile. The lighter the object and the larger its surface area, the more it is affected by air resistance. In heavy, slow-moving objects like a 16 pound shot, the air resistance is negligible, but light missiles tend to drop to the ground quickly due to a loss of horizontal force. This is the reason a player shifting from one sport to another finds it so difficult at first to judge the flight of the missile.

INERTIA

According to Newton's first law, a body at rest tends to remain at rest, and a body in motion tends to remain in motion in a straight line at constant velocity, unless it is compelled to change its state by the action of external forces upon it. This tendency to resist change is known as *inertia*, and accounts for the fact that an athlete finds it difficult to change direction when running at full speed. Any motion or change of motion results only from an applied force.

FORCES

The forces causing human motion may be either internal or external in origin. Of the internal forces, only that of muscular contraction is important in analyzing gross movements, although capillary attraction, osmotic pressure, and others may be important in medicine and physiology. Thus isometric strength may be thought of as potential force; isotonic strength as kinetic force.[1] Of the external forces, that of gravity is usually singled out for special attention, because of its constancy, uniformity, and unchanging direction.

Motion is better understood, and problems are simplified, if some time is devoted to the study of special characteristics of forces and their measurement. In mechanics, two kinds of quantitative measurements are encountered.

Scalar Quantities. *Scalar quantities* have magnitude only, and may be added arithmetically. Speed, mass, area, and volume are scalar quantities. If a person whose body volume is 6 cubic feet jumps into a swimming pool carrying a stone whose volume is 1.5 cu. ft., a total of 7.5 cu. ft. of water is displaced. *Vector quantities* have both magnitude and direction as definitive attributes, and should be added vectorially if maximum information is to result. Displacement, velocity, acceleration, momentum, and force are examples of vector quantities.

Vector Quantities. A vector quantity may be expressed graphically by an arrow whose length indicates its magnitude according to some convenient scale, and whose head indicates its direction. Suppose that a channel swimmer swims 4 miles north in a calm sea. His displacement can be represented by drawing an arrow 4 inches long in a direction representing north. Suppose now this same swimmer is affected by a tidal current sufficient to displace him

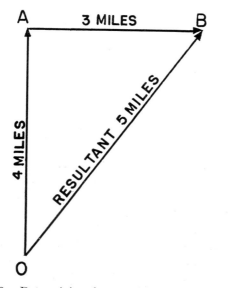

Fig 7-3. Determining the actual track of a swimmer by the addition of vector quantities.

3 miles to the east. This displacement could be represented by drawing another arrow 3 inches long in a direction representing east, starting at the terminal point of the first arrow. If these two quantities are added arithmetically, the total distance is indicated as 7 miles. But will the man be found at a point 7 miles from his starting point? As indicated in Figure 7–3, if arrow OB is drawn and measured, his actual displacement is found to be 5 miles from the starting point. OB is the vectorial sum of vectors OA and AB. Since OB is a vector, it is appropriate to apply a protractor and determine its direction, which is found to be about 37° east of north.

If a mathematical solution to such problems is preferred, the Pythagorean Theorem may be utilized. This states that the square of the hypotenuse of a right triangle is equal to the sum of the squares of the other two sides. Hence:

$$\overline{OB}^2 = \overline{OA}^2 + \overline{AB}^2$$

$$\overline{OB}^2 = 4^2 + 3^2 = 16 + 9 = 25$$

$$OB = \sqrt{25} = 5 \text{ miles.}$$

The direction may be determined from the Law of Sines. The sine of an acute angle of a right triangle is the ratio of the side opposite the angle to the hypotenuse. This ratio is constant for any given angle:

$$\text{Sin AOB} = \tfrac{3}{5} = 0.6.$$

Consulting the table of sines on page 574, and interpolating, a sine of 0.6 is found to correspond to an angle of 36.9°, and by inspection of the diagram that is seen to be east of north.

A typical example of the use of such computations in kinesiological problems is found in a study by Pugh *et al.*[2] in which it was necessary to determine the distances actually swum by participants in the 1955 race across the English Channel. One of the first contestants to finish was found to have actually covered 25.8 miles, although the displacement through the water was only 21.5 miles. Slower swimmers suffered more from tidal effects and were forced to swim greater distances, the result being that most of them failed to finish.

Composition of Vectors. Such problems as that of the swimmer affected by the cross-current, in which two forces are known and the resultant must be calculated, are solved by the method of *composition (or combination) of vectors.* In such problems it is customary to use the *parallelogram* method instead of the triangle method employed above.

Suppose two muscles with a common insertion but with different angles of pull contract simultaneously (Fig. 7–4). Point O represents the common insertion of the lateral and medial heads of the quadriceps on the patella (see Fig. 16–6). OA is a vector depicting the magnitude and direction of the pull of the lateral head; OB indicates the magnitude and direction of the pull of the medial head. From point A, the line AC is drawn parallel to OB; from point B, the line BC is drawn parallel to OA. The resultant represents the combination of the forces developed by the two muscles, and might be regarded as a hypothetical muscle pull which could replace the original muscles' pull without changing the effect of their action on the bone to which they are attached.

If there were three muscles pulling on a common point of insertion (as in the case of the three parts of the deltoid muscle), the composition of all could be found by determining the resultant from any two, and then combining it with that of the third muscle in order to get the final resultant. Any number of forces acting at a given point can thus be combined by taking two at a time.

Resolution of Vectors. In dealing with the composition of vectors, the problem is to find the resultant of two or more component vectors. Sometimes the opposite problem must be solved—a single

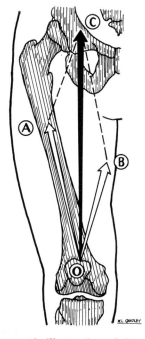

FIG. 7–4. Diagrammatic illustration of the composition of forces by the parallelogram method.

6

vector is known, and its components must be found. This is a
problem in *resolution of vectors*.

The kinesiologist is often interested in the resolution of muscle
forces. For example, suppose that a muscle is pulling with a force
of 100 lbs. at an angle of 50° to the long axis of the bone on which it
inserts. In Figure 7–5, OM is the vector representing the pull of the
muscle on bone XO. This force OM can be analyzed into two components, OR or OS. OR is the rotary component, acting at right
angles to the bone and representing the force which tends to turn
the bone around the fulcrum X. OS is the stabilizing component,
acting along the long axis of the bone and tending to pull it tightly
into the socket at X. The point R is located by erecting a line
from O perpendicular to XO, and by then drawing a line parallel to
XO from M to R. The point S is located by dropping a line from M
perpendicular to XO and parallel to OR. Knowing the magnitude
of OM to be 100 lbs. and the angle MOS to be 50°, the magnitude
of OR and OS can be computed as follows:

OR = OM × sin 50°	or	OR = OM × cos 40°
= 100 × 0.766		= 100 × 0.766
= 76.6 lbs.		= 76.6 lbs.
OS = OM × sin 40°	or	OS = OM × cos 50°
= 100 × 0.643		= 100 × 0.643
= 64.3 lbs.		= 64.3 lbs.

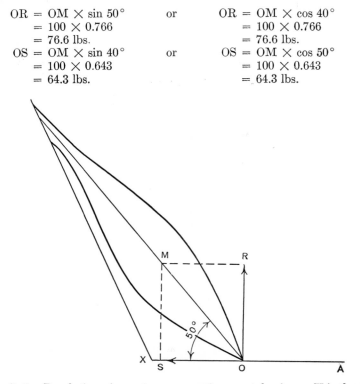

Fig. 7–5.   Resolution of a vector representing muscular force. X is the center of
the joint, around which bone XA turns. OM is a vector representing a muscle
pulling with a force of 100 lbs. at an angle of 50° to the bone. OR is the rotary
component; OS is the stabilizing component.

Except in research work, exact numerical values for the components of muscle force are seldom needed. However, any student of human performance will be interested in determining the relative values of the rotary and stabilizing components for muscles pulling at various angles. Such considerations indicate the usefulness of composition and resolution of vectors. Further applications are suggested in Chapter 8.

KINEMATICS

Kinematics is essentially the descriptive geometry of motion with respect to time, ignoring the causes of motion and ignoring the concepts of mass, force, momentum, and energy. In pure form, kinematics refers to the motion of an infinitesimally small massless particle. However, the kinematics of a rigid body of finite mass may be analyzed if its mass is considered to be concentrated at one point. Even a deformable mass, like the human body, under some circumstances can be treated as a particle by analyzing the motion of its center of gravity. In studying the motion of a runner, for example, we ordinarily are interested in the motion of his center of gravity, and not in the irrelevant flapping of a lock of his hair, shoelace, or wrist. Nevertheless, if there is some reason to be interested in the motion of his wrist, *per se*, there is no reason why we cannot follow its motion as a point, so long as we do not pretend that the analysis describes the overall motion of his body.

Displacement (d) is the change in position of a particle, with reference to some set of coordinate axes, and d is a vector, since it has a positive or negative direction. *Distance* is a scalar quantity describing the length of path traversed, including actual changes in direction; thus, it is always positive. With reference to some arbitrary x-axis, d is the difference between the terminal and initial coordinates of the particle on the scale:

$$d = x_t - x_i.$$

Velocity. *Average velocity* (v_{avg}) is the displacement divided by the elapsed time,

$$v_{avg} = \frac{x_t - x_i}{t_t - t_i} = \frac{d}{t}$$

If the coordinate x_i is numerically greater than x_t, on the scale being used, both displacement and velocity will be negative, indicating motion in a "backward" direction. When the elapsed time is very

small (as between frames of a slow motion movie), average velocity
may be treated as though it were *instantaneous velocity* without introducing serious error for most purposes in human motion analysis.
Of course, if velocity is constant (or uniform), average velocity and
instantaneous velocity have the same value.

Note that *average speed* is the total distance traversed, divided by
the elapsed time, and is different from average velocity. If a
champion sprinter runs the 100-yd. race in 9.3 sec., his average
velocity is $d/t = 100/9.3 = 10.75$ yd./sec. Here we are interested
in the average linear velocity and not in the average speed traversed by the runner's center of gravity as it wandered from side to
side and up and down, nor in the response time between the go-
signal and his first movement, although these are important factors
from the point of view of the athlete and his coach.

Acceleration is the time rate of change in velocity. When motion
is characterized by fluctuating velocity, analysis is complex unless
the motion is broken down into its component parts. But motion
characterized by constant acceleration is subject to analysis by
relatively simple equations. The remainder of this discussion will
pertain only to conditions of constant or uniform acceleration, of
which there are two sub-conditions. When constant acceleration is
zero, velocity is constant, and a graph of displacement plotted against
time is a straight line with a slope proportional to the constant
velocity. When acceleration is constant but not zero, the graph of
velocity against time will take the shape of part of a parabola. In
this instance, the acceleration may be positive or negative, with the
former indicating an increase of velocity with time, and the latter
indicating a decrease of velocity with time. Negative acceleration
is also called, non-technically, deceleration. For constant acceleration, the plot of acceleration against time is a horizontal straight
line, with its magnitude or height proportional to the degree of slope
of the plot of velocity against time.

The motion of a particle under constant acceleration may be described by the following equations, in which v_0 = initial velocity at
time $t_0 = 0$, v = terminal velocity, t = elapsed time from time
$t_0 = 0$, and d = displacement.

$$a = \frac{v - v_0}{t}$$

$$d = \tfrac{1}{2}(v_0 + v)t, \quad \text{or (if } v_0 = 0\text{)} \ d = \tfrac{1}{2}at^2$$

$$d = \tfrac{1}{2}(v_0 + v)t, \quad \text{or (if } v_0 = 0\text{)} \ d = \tfrac{1}{2}vt, \quad \text{or } d = v_{avg}t$$

$$v = v_0 + at, \quad \text{or (if } v_0 = 0\text{)} \ v = at$$

$$v^2 = v_0^2 + 2ad, \quad \text{or (if } v_0 = 0\text{)} \ v^2 = 2\,ad$$

The above equations contain a total of four variables, v, d, a, and t. Each of the equations lacks one of these, but contains the other three. Therefore, if v_o and any two of the other four variables are known, the remaining two unknown factors may be determined by selecting and solving two equations, each of which contains only one of the two unknowns. For example, if an automobile is known to accelerate uniformly from 15 m.p.h. (22 ft./sec.) to 30 m.p.h. (44 ft./sec.) in ten seconds, its acceleration is $\quad a = \dfrac{v - vo}{t}$

$$a = \frac{44 \text{ ft./sec.} - 22 \text{ ft./sec.}}{10 \text{ sec.}} = 2.2 \text{ ft./sec./sec., or } 2.2 \text{ ft./sec.}^2$$

The result is read as "2.2 feet per second per second" or "2.2 feet per second squared." This indicates that the velocity increases by 2.2 ft./sec. each second.

The preceding chapter cited the example of a gymnast who lost his handgrip and fell, from a stationary position ($V_o = O$), to the ground in 0.75 sec. We know that g, the acceleration of gravity, is equal to 32.2 ft./sec.^{2} His velocity upon impact is

$$v = at = (32.2 \text{ ft./sec.}^2)\ (0.75 \text{ sec.}) = 24.15 \text{ ft./sec.}$$

From another equation, we can find the distance he fell, as follows:

$$d = \tfrac{1}{2}vt = \frac{(24.15 \text{ ft./sec.})\ (0.75 \text{ sec.})}{2} = 9.05 \text{ ft.}$$

Rotary Motion. The same concepts set forth above are employed in measuring rotary motion. Assume that in a given time (t) a point advances from A to B on a circle (Fig. 7–6). The angle AOB which subtends arc AB is termed angular displacement, and may be measured in radians (θ), degrees or number of revolutions. This may be expressed as

$$\theta = \omega t$$

where θ = angular displacement in radians, ω = average angular velocity in radians/sec., and t = time. Similarly, $\quad \omega = \dfrac{\theta}{t}$.

Angular acceleration is found by

$$a = \frac{\omega - \omega_0}{t}$$

where a = angular acceleration in radians/sec.^{2}, ω = angular velocity in radians/sec., and t = time.

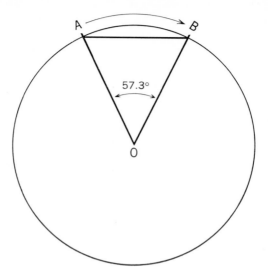

FIG. 7–6. Diagrammatic illustration of a radian. Arc AB is equal in length to the radius of the circle. A radian is defined as "the angle subtended by an arc on a circle equal in length to the radius of the circle," and is equivalent to 57.3°. 2π radians = one revolution, or 360°. This seeming arbitrary measurement is used because it relates linear velocity to angular velocity and linear displacement to angular displacement. Consequently, equations such as those for linear and angular acceleration can be expressed identically except for the distinguishing symbols.

Such problems are solved in the same manner as those for linear movement except that the answers are expressed in degrees or radians rather than in feet. Assume that the tumbler in Figure 7–1 performs a standing somersault in .5 sec. at a uniform velocity. The average velocity of his turn in radians may be determined as

$$\omega = \frac{\theta}{t}$$

$$= \frac{2\pi \text{ radians}}{.5 \text{ sec.}} = 4\pi \text{ rad./sec.} = 12.58636 \text{ rad./sec.}$$

Conversely, since his velocity is 0 when he starts the somersault and 12.58636 rad./sec. at the end of .5 sec., his angular displacement is

$$\theta = \omega t$$

$$\theta = 12.58636 \times .5 = 6.29318 \text{ rad.} = 2\pi \text{ rad.}$$

It is obvious from Figure 7–6 that the angular velocity is increased as the radius is shortened. This is the mechanical basis of the need for a tight tuck in the triple somersault and similar events. However, technically correct kinetic analysis requires accurate data on the mass, centers of gravity, and the moments of inertia of the body segments. Only limited data of this type exist for American males; none are available for American females.[3]

KINETICS

The stilted and now largely archaic English in which Newton's Laws were originally cast makes it difficult for the student to realize that they have any actual connection with the events of daily life. These laws, and the equations derived from them underlie and explain many of the expressions commonly heard on the athletic field.

Newton's First Law. Newton's first law states that a body remains in a state of rest or of uniform motion unless it is acted upon by some other body. When the total of all forces acting on an object is 0, the body is in a state of equilibrium. This state changes only when an unbalanced force enters the picture. A projectile like a ball or a missile would travel indefinitely through space in a straight line, were it not for the forces of gravitation, friction, air resistance, etc., which alter its course or bring it to a halt. As will be seen later, Newton's first law is simply a special application of his more generalized second law.

Newton's Third Law. Newton's third law states that whenever one body acts upon another, the second exerts an equal and opposite reaction on the first. An excellent example is found in the recoil of a gun. The force exerted upon the bullet and the gun are equal and opposite, but the greater weight of the firearm causes it to move relatively little as compared with the projectile. An even more extreme example is the "take off" of the jumper. The push which the athlete makes against the earth causes an equal and opposite reaction from the ground. Because of the difference in size, the earth is not moved, but its reaction pushes the jumper up into the air.

Newton's Second Law. Newton's second law describes the relationship between applied force, mass, and acceleration,

$$F = ma.$$

Since both F and a are vector quantities, this is also a vector equation. Mass $\times$ velocity (mv) = momentum. As a is the rate at which a change in velocity occurs, the difference in momentum may be substituted for a in the foregoing equation:

$$F = \frac{mv - mv_0}{t}.$$

Force then becomes defined as the change in the momentum of the moving object in a given unit of time. If the F be multiplied by the time during which it is applied, $Ft = mv - mv_0$, which is the so-called Impulse-Momentum equation. This is a vector quantity which serves as a measure of the force acting on the object over the unit of time.

This relationship is useful in the solution of problems where force is applied to an object for a given period of time and produces a change in the momentum of the object. Typical examples are those in which balls are struck with various sports implements.

Assume a standard 1.6 oz. golf ball is struck with a club and given a velocity of 200 feet per second. If it is known that the club head is in contact with the ball for 0.0005 second, by using the Impulse-Momentum equation, it is possible to calculate the force in pounds with which it is struck.

$$Ft = \frac{W}{g}v - \frac{W}{g}v_0$$

$$F = \frac{\frac{W}{g}v - \frac{W}{g}v_0}{t}.$$

The second term in the numerator disappears because the ball starts from rest and its initial velocity is zero.

Converting ounces to pounds,

$$F = \frac{\frac{0.1}{32.2} \times 200}{0.0005} = 1242 \text{ lbs.}$$

It is also possible to calculate the distance through which the club head is in contact with the ball.

$$\text{Average velocity} = \frac{v - v_0}{2} = \frac{200 - 0}{2} = 100 \text{ ft. per sec.}$$

$$\text{Distance} = vt = 100 \times 0.0005 = 0.05 \text{ feet.}$$

When the results of physical efforts in terms of change of momentum of objects thrown or struck are known, it is possible to calculate the minimum force which contraction of the muscles must produce to cause such changes. The experimental determination of the values of trunk, limb, and missile accelerations would make it possible to explore the kinetics of complicated movements such as throwing a ball, discus, or javelin or swinging a bat, racket, or golf club. Here is a whole field of kinesiology, little explored as yet, which in the future may yield much information concerning the performance of the human body.

From the foregoing equations it is apparent that the racket of a tennis player strikes the ball with a momentum proportional to its mass and the velocity with which it is moving. The player can hit the ball harder by "getting his body" into the serve, and thus increasing the mass, or by increasing the velocity with which the racket moves, and hence the velocity which it imparts to the ball. In either case, in order to produce a larger mv in the object, a larger Ft must be applied to the object. This is precisely the purpose of "follow-through" (Fig. 7–7). The bat is kept in contact with the ball just as long as is possible in order to impart the greatest possible Ft and hence velocity to the ball. Conversely, when a boxer "rolls with a punch" he seeks to increase the time during which it decelerates and thus reduce the force of its impact.

In physical contact sports these relationships are especially important. If a relatively small half-back must block a big lineman, his principal hope lies in moving fast enough so that he develops an mv great enough to overcome his adversary's advantage in mass. Again referring to the falling gymnast, the mv with which he strikes the floor will be equal to

$$\text{mv} = \frac{150 \text{ lb.}}{32.2 \text{ ft./sec.}^2} \times 24.15 \text{ ft./sec.} = 112.49 \text{ lb. sec.}$$

Conservation of Momentum. When one moving body strikes another, the momentum involved is said to be "conserved," that is, the total mv after the collision of two bodies is exactly equal to the total of the two momentums before the impact. If a heavy man is tackled by a light man, he may be slowed down, but keep moving. In such cases his loss of velocity is offset by the fact that he has gained in mass by the addition of the tackler to the moving body. When a runner is tackled head-on by a man possessing equal momentum, both come to a halt because the momentums were in opposite directions.

Fig. 7–7. Mickey Mantle hitting his 524th homer (and second of the day) on May 30, 1968. This illustrates the application of the Impulse-Momentum equation. From the time the ball leaves the pitcher's hand the batter has about $\frac{2}{5}$ sec. to decide whether to swing at it. The velocity imparted to the ball by the batter is proportional to the force and the time of its application. The swing of the bat is nearly level to contact the ball at 90° from the direction of the pitch. The arms are nearly fully extended to increase the arc through which the bat moves. Note that the force is developed by the step to meet the ball and the rotation of the hips, trunk, and shoulders. The wrists are seen to be unbroken at the moment of impact, although the left wrist rotates forcefully on the follow through. Consequently the power is applied before the wrists roll. The strongly emphasized follow through can triple or quadruple the time of application of the force. In contrast, follow through is minimized in bunting, as is the resulting velocity. (Wide World Photos, Inc.)

KINETICS OF ROTARY MOTION

In the kinetics of rectilinear motion, the concepts of force and mass were introduced. In the kinetics of rotary motion, the comparable concepts are *torque** and *rotational inertia*, respectively.

Torque. Torque may be thought of as the magnitude of twist around a center of rotation. More properly, it is a force multiplied by the perpendicular distance from the center of rotation to the line of application of the force, or

$$T = Fd.$$

F is the magnitude of the force in pounds (or kilograms); d is the distance in feet (or centimeters), and is often called the *lever arm* or *force arm*; and T is the torque in foot-pounds (or kilogram-centimeters). Elftman[4] comments that since the human body moves by a series of rotations of its segments, the amount of torque which a muscle can develop is the most useful measure of its effect.

The concept of perpendicular distance is sometimes confusing to beginning students. Consider the situation illustrated by Figure 7–5 which has been discussed previously. Assume that XO is 3 inches, or 0.25 feet. Although the actual force developed in the muscle is 100 lbs., the torque is not 100×0.25, because XO is not perpendicular to the line of the force. There are two alternative methods of determining the torque. The first, which was previously indicated, requires the resolution of the actual muscle force into components, one of which was OR, the "rotary component," which was calculated to be 76.6 lbs. Since this rotary component is perpendicular to the lever arm XO, the torque is given by

Torque = Rotary component $\times$ perpendicular distance

$$T = 76.6 \times 0.25$$
$$= 19.15 \text{ foot-pounds.}$$

In the method just described, torque was computed by taking the component of force which is perpendicular to the lever arm. The second method modifies the lever arm. In effect, a derived lever arm that is perpendicular to the original force is computed. Figure 7–8 illustrates the method. From center of rotation X, draw XL perpendicular to OL. The length of XL may be determined as follows:

$$XL = XO \times \sin 50°$$
$$= 0.25 \times 0.766$$
$$= 0.1915 \text{ feet.}$$

* The terms "torque" and "rotational inertia" have largely replaced the older terminology "moment of force" and "moment of inertia" respectively, especially in engineering usage.

Then, torque is given by

$$T = 100 \times 0.1915$$
$$= 19.15 \text{ foot-pounds,}$$

which agrees with the result obtained by the first method.

Rotational Inertia. Rotational inertia in angular motion is comparable to the mass in rectilinear motion. For relatively small objects centered at a relatively great distance from the center of rotation (like a stone being swung at the end of a string, or a person swinging on the flying rings), rotational inertia is approximately equal to the mass of the object multiplied by the square of its distance from the center of rotation. In most kinesiological and athletic problems, this special situation does not hold, because the mass of the body or segment is distributed over a large volume and is close to (or contains) the center of rotation. In such a case, it is necessary to take the mass of each elementary particle and multiply by the square of its distance from the center of rotation, and then to sum all such products, in order to calculate rotational inertia. Such a task is impractical; therefore, short-cut approximations are em-

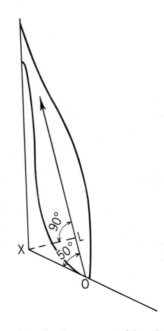

FIG. 7–8. Torque is equal to the force exerted by the muscle in direction OL, multiplied by the perpendicular distance from the center of rotation (X) to the line of the force (OL).

ployed. For example, the body is divided into segments, each of which is typified by a standard geometrical shape. The head is considered to be a sphere, the upper arm a cylinder, the forearm a truncated cone, etc. Physics books give formulas for computing rotational inertia for each idealized segment, and these are summed to determine roughly rotational inertia. Whenever the human body moves, its mass is redistributed, and rotational inertia changes, requiring a re-calculation. Because of these complexities, rotational inertia of the human body is rarely computed.

Rotational inertia is mentioned here only because of its relation to the phenomenon of conservation of angular momentum. In this regard, understanding of the concept of rotational inertia is important even though it cannot be quantified.

Angular Momentum. Angular momentum is analogous to rectilinear momentum (mv). Angular momentum is rotational inertia (J) multiplied by the angular velocity (ω).

$$\text{Angular momentum} = J\omega$$

Conservation of Angular Momentum. The principle of conservation of angular momentum is comparable to the principle of conservation of momentum in rectilinear motion. It is sufficient here to point out that $J\omega$, once established, will remain constant until outside forces act to change it. If a weight on the end of a string is swung around one's head, a certain angular momentum is established. If the string is drawn in so that it is shortened by 50 per cent, the angular velocity is increased to four times its original value. Shortening the radius by 50 per cent diminishes the rotational inertia (J) by 400 per cent; therefore, angular velocity (ω) must be increased 400 per cent so that the angular momentum ($J\omega$) remains constant.

This principle is a common and important consideration in a great variety of sports skills, and Chapter 22, "Kinesiological Principles of Sports and Games," presents a detailed explanation illustrated by practical examples.

Tangential Velocity. When a weight on the end of a string is swung in a circle, each mass particle has, at any instant, a tendency to fly off in a direction tangent to the circle. If the string breaks (cf. the release of a discus or a thrown ball), the weight flies away tangentially at a velocity termed the *tangential velocity*. In Figure 7–9, the vector for tangential velocity is labeled v_t. The magnitude of v_t is equal to the radius of the circle multiplied by the angular velocity.

$$v_t = R\omega$$

The equation indicates clearly why a discus thrower (Fig. 22–14) emphasizes speed of rotation, and why he moves the discus through an arc having the largest possible radius.

Radial Acceleration. Newton's first law indicates that an object in motion will tend to remain in motion in a straight line, unless some other force acts upon it. In Figure 7–9, the "straight line" is represented by the vector for tangential velocity, v_t. But since the object actually moves in a circle before its release, it is obvious that some force is constantly accelerating it toward the center of the circle. This is called *radial acceleration*, and is represented in Figure 7–9 by the vector labeled a_r. The magnitude of a_r at any moment is expressed by

$$a_r = \frac{v_t^2}{R}$$

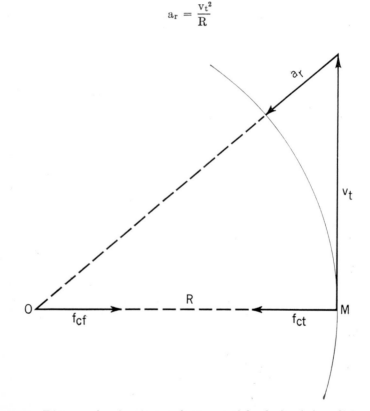

Fɪɢ. 7–9.   Diagram showing vectors for tangential velocity (v_t), radial acceleration (a_r), centripetal force (f_{ct}), and centrifugal force (f_{cf}) resulting from constant circular motion of mass-particle M in the counter-clockwise direction. O is the center of rotation. The line OM = R is a constraining thread with infinitely small mass. If the thread has mass, then each of its own mass-particles will generate vector quantities like those of mass-particle M.

which shows that radial acceleration is directly proportional to the square of the instantaneous tangential velocity and inversely proportional to the radius of the circle.

Centripetal and Centrifugal Force. The force which produces radial acceleration is called centripetal force, and is expressed by the following formula:

$$F = m \frac{v_t^2}{R} = \frac{W \, v_t^2}{g \, R}.$$

Centripetal force appears as tension in the structure connecting the object with the center of rotation, pulling the object toward the center of rotation. It is matched by a reactive force equal in magnitude and opposite in direction, the *centrifugal force*. The formula for centrifugal force is the same as that for centripetal force.

In the common problems of kinesiology and sports analysis, it is not ordinarily necessary to compute centrifugal and centripetal force, but the student should understand that these forces are directly proportional to the mass (or weight) of the object and the square of their tangential velocity.

In sports performance, centrifugal forces often reach tremendous magnitudes. The maximum momentary centrifugal force generated during a giant swing on the horizontal bar, at the bottom of the swing, has been calculated to be 438 pounds for an expert performer weighing about 160 pounds, making the total force directed away from the bar about 600 pounds.[5]

ACTION OF MECHANICAL FORCES ON MISSILES

Curves. If a ball is thrown with a spin, or hit off center so that it spins, aerodynamic effects may cause it to curve in its flight. The degree of curving will be positively related to three factors—the speed of the spin, the weight of the ball, and the roughness of its surface. The direction of the spin determines the direction in which the ball tends to curve.

An adequate mechanical analysis of curving requires reference to the complex laws of aerodynamics with consideration of different qualities of turbulence created on opposite sides of the spinning ball. The following is a more casual explanation: as the ball rotates, the roughness of its surface creates a greater air resistance on the side of the ball which is turning toward its path through space, and a lesser air resistance on the side turning away from its path in space. This difference results in a force action on the ball at right angles to its main direction, and the resulting lateral displacement produces the curved path (Fig. 7–10).

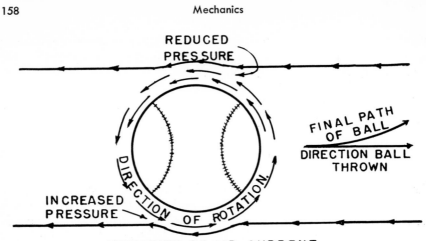

Fig. 7–10. A spinning ball is deflected from its straight path by dragging a "boundary layer" of air along with it in the direction of its rotation. This creates different pressures on opposite sides of the ball.

Gravity tends to produce a parabolic downward curve in the path of the ball. Thus, in throwing a down-curve (drop), gravity accentuates the curve; in throwing a pure side-curve (in-shoot or out-shoot), gravity has no effect on the extent of lateral curving; and in throwing an up-curve (up-shoot or hop), gravity tends to counteract the extent of curving, and vice versa. As a result, a drop is the easiest curve to throw, and an up-shoot is most difficult.

A new tennis ball, because of its light weight and fuzzy surface, and a golf ball, because of its dimples, curve much more readily than a baseball.

Rebound Angles. When a beam of light is reflected from a surface, its angle of incidence with the surface will be equal to its angle of reflection from the surface. Rebounding balls tend to react in much the same manner, although the relationship is subject to several discrepancies. Rotation of the ball, the area of contact, the degree of penetration of the ball into the surface or of the surface into the ball all cause the angle of rebound to differ from the angle of incidence. Roughly, however, we may assume that the angles of incidence and rebound are equal if the ball is not spinning and if both the ball and the surface are hard. If the ball is spinning when it hits the surface, the angle of rebound is markedly affected by the amount of direction of the spin. Figure 7–11 illustrates the effect of back and top spin on the rebound of a tennis ball. A cut or side spin will cause it to break to one side when it rebounds from the court.

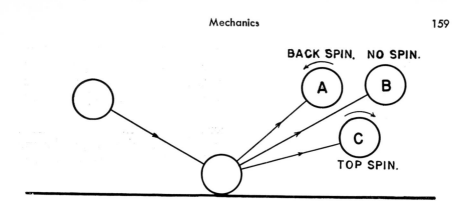

F<small>IG</small>. 7–11. Illustrating the effect of spin on the angle of rebound of a ball striking a horizontal plane surface. Back spin increases the angle of rebound of *A*. When no spin is present, as in *B*, there is no change in the angle of rebound, it being equal to the angle of impact. Top spin decreases the angle of rebound of *C*. A detailed discussion of the bounce of the ball is presented by Broer.[6]

Gyroscopic Action. The spin of an object in flight produces a stabilization against end-over-end tumbling and other erratic behavior. This is called gyroscopic action. The laws of gyroscopic action cannot be explained here, but it may be said that the result is beneficial to the flight path of such sports implements as a football or a discus.

Air Resistance. Small, heavy, smooth objects traveling at moderate speeds are affected very little by air resistance. Large, light, irregular objects traveling at fast speeds may be deterred significantly in their flight path by air resistance. Thus, a baseball or shot is seldom affected, whereas a badminton bird or ping pong ball reacts obviously to air resistance.

The object's speed, referred to above, means its speed with respect to the airstream. Wind resistance has the same effect as increasing the object's speed, or in the case of a tail wind, as decreasing the object's speed. The surface area of the human body is not great enough to cause great retardation due to air resistance at ordinary speeds of self-propulsion on a still day. Pugh[7] concluded that air resistance accounts for about 7.5 per cent of the net energy cost of running at middle distance speeds and about 13.6 per cent of the cost of sprinting.

In the event of a strong head wind, the relative speed of the body with respect to the airstream becomes large enough to cause significant retardation. Strong winds also affect the path of small objects such as a baseball or football. Records made in track and field events are disallowed if the runner is aided by a tailwind of greater than a stated magnitude.

Center of Percussion. Tennis and baseball players know from experience that if a ball is hit at a certain spot on a racket or bat, no vibrations are transferred to the hands and arms of the player. In sports terminology, this area is known as the "sweet spot"; in physics it is known as the center of percussion or center of oscillation of a compound pendulum.

If a ball hits a racket or bat at other than the center of percussion, the resulting vibrations in the implement are unpleasant, and some of the energy of the swing is inefficiently dissipated in setting up the vibrations.

References

1. Eckert, Helen: A Concept of Force-Energy in Human Movement. J. Am. Phys. Ther. Ass., 45, 213–218, 1965.

2. Pugh, L. G. C. E., et al.: A Physiological Study of Channel Swimmers. Clin. Sc., 19, 257–273, 1960.

3. Drillis, Rudolfo, Contini, Renato, and Bluestein, Maurice: Body Segment Parameters. A Survey of Measurement Techniques. Artif. Limbs, 8, 44–66, 1964.

4. Elftman, Herbert: Biomechanics of Muscle. J. Bone Joint Surg., 48-A, 363–377, 1966.

5. Burke, Roger K.: The Identification of Principles of External Mechanics Affecting the Performance of a Selected Gymnastic Movement. Unpublished master's thesis, University of California at Los Angeles, 1950, p. 97.

6. Broer, Marion R.: *Efficiency of Human Movement*, 2nd Ed. Philadelphia: W. B. Saunders Co., 1966. Chapters 8 and 19.

7. Pugh, L. G. C. E.: The Influence of Wind Resistance in Running and Walking and the Mechanical Efficiency of Work Against Horizontal or Vertical Forces. J. Physiol., 213, 255–270, 1971.

Recommended Reading

8. Amar, Jules: *The Human Motor*. Abridged in *Human Mechanics*. AMRL-TDR-63-123. Wright-Patterson Air Force Base: Aerospace-Medical Research Laboratories, 1963.

9. Williams, Marian and Lissner, Herbert R.: *Biomechanics of Human Motion*. Philadelphia: W. B. Saunders Co., 1962.

10. Rogers, E. M.: *Physics for the Inquiring Mind. The Methods, Nature, and Philosophy of Physical Science*. Princeton: Princeton University Press, 1960.

11. *Sir Isaac Newton's Mathematical Principles of Natural Philosophy and His System of the World*. July 5, 1668. English translation by Andrew Motte, 1729; revision by Florian Cajori. Berkeley: University of California Press, 1948.

Laboratory Exercises

1. Take the world's records for running distances for 100 yds. to 2 miles. Calculate the average speed in each event and plot on a graph. Which race has the fastest average speed?

2. When a karate expert strikes with one arm, he simultaneously pulls the other one back. What principle is he seeking to invoke and for what purpose?

3. In punting into a head wind, what adjustment should the kicker make in the angle of projection of the ball? If kicking with a tail wind? Why?

4. A boat sails due north for half an hour at 5 knots (1 knot = 1 nautical mile per hour.) Simultaneously it is set due east by a tidal current running at 1 knot. Find its speed and velocity.

5. In *How to beat better tennis players* (Garden City, N.Y., Doubleday & Co., Inc., 1970, p. 154) Loring Fiske indicates that Pancho Gonzales' serve travels at 112 m.p.h., while that of the average player does not exceed 80 m.p.h. Assume that the ball is struck at a height of 9.5 feet, and follows a linear trajectory until it lands in the service court at a point 58 feet horizontally away from the server. What is the linear displacement of the ball? Assuming average velocities cited above, what are the time intervals between impacts of the rackets and impacts of the balls with the ground? Actually, the balls fall off a linear trajectory, because they are acted upon by gravity during flight. Using the calculated time-of-flight estimates, how far will each player's ball fall under the influence of gravity? Which player's ball will have to be projected at the greater angle to the ground, and why?

6. In 1926 the coach of the Jesus College Boat Club pitched the crews' slides forward with a drop of about 2″ in the 14″ travel. His idea was to "get the weight on to the feet" during the forward travel. Wherein lay the fallacy?

Chapter 8

The Body as a Lever System

In Chapter 2 the skeleton was presented as a supportive structure composed of articulated bones. This is the classical anatomical approach. Today scientists involved with problems of human engineering speak of links and hinges rather than of bones and joints. Links are defined as straight lines extending through a body segment between adjacent hinge points. These are functional rather than structural entities, and they cannot be accurately measured from surface landmarks, but this concept justifies our representing the body by a stick diagram for the purposes of mechanical analysis (Fig. 8–1). The joints are the hinges, and the contraction of the muscles results in the movement of the links around their centers of rotation. Movement can take place only in the direction or directions and to the extent permitted by the configuration of the joints and their cartilages. All joint movements are rotational and may be measured in degrees or radians. Dynamic measurements of joint ranges are as yet very incomplete and little is known about the effect of training and exercise upon them.[1] In general, however, they are greater in females than in males and asthenic males than in muscular ones. The body's shape and functioning are largely determined by mechanical considerations. The principles of the conservation of energy require that the bulk of the muscle mass be concentrated at the proximal end of a lever rather than at the distal end. Thus the segments of the body tend to assume the shape of a inverted truncated cone. Single rotatory movements of these segments result in flexion or extension; a combination of two or more rotatory motions moving in the same direction, so that the total of all angles of rotation is zero, results in translatory progress. The various possible combinations of links and hinges give the body a wide variety of movements.

An understanding of leverage and the various kinds of levers is essential in comprehending the movements of the body.

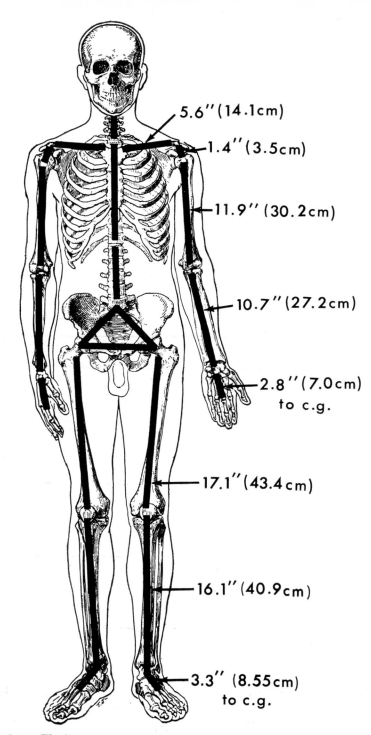

5.6″ (14.1cm)

1.4″ (3.5cm)

11.9″ (30.2cm)

10.7″ (27.2cm)

2.8″ (7.0cm)
to c.g.

17.1″ (43.4 cm)

16.1″ (40.9cm)

3.3″ (8.55cm)
to c.g.

Fig. 8–1.   The link system of the human body.   The straight black lines indicate the effective levers for rotatory actions between one joint center and the next in sequence.   Length dimensions are means for 50 centile of Air Force flying personnel. (After Dempster.)

A lever is a rigid bar revolving about a fixed point called the axis or fulcrum. That part of the lever between the fulcrum and the weight or resistance is termed the weight-arm; that part of it between the fulcrum and the applied force is termed the force-arm. The mechanical advantage of a lever is the ratio of the length of the force-arm to that of the resistance-arm. The usual function of a lever is to gain a mechanical advantage whereby a small force applied force applied over a large distance at one end of a lever produces a greater force operating over a lesser distance at the other, or whereby a given speed of movement at one end of a lever is greatly increased at the other. In the human body, the action of contracting muscles normally constitutes the force, the resistance is furnished by the center of gravity of the segment moved plus any additional weight which may be in contact with that segment, and the axis is the joint at which the movement takes place. In most cases the force-arm in the human body is shorter than is the resistance-arm, resulting in a mechanical disadvantage. The law of the conservation of energy implies that what is lost in force is gained in distance (and vice versa). When a lever turns on its axis, all points on the lever move in arcs of a circle, and the distance through which any given point moves is proportional to its distance from the axis. Since these different distances are traversed in the same period of time, it follows that the points more distant from the axis move faster than do those closer to it. Thus a gain in distance is also a gain in speed.

The penniform arrangement of the muscles gives a comparatively

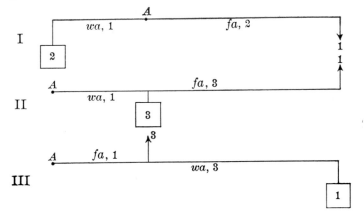

FIG. 8–2. The three classes of levers. The long straight lines are the levers; A is the axis; the squares represent the weight or resistance and the arrows the force or pull of muscle; fa, force-arm; wa, weight-arm. Numerals in the squares and beside the arrows are the magnitudes of the weights (or resistances) and of the effort forces respectively. The other numerals indicate the length of the lever arm.

large amount of force, and the arrangement of the bony levers gives distance of movement and speed. Since the force is usually applied with a short force-arm and a long resistance-arm, the muscles lie close to the bones and a compact structure is achieved. Baseball bats, hockey sticks, tennis rackets, and similar instruments represent artificial extensions of the resistance arms of body levers, thus increasing the speed at the striking point while requiring an increase in muscular force. On the other hand, wheelbarrows, pliers, and crowbars are designed to decrease the resistance arms and increase the force arms, thus increasing the mechanical advantage and allowing a greater application of effort with a small muscular force, but with loss of speed.

Levers are divided into three classes, depending upon the relative positions of the force, the axis, and the resistance (Fig. 8–2). In all three cases the force exactly balances the resistance when the product of the force times the length of the force arm is equal to the product of the resistance times the length of the resistance arm (f × fa = r × ra). It should be emphasized that f and r in the formula refer only to rotary components of the actual forces. These components are directed at 90° to the lever arms. Each side of this formula represents a torque:

$$f \times fa = \text{force torque.}$$
$$r \times ra = \text{resistance torque.}$$

Graphic and computational techniques for determining such torques were discussed in Chapter 7. The application of any additional force will cause the lever to move; and the effects of changes in any of the components of the lever may be easily determined by substituting in the above formula.

First Class Levers. Levers of the first class have the fulcrum located between the force and the resistance. As a consequence the two arms of the lever move in opposite directions, as in a crowbar, a pair of scissors, or a teeter-totter. Such levers often sacrifice force to gain speed. A typical example is the triceps (Muscle I, in Fig. 8–3). Assume the elbow is at the side, flexed at an angle of 90°, and the palm is exerting a force of 10 pounds against a table top. The palm is 12 inches from the elbow joint (fulcrum) and the triceps is inserted 1 inch from the opposite side of the fulcrum. What is the rotary force of contraction of the triceps?

$$f \times fa = r \times ra$$
$$f \times 1 = 10 \times 12$$
$$f = 120 \text{ pounds.}$$

Kinesiologists have variously presented the act of rising on tiptoe as an example of the functioning of first, second, and third class levers. In static equilibrium, however, any point may be chosen as the fulcrum and the sum of clockwise and counterclockwise torques about a point will be equal. Therefore, the designation of the class lever becomes arbitrary, and the type of lever advocated is immaterial provided that all torques involved are considered.

Second Class Levers. In levers of the second class the resistance is between the fulcrum and the force. Here speed is sacrificed to gain power. Examples are found in the wheelbarrow and the nutcracker. Almost no levers of this type are found in the body, but opening the mouth against resistance is an example.

Third Class Levers. In third class levers the force is applied between the fulcrum and the resistance. A common example is found in the spring which closes a screen door. This class of lever is the one most common in the body, since it permits the muscle to be inserted near the joint and to produce distance and speed of movement, although at a sacrifice of force.

A typical example is found in the biceps flexing the forearm against resistance (Fig. 8–3). Assume that the elbow is flexed at 90° and that a 16 lb. shot is held in the hand. The fulcrum is at the elbow joint. If the biceps is assumed to be inserted two inches from

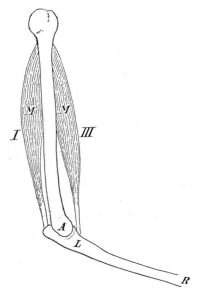

Fig. 8–3. Illustration of first class and third class levers by muscles acting on the elbow-joint. The bone AR is the lever, with the axis at A, the weight or resistance at the hand, which is beyond R. M, M are the muscles and L is the insertion of the muscle III.

the fulcrum and the distance from the fulcrum to the center of the shot is 14 inches, then the rotary force exerted by the biceps in supporting the shot can be calculated by the previous formula:

$$f \times fa = r \times ra$$
$$f \times 2 = 16 \times 14$$
$$f \times 2 = 224$$
$$f = 112 \text{ pounds.}$$

In this example, however, the weight of the forearm has been neglected. If we wish to include it we must know its weight and the location of its center of gravity. If we assume the weight of the forearm and hand to be 4 pounds and the center of gravity to be 6 inches from the fulcrum, the torque (moment of force, *i.e.*, force times perpendicular distance) about the elbow from this source is equal to:

$$4 \times 6 = 24 \text{ pounds.}$$

Since the torque of the shot equals 224 pounds, a total torque of 248 pounds results. In order to keep the forearm and the shot in equilibrium, the rotary force exerted by the contraction of the biceps must also equal 248. Since

$$force = \frac{\text{Resistance torque}}{\text{Force arm}} = \frac{r \times ra}{fa}$$

$$f = \frac{248}{2} = 124 \text{ lbs. force exerted by biceps.}$$

A more complicated example of a third class lever is seen in the Monteggia or so-called "night stick fracture," shown in Figure 8–4.

Effect of the Angle of Pull. Figure 8–5 shows how the angle of pull changes as the muscle contracts. When the bony lever is in position BC, the angle of pull (DEB) is 12°; in the position BC_1, it is 20°; at BC_2, 25°. The smaller the angle of pull, the farther and faster a given amount of muscular contraction moves the bone. In Figure 8–5 the muscle DE is represented as making four successive contractions, each one equivalent to one-eighth of the muscle's length. Starting at position BE, where the angle of pull is only 12°, the first contraction moves the bone BE through an angular distance of 32°; as the angle of pull increases, the same amount of contraction turns it 25°, 21°, and 19° respectively. When the angle of pull is 10° to 12°, movements are about the same.

FIG. 8–4.   Monteggia Fracture.   The fulcrum formed by the fractured ulna causes the head of the radius to dislocate at the elbow.   These fractures result from direct trauma to the arm when in pronation and elevation, as in defending one's head from a blow from a night stick.

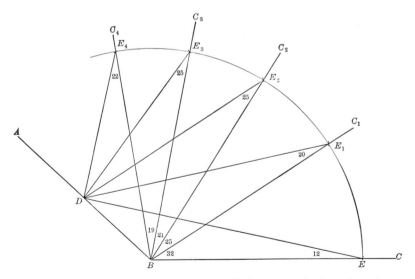

FIG. 8–5.   Diagram to show how angle of pull changes as the bony lever is moved by the muscle: AB is a stationary bone with axis at B; DE is the muscle and BC the moving bone, coming to positions BC_1, BC_2, etc., as the muscle shortens, the muscle coming to positions DE_1, DE_2, etc., DEB is the angle of pull.

From the standpoint of force alone, the optimal angle of pull for any muscle is 90°, since at this angle the entire force of the muscle is acting to rotate the bony lever around its axis. This is the only case in which the force arm is equal to the perpendicular distance. At angles of less than 90°, part of the muscular pull acts to pull the bone lengthwise into the joint, thereby increasing the friction of the joint and reducing the amount of pull available to perform external work. At angles greater than 90°, part of the pull tends to pull the bone out of the joint, again reducing the amount for external work. As a result, the increased distance and speed of movement at small angles of pull is achieved only at the sacrifice of power, and the actual movement at angles other than 90° is the resultant of two forces.

In the case of the biceps acting at the elbow, when the joint is flexed at an angle of less than 90°, the stabilizing component tends to pull the end of the bony lever out of the joint, thereby decreasing its stability. In such cases it may still be termed a stabilizing component, but has a negative value. Stabilization is of particular importance in the case of the shoulder, where the head of the humerus is only loosely held in place. In the absence of a relatively large stabilizing force, certain strenuous efforts might cause the joint to dislocate. In the upper range of movement where this is a definite possibility, the supraspinatus aids greatly by providing a relatively large force for this purpose. In the case of the hip, the stabilizing component need not be large because the socket is deep and the head of the femur is held firmly in place by strong taut ligaments. In many positions the weight of the body also tends to hold the head of the femur in the socket.

Because the stabilizing component of force cannot be utilized to do useful work, it represents wasted energy insofar as mechanical efficiency of the machine is concerned. In any movement in which the stabilizing force is relatively large compared to the rotary force, the efficiency of movement must be low.

As will be discussed later in this chapter, in some cases the body has endeavored to overcome this situation by the introduction of pulleys into the mechanical system.

Effect of Angle of Resistance. When an object is moved, the resistance which is overcome is usually the force of gravity. This is always effective vertically downward from the center of gravity of the object. As a muscle contracts and moves an object through space, the angle of the resistance to the force continually changes, just as has been shown to be true for the angle of pull of a muscle. As a result two calculations are necessary before the force required at any given stage in a movement can be calculated. Assume a weight lifter curls a 100 pound barbell. The perpendicular distance between the axis and the intersertion of the biceps is 2 inches; the angle of pull of the elbow flexors is 75°, the distance from the axis to the weight is 14 inches, and the angle between the forearm and the line of gravity of the barbell is 82°. The torque developed by this weight is equal to the amount of weight (100 lbs.) times the sine of the angle of the weight (sin 82° = .99027) times the length of the resistance arm (14 inches), or 1386.38 inch pounds. To this must be added the torque developed by the weight of the forearm itself— say 25 inch pounds—for a total torque of 1411.38 inch pounds. By use of the formula

$$f = \frac{\text{Resistance torque}}{\text{Force arm}}$$

we find the force of the muscular contraction necessary to offset this torque is 705.5 inch pounds. This is the *rotary force* which must be produced by the muscle pulling at an angle of 75°. The *entire force* of contraction which will be needed must now be found. Substituting known quantities in the formula

$$f = F \times \text{sine angle of pull}$$
$$705.5 = F \times 0.966$$
$$F = \frac{705.5}{0.966}$$
$$= 730.33 \text{ pounds.}$$

While the student should understand how such calculations are made, they are not normally used by any except specialists. Ordinarily several muscles act on a joint at once, necessitating very complex computations. Usually the distances from the axis, the angle of muscle pulls, and the weights of the body segments cannot be determined with any degree of accuracy. Even allowing for these inherent inaccuracies, however, such studies clearly show the extent to which the third class lever system of the body sacrifices force for speed, and, conversely, the great amount of force required to lift relatively light weights. Morris, *et al.*, have demonstrated that when a 170 pound man performs a straight-legged dead lift of 200 pounds, the forces of the weight lifted, the weight of the upper body, and the contraction of the deep muscles of the spine generate a theoretical reaction of 2,071 pounds at the lumbrosacral disc, although certain compensating mechanisms in the torso reduce this to 1,483 pounds.[2] Examples of this type clarify the reason such movements occasionally result in serious trauma, and emphasize the need for proper body mechanics.

In the human body maximal muscular effort produces relatively constant moments regardless of the angular position of the articulating levers, and in spite of the fact that the tensions developed by a muscle become less as the muscle shortens and greater as it lengthens. This effect is produced by a reciprocating arrangement of the muscles and levers by which changes in the torque which muscles can develop about a joint are offset by changes in the lengths of the effective lever arms, so that the force produced remains relatively constant. It has not been sufficiently emphasized that functional aberrations of the muscles will reflect modifications in the leverage system, and vice versa.[3] Isometric joint torques are not actually identical at all points within the arc of movement, but it is probably true that the compensatory arrangements tend to limit the degree of difference which would otherwise be present and to some degree equates muscular tension throughout the arc of movement.

WHEEL AND AXLE ACTION

A modification of the lever is found in the wheel and axle principle, which is used in the body to effect or prevent rotation of a segment. In trunk twisting exercises, for example, the oblique abdominal muscles pull on the trunk as though it were the rim of a wheel, and the trunk is turned in the direction of the pull. This actually constitutes a lever of the second class.

Usually rotation is the result of the synergic action of many muscles, whose pull is oblique rather than direct. Frequently a muscle inserts on a tuberosity, or bony process. This increases the torque by increasing the length of the lever arm.

PULLEY ACTION

The pulley provides a means of changing the direction of a force, thereby applying it at a different angle and perhaps resulting in a line of movement quite different from that which would otherwise have occurred. The tendon of insertion of the peroneus longus offers a good example. This tendon goes directly down the lateral aspect of the leg, passes around the external malleolus, goes to a notch in the cuboid bone, turns under the foot and inserts in the medial cuneiform and the first metatarsal. The pulley action of the external malleolus and the cuboid bone thus accomplishes two changes of direction which would otherwise be impossible. The result is that contraction of this muscle plantar-flexes the foot; without the pulleys it would insert in front of the ankle and on top of the foot, so that it would dorsi-flex that segment.

By changing the direction of the application of force, a pulley may provide a greater angle of insertion than would otherwise be possible. An example is found in the patella. By passing over this sesamoid bone, the patellar ligament inserts at a greater angle, which increases the rotary component of force of the quadriceps femoris and decreases the stabilizing component. In this case a change of direction of force achieves an increased effective force in the movement.

WORK

The purpose of the muscles and the levers upon which they act is to accomplish work. In solving problems of muscular work the kinesiologist ordinarily seeks answers to four questions: (1) How much work was accomplished? (2) What was the energy expenditure involved? (3) How much horsepower was developed by the worker? (4) What was the mechanical efficiency with which the work was done? Fortunately the formulae involved are not complex. First,

$$W_d = F \times d$$

where W_d = Dynamic Work, F = Force, and d = the displacement of the resistance in the direction of the force.

The answer may be expressed in foot-pounds, that is, in units of one pound moved through a distance of one foot, or in kilogram-meters. Suppose a weight lifter snatches (Figs. 16–13, 14, 15) 200 pounds from the floor to a height of 4.5 feet.

$$W_d = 200 \text{ lbs.} \times 4.5 \text{ ft.} = 900 \text{ ft. lbs.}$$

While technically no work is accomplished during static contractions, the physiological significance of the energy expended may be expressed by

$$W_s = F \times t$$

where t = time the effort was sustained.

The energy expended is usually measured by collecting the subject's expired air during work. The respiratory quotient (R.Q.) is determined by computing the ratio of carbon dioxide expired to the oxygen inspired $\left(\frac{CO_2}{O_2}\right)$. This figure may vary from 4.686 calories to 5.04 calories, depending on the combination of protein, carbohydrate, and fat in the diet. Tables or charts may be used to determine the caloric equivalent of 1 liter of oxygen for any given R.Q. If the oxygen alone has been measured, it is customary to use a conversion factor of 4.86, which is based on an R.Q. of 0.85, assumed to be that of an ordinary mixed diet. Thus the conventional formula for the conversion of oxygen consumption to energy expenditure in calories is

$$C = 4.86 \times \text{liters O}_2 \text{ used.}$$

Assuming that the lifter in question used 1.771 liters of oxygen in completing his lift and that he was on an ordinary mixed diet, his gross energy expenditure in calories would be

$$C = 1.771 \times 4.86 = 8.607.$$

To obtain the total net energy per minute cost of the work the kinesiologist has to add to the cost of the work the amount of oxygen used during recovery from the work (oxygen debt) and to subtract from this total the resting oxygen, that is, the amount of oxygen which the lifter would have used for physiological purposes even if he had done no work at all. Some writers also make a deduction for the specific dynamic action of foods. Either way the resulting figure may then be converted to a per minute basis. The expanded equation thus becomes:

$$E = \frac{\text{work O}_2 + \text{recovery O}_2 - \text{resting O}_2}{\text{total time}}.$$

Suppose the snatch takes 7 seconds to complete, the lifter uses 38.515 liters O_2 during a recovery period of 1 m. 53 sec. and that his resting consumption of oxygen is 250 ml./min. Then

$$E = \frac{1.771 + 38.515 - 500}{2 \text{ m}} - \frac{38.015}{2} = 19.007 \text{ liters O}_2.$$

Unfortunately the student will find energy expenditure reported in a number of different ways in the literature, which often makes it extremely difficult to compare data from different investigations. It appears preferable to give the results of such studies in gross cal./min. Energy requirements for a large number of sport and work activities have been measured and are readily available in the literature.[4-6]

Since the various forms of energy are interchangeable, mechanical work may be converted to calories on the basis that 3086 ft.-lbs. (426.7 kg-m) equals one calorie. Similarly work or calories may be converted to horsepower on the basis that 1 hp. equals 33,000 ft.-lbs., per minute (4562.4 kg-m/min), or 10.7 cal/min, or 2.1 liters O_2/min. For most purposes it is acceptable to use 15,000 ft.-pounds as the equivalent of 1 liter O_2.

The work efficiency (ratio of useful work output to total work input) is usually expressed in percentage form according to the formula

$$W.E. = \frac{W(in\ ft.-lbs.) \times 100}{liter\ O_2 \times (approximately)\ 15,000\ ft.-lbs.}.$$

The theoretical muscular efficiency is about 49 per cent, but even under favorable conditions the efficiency of the human machine seldom exceeds 29 per cent.[7] For the step test it is about 16 per cent,[8] and for the snatch it is only 6.3 per cent.[9] Mechanical efficiency may vary with speed, training, diet, type of work performed, duration of work, sex, age, height, weight, and other similar factors. It is greatest at about 1/5 of the muscles' maximum speed.[10]

When oxygen measuring apparatus is not available, the student may find it convenient to follow Bonjer's recommendation:

$$"Personal\ capability\ for\ a\ given\ task"\ quotient = \frac{Work}{Total\ heart\ beats}.$$

Within certain limitations there is a linear relationship between pulse rate and the oxygen consumed and the work load. Consequently, "personal capability" is essentially the same as work efficiency.[11]

STRENGTH

The term "strength" appears in various contexts in the literature. It may refer to the ability to overcome a resistance (concentric, isotonic, or dynamic strength), to resist extension (eccentric strength), or to support a load (isometric or static strength). The correlation between strengths measured in any of these ways is high but the scores and positions of maximal force are not identical[12] (Fig. 8–6).

POWER

Power is often confused with strength, but actually is the *rate* at which work is done. It is determined by dividing the work by the time required to do the work:

$$P = \frac{W}{t}.$$

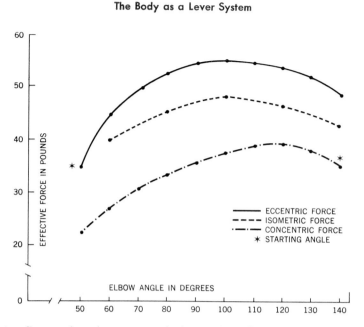

FIG. 8–6.   Curves of maximum eccentric, isometric, and concentric forces of forearm
    flexors. (Singh and Karpovich, by permission J. Appl. Physiol.)

Thus the power developed by our hypothetical weight lifter, as
determined by substituting in the above formula, is

$$P = \frac{200 \text{ lbs.} \times 4.5 \text{ ft.}}{7 \text{ sec.}} = 128.6 \text{ ft.-lbs./sec.}$$

Since power is usually expressed in horsepower (550 ft.-lbs./sec.)
rather than in foot-pounds,

$$P = \frac{128.6}{550} = 0.23 \text{ h.p.}$$

Some physiologists[13] suggest that human work output should be calculated in terms of "manpower." On the basis of comparative work
performance they compute 1 m.p. = .187 h.p.

A muscle develops its maximal power when contracting against a
load equal to approximately one-third of the maximal tension which
it can generate.

Wilkie[14] reviewed the literature dealing with the mechanical
power output of champion athletes under various conditions and
concluded the output is limited:

1. To less than 6 h.p. in single movements having a duration of
less than 1 sec., due to the intrinsic power production of muscle and

FIG. 8–7. *(Legend on opposite page)*

by the difficulty of coupling a large mass of muscle to a suitably matched load.

2. To 0.5 to 2 h.p. in bouts of exercise of 1 to 5 minutes' duration, due to the restricted availability in the muscles of stores of energy-yielding substances.

3. To 0.4 to 0.5 h.p. in steady state work of 5 to 150 mins. or more, due to the restricted ability of the body to absorb and transport oxygen.

4. To perhaps 0.2 h.p. in long-term work, due to wear and tear of muscles, the need to eat, etc.

In ordinary healthy individuals, the output is probably 70 to 80 per cent of these figures.

At this point the student may well feel that all this discussion of levers, torques, and other mechanical principles is highly abstract and has little or no practical application. Actually the converse is true. Figure 8–7 shows a typical example of human movement in athletics.

The caption describes how mechanical analysis can be applied to such an activity, and the results may be used to produce improved performance by showing the athlete exactly what he is trying to do, why he is trying to do it, and the most efficient means of accomplishing his ends. Similar analysis can be applied to any other example of movement, and may point the way to more effective performance.

––––––––––

FIG. 8–7. Okuri-ashi-harai (Sweeping ankle throw), a judo throw. A, The judoka on the right may be thought of as essentially a second class lever, with the fulcrum at his feet, his weight at his center of gravity, and a force couple applied at feet and chest. B, The mv with which the right foot of the opponent sweeps against his left ankle as he steps sideward develops an F which moves his foot against the right ankle (Newton's first law), thus narrowing his base of support to his right foot alone. Simultaneously the combined Fs of the lift-push of the opponent's left arm and the pull of the right arm rotate him on his narrowed base (Newton's second law) and cause his line of gravity to fall outside of his base. If the F of the opponent's foot is great enough, it overcomes the friction between the man's supporting foot and the mat and sweeps his base out from under him. C, The torque created by the force couple (F $\times$ d center of gravity to ankle + F $\times$ d center of gravity to chest) developed by the combined leg and arm maneuvers causes him to rotate around his center of gravity and crash to the mat on his back. By landing on his back (and by the preliminary slap of his right arm on the mat) the thrown judoka receives the landing shock on the padded parts of the body and minimizes the impact per square inch by dissipating it over as large an area as possible. A similar analysis of aikido throws will show that this art depends to a much greater extent on the use of centrifugal force. (Photos reproduced from Modern Judo, Volume I, by Charles Yerkow, with permission of the publishers. The Stackpole Company, Harrisburg, Pa.)

References

1. Dempster, Wilfrid Taylor: *Space Requirements of the Seated Operator*. Washington, D. C. U. S. Department of Commerce, July, 1955.

2. Morris, J. M., Lucas, D. B., and Bresler, B.: Role of the Trunk in Stability of the Spine. J. Bone Joint Surg., *43-A*, 327–351, 1961.

3. Inman, Vern T. and Ralston, H. J.: The Mechanics of Voluntary Muscle. In Paul E. Klopsteg and Philip D. Wilson, editors, *Human Limbs and Their Substitutes*. New York: McGraw-Hill Book Company, Inc., 1954, pp. 296–317.

4. Seliger, V.: Energy Metabolism in Selected Physical Exercises. Int. z. angew. Physiol. einschl. Arbeitphysiol., *25*, 104–120, 1968.

5. Durnin, J. V. G. A. and Passmore, R.: *Energy, Work and Leisure*. London: Heinemann Educational Books, Ltd., 1967.

6. Gordon, Edward E.: Energy Cost of Activities in Health and Disease. A.M.A. Arch. Int. Med., *101*, 702–713, 1958.

7. Whipp, Brian J. and Wasserman, Karlman: Efficiency of Muscular Work. J. Appl. Physiol., *26*, 644–648, 1969.

8. Rhyming, Irma: A Modified Harvard Step Test for the Evaluation of Physical Fitness. Arbeitsphysiologie, *15*, 235–250, 1953.

9. Leggett, Leslie R.: Physiological Measures of Selected Weight Lifting Activities. Unpublished Master's Thesis, Springfield College, 1958, p. 74.

10. Hill, A. V.: Voluntary Muscle—The Mechanics of Its Active State. The Times Review of the Progress of Science, *1*, 13, 1951.

11. Bonjer, F. H.: The Effect of Aptitude, Fitness, Physical Working Capacity, Skill and Motivation on the Amount and Quality of Work. Ergonomics, *2*, 254–261, 1959.

12. Singh, Mohan and Karpovich, Peter V.: Isotonic and Isometric Forces of Forearm Flexors and Extensors. J. Appl. Physiol., *21*, 1435–1437, 1966.

13. Balke, Bruno: Physiological Background for the Assessment, Evaluation and Classification of Physical Fitness. In *Proceedings of the First Canadian Fitness Seminar*. Saskatoon: University of Saskatchewan, 1963, pp. 5–14.

14. Wilkie, D. R.: Man as a Source of Mechanical Power. Ergonomics, *3*, 1–8, 1960.

Laboratory Exercises

1. Show that sprinters on their marks have adjusted the joints so that the angles of insertion of leg muscles are nearly optimal. Compare this with the ready positions of football players, swimmers, wrestlers.

2. In an attempt to explain the increase in rupture of the achilles tendon among skiers during the last few years, Dr. Heinz Schonbauer assumed that the force of the falling body is proportional to the sine of the angle formed by the ski and the lower leg. With the modern type of safety binding this angle is at least 60°; with the old-type, which permitted the heel to lift, it was only 30°. By what proportion has the new binding increased the stress on the achilles tendon during a forward fall?

3. In the 1955 race across the English Channel, the winner covered 25.8 miles at an average speed of 1.78 m.p.h. If he had an oxygen intake of 3.3 l./min. and were on an ordinary mixed diet, what was his gross energy expenditure in calories?

4. In an article entitled "Wrestling's Parallel-Perpendicular Axiom," (Scholastic Coach, XLV:8–11, 1965) William C. Garguilo states: "On the mat our wrestlers follow the parallel-perpendicular rule. When on top always work perpendicular to the opponent. When on the bottom always work parallel to the opponent." Explain the laws of leverage underlying this axiom.

5. A typical stiletto heel used as a weapon inflicts a circular puncture wound approximately 0.08 sq. in. in area.   Assume a woman stamps her heel on an assailant's instep with a force of 120 pounds.   What would be the force per square inch exerted on the area under the heel?

6. In *Use Your Head in Tennis* (London: Phoenix House Limited, 1959, p. 159) Bob Harman comments, "Ladies can't run or hit very well.   They simply aren't built for it."   What kinesiological considerations would cause you to agree or disagree with Harman's views?

7. A boat sails due north for half an hour at 5 knots (1 knot = 1 nautical mile per hour).   Simultaneously it is set due east by a tidal current running at 1 knot. Find its speed and velocity.

8. How long will it take a runner to go 2 miles if he averages 18 feet per second?

9. If a runner covers 1 mile in 4 minutes 8 seconds, what is his average speed in feet per second?

10. A sprinter running 100 yards reaches his maximum speed of 30 feet per second at the 10-yard mark.   He maintains this speed to the finish.   If it takes him 10.5 seconds to run the total distance, what is his average speed for the first 10 yards? What is his average acceleration for the first 10 yards?

11. What is the momentum of a 198-pound full back moving at the rate of 23 feet per second?   Will his forward momentum be stopped if he is hit headon by a 221-pound tackle moving at 19 feet per second?

12. A muscle inserts at an angle of 10°.   Is it better suited for moving the bone to which it is attached or for stabilizing the joint which it crosses?   If it inserts at an angle of 30°? 45°? 60°? 80°?

13. What are the typical physical attributes of the modern discus thrower?   How do each of these—height, weight, mass, strength, length of bones, height of center of gravity, etc.—contribute to success in this activity?   High jumper?   Gymnast? Football lineman?   Baseball pitcher?

14. Assume a wrestler supine on the mat pushes upward against his opponent's head with a force of 200 pounds.   What is the effect on the wrestler himself?   Why?

15. On June 19, 1963 Lt. Cliff J. Judkins, U.S.M.C., fell 15,000 feet into the ocean when his parachute failed to open.   He received a compression fracture of the back, a hairline fracture of the pelvis, and two broken ankles.   Assume the flier weighed 170 lbs.   What was his acceleration?   The time of his fall?   His speed at the time of impact?   His velocity at the time of impact?   The momentum with which he landed?   The force with which he struck?

Chapter 9

Movements of the Shoulder Girdle

The shoulder girdle* consists of two pairs of bones, a *clavicle* and a *scapula* on each side. The only bony connection of the arms and shoulder girdle with the axial skeleton is through the clavicles, whose medial ends articulate with the manubrium of the sternum (Fig. 9–1). Such a precarious system of bony connections indicates that stresses and weights borne by the upper limbs must be transferred to the central weight-bearing column of the spine mainly by the extensive shoulder girdle musculature.

The clavicle, which is about 6 inches long, appears straight when viewed from the front, but is curved like an italic *f* when seen from above. The *sternal end* is convex anteriorly, and the *acromial end* is convex posteriorly. The upper surface is smooth and the under surface rough; the sternal end is the thicker, and the acromial end more flattened. The *conoid tubercle*, the *trapezoid line*, and the *impression for the costoclavicular ligament* are landmarks for locating the attachment of ligaments (Figs. 9–2, A–1, A–2).

The scapula is a flat triangular bone with two surfaces, the *costal* (next to the ribs) and the *dorsal*; three borders, the *medial*, the *lateral*, and the *superior*; and three angles, the *superior*, the *lateral*, and the *inferior*. The *spine of the scapula*, on the *dorsal* surface, terminates in the flattened *acromion*, with the junction of the two being marked by easily palpable *acromial angle*, which is an important landmark for making postural and surgical measurements. Above the spine is the deep *supraspinous fossa*; below it is the shallow *infraspinous fossa*, which should not be confused with the *subscapular fossa* located on the costal surface of the scapula. The *coracoid process*, shaped like a bent finger, projects forward under the clavicle

---

* Some kinesiologists object that the term "shoulder girdle" is a misnomer, since the scapulae are not linked to each other. However, the term is so generally used that it is probably futile to attempt to discard it now.

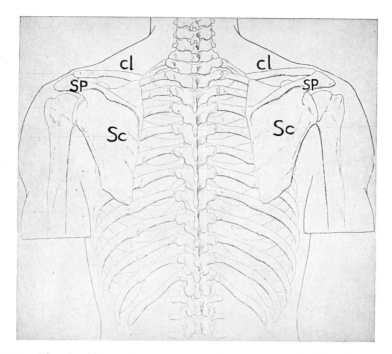

Fɪɢ. 9–1.   The shoulder girdle, rear view: *Sc*, scapula; *cl*, clavicle; *Sp*, spine of
scapula.   (Richer.)

and toward the head of the humerus, providing attachments for
ligaments to the clavicle, the acromion, and the humerus. There
are two articular surfaces, one on the acromion to receive the clavicle,
and one at the lateral angle, the shallow *glenoid cavity*, which receives the head of the humerus (Figs. 9–1, 9–3, A–3, A–4). The
greatest vertical length of the scapula in man is about 6 inches;
its greatest breadth is about 4 inches. This is a marked exception
to the general rule in vertebrate animals, most of whom have the
long axis of the scapula in line with its spine, so that the glenoid
fossa is at the end of the scapula instead of at the side.

The clavicle is joined to the sternum by a double joint, the two
bones being separated by a cartilage, with one articulation between
the sternum and the cartilage and another between the cartilage and
the clavicle. The cartilage serves as an elastic buffer in case of
shocks received in the arm or shoulder, and the joint permits the
outer end of the clavicle to be moved up and down, forward and
backward, or any combination of these movements; it also permits
slight rotation of the clavicle on its long axis. The capsular ligament
of the joint is strengthened by thickened bands at the front and

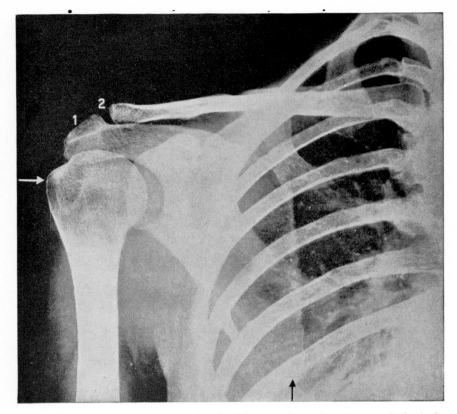

FIG. 9–2. X-ray photograph of a shoulder. 1, Acromion; 2, acromioclavicular joint. The lower arrow indicates the inferior angle of the scapula; the upper arrow the greater tuberosity. (*Gray's Anatomy*.)

rear; injury of the joint is further prevented by the *interclavicular* ligament, which joins the two clavicles, and by a ligament called the *costoclavicular*, which connects the under surface of each clavicle with the rib below it (Fig. 9–3).

The outer end of the clavicle is joined to the anterior border of the acromion by the *acromioclavicular* ligament, strengthening the capsular ligament on the upper side. The main protection against injury to the joint is the *coracoclavicular* ligament, two strong bands of fibers, the *conoid* and the *trapezoid* ligaments, connecting the top of the coracoid with the under surface of the clavicle (Fig. 9–3).

All movements of the shoulder girdle may be properly called movements of the scapula, since the position of the clavicle does not permit it to move independently. These movements always involve both of the joints just described, the clavicle moving so as to allow the scapula to assume its proper relation to the chest wall.

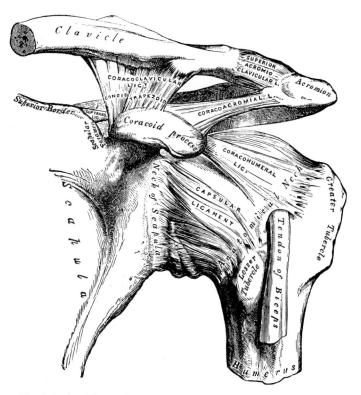

FIG. 9–3.   The left shoulder and acromioclavicular joints, and the proper ligaments of the scapula.   (*Gray's Anatomy.*)

In everyday life most movements of the scapula are closely integrated with and secondary to movements of the arm.   The scapula serves as a mobile base from which the arm operates.   Whatever action or position is required of the arm to accomplish a given task, the scapula moves to align the glenoid cavity so it will be in the best possible position to receive the head of the humerus.   Muscle function plays a critical role in determining the shape of the medial border of the scapula, the size of the scapular spine, and the size of the glenoid cavity.[1]   The mobility of the scapula makes possible a much wider range of movement of the arm than it would have otherwise.

The fundamental movements of the shoulder girdle described as scapular movements may be classified as follows:

1. *Adduction* is the movement of the scapula medially toward the spinal column.   *Abduction* is the opposite motion, in which the scapula slides laterally and forward along the surface of the ribs.

2. *Elevation* and *depression* are, respectively, the upward and

downward motions of the whole scapula without any rotation. All
parts of the scapula move the same distance. Pure elevation is a
relatively rare movement, exemplified by shoulder-shrugging, picking up a suitcase, and a few other tasks in which the upper limb is
not moved forward or sideward away from the body.

3. *Upward rotation* of the scapula involves an upward turning of
the glenoid cavity and the lateral angle in relation to the superior
angle and medial border, which turn downward. The rotation takes
place through an angle of 60° or more. The center of rotation is
within the scapula itself. Downward rotation is the reverse of upward rotation. Upward and downward rotation are distinguished
sharply from elevation and depression, which are not accompanied
by any rotation.

Since the clavicle is attached to the sternum, which is comparatively stationary, the acromion must always move in a curve with
the clavicle as a radius. Almost any movement away from the
anatomical position tends to narrow the width of the shoulders.

4. *Forward tilt* of the scapula occurs when the inferior angle moves
backward away from the rib cage. *Backward tilt* is the opposite
movement, in which the inferior angle and the costal surface return
to the surface of the rib cage. Since forward and backward tilt are
specialized movements of small extent and of little significance to
normal function, they are not discussed further in this chapter.

The following six muscles connect the shoulder girdle with the
main skeleton, hold it in normal position, and give rise to the movements just described. Anterior: subclavius, pectoralis minor,
serattus anterior. Posterior: levator scapulae, trapezius, rhomboid.

TRAPEZIUS

The trapezius muscle is a flat sheet of muscular fibers located on
the upper part of the back and lying immediately beneath the skin.

Origin. Base of the skull, ligament of the neck, and the row of
spinous processes of the vertebrae from the seventh cervical to the
twelfth thoracic inclusive (Fig. 9–4).

Insertion. Along a curved line following the outer third of the
posterior border of the clavicle, the top of the acromion, and the
upper border of the spine of the scapula (Figs. A–2 and A–4 [Appen-
dix]).

Innervation. The spinal accessory nerve (spinal portion of 11th
cranial nerve), and branches from anterior rami of 3rd and 4th
cervical nerves.

Structure. Best studied in four parts, passing from above downward.

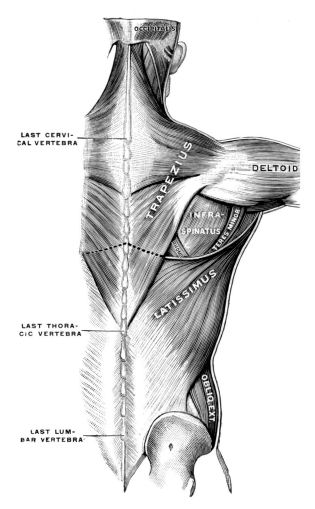

OCCIPITALIS

LAST CERVI-
CAL VERTEBRA

TRAPEZIUS

DELTOID

INFRA-
SPINATUS

TERES MINOR

LATISSIMUS

LAST THORA-
CIC VERTEBRA

OBLIQ. EXT.

LAST LUM-
BAR VERTEBRA

FIG. 9–4.   Superficial muscles of the back.

Part one is a thin sheet of parallel fibers starting downward from the base of the skull and then curving somewhat sideward and forward around the neck to the insertion on the clavicle. It is so thin and elastic that when it is relaxed one or two finger-tips can be pushed down behind the outer third of the clavicle with ease, stretching the muscle before it and forming a small pocket; when it contracts the fingers are lifted out and the pocket disappears. This enables us to test the action of part one of the trapezius, which is too thin to be seen and felt in the usual way.

Part two, extending from the ligament of the neck to the acromion, is a much thicker and stronger sheet of fibers, tendinous at the origin and converging to the narrower insertion.

Part three is similar to part two and still stronger, and includes the fibers that arise from the seventh cervical and the upper three thoracic vertebrae; these converge somewhat to the insertion on the spine of the scapula.

Part four, the lowest, is not so strong as the two middle portions, but stronger than the first; the fibers converge from their origin on the lower thoracic vertebrae to join a short tendon attached to the small triangular space where the spine of the scapula ends, near the medial border.

Action. When the head is free to move, contraction of part one of the trapezius will lower the back of the skull and turn it to the side; since the skull is posed freely on a pivot at its base, this will tilt the chin up and turn the face to the opposite side. When part one of right and left sides contract at once, evidently they will neutralize the tendency to rotate the head and will tilt the chin up with double force. However, electromyographic studies indicate that the trapezius functions in such movements as an accessory muscle, and is involved only when they are performed against strong resistance.[2] The upper trapezius, levator scapulae and upper digitations of the serratus anterior form a unit which provides passive support of the shoulder, elevation of the shoulder, and the upper component of the force couple necessary for scapular rotation.

With the head held still and the shoulder girdle free to move, contraction of part one of the trapezius will elevate the clavicle and scapula, but with little force, because the muscle is thin and weak.

Action of part two will elevate, upward rotate, and assist with adduction of the shoulder girdle.

Part three pulls in nearly a horizontal line upon the spine of the scapula, drawing it toward the spinal column. It is a prime mover for adduction of the scapula.

Part four rotates the scapula upward and assists with adduction.[3]

When all the parts of the trapezius contract at once, it is important to notice that they act upon the upper rather than the lower portion of the scapula; since they at the same time elevate the acromion, adduct the spine, and depress the vertebral border, they must by their combined action rotate the bone so as to turn the glenoid fossa upward rather than to move the whole bone any considerable distance in any direction.

Electromyographic studies suggest that it is mainly the third and fourth parts of the trapezius that are responsible for holding the scapula in adduction and the third part that keeps it up to normal height. If the trapezius is weak, the point of the affected shoulder

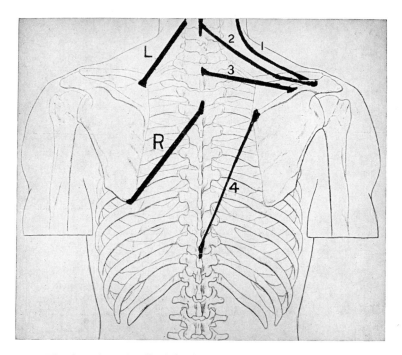

FIG. 9–5.   The direction of pull of the four parts of the trapezius on the right and
of the levator (*L*) and rhomboid (*R*) on the left.

becomes lowered. If the trapezius becomes paralyzed early in life,
the serratus anterior may be hypertrophied to perform the scapular
rotation necessary for humeral elevation.[3]

Since the trapezius lies immediately beneath the skin, it is comparatively easy to test its action in various movements by observing
the thickening and hardening of its fibers during contraction. As
shown in Figure 9–6, the lower three parts show this effect plainly,
the upper part indistinctly. The bulge labelled T1 may in part be
due to contraction of the underlying levator scapulae. The upper
part of the trapezius illustrates well why it is necessary to study the
muscles on the living model.

The effect of the posture on the action of the trapezius should be
noticed. When the shoulder is lifted as high as possible or when a
weight is held on the shoulder, the subject standing erect, part two
contracts strongly and part three slightly if at all; if he does the
same thing in a stooping posture, as when one lifts a pail of water
from the ground, parts two, three, and four all act at once, and the
lower parts relax as the erect position is reached. Here the action
meets the need exactly, and the person unconsciously brings into

FIG. 9–6. This picture of Otis Johnson contains several points of interest. The digitation of the deltoids is unusual, though not rare, and represents a continuance of the embryonic condition. The muscle marked *TM* is anomalous and probably contains fibers from the infraspinatus. (Hasse.) (*T*, trapezius; *D*, deltoid; *TM*, teres major.)

action the adducting and the elevating portions when they can do the most good.

All parts of the trapezius come into action at the same time in raising the arms sideward, and especially in raising them above the shoulder level, as shown in the above figure.

LEVATOR SCAPULAE

This is a small muscle on the back and side of the neck beneath the first part of the trapezius (Fig. 9–7).

Origin. The transverse processes of the upper four or five cervical vertebrae.

Insertion. The medial border of the scapula, from the spine to the superior angle (Fig. A–4).

Innervation. The cervical plexus supplies branches from the 3rd and 4th cervical nerves and by the dorsal scapular nerve with fibers from the 5th cervical nerve.

Structure. A thick band of parallel fibers, tendinous near the origin. In primitive mammalian forms the levator scapulae and the serratus anterior constitute a single sheet of muscle.[4]

Action. If the line (see Fig. 9–5) indicating the direction of pull of the levator is extended across the scapula, it is seen to pass very

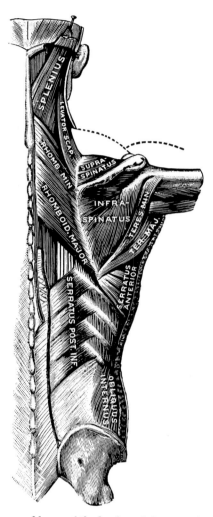

FIG. 9–7.   Muscles of second layer of the back and those on the back of the shoulder.

nearly through the center of the bone, and therefore the levator appears to be so situated as to draw the scapula upward and inward as a whole rather than to rotate it.   When, however, the levator is stimulated by electricity it lifts the vertebral edge of the scapula first and then moves the bone as a whole, giving a combination of elevation and downward rotation.   This is explained by the fact that the arm weighs down the acromial side of the scapula.   Study of the living model shows that the levator and the upper portion of the trapezius do the work in shrugging the shoulders and lifting or carrying weights in the hand or on the shoulder, as in case of a hod-carrier, postman, or ice man. The levator can be felt through the upper trapezius, and on a favorable subject one can observe that part two of the trapezius acts alone when a weight is held in the hand unless the shoulder is lifted; but as soon as the shoulder is raised by the slightest amount the levator springs instantly into action. This observation is made all the more interesting by beginning the movement in stooping posture and noting the shifting action of the muscles as the body is raised to the erect position.

The levator is an important support to the scapula in habitual posture, aiding the second part of the trapezius in holding it up to normal level. Subjects who have lost the use of the levator have the shoulder depressed, the deformity being most marked when both levator and second part of the trapezius are lacking. Loss of these two main supports is characterized by a thin neck and sloping shoulders. If the trapezius is paralyzed, the levator scapulae forms a prominent ridge on the neck when in action.

RHOMBOID

The rhomboid is named from its shape, that of an oblique parallelogram. It lies beneath the middle of the trapezius (Fig. 9–7).

Origin. The row of spinous processes of the vertebrae, from the seventh cervical to the fifth thoracic inclusive.

Insertion. The medial border of the scapula, from the spine to the inferior angle (Fig. A–4).

Innervation. The dorsal scapular nerve from the brachial plexus. The fibers come from the 5th cervical nerve.

Structure. Parallel fibers extend diagonally downward and sideward from the origin. The upper part, usually separate from the lower and described separately as the rhomboid minor, is thin and weak, while the lower part, the rhomboid major, is thick and strong. The attachment to scapula is peculiar, the fibers joining a tendon of insertion that is scarcely attached to the scapula at all for its upper two-thirds; sometimes the middle half is entirely free from the edge of the scapula, bringing the pull to bear on the lower angle alone.

Action. The structure of the rhomboid and its manner of insertion gives it a line of pull as shown in Figure 9–5. It adducts the lower angle of the scapula without adducting the upper angle at all, and so rotates the scapula downward. The action of the rhomboid when combined with that of the latissimus is to turn the scapula so that the glenoid cavity is turned downward to such a degree that the arm cannot be raised above the level of the shoulder.

The part played by the rhomboid in maintaining normal posture, as shown by defective cases, consists in moderating the upward rotation of the scapula produced by the trapezius, so as to keep the acromion down and in holding the lower angle close to the ribs. Subjects who have lost the use of the rhomboid have this angle of the scapula projecting conspicuously from the back, with a deep gutter beneath its edge—a position due to the pull of muscles that attach to the upper part of the bone.

Since downward rotation of the scapula usually accompanies any

FIG. 9–8.   Minaev, of the U.S.S.R., jerking 314 pounds in winning the 132 pound weight lifting title in the 1960 Olympic Games. This is an exceptionally fine photograph of the serratus anterior (SA) in action. (Kirkley, courtesy *Iron Man*.)

adduction or extension of the humerus, the rhomboid will act whenever these movements are performed forcefully or against gravity.

SERRATUS ANTERIOR

This muscle, named from its serrated or saw-toothed anterior edge, lies on the outer surface of the ribs at the side, covered by the scapula at the rear and the pectoralis major in front. It lies immediately beneath the skin for a space a little larger than the hand just below the axilla or armpit, its five lower sections showing plainly through the skin when the arm is raised against resistance, as in Figure 9–8.

Origin. The outer surfaces of the upper eight or nine ribs at the side of the chest.

Insertion. The anterior surface of the medial border of the scapula, from the superior to the inferior angle (Figs. 9–9 and A–3).

Innervation. Long thoracic nerve from anterior branches of 5th, 6th and 7th cervical before they enter the brachial plexus.

Structure. In two separate parts, the upper and lower. The upper part includes the fibers arising from the three upper ribs and diverging slightly to be inserted along the whole length of the scapula below the spine; the lower part is fan-shaped, the fibers arising from the lower six attachments on the ribs converging to be inserted together at the inferior angle. The lower part is thicker and stronger than the upper.

Action. The fibers of the serratus extend too nearly lengthwise of the ribs to exert much pull to move them unless the scapula is elevated. Its upper fibers are well situated for abducting the scapula foward as a whole, without rotation. The lower fibers of the serratus anterior and the lower part of the trapezius constitute the lower component of the force couple necessary for scapular rotation (Fig. 10–6).

Loss of the serratus has little effect on habitual posture of the scapula, but it interferes seriously with forward movements of the shoulder and arm. Subjects lacking the serratus find it difficult or impossible to elevate the arm above 100 degrees,[5] and when they try to do so the medial border of the scapula projects backward ("winging of the scapula") instead of lying close to the chest wall, as it does when the serratus acts normally in the movement. Generally the shoulder is displaced forward and drops to some extent. This may be accompanied by painful tightness of certain antagonists, such as the rhomboid and pectoralis major. Weakness of this muscle may be partly compensated for by hypertrophy of the lower part of the trapezius. In the case of paralysis, winged scap-

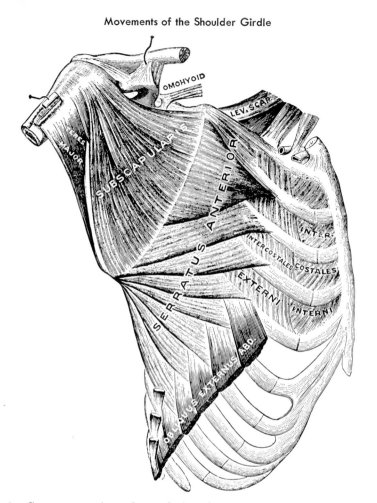

FIG. 9–9.   Serratus anterior, subscapularis and teres major. Notice that the clavicle
is cut apart and the scapula turned back away from the chest wall.

ulae have been corrected by transplanting the pectoralis minor, the
pectoralis major, the rhomboid, the teres major, or other muscles
(Fig. 9–10).

Study of the serratus on the normal living body shows its action
in a very clear and interesting way. Whenever the subject pushes or
reaches forward, the scapula can be seen and felt to glide forward
over the surface of the chest, and the distance it moves is surprising
to all who have not observed it before. When the arms are raised,
the trapezius can be felt to contract as soon as they begin to move,
but one can also see that this contraction does not rotate the scapula;
the lower serratus does not begin to contract until the arms have
been raised through at least 20 degrees and sometimes through 45

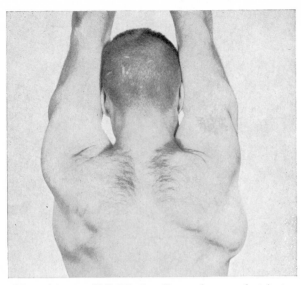

F<small>IG</small>. 9–10. The subject, a U.S. Marine Corps close combat instructor, suffered a traumatic paralysis of the nerve to the right serratus anterior. Assistance from the left hand was required to elevate the right arm to the perpendicular. A year later he was able to elevate the right arm without assistance and the winging of the scapula was reduced to about 50 per cent of that shown above. (U.S. Marine Corps photograph.)

degrees. This can be tested by placing the fingers on the lower angle of the scapula and noticing when it begins to move forward.

Another interesting case in which the lower serratus fails to act when it would be of use is when a weight is lifted or carried on the shoulder. Although the lower serratus can lift the acromion with great force, as we have seen, it never acts in lifting with the shoulder or carrying a heavy weight on it, the work in this case being done by the middle trapezius and levator so long as the arm hangs at the side. As soon as the arm is raised 30 degrees or more from the side it at once springs into action. This shows a reason why one who carries a heavy weight on the shoulder finds it restful to hold the arm in various positions—sometimes down by the side and sometimes raised.

PECTORALIS MINOR

A small muscle located on the front of the upper chest, covered by the pectoralis major.

Origin. The outer surfaces of the third, fourth and fifth ribs at a point a little sideward from their junction with the costal cartilages (Fig. 9–11).

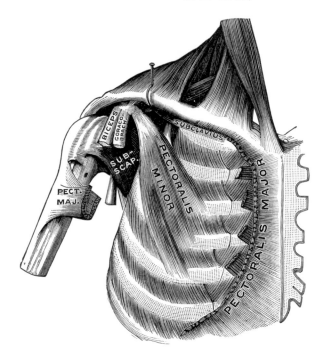

FIG. 9–11.   The pectoralis minor and subclavius.

Insertion.   The end of the coracoid.

Innervation.   The medial anterior thoracic nerve originating in the brachial plexus.   The fibers are from the 8th cervical and 1st thoracic nerves.

Structure.   Three groups of nearly parallel fibers that converge to join a single small tendon at the upper end.

Action.   The line of pull of the pectoralis minor may be represented on a mounted skeleton by a rubber band stretched from the coracoid to the fourth rib at a point about an inch from its junction with the costal cartilage.   When the scapula is in normal position, the direction of pull on the coracoid will be seen to be forward, downward and inward at nearly equal angles.   The inward pull is prevented from acting on the scapula by the position of the clavicle, so that contraction of the muscle is calculated to produce a combination of abduction and downward rotation of the scapula.   It can also be seen that the pull of the pectoralis minor, by prying across the chest, tends to lift the medial border and especially the inferior angle of the scapula away from the ribs.   This is sometimes called "winged scapula" or forward tilt.

When the scapula is held still, it is evident that action of this muscle will lift on the middle ribs, especially when the shoulder is raised in preparation for it, as one unconsciously does in taking a deep breath.

While normally the pectoralis minor is deeply covered, Duchenne reported cases in which, because of complete atrophy of the pectoralis major, it lay immediately under the skin and could be stimulated by electric current. The isolated action secured in this way is the same as that stated above. It is possible in favorable subjects to feel the contraction of the pectoralis minor through the muscle that covers it by proceeding as follows: have the subject hold the arms close to the sides and a little to the rear, which inhibits any action of the pectoralis major; then have him inhale deeply, first lifting the shoulders slightly. This puts the pectoralis minor into vigorous action and its lateral swelling may be felt and even seen as it lifts the relaxed tissue covering it.

To summarize, it may be said that the pectoralis minor acts in deep and forced breathing, but probably not in quiet breathing; it is placed in a position to help in all movements involving abduction and downward rotation of the scapula, which occurs in striking forward and downward as in chopping and also in supporting a part of the body weight on the arms. The pectoralis minor, along with trapezius 4, prevents upward displacement of the shoulder girdle when the arm exerts downward pressure against resistance. In most of these cases actual test of its action is rendered impossible because of the contraction of the large muscle covering it.

SUBCLAVIUS

This is the smallest of this group of muscles; located, as its name indicates, beneath the clavicle (Fig. 9–11).

Origin. The upper surface of the first rib, just where it joins its cartilage.

Insertion. A groove extending along the middle half of the under side of the clavicle.

Innervation. By a nerve from the brachial plexus, the fibers coming from the 5th and 6th cervical nerves.

Structure. Fibers radiating fanwise from the small tendon of origin to the much wider insertion.

Action. The action of the subclavius can only be inferred from its position, as it is neither readily felt nor stimulated from without. It is in a position to depress the clavicle, but its small size and angle of insertion indicate that its torque for depression must be negligible. Since the direction of its pull deviates only slightly from the long axis of the clavicle, its most important function is to pull the clavicle medially, protecting the sterno-clavicular joint from separation in such activities as hanging by the hands.

POSTURE OF THE SHOULDERS

The shoulder girdle is so freely movable that its habitual position depends on the relative tension of the six muscles discussed above, together with that produced by the pectoralis major and latissimus dorsi, which act indirectly on it through the arm. Whenever some of these muscles are absent or inactive because of disease, when the clavicle or scapula is deformed by disease or accident, or when any of the muscles fail for any reason to exert the right amount of tension, abnormal posture of the shoulders is the result.

It is generally assumed by anatomists, as previously stated, that for normal posture of the shoulder girdle the clavicles should be approximately horizontal, which places the scapulae at a height extending from the second to the seventh rib, and that they should lie flat against the chest wall on the back.

HELPING SYNERGISTS

When two muscles in simultaneous contraction both perform one action while mutually neutralizing all the rest of each other's actions, they are said to be *helping synergists*. The following helping synergies may be identified among the muscles of the shoulder girdle:

1. Trapezius II and trapezius IV both perform adduction and upward rotation, while their respective tendencies to perform elevation and depression are mutually neutralized.

2. Trapezius II and the serratus anterior both perform upward rotation, while their respective tendencies to perform adduction and abduction are mutually neutralized.

3. Trapezius II, trapezius IV, and the rhomboid all perform adduction. The tendency of trapezius II and trapezius IV to perform upward rotation is neutralized by the tendency of the rhomboid to perform downward rotation and vice versa.

4. Trapezius IV and the pectoralis minor both perform depression. The tendency of trapezius IV to perform upward rotation and adduction is neutralized by the tendency of the pectoralis minor to perform downward rotation and abduction, and vice versa.

More complicated combinations may be worked out if more than two muscles are considered, or if additional muscles are introduced to contribute only a stabilization or fixation function. For example, both the serratus anterior and the pectoralis minor perform abduction. The tendency of the serratus anterior to perform upward rotation is neutralized by the tendency of the pectoralis minor to perform downward rotation, and vice versa. But the pectoralis minor, upon contraction, also tends to perform depression—this could be neutralized by introducing a contraction of the levator scapulae, whose only function in this situation would be elevation. From the appropriately graded contraction of these three muscles, pure abduction would result.

In the illustrative examples given above, the synergies and neutralizations were worked out theoretically from a knowledge of the actions of various muscles. A more practical situation occurs when a given exercise is considered, and the starting point is a knowledge of what action occurs. By analysis, the probable contractions of various muscles necessary for performing the exercise can be determined.

IMPLICATIONS FOR ATHLETIC TRAINING

Fractures of the clavicle are probably the most common incapacitating athletic injuries to the shoulder girdle. Usually they are due

Fɪɢ. 9–12.   Dee Andrews, of Long Beach City College, being tackled by players from Tyler, Texas, in the 1960 Little Rose Bowl Game. Carlsöö and Johansson[6] suggest that extension of the arm to break a fall is a reflex muscle reaction due in part to the influence of the labyrinthine and neck righting reflexes (see pp. 439–442).

to falling on the outstretched hand and arm, so that the shock is transmitted through the acromioclavicular joint to the bone and muscles of the shoulder girdle (Fig. 9–12). The player must be coached to avoid falling in the manner shown and to utilize a body roll to absorb some of the impact forces.

The acromioclavicular joint may be sprained or dislocated as the result of falling on the point of the shoulder or of football blocks and tackles. This is commonly referred to as a "knock-down shoulder," or acromioclavicular separation, and may occur in varying degrees of severity. Rotating the shoulder or raising the arm causes local pain at the joint, and a distinct bump (representing the elevated acromial end of the clavicle) may be felt or seen. The injured shoulder may droop, and the mere weight of the dangling arm may intensify the pain and hinder healing. Even mild cases should be referred to a physician, since the acromion may also be fractured, requiring x-ray diagnosis. Weight throwers may experience sprains or tears of the muscles attached to the vertebral border of the scapula.

TABLE 9–1. Shoulder Girdle Muscles and Their Actions†

	Eleva-tion	Depres-sion	Abduc-tion	Adduc-tion	Upward Rotation	Downward Rotation
Subclavius		P.M.*				
Pectoralis minor		P.M.	P.M.			P.M.
Serratus anterior			P.M.		P.M.	
Trapezius I	P.M.					
Trapezius II	P.M.			Asst.**	P.M.	
Trapezius III				P.M.		
Trapezius IV		P.M.		Asst.	P.M.	
Levator	P.M.					
Rhomboid	P.M.			P.M.		P.M.

* P.M. = Prime Mover   ** Asst. = Assistant Mover
† Under certain circumstances the pectoralis major and latissimus dorsi indirectly influence shoulder girdle action. (See pp. 214–215.)

References

1. Wolffson, David M.: Scapula Shape and Muscle Function with Special Reference to the Vertebral Border. Amer. J. Phys. Anthrop., *8*, 331–338, 1950.

2. Yamshon, Leonard J. and Bierman, William: Kinesiologic Electromyography I. The Trapezius. Arch. Phys. Med., *24*, 647–651, 1948.

3. Wiedenbauer, M. M. and Mortensen, O. A.: An Electromyographic Study of the Trapezius Muscle. Amer. J. Phys. Med., *31*, 363–373, 1952.

4. Inman, Verne T., *et al.*: Observations on the Function of the Shoulder Joint. J. Bone Joint Surg., *26*, 1–30, 1944.

5. Duvall, Ellen Neall: Critical Analysis of Divergent Views of Movement at the Shoulder Joint. Arch. Phys. Med., *36*, 149–154, 1955.

6. Carlsöö, S. and Johansson, O.: Stabilization of and Load on the Elbow Joint in Some Protective Movements. Acta Anat., *48*, 224–231, 1962.

Recommended Reading

7. Horwitz, Thomas: Isolated Paralysis of the Serratus Anterior Muscle. Orthop., *1*, 100–103, 1959.

8. Basmajian, John V.: Recent Advances in the Functional Anatomy of the Upper Limb. Amer. J. Phys. Med., *48*, 165–177, 1969.

Laboratory Exercises

1. Identify the movements of the shoulder girdle in the various phases of the basketball chest shot, pullups, pushups, shot put.

2. Analyze the value of various swimming strokes in the treatment of abducted shoulders.

3. Measure the distance from the spine to the vertebral border of the scapulae of a number of subjects. Determine whether the difference results from variations in body type or from functional factors.

4. In general should inward or outward rotation of the arms be specified in corrective exercises? Why?

5. Is it possible to eliminate special corrective exercises and substitute sports competition as a means of correcting faulty posture or to prevent poor posture? State the basis by which you justify your answer.

6. What action results from simultaneous contraction of parts 1, 2, 3, and 4 of the trapezius and the rhomboids? In this action, what actions of what muscles are mutually neutralized? Can two muscles (or parts of two muscles) work cooperatively and antagonistically at the same time?

7. List the muscles covered in this chapter. Describe the best progressive resistance exercise to strengthen and hypertrophy each one.

8. List the joint actions covered in this chapter and describe the best joint mobilization exercise for each one.

9. Pick out one muscle or one group of muscles. Describe an exercise in which the muscle contracts eccentrically and one in which it contracts concentrically.

Chapter 10

Movements of the Shoulder Joint

The shoulder joint, formed by the articulation of the humerus with the scapula, is the most freely movable of the ball-and-socket joints. The shallow glenoid cavity is deepened by a cup of cartilage, the *glenoid labrum*, attached firmly to the inner surface of the fossa, and the head of the humerus fits into the cup. The joint is surrounded by the usual *capsular ligament,* which is reinforced on the front side by a strong band of fibers connecting the humerus with the coracoid and called the *coracohumeral ligament.* Tendons of the subscapularis, the supraspinatus, the infraspinatus, the long head of the biceps and the long head of the triceps have an intimate relation to the capsule and add materially to its strength. The capsule is so loose that it permits the head of the humerus to be drawn out of the socket about one inch, but the tendency of the weight of the arm to pull it far out is resisted by the tone of the muscles. The joint is protected by the acromion, which projects over it, by the coracoid in front, and by the *coracoacromial, coracohumeral, transverse humeral,* and *glenohumeral ligaments* (Figs. 9–3 and 10–1).

Starting from the resting position at the side of the body, movement of the arm away from the body in any direction may be called *elevation.* This term is ambiguous; therefore, separate terms are given to elevations in different directions, and other terms apply to the corresponding depressions. From anatomical position, a forward elevation of the arm is called *flexion*; the return movement is *extension.* Backward elevation, which is a continuation of extension, is called *hyperextension.* *Abduction* is sideward elevation of the arm; *adduction* is the return movement. The extreme terminal position for abduction is the same as that for flexion, although it should be noted that an upward rotation of the shoulder girdle must be added to the shoulder joint movements in order to achieve this vertical position. It is possible to elevate the arm in diagonal planes

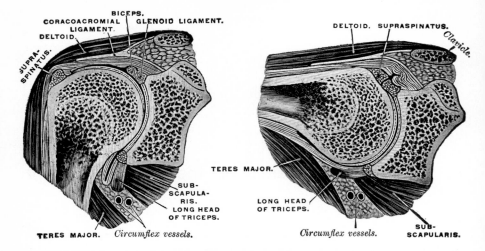

FIG. 10–1. Vertical section through the right shoulder joint, seen from the front, showing how sideward elevation of the arm is limited to 90 degrees. (*Gray's Anatomy.*)

between abduction and flexion, and between abduction and hyperextension, but there is no standard terminology for these diagonal movements.

Inward rotation is the turning of the humerus around its long axis so that its anterior aspect moves medially. *Outward rotation* is the opposite, with the anterior aspect moving laterally. When the arm is in other than the anatomical position, a beginning student may find it difficult to determine whether rotation is inward or outward. It is helpful to look along the long axis of the right arm toward the elbow—then, any counter-clockwise rotation is inward, and any clockwise rotation is outward.

If the arm is flexed to the horizontal, it may then be moved horizontally backward. This movement is called *horizontal extension-abduction* (which may be abbreviated to either *horizontal extension* or *horizontal abduction*). The opposite of this movement, a movement of the arm horizontally forward, is called *horizontal flexion-adduction* (which may be abbreviated to either *horizontal flexion* or *horizontal adduction*). Although unwieldy, these terms are most helpful in describing shoulder joint movements. The beginning student should not be confused when these terms are applied to shoulder joint movements when the body is in the supine position or some other non-erect position. They are still called "horizontal" movements, because terms are always defined with reference to erect anatomical position.

Another possible source of confusion to the beginner is the failure to distinguish elbow or forearm movements from shoulder joint movements. Shoulder joint rotation is often confused with forearm pronation and supination.

Circumduction is not a pure movement like the aforementioned, but is a combination of movements causing the elbow to describe a circle.

Movements of the shoulder joint are produced by eleven muscles. Two of these (the biceps and triceps) are primarily designed to act on the elbow joint, but they also cross the shoulder joint and are therefore known as two-joint muscles. The long and short heads of the biceps act as two different muscles at the shoulder joint. Of the three heads of the triceps, only the long head acts at the shoulder. The structure and function of the triceps and biceps will be discussed on pp. 223–224 and 225–228.

	Two-Joint Muscles	*Large Muscles*	*Small Associates*	*Rotators of Humerus*
Above	Biceps(long head)	Deltoid	Supraspinatus	Infraspinatus
Front	Biceps (short head)	Pectoralis major	Coracobrachialis	Subscapularis
Rear	Triceps (long head)	Latissimus dorsi	Teres major	Teres minor

DELTOID

This is a triangular multipennate muscle located on the shoulder, with one angle pointing down the arm and the other two bent around the shoulder to front and rear (Figs. 9–6, 10–3 and 10–4). It is proportionately far larger in man than in primitive mammalian forms.[1]

Origin. Along a curved line following the outer third of the anterior border of the clavicle, the top of the acromion, and the posterior border of the scapular spine.

Insertion. On the deltoid tuberosity of the humerus just above its center.

Innervation. The axillary nerve from the brachial plexus. The fibers are from the fifth and sixth cervical nerves.

Structure. In three parts—anterior, middle, and posterior. The anterior and posterior portions are simple penniform, while the middle is multipennate. The tendon of insertion divides near the humerus into five strands; the outer two, placed anteriorly and posteriorly, receive the fibers of the front and rear portions of the

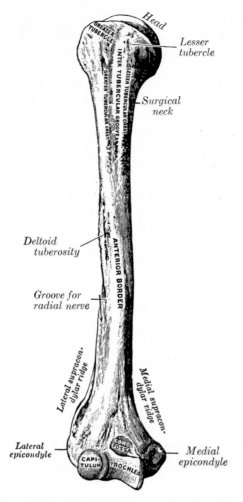

Fig. 10–2.   The right humerus, anterior view.

muscle, which arise directly from the bones above; the middle has
four tendons of origin passing down from the acromion and the
three tendons of insertion passing up from below alternate between
them; the muscular fibers of the middle portion pass diagonally
across between the seven tendons.   The result of the arrangement is
that the middle part has more power and less extent of contraction
than do the other two parts.

Action.   Functionally the three parts of the deltoid should be
considered as separate muscles.

The *anterior portion* is a prime mover for flexion and horizontal
flexion, and an assistant mover for inward rotation and abduction.

Fig. 10–3. The three parts of the deltoid in action: *D1*, anterior; *D2*, middle; *D3*, posterior. *T*, trapezius. Posed by Bill Pearl, 1953 Mr. America. (Stern.)

The *middle portion* is a prime mover for abduction, and (except for the most anterior fibers) for horizontal extension. Its anterior fibers normally function as assistors to the anterior deltoid, and its posterior fibers serve a similar function with the posterior deltoid.

The *posterior portion* is a prime mover for horizontal extension and an assistant mover for extension and outward rotation. It may be active during adduction or abduction, apparently acting not as a mover but as a stabilizer against the tendency of movers to produce unwanted inward rotation or horizontal flexion.[2]

This muscle is relatively ineffective for abduction when the arm is at an angle of less than 60 degrees and displays its greatest activity between 90 and 180 degrees. When the arm is hanging at the side, contraction of the deltoid tends to pull the humerus upward in the direction of its long axis. This tendency is offset by the downward pull of the short rotators (subscapularis, infraspinatus, and teres minor). However, all parts of the muscle are active in all movements of the shoulder.[3] This might seem to indicate that the muscle works against itself, but the action potentials in the part producing the given movement are of greater amplitude and frequency. It has been suggested that the purpose of this overall contraction is to stabilize the joint and to hold the head of the humerus in the glenoid cavity during movement.[4] With the deltoid thus prevented from dissipating its force in vertical movement, the combined action of the two groups of muscles tends to produce downward rotation of the head of the humerus and upward rotation of the shaft of the humerus.[1]

Loss of one or more of the three portions of the deltoid interferes so seriously with all movements involving elevation of the arm that subjects with this defect have much difficulty in feeding and dressing themselves. Loss of the posterior deltoid makes it impossible to put the hand behind the body at the waistline; if it is the front part, the subject cannot bring his hand up to his face or put on his hat without bending the head far forward; if it is either the front or middle portion, the arm cannot be lifted above the shoulder level in any direction. When it is paralyzed, the supraspinatus and other elevators may be hypertrophied to take its place as an abductor, although the force of the movement will be greatly reduced.[5]

SUPRASPINATUS

A small but relatively powerful muscle filling the supraspinous fossa and covered by the second part of the trapezius (Figs. 9–7 and A–5).

Origin. The inner two-thirds of the supraspinous fossa.

Insertion. The top of the greater tubercle of the humerus.

Innervation. A branch of the suprascapular nerve from the brachial plexus. The fibers come from the fifth cervical nerve.

Structure. Penniform, the fibers arising directly from the bone and joining the tendon of insertion obliquely as it passes through the center of the muscle, much as the seeds of a pine cone join their stem.

Action. The supraspinatus is a prime mover for abduction, and assists with horizontal extension. In abduction, it creates a lever of the first class. Its line of action gives it good mechanical efficiency, and simultaneously it tends to pull the head of the humerus directly into the glenoid fossa, protecting the joint from dislocation in a manner which cannot be performed by the middle deltoid at most points in the range of movement. Even when the deltoid is paralyzed, the supraspinatus can carry the arm through a complete range of abduction.

When the arm is along the side of the body, the angle of pull of the supraspinatus is much superior to that of the deltoid in initiating abduction. When the supraspinatus is paralyzed with a local anesthetic, the subjects can move the arm through its full range in the shoulder joint, though the force and endurance during abduction are reduced. If the supraspinatus has been injured, there may be a tendency for the head of the humerus to slip downward in abduction movements.

PECTORALIS MAJOR

A large multipennate muscle lying immediately beneath the skin over the front of the chest (Fig. 10–4). The pectoral muscles originally comprised a single mass, of which the pectoralis major was the superficial layer and the minor the deeper layer.[1] Occasionally a pectoralis minimus, extending from the first rib cartilage to the coracoid process, may be found.[6]

Origin. The inner two-thirds of the anterior border of the clavicle, the whole length of the sternum, and the cartilages of the first six ribs, near their junction with the sternum.

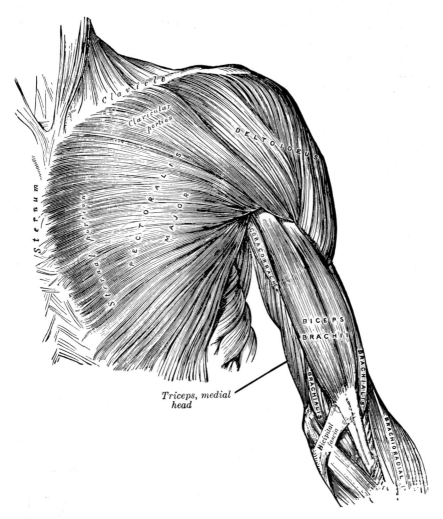

Fɪɢ. 10–4. Superficial muscles of the chest and front of the arm. (*Gray's Anatomy.*)

8

Insertion. By a flat tendon about 3 inches wide into the ridge that forms the outer border of the bicipital groove of the humerus, extending from just below the tuberosities nearly down to the insertion of the deltoid (Fig. A–5).

Innervation. Both the medial and lateral anterior thoracic nerves coming from the brachial plexus. Fibers come from the fifth cervical to the first thoracic nerves.

Structure. The fibers arise directly from the bone and converge to join the tendon of insertion. Near its insertion it is twisted through 180 degrees, the lower part passing beneath to be inserted near the head of the humerus while the fibers from the clavicle pass across them on the outside and join the humerus lower down (Fig. 10–4). The sternal head of this muscle spirals so that the fibers which have the lowest origin have the highest insertion. When the humerus is elevated above the head, the muscle is "unwound."

Action. The clavicular portion of the pectoralis major is a prime mover for flexion, and an assistant mover for abduction after the arm has been abducted to horizontal. The sternal portion is a prime mover for extension and adduction. Both parts act strongly in horizontal flexion, and are assistant movers for inward rotation.

In a study of amputees, Inman and Ralston[7] found that this muscle could exert a force of 1.63 kg. per sq. cm. of cross section.

Loss of the pectoralis major disables one much less than loss of the anterior deltoid, except in movements where great force is required. When the deltoid is intact, the subject can raise his hand to any position in front of the trunk, fold his arms, place the hand on the opposite shoulder, etc., even if the pectoralis major is lacking. The force of gravitation enables him also to lower the arm to or through any position with the aid of the deltoid; but the power in forward and downward movements of the arm is lacking unless the pectoralis can help. A study by Jokl[8] of the incidence of the congenital absence of different muscles among athletes has revealed that the pectoralis is by far the one most commonly affected.

Figure 10–5 shows the antagonistic actions of the clavicular and sternal parts of the pectoralis major. The subject is attempting shoulder joint extension with his right arm, bring the sternal portion into strong contraction, and shoulder joint flexion with his left arm, bringing the clavicular portion into strong contraction. In the classroom, this may be demonstrated by having the subject clasp his hands together at chest level in front of the body. Right shoulder joint extension against the resistance of left shoulder joint flexion will duplicate the situation in Figure 10–5. By alternately reversing the actions, the sternal and clavicular parts will jump in and out of action in reciprocal fashion. The inactive parts remain

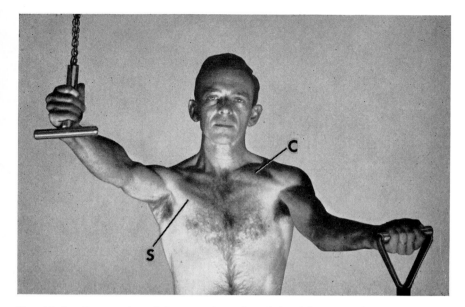

FIG. 10–5.   Contraction of the sternal portion of the right pectoralis major (S) and
the clavicular portion of the left pectoralis major (C).

flaccid, under the influence of the mechanism of reciprocal innervation. However, if the subject presses his hands together stongly,
both parts of both muscles come into action simultaneously, since
both parts are prime movers for horizontal flexion.

CORACOBRACHIALIS

A small muscle named from its attachments and located deep
beneath the deltoid and pectoralis major on the front and inner side
of the arm (Fig. 10–6).

Origin.   The coracoid process of the scapula.

Insertion.   Antero-medial surface of the humerus, opposite the
deltoid.

Innervation.   Musculocutaneous nerve with the fibers coming
from the sixth and seventh cervical nerves.

Structure.   The fibers arise from a short tendon and are inserted
directly into the humerus.   Attachment to the tendon is penniform.

Action.   This muscle is a prime mover for shoulder joint horizontal flexion and an assistant for flexion.   Because of its small size
it cannot act as an effective substitute in flexion if the prime movers
are paralyzed.   It stabilizes the shoulder joint, tending to prevent
downward displacement of the humerus.   When the arm is in a

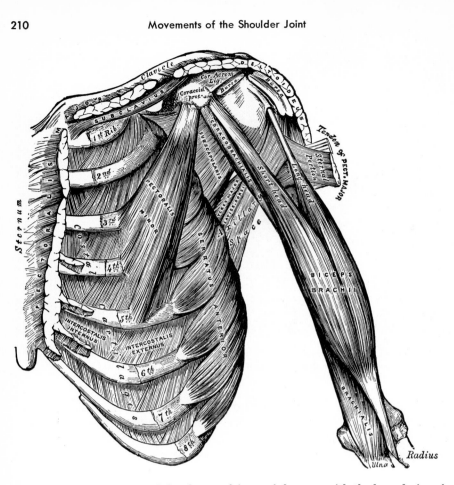

FIG. 10–6.   Deep muscles of the chest and front of the arm, with the boundaries of
the axilla.   (*Gray's Anatomy.*)

position of outward rotation, the coracobrachialis will rotate it inward to the neutral point; when the arm is in a position of inward rotation, this muscle will rotate it outward to the neutral point.

LATISSIMUS DORSI

A very broad muscle, as its name indicates, situated on the lower half of the back and lying immediately beneath the skin except for a small space, where it is covered by the lower trapezius (Fig. 9–4).

Origin.   The spinous processes of the six lower thoracic and all the lumbar vertebrae, the back of the sacrum, the crest of the ilium, and the lower three ribs.

Insertion.   The bottom of the intertubercular groove of the humerus, by a flat tendon attached parallel to the upper three-fourths of the insertion of the pectoralis major (Fig. A–5).

Innervation. The thoracodorsal nerve from the brachial plexus. The fibers come from the sixth, seventh and eighth cervical nerves.

Structure. The fibers converge from their wide origin much like the pectoralis major, and like the latter its flat tendon is twisted so that the upper fibers go to the lower insertion, and *vice versa*. The muscle is joined to the lower vertebrae and the sacrum by the *thoracolumbar fascia*, which also gives attachment to several other muscles.

Action. The latissimus is a prime mover for adduction, extension, and hyperextension of the shoulder joint. It assists in horizontal extension and inward rotation. In rope climbing and similar activities it acts to draw the trunk up toward the humerus. It is powerfully involved in swimming and rowing.

Loss of the latissimus results in a forward displacement of the shoulder, due to the pull of the pectoral muscles, major and minor. It noticeably weakens all downward movements of the arm. When

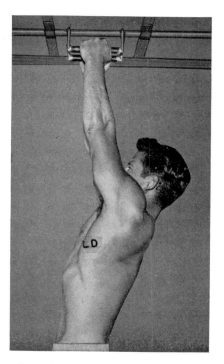

Fig. 10–7. The latissimus dorsi (LD) in action. Bill Golumbick, Mr. America and Mr. Universe contestant, in the starting position for under bar chins. (Courtesy Rader.)

both the latissimus and pectoralis major are lost the shoulder is apt
to be too high, because of the lifting action of the trapezius and
rhomboid.

TERES MAJOR

A small round muscle lying along the axillary border of the scapula
named "larger round" in comparison with the teres minor or
"smaller round muscle" (Figs. 9–7, 9–9, and 10–6).

Origin.   The dorsal surface of the scapula at the lower end of its
lateral border.

Insertion.   The ridge that forms the inner border of the bicipital
groove of the humerus, parallel to the middle half of the insertion of
the pectoralis major (Fig. A–5).

Innervation.   The lower subscapular nerve from the brachial
plexus.   Fibers come from the fifth and sixth cervical nerves.

Structure.   Fibers arising directly from the scapula and inserted
into the tendon in a penniform manner.

Action.   In their penetrating studies of muscular function at the
shoulder joint, Inman, et al.[1] found that the teres major was never
active during abduction and flexion movements, but that it contracted statically with tension proportional to the load on the arm
whenever a stationary position was reached.

Except for this special function of the teres major, its actions on
the arm appear to be the same as those of the latissimus dorsi, and
it has been called "the latissimus dorsi's little helper."[9]   However,
it is a prime mover rather than an assistant mover for inward
rotation.

INFRASPINATUS AND TERES MINOR

These two muscles, located on the back of the scapula, have identical action, and hence will be studied together (Fig. 9–7).   Morphologically the teres minor is a portion of the deltoid; it is absent in
primitive mammalians.[1]

Origin.   Infraspinatus: Medial two-thirds of the infraspinatous
fossa; teres minor: dorsal surface of the lateral border of the scapula.

Insertion.   Infraspinatus: on middle of greater tubercle of the
humerus; teres minor: on lower part of greater tubercle and adjacent shaft of the humerus.

Innervation.   The nerve supply of the infraspinatus is from the
suprascapular nerve from the brachial plexus with its fibers coming
from the fifth and sixth cervical nerves.   The teres minor is innervated by the axillary nerve with its fibers coming from the fifth
cervical nerve.

Structure.   Longitudinal converging fibers.

Action.   The infraspinatus and teres minor are prime movers for outward rotation and horizontal extension of the shoulder joint. An additional function, not traditionally listed, is their important participation in the force couple for abduction and flexion, as noted in the discussion of deltoid actions.

SUBSCAPULARIS

Named from its position on the costal surface of the scapula, next to the chest wall (Figs. 9–9 and 9–11). In primitive forms it is the largest muscle of the scapulo-humeral group.[1]

Origin.   The whole costal surface of the scapula except a small space near the joint (Fig. 10–6).

Insertion.   The lesser tubercle of the humerus (Fig. 10–2).

Innervation.   The subscapular nerves from the posterior cord of the brachial plexus.

Structure.   Multipennate. Its volume is approximately equal to that of the infraspinatus and teres minor combined.

Action.   The subscapularis forms a functional group with the infraspinatus and teres minor in the force couple for abduction and flexion, as noted in the discussion of deltoid actions. It acts as a prime mover for inward rotation of the humerus, being antagonistic to the infraspinatus and teres minor in this respect. The subscapularis plays an important role in preventing dislocation of the shoulder joint.

FUNDAMENTAL MOVEMENTS OF
SHOULDER JOINT AND SHOULDER GIRDLE

Much of the preceding material on the movements of the shoulder girdle and the shoulder joint has dealt with individual bones, joints, and muscles. The analytical study of individual components, whether they be anatomical parts or phases of a movement, is necessary for adequate comprehension of the pattern of which they are a part. However, as was stated in Chapter 3, a muscle seldom, if ever, acts alone. From the practical standpoint the kinesiologist is usually interested primarily in the total movement which is the resultant of these individual actions. The following paragraphs will emphasize certain important relationships resulting from the interaction of the individual muscles comprising the shoulder girdle and the shoulder joint.

The ultimate purpose of all shoulder motion is to increase the area through which the hand may move. In nearly every arm movement there is an associated movement in the shoulder girdle; and when the arm is held in a static position, there must be a stabilization of the shoulder girdle in order to support it. In most natural movements, there is a consistent and predictable pattern of shoulder girdle movement that accompanies any given movement of the shoulder joint. This pattern can be altered by conscious attention to the process, but this is not usually done in the activities of work, sport, and daily life.

Elevation of the Arm. Both flexion and abduction of the arm are accompanied by upward rotation of the shoulder girdle. During the first 30 to 60 degrees of arm elevation, the scapula may remain stationary or it may perform upward rotation in a pattern which depends upon the nature of the starting position, the speed of movement, the amount and direction of resistances, and other variable aspects of the situation. After abduction has taken place through 30 degrees, or after flexion has taken place through 60 degrees, the relationship of arm elevation to upward rotation of the scapula becomes remarkably consistent, with 2 degrees of shoulder joint movement being associated with every 1 degree of scapular rotation. Demonstration of this by Inman and his associates,[1] who inserted pins into the bones of living subjects and employed x-ray pictures, has served to resolve the many conflicting opinions regarding the movements in question.

Backward elevation of the arm (hyperextension) is seldom accompanied by upward rotation of the scapula, but is often accompanied by elevation of the shoulder girdle.

Flexion of the shoulder joint normally involves an associated abduction of the shoulder girdle, along with upward rotation, especially if the movement is a reaching or pushing action. The serratus anterior is of great importance in movements of reaching and pushing, since it is the only muscle which can simultaneously abduct and upward rotate the shoulder girdle.

Depression of the Arm. Extension of the shoulder joint is usually accompanied by downward rotation and adduction of the shoulder girdle; adduction alone usually involves only downward rotation. If the resistance consists only of the weight of the upper extremity, with or without the weight of an object held in the hand, and if the trunk is in an upright position, the movement is ordinarily performed by eccentric contraction of the upward rotators of the shoulder girdle and the elevators of the shoulder joint. If other kinds of forces are present, as in the case of pulling on a horizontal rope, the shoulder girdle downward rotators and adductors and the shoulder joint extensors may have to contract concentrically. In this latter example, the latissimus dorsi will also contract, and it has an indirect tendency to adduct and rotate the shoulder girdle downward as it extends the shoulder joint. In forceful adduction of the shoulder joint against resistance, the latissimus is joined by the sternal portion of the pectoralis major in causing shoulder joint adduction along with downward rotation of the shoulder girdle, and the tendencies of these muscles to cause anterior and posterior deviations of the arm and shoulder girdle are mutually neutralized (Fig. 10–8). The contributions of the latissimus dorsi and the pectoralis major to shoulder girdle action are clearly demonstrated when doing dips (sometimes called "pushups") on the parallel bars, and when arising from a chair by pushing down upon its arms.

Rotation of the Arm. Inward rotation of the shoulder joint is ordinarily accompanied by shoulder girdle abduction; outward rotation is ordinarily accompanied by shoulder girdle adduction. These tendencies are most marked when rotation is carried to its extreme. In devising corrective exercises for abducted shoulders, these natural tendencies should be taken into consideration.

Horizontal Arm Movements. Horizontal flexion at the shoulder joint is usually accompanied by shoulder girdle abduction; horizontal extension is usually accompanied by shoulder girdle adduction.

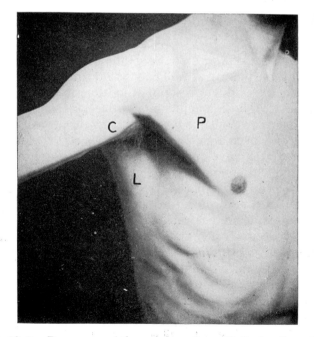

Fig. 10–8. Depressors of the arm in action. *P*, Pectoralis major; *C*, Coracobrachialis; *L*, Latissimus dorsi.

The Range of Arm Abduction. An interesting relationship between arm abduction and arm rotation can be demonstrated by the following exercise: From standing position with arms hanging at the sides, palms toward the thigh, abduct the arm as far as possible without rotating it. Then rotate the arm outward, and notice how much further the abduction can be continued. Finally, with the arm extremely abducted, notice that it cannot be rotated inward to any significant extent. Many authors have commented upon the limited abduction when the arm is not rotated outward; several reasons have been advanced to account for it. Some have suggested that ligaments are responsible for stopping the movement, and that outward rotation makes them slack so that abduction can be continued. Most, however, think that the greater tubercle of the humerus impinges upon the top of the glenoid cavity or upon soft tissues which are pinched between it and the top of the glenoid cavity. X-ray studies have shown that the bony parts remain distinctly separated, making it very likely that the abduction is limited by the pinching of soft tissues between the greater tubercle of the humerus and the glenoid cavity. This relationship is shown in Figure 10–1. As the humerus is rotated outward, so is the greater tubercle, and abduction can be continued until muscles and ligaments on the inferior aspects of the joint become tight.

SHOULDER JOINT DISLOCATION

The arrangement of bones at the shoulder joint allows rather free movement in three planes, as well as marked rotation of the humerus around its long axis. Such freedom of motion occurs at the sacrifice of joint stability. The ligaments and muscles, rather than the bones, must be primarily responsible for preventing dislocation. When the ligaments become permanently elongated as a result of repeated dislocations, even well-developed muscles are inadequate to prevent frequent further dislocation.

The humerus can be displaced backward (subspinous dislocation), downward (subglenoid dislocation), or forward (subcoracoid dislocation). The subcoracoid dislocation is most likely to become chronic, and it usually occurs when the arm is abducted and rotated outward. The joint capsule is loose, relatively thin, and without reinforcements at its antero-inferior aspect.

Muscular pulls on the humerus by the pectoralis major may sometimes be responsible for subcoracoid dislocation. This happens relatively often in sports, especially when the humerus is outward rotated so that the tendon of insertion of the pectoralis major is stretched. Forceful overhand throwing, quick forward-downward striking at a resistant object, and blocking with the forearms in football lineplay are examples of activities which combine strong contractions of the pectoralis major with a position of anatomical vulnerability.

IMPLICATIONS FOR ATHLETIC TRAINING

Because the intricate musculature and comparatively loose construction of the shoulder joint make it an instrument possessing a great range of movement but comparatively little resistance to

TABLE 10–1. Shoulder Joint Muscles and Their Actions

	Flex.	Ext.	Abd.	Add.	Inw. Rot.	Outw. Rot.	Hor. Flex.	Hor. Ext.
1. Anterior Deltoid	P.M.		Asst.		Asst.		P.M.	
2. Middle Deltoid			P.M.					P.M.
3. Posterior Deltoid		Asst.				Asst.		P.M.
4. Supraspinatus			P.M.					Asst.
5. Pect. Major, clavicular	P.M.		Asst.*		Asst.		P.M.	
6. Pect. Major, sternal		P.M.		P.M.	Asst.		P.M.	
7. Coracobrachialis	Asst.		Asst.*	Asst.*	Asst.†		P.M.	
8. Subscapularis	Asst.#		Asst.#	Asst.*	P.M.		Asst.#	
9. Latissimus dorsi		P.M.		P.M.	Asst.			Asst.
10. Teres major		P.M.		P.M.	P.M.			Asst.
11. Infraspinatus						P.M.		P.M.
12. Teres minor						P.M.		P.M.
13. Biceps, long head			Asst.					
14. Biceps, short head	Asst.			Asst.	Asst.		Asst.	
15. Triceps, long head		Asst.		Asst.				

* Indicated action takes place only when arm is above the horizontal.
† Indicated action takes place only from a position of rotation to the neutral point.
# Assistant actions vary with joint position and activity of synergic muscles.

traumatic forces, it may be literally knocked apart in such a sport as football or twisted apart in such a sport as wrestling. The study of injuries in athletics very clearly points up the necessity for a vigorous exercise schedule aimed at strengthening this part of the body as an integral part of the preseason conditioning program preceding participation in physical contact sports. Even this may not be an unmixed blessing. Instances are recorded in which the humerus has been broken by muscular violence alone while the individual was throwing a ball. This is believed to result from torsional stresses developing within the humerus, arising from the tendency of certain muscles to hold the head of the humerus in static position while other muscles, aided by the leverage of the bent forearm, tend to rotate the distal end inward.[10]

The typical painful shoulder of the pitcher or passer is characterized by tenderness over the lesser tuberosity of the humerus. Throwing requires elevation, abduction, and external rotation, followed by a forceful forward flexion, adduction, and internal rotation. The basic muscles involved are those of the *rotator cuff*—subscapularis, supraspinatus, infraspinatus, and teres minor. The injury is commonly a localized tendinitis at the insertion of the subscapularis, resulting from overstretch of this muscle at the "drawback," followed imediately by the explosive force of the throw.

Following trauma, the shoulder joint is especially susceptible to "freezing" and every effort should be made to keep it mobilized, even though activity is accompanied by some discomfort. Heat, massage, and exercise are useful in overcoming any tendency to ankylosing fibrosis. Once a shoulder joint has sustained severe damage it tends to become susceptible to recurrent dislocation ("trick shoulder") and a restrictive harness designed to prevent the athlete from raising his arm higher than 85 degrees may become a necessity if he is to continue to participate in his chosen activities.

References

1. Inman, Verne T., *et al.*: Observations on the Function of the Shoulder Joint. J. Bone Joint Surg., *26*, 1–30, 1944.

2. Shevlin, M. Geraldine, *et al.*: Electromyographic Study of the Function of Some Muscles Crossing the Glenohumeral Joint. Arch. Phys. Med., *50*, 264–270, 1969.

3. Yamshon, Leonard J. and Bierman, William: Kinesiologic Electromyography. III. The Deltoid. Arch. Phys. Med., *30*, 286–289, 1949.

4. Scheving, Lawrence E. and Pauly, John E.: An Electromyographic Study of Some Muscles Acting on the Upper Extremity of Man. Anat. Rec., *135*, 239–245, 1959.

5. Duvall, Ellen Neall: Critical Analysis of Divergent Views of Movement at Shoulder Joint. Arch. Phys. Med., *36*, 149–154, 1955.

6. Hasan, Mahdi: Pectoralis Minimus Muscle. J. Anat. Soc. India, XI, 89, 1962.

7. Inman, Verne T. and Ralston, H. J.: The Mechanics of Voluntary Muscle. In Paul E. Klopsteg and Philip D. Wilson, editors, *Human Limbs and Their Substitutes*. New York: McGraw-Hill Book Company, Inc., 1954, pp. 296–317.

8. Jokl, Ernst: Studies in the Clinical Physiology of Exercise. I. Congenital Absence of Pectoral Muscle in Athletes. J. Ass. Phys. Men. Rehabil., *12*, 86 *et seq.*, 1958.

9. Wells, Katharine F.: *Kinesiology*, 4th Ed. Philadelphia: W. B. Saunders Co., 1966, p. 237.

10. Peltokallio, Pekka, *et al.*: Fractures of the Humerus from Muscular Violence. J. Sport. Med., *8*, 21–25, 1968.

Recommended Reading

11. Kent, Barbara E.: Functional Anatomy of the Shoulder Joint. Phys. Ther., *51*, 867–887, 1971.

Laboratory Exercises

1. Analyze (*a*) the up-movement, and (*b*) the down-movement of pullups. Name the shoulder girdle and shoulder joint actions, specific muscles active, and kind of contraction.

2. Assume that a man in the supine position is pressing a barbell to arm's length. (*a*) What shoulder joint muscles are involved? (*b*) What will be the difference in the effect upon them resulting from keeping the hands wide apart or bringing them close together?

3. Make a list of the muscles covered in this chapter and describe progressive resistance exercises best calculated to strengthen and hypertrophy each one.

4. Why is it efficient to have simple penniform arrangement of the fibers in the anterior and posterior deltoids, but multipenniform arrangements of the fibers in the middle deltoid?

5. The ancient Romans are said to have been particularly interested in the development of large deltoids. What sports might they have found especially useful for this purpose? Give reasons for your answer.

6. In hand-to-hand combat a soldier might desire to dislocate an opponent's shoulder. How might he apply force for this purpose? And in what direction?

7. Analyze the different types of swimming strokes and evaluate the role of the latissimus dorsi in each one.

8. Assume that a man is lying supine, holding dumbbells in his hands. He first stretches his arms to the side and repeatedly brings the dumbbells together (lateral raise). He then stretches his arms overhead and repeatedly raises them to the vertical position (pull over). Analyze these two exercises and determine the difference in the effect on the muscles which are involved. Will the muscular actions be the same if he is lying on a low bench instead of on the floor?

9. Analyze the role of the pectoralis major in delivering a left hook.

Chapter 11

Movements of Elbow and Radio-Ulnar Joints

Functionally, there is a distinct separation of the elbow joint and the radio-ulnar joints, the former allowing flexion and extension of the radius and ulna with respect to the humerus, and the latter allowing pronation and supination of the forearm.

Elbow flexion and extension take place through a range of approximately 150 degrees, depending upon individual variations in anatomy and use of the joint. Flexion is limited by contact of the soft tissues of the arm and forearm; extension is limited by contact of the olecranon process of the ulna with the humerus. Either may be hindered by the tightness of ligaments and muscles on the opposite aspect of the joint. Some individuals can hyperextend the elbow, thus allowing it to be "locked" when supporting the body weight on the upper limbs or when pushing. Most women can hyperextend the elbow, and this is sometimes taken as evidence of a skeletal sex difference. However, it should be noted that many gymnasts, weightlifters, and others who often perform complete forceful extensions can also hyperextend the joint.

When the elbow is extended, inward and outward rotation of the arm at the shoulder joint may accompany pronation and supination, respectively, thus greatly increasing the amount of forearm rotation allowed by pronation and supination alone. The total combined range of the movement in the two joints may approach 270 degrees. In kinesiological analysis and in muscle testing, the rotary movements of the shoulder joint and of the radio-ulnar joints should be carefully distinguished.

The Elbow Joint. The elbow is a double ginglymus or hinge joint, whose articular surfaces are (1) the *trochlear notch* of the ulna against the *trochlea* of the humerus, where most of the weight is borne, and (2) the proximal surface of the *head* of the radius against the *capitulum* of the humerus (Figs. A–5, A–6, and A–7). A capsule and synovial membrane enclose both of these articular pairs, and also the proximal articulation between radius and ulna. Pinching of the fringes of the synovial membrane in the joint has been suggested as a cause of "tennis elbow."[1] Longitudinal thickenings of this capsule are designated as the *anterior, posterior, radial collateral*, and *ulnar collateral ligaments*.

The Radio-ulnar Joint. There are three distinct radio-ulnar joints. The *proximal radio-ulnar joint* is a pivot joint between the head of the radius and the *radial notch* of the ulna. It shares the synovial membrane and capsule of the elbow joint. The *anular ligament* (Fig. 11–1) encircles the head of the radius, with both of its ends attaching to the ulna near the radial notch, thus holding the head of the radius firmly in place. During supination and pronation, the radial head rotates axially within the anular ligament and the radial notch.

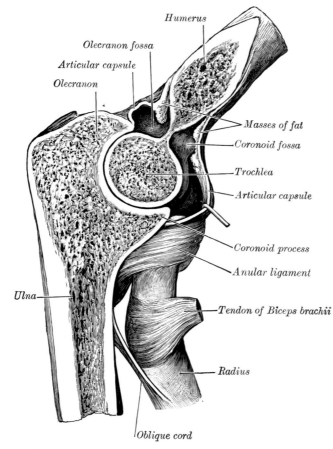

FIG. 11–1.   Sagittal section through the left elbow joint. (*Gray's Anatomy*.)

The *middle radio-ulnar joint* is a slightly movable ligamentous joint without a cavity. The medial borders of the shafts of the radius and ulna are connected by a ligamentous sheet, the *interosseous membrane,* and the small *oblique cord.* The fibers of the interosseous membrane run diagonally, the attachment on the radius tending to be more proximal than that on the ulna. Thus, in addition to preventing undue separation of the bones, it functions to transmit and to cushion the longitudinal forces of weight-bearing. In arm support positions, the body weight is transferred from the humerus primarily to the ulna; the force of resistance from the hand is transferred primarily to the radius at the wrist joint. It remains largely for the interosseous membrane to resist the resulting tendency of the radius and ulna to slide past each other longitudinally.

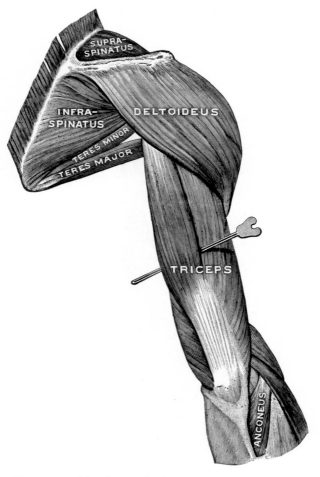

FIG. 11–2.   Muscles on the back of shoulder and arm.

The *distal radio-ulnar joint* is a pivot joint between the (distal) *head* of the ulna and the *ulnar notch* of the radius. The articular capsule and the ligamentous *articular disk*, which connects radius and ulna while separating the distal end of the ulna from the carpal bones, protect the joint. The distal radio-ulnar joint has its own synovial cavity and thin capsule. In pronation and supination, the end of the radius glides around the head of the ulna and rotates on its long axis to keep its articular surface toward the articulating surface of the ulna.

TRICEPS BRACHII

The triceps is on the posterior side of the upper arm, and, as its name implies, has three separate places of origin (Figs. 11–2, A–3, and A–6).

Origin. (1) The long head, from the scapula, just below the shoulder joint; (2) the lateral head, from a space half an inch wide on the back of the humerus, extending from the middle of the shaft up to the greater tubercle; (3) the medial head, from the lower part of the back of the humerus, over a wide space extending nearly two-thirds of the length of the bone.

Insertion. The end of the olecranon process of the ulna, via a common tendon.

Innervation. The radial nerve from the brachial plexus with fibers from the seventh and eighth cervical nerves.

Structure. The long head has a short tendon of origin; the fibers of the other two parts arise directly from the humerus. The tendon of insertion is flat, and as it leaves the ulna it broadens into a thin sheet that extends far up the external surface of the muscle and the muscular fibers attach obliquely to its deeper surface. The long head passes up between the teres major, lying in front, and the teres minor, behind it.

Action. The olecranon process of the ulna extends past the elbow joint and the triceps is inserted into the end of it, making the ulna a lever of the first class. Thus the triceps is the prime mover for extension of the elbow joint. The leverage is short, favoring speed rather than power. The angle of pull is nearly 90 degrees through a large part of its movement, the tendon passing over the lower end of the humerus as a pulley; the great number of short fibers in its structure, together with its large angle of pull, gives the muscle great power as well as speed. The origin of the long head on the scapula enables that part to act on the shoulder joint as well as the elbow; a rubber band looped around the olecranon and held at the point of origin shows plainly that its pull is chiefly lengthwise of the

Fɪɢ. 11–3. The triceps, T, with the elbow joint in the extended and the flexed positions. LaH, Lateral Head; LgH, Long Head; MH, Medial Head; IS, Intermuscular Septum. The strap-like appearance of the common tendon of insertion as it passes over the olecranon process in the elbow flexed position is remarkable. Posed by Tom Sansone, Mr. America, 1958, Mr. Universe, 1963. (Courtesy Rader.)

humerus, lifting its head up into the glenoid cavity. If the humerus is lifted, the tension on the rubber band is increased, showing that it is able to aid in depressing the arm, but its angle of pull is here very small.

Loss of the triceps destroys a person's ability to extend the elbow forcibly, but does not disable him for light tasks, since the weight of the forearm will extend the elbow when there is no resistance, making it possible to use the hands in any position when the movement requires little force.

Contraction of the different parts of the triceps causes extension of the elbow, but the medial head is the prime mover.[2] Contraction of the long head alone assists in adduction, extension, and hyperextension of the humerus at the shoulder joint. In a study of amputees, Inman and Ralston found that this muscle could exert a force of 1.31 kg. per sq. cm. of cross section.[3]

ANCONEUS

A small triangular muscle on the back of the arm (Fig. 11–2). It appears to be a continuation of the triceps.

Origin.   Posterior aspect of lateral epicondyle of the humerus.

Insertion.   Lateral side of olecranon process and upper part of posterior aspect of the ulna.

Innervation.   A branch of the radial nerve containing fibers from the seventh and eighth cervical nerves. It will be noted that this innervation is identical with that of the triceps. As a result the two muscles are usually disabled simultaneously in cases of neurological disease.

Action.   Extension of the elbow and weak abduction of the ulna during resisted pronation.[4]   The latter is an easily overlooked movement of the ulna alone at the proximal radio-ulnar joint, occurring during pronation if the central long axis of the forearm remains stationary (as, for example, in turning a doorknob).

BICEPS BRACHII

A prominent muscle on the front side of the upper arm with two separate places of origin (Fig. 10–6). It is fusiform.

Origin.   (1) The long head, from the scapula at the top of the glenoid cavity, the tendon passing over the head of the humerus and blending with the capsular ligament of the shoulder joint; (2) the short head from the coracoid.

Insertion.   The tuberosity of the radius (Fig. 11–4).

Innervation.   The musculocutaneous nerve from the brachial plexus. Fibers come from the fifth and sixth cervical nerves.

Structure.   The tendon of the long head is long and slender and lies in the intertubercular groove of the humerus, becoming muscular at the lower end of the groove. The tendon of the short head is shorter, the muscular fibers of the two parts being of equal length. The tendon of insertion is flattened as it joins the muscle and passes up as a septum between the two parts and receives the fibers in a penniform manner from both sides. The only cross sectional count of biceps fibers ever published was based on the dissection of three males. The fiber count ranged from 199,240 fibers to 316,243. The individual fascicles numbered from 1726 to 3371. The mean fiber diameter was 22.54 μ for the smallest subject and 42.26 μ for the largest.[5]

Action.   The biceps is in a position to act on three joints: shoulder, elbow, and radio-ulnar (Figs. 11–4 and 11–5). At the shoulder joint, contraction of the long head of the biceps stabilizes the articulation and possibly assists with abduction. Contraction of the short

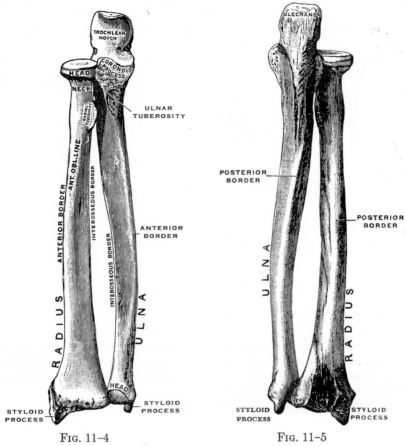

Fig. 11–4   Fig. 11–5

The radius and ulna.

head assists with flexion, abduction, inward rotation, and horizontal flexion. Inman and Ralston found that the biceps can exert a force of 2.38 kg. per sq. cm. of cross section.[3] Both parts act to flex the elbow, the power arm being somewhat over an inch in length and the angle variable from 15 or 20 degrees in the position of complete extension up to 90 degrees when the elbow is flexed to about a right angle and diminishing again as flexion continues. When the hand is placed in extreme pronation, the tuberosity of the radius is turned inward and downward, wrapping the tendon of the biceps more than half-way around the bone; contraction of the muscle will evidently tend to unwrap it and thus supinate the hand. When the forearm is in a pronated position, the recorded electromyographic potentials from the biceps are lower than when the arm is in the supinated position.[6]

Fig. 11–6. The marked groove between the long and short heads of the biceps is seldom seen except in men who have trained very hard and who have very little subcutaneous fat, as is the case with Otis Johnson. The underlying brachialis may also be seen. (Hasse.)

With the forearm extended, supination does not produce any evidence of biceps potentials if rotation of the arm at the shoulder is prevented, unless supination is firmly resisted.[7,8]

Loss of the biceps does not necessarily result in inability to flex the elbow, since there are other muscles able to perform this movement. Those who retain the use of the other flexors but lack the biceps can do light work readily, but when they try to lift heavy objects the weight pulls the head of the humerus down out of its socket, causing pain and quick fatigue. When all the flexors are lost, the use of the arm is practically abolished, since the subject cannot lift the hand to the face nor touch the body with the hand above the middle of the thigh.

Because the biceps acts as an important prime mover for elbow flexion and an assistant for forearm supination,[9] a classic example of true synergy arises when strong supination without elbow flexion is desired, as in driving a screw with a screwdriver or in turning a resistant doorknob. In these tasks, the biceps is needed as a supinator, but its simultaneous tendency to produce elbow flexion would cause the hand to be removed from the site of the work if flexion actually occurred. The problem is solved by simultaneous contraction of the triceps, which as an elbow extensor effectively neutralizes the flexion tendency of the biceps while allowing its supinatory action to take place unhindered. An easy classroom demonstration of this can be performed as follows: With the elbow partially flexed, shake hands with a partner, allowing him to turn his forearm to a position of extreme pronation. With your left hand, grasp his upper arm so that fingers are on his triceps and thumb is on his biceps. Ask the partner to supinate his hand forcefully while you resist the motion. Notice that his triceps springs into action at the same time as the biceps, in order to counteract the flexion tendency of the biceps as it supinates.

There is sharp disagreement among electromyographers regarding the action of the biceps when the forearm is pronated. It has been stated that the biceps plays little, if any, role in flexion at this time. This has been explained by the assumption that in order to maintain the prone position against the biceps' tendency to supinate the forearm during contraction, afferent impulses from the pronating muscles, working through the central nervous system, result in a negative feedback to the spinal centers controlling the biceps.[7] However, some students have contended that when the forearm is pronated, the long head may contract while the short head may fail to show any signs of electrical activity.[8] It is evident that much further study will be required to reconcile such discrepancies.

BRACHIORADIALIS

"Brachium" is the Latin for the upper arm; hence the name indicates that the muscle is attached to the humerus and to the radius. It is a fusiform muscle situated on the outer border of the forearm and gives rise to the rounded contour from the elbow to the base on the thumb (Fig. 11–7).

Origin. The upper two-thirds of the lateral supracondyloid ridge of the humerus and from the lateral intermuscular septum.

Insertion. The lateral surface of the radius at the base of the styloid process.

Innervation. A branch of the radial nerve from the brachial plexus. The fibers are from the fifth and sixth cervical nerves.

Structure. Arising directly from the humerus, the fibers join the lower tendon in a penniform manner.

Action. The position of the brachioradialis indicates it as a flexor of the elbow; its leverage is long but its angle of pull very small; computation shows that when both are taken into account it has better mechanical advantage than the biceps.   As a result, flexion of the elbow is possible when a lesion of the musculocutaneous nerve results in paralysis of both the biceps and the brachialis.   Electromyographers disagree about the role of this muscle in supination and pronation.   Basmajian[8] holds that it assists in these movements

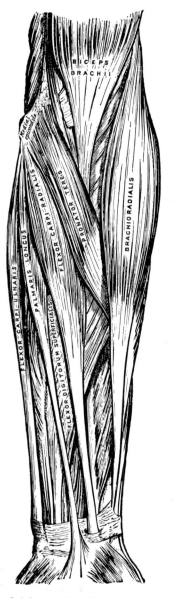

FIG. 11–7.   Anterior superficial muscles of the left forearm.   (*Gray's Anatomy.*)

when resistance renders it necessary to exert force; De Sousa *et al.*[10] argue that it does not come into activity regardless of the resistance. No decision between these conflicting views can be made at this time.

BRACHIALIS

Literally translated, "muscle of the upper arm." It is located between the biceps and the humerus near the elbow (Figs. 10–4 and 10–6).

Origin. Anterior surface of the lower half of the humerus and the intermuscular septa.

Insertion. Tuberosity of the ulna and the anterior surface of the coronoid process.

Innervation. Primarily by the musculocutaneous nerve from the brachial plexus, with the fibers coming from the fifth and sixth cervical nerves. A small branch of the radial nerve is usually present; a branch of the median nerve may be.

Structure. The tendon of insertion flattens into a thin sheet and the muscular fibers, arising from the humerus, are attached obliquely to its deeper surface.

Action. Simple flexion of the elbow. It is equally effective in the supine, mid, or prone positions of the forearm, since its line of pull does not change with rotation of the forearm. The brachialis has been described as "the workhorse among the flexor muscles of the elbow."[7]

PRONATOR TERES

A small spindle-shaped muscle lying obliquely across the elbow in front and partly covered by the brachioradialis (Figs. 11–7, 12–3).

Origin. Two heads, one from the medial epicondyle of the humerus and the other from the coronoid process of the ulna.

Insertion. Lateral surface of the radius near its center.

Innervation. A branch of the median nerve, containing fibers from the sixth and seventh cervical nerves.

Action. Assists the pronator quadratus in pronation of the forearm whenever speed of movement is required or resistance is encountered. Participation of this muscle is not required in flexion of the unloaded forearm.[11] In pure flexion against resistance it may act with the biceps, its pronating action neutralizing some of the supinating action of the larger muscle.

PRONATOR QUADRATUS

A thin square sheet of parallel fibers lying deep on the front of the forearm near the wrist (Fig. 11–8).

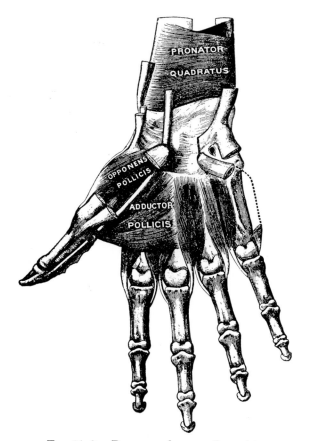

Fig. 11–8.   Deep muscles near the wrist.

Origin.   Lower fourth of the anterior surface of the ulna.

Insertion.   Lower fourth of the anterior surface of the radius.

Innervation.   The anterior interosseous nerve, which branches from the median nerve.   The fibers come from the eighth cervical and first thoracic nerve by way of the brachial plexus.

Structure.   Parallel fibers attached directly to the bones.

Action.   Prime mover in pronation of the forearm, regardless of the angle of the elbow joint.[11]

SUPINATOR

A broad muscle situated under the brachioradialis and the extensor muscles attached to the lateral epicondyle (Figs. 11–9, 12–3).

Origin.   Lateral epicondyle of the humerus, supinator crest of the ulna (Fig. A–8), ligaments between.

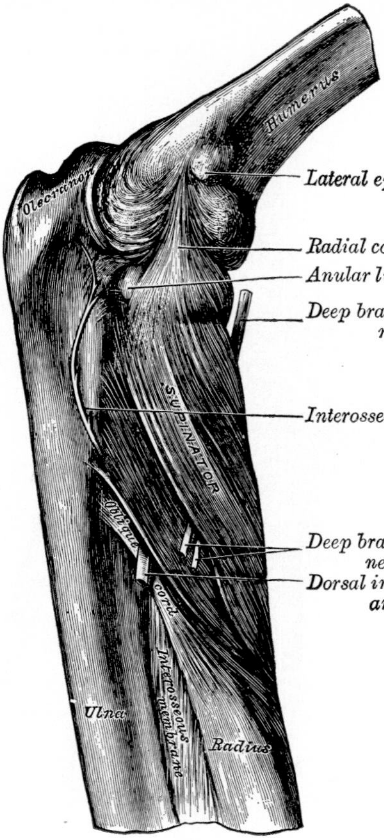

Fig. 11-9. The supinator. (*Gray's Anatomy*.)

Insertion.   Lateral surface of the upper third of the radius.

Innervation.   Posterior interosseous branch of the deep radial from the brachial plexus.   Fibers come from the sixth cervical nerve.

Structure.   Mostly parallel fibers.

Action.   Acts alone in slow, unresisted supination, or in fast supination with the elbow extended.   Requires the assistance of the biceps during supination against resistance or during fast supination with the elbow flexed.[12]

FUNDAMENTAL MOVEMENTS

The fundamental movements of the elbow and the radio-ulnar articulations are flexion, extension, pronation, and supinations Almost every movement of the arm in such fundamental skills as pushing, pulling, throwing, and striking involves not only the joint.

mentioned above but the shoulder and wrist as well. While it is necessary to study their isolated movement at this time, this is rarely the case in concrete situations. In the analysis of simple skillful motions executed by the arm and involving these joints, it is necessary to consider their actions as they are related to the adjacent parts.

Some baseball pitchers who depend on curves, inshoots, and screwballs are troubled with recurring sore arms. Such trauma is not surprising in view of the small size of most of the muscles of pronation and supination, and the tremendous limb velocity which is generated prior to the final snapping of the arm into a pronated or supinated position.

In the average person the flexors of the elbow are about one and one-half times as effective as the extensors.

Bankov and Jørgensen[13] have calculated the torque developed by each of the various muscles involved in a maximal isometric flexion of the supinated forearm against a strain gauge. Their determinations, based in part on anthropometric data collected by Braune and Fischer, are shown in Table 11–1. They computed that the torque developed with the forearm pronated was about 82 per cent of the above.

An earlier investigation of actual dumbbell lifting had concluded that a subject could handle about two-thirds as much weight with the forearms pronated as he could with them supinated.[14]

Similar findings by Provins and Salter[15] have been explained on the following basis: The difference in the strength of flexion at the various forearm positions must be due principally to changes in the length of and mechanical efficiency exerted by the biceps, brachialis, brachioradialis, and pronator teres. Of these the brachialis is unaffected by rotation of the forearm. As the forearm is rotated from supination to pronation, the length of the biceps becomes progressively longer, but the mechanical advantage decreases as the tendon is wrapped around the radius and the effective lever arm is reduced. The brachioradialis has its greatest mechanical advantage

TABLE 11–1. Torque Developed During Maximal Isometric Flexion of the Forearm at a 90° Angle.

Muscle	Torque
Pronator teres	3.62 kp. × cm
Extensor carpi radialis longus . . .	10.38
Brachialis	28.01
Biceps brachii	29.75
Brachioradialis	16.65

at the midposition, but as its mechanical advantage increases in turning from supination or pronation, its length decreases. These two factors probably cancel each out to a large extent. The pronator teres, however, is at its shortest length and its mechanical ad-

TABLE 11–2.   Elbow and Radio-Ulnar Articulation Muscles and Their Actions

Muscle	Flexion	Extension	Pronation	Supination
Biceps brachii	P.M.			Asst.
Brachialis	P.M.			
Brachioradialis	P.M.		Asst. (?)*	Asst. (?)*
Pronator teres	Asst.		Asst.	
Pronator quadratus			P.M.	
Triceps brachii		P.M.		
Anconeus		Asst.	Asst.	
Supinator				P.M.
Flexor carpi radialis	Asst.		Asst.	
Flexor carpi ulnaris	Asst.			
Palmaris longus	Asst.			
Extensor carpi radialis longus		Asst.		Asst.
Extensor carpi radialis brevis		Asst.		
Extensor carpi ulnaris		Asst.		
Flexor digitorum superficialis	Asst.			
Extensor digitorum		Asst.		
Extensor digiti minimi		Asst.		
Extensor pollicis longus				Asst.
Abductor pollicis longus				Asst.

* To the mid-position.   (See p. 229.)

vantage is relatively poor in the pronated position. The overall effect, then, may be largely due to the changes in the pronator teres.

IMPLICATIONS FOR ATHLETIC TRAINING

Trauma to the elbow joint is relatively common in body contact sports, such as football and wrestling, in activities where the body is subject to impact forces, such as gymnastics and tumbling, and as a result of movements requiring sudden forcible hyperextension of the forearm, as in tennis serving, baseball pitching, and javelin throwing. It is often immobilized, or semi-immobilized, during the acute period. Passive exercises and underwater exercises are often very useful aids to its remobilization.

"Tennis elbow" and "golfer's elbow" are among the most common athletic injuries. There is a good deal of controversy concerning their etiology and it seems likely that these are merely generic names covering several different ailments. Many cases of the former appear to involve strains or tears of the extensor carpi radialis brevis, while it is probable that the latter often results from strains of the flexor carpi ulnaris[1] (see Chapter 12).

References

1. Rasch, Philip J. and Brubaker, Merlin L.: The Problem of Tennis Elbow. J. Amer. Osteopath. Ass., *57*, 268–271, 1957. *Idem*: Tennis Elbow: A Second Look. *Ibid.*, *59*, 265–267, 1959.

2. Travill, A. A.: A Study of the Extensor Apparatus of the Forearm. Anat. Rev., *144*, 373–376, 1962.

3. Inman, Verne T. and Ralston, H. J.: The Mechanics of Voluntary Muscle. In Klopsteg, Paul E. and Wilson, Philip D., editors: *Human Limbs and Their Substitutes*. New York: McGraw-Hill Book Company, Inc., 1954, pp. 269–317.

4. Pauly, John B., *et al.*: An Electromyographic Study of Some Muscles Crossing the Elbow Joint. Anat. Rec., *159*, 47–54, 1967.

5. Etemadi, A. A. and Hosseini, F.: Frequency and Size of Muscle Fibers in Athletic Body Build. Anat. Rec., *162*, 269–273, 1968.

6. Larson, Robert F.: Forearm Positioning on Maximal Force. Phys. Ther., *49*, 748–756, 1969.

7. Bierman, William and Yamshon, Leonard J.: Electromyography in Kinesiologic Evaluations. Arch. Phys. Med., *29*, 206–211, 1948.

8. Basmajian, J. V.: *Muscles Alive. Their Functions Revealed by Electromyography*, 2nd Ed. Baltimore: The Williams & Wilkins Co., 1967, pp. 172–177.

9. Travill, Anthony and Basmajian, John V.: Electromyography of the Supinators of the Forearm. Anat. Rec., *139*, 557–560, 1960.

10. DeSousa, O. Machado, *et al.*: Electromyographic Study of the Brachioradialis Muscle. Anat. Rec., *139*, 125–131, 1961.

11. Basmajian, J. V.: *Op. cit.*, pp. 178–182.

12. *Ibid.*: pp. 182–184.

13. Bankov, Stephan and Jørgensen, Kurt: Maximum Strength of Elbow Flexors with Pronated and Supinated Forearm. Communications from the Danish National Association for Infantile Paralysis. No. 29, 1969.

14. Rasch, Philip J.: Effect of the Position of Forearm on Strength of Elbow Flexion. Res. Quart., *27*, 333–337, 1956.

15. Provins, K. A. and Salter, Nancy: Maximum Torque Exerted About the Elbow Joint. J. Appl. Physiol., *7*, 393–398, 1955.

Laboratory Exercises

1. Demonstrate the peculiar action of the radius with reference to the ulna in movements of pronation and supination. List some common activities which would be virtually impossible if the forearm could not be pronated and supinated.

2. Classify and analyze the bone-muscle levers at the elbow. Are they designed for producing speed or power?

3. In what positions should the elbow and shoulder joints be held in order to make possible the delivery of maximal supinatory force?

4. Note that inward and outward rotation of the shoulder joint are effective in "adding to" the forearm motions of pronation and supination, respectively, when the elbow joint is fully extended. In turning a knob, the total *range of motion* would be greater if the knob were at arm's length and the elbow joint were extended. Greater turning *force* would be available, however, if the elbow joint were flexed to 90 degrees, so that the biceps tendon would be working at an optimal angle of insertion for exerting supinatory force. Discuss the importance of such kinesiological considerations in designing machinery and instrument panels.

5. Analyze the action of the muscles of the shoulder and arm in throwing a curve ball.

6. Using a goniometer, measure the range of movement of the elbow joint of as many subjects as possible. Note the amount of flexion and extension possible for each subject. Tabulate and determine the average value for both sexes. Account for the difference.

7. The motion of the elbow joint is pure flexion and extension; however, the biceps, a powerful flexor, also supinates, which modifies its action.

   a. Flexion. With the arm horizontal and supported through its entire length to avoid the action of gravity on the long head of the biceps, flex the forearm with the hand in (1) supination, (2) pronation, and (3) midposition. Palpate to determine which muscles flex the forearm with no resistance and with moderate resistance.

   b. Extension. Stand facing a wall. Place the palm of the hand, fingers pointing upward, against the wall, and with the elbow at 90 degrees push against the wall. Palpate to determine which muscles act to extend. Next place the back of the hand against the wall with the elbows at 90 degrees and repeat the efforts to extend the elbow by pressing against the wall. Palpate to determine which muscles contract. Explain any differences.

   c. Supination. Grasp a doorknob, thumb up, with the elbow bent at 90 degrees. Twist the doorknob to supinate the hand. Palpate to determine the active muscles.

8. Determine the difference in muscular stresses during the pullup (hands turned out) and the chin (hands turned in).

Chapter 2

Movements of the Wrist and Hand

The human hand represents a generalized anatomical structure, as compared with the narrowly specialized forefoot of the horse or other animal. It is, however, a highly specialized organ of tactile sensibility, through which man learns surface texture, shape, dimensions, weights, hardness, and other qualities. Consequently a comparatively large area is provided in the cerebral cortex for movements of the hand. Clinically, damage of the motor areas is apt to be followed by incomplete and long delayed recovery of the hand.

The hand includes twenty-seven bones and over twenty joints, while its action involves the use of thirty-three different muscles. The larger muscles acting on the hand are located in the forearm and are connected with their insertions by long slender tendons. These tendons are held within a small space at the wrist by a deep concavity on the anterior surface of the carpal bones and by a flat encircling band of connective tissue known as the anular ligament of the wrist. There are several small muscles in the hand itself, the largest group making up what is known as the thenar eminence on the thumb side of the palm, and a smaller group forming the hypothenar eminence on the ulnar side.

The twenty-seven bones of the hand form three groups: (1) the carpal bones, eight in number, in two rows of four bones each; (2) the five metacarpal bones, numbered beginning at the thumb, and (3) the fourteen phalanges, in three rows, the proximal and distal rows containing five each and the second row four, the phalanx of the middle row being absent in the thumb (Figs. 12–1 and 12–2). The carpal or wrist bones are very irregular in shape and are named as follows, beginning on the thumb side:

First row: scaphoid, lunate, triquetrum, and pisiform.
Second row: trapezium, trapezoid, capitate, and hamate.

The metacarpals are considerably larger and longer than any of the phalanges, and the latter decrease in size toward the tips of the fingers. The phalanges of the distal row are small and pointed. The thumb is separated from the first or index finger more widely than the other fingers are from one another, and is turned on its axis so that flexion is somewhat toward the others rather than in the same plane. The ends of the metacarpals and phalanges have rounded articular surfaces.

The wrist, which connects the rest of the hand with the forearm,

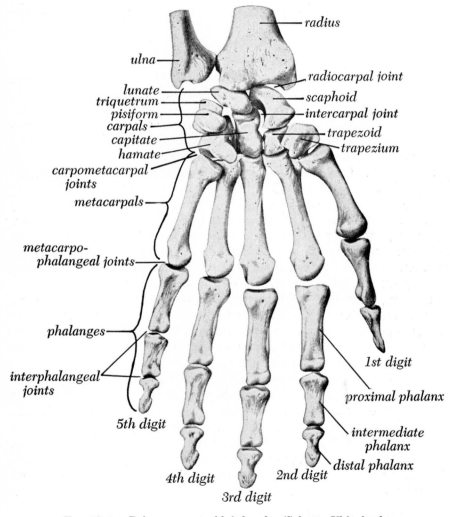

FIG. 12–1. Palmar aspect of left hand. (Sobotta-Uhlenhuth, courtesy Hafner Publishing Co., New York–London.)

has three distinct joints permitting an unusual amount of freedom of movement of the hand:

(1) The radiocarpal joint lies between the end of the radius and three of the first row of carpal bones, the scaphoid, the lunate, and the triquetrum. Neither the ulna or pisiform bone participate, the ulna being separated from the carpal bones by an articular disk of fibrocartilage. The three carpal bones slide across the end of the radius, the direction depending upon the nature of the movement.

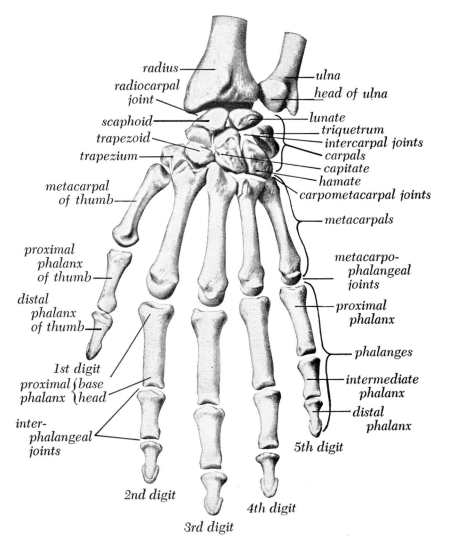

FIG. 12-2. Dorsal aspect of left hand. (Sobotta-Uhlenhuth, courtesy Hafner Publishing Co., New York–London.)

9

The radiocarpal joint is enclosed in a strong but loose capsule strengthened by four strong areas of ligamentous tissue joining the proximal edges of the carpal bones to the bones of the forearm. These ligaments are the *palmar* and *dorsal radiocarpal ligaments* and the *radial* and *ulnar collateral ligaments*. The joint permits all classes of movement except rotation.

(2) The intercarpal articulation is a gliding joint between the two rows of carpal bones. It has its own synovial sac which often includes portions of the carpometacarpal joint. The pisiform bone is joined to the triquetrum in a separate synovial sac. The joint is supported by the palmar ligaments which join the palmar surface of the first row to the palmar surface of the capitate. The dorsal ligaments join the first and second rows; and the ulnar and radial collateral ligaments join the scaphoid with the trapezium and the triquetrum with the hamate. They may be regarded as extensions of the corresponding ligaments of the radiocarpal joint. The small amount of gliding possible in the joint permits some flexion and slight extension.

The bones of each row also articulate between others of the same row by arthrodial joints and are joined to each other by strong ligaments. The three bones of the first row are joined by palmar, dorsal, and interosseous ligaments. The pisiform is not included but does have two palmar ligaments, one joining it to the hamate and the other joining it to the fifth metacarpal. The second row has three dorsal and three palmar ligaments joining the four bones as well as the usual interosseous ligaments.

(3) The carpometacarpal joints are also arthrodial. Each metacarpal is united by two strong dorsal ligaments to the adjacent carpal bones except the fifth which has only one. The palmar aspect has a somewhat similar arrangement except that the third metacarpal is attached to the adjacent carpals by three ligaments. Interosseous ligaments also strengthen the joint.

DEFINITIONS OF JOINT ACTIONS

Together the wrist joints permit abduction, adduction, circumduction, flexion, and extension. The free rotation of the shoulder and radio-ulnar joints give the hand freedom to turn through 270 degrees. Starting from the straight extended position the wrist can be flexed through from 60 to 90 degrees. The first and fifth metacarpals can be flexed farther than those between, making it possible to draw the two sides of the palm toward each other, forming a cup-shaped depression in the middle of the palm.

The first carpometacarpal joint (that of the thumb) is atypical. It is a saddle joint, with a strong but loose capsule, permitting much more freedom of movement than do the other carpometacarpal joints. From anatomical position, a lateral separation of the first metacarpal bone from the second is called *abduction of the thumb*; the return movement is called *adduction* (and, when it is continued across the palm, *hyperadduction*). A movement of the first metacarpal bone forward from anatomical position, approximately in the antero-posterior plane, is called *flexion of the thumb*; the return movement is *extension*. In addition, the first metacarpal bone may execute a peculiar partial circumduction and rotation which is called *opposition*, because it brings the tip of the thumb around in position to face or oppose the fingertips. The return movement from opposition is known as *reposition*.*

The metacarpophalangeal joints each have a capsule, one volar ligament, and two collateral ligaments. The first metacarpophalangeal joint (that of the thumb) is a hinge joint, capable only of flexion and extension through about 90 degrees. The second through fifth metacarpophalangeal joints are condyloid, permitting movement in two planes: First, flexion and extension may occur through about 90 degrees, and, in addition, hyperextension may occur, varying from a few degrees to as much as 40 degrees in the second and fifth fingers. Second, lateral movements (abduction and adduction) are possible. The terminology for these lateral movements is variable, depending upon the textbook consulted. In this text, the movements are defined consistently with the general scheme for naming abduction and adduction in other parts of the body. Therefore, it is first assumed that the body is in anatomical position (erect, arms hanging at the sides, palms turned forward). From this position, when any of the four fingers is moved laterally (*away from the midline of the whole body*), the movement is called abduction; and when any of the four fingers is moved medially (*toward the midline of the whole body*), the movement is called adduction. It should be noted that some texts define abduction as a spreading of the fingers away from the middle finger, and adduction as a closing of the fingers toward the middle finger, in which case some special terms, such as radial flexion and ulnar flexion, must be introduced to name the movements of the middle finger. Again, definitions must be checked in each individual textbook which is consulted.

The interphalangeal joints are capable only of flexion and extension, being hinge joints. Each has a capsule reinforced by one palmar and two collateral ligaments.

---

* Some older textbooks interchange the definitions of abduction-adduction with those for flexion-extension. When consulting various texts, the authors' definitions should be checked.

MUSCLES ACTING ON THE WRIST JOINT

There are six principal muscles acting on the wrist joint, grouped as follows:

Flexor carpi radialis   Extensor carpi radialis longus
Palmaris longus   Extensor carpi radialis brevis
Flexor carpi ulnaris   Extensor carpi ulnaris

In addition, the extrinsic muscles of the hand which cross the wrist may act as assistant movers for wrist motions.

Abduction of the hand is produced by the combined action of the radial flexor and extensor, while the ulnar flexor and extensor together adduct it.

FLEXOR CARPI RADIALIS

This fusiform muscle lies on the upper half of the front of the forearm just beneath the skin, half-way from the brachioradialis to the ulnar side (Fig. 11–7).

Origin. The medial epicondyle of the humerus.

Insertion. The anterior surface of the base of the second metacarpal, with a slip to the base of the third metacarpal.

Innervation. The median nerve, with its fibers coming from the sixth and seventh cervical nerves by way of the brachial plexus.

Action. Flexion and abduction of the wrist.

PALMARIS LONGUS

A slender muscle lying just on the medial side of the preceding. It is absent in about 13 per cent of the individuals (Fig. 11–7).

Origin. The medial epicondyle of the humerus.

Insertion. The anular ligament of the wrist and the palmar aponeurosis.

Innervation. The median nerve, with its fibers coming from the sixth and seventh cervical nerves by way of the brachial plexus.

Action. Tightens fascia of the palm. Because of its small size it assists weakly in wrist flexion. The palmaris longus tendon should not be confused with the larger flexor digitorum superficialis tendon (Fig. 11–7).

FLEXOR CARPI ULNARIS

Located on the medial side of the forearm (Fig. 12–3).

Origin. The medial epicondyle of the humerus and medial margin of the olecranon and upper two-thirds of the dorsal border of the ulna.

Insertion. The palmar surfaces of the pisiform and hamate bones and of the fifth metacarpal.

Innervation. The ulnar nerve from the brachial plexus. Fibers are from the eighth cervical and first thoracic nerves.

Action. Flexion and adduction of the wrist. Electrical stimulation of the flexor carpi ulnaris does not adduct the hand, but in voluntary adduction it contracts along with the extensor carpi ulnaris, probably to prevent the hyperextension the latter would otherwise produce.

By flexing the wrist strongly against a resistance, the tendons of the three flexor muscles can be easily felt.

EXTENSOR CARPI RADIALIS LONGUS

This muscle is on the radial side of the upper forearm, just posterior to the brachioradialis (Fig. 12–3).

Origin. The lower third of the lateral supracondylar ridge of the humerus.

Insertion. The dorsal surface of the base of the second metacarpal.

Innervation. The radial nerve from the brachial plexus. Fibers come from the sixth and seventh cervical nerves.

Action. Extension and abduction of the wrist.

EXTENSOR CARPI RADIALIS BREVIS

Situated just beneath the preceding muscle (Fig. 12–3).

Origin. The lateral epicondyle of the humerus.

Insertion. The dorsal surface of the base of the third metacarpal.

Innervation. The radial nerve from the brachial plexus. Fibers come from the sixth and seventh cervical nerves.

Action. Extension and abduction of the wrist.

EXTENSOR CARPI ULNARIS

Situated on the back and ulnar side of the forearm (Fig. 12–3).

Origin. The lateral epicondyle of the humerus and the middle third of the narrow ridge on the dorsal border of the ulna.

Insertion. The posterior surface of the base of the fifth metacarpal.

Innervation. Posterior interosseous branch of the deep radial nerve from the brachial plexus. Fibers are from sixth, seventh, and eighth cervical nerves.

Action. Extension and adduction of the wrist.

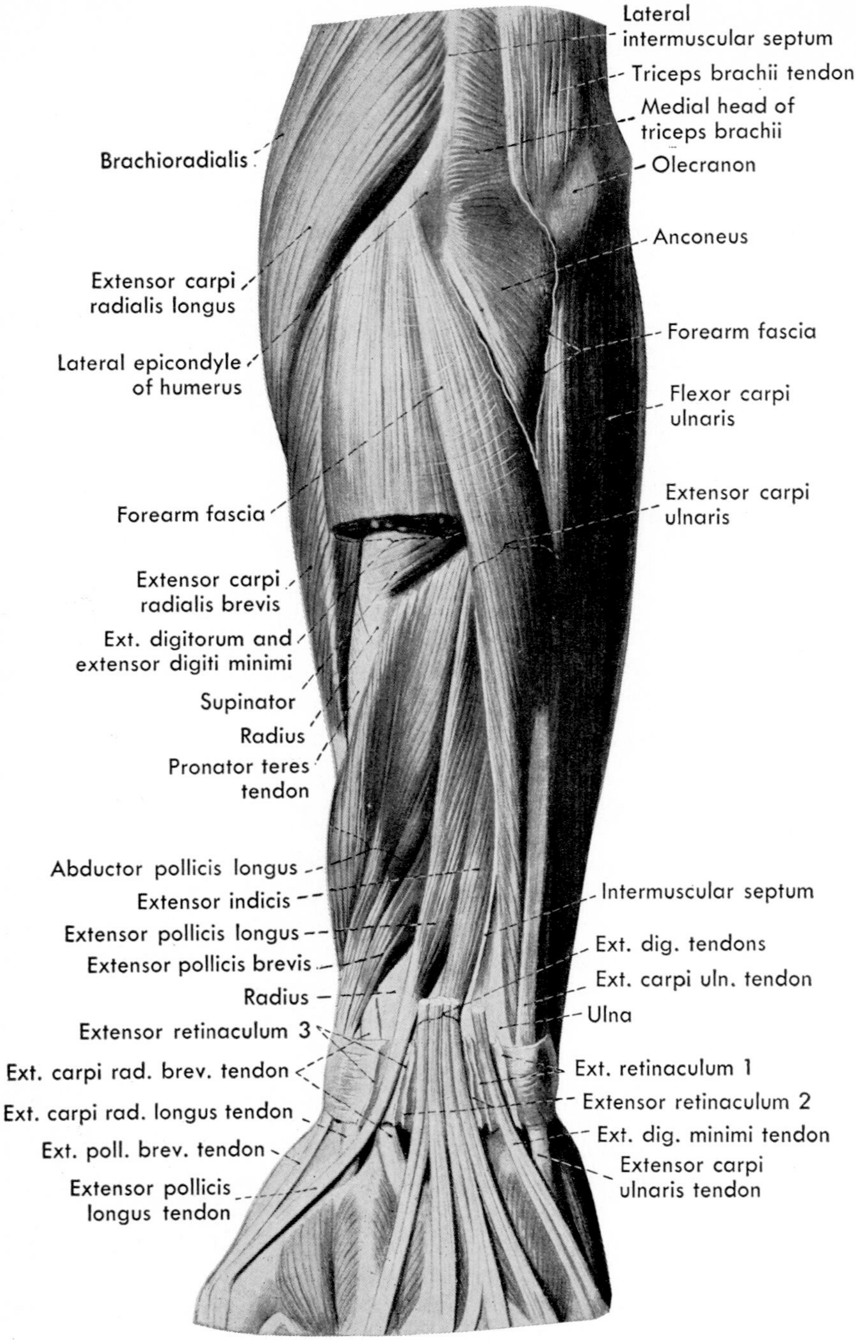

Lateral
intermuscular septum

Triceps brachii tendon

Medial head of
triceps brachii

Olecranon

Anconeus

Forearm fascia

Flexor carpi
ulnaris

Extensor carpi
ulnaris

Intermuscular septum

Ext. dig. tendons

Ext. carpi uln. tendon

Ulna

Ext. retinaculum 1

Extensor retinaculum 2

Ext. dig. minimi tendon

Extensor carpi
ulnaris tendon

Brachioradialis

Extensor carpi
radialis longus

Lateral epicondyle
of humerus

Forearm fascia

Extensor carpi
radialis brevis

Ext. digitorum and
extensor digiti minimi

Supinator

Radius

Pronator teres
tendon

Abductor pollicis longus

Extensor indicis

Extensor pollicis longus

Extensor pollicis brevis

Radius

Extensor retinaculum 3

Ext. carpi rad. brev. tendon

Ext. carpi rad. longus tendon

Ext. poll. brev. tendon

Extensor pollicis
longus tendon

FIG. 12-3.   Posterior aspect of left forearm.   (Sobotta-Uhlenhuth,
courtesy Hafner Publishing Co., New York–London.)

MUSCLES MOVING THE FINGERS

There are three muscles in the forearm that act on all four fingers at once, two of them flexors and one an extensor. They are named—

Flexor digitorum superficialis
Flexor digitorum profundus
Extensor digitorum.

Each of these muscles has four tendons going to the four fingers, beginning at the lower fourth of the forearm, and each tendon is acted upon by separate groups of muscle fibers, making it possible to flex and extend the fingers separately as well as all at once. The wide difference seen in the abilities of different persons to do this is due to differences in coordination resulting from various amounts and kinds of training and not from differences in the structure of the muscles.

FLEXOR DIGITORUM SUPERFICIALIS

Situated just beneath the flexor carpi radialis and the palmaris longus on the anterior side of the forearm. This muscle is subject to considerable variation and is seldom seen in identical form in any two subjects (Fig. 11–7).

Origin. The medial epicondyle of the humerus, the coronoid process of the ulna, and a long oblique line on the middle half of the anterior surface of the radius.

Insertion. By four tendons which separate after passing the wrist and go to the four fingers. Opposite the proximal phalanx each tendon splits into two parts, which are inserted into the sides of the base of the middle phalanx (Fig. 12–5).

Innervation. The median nerve from the brachial plexus. Fibers come from the seventh and eighth cervical and the first thoracic nerves.

Action. Primary flexor of the middle and proximal phalanges; assists in wrist flexion.

FLEXOR DIGITORUM PROFUNDUS

Located just beneath the flexor superficialis (Fig. 12–4).

Origin. The upper three-fourths of the anterior and medial surfaces of the ulna.

Insertion. By four tendons which separate after passing the wrist and go to the four fingers. Each tendon passes through the split in the corresponding flexor digitorum superficialis tendon and is inserted into the dorsal surface of the base of the distal phalanx (Fig. 12–5).

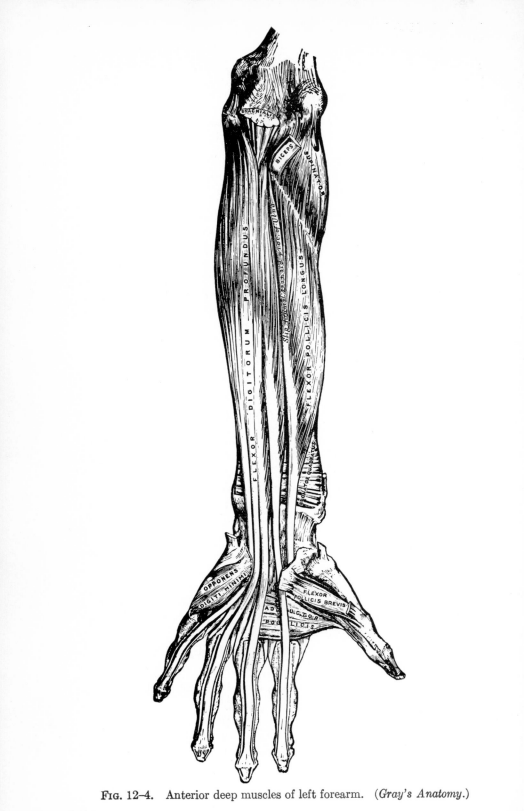

Fig. 12–4. Anterior deep muscles of left forearm. (*Gray's Anatomy*.)

Innervation. The anterior interosseous nerve, the fibers of which come from the brachial plexus by way of the median and ulnar nerves. Fibers are from the eighth cervical and first thoracic nerves.

Action. Flexes all the phalanges; assists in wrist flexion.

EXTENSOR DIGITORUM

A fusiform muscle, situated on the middle of the dorsal surface of the forearm (Fig. 12–3).

Origin. The lateral epicondyle of the humerus.

Insertion. By four tendons which separate after passing the wrist and go to the four fingers. Each tendon is attached by fibrous slips to the dorsum of the proximal phalanx and then divides into three parts; the middle part is inserted into the dorsal surface of the base of the middle phalanx and the two collateral parts into the dorsal expansion of the finger extensor tendons. The tendon to the little finger is commonly replaced with a junctura tendinii connecting the common extensor tendon of the ring finger to the dorsal expansion of the little finger.[1]

Innervation. Posterior interosseous branch of the deep radial nerve from the brachial plexus. Fibers come from the sixth, seventh, and eighth cervical nerves.

Action. Contraction of the extensor digitorum extends the proximal phalanx and the wrist. If the proximal phalanx is held flexed, the muscle will extend the other phalanges; but if the proximal phalanx or the wrist are allowed to extend, its contraction has little effect on the last two phalanges. This is partly due to the insertion of the tendons into three successive segments of the finger and partly to leverage and slack, as explained in case of the flexors. Since the extensor digitorum has the best leverage on the wrist, strong extension of the fingers is impossible unless the wrist is prevented from hyperextending as the muscle contracts.

EXTENSOR INDICIS

A long thin muscle medial to and paralleling the extensor pollicus longus.

Origin. Dorsal surface of the lower half of the body of the ulna and the interosseous membrane (Fig. 12–3).

Insertion. Into the ulnar side of the tendon of the index finger of the extensor digitorum, and into the dorsal expansion of the finger extensor tendons.

Innervation. Posterior interosseous branch of the deep radial nerve of the brachial plexus. Fibers arise from the sixth, seventh, and eighth cervical nerves.

Action. Extends and assists with adduction of the proximal phalanx of the index finger; assists with wrist extension. Acting through the dorsal expansion, it extends the middle and distal phalanges, especially when the phalanx is held in flexion.

EXTENSOR DIGITI MINIMI

A long thin fusiform muscle medial to and paralleling and often attached to the extensor digitorum (Fig. 12–3).

Origin. Arises from the common tendon of the extensor digitorum.

Insertion. Into the tendon of the extensor digitorum at the proximal phalanx of the little finger, and into the dorsal expansion of the finger extensor tendons.

Innervation. Posterior interosseous branch of the deep radial nerve of the brachial plexus. Fibers arise from the sixth, seventh, and eighth cervical nerves.

Action. Extends the proximal phalanx of the little finger, and assists with wrist extension. Acting through the dorsal expansion, it extends the middle and distal phalanges, especially when the proximal phalanx is held in flexion.

MUSCLES IN THE HAND

There are three groups of small muscles placed in the hand itself that help to flex and extend the fingers and also to adduct and abduct them. There are eleven of these muscles, as follows:

> Four lumbricales
> Four dorsal interossei
> Three palmar interossei.

In addition there are three muscles which act on the little finger alone, their action contributing to some of the unusual features of the hand.

The lumbricales are in the palm and the interossei lie between the metacarpal bones. All eleven act to flex proximal phalanges and to extend middle and distal phalanges.

THE LUMBRICALES

Four little spindle-shaped muscles, named from their resemblance to an earthworm (lumbricus) (Fig. 12–5).

Origin. The tendons of the flexor digitorum profundus.

Insertion. The tendon of each muscle turns around the radial side of the metacarpal bone and is inserted into the dorsal expansion of the finger extensor tendons.

Innervation.   The first two lumbricales from the third and fourth digital branches of the median nerve, containing fibers from the sixth

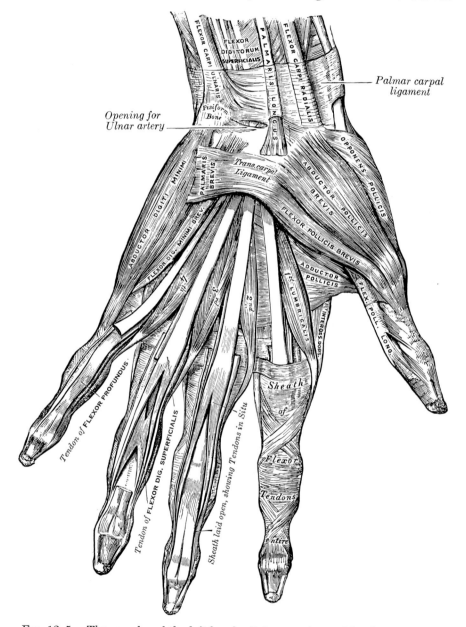

Fig. 12–5.   The muscles of the left hand. Palmar surface. (*Gray's Anatomy.*)

and seventh cervical nerves. The third and fourth lumbricales from branches of the palmar branch of the ulnar nerve, containing fibers from the eighth cervical nerve.

Action. The lumbricales are weak flexors of the metacarpophalangeal joints during interphalangeal extension, and the principal extensors of the interphalangeal joints in association with the extensor digitorum. When the metacarpophalangeal joints are stabilized with regard to flexion and extension, the lumbricales abduct the proximal phalanges.[2]

THE DORSAL INTEROSSEI

Four small bipennate muscles lying between the five metacarpal bones at the back of the hand (Fig. 12–6).

Origin. Each from the two bones between which it lies.

Insertion. Proximal phalanges of the second, third, and fourth digits and the dorsal expansion of the finger extensor tendons.

Innervation. The palmar branch of the ulnar nerve with fibers coming from the eighth cervical and first thoracic nerves by way of the brachial plexus.

Action. The first and second abduct the index finger and middle fingers. The third and fourth adduct the middle and ring fingers. All assist in flexing the proximal phalanges of the index, middle, and

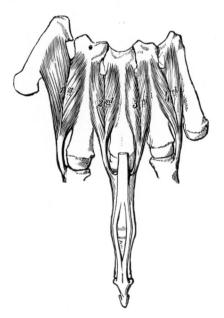

Fig. 12–6. Dorsal interossei of the left hand. (*Gray's Anatomy.*)

ring fingers, and assist in extending the middle and distal phalanges of the same fingers.

THE PALMAR INTEROSSEI

Three small muscles in the palm, on the central sides of the second, fourth, and fifth metacarpals (Fig. 12–7).

Origin.   Sides of the metacarpals except the first and third.

Insertion.   The base of the proximal phalanges of the index, ring, and little fingers.

Innervation.   The palmar branch of the ulnar nerve with fibers coming from the eighth cervical and first thoracic nerves by way of the brachial plexus.

Action.   The first palmar interosseous muscle adducts the proximal phalanx of the index finger.   The second and third interosseus muscles abduct the proximal phalanx of the ring and little finger. All three assist in flexing the proximal phalanges of the index, ring, and little fingers respectively, and in extending the middle and distal phalanges of the same fingers.

ABDUCTOR DIGITI MINIMI

Easily palpated on the ulnar border of the hand (Fig. 12–5).

Origin.   Arises from the pisiform bone and from the tendon of the flexor carpi ulnaris.

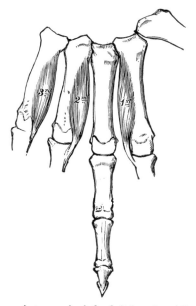

FIG. 12–7.   Palmar interossei of the left hand.   (*Gray's Anatomy.*)

Insertion. Two slips; one inserted into the ulnar side of the base of the proximal phalanx of the little finger; the other into the ulnar border of the aponeurosis of the extensor digiti minimi brevis, with connections from each to the dorsal expansion of the finger extensor tendons.

Innervation. The deep branch of the ulnar nerve from the brachial plexus with fibers from the eighth cervical nerve.

Action. Under the classification system used in this text (see pp. 36 and 241) this muscle adducts the little finger. It also assists in flexing its proximal phalanx.

FLEXOR DIGITI MINIMI BREVIS

Because its fibers of origin merge with those of the adjacent abductor digiti minimi, the flexor digiti minimi brevis is in effect a part of that muscle (Fig. 12–5).

Origin. The hamate bone and the contiguous parts of the transverse carpal ligament.

Insertion. The ulnar side of the proximal phalanx of the little finger.

Innervation. The deep branch of the ulnar nerve from the brachial plexus. Fibers from the eighth cervical and first thoracic nerves.

Action. Flexes the proximal phalanx of the little finger.

OPPONENS DIGITI MINIMI

A triangular muscle immediately beneath the preceding muscles (Fig. 12–4).

Origin. Convex surface of the hamate bone and the contiguous portion of the transverse carpal ligament.

Insertion. The ulnar margin of the entire length of the metacarpal bone of the little finger.

Innervation. The deep branch of the ulnar nerve from the brachial plexus with fibers from the eighth cervical and first thoracic nerves.

Action. Slight flexion and rotation of the fifth metacarpal in "cupping" the hand.

MUSCLES MOVING THE THUMB

Of the eight muscles moving the thumb, four are in the forearm and four in the thenar eminence. Some of these muscles correspond to muscles that act on the fingers, and it will help in understanding and remembering the new ones to keep such resemblances in mind.

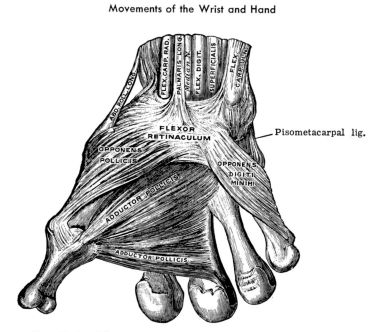

Fɪɢ. 12–8.   The muscles of the thumb.   (*Gray's Anatomy.*)

EXTENSOR POLLICIS LONGUS

The extensor pollicis longus lies on the back of the forearm next to the extensor indicis and like it may be considered to be a part of the extensor digitorum (Fig. 12–3).   It forms the ulnar boundary of the "anatomical snuff box."   It is a specialized portion of the abductor longus.

Origin.   Posterior surface of the middle third of the ulna and the interosseus membrane.

Insertion.   The posterior surface of the base of the distal phalanx of the thumb.

Innervation.   Posterior interosseous branch of the deep radial nerve with fibers from the sixth, seventh, and eighth cervical nerves by way of the brachial plexus.

Action.   It extends the distal phalanx of the thumb and then if the movement is continued it extends the other joints, drawing the thumb into the plane of the rest of the hand.   May assist in extending the wrist.

EXTENSOR POLLICIS BREVIS

This muscle lies deep beneath the extensor digitorum on the back of the forearm.   Its tendon forms the radial boundary of the "anatomical snuff box" (Fig. 12–3). It is found only in man and the gorilla.

Origin. Small spaces on the dorsal surfaces of both radius and ulna near their middle.

Insertion. The posterior surface of the base of the proximal phalanx of the thumb.

Innervation. Posterior interosseous branch of deep radial nerve with fibers from the sixth and seventh cervical nerves by way of the brachial plexus.

Action. Extends the proximal phalanx of the thumb and, by continued action, abducts the first metacarpal and the wrist.

ABDUCTOR POLLICIS LONGUS

This, the last of the long extensors, acts, as its name indicates, on the metacarpal bone of the thumb. It lies just below the supinator and is sometimes united with it (Fig. 12–3).

Origin. A small space on the ulnar side of the radius near its middle, the lateral part of the dorsal surface of the body of the ulna just below the insertion of the anconeus and the interosseous membrane.

Insertion. The radial side of the base of the first metacarpal.

Innervation. Posterior interosseous branch of the deep radial nerve with fibers from the sixth and seventh cervical nerves by way of the brachial plexus.

Action. Abducts the thumb, and, by continued action, the wrist.

FLEXOR POLLICIS LONGUS

This is the only flexor of the thumb located in the forearm. Since the thumb lacks the middle phalanx, the flexor superficialis, flexor of the middle phalanx of the fingers, naturally has no counterpart among the thumb muscles. The flexor pollicis longus lies beside the flexor profundus in the forearm and is attached to the distal phalanx like the latter. It can therefore be considered as a part of the deep flexor (Fig. 12–4). This muscle is absent in some primates, which suggests that it was acquired comparatively recently in the evolutionary process.[3] It is unipennate.

Origin. Anterior surface of the middle half of the radius and adjacent parts of the interosseous membrane.

Insertion. The anterior surface of the base of the distal phalanx of the thumb.

Innervation. The anterior interosseous nerve from the median. Fibers come from the eighth cervical and first thoracic nerves.

Action. Flexes the distal phalanx of the thumb. Continued action flexes the proximal phalanx and flexes and adducts the metacarpal and wrist.

FLEXOR POLLICIS BREVIS

This is the inner of the two short flexors (Figs. 12–4 and 12–9).

Origin. A superficial head arises from the crest of the trapezium, and a deep head from the trapezoid and capitate bones and the palmar ligaments of the distal row of carpal bones.

Insertion. Base of the proximal phalanx of the thumb on the radial side.

Innervation. Superficial head supplied by fibers from the median nerve; deep head supplied by fibers from the ulnar nerve.

Action. Flexion of the proximal phalanx, flexion and adduction of the metacarpal of the thumb.

OPPONENS POLLICIS

A small triangular muscle beneath the abductor pollicis brevis (Fig. 12–8).

Origin. The trapezium and transverse carpal ligament.

Insertion. The shaft of the first metacarpal bone on its radial side.

Innervation. The median nerve with fibers from the sixth and seventh cervical nerves.

Action. Opposition, which is a partial circumduction of the metacarpal of the thumb. By its use the tip of the thumb can be made to meet the tips of the four fingers in turn.

ABDUCTOR POLLICIS BREVIS

This is the most superficial muscle of the lateral part of the thenar eminence (Figs. 12–5 and 12–9). It is fusiform in shape and bipartite.

Origin. The tuberosity of the scaphoid and the ridge of the trapezium. Another slip originates from the transverse carpal ligament.

Insertion. The lateral surface of the base of the proximal phalanx of the thumb.

Innervation. The median nerve with fibers from the sixth and seventh cervical nerves.

Action. Flexion and medial rotation of the metacarpal of the thumb.

ADDUCTOR POLLICIS

This is the deepest of the thenar muscles (Figs. 12–5, 12–8 and 12–9).

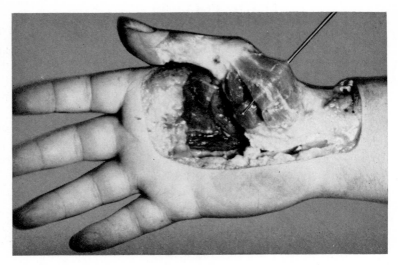

Fig. 12–9. Dissection showing the abductor pollicis brevis (over the probe) and the flexor pollicis brevis (under the probe). The adductor pollicis is seen just distal to the latter. (McFarlane, reprinted with permission from J. Bone Joint Surg., *44-A,* 1073–1088, 1962.)

Origin. The oblique head arises from the capitate bone, the bases of the second and third metacarpals and the intercarpal ligaments. The transverse head arises from the lower two-thirds of the palmar surface of the third metacarpal bone.

Insertion. The medial surface of the base of the proximal phalanx of the thumb.

Innervation. The deep palmar branch of the ulnar nerve. Fibers come from the eighth cervical and first thoracic nerves.

Action. Adduction and hyperadduction of the metacarpal of the thumb. If the thumb is in a position of flexion and hyperadduction, it will extend the first metacarpal, bringing it to the surface of the palm.

WRIST MOVEMENTS

Actions of the Prime Movers. Considering only the prime movers for wrist movements, one prime mover is in excellent position to perform each of the four "diagonal" movements:

Flexor carpi radialis . . .	Flexion and abduction
Flexor carpi ulnaris. . . .	Flexion and adduction
Extensor carpi radialis (longus & brevis considered as one).	Extension and abduction
Extensor carpi ulnaris . . .	Extension and adduction

None of these prime movers is capable of producing "pure" flexion, extension, abduction, or adduction. When such pure movements are desired, there must be helping synergy involving a pair of these prime movers. (In *helping synergy*, two muscles contract, each co-operating to produce the desired movement, and each neutralizing an undesired secondary action of the other.)

Flexion—The flexor carpi radialis and the flexor carpi ulnaris both produce flexion. The tendency of the former to perform abduction is neutralized by the tendency of the latter to perform adduction, and vice versa.

Extension—The extensor carpi ulnaris and the extensor carpi radialis (longus and brevis considered as one) both produce extension. The tendency of the former to perform adduction is neutralized by the tendency of the latter to perform abduction, and vice versa.

Abduction—The flexor carpi radialis and the extensor carpi radialis (longus and brevis) both produce abduction. The tendency of the former to perform flexion is neutralized by the tendency of the latter to perform extension, and vice versa.

Adduction—The flexor carpi ulnaris and the extensor carpi ulnaris both produce adduction. The tendency of the former to perform flexion is neutralized by the tendency of the latter to perform extension, and vice versa.

Actions of the Assistant Movers. It is a rule that when a multi-joint muscle (*i.e.*, one which crosses more than one joint) contracts, it tends to perform movements at each of the joints it crosses. A number of long muscles, which are primarily designed to cause actions at the more distal joints, have their origins on the radius, ulna, or humerus, and thus cross the wrist joint, where they tend to perform assistant mover actions. The most important are the flexor digitorum superficialis, the flexor digitorum profundus, and the extensor digitorum. The potential actions of these long flexors and extensors are summarized as follows (with prime mover actions in upper case):

Flexor digitorum superficialis—wrist flexion, META-CARPOPHALANGEAL FLEXION, FIRST INTER-PHALANGEAL FLEXION.

Flexor digitorum profundus—wrist flexion, metacarpo-phalangeal flexion, first interphalangeal flexion, SECOND INTERPHALANGEAL FLEXION.

Extensor digitorum—wrist extension, METACARPO-PHALANGEAL EXTENSION, FIRST INTERPHA-LANGEAL EXTENSION, SECOND INTERPHALAN-GEAL EXTENSION.

According to the usual rule, these muscles would be expected to perform all of their potential actions when they contract individ-

ually.   However, the long flexors and the long extensor interfere
with one another, as demonstrated in the following experiments:

> 1. With the wrist in full flexion, attempt to perform full finger flexion. This
> is usually impossible because the extensor digitorum is not long enough to per-
> mit full flexion in all of the joints it crosses.
>
> 2. With the wrist in full hyperextension, attempt to perform full finger exten-
> sion. This is usually impossible because the flexor digitorum superficialis and
> the flexor digitorum profundus are not long enough to permit full extension in
> all of the joints they cross.

These situations are avoided by use of the prime movers for wrist
actions, as demonstrated in further experiments:

> 1. Ask a person to make a tight fist (to perform forceful and complete finger
> flexion). Notice that he unconsciously keeps his wrist in an extended position
> while doing this. Upon palpation, the extensor carpi ulnaris and the extensor
> carpi radialis longus and brevis will be found to be contracting statically. These
> wrist extensors neutralize the tendency of the long finger flexors to produce
> wrist flexion, thereby preventing a limitation of finger flexion due to the short-
> ness of the extensor digitorum.
>
> 2. Ask a person to extend his fingers forcefully and completely. Notice that
> he unconsciously keeps his wrist in a slightly flexed position, or at least avoids
> hyperextension at the wrist. Upon palpation, the flexor carpi radialis and the
> flexor carpi ulnaris will be found to be contracting statically. These wrist flexors
> neutralize the tendency of the extensor digitorum to produce wrist extension,
> thereby preventing a limitation of finger extension due to shortness of the long
> finger flexor muscles.

In both of the foregoing examples, the prime movers for wrist
flexion or extension are contracting as true synergists.

Regarding these phenomena, some practical observations may be
made. When either strong finger flexion or strong finger extension
is desired, the most stable position of the wrist is that of extension,
avoiding any marked flexion or hyperextension. The extended (but
not hyperextended) position of the wrist provides the most stable
anatomical position for the boxer's tightly-closed fist, for grasping a
bat, hammer, axe, tennis racket, or other implement, and for with-
standing the impacts of wrestling, boxing, or judo. The position is
natural, but in sports an occasional performer needs to be coached
with regard to his wrist position. Therapists will note that paralysis
of the main wrist extensors prevents effective grasping of small objects with the fingers, although custom-made braces to hold the
wrist in extension may be useful in restoring the function.

FINGER MOVEMENTS

The Dorsal Expansion, or Extensor Expansion. The mechanism
of finger extension cannot be explained rationally if only the direct

bony insertions of the finger muscles are considered. It is necessary to understand complex and highly specialized tendinous branchings known as the *dorsal expansion* or *extensor expansion*.

An extensor expansion is found on the dorsal aspect of each digit, with a somewhat modified structure for the thumb. A diagram of the essential architecture of the extensor expansion is shown in Figure 12–10.

The structure consists of systematic ramifications of the tendons of insertion of the extensor digitorum, the interosseous muscles, the lumbricales, and some of the thenar and hypothenar muscles. It is basically triangular, with a broad base or *hood* created from lateral slips spreading from the extensor digitorum tendon at the level of the metacarpophalangeal joint. This hood is partly wrapped around the sides of the base end of the proximal phalanx, enclosing the direct bony insertion of the interosseous muscles. Just distal to the hood, the interosseous muscles each send a tendon into the extensor expansion, forming the sides of the triangle, called the *lateral bands*. Just distal to these, at the shaft of the proximal phalanx, the lum-

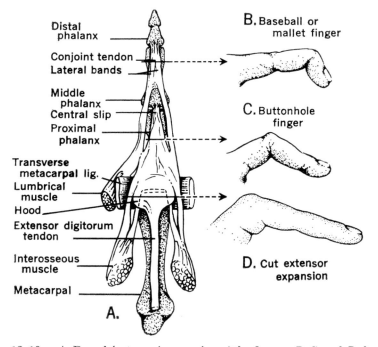

FIG. 12–10.   *A*, Dorsal (extensor) expansion of the fingers; *B, C,* and *D* show the type of injury resulting from trauma to the expansion mechanism at the levels indicated; *B*, severed conjoint tendon; *C*, severed central slip; *D*, severed extensor expansion. (Adapted from Entin, M. A.: Repair of extensor mechanism of the hand. Surg. Clin. North America, April, 1960, pp. 275–285.)

bricales also insert into the extensor expansion. The lateral bands converge distally and attach to the dorsal surface of the proximal end of the distal phalanx. The main tendon of the extensor digitorum forms the centrally located *middle slip* of the extensor expansion, which inserts on the dorsal surface of the base of the middle phalanx. The middle slip also receives fibers from the interossei and the lumbricales; likewise, the extensor digitorum tendon expands outward and contributes to the lateral bands.

The extensor expansion permits the extensor digitorum to extend the distal phalanges of the digits as well as the more proximal middle and proximal phalanges. The lumbricales and interossei, however, enter the extensor expansion at the lateral bands and at the part of the hood which is curved around the sides of the bases of the proximal phalanx, in such a manner as to cause flexion of the proximal phalanx (at the metacarpophalangeal joint) and extension of the middle and distal phalanges. Only because of this mechanism are such acts as writing and needle-threading possible. These activities require metacarpophalangeal flexion and interphalangeal extension. These actions can be performed by the lumbricales and interossei, but not by the extensor digitorum. Paralysis of the lumbricales and interossei leaves only the extensor digitorum to extend the interphalangeal joints. Their unaided action causes simultaneous extension of the metacarpophalangeal joint ("claw hand"), making impossible the many fine hand actions requiring extension of the distal phalanges along with flexion of the proximal phalanx. In other words, such paralysis leaves only the possibility of flexion of all the phalanges by the long finger flexors, or extension of all the phalanges by the long finger extensor.

If it is desired to perform extension of the proximal phalanx with simultaneous flexion of the middle and distal phalanges, contraction of the extensor digitorum and of the long finger flexors will produce the wanted result.

Individuality of Finger Flexion and Extension. The flexor digitorum superficialis and the flexor digitorum profundus each are composed of separate bundles of fibers which may be stimulated separately to activate the long flexor tendons of the four fingers individually. Typing and playing some musical instruments depend upon learning these individuations. The extensor digitorum is unable to move the fingers independently to the same degree as the flexors, because of three fibrous bands which interconnect the extensor tendons across the back of the hand (Fig. 12–3). The ring finger is especially limited in this way. However, the index finger and the little finger are provided with their own small extensor muscles, the extensor indicis and the extensor digiti minimi, respectively. These small muscles are inserted into the corresponding tendon of the extensor digitorum and into the extensor expansions, along with other small individual finger muscles, thus permitting an amazing versatility of fine finger movements. Paralysis of even a few of the various finger muscles will reduce the functional ability of the hand to that of a paw.

Extensors of the Interphalangeal Joints. When the metacarpophalangeal joint is held in extension, the extensor digitorum muscle is primarily responsible, but it does not have sufficient shortening ability to extend the two interphalangeal joints at the same time. Under these conditions, the lumbricales and the interossei, being on stretch because of the metacarpophalangeal extension, become prime movers for extension of the interphalangeal joints.

The situation is reversed when the metacarpophalangeal joint is held in flexion. Then, the lumbricales and interossei have expended their shortening ability in causing metacarpophalangeal flexion, and are able to contract further so as to cause extension at the interphalangeal joints. However, the extensor digitorum is on stretch because of the metacarpophalangeal flexion, and therefore can use its shortening power to become a prime mover for the interphalangeal extension.

Since both the extrinsic and intrinsic muscles of the fingers span more than one joint, the contribution of a given muscle to any of the four basic positions of the finger (Fig. 12–11) can be determined only by a consideration of the positions of the several joints, as well as of the muscles.

McCue has provided a kinesiologically instructive insight in his comment that the proximal interphalangeal joint of the finger is frequently injured because of "its relatively long proximal and distal

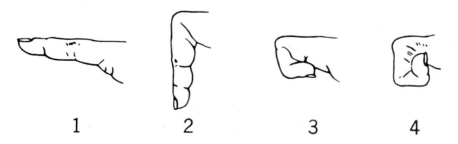

1   2   3   4

Fig. 12–11.   Four basic positions of the finger. *1*, Full extension. MP (metacarpophalangeal) extension, IP (interphalangeal) extension. *2*, Lumbrical position. MP flexion, IP extension. *3*, Hook. MP extension, IP flexion. *4*, Full flexion. MP flexion, IP flexion. In positions *1* and *2*, the lumbricales are contracted; in *3* and *4*, they are relaxed. The interossei contract actively in *2*, and contribute to MP flexion in position *4* because they are under passive stretch. (After Stack.[4])

lever arms which transmit lateral and torque stresses without allevi-
ation by some lateral flexibility."[5]

The anatomy and function of the separate and combined actions
of the extensor digitorum, interosseous, and lumbrical muscles have
been thoroughly discussed by anatomists.[6] Sunderland[7] includes
observations of lesions of the radial, ulnar, and medial nerves, separately and in combination.

THUMB MOVEMENTS

Opposition of the thumb to the fingers is a unique action. Although the adductor pollicis and the flexor pollicis longus and brevis
participate in opposition, the contraction of the opponens is the
crucial factor. When the opponens is paralyzed, true opposition is
impossible, even though thumb adduction and thumb flexion at both
metacarpophalangeal and interphalangeal joints are unaffected.

When forcibly closing the fist, or in the simple use of the hand,
such as grasping the handle of a hammer, the abductor pollicis
draws the thumb away from the hand while the opponens pollicis
rotates the metacarpal of the thumb bringing it out in front of the
palm to face the fingers. The fingers are flexed by contraction of the
flexors superficialis and profundus. This is accompanied or closely
followed by contraction of the adductor pollicis and the flexors of the
thumb, together with extension of the wrist to complete the movement.

In chopping and in using a hammer there is also strong adduction
of the wrist. In the use of coarse tools, such as the axe, hammer,
saw, plane and wrench, it is mainly the three flexors of the thumb
that come into action. In finer work, such as the use of a pen,
pencil, needle, or other small instruments, where the tips of the
thumb and fingers must be brought together, it is necessary to keep
the thumb in opposition and flex the proximal phalanx of the fingers
to nearly a right angle, because the thumb is so much shorter than
the fingers.

Writing with a pen or pencil and using the so-called "finger movement" requires the use of many muscles. The grasping of the pen
between the thumb and the next two fingers calls into action the
flexors profundus and superficialis. The three flexors of the thumb
along with the abductor are likewise required. To make an up-
stroke with the pen the lumbricales and interossei contract and extend the last two phalanges while still further flexing the first; in the
thumb a similar movement takes place, the metacarpal bone being
flexed on the wrist and the other joints extended. Then to make a
down-stroke the two flexors of the fingers join with the extensor

digitorum in order to pull the finger tips closer to the palm, while the abductor pollicis longus acts with the flexors longus and brevis pollicis to accomplish the same result on the thumb side.

Experts on accident insurance estimate the value of the thumb at half that of the whole hand. Its usefulness is largely due to its position of opposition to the fingers and the resulting ability to grasp and hold objects between them. In the finer work in which man excels all other animals certain tools are manipulated by action of the fingers and thumb. In such work the muscles of the thenar eminence are of greatest value in moving the thumb. The hand of man differs from that of the anthropoid apes mainly in the greater development of the muscles of the thenar eminence and in the habitual position of the thumb, which is one of much more nearly complete opposition to the fingers. It has been theorized that every skilled musician, instrument maker, sleight-of-hand artist, and pickpocket must have hands that are constructed in such a way as to make them adaptable to his peculiar task.[8] This suggestion needs to be investigated, but there is no movement of the hand which a man can make that a monkey cannot. The difference lies in the fact that man is more capable of purposive actions. Human skill is a result of an elaboration of the central nervous system and not of a specialization of the hand, which is actually a relatively primitive structure.[9]

PREHENSILE MOVEMENTS

The nature of the grip is actually dictated by the nature of the intended activity. Napier[9] contends that all movements of the hand may be divided into two main groups: prehensile movements, in which an object is seized and held wholly or partly within the grasp of the hand, and nonprehensile movements, in which objects are manipulated by pushing or lifting. Prehensile movements may be further subdivided into a power grip, in which the object is clamped by the partly flexed fingers and palm, with counter pressure applied by the thumb lying more or less in the plane of the palm, and a precision grip, in which the object is pinched between the fingers and the opposing thumb. The position of the thumb shows a fundamental difference in the two prehensile grips. In the power grip it is adducted at both the metacarpophalangeal and carpometacarpal joints. The hand is deviated toward the ulnar side, and the wrist is held in the neutral position. In the precision grip the thumb is abducted and medially rotated, the hand is held midway between radial and ulnar deviation, and the wrist is markedly dorsiflexed. However, very heavy objects are often held in the clenched fist, with the thumb fully adducted.

TABLE 12–1. Actions of the Wrist and Hand Muscles

	WRIST				METACARPO-PHALANGEAL				INTER-PHALANGEAL 1st		INTER-PHALANGEAL 2nd		CARPOMETACARPAL OF THUMB				
	Flexion	*Extension*	*Abduction*	*Adduction*	*Flexion*	*Extension*	*Abduction*	*Adduction*	*Flexion*	*Extension*	*Flexion*	*Extension*	*Flexion*	*Extension*	*Abduction*	*Adduction*	*Opposition*
Flexor carpi radialis	P.M.		P.M.														
Flexor carpi ulnaris	P.M.			P.M.													
Palmaris longus	Asst.																
Extensor carpi radialis longus		P.M.	P.M.														
Extensor carpi radialis brevis		P.M.	P.M.														
Extensor carpi ulnaris		P.M.		P.M.													
Flexor digitorum profundus	Asst.				Asst.				P.M.		P.M.						
Flexor digitorum superficialis	Asst.				P.M.				P.M.								
Extensor digitorum		Asst.				P.M.				P.M.		P.M.					
Extensor indicis		Asst.				P.M.		Asst.		P.M.		P.M.					
Extensor digiti minimi		Asst.				P.M.				P.M.		P.M.					

Muscle								
Lumbricales			P.M.	P.M.				
1st & 2nd Dorsal Interossei			Asst.	Asst.				
3rd & 4th Dorsal Interossei			Asst.	Asst.				
1st Palmar Interosseous		P.M.	Asst.	Asst.				
2nd & 3rd Palmar Interossei		P.M.	Asst.					
Abductor digiti minimi		P.M.	Asst.					
Flexor digiti minimi brevis			P.M.					
Opponens digiti minimi			P.M.					
Extensor pollicis longus	Asst.	Asst.						
Extensor pollicis brevis		Asst.	P.M.	P.M.				
Abductor pollicis longus	Asst.					P.M.		
Flexor pollicis longus		P.M.				P.M.	P.M.	
Flexor pollicis brevis		P.M.				P.M.	P.M.	
Opponens pollicis						P.M.		P.M.
Abductor pollicis brevis			P.M.			P.M.		P.M.
Adductor pollicis						P.M.	P.M.	P.M.

A more detailed analysis of the various types of prehension is shown in Figure 12–12. In all these grips the hand assumes a fixed position and is maintained therein by the cocontraction of the opposing muscles. Each of the muscles of the wrist functions as an agonist, a stabilizer, or an antagonist as the load shifts. The maximum prehensile force is obtained at a wrist angle of about 145 degrees. In extreme positions of wrist angle the marked stretching or slackening of the wrist muscles results in a reduction of strength. In rest, with the hand hanging loosely at the side, the wrist takes a mid-position and the hand is dorsiflexed 35 degrees with respect to the extended forearm axis. This is its position of greatest prehensile force.[10]

Taken over the whole range of rotation, pronation of the wrist and hand is on the average stronger than is supination, although there are certain shoulder-elbow positions in which the converse is true.

Grip Strength. In a study of 1,182 male industrial workers, the mean grip strength of the preferred hand was 113.1 lbs., while that of 80 female workers was 69.8 lbs.[11] The maximum grip strength is found during the mid-twenties; by age sixty there is a decline of 16.5 per cent.[12] The limiting factor in grip strength appears to be the ability of the thumb to oppose the force of the fingers. Correla-

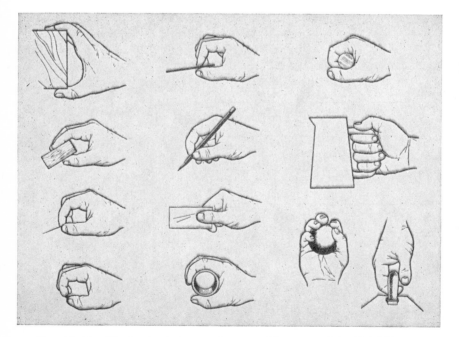

FIG. 12–12. Twelve basic types of grasp. (Courtesy of Artificial Limbs. After Schlesinger.)

tions between forearm girth and grip strength are positive but low, being on the order of r = .3 to .6.[13] Possibly the explanation is that tests of grip strength are said to be largely tests of the strength of the muscles of the thenar eminence.[14] Presumably this is the reason that such tests do not give a satisfactory indication of general strength.[15]

IMPLICATIONS FOR ATHLETIC TRAINING

Williams[16] suggests that variations in the size, strength, attachments, presence or absence of various muscles of the wrist and hand, and similar factors may be responsible for individual differences in the way rackets, clubs, or bats are held, footballs passed, and other apparent idiosyncrasies in athletic technique. Traumata to the hands are relatively frequent in such sports as boxing, football, and baseball. Fractures of the finger and hand bones are the most common of all fractures resulting from sports activities. Inflammation of the long extensor tendon of the thumb, resulting from the dorsiflexion of the wrist in feathering the oar, is said to be the most common lesion among crewmen. The classic picture following a hand injury is a loss of tone in the extensor carpi radialis brevis, resulting in wrist drop. Surgeons emphasize the importance of preventing wrist flexion and the consequent loss of the prime function of the wrist extensors. The metacarpophalangeal and interphalangeal joints are especially subject to degenerative fibrotic changes when the hand is immobilized. At the first appearance of circulatory stasis or stiffness in the fingers, moist heat, massage, and exercise should be started. Squeezing of small rubber balls is often recommended, but these are usually of such a size that only partial flexion of the fingers is achieved. Foam rubber or plastic putty are more useful. All too often flexion exercises are prescribed when the fingers are already in a state of partial contracture and the actual need is for a strengthening of the extensors and a stretching of the flexors.

References

1. Schenck, Robert R.: Variations of the Extensor Tendons of the Fingers. J. Bone Joint Surg., *46-A*, 103–110, 1964.

2. Long, Charles and Brown, Mary Eleanor: Electromyographic Kinesiology of the Hand: Muscles Moving the Long Finger. J. Bone Joint Surg., *46-A*, 1683-1706, 1964.

3. Mangini, Uberto: Flexor Pollicis Longus Muscle. J. Bone Joint Surg., *42-A*, 467–470, 1960.

4. Stack, H. Graham: Muscle Function in the Fingers. J. Bone Joint Surg., *44-B*, 899–909, 1962.

5. McCue, Frank C.: Athletic Injuries of the Proximal Interphalangeal Joint Requiring Surgical Treatment. J. Bone Joint Surg., *52-A*, 937–956, 1970.

6. Eyler, Don L. and Markee, Joseph E.: The Anatomy and Function of the Intrinsic Musculature of the Fingers. J. Bone Joint Surg., *36-A*, 1–20, 1954.

7. Sunderland, Sydney: The Actions of the Extensor Digitorum Communis, Interosseous and Lumbrical Muscles. Amer. J. Anat., *77*, 189–209, 1945.

8. Williams, Roger J.: Chemical Anthropology—An Open Door. Amer. Scientist, *46*, 1–23, 1958.

9. Napier, J. R.: The Prehensile Movements of the Human Hand. J. Bone Joint Surg., *38-B*, 902–913, 1956.

10. Taylor, Craig L. and Schwartz, Robert J.: The Anatomy and Mechanics of the Human Hand. Artif. Limbs, *2*, 22–35, 1955.

11. Schmidt, Reynold T. and Toews, J. V.: Grip Strength As Measured by the Jamar Dynamometer. Arch. Phys. Med., *51*, 321–327, 1970.

12. Fisher, M. Bruce and Birren, James E.: Age and Strength. J. Appl. Physiol., *31*, 490–497, 1947.

13. Rasch, Philip J.: Hand Grip Exercises: Effect on Strength and Forearm Hypertrophy. Arch. Phys. Med., *44*, 507–510, 1963.

14. Bechtol, Charles O.: Grip Test. J. Bone Joint Surg., *36-A*, 820–824, 1954.

15. Rasch, Philip J. *et al.*: A Study of the Total Proportional Strength of Young Adult Males. Rev. Canad. Biol., *19*, 369–376, 1960.

16. Williams, Roger J.: Medical Tribune, July 7, 1965.

Recommended Reading

17. Marzke, Mary Walpole: Origin of the Human Hand. Am. J. Phys. Anthrop., *34*, 61–84, 1971.

Laboratory Exercises

1. Study the number of tendons, nerves, and blood vessels which traverse the wrist and hand areas. Are these well protected from possible incisions?

2. With the wrist completely hyperextended, try to extend the fingers completely. Discuss the reasons why this is difficult or impossible.

3. Completely flex the wrist and attempt to flex the fingers completely. Why is this impossible?

4. Extend the fingers. Explain why they tend to spread apart.

5. Using a goniometer, measure the amount of abduction and adduction of the wrist. Measure the amount of flexion and extension of the wrist with the fingers extended and with the hand tightly clenched.

6. Grasp a stick having about the same diameter as a broom handle. Have a laboratory partner forcibly flex your wrist and measure the angle of flexion when you are obliged to release the stick.

7. Using a hand dynamometer, measure the strength of the grasp in wrist hyperextension, neutral position, and flexion.

8. Using a goniometer, measure the entire range of rotation of the extended arm. There is some rotation in the midcarpal joint. Does the value just measured exceed the sum of shoulder joint rotation and radio-ulnar pronation-supination?

9. The tenth position shown in Figure 12–12 is known to surgeons as the "position of function" and is recommended by them as the best position in which a severely injured hand can become stiff. What are the kinesiological reasons for this? (Suggestion: See William L. White: Restoration of Function and Balance of the Wrist and Hand by Tendon Transfers. Surg. Clin. North America, *40*, 427–459, 1960.)

Chapter 13

Movements of the Spinal Column

The bony axis of the trunk, called the spinal column, consists of 33 vertebrae; 24 of these are joined to form a flexible column. Seven vertebrae are in the neck and are called cervical vertebrae; 12 are in the region of the chest and are called thoracic or dorsal vertebrae; 5 are in the lumbar region; 5 are fused together to form the sacrum, the rear portion of the pelvis; the lower 4 are only partially developed and form the coccyx. The spinal column is flexible above the sacrum, upon which the flexible portion rests. Each vertebra bears the weight of all parts of the body above it, and since the lower ones have to bear much more weight than the upper ones, the former are much the larger. The flexibility of the column makes it possible to balance the weight upon the vertebrae in sitting and standing.

Each vertebra has several points of interest. The body is the largest portion and the most important, since the weight is transmitted through it; passing to the rear are the two pedicles, then the two laminae, the five enclosing the vertebral foramen. A spinous process extends to the rear, and a transverse process from each side. Four articular processes, two above and two below, have articulations with the next vertebrae. Beneath each pedicle is an intervertebral notch, leaving a place for nerves to leave the spinal cord. Besides these points, to be found on all vertebrae, the thoracic vertebrae also have four articular processes or facets for the attachment of the ribs (Fig. 13–1).

The skeleton of the chest or thorax includes the sternum and twelve pairs of ribs, a pair for each thoracic vertebra. The ten upper ribs are attached to the sternum by the costal cartilages, the lower two being attached only to the vertebrae.

The vertebrae are separated by elastic disks of cartilage called the *intervertebral disks*, which are firmly joined to the bodies of the vertebrae and which permit movement of the column because of

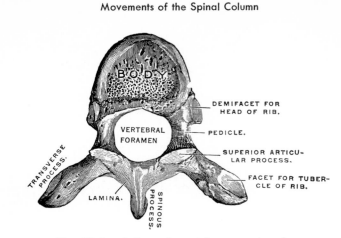

FIG. 13–1. A thoracic vertebra, superior view.

their elasticity. These disks are composed of a centrally located gel-like mass, the *nucleus pulposus,* which is surrounded by a heavy and strong layer of fibrocartilage, the *anulus fibrosus,* whose obliquely directed fibers prevent excessive movement in any direction. The deformable disk permits motion between the vertebrae while providing a cushion for them. When the nucleus pulposus is compressed, it exerts considerable centrifugal force on the fibers of the anulus, so that these are stretched, not compressed, on weight bearing. This can lead to herniation of the nucleus pulposus. The ends of each disk are closed by thin cartilaginous plates which adhere tightly to the bony surfaces of the vertebrae. Besides the union through the disks the vertebrae are joined by ligaments; the bodies by an anterior and a posterior common ligament extending from the skull to the sacrum along their front and rear surfaces and by short lateral ligaments joining the bodies of adjacent vertebrae; the laminae are joined by the ligamentum flava, which enclose the spinal canal, and the spinous processes by the interspinous ligaments. In the cervical region these processes are short and the interspinous ligaments are replaced by a single strong elastic ligament, the ligamentum nuchae or ligament of the neck. In quadrupeds this ligament has to support the weight of the head and is much larger than in man (Fig. 13–2).

The normal spinal column is approximately straight when viewed from the front to rear; it has a slight curve to right in the thoracic region, supposed by some to be due to the pressure of the aorta and by others to the pull of the right trapezius and rhomboid, which are used more than the muscles of the left side by right-handed individuals. This deviation from a straight line is too slight to be observed in the normal living subject.

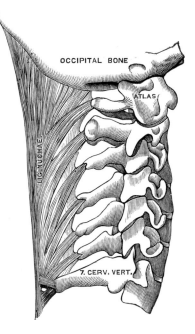

FIG. 13–2.   The ligament of the neck.

When the spinal column is viewed from the side, it presents four so-called normal curves: cervical and lumbar curves, concave to the rear, and thoracic and sacral curves, convex to the rear. These curves merge gradually into one another, the only approach to an angle being where the last lumbar vertebra joins the sacrum; the sharp bend here is due to the fact that the top of the sacrum slants forward about 45 degrees with the horizontal, giving the sacral angle (Fig. 13–3).

The thoracic curve exists before birth, and is chiefly due to the shape of the bodies of the vertebrae, which in this region are slightly thinner at their front edges (see Fig. 13–3). The cervical and lumbar curves are not present in the infant, which has a single curve convex to rear through the entire extent of the spine. The cervical curve is formed by the action of the infant's muscles when he begins to sit up and hold his head erect, and later to a more marked extent when he raises his head to look forward while creeping. The lumbar curve is formed in a similar way when he first stands on his feet. Up to this time the child's hip joints are kept flexed to a considerable extent; even when he lies on his back he seldom extends the hips fully. When he begins to stand on his feet the iliofemoral band is put on a stretch for the first time, holding the pelvis tilted forward; to rise to erect position he has to fully extend the spine in the lumbar region, which gives the normal curve. Until he develops more strength in

10

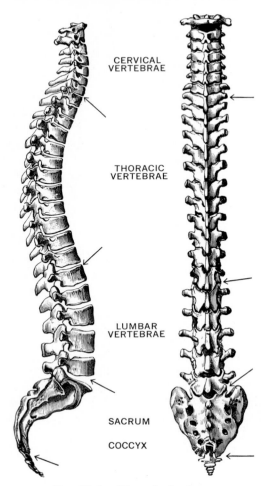

CERVICAL
VERTEBRAE

THORACIC
VERTEBRAE

LUMBAR
VERTEBRAE

SACRUM

COCCYX

FIG. 13–3.　The spinal column.

his legs and in the lumbar region and perfects the coordination, his position is somewhat stooped.

Movements of the spinal column take place by compression and traction of the elastic disks and by gliding of the articular surfaces upon each other. Bending the trunk forward, bringing the face toward the pubes, is called flexion; the opposite movement as far as the normal position is called extension; backward movement beyond a normal posture is hyperextension; bending sidewise is called lateral flexion and rotation on a vertical axis is called rotation or torsion.

Except for the first two cervical vertebrae there is relatively little movement in each individual joint although the total movement of all the joints may appear to be large. The ligaments joining the individual vertebrae are strong, thick, and taut, and permit little movement. Some regions are more mobile than others, partly because the ligaments are less taut. If the intervertebral disks are thick, more compression is possible, yielding a greater range of motion. In the thoracic region the overlapping and close proximity of the downward deflected spinous processes limit hyperextension, and the ribs, which make the spine a part of a semi-rigid cage, limit anterior and lateral movement. The position of the articular facets govern the direction and to some extent the amount of motion.

Flexion takes place in all regions of the spine but is most free in the lumbar region. By voluntary flexion young subjects can usually obliterate the lumbar and cervical curves and increase the thoracic curve. The shape of the articular processes in the lumbar region permits flexion and extension, while limiting other movements. The total amount of flexion possible in the spine is apt to be overestimated because the movements in the hip and in the joint between the head and the spine are easily mistaken for actual flexion of the trunk.

Extension is free in normal subjects; hyperextension is possible to a slight extent in the cervical and thoracic regions and to a much greater extent in the lumbar region and in the lower two thoracic segments.

Lateral flexion is possible to a slight degree at all levels, but is most free at the junction of the thoracic and lumbar regions. The ribs prevent much lateral movement in the region of the chest, and the interlocking processes prevent it in the lumbar region. Considerable lateral movement is possible in the neck.

Rotation is most free in the upper parts of the spine and less free as we pass downward, being prevented in the lumbar region by the processes. The shape of the articular processes permits rotation above, the limitation in the chest region being due to the ribs. Rotation is said to be to right or left according to the way it would turn the face. When the pelvis is fixed, as in standing or sitting, right rotation of the spine occurs if the head and shoulders are turned to the right. However, if the upper part of the spine is fixed, and the pelvis is turned to the *left* (as may occur while hanging by the hands from a horizontal bar), the action in the spinal column is still called *right* rotation. In this latter example, even though the head and shoulders were stationary, it is *as if* they had been turned to the right with respect to the pelvis.

Lateral flexion and rotation of the spine are usually described separately by authors on anatomy although the two movements never occur separately: lateral flexion of the trunk always involves rotation, and rotation of the trunk always involves lateral flexion.

The presence of rotation, accompanying all lateral flexion of the trunk, is explained by a law of mechanics stating that if a flexible rod is bent first in one plane and then, while it is in this bent position, it is bent again in a plane at right angles to the first, it always rotates on its longitudinal axis at the same time. When the subject bends forward, giving a condition always present in the thoracic region, it puts a tension on the ligaments at the rear (flava and interspinous) that makes them resist lateral flexion more than usual, while the weight, bearing down on the front edges of the bodies aids in the lateral bending. The result is that the bodies of the vertebrae go farther away from the vertical than do the spinous processes during lateral flexion. The general principle, which is self-evident and which helps one to remember in which direction the rotation will be, is that the concave side of the normal curve, being under pressure, turns to a convex side of the lateral curve. It follows that in the thoracic region a lateral bend rotates the spinous processes to the concave side and in the lumbar region to the convex side. The rotation which accompanies lateral flexion is a passive mechanical phenomenon, and does not require active contraction of rotator muscles. Furthermore, it is a local effect which seldom achieves sufficient magnitude to produce an externally-visible turning of the shoulders in relation to the hips.

The first and second cervical vertebrae deserve special attention because of their unique structure and function. The first, called the *atlas*, has no body but is a bony ring surrounding the spinal foramen. The spinous process is flattened but the two transverse processes are long. On its upper surface it has two large concave articular surfaces which accommodate the occipital condyles of the skull. These atlanto-occipital joints allow considerable flexion and extension of the head. The joint has a loose capsule but is spanned by two strong ligaments, the anterior and posterior atlanto-occipital ligaments.

The second vertebra, called the *axis*, has a short peg, called the *dens*, which extends vertically from its body into the vertebral foramen of the atlas where a very large ligament separates it from the spinal cord. This process serves as a pivot around which the atlas rotates rather freely, making it possible to rotate or shake the head from side to side. Movement in these two joints is relatively free compared to the other intervertebral articulations.

The muscles which produce spinal movements exist in bilateral pairs. Except for the quadratus lumborum, all spinal muscles are movers for either flexion or extension, in accordance with the following classification:

Pure Lateral Flexor—Quadratus lumborum

Flexors—
        Rectus abdominis
        External oblique
        Internal oblique
        Sternocleidomastoideus
        3 Scaleni
        Longus colli
        Longus capitis
        Rectus capitis anterior
        Rectus capitis lateralis
        Psoas

Extensors—
        Intertransversarii
        Interspinales
        Rotatores
        Multifidus
        Semispinalis thoracis
        Semispinalis cervicis
        Semispinalis capitis
        Iliocostalis lumborum
        Iliocostalis thoracis
        Iliocostalis cervicis
        Longissimus thoracis
        Longissimus cervicis
        Longissimus capitis
        Spinalis thoracis
        Spinalis cervicis
        Splenius cervicis
        Splenius capitis
        4 Suboccipital muscles

MUSCLE GROUPS

In medicine, surgery, and therapeutics, a knowledge of individual muscles is sometimes essential. For general analysis of movement, including nonmedical aspects of body mechanics, muscles may be studied in groups, thereby simplifying the material without any important loss of understanding. In Table 13–1, at the end of this chapter, muscles have been classified into two basic subdivisions: (1) those acting on the cervical spine, and (2) those acting on the thoracic and lumbar areas of the spine.

Muscles which produce, essentially, the same joint actions may also be grouped. The *abdominal group* includes the rectus abdominis, external oblique, and internal oblique muscles, which in common produce spinal flexion and lateral flexion, although their functions in rotation are different. Some anatomists would also include the transversalis, but this is a muscle of respiration which does not act on the spine. The *erector spinae group* includes the iliocostalis cervicis, longissimus cervicis, longissimus capitis, spinalis cervicis, iliocostalis thoracis, iliocostalis lumborum, longissimus thoracis, and spinalis thoracis, which act together to produce spinal flexion, lateral flexion, and rotation to the same side. The *deep posterior spinal group* includes the intertransversarii, interspinales, rotatores, and multifidus, which act together to produce spinal flexion, lateral flexion, and rotation to the opposite side. Functionally, the semispinalis thoracis is also a member of this group. Such groupings, which are indicated in Table 13–1, materially reduce the number of elements to be mastered or to be listed in activity analysis.

PURE LATERAL FLEXOR
QUADRATUS LUMBORUM

The "four-sided muscle of the loins" is a flat sheet of fibers on each side of the spinal column beneath the iliocostalis (Fig. 13–8).

Origin. The crest of the ilium, the ligament, and the transverse processes of the lower four lumbar vertebrae.

Insertion. The transverse processes of the upper two lumbar vertebrae and the lower border of the last rib.

Innervation. Branches of the twelfth thoracic and first lumbar nerves.

Structure. A flat sheet of fibers directed mainly in a vertical direction.

Action. Prime mover for lateral flexion to the same side. When both of these muscles act together, they depress the last ribs and assist in holding them down when the diaphragm contracts. Knapp[1] believes that its function is largely to stabilize the spine. Paralysis of the oblique fibers on one side causes a drop pelvis on the opposite side and is one cause of scoliosis.

THE FLEXORS OF THE SPINE
RECTUS ABDOMINIS

A rather slender muscle extending vertically across the front of the abdominal wall. The right and left recti are separated by a tendinous strip about an inch wide called the *linea alba* (white line) (Fig. 13–4).

Origin. The crest of the pubis.

Insertion. The cartilages of the fifth, sixth, and seventh ribs.

Innervation. Branches of the seventh to the twelfth intercostal nerves.

Structure. Parallel fibers, crossed by three tendinous intersections. The lower end of the rectus passes through a slit in the transversalis and lies beneath it.

Action. Prime mover for spinal flexion; contraction of one rectus abdominis alone assists with lateral flexion to the same side. In standing position, with the pelvis as the fixed point, the rectus will pull downward on the front of the chest, exerting its force on two sets of joints; those of the ribs and those of the spinal column. If the ribs are free to move, they will be depressed; if they do not move or after they have moved as far as they can move, it will flex the trunk. Unlike most muscles previously studied, the rectus abdominis usually follows a curved line when at rest and the first effect of its action will be to flatten the abdominal wall so as to bring it into a straight line.

Electromyographic studies[2] indicate that the contraction of the

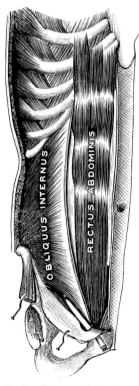

Fig. 13–4. Rectus abdominis and internal oblique.

Fig. 13–5. External oblique.

rectus abdominis and external oblique muscles is an important factor limiting the depth of voluntary maximal inspiration. It is believed that these muscles complete expiration rather than initiate it.

EXTERNAL OBLIQUE

This muscle covers the front and side of the abdomen from the rectus abdominis to the latissimus (Figs. 13–5 and 13–11).

Origin. By saw-tooth attachments to the lower eight ribs, in alternation with those of the serratus anterior and latissimus.

Insertion. The front half of the crest of the ilium, the upper edge of the fascia of the thigh, the crest of the pubis and the linea alba.

Innervation. Branches of the eighth to twelfth intercostal nerves, and iliohypogastric and ilioinguinal nerves.

Structure. A sheet of parallel fibers extending diagonally sideward and upward from the origin, the fibers of the pair forming a letter V on the front of the abdomen.

Action. Prime mover for flexion, lateral flexion to the same side, and rotation to the opposite side. The line of pull is too nearly coincident with the line of the rib it joins to give it much power to depress the chest. If the muscle of one side acts alone it will pull the origin forward and downward, causing a combination of flexion, lateral flexion, and rotation to the opposite side; if both muscles of the pair act at once the lateral pulls and the rotational tendencies are neutralized, giving pure flexion of the spinal column. The external oblique will tend to flatten the abdomen even more than the rectus because of its curved position around the side and front of it.

INTERNAL OBLIQUE

Situated beneath the externus, with fibers running at nearly right angles to those of the outer muscle (Fig. 13–4).

Origin. The lumbar fascia, the anterior two-thirds of the crest of the ilium, and the lateral half of the inguinal ligament.

Insertion. The cartilages of the eighth, ninth, and tenth ribs and the linea alba.

Innervation. Branches of the eighth to twelfth intercostal nerves, and the iliohypogastric and ilioinguinal nerves.

Structure. A sheet of slightly radiating fibers forming with the opposite muscle an inverted V on the front of the abdomen.

Action. Prime mover for flexion, lateral flexion to the same side, and rotation to the same side. Pulling downward and sideward on the front of the chest and abdomen, the internal oblique of one side will flatten the abdomen, rotate to the same side, and flex the trunk; working with its fellow it will cause pure flexion.

The rectus and the two oblique muscles of the abdomen act together in all movements of vigorous flexion of the trunk, as in rising to erect sitting position when lying on the back. When the movement begins slowly, the head being lifted first, the rectus acts alone, the obliques joining in when the shoulders begin to rise. In lateral flexion the abdominal muscles of one side act; in rotation, the external of the opposite side acts with the internal oblique of the same side.

Paralysis of the abdominal muscles gives rise to an excessive lumbar curve, produced by the unopposed action of the extensors. In the erect position these muscles are in continual contraction, possibly to protect the inguinal region from rupture,[3] in addition to assisting in the maintenance of the posture.

STERNOCLEIDOMASTOID

A pair of prominent muscles forming a letter V down the front and sides of the neck.

Origin. The anterior aspect of the sternum and medial (inner)

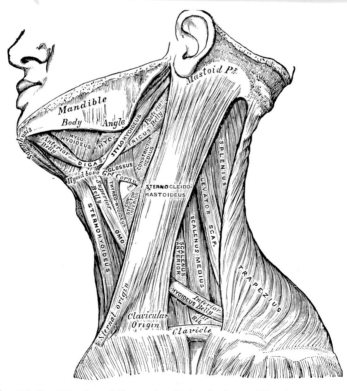

Fig. 13–6. Muscles of the neck. Lateral view. (*Gray's Anatomy.*)

third of the superior and anterior surfaces of the clavicle ("cleido" is the Latin root referring to the clavicle) (Fig. 13–6).

Insertion. The mastoid process of the skull.

Innervation. The spinal portion of the accessory nerve and branches from the anterior rami of the second and third cervical nerves.

Structure. Two bundles of parallel fibers uniting into a single bundle above the center.

Action. Acting on the head and cervical spine, it is a prime mover for flexion, lateral flexion, and rotation to the opposite side. If the head is stabilized, it may act as a muscle of respiration. This will be discussed further in the following chapter.

SCALENI

Three muscles, the scalenus anterior, scalenus medius, and scalenus posterior, named from their relative positions and their triangular form as a group (Fig. 13–7).

Origin. The transverse processes of the cervical vertebrae.

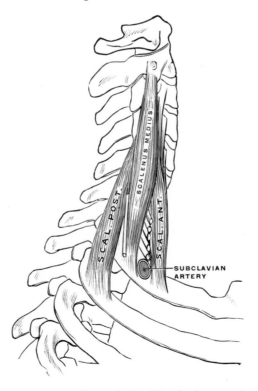

Fig. 13–7. The scaleni. (*Gray's Anatomy.*)

Insertion. The scalenus anterior and scalenus medius insert on the superior surface of the first rib; the scalenus posterior on the second rib.

Innervation. The scalenus anterior and scalenus medius receive branches from the lower cervical nerves. The posterior scalenus receives fibers from the anterior rami of the last three cervical nerves.

Structure. Longitudinal fibers, tendinous at each end.

Action. Prime mover for lateral flexion and assistant mover for flexion of the cervical spine. If the head is stabilized, it may act as a muscle of respiration. This will be discussed further in the following chapter.

LONGUS COLLI

Origin. Anterior tubercles of the transverse processes of the third to fifth cervical vertebrae and the anterior surface of the bodies of the last three cervical and first three thoracic vertebrae.

Insertion. The tubercle on the anterior arch of the atlas, the anterior surfaces of the bodies of the second through fourth cervical vertebrae, and the transverse processes of the fifth and sixth cervical nerves.

Innervation. Branches of the second to seventh cervical nerves.

Action. Assistant mover in flexion and lateral flexion of the cervical spine.

LONGUS CAPITIS

Origin. The anterior tubercles of the transverse processes of the third to sixth cervical vertebrae.

Insertion. Inferior surface of the basilar part of the occipital bone.

Innervation. Branches from the first three cervical nerves.

Action. Assistant mover for flexion and lateral flexion of the head and cervical spine.

RECTUS CAPITIS ANTERIOR

Origin. Anterior surface of the lateral mass of the atlas and the root of its transverse process.

Insertion. The inferior surface of the occipital bone anterior to the foramen magnum.

Innervation. Branches of the first and second cervical nerves.

Action. Assistant mover for flexion of the head.

RECTUS CAPITIS LATERALIS

Origin.   Superior surfaces of the transverse process of the atlas.
Insertion.   Inferior surfaces of the jugular process of the occipital bone.
Innervation.   Branches of the first and second cervical nerves.
Action.   Assistant movement for lateral flexion of the head.

THE EXTENSORS OF THE SPINE
INTERTRANSVERSARII

Pairs of small muscles, anterior and posterior, on each side of the spine, joining the transverse processes of adjacent vertebrae. They extend from the atlas to the first thoracic vertebra and from the tenth thoracic vertebra to the last lumbar vertebra.   The nerve supply is from both the anterior and posterior rami of the spinal nerves.

Action.   Prime mover for lateral flexion of the spine. If both sides act together, they are prime movers for extension and hyperextension of the spine.

INTERSPINALES

Pairs of small muscles joining the spinous processes of adjacent vertebrae, one on each side of the interspinal ligament.   Continuous in the cervical region extending from the axis to the second thoracic vertebra and in the lumbar region from the first lumbar vertebra to the sacrum.   They are innervated by the posterior rami of the spinal nerves.

Action.   Prime movers for extension and hyperextension of the spine.

ROTATORES

A series of pairs of small muscles extending from the sacrum to the axis.   Their fibers run upward and medially.

Origin.   The transverse processes of the vertebrae.
Insertion.   The bases of the spinous processes of the first and second vertebrae above.
Innervation.   Posterior rami of the spinal nerves.
Action.   Prime movers for rotation of the spine to the opposite side. If both sides act together, they are prime movers for extension and hyperextension of the spine.

MULTIFIDUS

A series of pairs of small muscles about 66 mm. long and 19 mm. wide found the full length of the spine just superficial to the rota-

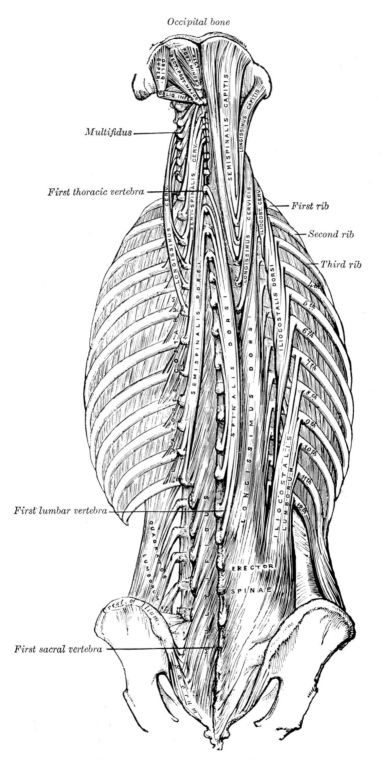

FIG. 13–8. Deep muscles of the back. (*Gray's Anatomy.*)

tores. The fibers run upward and medially, spanning two or three intervertebral spaces before inserting (Fig. 13–8).

Origin. The back of the sacrum, the dorsal end of the iliac crest, the transverse processes of the lumbar and the thoracic vertebrae, and the articular processes of the fourth to seventh cervical vertebrae.

Insertion. Spinous processes of all the vertebrae except the atlas.

Innervation. The posterior rami of the spinal nerves.

Action. Prime mover for lateral flexion, and rotation to the opposite side. If both sides act together, they are prime movers for extension and hyperextension of the spine.

SEMISPINALIS THORACIS

Origin. The transverse processes of the sixth to tenth thoracic vertebrae (Fig. 13–8).

Insertion. The spinous processes of the four upper thoracic and two lower cervical vertebrae.

Innervation. Posterior rami of thoracic nerves.

Action. Prime mover for lateral flexion, and rotation to the opposite side. If both sides act together, they are prime movers for extension and hyperextension of the spine.

SEMISPINALIS CERVICIS

Origin. The transverse processes of the upper five or six thoracic vertebrae (Fig. 13–8).

Insertion. The spinous processes from the axis to the fifth cervical vertebra.

Innervation. Posterior rami of the cervical nerves.

Action. Prime mover for lateral flexion, and rotation to the opposite side. If both sides act together, they are prime movers for extension and hyperextension of the spine.

SEMISPINALIS CAPITIS

Origin. Articular processes of the fourth through sixth cervical vertebrae and the transverse processes of the seventh cervical and first six thoracic vertebrae (Fig. 13–8).

Insertion. Between the superior and inferior nuchal lines of the occipital bone.

Innervation. The posterior rami of the cervical nerves.

Action. Prime mover for lateral flexion of the head and cervical spine. Prime mover for extension and hyperextension of the head and cervical spine when both sides act together.

ILIOCOSTALIS LUMBORUM

Origin. The posterior aspects of the sacrum, the spines of the lumbar vertebrae, and the iliac crest (Fig. 13–8).

Insertion. The inferior borders of the angles of the lower six or seven ribs.

Innervation. Posterior rami of the spinal nerves.

Action. Prime mover for lateral flexion, and rotation to the same side. If both sides act together, they are prime movers for extension and hyperextension of the spine.

ILIOCOSTALIS THORACIS

Origin. The upper borders of the angles of the last six ribs (Fig. 13–8).

Insertion. The upper borders of the angles of the upper six ribs.

Innervation. Posterior rami of the spinal nerves.

Action. Prime mover for lateral flexion, and rotation to the same side. If both sides act together, they are prime movers for extension and hyperextension of the spine.

ILIOCOSTALIS CERVICIS

Origin. The upper borders of the angles of the third to sixth ribs (Fig. 13–8).

Insertion. The transverse processes of the fourth to sixth cervical vertebrae.

Innervation. Posterior rami of the spinal nerves.

Action. Prime mover for lateral flexion, and rotation to the same side. If both sides act together, they are prime movers for extension and hyperextension of the spine.

LONGISSIMUS THORACIS

Origin. The posterior aspects of the sacrum, the spines of the lumbar vertebrae, and the iliac crest (Fig. 13–8).

Insertion. Accessory processes of the first to the fifth lumbar vertebrae, transverse processes of the first thoracic to the fifth lumbar vertebrae, and into the second to twelfth ribs between their tubercles and angles.

Innervation. Posterior rami of the spinal nerves.

Action. Prime mover for lateral flexion, and rotation to the same side. If both sides act together, they are prime movers for extension and hyperextension of the spine.

LONGISSIMUS CERVICIS

Origin. The transverse processes of the first four to six thoracic vertebrae (Fig. 13–8).

Insertion. The transverse processes of the second to sixth cervical vertebrae.

Innervation. Posterior rami of the spinal nerves.

Action. Prime mover for cervical spine extension, hyperextension, and rotation to the same side. Possible assistant mover for lateral flexion.[4]

LONGISSIMUS CAPITIS

Origin. The transverse processes of the first four thoracic and the articular processes of the last four cervical vertebrae (Fig. 13–8).

Insertion. Mastoid process of the skull.

Innervation. The posterior rami of the spinal nerves.

Action. Prime mover for rotation of the head, and lateral flexion of the head and cervical spine. Prime mover for extension and hyperextension of the head when both sides act together.

SPINALIS THORACIS

Origin. The spines of the first two lumbar and last two thoracic vertebrae (Fig. 13–8).

Insertion. The spines of the upper thoracic vertebrae, the number varying from four to eight.

Innervation. Posterior rami of the spinal nerves.

Action. Prime mover for lateral flexion. If both sides act together, they are prime movers for extension and hyperextension of the spine.

SPINALIS CERVICIS

This muscle is often absent.

Origin. Lower part of the ligamentum nuchae, spinous process of the seventh cervical vertebra, and sometimes from the spinous processes of the first and second thoracic vertebrae.

Insertion. The spinous process of the axis, and occasionally the spinous processes of the second and third cervical vertebrae.

Innervation. Posterior rami of the lower cervical nerves.

Action. Prime mover for lateral flexion. If both sides act together, they are prime movers for extension and hyperextension of the spine.

SPLENIUS CERVICIS

A broad sheet of muscle whose fibers pass upward and laterally to the cervical spine (Fig. 13–9).

Origin.   Spinous processes of the third to the sixth thoracic vertebrae.

Insertion.   Transverse processes of the upper two or three cervical vertebrae.

Innervation.   Posterior rami of the lower cervical nerves.

Action.   Prime mover for lateral flexion and rotation to the same side.   If both sides act together, they are prime movers for extension and hyperextension of the spine.

SPLENIUS CAPITIS

A broad sheet of muscle whose fibers pass upward and laterally to the skull.   The greater portion of the muscle is covered by the trapezius, and it covers the semispinalis capitis (Figs. 13–6 and 13–9).

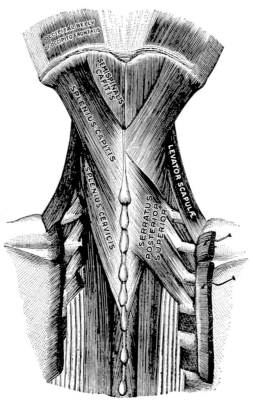

FIG. 13–9.   The splenius and the serratus posterior superior.

Origin. The lower half of the ligamentum nuchae, and the spinous processes of the seventh cervical and the upper three or four thoracic vertebrae.

Insertion. Occipital bone and mastoid process of the temporal bone.

Innervation. Lateral branches of the posterior rami of the middle and lower cervical nerves.

Action. Prime mover for rotation to the same side, and lateral flexion of the head and cervical spine. Prime mover for extension and hyperextension of the head and cervical spine when both sides act together.

SUBOCCIPITAL MUSCLES

Four muscles: rectus capitis posterior major, rectus capitis posterior minor, obliquus capitis superior, and obliquus capitis inferior (Fig. 13–8).

Origin. Posterior surfaces of the atlas and axis.

Insertion. The first three, deep on the occipital bones; the last, the transverse process of the atlas.

Innervation. Branches of the suboccipital nerve.

Action. Assistant movers for lateral flexion of the head, and for rotation of the head to the same side. Assistant movers for extension and hyperextension of the head when both sides act together.

MOVEMENTS OF THE TRUNK

The muscles of the spine occur in pairs, placed in bilateral symmetry. Lateral stability is maintained by intermittent contraction of the muscles each side of the center line, with the muscles of one side counteracting any tendency to fall toward the opposite side. The quadratus lumborum, internal and external obliques, and erector spinae group are the main lateral stabilizers (Fig. 13–10). Under the stress of load carrying the short deep muscles of the back stabilize the individual joints and tend to reduce lumbar lordosis. If the line of gravity falls anterior to the axis of the lumbosacral joint, any increase in the load will cause an increase in the contraction of the superficial long back muscles; if the line of gravity falls behind this axis, the abdominal muscles will contract.[5] Electromyographic studies,[3,6,7] have confirmed this pattern of postural stabilization, with intermittent and finely graduated contractions appearing to be correlated with body sway. Erect posture is not a firm, rigid position, but the result of a precisely integrated series of continuous dynamic adjustments which are appropriately graded by the feedback from

Fig. 13–10.   The back of Paul Wynter, 1960 Professional Mr. Universe.   His unusually massive erector spinae (ES) muscles must have played an important role in his winning of the title.   (Courtesy Rader.)

kinesthetic sensations originating in muscles, ligaments, tendons, labyrinths, and oculomotor apparatus.

Erect Standing Position.   The problem of stabilizing the body at the spinal joints is more difficult than is the problem of stabilizing it at the knee and hip joints.   The fact that there are two lower limbs to act as weight bearing extremities simplifies the stabilization of the body in the lateral plane.   The spine is a single weight bearing column which depends entirely upon muscular strength for both lateral and anterior-posterior stabilization.   The knee and hip joints may be "locked" in slight hyperextension, allowing the small gravitational torques tending to destroy balance to be borne by the ligaments; but in the spine the joints cannot be locked, and the normal antero-posterior curves are constantly subject to gravitational torques which tend to increase them and thus destroy upright stability.   If the spinal muscles are weak or if they lack endurance, curvature in any direction may increase markedly, and ligaments may be subject to acute or chronic stresses.   These excessive curvatures become pathological in geometric proportion to their extent.

Movements from Standing Position.   From an erect standing position, in which momentary perfect balance is assumed, a voluntary spinal movement in any direction is initiated by momentary concentric contraction of the movers for that joint action.   With equilibrium thus destroyed, gravitational force enters as the "prime mover" for continuance of the movement; that is, the trunk tends to fall in that direction.   In the fraction of a second that the gravitational movement commences, the muscles antagonistic to the movement spring into action, contracting eccentrically to modify or "brake" the gravitational acceleration and to lower the trunk under control in the desired direction. As the movement continues, the eccentrically-contracting muscles are elongated until ligaments (and sometimes also fascial bands) become taut. If the momentum of the movement is sufficiently great, these ligaments may be torn, but usually they are strong enough to absorb the stress and to stop the movement. At the point at which ligaments take over the stresses of gravity, the muscles relax and the individual's torso may literally hang from his intervertebral ligaments. A small amount of further motion may be possible if the prime movers for the particular joint action contract strongly and force the ligaments to extend slightly.

From the position of trunk flexion the return to the erect position is begun by extension of the hip joint, initiated by the muscles of the buttocks and legs. In dead lifting (the "derrick lift") the lifting effort is usually accompanied by contraction of the gastrocnemius and soleus, with a resultant tendency for the heels to rise from the ground. This tendency is counterbalanced by an opposing moment produced by the body weight. In most practical lifting operations the maximum lifting force is limited by the maximum counterbalancing moment which the body weight can provide, and that only in exceptional cases will the muscular strength of the trunk extensors be the limiting factor.[8] Body proportions may also be of some importance.

The common industrial injury to the back is usually a simple myofascial strain, but a suddenly increased stress, such as is encountered in lifting a weight in this position, may rupture the anulus fibrosus or other intervertebral ligaments. Back disorders resulting from lifting are responsible for as much as 12 per cent of all industrial injuries. Between 85 and 99 per cent of all serious back injuries occur at the L4/L5 and L5/S1 levels.[9] Many weight trainers utilize a springy platform known as a "hopper" to reduce the danger of back injuries while performing dead lifts.

Between 80 and 90 per cent of all backaches result from faulty mechanical and postural habits.[10] These aggravate lumbar and sacral structures by placing them under relatively mild, but continuous, stress. Probably most of these trace to a continued mild overstretching of the ligaments and muscles involved.

A kinesiologically instructive injury is seen in "shoveler's fracture." It occasionally happens that the load sticks to a shovel when it is swung and, if the man has a firm footing, draws his arms forward with considerable force. This force is transmitted from the arms to the shoulder girdle, thence to the trapezius, rhomboids, and other powerful back muscles, and finally to the spinous processes, which may be fractured. It is possible that the pull of the ligamentum nuchi and the interspinal ligaments may produce a similar trauma in cases of whip lash injury.[11]

Long Sitting Position. In this position, the knees are extended so that the calf and hamstring muscles are flat against the floor, and the trunk is held perpendicularly erect. So long as the hands are not placed on the floor to help support the trunk, this position cannot be held passively but requires marked static contraction of several muscle groups. The taut hamstrings tend to tilt the pelvis backward; this tendency must be counteracted by static contraction of hip flexors and abdominal muscles. The downward pull of the abdominals on the rib cage tends to flex the thoracic spine; this tendency must be counteracted by marked static contraction of the extensors of the thoracic spine. While holding the position, the hamstrings and lumbar spine extensors are being stretched. Thus, the position has general postural corrective values.

Hook Sitting Position. This is similar to long sitting position, except that the knees are flexed and the heels are drawn up toward the buttocks, with soles flat on the floor. The knee flexion removes almost all tension in the hamstrings, and the hip flexion slackens the iliopsoas so much that it is unable to shorten sufficiently to pull on the pelvis. Therefore, the pelvis assumes a natural backward tilt, being restrained only by the stretched rectus femoris. The lumbar curve tends to be obliterated under the influence of static contraction in the abdominals, which are contracting in order to hold the trunk erect. The abdominals pull downward on the rib cage, necessitating contraction of the extensors of the thoracic spine. Compared to long sitting position, the hook sitting position has the additional value of minimizing activity by the iliopsoas and of providing a greater stretch for the lumbar spine extensors.

Long Lying Position, Supine. With the knees, hips, and spine extended in this position, gravity tends to eliminate or minimize all spinal curves. The iliopsoas and the Y-ligament are moderately stretched, as are lumbar spine extensors, thoracic spine flexors, and shoulder girdle abductors. Circulatory stasis in the great veins of the lower extremity and abdominal cavity is discouraged because the return of venous blood to the heart is much easier in the horizontal position.

The great disadvantage of the long lying position results from the tension which is applied to the iliopsoas and the Y-ligament. In the individual who has excessive lumbar curvature (lordosis), the tension in the iliopsoas and the Y-ligament combines with the tension produced by the short lumbar extensor muscles to cause forward pelvic tilt. Gravity may only partly remedy this, and in some individuals there may be up to 4 inches or more of vertical space between the floor and the highest point in the lumbar curve. Such excessive curvature elongates and stretches the abdominals, and may make it impossible to perform curling situps. In milder cases of lumbar curvature, voluntary contraction of the abdominal muscles may be sufficient to flatten the lumbar curve. Such lumbar flattening (or backward pelvic tilt) is itself a good corrective exercise, since the abdominals are strengthened while the lumbar extensors and iliopsoas are stretched.

Hook Lying Position. This is similar to long lying position, except that the knees are flexed and the heels are drawn up toward the buttocks, with soles flat on the floor. The hook lying position has all the advantages of the long lying position, without the undesirable tension on the hamstrings, iliopsoas, and Y-ligament, which are made slack by the knee and hip flexion. The hook lying position, when used as a starting or terminal position for exercise, minimizes the activity of the iliopsoas, provided that the legs are not held down by a partner, strap, or other apparatus.[12]

ANALYSIS OF MOVEMENTS IN TRUNK EXERCISES

The Trunk Curl. From the long lying position, supine, a trunk curl commencing at the upper levels of the spine will carry the trunk about one-third of the way toward the sitting position. (The rest of the situp consists primarily of hip flexion.) As the head is lifted at the start of the curl, the rectus abdominis springs into action simultaneously with the sternocleidomastoid. The oblique abdominals come into action almost immediately afterwards, as the curl is continued, but the intensity of their activity never approaches that of the recti[3] unless exceptional resistance is encountered. The curl is valuable because it activates abdominals without requiring significant activity in the hip flexors. Walters and Partridge[12] demonstrated greater activity in the *upper* portions of the rectus abdominis when no resistance other than body weight was employed, but an equal activity in upper and lower portions when an extra 10-pound weight was harnessed to the shoulders.

The Reverse Trunk Curl. In this exercise, knees and hips are flexed, and knees are drawn toward the chest so that the curl commences at the lower spinal levels. All abdominals are active, and Walters' and Partridge's[12] experiment showed that activity was greater in the lower portions of the rectus abdominis than in the upper portions. There is reason to believe that the obliques are more active in reverse curls than in regular curls. Because of the flexed knees and hips, the hip flexors do not encounter great resistance in reverse curls. The amount of resistance to contraction of the abdominals may be increased by performing reverse curls from a position of hanging by the hands from a bar.

Double Leg Raising. Raising the straight legs requires contraction of abdominals against strong resistance, but the contraction tends to be static. Hip flexion predominates over spine flexion, making the exercise better suited for developing the iliopsoas than the abdominals. In weaker individuals, the abdominals may be unable to stabilize the pelvis, and lumbar hyperextension may actually be increased.

Single Leg Raising. Muscle contraction is similar to that involved in double leg raising, except that the intensity of activity is much less. The abdominal muscles on the same side as the lifted leg are more active than their opposite counterparts, and the internal oblique is more active than the other abdominals.[3]

Double Leg Circling. This exercise starts from supine lying position with knees drawn up to the chest. The legs are dropped to one side, knees and hips are extended, and the legs are circled through long lying position around to the opposite side, whereupon hips and knees are again flexed and returned to starting position. The pattern of muscular contraction is almost opposite to that of regular trunk curls—although all abdominals contract, the external oblique is markedly more active than the rectus abdominis. The long lever of the extended legs offers considerable resistance to the iliopsoas.

Situps. The complete situp adds an important hip-flexion phase to trunk curling. There is little reason to believe that the whole situp is superior to trunk curls from the standpoint of abdominal development, since an emphasis upon contraction of the iliopsoas is usually considered undesirable. Electromyographically, the abdominals are involved more and more strongly as the starting position is changed from long lying to hook lying.[12] The first 30 degrees of hip flexion in the situp in the long lying position are performed with little activity in the iliopsoas. In the hook lying position the iliopsoas is electrically active through the entire range of hip movement, but is required to exert but little force, as the pelvis is stabilized by the rectus femoris.[13] Whether in long lying or hook lying position, the activity of the hip flexors is increased when the feet are held down, and the activity of the abdominals is increased when they are not held down.

Arm flinging makes it easier to perform situps because the momentum of the arms is transferred to the trunk, substituting for contraction of hip and spine flexors. If the object is to sit up with the least expenditure of energy, arm flinging should be employed; if the object is development of muscles, it should be eliminated.

A trunk twist may be added to the situp exercise, touching one hand to the opposite foot, after the situp is complete. Electromyographic studies show that this extra twisting results from the contraction of both the internal obliques[12] and the external obliques.[14]

ACTION OF THE PSOAS ON THE SPINE

The psoas is primarily a flexor of the hip, although it is also listed as a flexor of the lumbar spine. The use of an articulated skeleton to study its origin and angle of pull is recommended, since two-dimensional drawings may be misleading.

Under special circumstances, the psoas may become a *hyperextensor* of the lumbar spine. This reversal of function is sometimes called the *psoas paradox*. It generally occurs when the body is in supine lying position. As the psoas contracts, it is joined by the iliacus in flexing the hip joint, and it tends to pull on the lumbar vertebrae in an anterior and inferior direction. If the abdominals contract simultaneously, forward tilt of the pelvis is prevented, and lumbar flexion and/or hip flexion will result. But if the abdominals are weak, the pelvis tilts forward under influence of the iliacus while the lumbar vertebrae are raised off the floor (lumbar hyperextension) by the psoas. The passive weight of the head and thorax prevent the trunk from flexing in response to the pull of the psoas. There is said to be a significant correlation between the cross-sectional area of the psoas and the degree of lumbar curvature.[15]

Adequate contraction of the abdominals would prevent the psoas from hyperextending the lumbar spine, but there is a fairly consistent tendency for abdominal strength to be inferior, functionally, to psoas strength. Furthermore, the human body tends to have pre-existing excessive lumbar curvature of an inflexible nature. Therefore, it is a principle of general therapeutic and conditioning exercise to emphasize abdominal development and to minimize iliopsoas development in an attempt to achieve a better balance between the two muscle groups. Many proposed "abdominal exercises," such as double leg lifting, activate the paradoxical function of the psoas as a lumber spine hyperextensor, and cause unwarranted stretch and stress in the abdominals.

Probably it is advisable for all people to avoid "psoas exercises," but it is particularly important for the weaker or undervitalized individual to do so. If, when attempting an exercise that calls for flexion of the lumbar spine, an individual's first effort is accompanied by lumbar hyperextension, that exercise is contra-indicated. Since the forward lunge applies the maximum mechanical leverage against the iliopsoas, it is an excellent exercise for stretching this muscle.

IMPLICATIONS FOR ATHLETIC TRAINING

A supporting column is normally rigid; in the human spine, how-ever, nature has sacrificed rigidity in order to secure a relatively wide range of movement. The result of this attempt to combine two incompatible qualities is an unstable structure which may be seri-ously deranged by sports as diverse as golf and weight lifting. Back injuries are particularly common in sports such as wrestling, trampoline, diving, and pole vaulting, in which strong rotational movements of the back are frequent, and weight lifting and pyramid building, where loads may be attempted which are too heavy for the muscles to tolerate. These injuries are very painful, slow to heal, and extremely liable to recurrence. The victim will complain that there is no position which he can assume with comfort. Usually the erector spinae muscle group is the one injured; occasionally the quadratus lumborum may be involved. Injuries of this type are commonly referred to as sacro-iliac strains; actually the construction of the bony framework of that area suggests that it is almost impos-sible to injure it in the course of normal activity. Probably most back injuries incurred in athletics are actually in the lumbosacral area. These muscles readily go into spasm from injury or inflam-

Fig. 13–11. Abdominal muscles of Bob Hinds. The development of the external obliques is unusual and is seen only in individuals who have exercised these muscles vigorously over a long period. In early physical training literature such hypertro-phied external obliques were often referred to by the poetic name "Girdle of Apollo." The "washboard" appearance of the rectus abdominis illustrates the persistence of myotomic segmentation in many human muscles. (Courtesy Rader.)

TABLE 13–1.   Spinal Muscles and Their Actions

CERVICAL SPINE

Muscles	Flexion	Extension	Lateral Flexion	Rotation to the Same Side	Rotation to the Opposite Side
Sternocleidomastoid	P.M.		P.M.		P.M.
The 3 scaleni	Asst.		P.M.		
The prevertebral group (Longus colli, longus capitis, rectus capitis anterior, rectus capitis lateralis)	Asst.		Asst.		
Splenius capitis and splenius cervicis		P.M.	P.M.	P.M.	
The erector spinae group (Iliocostalis cervicis, longissimus cervicis, longissimus capitis, and spinalis cervicis)		P.M.	P.M.	P.M.	
Semispinalis cervicis		P.M.	P.M.	P.M.	
Semispinalis capitis		P.M.	P.M.		
The deep posterior spinal group					
Intertransversarii		P.M.	P.M.		
Interspinales		P.M.			
Rotatores		P.M.			P.M.
Multifidus		P.M.	P.M.		P.M.
The suboccipital group		Asst.	Asst.	Asst.	

THORACIC AND LUMBAR SPINES

Muscles	Flexion	Extension	Lateral Flexion	Rotation to the Same Side	Rotation to the Opposite Side
The abdominal group					
Rectus abdominis	P.M.		Asst.		
External oblique	P.M.		P.M.		P.M.
Internal oblique	P.M.		P.M.	P.M.	
Psoas	Asst.	Asst.*			
Quadratus lumborum			P.M.		
The erector spinae group					
Iliocostalis thoracis		P.M.	P.M.	P.M.	
Iliocostalis lumborum		P.M.	P.M.	P.M.	
Longissimus thoracis		P.M.	P.M.	P.M.	
Spinalis thoracis		P.M.	P.M.		
Semispinalis thoracis		P.M.	P.M.		P.M.
The deep posterior spinal group					
Intertransversarii		P.M.	P.M.		
Interspinales		P.M.			
Rotatores		P.M.			P.M.
Multifidus		P.M.	P.M.		P.M.

* Under special circumstances (which are described in the text), the psoas may become a hyperextensor of the lumbar spine. The iliacus may contribute to this action, indirectly, by tilting the pelvis forward.

mation and become acutely painful. The application of heat and supportive adhesive strapping or supportive belts to the affected area will give relief. In mild cases slow but extensive gentle stretching may ease the spasm.

In instances in which an individual complains of low back pain without the occurrence of an injury, the kinesiologist should carefully examine the length of the legs and the height of the iliac crests to determine whether they are even. If they are not, this may be the source of the difficulty.

Strong abdominal musculature is necessary to resist successfully blows which might otherwise reach the vital organs. At the least such blows may cause an interruption in respiration, as in the "solar plexus" punch; at worst they may cause hemorrhage or an actual lesion in one of the underlying organs. The fact that these muscles are so little employed in ordinary activity necessitates the use of very specific exercises. In many cases the exerciser works the frontal muscles to a satisfactory degree, but overlooks the fact that the side muscles need equally vigorous training. Major ruptures of the abdominal wall, as sometimes result from pushing, throwing, or boxing, require surgical repair.

The question of whether the development of the abdominal musculature aids in the prevention of hernia is a matter for argument. In the opinion of some surgeons, hernia results from an innate defect in the abdominal wall, and it seems unlikely that any appreciable benefit is derived from preventive exercises. On the other hand many therapists with a good deal of experience with exercise are convinced that abdominal development contributes to the prevention of this condition. The answer probably lies in the cause of the individual injury.

References

1. Knapp, Miland E.: Function of the Quadratus Lumborum. Arch. Phys. Med., *32*, 505–507, 1957.

2. Campbell, E. J. M.: *The Respiratory Muscles and the Mechanics of Breathing.* Chicago: Year Book Publishers, Inc., 1958, p. 41.

3. Floyd, W. F. and Silver, P. H. S.: Electromyographic Study of Patterns of Activity of the Anterior Abdominal Wall Muscles in Man. J. Anat., *84*, 132–145, 1950.

4. Fountain, Freeman P., *et al.*: Function of Longus Colli and Longissimus Cervicis Muscles in Man. Arch. Phys. Med., *47*, 665–669, 1966.

5. Klausen, Klaus: The Form and Function of the Loaded Human Spine. Acta Physiol. Scand., *65*, 176–190, 1965.

6. Morris, J. M., *et al.*: An Electromyographic Study of the Intrinsic Muscles of the Back in Man. J. Anat., *96*, 509–520, 1962.

7. Portnoy, Harold and Morin, F.: Electromyographic Study of Postural Muscles in Various Positions and Movements. Amer. J. Physiol., *186*, 122–126, 1956.

8. Whitney, R. J.: The Strength of the Lifting Action in Man. Ergonomics, *1*, 101–128, 1958.

9. Chaffin, Don B.: A Computerized Biomechanical Model—Development of and Use in Studying Gross Body Actions. J. Biomech., *2*, 429–441, 1969.

10. Flint, M. Marilyn: Effect of Increasing Back and Abdominal Strength on Low Back Pain. Res. Quart., *29*, 160–171, 1958.

11. Budin, Earl, *et al.*: Shoveler's Fracture—A Changing Concept. J. Einstein Med. Center, *2*, 109–112, 1954.

12. Walters, C. Etta and Partridge, Miriam J.: Electromyographic Study of the Differential Action of the Abdominal Muscles During Exercise. Amer. J. Phys. Med., *36*, 259–268, 1957.

13. Partridge, Miriam J. and Walters, C. Etta: Participation of the Abdominal Muscles in Various Movements of the Trunk in Man. Phys. Ther. Rev., *39*, 791–800, 1959.

14. LaBan, Myron M., *et al.*: Electromyographic Study of Function of Iliopsoas Muscle. Arch. Phys. Med., *46*, 676–679, 1965.

15. Aaron, C. and Gillot, C.: Muscles psoas et courbures lombaires. C. R. Ass. Anat., *116*, 159–169, 1963.

Recommended Reading

16. Brown, Isadore: Intensive Exercises for the Low Back. Phys. Ther., *50*, 487–498, 1970.

Laboratory Exercises

1. In a feature article in the Los Angeles *Times* for July 10, 1960 a drama coach recommends picking things up by bending at the waist while keeping the knees straight, thus, "you stretch and strengthen the muscles of the lower back and legs so that the body can go into the correct alignment." Discuss the kinesiology of this advice. Why do many kinesiologists believe that such actions contribute to poor posture, if not trauma?

2. Weight trainers sometimes place a heavy barbell on their shoulders and then twist the trunk alternately to the right and the left. What is the danger of this exercise?

3. Analyze the differences in the function of the spine in an erect biped and in a quadruped. (Suggestion: See Napier, John: The Antiquity of Human Walking. Scientific Amer., *216*, 56–66, 1967.)

4. What sort of exercises might be recommended for a person known to be subject to low back disability?

5. What would be the difference in muscular development achieved through practice of the wrestler's bridge in the supine position as compared with practice of it in the prone position?

6. What are the disadvantages to sleeping in a excessively soft bed? Why is a person with a back injury more comfortable on a firm surface than on a yielding one?

7. Compare the effects of leg raising and situps on the floor with those of the same exercise done on an inclined board.

8. Aikido students are often taught the following exercise "to strengthen their abdominal muscles": The student kneels down, bends over backwards until his back is on the mat, and then straightens up again. Analyze the kinesiology of this movement. What muscles are principally affected? Would you consider it a desirable exercise? Why?

9. Toe touching from the erect position is sometimes recommended for the development of the abdominal musculature. Analyze the value of this recommendation.

10. Have a subject lie supine on a bench. Have another student straddle the bench and hold the subject's hips firmly in contact with it. Instruct the subject to sit up. Measure the angle through which he can move.

11. Spinal rotation is named right or left according to the direction in which the face is turned. If the upper part of the spine is stabilized and the lower part of the spine is turned, the rotation is called right or left according to which direction the face would have turned had it been the moving part. Specify the direction of spinal rotation in the following exercises:

(a) From erect standing position, turn head and shoulders to the left.

(b) From a position of hanging by the hands from a bar, turn the pelvis and legs to the left.

(c) From supine lying with legs raised to vertical, lower both legs sideways left to the floor while keeping the shoulders flat on the floor.

Chapter 14

Muscles of the Thorax and Respiration

The framework of the thorax includes the twelve thoracic vertebrae, twelve pairs of ribs, the costal cartilages, and the sternum.
The *head* of each rib articulates with the body of the similarly numbered thoracic vertebra by means of a synovial joint with a ligamentous capsule, and (except for the first, tenth, eleventh, and
twelfth ribs) with the body of the thoracic vertebra immediately
above. Each rib has a *tubercle* which makes a synovial articulation
with the tip of the transverse process of its own vertebra. The part
between the head and the tubercle is called the *neck*. The remainder
of the rib is the long curving body, and its point of sharpest curvature is called the *angle*. The ends of the ribs are continuous with the
costal cartilages. These hyaline bars are normal epiphyseal cartilage. They may ossify partially or completely after puberty. The
first seven costal cartilages join the sternum either directly or by
means of an interposed synovial joint. The eighth through tenth
costal cartilages do not join the sternum, but are continuous with the
costal cartilage immediately above. The eleventh and twelfth costal
cartilages are free; their ribs are known as "floating ribs." The
sternum is made up of three parts, named, from above down, the
manubrium, the *body*, and the *xiphoid process*. They are joined by
epiphyseal cartilages which do not ossify until after middle age. In
youth, the body has four parts separated by epiphyseal cartilages.

The ribs may be raised and lowered by means of motion in the
synovial articulations with the vertebrae; in addition, the thin
shafts, the costal cartilages, and the sternum are rather markedly
deformable. The sum of these possible movements is appreciable.
Rib cage movements are usually considered as a whole, and are
called *elevation* and *depression* (Fig. 14–1). The movements of elevation and depression should not be confused with the general
raising and lowering of the entire thorax caused by extension and

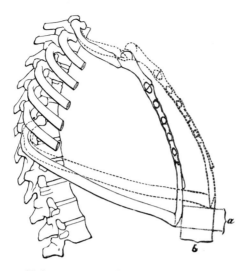

Fig. 14–1.   Enlargement of the chest by elevation of the ribs.

flexion of the thoracic spine.   Likewise, adduction of the shoulder girdle gives the appearance of chest expansion which should not be confused with true movements of the rib cage.   Technically, elevation and depression of the rib cage occur only in conjunction with breathing movements.

Breathing is the flow of air in or out of the lungs (inspiration and expiration) associated with elevation and depression of the rib cage and with the descent and return of the floor of the thorax resulting from contraction and relaxation of the diaphragm muscle.

Within the rib cage are the right and left *pleural cavities*, separated medially by the mediastinum, a partition containing the heart in its pericardial sac, blood vessels, nerves, lymph vessels, thymus gland, esophagus, trachea and bronchi, connective tissue, and the two lungs.   The lungs may be thought of as having grown out of the mediastinum and invaded the right and left pleural cavities until the cavities are obliterated by the pushing of their medial wall against their lateral walls.   Thus the pleural cavities have no air space within them, but only potential spaces containing a slight amount of fluid.   Actually, the idea of the lungs "pushing outward" is false, for the lungs have a marked elasticity which constantly tends to make them contract or shrivel.   Since the pleural cavities are completely self-inclosed, air cannot enter them, and their slight negative pressure (loosely called a "partial vacuum") allows the atmospheric pressure of air in the lungs to overcome the natural contractile tendency of the lungs and to push the walls of the lungs outward against the rib cage, virtually obliterating the pleural cavities. If the thorax is punctured from the outside, air rushes into the pleural cavity until atmospheric pressure is established, equalling the atmospheric pressure of the air within the lungs. Because the natural elasticity of the lungs is now unopposed, the lung shrivels up around its root in the mediastinum.

During inspiration, the ribs are elevated, enlarging the antero-posterior diameter of the thorax (Fig. 14–1). The bodies of the ribs, especially the lower ones, also move laterally, increasing the lateral thoracic diameter. Simultaneously, the dome-shaped diaphragm contracts and flattens the floor of the thorax, increasing the vertical diameter. With the thoracic volume thus enlarged, atmospheric pressure causes air to enter the lungs and expand them. Muscular contraction, then, is necessary for even the smallest amount of inspiration.

At resting levels of breathing, no muscular contraction is necessary for expiration. The muscles relax, and the weight of the thorax causes depression of the ribs. The natural elasticity of the lungs draws the diaphragm back up to its domed position, with the assistance of pressure caused by the residual resting tension in the muscles and connective tissues of the abdominal wall. Forced expiration, on the other hand, such as occurs in deep or rapid breathing, requires definite contraction of abdominal musculature and of rib cage depressors. Modern research has left unchanged this historic concept of breathing mechanisms, although there remains much confusion and doubt about the role of specific muscles.

The muscles primarily involved in the respiratory movements include the following:

> Intercostales Externi
> Intercostales Interni
> Diaphragm
> Levatores Costarum
> Serratus Posterior Superior
> Transversus Abdominis
> Serratus Posterior Inferior

INTERCOSTALES EXTERNI

Eleven sheets of muscular fibers located in the spaces between the ribs (Fig. 14–3).

Origin.   The lower borders of the first eleven ribs.

Insertion.   The upper borders of the last eleven ribs.

Innervation.   The intercostal nerves.

Structure. Short parallel fibers extending diagonally forward and downward, in the direction of the external oblique. They extend from the spinal column forward to the costal cartilages, being absent next to the sternum.

Action. Although the action of the intercostals has long been a matter of dispute, it is now generally agreed that the intercostales externi act to lift the ribs in inspiration, with the upper ribs fixed by the scaleni. Electromyographic studies indicate that during quiet breathing the external intercostal muscles contract only during inspiration, but it is possible that they contract strongly during voluntary expiratory efforts and in coughing if the lower ribs are held down by contraction of the abdominal muscles and the quadratus lumborum.

INTERCOSTALES INTERNI

Eleven muscular sheets just beneath the intercostales externi (Fig. 14–3).

Origin. The ridge on the inner surface of a rib or the corresponding costal cartilage.

Insertion. The upper border of the rib below.

Innervation. Intercostal nerves.

Structure. Short parallel fibers extending diagonally downward and backward, opposite in direction to the intercostales externi. They commence at the sternum, between the true ribs and at the anterior extremities of the cartilages of the false ribs and backward as far as the angles of the ribs.

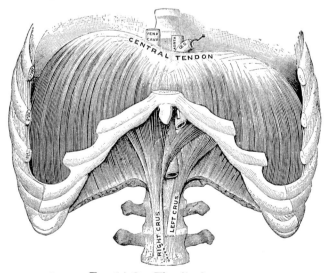

FIG. 14–2. The diaphragm.

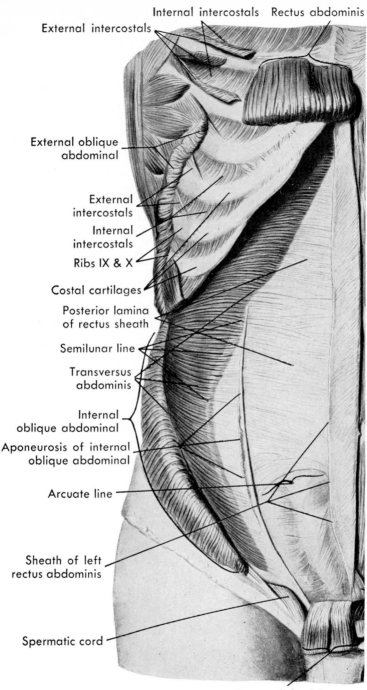

Internal intercostals   Rectus abdominis

External intercostals

External oblique
abdominal

External
intercostals

Internal
intercostals

Ribs IX & X

Costal cartilages

Posterior lamina
of rectus sheath

Semilunar line

Transversus
abdominis

Internal
oblique abdominal

Aponeurosis of internal
oblique abdominal

Arcuate line

Sheath of left
rectus abdominis

Spermatic cord

Rectus abdominis

FIG. 14–3. Abdominal and anterior thoracic muscles.

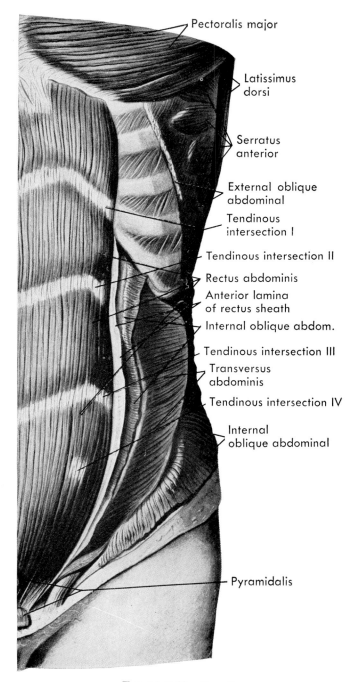

Pectoralis major

Latissimus dorsi

Serratus anterior

External oblique abdominal

Tendinous intersection I

Tendinous intersection II

Rectus abdominis

Anterior lamina of rectus sheath

Internal oblique abdom.

Tendinous intersection III

Transversus abdominis

Tendinous intersection IV

Internal oblique abdominal

Pyramidalis

Fig. 14–3 *(Continued)*

(Sobotta-Uhlenhuth, courtesy of Hafner Publishing Co., New York–London.)

Action. These muscles show only very restricted activity during quitet breathing, but function as expiratory muscles during vigorous respiratory efforts. This will be discussed in more detail later in this chapter.

THE DIAPHRAGM

A dome-shaped sheet, partly muscular and partly tendinous, forming a partition between the thoracic and abdominal cavities The tendon is at the summit of the dome and the muscle fibers along sides (Fig. 14–2).

Origin. An approximately circular line passing entirely around the inner surface of the body wall. It is attached at the back to the upper two lumbar vertebrae and the lumbar fascia; on the sides for a variable distance, to the sternum.

Insertion. The central tendon, which is an oblong sheet forming the summit of the dome.

Innervation. The phrenic nerve from the cervical plexus, with fibers largely from the fourth but also from the adjacent cervical nerves.

Structure. The fibers pass vertically upward for some distance from the origin, and then turn inward to their insertion. The fibers of the sternal portion are shortest; the lateral portion has saw-toothed attachments to the ribs and cartilages, in alternation with those of the transversalis, which is a muscle of expiration.

Action. The diaphragm is the principal muscle of inspiration and during quiet breathing may be the only respiratory muscle in action.[1,2] Contraction of its fibers pulls down on the central tendon and up on the ribs and sternum. The ribs are lifted slightly, but the central tendon is depressed as the principal movement. In quiet respiration the total diaphragmatic movement is about 1.5 cm.; in deep respiration the total diaphragmatic excursion is between 7 and 12 cm.[3] In normal breathing there is close cooperation between the movements of the diaphragm and of the intercostals. As the diaphragm descends it flattens and creates more room in the chest. The relation of the diaphragm to the abdomen, as well as to the chest, is of importance. When it descends it must, of course, displace the abdominal cavity just as much as it adds to the thoracic cavity. It pushes the stomach, liver, and other abdominal organs before it, and since these organs are soft and pliable but not easily compressible, they crowd out against the abdominal wall. The soft and flexible abdominal wall gives way, expanding on the front and somewhat at the side to make the needed room. If the abdominal wall is thick and strong, it offers considerable resistance to the descent of the diaphragm, and this will increase the upward pull of the latter on the ribs.

LEVATORES COSTARUM

Twelve small muscles on each side of the spine (Fig. 13–8).

Origin. The transverse processes of the last cervical and the first eleven thoracic vertebrae.

Insertion. The outer surfaces of the ribs between the tubercle and the angle.

Innervation. Branches of the intercostal nerves.

Structure. These muscles pass obliquely downward and laterally similar to the external intercostals. They insert into the rib beneath, except that the lower four divide, one part attaching to the rib beneath and the other to the second rib below its origin.

Action. No adequate studies of the functions of these muscles in man have been reported. Their anatomical position suggests that they raise the ribs, increasing the thoracic cavity, and, in the vertebral column, cause extension, lateral flexion, and slight rotation to the opposite side.

SERRATUS POSTERIOR SUPERIOR

A flat rhomboidal sheet of muscular fibers lying beneath the upper half of the scapula (Fig. 13–9).

Origin. The ligamentum nuchae and the spinous processes of the seventh cervical and the first three thoracic vertebrae.

Insertion. The second to the fifth ribs inclusive, beyond their angles.

Innervation. Branches of the anterior rami of the four upper thoracic nerves.

Structure. Longitudinal arrangement with the ends tendinous.

Action. The serratus posterior superior lies so deep beneath the scapula and the trapezius and rhomboid that its action has not been observed. Its position and attachments are such that it is able to lift the ribs.

TRANSVERSUS ABDOMINIS

This muscle forms the third layer of the abdominal wall next to its inner surface, lying immediately beneath the obliquus internus (Fig. 14–3).

Origin. Lateral third of the inguinal ligament, anterior three-fourths of the iliac crest, the lumbodorsal fascia, and the cartilages of the lower six ribs.

Insertion.   Linea alba.

Innervation.   Branches from the seventh to twelfth intercostal, the iliohypogastric, and ilioinguinal nerves.

Structure.   A thick sheet of parallel fibers crossing the abdomen horizontally.   Its middle part is thickest and also has the longest fibers.   Like internal and external obliques, its muscular fibers are placed chiefly at the sides of the abdomen.   The front tendons of the three fuse to form a single tendon which is slit down the center to form a sheath for the rectus abdominis.

Action.   Constricts the abdomen, compressing the contents and assisting in micturition, defecation, emesis, parturition, and forced expiration.   During weight lifting in the flexed position the weight of the object is transmitted from the trunk by the latissimus dorsi to the lower back.   The abdominal muscles and the diaphragm contract to raise the intra-abdominal pressure and stabilize the thoracic cage against the compression effect exerted by the latissimus dorsi.[4]

SERRATUS POSTERIOR INFERIOR

Named from its position and its saw-toothed insertion (Fig. 9–7).

Origin.   The spines of the last two thoracic and the first two or three lumbar vertebrae.

Insertion.   The lower four ribs, beyond their angles.

Innervation.   Branches of the anterior rami of the ninth to twelfth thoracic nerves.

Structure.   The inner half is a tendinous sheet blended with the tendons of the latissimus and erector spinae.   The muscular fibers are inserted directly into the ribs.

Action.   The fibers of the serratus posterior inferior are in a position to depress the ribs and the angle of pull is large.   It is therefore generally considered a muscle of expiration.

ANALYSIS OF RESPIRATORY MOVEMENTS

Although the general nature of breathing movements is well understood the individual contributions of the specific muscles is still the subject of great disagreement.   One reason for the confusion is the fact that the conditions of breathing vary from person to person and from situation to situation.   Individual differences in structure are startling—the number of ribs, the nature of their articulations, the general body build of the person and the amount of superincumbent fat are widely variable.   In females, the relative size of the breasts and the occurrence of pregnancy are variables.   Mobility and flexibility of structures vary with age and degree of ossification of cartilages. The chest is relatively deep and narrow in infancy and becomes broadened and flattened as the individual matures, apparently as a result of the normal activity of the body. The degree of muscular development and the extent of restriction of movement by postural defects cover a wide range. Aside from individual variations, it is known that the problem of breathing depends upon upright or recumbent position, the load carried on shoulders or arms, water pressure during submersion, amount of stabilization of the chest required to provide a firm base for arm and shoulder girdle movements, external forces produced in crutch-walking and contact sports such as wrestling, and similar factors. Quiet and vigorous breathing are entirely different conditions. The ventilation during maximal work is not limited by the strength of the respiratory muscles, but is regulated through the central nervous system.[5]

Sports writers frequently describe athletes as being "barrel-chested." Actually, studies of the thoracic indices of successful competitors indicate that they show a tendency toward wide flat chests rather than round ones.[6,7] According to Seltzer,[8] in exhausting work the flat-chested individuals display greater capacities for supplying oxygen to the tissues, indicative of more efficient respiratory and cardiovascular mechanisms. There is little to indicate that the successful athlete needs an unusually large chest. The vital capacity in most of the runners participating in the 1924 Boston marathon was found to be normal,[9] and the pulmonary functions of the 1956 United States Olympic Free Style Wrestlers did not significantly exceed the norms for young men of similar stature.[10] Perhaps the respiratory superiority of the trained athlete lies largely in the increased strength and contractility of his respiratory muscles.[11]

Diaphragm. The diaphragm is the single most important muscle of inspiration. The flattening of its dome during inspiration is probably responsible for the greater part of the tidal volume during normal inspiration. At maximal inspiration the abdominal muscles contract to counterbalance the action of the diaphragm and thus limit further expansion of the lungs.[12] In normal subjects, it is invariably active during inspiration, and in some subjects may be the only respiratory muscle active during quiet breathing. However, it is not essential, and respiration can go on unhindered even when it is paralyzed. The blow which "knocks the wind out" probably paralyzes and causes temporary spasm of the diaphragm. In the trained athlete the diaphragm plays a relatively larger role in respiration than it does in the untrained man. This enables him to avoid the muscular fatigue which accompanies the enlargement of the chest wall characteristic of costal breathing.

Intercostals. As has been indicated earlier in this chapter, the function of the intercostals has been a matter of dispute and their mechanical action is yet to be definitely established. The external intercostals are probably second only to the diaphragm in importance as inspiratory muscles, whereas the internal layer largely functions as an expiratory muscle during vigorous expiratory efforts. It has been suggested that the external intercostals exert a rotational couple on each rib, tending to evert it on the one above and thus help to expand the chest, while the internal intercostals exert a turning couple which inverts each rib on the one above. During vigorous breathing, reciprocal innervation has been observed in these two sets of muscles.[13]

It is questionable whether the internal intercostals normally have any important respiratory function, but it should be noted that Duchenne[14] reported a case in which a subject with paralysis of the diaphragm and stenocleidomastoids and with the scalenes about two-thirds wasted away continued to breathe by use of the intercostals alone. Since the intercostals tend to pull the adjacent ribs together, they may function differently depending upon whether the upper or the lower ribs are stabilized. Koepke and his associates[2] have demonstrated that the diaphragm is always active, and is the first muscle to come into action in quiet breathing; that the first intercostals are usually active; that the second intercostals are occasionally active; and that the remaining intercostals are never active. As deeper and deeper breaths were taken, successive intercostals were recruited, from the top down.

Sternomastoid. The sternomastoids are important auxiliary muscles of inspiration, provided that the cervical spine is extended and held firm to give them a base to pull upon. Their action is to elevate the sternum, thus increasing the antero-posterior diameter of the thorax. However, it is difficult to evaluate the mechanical importance of this. They display a surprisingly slight amount of respiratory activity in normal subjects, but become important when the respiratory level is elevated and the ordinary muscles of inspiration are operating at a greatly reduced mechanical advantage. Duchenne[14] observed a young male patient with cervical transection of the spinal cord as a result of a fall during the practice of gymnastics who was able to breathe for some weeks by means of his sternomastoids alone.

Scaleni. Anatomical considerations suggest that the three scaleni have the same fundamental actions. They are not necessarily activated during quiet breathing of normal persons, but during augmented ventilation are possibly the most important accessory muscles of respiration.[15,16] Their action at times may be to fix the upper ribs and prevent the thoracic cage from being pulled downwards by the abdominal muscles, or to provide support for the apex of the lung to prevent it from bulging upward.

Abdominals. During quiet respiration, the abdominals are inactive. The external and internal obliques (and presumably the transversus, which is inaccessible to or undifferentiated by electromyography) participate vigorously in forced expiration, coughing, singing, straining, vomiting, and defecation, in proportion to the severity of the activity. The rectus abdominis is relatively inactive, provided that there is no concurrent tendency toward spine flexion. The abdominals are considered by Campbell[17] to be the most important muscles of forced expiration. His studies demonstrated that in the erect position they do not contract very forcefully until the pulmonary ventilation exceeds 70 to 90 l./min. Their effect upon the respiratory system probably reflects the changes of intraabdominal pressure resulting from their contraction and relaxation, which, in turn, affects the position and movement of the diaphragm. During quiet breathing the effects of gravity and the elastic recoil of the thoracic cage appear sufficient to produce expiration.

Other Muscles. The quadratus lumborum and the serratus posterior inferior muscles are often mentioned as assistants in forced expiration, as are the serratus posterior superior, levatores costarum, erector spinae, and oblique spine extensors for forced inspiration. Their importance is debatable. At moments of extreme respiratory distress (dyspnea), the thoracic and cervical spine extensors, the thoracohumeral muscles such as the pectoralis major, and the thoracoscapular muscles such as the serratus anterior may be effectively utilized to stabilize the spine and keep the rib cage in an elevated position.

The rationale for the utilization of this is based on Wade's[3] discovery that chest circumference is increased at the beginning of forced breathing and that subsequent thoracic movements are relatively small around this position. This suggested to him that an expanded chest position increases the effective area of the diaphragm, thereby improving ventilation. This finding confirms the importance of keeping the thorax high and free from hindrance during severe exercise and recovery. Runners, for example, should avoid restricted arm movements and excessive tension in the musculature of arms and shoulder girdle.

Grasping some supporting object, particularly one overhead, after vigorous exertion permits the thoracohumeral muscles to relieve the inertia of the arms and thus reduce the resistance against which the respiratory muscles must act. Teammates who assist a staggering runner after his race should throw his arms over their shoulders and let him continue to walk while his shoulder girdle is kept high. In this way, forced breathing is facilitated (and the continued attempts at voluntary locomotion will help maintain adequate return of venous blood to the heart). If the exhausted athlete collapses, he should be placed in supine lying position with his arms in complete abduction, so that the stretched pectoralis major will help to keep the rib cage elevated and the taut sternomastoids can effectively participate in breathing movements.

Some investigators[18] have concluded that singers may develop selective control of the actions of the diaphragm and other inspiratory muscles. In normal subjects, excursion of the diaphragm is governed exclusively by the depth of breathing. Campbell[17] found no convincing differences in the activity of the intercostal muscles during attempts at predominantly thoracic and predominantly abdominal breathing. Thoracic cage movements may indeed be regulated voluntarily, but much of the observed elevation of the rib cage is a product of extension of the thoracic spine, a movement which lifts not only the ribs but also the diaphragm, thus contributing no extra intrathoracic volume. However, Stigol and Cuello[19] have demonstrated that at least some individuals can be taught to inspire actively without contracting the diaphragm. In such cases the diaphragm simply acts as a passive membrane.

Breathing Exercises. The nineteenth century gymnastic systems included deep breathing exercises in the "Day's Order," the rationale being based on the incomplete and faulty physiological knowledge of the previous century. Haphazard early American variations destroyed whatever postural benefit might have been involved in these exercises. Williams, in his early editions of *Principles of Physical Education,* was almost singlehandedly responsible for popularizing the viewpoint that ". . . except for corrective purposes in defective cases, breathing exercises are unscientific, and probably harmful."[20] Williams' view was based primarily on the facts that increased ventilation upset the normal partial pressures of blood gases and that effective gas exchange results from physiological needs rather than from increased ventilation. Physical educators were so impressed that they tended to ignore the qualification "except for corrective purposes," and it is probable that the values of deliberate breathing in some exercise circumstances have been under-emphasized.

In the absence of physiological or kinesiological needs, taking voluntary deep breaths as an arbitrary exercise is valueless. Further, many coaches and exercise physiologists are convinced that conscious attempts by athletes to regulate breathing usually interfere with performance. Ordinarily, deep breathing is useful only when it results from the stimulation of the breathing mechanisms by hard work. Nevertheless, voluntary regulation may be warranted under certain circumstances, some of which are listed below:

(1) After voluntary hyperventilation, the breath can be held longer, yielding an advantage in competitive swimming and underwater recreation. However, it may result in suspending breathing long enough to reduce O_2 pressure to hypoxia levels, followed by loss of consciousness and possible drowning.[21]

(2) Taking a deep breath tends to improve general posture, and may facilitate the learning of optimal postural positions.

(3) The correction of various chest deformities such as "chicken breast" and "funnel chest" may be aided by maximal inspirations, which are inefficiently achieved through natural activities.

(4) The undesirable tendency to "strain" (known as the *Valsalva effect*—an expiratory effort with the glottis closed) while doing heavy work can be prevented only by conscious attention to continuous breathing. Some gymnasts participating in arm-supporting events exhibit repeated Valsalva effects, and are unable to complete their routines unless they are taught to breathe consciously throughout their event.

(5) The accuracy of precise movements, such as free-throwing in basketball and pistol shooting, may be increased if the breath is held and the rib cage is stabilized at the end of the last normal inspiration preceding the performance.

(6) Singers and speakers are taught to maintain a high chest position, primarily because the expanded chest serves better as a sounding-box and permits longer intervals between inspirations.

(7) Those who must talk loudly in their occupation can improve the quality of their voices by taking preliminary deep breaths and by "huffing out" and unusual amount of air. Failure to do this may cause a feeling of strain on the vocal cords.

Cost of Ventilation. The mechanical efficiency of breathing appears to be about 19 to 25 per cent, which is of the same order of magnitude as has been found for other forms of muscular work.[22] The cost of resting breathing has been estimated to be about 0.6 to 1.4 cal./min., which is a negligible factor in the total energy output. Under a work load it may approximate 3 per cent of the total energy expenditure.[23] During muscular exercise ventilation usually bears an approximately linear relationship to the oxygen consumption until the steady state is exceeded, when pulmonary ventilation becomes excessive. Hyperventilation is accompanied by little increase in actual pulmonary ventilation. This may reflect a decrease in the mechanical efficiency of breathing, an increase in the mechanical work required per unit of ventilation, or muscular effort not directly associated with respiratory movements. The men who have run the mile in under four minutes probably possess a unique ability to achieve a large ventilation volume at a relatively small cost.

IMPLICATIONS FOR ATHLETIC TRAINING

The thoracic cage must function to protect the heart and lungs from the trauma of physical contact. The curvilinear design of the ribs, their flexibility, and the network of muscles holding them in position makes these seemingly fragile bones surprisingly resistant to trauma. In the young person, however, the flexibility of the ribs may be sufficient to permit the thorax to be distorted to the point that the heart can be injured without fracture of the ribs or sternum. Injuries of this sort may be considerably more common in boxing than is generally realized. The possibility of traumata of this type should be carefully considered before permitting young persons to engage in physical contact activities.

Young athletes quite frequently complain to their coaches that

TABLE 14–1. Respiratory Muscles and Their Actions

MUSCLES	INSPIRATION		EXPIRATION	
	Resting	*Forced*	*Resting*	*Forced*
Diaphragm	P.M.	P.M.		
The 3 scaleni	Asst.*	P.M.*		Asst. (?)‡
External and internal intercostals .	P.M.†	P.M.†		Asst. (?)‡
Sternocleidomastoid		Asst.*		
Levatores costarum	Asst. (?)	Asst. (?)		
Serratus posterior superior . .	Asst. (?)	Asst. (?)		
Erector spinae and other oblique spinal extensors		Asst.¶		
Pectoralis major and minor, and serratus anterior		Asst.‖		
Transversus abdominis . . .				P.M.
External and internal oblique abdominals				P.M.
Serratus posterior inferior. . . .				Asst. (?)
Quadratus lumborum				Asst.

(?)—Indicates that the action has not been verified electromyographically, or is otherwise in dispute.

*—When the cervical spine is stabilized by extensor muscles.

†—When the upper ribs are stabilized by the scaleni.

‡—When the lower ribs are stabilized by the abdominals and the quadratus lumborum.

¶—Stabilizing the spine in extended position.

‖—When the arms and shoulder girdle are stabilized in a position of elevation.

they have experienced a sharp pain in the region of the heart accompanied by a "catch in the breath" and are worried about the possibility of having suffered a mild heart attack. In the great majority of cases these pains represent nothing more serious than a slight tearing of an intercostal muscle, but the coach or trainer should refer such cases to the team physician for consultation rather than simply reassure the athlete and send him on his way.

Rib muscle strains are quite common in such sports as wrestling, in which the hips may be held in one position while the upper body is twisted to another. Such injuries are painful during movements of the body, but are seldom serious. Fractured ribs, such as may result from trauma sustained in football, skiing, boxing, and similar activities, are quite another matter, since the possibility always exists that the broken rib, or a splinter from it, may penetrate the pleural cavity.

Unfortunately, there appears to be comparatively little that the athlete himself can do to prevent such injuries. The design of the body does not lend itself to exercises which will develop muscles which will hold the thoracic cage in place or shield it from injury. Prevention of thoracic injuries lies primarily in the design of protective equipment, formulation of rules of the game, and the teaching of proper techniques and skills.

References

1. Rankin, John and Dempsey, Jerome A.: Respiratory Muscles and the Mechanisms of Breathing. Amer. J. Phys. Med., 46, 198–244, 1967.

2. Koepke, George H., et al.: Sequence of Action of the Diaphragm and Intercostal Muscles During Respiration: I. Inspiration. Arch. Phys. Med., 39, 426–430, 1958.

3. Wade, O. L.: Movements of the Thoracic Cage and Diaphragm in Respiration. J. Physiol., 124, 193–212, 1954.

4. Bearn, J. G.: The Significance of the Activity of the Abdominal Muscles in Weight Lifting. Acta Anat., 45, 83–89, 1961.

5. Consolazio, C. Frank, et al.: Respiratory Function in Normal Young Adults at Sea Level and at 4300 Meters. Mil. Med., 133, 96–105, 1968.

6. Weisman, S. A.: Track Stars Are Not Barrel Chested. J. Lancet, 73, 280, 282, 1953.

7. Rasch, Philip J.: Indices of Body Build of United States Free Style Wrestlers. J. Ass. Phys. & Ment. Rehabil., 12, 91–94, 1958.

8. Seltzer, Carl C.: Body Build and Oxygen Metabolism at Rest and During Exercise. Amer. J. Physiol., 129, 1–13, 1940.

9. Gordon, Burgess, et al.: Observations on a Group of Marathon Runners. Arch. Int. Med., 33, 425–434, 1924.

10. Rasch, Philip J. and Brant, John W. A.: Measurements of Pulmonary Function in United States Olympic Free Style Wrestlers. Res. Quart., 28, 279–287, 1957.

11. Shapiro, William, *et al.*: Maximum Ventilatory Performance and Its Limiting Factors. J. Appl. Physiol., *19*, 199–203, 1964.

12. Agostoni, Emilio and Rahn, Hermann: Abdominal and Thoracic Pressures at Different Lung Volumes. J. Appl. Physiol., *15*, 1087–1092, 1960.

13. Taylor, A.: The Contribution of the Intercostal Muscles to the Effort of Respiration in Man. J. Physiol., *151*, 390–402, 1960.

14. Duchenne, G. B.: *Physiology of Motion*, translated and edited by Emanuel B. Kaplan. Philadelphia: W. B. Saunders Co., 1959, pp. 469 and 481–485.

15. Thompson, W. T., *et al.*: Observations on Scalene Respiratory Muscles. Arch. Int. Med., *113*, 856–865, 1964.

16. Raper, A. Jarrell, *et al.*: Scalene and Sternomastoid Muscle Function. J. Appl. Physiol., *21*, 497–502, 1966.

17. Campbell, E. J. Moran: *The Respiratory Muscles and the Mechanics of Breathing*. Chicago: The Year Book Publishers, Inc., 1958.

18. Bouhuys, Arend, *et al.*: Kinetic Aspects of Singing. J. Appl. Physiol., *21*, 483–496, 1966.

19. Stigol, Luisa C. and Cuello, Alfredo C.: Voluntary Control of the Diaphragm in One Subject. J. Appl. Physiol., *21*, 1911–1912, 1966.

20. Williams, Jesse Feiring: *The Principles of Physical Education*, 3rd Ed. Philadelphia: W. B. Saunders Co., 1939, p. 107.

21. Craig, Albert B., Jr.: Cause of Loss of Consciousness During Underwater Swimming. J. Appl. Physiol., *16*, 583–586, 1961.

22. Margaria, R. G., *et al.*: Mechanical Work of Breathing During Muscular Exercise. J. Appl. Physiol., *15*, 354–358, 1960.

23. Milic-Emili, G. and Petit, J. M.: Mechanical Efficiency of Breathing. J. Appl. Physiol., *15*, 359–362, 1960.

Laboratory Exercises

1. There is evidence that the administration of oxygen to swimmers just before a race improves their times. What is the reason for this? Why is it not equally valuable for runners?

2. In lifting a heavy weight overhead, a lifter usually takes a full inspiration while the barbell is at the shoulders and then holds his breath as he presses it to arms' length. What is the rationale for this? What undesirable effects may follow?

3. In his text *The Physiology of Physical Education* (p. 518) Percy M. Dawson noted that ex-wrestlers and weight lifters may be "stiff chested," with little or no chest expansion. How does this condition come about and what is its significance so far as performance is concerned?

4. Assume that a mature individual undertakes a program of weight training and finds that as a result his normal chest circumference is 3 inches larger than it was before he started to exercise. How do you account for this change? What would you expect to find true about his chest expansion?

5. What is the effect of pressure on the thorax, such as applied in the "bear hug" in wrestling, on respiration? What is the purpose of the wrestler's "expiratory grunt"?

6. Partially paralyzed patients may be taught a respiratory technique known as "frog breathing." Determine how this is done and analyze the kinesiological actions involved.

7. What may result if an individual practices deep breathing exercises when there is no physiological need for increased respiration?

8. What value should be attached to spirometric tests of lung capacity? What were the reasons for the objections made to the inclusion of this in the Rogers Strength Test?

9. In the Flack Test the subject exhales against a standard resistance of 40 mm. of mercury for as long as possible. What is revealed by this test? (Suggestion: See T. J. Powell and Sunahara, F. A., A Physiologic Evaluation of the Flack Test. J. Aviat. Med., *29*, 444–453, 1958.)

10. Analyze the effects of movements of the spinal column, such as backward bending, forward bending, and lateral bending, on the respiration. Which position appears most advantageous for efficient respiration?

11. Have a subject hold his breath at the end of a normal inspiration. Compare chest circumference measurements in slumped, normal, and exaggerated military posture.

Chapter 15

Movements of the Pelvic Girdle and the Hip Joint

Everyone is familiar with resemblances between the upper and lower limbs. However, the pelvic girdle, which corresponds to the shoulder girdle, is not movable in the same manner as the latter, with the consequence that the entire set of movements and muscles studied in Chapter 9 has no counterpart in the lower limb.

THE PELVIS

Each half of the pelvic girdle consists of three bones, the *ilium* above at the side of the hip, the *pubis* below and forward, and the *ischium* below and to the rear. They are separate in early life, but in the adult are joined to form one solid structure, the *os coxae* or hip bone. The pelvic basin is closed posteriorly by the sacrum, which is wedged between and attached to the two hip bones. The joint formed by the sacrum and the ilium is cartilaginous, held by three of the strongest ligaments in the human body: the anterior and posterior sacroiliac and the interosseous ligaments. The possibility of movement in the sacroiliac joint is greatly reduced by the presence of interlocking convolutions on the two articulating surfaces. So immobile are the joints the sacrum forms with the two hip bones that for most purposes the entire structure may be regarded as one single bone.

The pelvis is tied together at the pubic symphysis, the two pubes being separated by a heavy disc of fibrocartilage. This is also a tight joint and is heavily reinforced by ligaments, the superior pubic above and the arcuate pubic beneath, and by ligamentous tissue associated with the interpubic disc. The ligaments of both the pubic and sacroiliac joints relax somewhat during pregnancy, due to hormonal influences which soften and relax the sacroiliac ligaments and the symphysis pubis. This permits some movement and expansion of the pelvis. A milder form of this same phenomenon is seen during menstruation.[1]

Because the pelvic girdle, including the sacrum, acts as a unit, the lumbosacral joint becomes the important articulation when the pelvis moves in relation to the spine. This joint is supported by ligaments in a manner quite similar to that of the other nearby intervertebral joints.

FUNDAMENTAL MOVEMENTS OF THE PELVIS

Most movements of the pelvis are for the purpose of aligning the pelvis in order to provide greater ease or range of motion of either the trunk or the lower extremities. When we bend over to tie a shoe lace, the pelvis tilts or rotates to accommodate the movement of the trunk. If the thigh is flexed on the trunk, as when punting a football, the pelvis rotates in order to increase the range of motion of the thigh with reference to the trunk. Movements of the pelvis are more properly considered as spinal movements occurring at the lumbosacral articulation. They may be conveniently classified as follows:

1. Forward rotation or tilt. Increased inclination resulting from lumbosacral hyperextension and, in the erect position, hip flexion.

2. Backward rotation or tilt. Decreased inclination resulting from lumbosacral flexion (reduction of hyperextension) and, in the erect position, hip extension.

3. Lateral tilt. The lowering or raising of one iliac crest with reference to its contralateral mate.

4. Rotation. Turning about a vertical axis either to the right or to the left.

THE HIP JOINT

The hip joint is formed by the articulation of the head of the femur with the *acetabulum* (Fig. 15–1), which is the name given to the socket on the outer surface of the hip bone just where the ilium, pubis and ischium join. It is a ball-and-socket joint, having less freedom of motion than the shoulder joint, the socket being deeper and the bones fitting so closely that much force is required to pull it apart. However, in a trained person a surprisingly large degree of flexibility can be demonstrated (Fig. 15–2). The usual capsular ligament is present and is thickened on the anterior side by the *iliofemoral band,* or the *inverted Y-ligament,* on the antero-inferior side the *pubofemoral ligament,* and on the posterior the *ischiofemoral ligament* (Fig. 15–3).

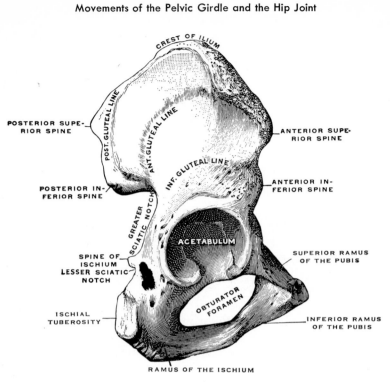

FIG. 15–1.   The hip bone of right side, lateral view.

FIG. 15–2.   Swami Vishnudevananda demonstrating the remarkable flexibility of the hip, knee, and ankle joints achieved from practice of yoga exercises. Roentgenographic examination of the pelvis, knees, ankles, and feet disclosed no evidence of traumatic or pathologic changes.[2]   (O'Connell, courtesy C.C.M.)

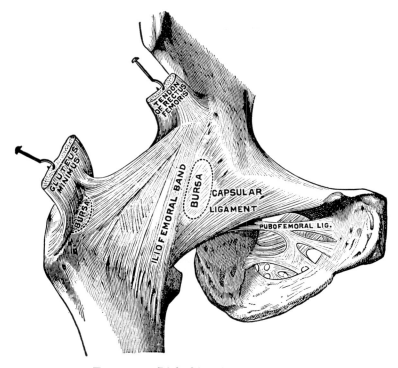

FIG. 15–3.   Right hip joint, anterior view.

FUNDAMENTAL MOVEMENTS OF THE HIP JOINT

The femur is the longest bone in the body and corresponds in a way to the humerus; like the humerus it has a head, shaft, and two condyles; in place of tuberosities it has two large prominences, the greater and lesser *trochanters*; along the back of the shaft is the *linea aspera,* or rough line (Fig. 15–4).

Flexion.   The hip joint permits movement of the femur most freely forward; this is called flexion; it can take place through 150 degrees or more, when it is stopped by contact of the thigh with the front of the trunk.   When the knee is extended the hip joint can be flexed only to the extent of a right angle, but this is due to tension of the hamstring muscles and not to the form of the joint.

Extension.   The reverse of flexion, movement of the femur downward and backward, is called extension, and is free until the limb is vertically downward in line with the trunk, when it is stopped by tension of the iliofemoral ligament and of the psoas and iliacus muscles, making any hyperextension of the hip joint impossible in normal subjects.   Careful examination will show that in apparent

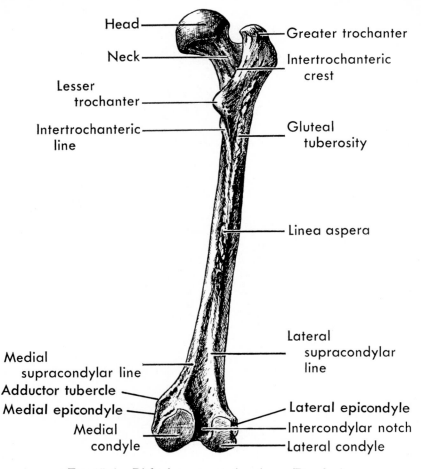

Head

Greater trochanter

Neck

Intertrochanteric crest

Lesser trochanter

Intertrochanteric line

Gluteal tuberosity

Linea aspera

Lateral supracondylar line

Medial supracondylar line
Adductor tubercle
Medial epicondyle
Medial condyle

Lateral epicondyle
Intercondylar notch
Lateral condyle

Fig. 15–4.   Right femur, posterior view.   (Douglas.)

hyperextension of the hip joint, which occurs when one pushes one limb as far back as possible while standing on the other limb, the pelvis tilts forward with the moving femur, the movement really being a slight flexion of the other hip joint and slight hyperextension of the spinal column in the lumbar region.   Horizontal flexion and horizontal extension of the hip joint can also be differentiated, but these have little practical application and will not be considered here.

Abduction.   Movement of one limb away from the other toward the side is called abduction, and is usually possible through 45 degrees or more.   The limitation here is due to resistance of opposing muscles, the joint itself permitting nearly 90 degrees of abduction, especially if the toes are turned outward.   Abduction may also take place by movement of the trunk; for example, the right hip joint is abducted by inclining the trunk to the right while standing on the right foot.

Adduction.   Adduction is limited by contact of the moving limb with the other limb; it can take place further when the moving limb is a little front or rear from the other, or when the trunk is inclined to the side, as in the last example; the right hip joint is also adducted when the left hip is dropped below the level of the right while standing on the right leg.

Circumduction.   Movement of the limb in a circular manner by a combination of the four movements above described is called circumduction; turning the limb on its central axis is called rotation. This axis is a line through hip and knee joints, passing considerably inside of the shaft of the femur because of the sharp bend of that bone near the trochanters.

Rotation.   Rotation is possible through about 90 degrees, and is said to be outward or inward according to the way the toes are turned. Because of the sharp bend of the femur just mentioned, the neck of the femur strikes the side of the socket and limits the movement called rotation of the limb. The way the bones come in contact explains why flexion is so free and why rotation is so limited.

MUSCLES ACTING ON THE HIP JOINT

The twenty-two muscles acting on the hip joint may be classified as follows:

Three *flexors;* psoas, iliacus, rectus femoris.

One *flexor-adductor;* pectineus.

Three *extensors;* biceps femoris (long head), semimembranosus, semitendinosus. These are twice the weight of the flexors.

One *extensor-outward rotator;* gluteus maximus.

One *abductor;* gluteus medius.

Four *adductors;* gracilis, adductor longus, adductor brevis, adductor magnus.

Two *inward rotators;* tensor fasciae latae, gluteus minimus.

Six *outward rotators;* pyriformis, obturator externus, obturator internus, gemellus superior, gemellus inferior, quadratus femoris.

One *flexor-abductor-outward rotator;* sartorius.

PSOAS

Nearly all the psoas lies in the abdominal cavity behind the internal organs, where it cannot be easily observed *in vivo* (Fig. 15–5). It is usually called the "psoas major" to distinguish it from

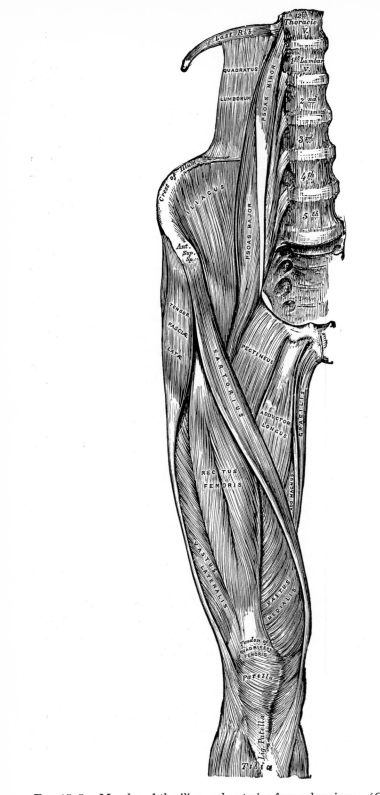

FIG. 15-5. Muscles of the iliac and anterior femoral regions. (*Gray's Anatomy*.)

a small muscle associated with it in most vertebrate animals and called the "psoas minor." The psoas is approximately 16 inches long.

Origin. The sides of the bodies of the last thoracic and all the lumbar vertebrae, and their intervertebral cartilages. The anterior surfaces and lower borders of the transverse processes of all the lumbar vertebrae.

Insertion. The lesser trochanter of the femur.

Innervation. Branches of the femoral nerve from the lumbar plexus which contain fibers from the second and third lumbar nerves.

Structure. Unipennate, with muscle fibers arising directly from the bodies of the vertebrae and attaching obliquely into the tendon of insertion.

Action. The psoas major is electrically silent at rest in both the sitting and standing positions, but is vigorously active in controlling deviations of the trunk from the rest position, particularly lateral bending and backwards leaning. It functions in hip flexion and in initiating advancement of the thigh early in the swing phase of walking.[3]

The psoas is especially well adapted to work where the hip joint and spinal column are flexed at the same time, as in rope climbing and similar exercises. It is practically impossible to observe its action in a normal subject, but the capacity of this muscle to act rapidly is extremely important in many athletic activities. If both psoas muscles are paralyzed, it is difficult to raise the body from a supine to a sitting position. The backward pull of a load carried low on the back is offset by a forward inclination of the trunk, resulting from the contraction of the psoas muscle.[4]

In about two-thirds of the people the psoas minor is missing or present on only one side. When it exists, it arises between the T–12 and L–1 vertebrae and inserts on the pubis. In some cases it remains too short and may produce contracture of the hip joint, sometimes serious enough to cause limping. This may be accompanied by limitation of inward rotation and abduction of the thigh. A lateral curvature of the spine and scoliosis may be produced. This condition is more common in the female, as her wider pelvis places the muscle under greater tension.[5]

ILIACUS

A flat, triangular muscle named from the bone on which it has its origin (Fig. 15–5).

Origin. The inner surface of the lilium and a part of the inner surface of the sacrum near the ilium.

Insertion.   Its tendon joins that of the psoas just where the latter crosses the front of the pelvis, to attach with it on the lesser trochanter.

Innervation.   Branches from the femoral nerve from the lumbar plexus.   Fibers come from the second and third lumbar nerves.

Structure.   Muscle fibers arising directly from the ilium and joining the tendon obliquely.

Action.   Hip joint flexion and stabilization.[6]   Since the psoas and iliacus have a common tendon of insertion, they function as a single bipennate muscle and are frequently referred to jointly as the iliopsoas.   However, the iliacus cannot act on the joints of the spine as does the psoas.   The two may easily develop a tensile pull in excess of 1000 pounds in an average adult.[6]

A striking example of the value of kinesiological observations has been reported from Britain.   Patients there complained of symptoms which appeared to be those of mild appendicitis.   However, a careful study revealed that the arrangements of the accelerator and brake pedals in their cars was such that the necessary leg movements produced fatigue in the right iliopsoas muscle, resulting in abdominal discomfort.[7]

SARTORIUS

The name means tailor's muscle, so-called because the ancient anatomists noticed that it is the muscle used in crossing the legs to take the position Oriental tailors assume at their work.   It is the longest muscle in the body, and is capable of a greater extent of contraction than any other (Fig. 15–5).   It is fusiform.

Origin.   The anterior superior iliac spine and the upper half of the notch just below it.

Insertion.   Lower anterior part of the medial surface of the tuberosity of the tibia.

Innervation.   Two branches from the femoral nerve containing fibers from the second and third lumbar nerves.   One branch serves the proximal portion of the muscle; the second branch the distal portion.

Structure.   The muscle lies between two layers of the fascia of the thigh, and some of its fibers are inserted into the fascia half-way down the thigh.   The muscle curves around the medial side of the thigh, passing behind the medial condyle and then forward to its insertion.

The fascia of the thigh is a thick sheet of fibrous connective tissue that envelops the thigh just under the skin.

Action.   Directly assists in flexion, abduction, and outward rotation of the thigh at the hip joint, knee flexion, and knee inward rotation.

RECTUS FEMORIS

This large bipennate muscle, named from its position straight down the front of the thigh, corresponds closely to the long head of the triceps on the arm, being the middle part of a three-headed extensor (Fig. 15–5).

Origin.   The antero-inferior spine of the ilium, between its tip and the hip joint, and a second head, the posterior, from a groove above the edge of the acetabulum.

Insertion.   The proximal border of the patella.

Innervation.   The femoral nerve fibers come from the second, third, and fourth lumbar nerves.

Structure.   The upper tendon passes down the middle of the muscle and the flattened lower tendon passes up beneath its deeper surface.   The muscle fibers cross obliquely from one tendon to the other.

Action.   The rectus femoris is a prime mover for hip joint flexion and assists with hip joint abduction.   It possesses a very short power arm and a pull nearly in line with the femur, favorable for speed but not for force; there is very little change in leverage when the limb is lifted.   Any force keeping the knee flexed will make the tension on the rectus femoris much greater.

Isolated action of the rectus femoris causes flexion of the hip and extension of the knee with great speed and power, giving the motion employed in kicking a football.   It is the only muscle that could do this alone and therefore might be properly called the "kicking muscle."   It forms a conspicuous ridge down the front of the thigh as it contracts, and can be seen and felt in action in all movements of combined flexion of the hip and extension of the knee.   Its action on the knee will be discussed further in connection with the muscles extending the knee.

PECTINEUS

A short thick muscle just below the groin, partly covered by the sartorius and the rectus femoris (Figs. 15–5, A–11, A–14).

Origin.   A space an inch wide on the front of the pubes, just below the rim of the pelvic basin between the iliopectineal eminence and the tubercle of the pubis.

Insertion.   A rough line leading from the lesser trochanter to the linea aspera.

Innervation.   A branch of the femoral nerve, with fibers from the second, third and fourth lumbar nerves.

Structure.   Penniform, both ends of the muscle having muscular and tendinous fibers intermingled.   It is twisted through 90 degrees as it passes from the origin to insertion.

Action.   The pectineus is a prime mover for hip joint flexion and adduction.   It is a weak assistant for outward rotation.   The power arm of the pectineus is several inches long and its angle of pull about 60 degrees, indicating lifting power rather than speed of movement. Leverage improves as the femur is moved forward and inward.

The pectineus can alone lift the thigh while the subject is sitting and place it across the other thigh.   It is used in practically all vigorous flexion of the hip, especially in motions requiring force rather than speed.

TENSOR FASCIAE LATAE

A small muscle at the front and side of the hip, called "tensor fasciae latae" from its action to tighten the fascia of the thigh.   It is peculiar in having no bony insertion (Fig. 15–5).

Origin.   The iliac crest in the region of the anterior-superior spine of the ilium.

Insertion.   The iliotibial tract of the fascia lata of the thigh, one-fourth of the way down the outside of the thigh.

Innervation.   A branch of the superior gluteal nerve from the femoral plexus.   It contains fibers from the fourth and fifth lumbar nerves and the first sacral nerve.

Structure.   The muscle lies between two layers of the fascia, and the longitudinal muscle fibers are inserted into these two layers.

Action.   A prime mover for inward rotation and an assistant for flexion and abduction of the hip joint.   This muscle may hypertrophy if the psoas is paralyzed.

The tensor fasciae latae affords a good example of the amazing strength of human muscle.   Parallel arrangement of heavy fiber, fascia, and tendon gives great strength in the direction in which the muscle is subject to strain.   In one group of cadavers the average tensile strength of this muscle was 7,000 pounds per square inch. This compares favorably with that of soft steel wire of the same weight.   The elasticity (capacity to return to original dimensions under limited maximum safe stress) of this muscle was above 91 per cent.[8]

GLUTEUS MAXIMUS

A very large fleshy muscle at the back of the hip (Figs. 15–6 and 15–7).   The great bulk of this muscle in man is peculiarly human, its development being associated with erect posture.

Origin.   The outer surface of the ilium along the posterior one-fourth of its crest, the posterior surface of the sacrum close to the ilium, the side of the coccyx, and the fascia of the lumbar region.

Insertion. A rough line about 4 inches long on the posterior aspect of the femur between the greater trochanter and the linea aspera, and the iliotibial tract of the fascia lata.

Innervation. The inferior gluteal nerve from the femoral plexus. Fibers come from the fifth lumbar and first and second sacral nerves.

Structure. Muscular fibers arising directly from the pelvis and making an oblique junction with the tendon of insertion, which is a flat sheet extending up from the femur and along the posterior edge of the muscle.

Action. Extension, outward rotation and abduction of the thigh at the hip joint.[9] Upper fibers assist with abduction; lower fibers assist with adduction. The gluteus maximus, being superficial, can easily be palpated. It contracts in raising the trunk from a position of inclination forward and from a position in which the knees are bent deeply, but it ceases to act before the erect position is reached. It can be observed similarly that it acts in raising the body from sitting to standing, and in walking up stairs or up a steep incline. It contracts vigorously in jumping, but in easy walking remains relaxed except as used to check the momentum of the limb at the end

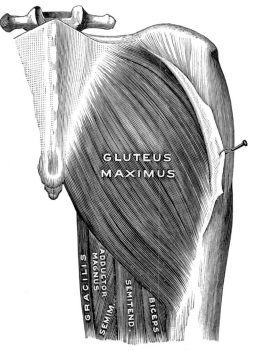

Fig. 15–6.   Gluteus maximus of right side.

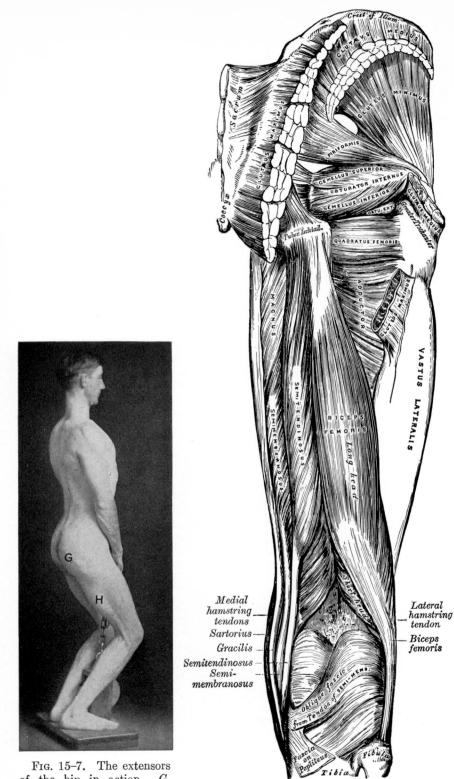

FIG. 15–7. The extensors
of the hip in action. *G*,
gluteus maximus; *H*, hamstring group.

FIG. 15–8. Posterior superficial muscles of
the thigh. (*Gray's Anatomy.*)

of the forward swing. These peculiarities in the action of the gluteus maximus are instances of the working of a rule governing the coordination of extension of the hip somewhat similar to one pertaining to the upward rotation of the scapula, in which the lower serratus anterior fails to work in certain positions. The rule seems to be that the gluteus maximus is not called into action in extension of the hip until the hip is flexed in excess of about 45 degrees, unless there is strong resistance, when the angle of limitation is less. The rule explains the tendency of bicyclists to stoop forward, the demonstrated advantage of the crouching start in sprint racing, and the tendency of old people to incline forward in going up stairs. In all such instances the position gives the person stronger use of the gluteus maximus.

Persons who have lost the use of the gluteus maximus walk normally, but cannot go up stairs nor up an incline without extreme fatigue, and running, jumping, or dancing quickly exhausts them.

BICEPS FEMORIS

Fusiform. Similar in several respects to the biceps brachii (Fig. 15–8).

Origin. The long head from the medial facet of the tuberosity of the ischium; the short head from the lateral lip of the linea aspera.

Insertion. The lateral condyle of the tibia and the head of the fibula. The tendon of insertion of this muscle forms the lateral hamstring.

Innervation. The long head is supplied by two branches from the tibial portion of the sciatic nerve and contains fibers from the first, second, and third sacral nerves. The short head is served by branches from the peroneal portion of the sciatic nerve and contains fibers from the fifth lumbar and the first and second sacral nerves.

Structure. The tendon of origin is long and flat and forms a septum between the biceps and the semitendinosus; the lower tendon extends half-way up the thigh. The muscle fibers are short and pass obliquely downward from the upper tendon and the femur to join the lower tendon.

Action. Only the long head acts at the hip joint. It is a prime mover for extension and an assistant for outward rotation. Both heads act as prime movers for flexion and outward rotation at the knee.

SEMITENDINOSUS

An unipennate muscle named from its long tendon of insertion, which reaches half-way up the thigh (Fig. 15–8).

Origin. The medial facet of the tuberosity of the ischium, by a common tendon with the biceps femoris.

Insertion. The upper part of the medial surface of the tibia, along with the sartorius. The tendon of insertion of this muscle forms one of the medial hamstrings.

Innervation. From two branches of the tibial portion of the sciatic nerve. Fibers come from the fifth lumbar and first and second sacral nerves.

Structure. The short muscle fibers pass diagonally downward from the tendon of origin to join the tendon of insertion, the bulk of the muscle being in the upper half of the thigh.

Action. Extends the thigh and assists in inward rotation of the hip joint. At the knee it is a prime mover for flexion and inward rotation.

SEMIMEMBRANOSUS

This unipennate muscle, which is named from its membranous tendon of origin, lies on the posterior and medial aspect of the thigh (Fig. 15–8).

Origin. The lateral facet of the tuberosity of the ischium.

Insertion. The posterior medial aspect of the medial condyle of the tibia. The tendon of insertion of this muscle forms one of the medial hamstrings.

Innervation. Branches from the tibial portion of the sciatic nerve. The fibers are from the fifth lumbar and first two sacral nerves.

Structure. Similar to the semitendinosus, but a longer upper tendon and a shorter lower one brings the muscular mass lower down so that the two muscles form a cylindrical mass. Since the belly of one is in contact with the tendinous part of the other, the action of one does not interfere with the action of the other.[10]

Action. Extends the thigh and assists in inward rotation of the hip joint. At the knee it is a prime mover for flexion and inward rotation.

GLUTEUS MEDIUS

A short thick muscle situated at the side of the ilium and giving the rounded contour to the side of the hip (Fig. 15–8).

Origin. The outer surface of the ilium near its crest between the posterior gluteal line above and the anterior gluteal line below.

Insertion. The oblique ridge on the lateral surface of the greater trochanter.

Innervation. Branches of the superior gluteal nerve from fibers of the fourth and fifth lumbar and first sacral nerves.

Structure.   The fibers arise directly from the ilium and converge to a penniform junction with the flat tendon of insertion.

Action.   The power arm of the gluteus medius, which is a straight line from the top of the trochanter to the center of the hip joint, is an unusually long one, and the muscle pulls upon it at almost a right angle, giving it great mechanical advantage.   The gluteus medius is a powerful abductor of the hip joint.   The anterior fibers assist with inward rotation and flexion; the posterior fibers with outward rotation and extension.   In the erect position, when a limb is raised off the ground the pelvis tends to drop on that side (Trendelenburg's sign).   This is prevented by contraction of the opposite gluteus medius.   The tensor fasciae latae and the gluteus medius are the most important postural thigh muscles.   This may reflect their role in the adjustment of sideways postural sway.[11]

GLUTEUS MINIMUS

A smaller companion of the preceding, lying just beneath it (Fig. 15–8).

Origin.   The lower part of the outer surface of the ilium.

Insertion.   The front part of the top of the greater trochanter.

Innervation.   Branches of the superior gluteal nerve from fibers of the fourth and fifth lumbar and first sacral nerves.

Structure.   Similar to the medius.

Action.   The anterior fibers cause strong inward rotation at the hip joint and assist with flexion.   The posterior fibers assist with outward rotation and extension.   The whole muscle assists with abduction.

GRACILIS

A slender muscle passing down the inner side of the thigh (Figs. 15–5, A–11, A–15).

Origin.   Anterior margins of the lower half of the symphysis pubis and the upper half of the pubic arch.

Insertion.   The upper part of the medial surface of the body of the tibia, below the condyle.

Innervation.   A branch from the anterior division of the obturator nerve which contains fibers from the third and fourth lumbar nerves.

Structure.   A thin flat tendon above with slightly converging fibers to a round tendon below.

Action.   Adduction at the hip joint.   Assists with flexion and inward rotation.   At the knee, assists with flexion and inward rotation.[12]

ADDUCTOR LONGUS

This muscle lies just to the inner side of the pectineus (Fig. 15–9).

Origin. The front of the pubis, just below the crest.

Insertion. The linea aspera in the middle third of the thigh.

Innervation. A branch of the anterior obturator nerve which contains fibers from the third and fourth lumbar nerves.

Structure. A thick triangular muscle, arising by a short tendon and diverging fanwise to its wide insertion.

Action. Adduction of the hip joint. Assists with flexion and outward rotation. Isolated action of the adductor longus is a combination of flexion and adduction, but it does not flex enough to lift the thigh over the other one while sitting, as the pectineus does.

ADDUCTOR BREVIS

A short triangular muscle behind and above the adductor longus (Fig. 15–9).

Origin. Outer surface of the inferior ramus of the pubis.

Insertion. The upper half of the linea aspera.

Innervation. A branch of the anterior obturator nerve which contains fibers from the third and fourth lumbar nerves.

Structure. A fan-shaped sheet similar to the longus but shorter.

Action. Adduction of the hip joint. Assists with flexion and outward rotation.

ADDUCTOR MAGNUS

One of the largest muscles of the body, situated on the medial side of the thigh (Fig. 15–9). It is pennate.

Origin. The front of the pubis, the tuberosity of the ischium, and the whole length of the ramus connecting the two.

Insertion. The whole length of the linea aspera and the medial supracondylar line and the adductor tubercle on the medial condyle of the femur.

Innervation. Branches from the posterior division of the obturator nerve which contains fibers from the third and fourth lumbar nerves, and also a branch from the sciatic nerve which innervates the lower fibers.

Structure. The fibers from the pubis pass horizontally across to the femur, much like those of the brevis; those from the ramus pass lower on the linea aspera; those from the tuberosity of the ischium go to the lower end of the medial supracondylar line.

Action. The whole muscle adducts the hip joint. The upper

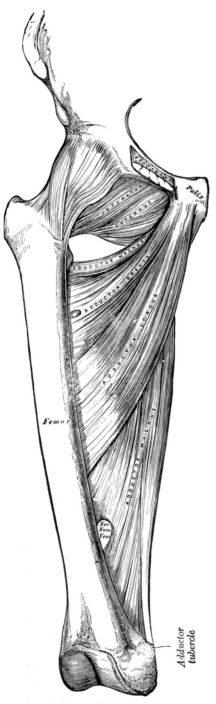

FIG. 15–9. Deep muscles of the medial femoral region. (*Gray's Anatomy*.)

fibers assist with outward rotation and flexion; the lower fibers assist with inward rotation and extension.

The ability of the adductor magnus to inward rotate the hip joint is utilized in such actions as "stemming" in skiing and in gripping the horse's sides while riding. Any strain of this muscle is colloquially termed "rider's strain," although among athletes such injuries are most commonly incurred by performers on certain pieces of gymnastic apparatus.

THE SIX OUTWARD ROTATORS

Of the numerous muscles capable of rotating the hip outward, only the group known as "the six outward rotators" perform this function without important side actions. Although it is sometimes necessary to study them individually in surgical and therapeutic applications, they can be considered as a unit for most problems in normal function (Fig. 15–8).

Origin. The posterior portions of the pelvis.

Insertion. The greater trochanter of the femur.

Innervation.

Piriformis—Branches from the first and second sacral nerves.

Obturator internus—A nerve from the sacral plexus, containing fibers from the fifth lumbar and first and second sacral nerves.

Obturator externus—A branch of obturator nerve. The fibers are from the third and fourth lumbar nerves.

Quadratus femoris—A nerve from the sacral plexus that contains fibers from the fourth and fifth lumbar and first sacral nerves.

Gemellus superior—Same as obturator internus.

Gemellus inferior—Same as quadratus femoris.

Action. Outward rotation. After the thigh has been flexed through 90 degrees, the six outward rotators can also produce horizontal extension.

ACTIONS OF THE HIP FLEXORS

Because of their common tendon of insertion and similarity of action, the psoas and the iliacus are often referred to as the *iliopsoas muscle*. Under certain conditions, the psoas has complex effects upon the lumbar spine (see detailed discussion in Chapter 13, p. 294). Both the psoas (indirectly) and the iliacus (directly) tend to tilt the pelvis forward if they contract when the femur is fixed, as in erect weight-bearing, or when an attempt is made to flex the hip against heavy resistance, as in the double leg-lift exercise from supine lying position. Thus, the psoas and iliacus may play a crucial role in faulty posture. Both muscles are ordinarily relatively well developed. They are called into action in nearly all activities requiring forceful hip flexion, since they are the only prime movers for hip flexion which have no other prime mover actions to distract from their effectiveness.

Habitually poor posture involving increased lumbar curvature and increased forward pelvic tilt often results in the development of abnormally short psoas and iliacus muscles. This condition may make it impossible for an individual to flatten the lumbar spine and extend the hip simultaneously.

Despite the importance of the iliopsoas group in forceful hip flexion, these muscles and the other hip flexors are usually found to be relaxed during erect standing. This is possible because the trunk is inclined backward very slightly, so that the line of gravity falls just to the rear of the femoral heads. The strong Y-ligaments (iliofemoral bands) of the hip joint prevent the trunk from falling backward in this situation, removing the need for anterior postural stabilization by the hip flexor muscles.

During simultaneous knee extension and hip flexion, as in kicking, the rectus femoris is an obvious mover; during simultaneous knee flexion and hip flexion, as in walking uphill in herringbone fashion on skis, the sartorius contracts vigorously. In situations such as these the iliopsoas group is important as a hip flexor.

Certain special aspects of the functioning of the two-joint muscles of the thigh are discussed on p. 356. The actions of the ilio-psoas group must usually be considered in relation to these special functions of the two-joint muscles. Since the location and activity of the psoas and iliacus cannot be studied by palpation or observation, and since two-dimensional pictures are inadequate to demonstrate the positional relationships, the beginning student should study descriptions of the attachments with unusual care, and should use elastic bands or other means to simulate the origin, course, and insertion on an articulated skeleton, if possible.

ACTIONS OF THE HIP EXTENSORS

The biceps, semitendinosus, and semimembranosus form a group known as the *hamstring muscles* (Fig. 15–10). These muscles, although smaller and less powerful extensors of the hip than the gluteus maximus, are much more useful for the ordinary purposes of life, because they act in walking and in standing, while the gluteus maximus does not. The consequence is that one who has lost the use of the gluteus maximus may stand and walk normally, while one who has lost the hamstring muscles can stand and walk only by throwing the weight of the trunk so far back that it tends to over-extend rather than to flex the hip, putting a tension on the ilio-femoral band. Such a position can be maintained without the use of the hamstring group while standing still and in walking carefully on a smooth and level place, but one who has lost the hamstring group cannot walk rapidly or irregularly, nor can he run, hop, jump, dance, or incline the trunk forward without falling.

When the trunk in a normal individual is inclined forward on the hip joints as an axis, the knees being kept extended and the trunk held as straight as it is in the erect position, the average adult can incline until the flexion in the hip joints is about 45 degrees; the hamstring muscles, somewhat shortened by contracting to sustain the weight of the trunk, permit no further flexion. One can flex one hip farther than this while standing on the other foot, because in this position the hamstring group is relaxed and therefore longer than in the preceding case. The same is true when one sits on the floor with the legs out straight in front; by using all the force of the flexors most people can hold the trunk erect, the stretched and relaxed hamstring muscles permitting a flexion of 90 degreees. While sitting on a chair or bench there is no difficulty in holding the trunk erect, because now the hamstring muscles are not only re-

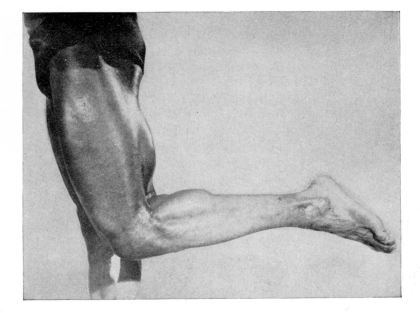

FIG. 15–10. Unusual hypertrophy of the biceps femoris, displayed by Bob Sheahy. (Courtesy Rader.)

laxed, but further slackened at the lower end by flexion of the knee; the hips will flex several degrees farther here and also in sitting on the floor if the knees are flexed, tailorwise. Persons who work sitting in an automobile or at a desk may develop contractures of the hamstrings and calf muscles strong enough to produce severe chronic backaches.

ACTIONS OF THE HIP ABDUCTORS

Whereas there are several assistant movers for hip abduction, only one muscle is listed as a prime mover—the gluteus medius. There are relatively few necessary life activities calling for a significant amount of forceful abduction of the femur away from the center line of the whole body and at first thought it may appear that development of the gluteus medius is of small importance. However, as pointed out in the preceding discussion of this muscle, the gluteus medius performs the crucial task of stabilizing the pelvis in a more or less level position atop the femur during periods of single-leg support in walking and all other forms of bipedal locomotion. If the gluteus medius be paralyzed, the Trendelenburg sign (lateral pelvic tilt or hip drop) occurs whenever there is unilateral support on the same side as the paralyzed muscle. During this unilateral support, not even momentary stabilization of the pelvis is possible; therefore, the paralyzed individual resorts to the characteristic *gluteus medius limp,* in which the trunk is tilted laterally to the same side until the center of gravity of the body parts above the hip is directly over the femoral head. The lateral waddle is very noticeable, and is accentuated in bilateral fashion if both gluteus medius muscles are affected.

Relaxed standing on one foot is usually accompanied by relaxation of the gluteus medius on the same side, resulting in hip drop on the opposite side, similar to the Trendelenburg sign. If such a stance is habitually assumed, the lateral ligaments of the hip and spine are stretched unilaterally, predisposing the persons to habitual lateral curvature of the spine. In healthy, active persons, such a purely functional scoliosis does not assume the danger attached to structural scoliosis caused by unilateral short leg or unilateral paralysis, but the habit of standing on one foot is nevertheless to be condemned from the standpoint of postural hygiene.

For normal individuals, special exercises for development of the hip abductors are usually unwarranted, since the natural activities of walking, running, skipping, hopping, kicking, and balancing will strengthen not only the gluteus medius, but also the lateral stabilizers of the spine and other joints. Sedentary adults and children who are deprived of vigorous natural activity, however, may be especially susceptible to lateral spine defects.

ACTIONS OF THE HIP ADDUCTORS

Paralysis of the adductors causes some difficulty in walking and running, but is not nearly so serious as the loss of the flexors, extensors, or abductors. Vigorous adduction of the hip is useful in riding horseback, climbing a rope or a tree, and similar activities, but one may wonder what causes the development of such large masses of muscle when there is apparently so little for them to do. The explanation is probably the fact that there are so many secondary actions for them to perform. Each adductor has at least two other possible actions on the hip joint, and some help with knee motions as well. The development of the adductor muscles is justified by the tremendous variety of combinations of movements which are required for versatile functioning of the body in many activities. For example, pivoting and cross-over steps in football and basketball require hip flexion or extension with inward or outward rotation and adduction. The adductors are needed to perform these movements, even when the adduction component involves very little resistance.

KINESIOLOGICAL EFFECTS ON THE FEMUR

Primitive peoples do a great deal more squatting, running, and jumping than is true of their civilized contemporaries. The muscular actions involved may result in certain structural alterations of the femur. Among such alterations reported in the literature are the following: The depth of the posterior end of the patellar groove is considerably greater in primitives, probably due to the pressure of the posterior cruciate ligament when the limb is in the squatting position. An articular facet may be found on the supero-lateral margin of the patellar surface. This is attributed to the action of the tendon of the quadriceps femoris muscle while the joint is fully extended. There is a very noticeable development of the adductor tubercle; it seems likely that this is connected with a greater development of the adductor magnus muscle, which is probably used in the squatting position to stabilize the limb.[13]

The head of the femur must sustain not only the pressure of the superincumbent body weight, but also the force of the abductor muscles and the tension on the iliotibial tract, which interact to hold the pelvis in equilibrium. This force is not normally borne vertically; rather it is transmitted to the femoral head at an angle, and the plane of the resulting force is in line with the medial trabeculae of the femur. The angle of this plane is approximately 165 to 170 degrees. In cases of early paralysis the weakened muscles do not permit the pelvis to be held in the normal position. The individual shifts his center of gravity by bending to the affected side and the resultant forces on the femoral neck shift more nearly to the vertical. In time a deformation of the neck of the femur (*coxa valga*—an increase in the angle between the neck and shaft of the femur) results. Individuals with certain hip diseases may also shift their centers of gravity over the hip, thus reducing the pull of the abductor muscles and decreasing the total load on the femoral head. The load is carried more vertically on the femur, giving rise to the so-called "antalgic" (pain relieving) gait, but this effects a change in the direction of the forces reacting on the femur. The result may be bone deformation or shearing stress on the epiphyseal plate.

TABLE 15–1.   Hip Joint Muscles and Their Actions

	Flex- ion	Exten- sion	Abduc- tion	Adduc- tion	Inward Rota- tion	Outward Rota- tion
Psoas	PM					
Iliacus	PM					
Sartorius	Asst.		Asst.			Asst.
Rectus femoris . . .	PM		Asst.			
Pectineus	PM			PM		Asst.
Tensor fasciae latae . .	Asst.		Asst.		PM	
Gluteus maximus . .		PM	Asst.*	Asst.**		PM
Biceps femoris . . (long head)		PM				Asst.
Semitendinosus . . .		PM			Asst.	
Semimembranosus . .		PM			Asst.	
Gluteus medius . . .	Asst.†	Asst.††	PM		Asst.†	Asst.††
Gluteus minimus . .	Asst.†	Asst.††	Asst.		PM†	Asst.††
Gracilis	Asst.			PM	Asst.	
Adductor longus . .	Asst.			PM		Asst.
Adductor brevis . . .	Asst.			PM		Asst.
Adductor magnus . .	Asst.*	Asst.**		PM	Asst.**	Asst.*
The six outward rotators						PM

* Upper fibers
** Lower fibers
† Anterior fibers
†† Posterior fibers

IMPLICATIONS FOR ATHLETIC TRAINING

The violent exertion, the gravitational load to be borne, the extreme range of movement, and the abrupt changes in direction required in athletics make the muscles of the hip joint peculiarly susceptible to injury.

Powerful contraction of the quadriceps femoris (see Chapter 16) coupled with a failure of the antagonists to relax quickly enough may result in tears of the hamstrings, usually the semitendinosus or semimembranosus (sprinter's strain). In certain styles of high jumping it is necessary to twist one leg and rotate the body, so that a severe strain is placed on the outward rotators (high jumper's strain). Trauma to the adductor muscles may result while horseback riding or in gymnastics (rider's strain). Dancers and acrobats are said to be subject to tearing of the fibers of the adductor longus muscle near its tendinous attachment to the pubis while performing the "split."

Injuries of this type are often slow to heal and tend to recur. There is a general belief among both athletes and dancers that they can best be prevented by slow, careful, stretching exercises before engaging in activity.

References

1. Colachis, Sam C., *et al.*: Movement of the Sacroiliac Joint in the Adult Male: A Preliminary Report. Arch. Phys. Med., *44*, 490–498, 1963.

2. Rasch, Philip J.: The Functional Capacities of a Yogi. J. Amer. Osteopath. Assn., *58*, 344–345, 1959.

3. Keagy, Robert D., *et al.*: Direct Electromyography of the Psoas Major Muscle in Man. J. Bone Joint Surg., *48-A*, 1377–1382, 1966.

4. Klausen, Klaus: The Form and Function of the Loaded Human Spine. Acta Physiol. Scand., *65*, 176–190, 1965.

5. Vos, P. A.: The Psoas Minor Syndrome. J. Inter. Coll. Surg., *44*, 30–36, 1965.

6. Michele, Arthur A.: *Iliopsoas*. Springfield: Charles C Thomas, 1962, pp. 119–126.

7. Beswick, Rhona E.: Ilio-psoas Fatigue in Car Drivers. Practitioner, *196*, 688–689, 1966.

8. Gratz, Charles Murray: Tensile Strength and Elasticity Tests on Human Fascia Lata. J. Bone Joint Surg., *13*, 334–340, 1931.

9. Karlson, Erling and Jonsson, Bengt: Function of the Gluteus Maximus Muscle. An Electromyographic Study. Acta Morph. Neerl. Scand., *VI*, 161–169, 1965.

10. Martin, B. F.: The Origins of the Hamstring Muscles. J. Anat., *102*, 345–352, 1968.

11. Jonsson, B. and Steen, B.: Function of the Hip and Thigh Muscles in Romberg's Test and "Standing at Ease." An Electromyographic Study. Acta Morph. Neerl. Scand., *5*, 269–276, 1963.

12. Jonsson, Bengt and Steen, Bertil: Function of the Gracilis Muscle. An Electromyographic Study. Acta Morph. Neerl. Scand., *VI*, 325–341, 1966.

13. Martin, C. P.: Some Variations in the Lower End of the Femur Which Are Especially Prevalent in the Bones of Primitive People. J. Anat., *66*, 371–383, 1932.

Recommended Reading

14. Fischer, Frederick J. and Houtz, S. J.: Evaluation of the Function of the Gluteus Maximus Muscle. Amer. J. Phys. Med., *47*, 182–191, 1968.

Laboratory Exercises

1. Compare the pelvic girdle with the shoulder girdle of a skeleton. Why do some kinesiologists insist that the pelvic girdle is properly designated but the shoulder should be referred to as a functional unit, not as a girdle?

2. Palpate the gluteus maximus. Is it brought into action more forcibly when the hip is flexed or when it is extended? Does it contract in normal walking? Does it contract in climbing stairs?

3. In what respects is the biceps femoris similar to the biceps brachii? In what respects does it differ?

4. Since women tend to suffer from lumbar lordosis, the use of iliopsoas stretching exercises in their conditioning programs are indicated rather than the commonly administered leg raises and sit ups. What exercises would you recommend for this purpose? (Suggestion: See Reference 6, p. 342.)

5. In the 1968 Olympic Games sprinter Charley Greene was hampered by a "bothersome hamstring." His trainer explained, "We put bands around his legs to keep the hamstring muscles from hitting together." (Washington, D. C. *Post,* October 20, 1968.) Evaluate this statement from the standpoint of kinesiology.

Chapter 16

Movements of the Knee Joint

The knee, the largest and most complex joint in the body, has probably evolved from three separate joints. In man there is a single joint cavity, but three separate articulations may be identified: between the medial condyles of the femur and tibia, between lateral condyles of the femur and tibia, and between patella and femur. Figures 16–1 through 16–8 illustrate the structures which are described below.

At the distal end of the femur, the following bony landmarks are important: The *medial* and *lateral condyles*, each provided with *epicondyles*, bear articular surfaces for contact with the tibia and its cartilages. Anteriorly, the condyles are separated by the shallow depression of the articular *patellar surface*, and posteriorly and inferiorly by the deeper *intercondylar* fossa (Fig. 15–4).

At the proximal end of the tibia, the following bony landmarks are important: The *medial* and *lateral condyles* are indistinctly separated except on the superior surface, where the *anterior* and *posterior intercondylar* areas and the *intercondylar eminence* occur between the two facets of the *superior articular surface*. Approximately one-half inch from the proximal end, the tibial *tuberosity* projects anteriorly. Laterally, the *head of the fibula* forms the *proximal tibiofibular articulation* with the lateral condyle of the tibia. Although this joint is separate from the knee joint, the head of the fibula has some functional relationships with the workings of the knee joint.

The *patella*, or knee cap, is a sesamoid bone (develops intramembranously) within the tendon of the quadriceps femoris muscle group. The patella is roughly triangular, with its apex projecting inferiorly and serving as the proximal attachment for the *patellar ligament*, which proceeds inferiorly to its distal attachment on the tuberosity of the tibia. Technically, the patellar ligament is appro-

priately named, since it joins bone to bone, but functionally it is a
tendon, being composed of fibers which are continuous with those
of the quadriceps tendon. The posterior surface of the patella bears
facets for artciulation with the patellar surface of the femur. The
patella protects the anterior aspect of the knee joint and acts as a
sort of pulley by increasing the angle of insertion of the patellar
ligament upon the tibial tuberosity, thus improving the mechanical
advantage of the quadriceps femoris muscle group.

On the superior articular surfaces of the tibia are the *medial* and
lateral menisci, or *semilunar cartilages*, composed of tough fibrocartilage. The cartilages serve to adapt the shapes of the femoral

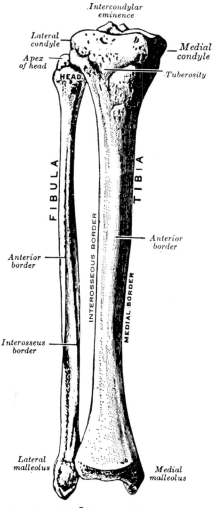

FIG. 16–1.   The right tibia and fibula, anterior view.

condyles to the articular surface of the tibia, to buffer the jars of walking and jumping, to prevent frictional wear, and, by deformation, to allow the motions of the knee joint. The menisci are roughly crescentic in shape, the lateral meniscus being smaller in circumference than the medial meniscus. Each is somewhat triangular in cross section, being much thicker at the peripheral border. The anterior ends of each meniscus are attached to the anterior inter-

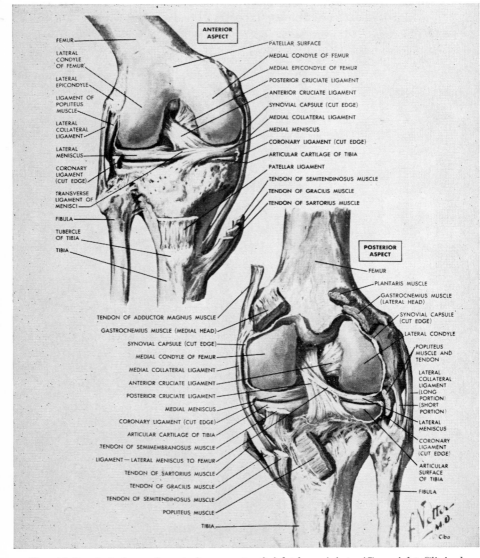

FIG. 16–2. Anterior and posterior aspects of right knee joint. (Copyright Clinical Symposia by Frank H. Netter, M.D., published by CIBA Pharmaceutical Company.)

condylar area of the tibia, and to each other by a *transverse ligament* which is sometimes absent. The posterior ends are attached to the posterior intercondyloid area. The peripheral borders of each meniscus are attached to the edges of the tibial condyles by *coronary ligaments* with vertical fibers; the inner borders of the menisci are free, as are the superior and inferior surfaces. The medial meniscus is attached at its periphery to the tibial collateral ligament; the lateral meniscus has no such attachment to the fibular collateral ligament, but its posterior end gives off the *posterior menisco-femoral ligament* to the medial condyle of the femur, just behind the posterior cruciate ligament. These anatomical details are important to the understanding of knee injuries, which will be considered later in this chapter.

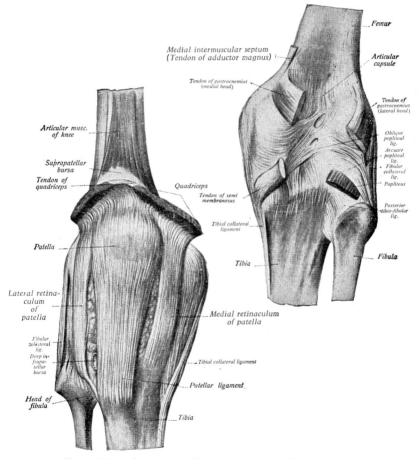

FIG. 16–3. Anterior and posterior views of knee joints
showing accessory ligaments. (Sobotta.)

The strong *anterior* and *posterior cruciate ligaments* are the main structures forming the incomplete *intercondylar septum* which partially divides the knee joint cavity into right and left halves. The anterior cruciate runs from the anterior intercondylar area of the tibia upward and backward to the intercondylar fossa of the femur; the posterior runs from the posterior intercondylar area of the tibia upward and forward to the intercondylar fossa of the femur.

The *tibial collateral ligament,* on the medial side of the knee, joins the medial condyles of the femur and tibia, merging on the way with the capsule of the joint and with the coronary ligament of the medial meniscus. The *fibular collateral ligament,* on the lateral side of the knee, joins the lateral condyle of the femur with the head of the fibula. The tendon of the popliteus muscle separates the fibular collateral ligament from the lateral meniscus and from the joint capsule proper.

On the posterior aspect of the knee joint, the *oblique popliteal ligament* connects the articular margins of the femur and tibia, and the *arcuate popliteal ligament* runs downward from the lateral condyle of the femur to the posterior surface of the joint capsule and, by two converging bands, to the head of the fibula.

All of the articular surfaces of the femur, tibia, and patella are covered with the usual hyaline cartilage. The ligamentous *joint capsule* is irregular and extensive. The capsule is lined with a *synovial membrane,* which invests both the upper and lower surfaces of the two menisci, excluding them from the joint cavity.

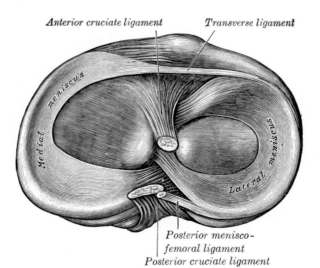

Anterior cruciate ligament   *Transverse ligament*

*Posterior menisco-
femoral ligament*
Posterior cruciate ligament

FIG. 16–4.   Head of right tibia, superior view, showing menisci and attachments of ligaments. (*Gray's Anatomy.*)

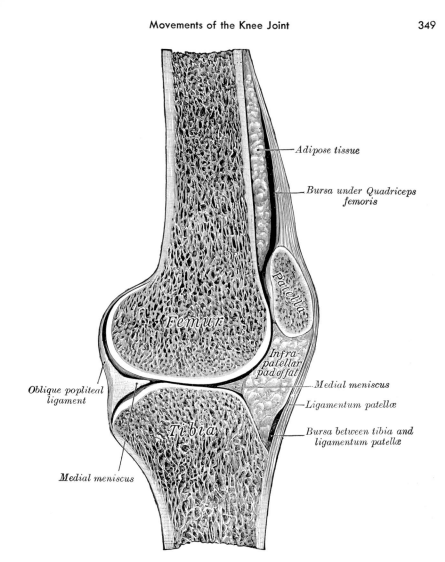

FIG. 16–5.   Sagittal section of right knee joint.   (*Gray's Anatomy.*)

Numerous bursae occur around the joint, some of them having connections with the main joint cavity in some or all individuals. The *prepatellar bursa* lies between the patella and the skin on the anterior aspect.   The *suprapatellar bursa* lies deep to the quadriceps tendon.   The *infrapatellar bursa* lies deep to the patellar ligament and superficial to the *infrapatellar fat pad*.   Another bursa lies subcutaneously over the tuberosity of the tibia; several others cushion the tendons of the popliteus, of both heads of the gastrocnemius, and of other two-joint muscles.

The fascia surrounding the knee joint merges with ligaments, and, when various muscles are tense, plays no small part in the stabilization of the joint. Tendons of the two-joint muscles (rectus femoris, the hamstrings, sartorius, gracilis, and gastrocnemius) participate vigorously in strengthening and protecting the joint against unnatural or excessive movements.

In the erect standing position, the tibia are almost exactly vertical, and the medial and lateral condylar articulating surfaces of both tibia and femur lie in a horizontal plane. The shafts of the femur are not vertical, since the knees are relatively close together while the femoral heads and trochanters are markedly spread apart. This obliquity of the shaft of the femur differs from person to person, depending upon heredity, sex (females have broader hips *in proportion to height*), nutrition and disease (especially during the growth period), occupational and recreational activity, muscular development, footgear, and other factors. Torsion in the shaft of the femur and angle between shaft and neck of the femur also vary. These differences may affect gait and other functions, and are important considerations in orthopedic medical practice and therapeutic programs.

There are twelve muscles acting on the knee joint. These may be divided into three groups:

Hamstring group: Semitendinosus, semimembranosus, biceps femoris.

Quadriceps femoris group: Rectus femoris, vastus lateralis, vastus intermedius, vastus medialis.

Unclassified group: Sartorius, gracilis, popliteus, gastrocnemius, plantaris.

Some of these have been discussed earlier; two (gastrocnemius and plantaris) will be described in the next chapter.

POPLITEUS

Origin. The lateral aspect of the lateral condyle of the femur (Figs. 16–2, 17–9).

Insertion. Medial posterior side of tibia, superior to the origin of the soleus.

Innervation. A branch of the tibial nerve which contains fibers from the fourth and fifth lumbar, and first sacral nerves.

Structure. A thin, flat, triangular muscle which forms the lower part of the floor of the popliteal space.

Action. Flexion and medial rotation of the tibia. Aids in unlocking the knee at the start of knee flexion. Assists in stabilizing the knee.[1]

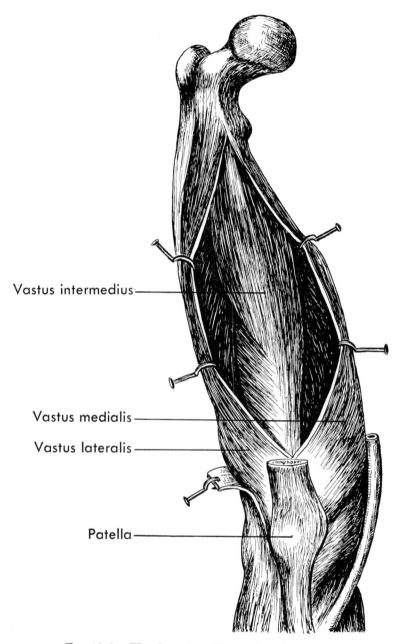

Vastus intermedius

Vastus medialis

Vastus lateralis

Patella

FIG. 16-6.   The three "vasti" muscles.   (Douglas.)
Compare Figure 16-7.

VASTUS LATERALIS

A large muscle located half-way down the outer side of the thigh and making the rounded eminence to be found there. It corresponds closely to the lateral head of the triceps brachii (Figs. 15–5, 16–6). It is bipennate.

Origin. The lateral surface of the femur just below the greater trochanter and the upper half of the linea aspera (Figs. A–13, A–14).

Insertion. The lateral and superior borders of the patella and the quadriceps femoris tendon.

Innervation. Branches from the femoral nerve which contain fibers from the second, third, and fourth lumbar nerves.

Structure. A small portion of the muscular fibers arises directly from the femur near the trochanter; the greater part arises from a tendon shaped much like a sheet of paper covering the outer surface of the muscle for its upper two-thirds, with its posterior edge attached to the linea aspera. The lower tendon is a flat sheet attached to the upper border of the patella and serving as a tendon of insertion

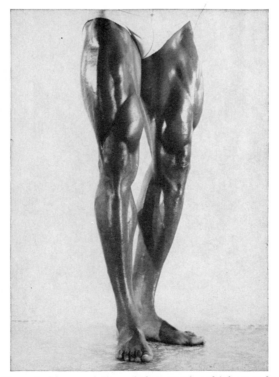

Fig. 16–7. Remarkable separation of the anterior thigh muscles; displayed by Robert Walker. The student will find identifying each of these muscles and their action an excellent aid to learning. (Hasse, courtesy *Strength and Health*.)

for the three "vasti" muscles; it lies beneath the vastus lateralis, and the muscle fibers pass obliquely downward and inward from the upper tendon to join it.

Action. Prime mover for knee extension. It needs a companion from the inner side to give a straight pull on the patella.

VASTUS MEDIALIS

This bipennate muscle, corresponding to the medial head of the triceps brachii, is located on the medial side of the thigh, somewhat lower than the lateralis and partly covered by the rectus and the sartorius (Figs. 15–5, 16–6).

Origin. The whole length of the linea aspera and the medial supracondylar line (Figs. 15–4, A–14).

Insertion. The medial border of the patella and the quadriceps femoris tendon.

Innervation. Branches from the femoral nerve which contain fibers from the second, third, and fourth lumbar nerves.

Structure. Similar to the vastus lateralis.

Action. Prime mover for knee extension. Its diagonal pull inward counterbalances the vastus lateralis' diagonal pull outward and the two muscles give a straight pull on the patella. The common belief that this muscle contracts strongly only during the last fifteen degrees of extension of the knee is not supported by recent studies of its function. The chore of completing the screw-home movement of the knee joint commonly assigned to it by clinicians seems more reasonably attributable to ligamentous and articular alignment. An important function of the muscle is the maintenance of patellar alignment against the lateral pull of the vastus lateralis[2] (Fig. 7–4).

VASTUS INTERMEDIUS

A companion of the two preceding muscles, lying between them and beneath the rectus femoris (Fig. 16–6). It is difficult to separate this muscle from the medialis, and the two may be continuous for part of their length.

Origin. Anterior and lateral aspect of the femur, except the inferior four inches.

Insertion. The superior border of the patella via the quadriceps femoris tendon.

Innervation. Branches from the femoral nerve which contain fibers from the second, third, and fourth lumbar nerves.

Structure. The muscle fibers arise directly from the bone and pass downward and forward to join the deeper surface of the sheet which serves as a tendon for the two preceding muscles.

Action.   Prime mover for knee extension.   Like the rectus femoris, its pull is directly upward on the patella.

ILIOTIBIAL BAND

The iliotibial band, or iliotibial tract, is a broad ligament connecting the ilium with the lateral tubercle of the tibia, the patella, the linea aspera, and the lateral condyle of the femur.   The tensor fasciae latae inserts into it, and the band itself inserts into the tibia and blends with fibrous expansions from the vastus lateralis and biceps femoris.   This tract has been found only in man; other animals have developed the tensor fasciae latae without simultaneously developing the iliotibial band.[3]   The tension of this tract strongly reinforces the lateral retention apparatus of the knee joint, and thus contributes importantly to the maintenance of erect posture.   However, in cases of pathological contractures, such as may follow poliomyelitis, it may produce severe deformities involving the hip and the knee joints.

MOVEMENTS OF THE KNEE JOINT

Flexion and Extension.   The fundamental movements of the knee joint are *flexion* and *extension*, but the knee is not a simple ginglymus or hinge joint.   With the knee fully extended, the femoral condyles project posteriorly from the line of the shaft of the femur.   As the knee is flexed, the femoral condyles would tend to roll like wheels off the posterior edge of the tibia if they were not restrained by the cruciate ligaments, the fascia lata, and other fascial and muscular structures.   As flexion progresses, the anterior cruciate ligament becomes taut and forces the femoral condyles to slide forward on the menisci.   Thus, there is the tendency for approximately the same spot on the tibia to make contact with progressively more posterior parts of the condyles of the femur.   From a position of full flexion, as extension occurs there would be a tendency for the femur to roll off the anterior edge of the tibia if the posterior cruciate ligament did not become taut and force the femoral condyles to slide backward on the menisci.

Flexion of the knee is possible through about 135 degrees, when it is brought to a stop by contact of the tissues on the back of the thigh and leg and by the capsular and cruciate ligaments.   Since the angle of the knee joint has a decided effect on strength scores, it is possible to compare leg lift figures only if they are recorded with the knee flexed to a specified degree.

The Normal Locking of the Knee.   The joint can be very slightly hyperextended. Further hyperextension is limited by the anterior cruciate ligament, and perhaps also by parts of the fascia lata, collateral ligaments, and other connective tissues. When the body is balanced in an erect position, the gravity line falls slightly in front of the tibiofemoral articular contact points. Thus, the quadriceps extensor muscles can relax, because the knees are effectively "locked" in hyperextension by the small gravitational torque.

Locking of the knee, while the body is in erect weight-bearing position, is not accomplished by extension alone, however. Figures 16–4 and 16–8 show that the diameters of the medial meniscus and femoral condyle are greater than the diameters of the lateral meniscus and femoral condyle. Knee extension reaches its limit when the lateral femoral condyle becomes close-packed (see page 34), but at this point the medial side is still loose-packed. Inward rotation of the femur on the tibia is still possible, and may be caused by continued contraction of the quadriceps femoris muscle group, aided by the forces of weight-bearing, until the joint is completely close-packed or "locked." The terminal inward rotation that seats the femur congruously into the menisci is sometimes called the "screw-home movement" of the knee. Some kinesiologists have not been able to detect the screw-home movement at the end of passive, non-weight-bearing knee extension. Perhaps this means that the knee does not necessarily have to lock when it is completely extended.

Action of the popliteus muscle is necessary to unlock the weight-bearing knee before flexing it. The popliteus is listed as a prime mover for inward rotation of the knee joint, the assumption being that the tibia is the moving part. But the tibia is well stabilized when weight is borne on the extremity, so contraction of the pop-

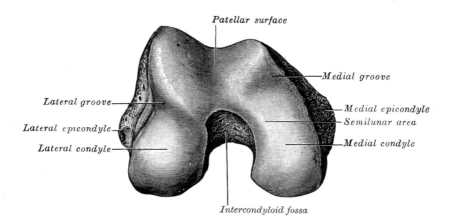

Patellar surface

Medial groove

Lateral groove

Medial epicondyle
Semilunar area

Lateral epicondyle

Lateral condyle

Medial condyle

Intercondyloid fossa

FIG. 16–8. Lower extremity of right femur viewed from below. (*Gray's Anatomy.*)

liteus acts to rotate the femur outward, effectively reversing the
screw-home movement. When weight is not being borne, unlocking
can occur passively as a by-product of knee flexion.

Rotation. When the knee is locked in extension, no rotation is
possible, although the foot may still be turned inward and outward
by rotation at the ankle and hip joints. As the knee is flexed, the
collateral ligaments and fascia become progressively more slack,
permitting *inward* and *outward rotation*. After about 90 degrees of
flexion, as much as 60 to 90 degrees of rotation may be possible. In
the extended knee, postural stability is encouraged by the lack of
rotation, but the joint is very vulnerable to injury from lateral
forces. During activity, when the knee is likely to be flexed to some
extent, the ability to rotate makes possible a wide variety of movements, such as pivoting, changing direction of location, grasping
objects between the soles (as in climbing a pole), and performing
inside- and outside-ankle kicks in soccer.

ACTIONS OF TWO-JOINT MUSCLES

The preceding analysis has shown that certain muscles act simultaneously on both the hip joint and the knee joint. The nerve endings in dogs suggest that one part of a two-joint muscle may shorten
while another lengthens, but electromyographic studies have demonstrated that this phenomenon does not occur in man under normal
conditions. In the latter when a two-joint muscle contracts, it pulls
at both ends at once. For example, the sartorius flexes both the hip
and the knee in withdrawing the foot from a painful stimulus, in
initiating the forward swing of the lower limb just after the vigorous
push-off of a crouch start in running, and in stepping up onto a high
bench. Similarly the rectus femoris both flexes the hip and extends
the knee in punting a football.

However, the action of the two-joint muscles of the hip and knee
is not as simple as these examples might indicate, and the study of
the functions of individual muscles is insufficient to account for all
of the observed phenomena of lower limb movement. During
normal body motions, muscles tend to act in groups and to effect a
coordinated movement. The composition of a group is not constant. The muscle-members are selected according to the needs of
the teamwork which is desired. Analogously, it might be compared
to a coach (the central nervous system) drawing on his past experience (conditioned reflexes) to send into the game (cause to contract)
various combinations of his players (muscles) according to the different game situations, such as general offense (hip flexion and knee
extension), defense against running attack (hip and knee flexion), or

defense against passing attack (hip and knee extension). The teamwork of muscles is complex even when it involves one-joint muscles
only. If two-joint muscles are involved, the complexity is greatly
increased, and a special analysis must be made.

Lombard's Paradox. While sitting in a chair, the student may
grasp his thigh so that the thumb palpates the belly of the rectus
femoris and the fingers palpate the bellies of the hamstring muscles.
As he arises from the chair by means of hip and knee extension, he
will feel both the rectus femoris and the hamstring muscles spring
into action. It may surprise him to find that all of these muscles are
active, since he will recall that while the rectus femoris tends to extend the knee, it also tends to flex the hip, and while the hamstrings tend to extend the hip, they also tend to flex the knee. He
might expect that the rectus femoris and the hamstrings would
mutually neutralize each other's action at both the hip and knee
joints. This seemingly contradictory situation is known as Lom-

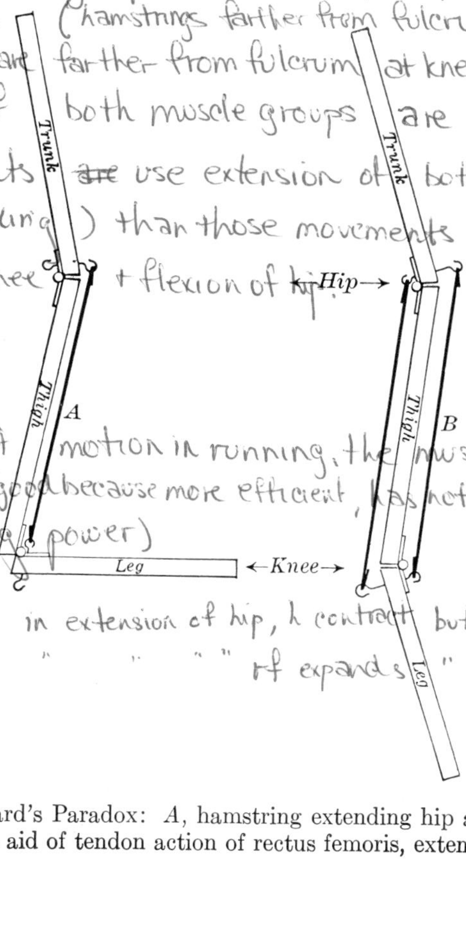

[handwritten annotations:]

both of the muscle group exert = force, but, due to distance from fulcrum (hamstrings farther from fulcrum at hip + rectus femoris, etc., are farther from fulcrum at knee), both go to extension if both muscle groups are stimulated equally.

More movements use extension of both joints (jumping, running, walking) than those movements (kicking) using extension of knee + flexion of hip.

In full range of motion in running, the muscles remain the same size (good because more efficient, has not used up all pulling or contracting power)

h.

in extension of hip, h contract but knee extends, making h expand
" " " " rf expands " " " " " rf contract

FIG. 16–9. Lombard's Paradox: *A*, hamstring extending hip and flexing knee;
B, hamstring with aid of tendon action of rectus femoris, extending both joints.

bard's Paradox, after W. P. Lombard,[4] who was one of the first scholars to analyze and explain clearly the problem.

Study of the action of the two-joint muscles of the thigh during simultaneous hip and knee extension may be approached step-by-step through the use of the simple model shown in Figure 16–9A and B. Figure 16–9A shows an elastic band placed so as to represent a hamstring muscle. If the elastic band is placed on the opposite side of the model, it represents the rectus femoris muscle. Now, if two elastic bands are employed, simulating simultaneous contraction of the hamstrings and the rectus femoris, as shown in Figure 16–9B, the paradox appears: extension takes place at both joints! Lombard's explanation, which is still accepted, in spite of alternative proposals, is based on anatomical measurements which have been deliberately duplicated in the model. At the hip joint, the lever arm (that is, the distance from the center of rotation of the joint to the point of attachment of the muscle) of the hamstrings for extension is greater than that of the rectus femoris for flexion. The rotational torque for each muscle is equal to the force of its pull multiplied by its perpendicular distance from the axis of rotation. Assuming that the forces developed within the two muscles are equal, the torque of the hamstrings for hip extension is greater than the torque of the rectus femoris for hip flexion, because of the difference in lengths of the lever arms. A similar but opposite situation exists at the knee joint. The torque of the rectus femoris for knee extension is greater than the torque of the hamstrings for flexion. Elftman[5] has presented the lengths of these lever arms in a representative individual, as shown in Table 16–1. These figures are cited here out of context, and should be interpreted only as rough approximations for comparative purposes.

In summary, it may be said that Lombard's Paradox is explained by the fact that the leverages of the bones comprising the joints prevent the fundamental antagonism of the muscles from completely neutralizing each other's actions.

Tendinous or Belt-Like Action of Two-Joint Muscles. The model in Figure 16–9 may be further utilized to illustrate another principle

TABLE 16–1.   Comparative Lengths of Lever Arms of
Two-Joint Muscles

| | *LENGTH OF LEVER ARMS* | |
	At Hip Joint	*At Knee Joint*
Rectus femoris	3.9 cm.	4.4 cm.
Hamstrings	6.7 cm.	3.4 cm.

of two-joint muscle action. If either one of the elastic bands is replaced with a taut cord, the working of the model is not altered. Extension at both joints still results. The action of the model in this instance may be explained by what is variously called the *tendinous action, belt-like action,* or *pulley action* of the two-joint muscles. Let us assume that the hamstrings are represented by the elastic band, and the rectus femoris by the cord. The tension within the elastic band (simulating contraction of the hamstrings) pulls the hip into extension. This movement causes a pull on the cord (rectus femoris), which is transmitted to the other end of the cord, causing extension of the knee, just as if a contracting muscle were operating. Extension of the knee would, of course, be opposed by the tension within the elastic band, but at each joint the long lever arms for extension determine the movement which takes place. In this situation, the passive function of the cord in transmitting the tension is similar to the function of a rectus femoris muscle whose connective tissue will not allow it to be stretched more than a certain amount, thus making it tight even though it is relaxed.

If *both* elastic bands on the model are replaced by taut cords, it is virtually impossible to tie them tight enough to introduce tension into the closed system. Hence the model no longer exhibits extension at both joints, but lies motionless in whatever position it is placed. However, the cords are sufficiently tight to compare with relaxed hamstring muscles, which are also notoriously taut in living individuals. Now if the model is grasped by the "trunk" member with one hand, and if the other hand is used to flex the "thigh" on the "trunk," the "leg" will also flex on the "thigh." The cords now act like an endless belt going around pulleys at the hip and knee joints. Hip flexion causes a pull on the hamstrings, which is transferred to the knee joint, flexing it. Knee flexion causes a pull on the rectus femoris, which is transferred to the hip joint, furthering the flexion which was originally induced by the outside force. Under similar circumstances, if the model is manipulated so as to extend the hip, then the knee is also extended. This same sort of tendinous action occurs in the intact human organism, provided that the muscles are naturally taut or that they are contracting enough to take up slack. It should be noted that the principle of tendinous action is different from, and independent of, the principle of differential leverage which was used to explain Lombard's Paradox. The two principles may be invoked simultaneously, but tendinous action would occur even if the lever arms were all of the same length.

A more nearly complete and realistic illustration of tendinous action of two-joint muscles in conjunction with action of one-joint muscles can be achieved with the slightly more complex model

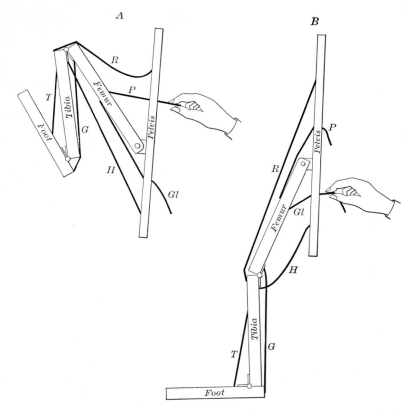

FIG. 16–10.   The so-called tendinous action of the two-joint muscles of the thigh:
R, rectus femoris; *P*, psoas; *Gl*, gluteus maximus; *H*, hamstring; *T*, anterior tibial;
G, gastrocnemius.   (Lombard.)

illustrated in Figure 16–10*A* and *B*.   Figure 16–10*A* shows hip
flexion caused by contraction of the psoas.   The rectus femoris is
slacked, allowing the natural tightness of the hamstrings to flex the
simulated knee by tendinous action.   The knee flexion allows the
gastrocnemius to go slack, which in turn permits a minimal contraction of the tibialis anterior to dorsiflex the ankle.*

If, while the three joints are in a position of flexion, the gluteus
maximus contracts, the result is that shown in Figure 16–10*B*.   The
gluteus maximus initiates hip extension, thus removing tension

---

* In the frog, the tibialis anterior is a two-joint muscle, extending above the knee.
Such an arrangement allows tendinous action to encourage dorsiflexion in the situation
described above.   In the opposite situation when multi-joint extension is taking place
during jumping, two-joint muscles enhance the activity, providing kinesiologists with
an extra erudite insight into Mark Twain's story of the jumping frogs of Calaveras
County.   It may be assumed that winning jumpers have exceptionally long lever arms
for extension.

from the hamstrings while stretching the rectus femoris. This results in knee extension, which in turn takes up the slack in the gastrocnemius, causing plantar flexion at the ankle.

The results of manipulating models should not be over-generalized. Although in most people the hamstring muscles are sufficiently tight to exert tendinous action at the slightest provocation, the majority of the other muscles are not. Tendinous action is minimized or disappears when the two-joint muscles are relaxed, although it will operate whenever these muscles are contracted sufficiently to make them taut. An understanding of Lombard's Paradox and the concept of tendinous action engenders appreciation of the teamwork potentiality and the versatility of the muscular system. The anatomical arrangements are beautifully designed to enhance the performance of natural activities, and are especially efficient in combating the pull of gravity which constantly threatens man's upright position.

Energy Conservation by Two-Joint Muscles. One-joint muscles are necessary in order to provide individuation of movement—that is, the performance of a single joint action separately from any other joint action. However, a two-joint muscle is much more efficient when some definite combination of actions at two different joints simultaneously is required. Elftman,[6] in a thorough determination of total and segmental energy exchange during running, found a stage in the forward swing of the leg, shortly before it contacted the ground, in which hip extensors were required to do positive work at the same time that knee flexors were required to decelerate the extension of the knee. At this moment the hamstring muscles receive kinetic energy from the momentum of the lower leg at the knee joint; at the same time they are expending energy at the hip joint. One-joint muscles could perform the task, but the energy received at the knee joint would be wasted (dissipated as heat), whereas two-joint muscles can apply at the hip joint the energy received at the knee. According to his calculations, the work of walking requires an expenditure of 2.61 h.p. by the limb muscles; if only single joint muscles were used, 3.97 h.p. would be needed. One result of this is that two-joint muscles preponderate in the thigh and largely determine its shape (Fig. 16–11).

This gain in efficiency, however, is achieved at the cost of greater vulnerability to injury. When a musculotendinous unit activates or crosses two joints, a full extension of both of them places a maximal stretch upon the muscle. The resulting tension may be great enough to tear some of its elastic components. A common example is seen in "tennis leg." When the knee is fully extended and the ankle is dorsiflexed, a sudden strain may result in a transverse

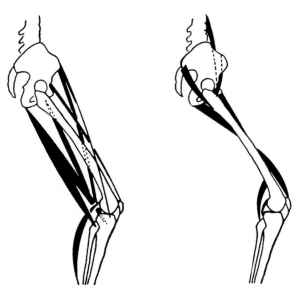

FIG. 16–11. This comparison of the two-joint muscles of the thigh (left) with the one-joint muscles (right) clearly shows the preponderance of the former and how this influences the shape of the thigh. (Reproduced by permission from Herbert Elftman: Body Dynamics and Dynamic Anthropometry. Ann. New York Acad. Sc.)

rupture of the medial gastrocnemius at the musculotendinous junction. The biceps femoris, semimembranosus, and rectus femoris are other muscles which are particularly susceptible to injury because of their two-joint nature.

Kinesiological Effects on the Tibia. In primitive people who do a great deal of running and leaping the tibia tends to become flattened in order to provide a larger surface of origin for the tibialis anterior. This results from the conditions causing hypertrophy of that muscle. The same conditions may be responsible for a prominence on the anterior aspect of the lateral condyle, where the anterior portion of the iliotibial tract attaches. *Retroversion* is a condition in which the diaphysis is straight but the proximal end is tilted slightly backwards, so that a pronounced concavity of the bone results. This is found mainly in mountaineers and may result from their habit of walking with the knees slightly flexed; it may also result from the act of squatting. In squatting the lateral meniscus moves somewhat backwards. This movement is facilitated by an increased convexity of the articular surface of the lateral condyle. Such convexity has been found to be much greater in savage races than in Europeans. In Europeans the anterior margin of the distal epiphysis is usually sharp, but in primitives it has an articular facet toward the fibular side. This fits together with a similar facet which is found on the neck of the talus. It is believed to be due to the extreme dorsiflexion of the ankle joint which occurs in squatting. Variations in the shape of the medial condyle also result from squatting. A groove in the tibiae deep to the patellar ligaments is characteristic of squatters. It is believed to result from tendinous pressure.[7] Torsion of the tibia may result from the habit of turning the foot laterally to improve the base of support when standing. The angle of torsion is about 19 degrees in modern Europeans, but is less in races which rest in the kneeling position with the feet turned medially under the buttocks so that the toes point towards each other.[8]

Muscle Substitution. It is the experience of every therapist that

FIG. 16–12. Use of the legs in lifting heavy weights overhead. Tommy Kono, former Olympic and World Light Heavyweight Weight Lifting Champion, in starting position for the two hands snatch. (Hasse, courtesy *Strength and Health.*)

unless a patient is closely supervised during the process of rehabilitation he will tend to substitute other muscle groups for those which he finds inefficient or painful to use. While these so-called "trick moments" may be annoying to the therapist, they are very instructive to the kinesiologist. Treatment of any condition affecting the knee joint will include quadriceps exercises. "Trick movements" enable the patient to achieve knee-extension without placing a proportionate share of the work on these muscles. When the patient lies supine, the knee is not fully extended, owing to the calcaneus and the posterior muscles being in contact with the surface upon which he is lying. Static muscle contractions do not necessarily work the quadriceps to the extent required, since the oblique posterior ligament and the contraction of the hamstrings may pull the femur downward and thus extend the knee. Lifting of the heel produces an apparently more active extension of the knee, but the action may be performed by hip-flexion. In the sitting position dorsi-flexion of the foot may transmit a pull to the gastrocnemius and plantaris muscles. Working with reversed origins, these may pull the femur backward. In leg-raising from the sitting position,

Fig. 16–13. Kono snatching in the squat style. (Hasse, courtesy *Strength and Health*.) For a mechanical analysis of the two styles of snatching see Arnold Scott Arsenault, *A Mechanical Analysis of the Two Weight Lifting Methods of Two Hands Snatching*. Unpublished Master's Thesis, Springfield College, August 1957.

fixation and stabilization of the knee joint may be partially accomplished by the gastrocnemius and plantaris, working eccentrically with reversed origins. These movements can be excluded by raising the thigh with a sandbag and thus increasing the degree of flexion at the knee joint to such an extent that only a more forceful contraction of the quadriceps will raise the leg from its support. This will also eliminate the possibility of leg raising by hip flexion.[9] A large number of similar "vicarious motions" used in other parts of the body are described by Wynn-Parry.[10]

Fig. 16–14. Norbert Schemansky, former Olympic and World Middle Heavyweight Weight Lifting Champion, snatching in the split style. (Kirkley.) Lifting as a heavyweight, Schemansky snatched 363.75 lbs. in the 1964 Olympic Weight-Lifting Championships. For physiological data on this style of snatching see Leslie R. Leggett, *Physiological Measures of Selected Weight Lifting Activities.* Unpublished Master's Thesis, Springfield College, June, 1958.

IMPLICATIONS FOR ATHLETIC TRAINING

Ligamentous injuries of the knee joint are relatively common in body contact athletics and are frequently permanently incapacitating. The lateral stability of the knee joint is maintained by the muscles and five other structures: both collateral ligaments, both cruciate ligaments, and the articular capsule. Anterior and posterior movement at the joint results when either of the cruciates is ruptured; an abnormal amount of rotation becomes evident when the collateral ligaments are torn. Collateral ligament injuries may have associated cruciate ligament injuries, and the menisci may or may not be involved. Most serious injuries to the knee joint can be remedied only by surgery; fortunately a normally functioning knee usually results after an operation for removal of the menisci.

Meniscus injuries ("football knees") are common. A meniscus may be split or cracked, broken into two or more pieces, or loosened by a tearing of its ligamentous attachments. Such injuries usually result from a lateral blow (the result of blocking or tackling) or from inadvertent "lateral flexion" (the result of turning an ankle, stepping in a hole, or running on an irregular surface). When the knee is in a completely-extended or nearly-extended position while weight is borne on the extremity, both the collateral and cruciate ligaments are taut and the anterior aspects of both menisci are secured between the condyles of the tibia and the femur. Trauma to the joint when the leg is in this position may have serious consequences (Fig. 16–15). Therefore, some football coaches advise players to flex the knee and remove weight from the extremity whenever lateral impact is anticipated.

The medial meniscus is injured much more frequently than the lateral. Since the medial meniscus is attached to the tibial collateral ligament, a tearing of that collateral ligament may pull the meniscus out of place or break it. The lateral meniscus does not attach to the fibular collateral ligament; furthermore, the posterior meniscofemoral ligament (Fig. 16–2) may provide extra stabilization.

Ski Injuries. Lower limb accidents involving turning are common among skiers. Usually a ski tip catches, momentum tries to carry the skier forward, he rotates on the fixed leg, and a tremendous torque is built up as the free leg crosses over in front of the body. Lateral-rotation stresses resulting in spiral fracture of the lateral malleolus (skier's fracture) or other trauma to the ankle, tibiofibular complex or the knee are responsible for the most requent fractures and ligamentous lesions of the lower extremity in skiing.[12]

Dislocations. A true tibiofemoral dislocation of the knee is comparatively rare in athletics. Usually a "dislocation of the knee" is actually a dislocation of the patella.

Fig. 16–15.   How typical football knee injuries occur.   Note that the left foot of
the player in the white uniform is fixed to the ground by the cleats of his shoe.   He is
turned away from the fixed foot, throwing the leg into external rotation at the same
time that a forcible blow is delivered on the outside of the knee, producing medial
bowing.   The result may be what O'Donoghue[11] has termed the "Unhappy Triad":
i.e., torn medial collateral ligament, torn medial meniscus, and torn anterior
cruciate.   This condition often results when a player is "mouse-trapped."   (Photo
courtesy *The Miami Herald*.)

Rehabilitation.   During the prolonged immobilization of the knee
joint associated with rehabilitation, ankylosis* may appear.   This is
often progressive and irreversible in nature.   Within twenty-four
hours after injury to the knee, disuse atrophy, wasting of the thigh
muscles, and a loss of coordination between the muscle groups involved may be notable.   This is possibly due to a reflex mechanism
which seeks to protect the articular synovial membrane.   A disproportionate atrophy of the vastus medialis is a familiar clinical picture.   Once a knee has become stiffened, restoration of strength to

* Ankylosis is the knitting together of two bones, resulting in a stiff joint.

13

the vastus medialis in particular and of mobility to the knee joint in general presents one of the most difficult problems in physical medicine and rehabilitation. Current practice holds that the first step in both the prevention and treatment of knee injuries is the development of quadriceps and hamstring strength. Excellent results in the treatment of various kinds of traumata to the knee have resulted from programs of progressive resistance exercise.

Shin Splints. Running or marching may cause a unique pain at or around the shin, known as "shin splints." The pain probably arises from irritation of the periosteum, but the cause may be any one of the following: (1) direct muscle and tendon pulls on the periosteal muscle attachment; (2) sprains and tears of the interosseous membrane, referred to its periosteal attachments on the tibia or fibula; (3) hairline stress fractures of the tibia, or (4) anterior tibial compartment syndrome. In mild cases the symptoms may disappear if the athlete continues light but gradually increasing exercise on softer surfaces. When the disability is more severe in any of the first three types, cessation of activity appears essential.

Stress fractures result from a bone's inability to withstand repeated subthreshold bending stress, such as occurs in running or marching on hard surfaces. They occur in the fibula less often than in the metatarsals, where the injury is termed "march fracture." Devas and Sweetnam[13] suggest that strenuous contraction of the powerful plantar and long toe flexors draws the fibula toward the tibia. The resultant to-and-fro movement is believed to cause fractures which most frequently occur near the inferior tibiofibular joint. Devas[14] has also suggested that strong calf muscles working at their maximum strength may cause the tibia to bow forward. It is possible that the tibial fractures which Burrows[15] observed in male ballet dancers are injuries of a similar nature, although a different mechanism appears to be involved. With rest and support, these fractures usually heal in three to six weeks.[16]

Anterior tibial compartment syndrome is relatively rare, but it requires special mention because permanent paralysis results unless surgery is instituted within a few hours of the occurrence of pain. The anterior tibial compartment is an unyielding cylinder composed of tibia, fibula, interosseous membrane, and crural fascia, enclosing the tibialis anterior and other muscles, with only small openings for the passage of tendons, nerves, and blood vessels. Strenuous exercise (as well as tibial fractures and other conditions unrelated to shin splints) may cause swelling within the compartment, compressing and obstructing the veins and initiating a cycle of increasing internal pressure. If surgical decompression is not performed, necrosis (death) of the enclosed soft tissue occurs. In one case, partial

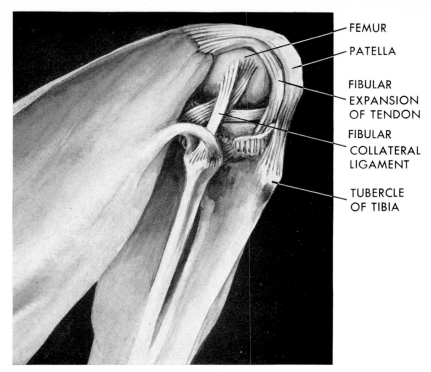

FEMUR

PATELLA

FIBULAR
EXPANSION
OF TENDON

FIBULAR
COLLATERAL
LIGAMENT

TUBERCLE
OF TIBIA

A

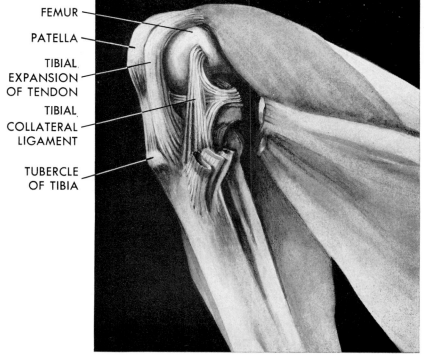

FEMUR

PATELLA

TIBIAL
EXPANSION
OF TENDON

TIBIAL
COLLATERAL
LIGAMENT

TUBERCLE
OF TIBIA

B

FIG. 16–16. The knee joint in full flexion during weight bearing. *A*, Lateral view. *B*, Medial view. (Drawing by Pauline G. West, courtesy Karl K. Klein, University of Texas.)

paralysis occurred even though surgery was performed only eighteen hours after pain occurred.[17]

A physical educator or trainer should lose no time in making a referral for medical diagnosis whenever a case of "shin splints" involves the following symptoms: Unrelenting pain even when the leg is at rest; skin red, hot, tense, and glossy over the anterior compartment; tenderness on palpation, and (especially) any loss of sensation at the base of the toes, or any loss of voluntary movement of the toes, foot, or ankle.

Osgood-Schlatter's Disease. In some individuals a pronation of the feet, inward displacement of the patella, or genu valgus (p. 452) may cause an abnormal angle of insertion of the tendon of the patella into the tubercle of the tibia. Consequently the force exerted on the patella by the quadriceps develops a shearing stress which causes the separation of fragments of cartilage and bone of the tubercle. Patients are usually in the eleven to fifteen years age group. Treatment consists primarily in raising the inner side of the heels of the shoes and of the elimination of running.[18]

The **deep knee bend,** the **full squat,** and **"duck waddle"** have been condemned by the National Federation of State High School Athletic Associations and the Committee on the Medical Aspects of Sports of the American Medical Association as potentially injurious to the internal and supporting structures of the knee joint. They postulate that when the foot is fixed normal rotation of the tibia cannot take place. The result is an increased stress on the ligaments

TABLE 16–2.   Knee Joint Muscles and Their Actions

Muscle	Flexion	Extension	Inward Rotation	Outward Rotation
Semitendinosus	P.M.		P.M.	
Semimembranosus	P.M.		P.M.	
Biceps femoris	P.M.			P.M.
Rectus femoris		P.M.		
Vastus lateralis		P.M.		
Vastus intermedius		P.M.		
Vastus medialis		P.M.		
Sartorius	Asst.		Asst.	
Gracilis	Asst.		Asst.	
Popliteus*	Asst.		P.M.	
Gastrocnemius	Asst.			
Plantaris	Asst.			

* "Unlocks" the knee at the start of knee flexion.

and cartilages of the flexed knee (Fig. 16–16). This, they argue, may stretch the supporting structures and predispose the joint to injury, or may even cause a tear of the medial semi-lunar cartilage.

It should be noted, however, that the common practice has been to conduct examinations for lateral instability with the knee fully extended. Hallen and Lindahl[19] divided the superficial and deeper portions of the tibial collateral ligament and the anterior and posterior cruciate ligaments in turn but were unable to demonstrate any instability in the fully extended joint unless there was a loss of substance in the condyles of the knee. They concluded that injuries to the ligaments, especially of the tibial collateral ligament, could be diagnosed only with the joint flexed about 20 degrees.

References

1. Kaplan, Emanuel B.: Some Aspects of Functional Anatomy of the Human Knee Joint. *Clinical Orthopaedics, 23*, 18–29. Philadelphia: J. B. Lippincott Co., 1962.

2. Lieb, Frederick J. and Perry, Jacquelin: Quadriceps Function. J. Bone Joint Surg., *50-A*, 1535–1548, 1968.

3. Kaplan, Emanuel B.: The Iliotibial Tract. J. Bone Joint Surg., *40-A*, 817–832, 1958.

4. Lombard, W. P. and Abbott, F. M.: The Mechanical Effects Produced by the Contraction of Individual Muscles of the Thigh of the Frog. Amer. J. Physiol., *20*, 1–60, 1907.

5. Elftman, Herbert: The Function of Muscles in Locomotion. Amer. J. Physiol., *125*, 357–366, 1939.

6. ————: The Work Done by Muscles in Running. Amer. J. Physiol., *129*, 672–684, 1940.

7. Kate, B. R. and Robert, S. L.: Some Observations on the Upper End of the Tibia in Squatters. J. Anat., *99*, 137–141, 1965.

8. Wood, W. Quarry: The Tibia of the Australian Aborigine. J. Anat., *54*, 232–257, 1920.

9. Hill, Ernest R.: Trick-Movements in Knee-Extensions. Physiotherapy, *44*, 137–138, 1958.

10. Wynn-Parry, C. B.: Vicarious Motions. In Sidney Licht, editor, *Therapeutic Exercise*. New Haven: Elizabeth Licht, 1958, pp. 116–126.

11. O'Donoghue, Don H.: *Treatment of Injuries to Athletes*. Philadelphia: W. B. Saunders Co., 1962, pp. 450–452.

12. Spademan, Richard: Lower-Extremity Injuries as Related to the Use of Ski Safety Bindings. JAMA, *203*, 445–450, 1968.

13. Devas, M. B. and Sweetnam, R.: Stress Fractures of the Fibula. J. Bone Joint Surg., *38-B*, 818–829, 1956.

14. Devas, M. B.: Stress Fractures of the Tibia in Athletes, or "Shin Soreness." J. Bone Joint Surg., *40-B*, 227–239, 1958.

15. Burrows, H. Jackson: Fatigue Infraction of the Middle of the Tibia in Ballet Dancers. J. Bone Joint Surg., *38-B*, 83–94, 1956.

16. McBryde, Angus, Jr., and Bassett, Frank H., III.: Stress Fracture of the Fibula. GP, *38*, 120–123, 1968.

17. Leach, Robert E., *et al.*: Anterior Tibial Compartment Syndrome. J. Bone Joint Surg., *49-A*, 451–462, 1967.

18. Willner, Philip: Osgood-Schlatter's Disease, *Clinical Orthopaedics and Related Research, No. 62.* Philadelphia: J. B. Lippincott Co., 1969, pp. 178–179.

19. Hallen, L. G. and Lindahl, O.: The Lateral Stability of the Knee Joint. Acta Orthop. Scandinav., *36*, 179–191, 1965.

Recommended Reading

20. Peterson, Thomas R.: The Cross Body Block, the Major Cause of Knee Injuries. J.A.M.A., *211*, 449–452, 1970.

Laboratory Exercises

1. It has been concluded that an important predisposing cause of falls in the aged is weakness of the quadriceps femoris. (Trevor H. Howell, Analysis of Falls in Old People, J. Amer. Geriat. Soc., *6*, 522–525, 1958.) Why is strength in this muscle especially important in the prevention of falls?

2. Assume that one man does deep knee bends or squats with a bar bell while another does leg presses. What differences in muscular development might result? Justify your answer.

3. What differences might be expected in the muscular development resulting from deep knee bends or squats and leg presses as compared with extensions of the knee done in the sitting position?

4. Analyze the two styles of lifting shown in Figs. 16–12, 16–13, and 16–14. From the kinesiological standpoint what are the advantages and disadvantages of each? Are there any structural factors involved in the selection of the style to be used by a given individual? Explain why Kono wears high heels but Schemansky does not.

5. In a duel in 1547 Jarnac defeated Chastaigneraie by slicing through the muscle behind the left knee. This is known in history as the *coup de Jarnac*. What muscles would be affected by such a cut and what would be the results?

Chapter 17

Movements of the Ankle and Foot

The relatively rigid structure comprising the human foot has evolved from the flexible grasping organ of the arboreal dwelling pre-human. Jones[1] considers it the most distinctively human part of man's anatomy, and comments that it is the hall-mark which separates him from all the other members of the animal kingdom. The foot includes twenty-six bones so grouped as to form a half-

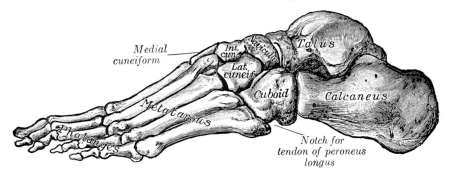

FIG. 17–1.   Lateral aspect of left foot.   (*Gray's Anatomy.*)

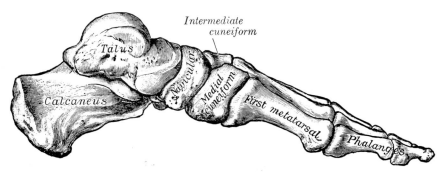

FIG. 17–2.   Medial aspect of left foot.   (*Gray's Anatomy.*)

373

dome. The base of this half-dome extends from the calcaneus along the lateral border of the foot to the distal ends of all five metatarsals. The arch which occurs in the vertical plane running from the calcaneus to the distal end of the first metatarsal is commonly known as the longitudinal arch. In walking weight is transmitted from the talus to all the peripheral weight-bearing parts of the foot. The bones are held together by ligaments and the half-domes are kept from flattening by ligaments, the plantar aponeurosis, the tendons of the extrinsic muscles of the foot, and the intrinsic muscles of the foot.

The bones of the foot are as follows:

Seven *tarsal* bones: talus, calcaneus, navicular, cuboid, and the medial, intermediate, and lateral cuneiform bones. The movements of these bones have been carefully analyzed by Shephard.[2]

Five *metatarsal* bones: numbered from within outward.

Fourteen *phalanges*: three for each toe except the first, which has two. The actions of these bones and their interrelations are well described by Steindler.[3]

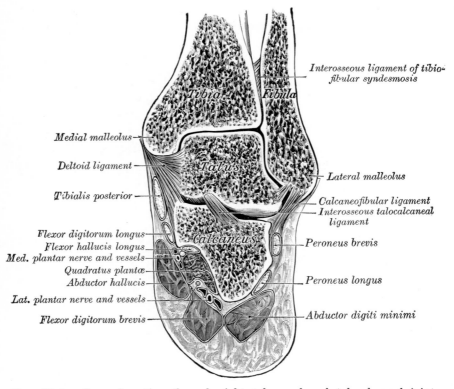

Fig. 17–3. Coronal section through right talocrural and talocalcaneal joints. (*Gray's Anatomy.*)

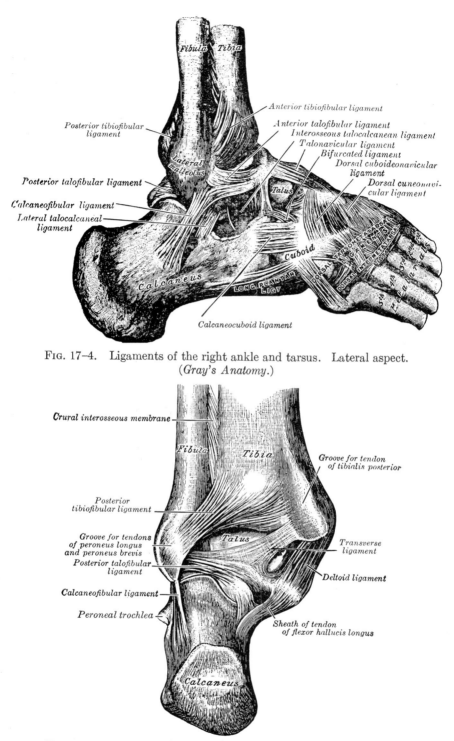

FIG. 17–4.   Ligaments of the right ankle and tarsus.   Lateral aspect.
(*Gray's Anatomy*.)

FIG. 17–5.   Posterior aspect of left ankle joint.   (*Gray's Anatomy*.)

The longitudinal arch is held in position primarily by the bowstring ligaments—the *long plantar ligament*, the *plantar calcaneocu-
boid ligament*, and the *plantar calcaneonavicular (or spring) ligament*
(Fig. 17–6). These are assisted by other ligaments and muscles of
the foot. Drew[4] has contrasted the great functional movement of
the arches of uncivilized peoples with the rigidity of those of civilized

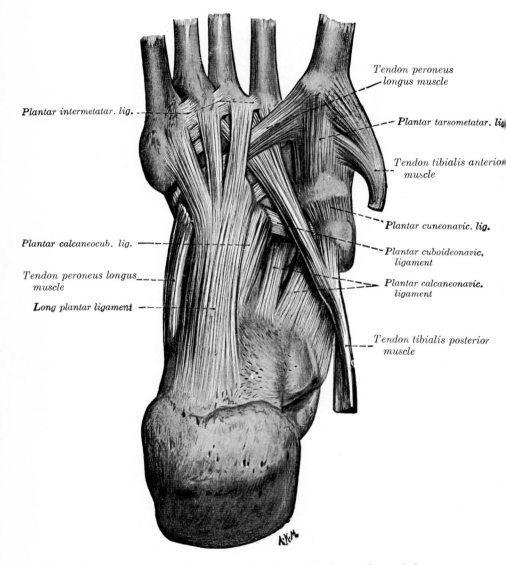

FIG. 17–6.   Ligaments of the sole of the foot, with the tendons of the peroneus
longus, tibialis posterior and tibialis anterior muscles.   (Quain.)

peoples. He attributes the latter to the splinting action of shoes, which effectively immobilize the joints of the foot of the wearer.

The movements of the foot take place in several different joints.

1. Talocrural (Ankle) Joint. A hinge joint, formed by the articulation of the tibia and fibula with the talus. The tibia and fibula are bound closely, chiefly by the *interosseous membrane* and ligaments, but also by the *anterior* (Fig. 17–4) and *posterior tibiofibular ligaments* (Fig. 17–5) and the *transverse ligament* (Fig. 17–5) which also articulates with the talus. The tibia transmits the body weight to the trochlea of the talus. A process of the tibia, the medial malleolus, articulates with the medial malleolar facet of the talus. The fibula bears little or no weight but passes down the lateral side of the talus, forming the lateral malleolus, which articulates with the lateral malleolar facet of the talus. In this way the talus fits up into a sort of flanged slot or mortise, which adds great stability to the joint. Medially the talus is bound to the tibia by the *deltoid ligament,* which attaches to the malleolus (Fig. 17–5). This ligament also has bands which connect the malleolus with the calcaneus and navicular bone, preventing either forward or backward displacement of the tibia. Laterally the joint is spanned by the *anterior* and *posterior talofibular ligaments* (Fig. 17–4) and the *calcaneofibular ligament* (Fig. 17–4). These ligaments are arranged not only to tie the joint together, but also to prevent forward or backward displacement of the fibula.

The ankle permits about 60 degrees of voluntary movement. The amplitude can be increased by using the weight of the body. Starting from standing position, the knees can be flexed until the tibia inclines forward 25 to 30 degrees with the foot flat on the floor; with further movement the heel is lifted by the posterior ligaments of the ankle joint. The front of the foot can be depressed through about 45 degrees. The axis of the ankle joint is parallel to that of the knee joint.

2. Intertarsal Joints. These are the articulations between the seven tarsal bones. Gliding movements are permitted by these arthrodial type joints.

3. Tarsometatarsal Joints. These are the articulations between the tarsal bones and the proximal ends of the five metatarsals. Gliding movements are permitted by these arthrodial type joints.

4. Metatarsophalangeal Joints. These are the articulations between the distal ends of the metatarsals and the proximal phalanges. The movements of these condyloid type joints are potentially the same as in the metacarpophalangeal joints of the fingers. Flexion and extension, and slight abduction and adduction, are permitted.

5. **Interphalangeal Joints.** These are hinge joints that permit flexion and extension of the toes.

The motions of the ankle and tarsal joints are conveniently named, and simultaneously described, by considering them as foot motions. There are four foot motions:

1. Foot *dorsiflexion* (also called *foot flexion*) consists of raising the foot toward the anterior surface of the leg. Dorsiflexion takes place mostly in the ankle joint, and slightly in the tarsal joints.

2. Foot *plantar flexion* (also called *foot extension*) consists of lowering the foot so as to bring its long axis in line with that of the leg. Plantar flexion takes place mostly in the ankle joint, and slightly in the tarsal joints.

3. Foot *eversion* takes place when the sole is turned laterally or "outward." Eversion cannot be accomplished without simultaneously displacing the long axis of the foot into the "toe-out" position. Eversion takes place only in the tarsal joints.

4. Foot *inversion* takes place when the sole is turned medially or "inward." Inversion cannot be accomplished without simultaneously displacing the long axis of the foot into the "toe-in" or "pigeon-toed" position. Inversion takes place only in the tarsal joints.*

There are twelve muscles which are involved in producing the movements of the foot described above:

Tibialis anterior	Soleus
Extensor digitorum longus	Peroneus longus
Peroneus tertius	Flexor digitorum longus
Extensor hallucis longus	Flexor hallucis longus
Gastrocnemius	Tibialis posterior
Plantaris	Peroneus brevis

In addition there are nineteen intrinsic muscles of the foot which aid in supporting the half-domes and which produce the fine movements of the toes.

EXTRINSIC MUSCLES OF THE ANKLE AND FOOT

TIBIALIS ANTERIOR

A slender muscle situated on the antero-lateral aspect of the tibia (Figs. 17–7 and 17–8).

Origin. The upper two-thirds of the lateral surface of the tibia

---

* Certain authors define *pronation* of the foot as a normal action composed of eversion in combination with abduction, and *supination* as a normal action composed of adduction in combination with inversion. In this text these terms have been reserved for use in consideration of foot defects, such as talipes valgus and talipes varus.

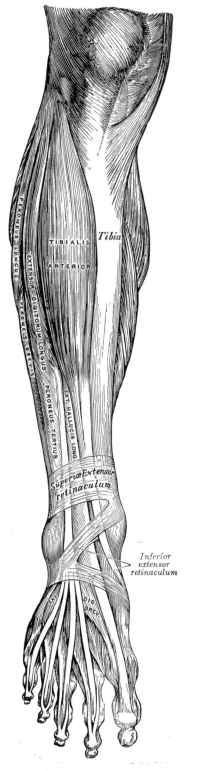

PERONEUS LONGUS

TIBIALIS ANTERIOR

Tibia

EXTENSOR DIGITORUM LONGUS

PERONEUS BREVIS

EXT. HALLUCIS LONG

PERONEUS TERTIUS

Superior Extensor retinaculum

Inferior extensor retinaculum

EXT. DIG. BREV.

FIG. 17–7. Muscles on anterior aspect of right leg. (*Gray's Anatomy.*)

and the corresponding portion of the interosseous membrane which joins the tibia and the fibula.

Insertion.   The medial and plantar surface of the medial cuneiform bone and the base of the first metatarsal.

Innervation.   A branch of the deep peroneal nerve with fibers coming from the fourth and fifth lumbar and first sacral nerves.

Structure.   The muscle fibers arise directly from the bone and are

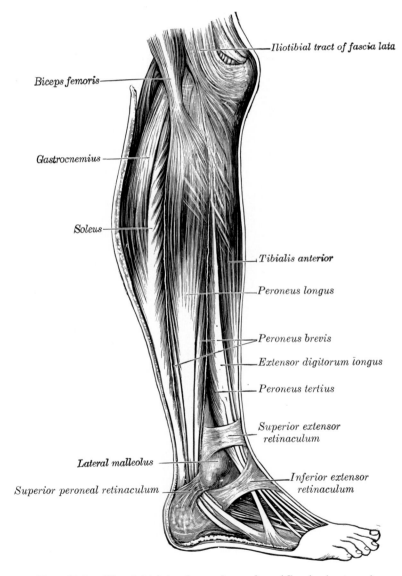

FIG. 17–8.   The right lateral crural muscles. (*Gray's Anatomy.*)

inserted obliquely into the tendon of insertion, which is held down at the ankle by the superior extensor retinaculum.

Action. Prime mover for dorsiflexion and inversion. When this muscle is paralyzed, the individual suffers from foot drop and may stub his toes on curbs or steps. Contrary to the implication of some texts, the muscle is not active as an invertor during plantar flexion.[5]

EXTENSOR DIGITORUM LONGUS

Similar to the preceding and situated just laterally to it (Figs. 17–7 and 17–8). It is unipennate.

Origin. Lateral condyle of the tibia, the upper three-fourths of the anterior surface of the fibula, and the adjacent interosseous membrane and covering deep fascia.

Insertion. Dorsal aspect of the four lesser toes and their extensor expansions.

Innervation. Branches of the deep peroneal nerve, containing fibers from the fourth and fifth lumbar and first sacral nerves.

Structure. A penniform muscle with a long tendon beginning at the middle of the leg. As it passes under the superior and inferior extensor retinacula the tendon divides into four slips which pass to the toes.

Action. Prime mover for toe extension, dorsiflexion, and eversion.

PERONEUS TERTIUS

Often described as a portion of extensor digitorum longus (Fig. 17–7). It has been found only in the feet of man and of the gorilla. Pennate.

Origin. The lower third of the anterior surface of the fibula and the lower portion of the interosseous membrane.

Insertion. The dorsal surface of the base of the fifth metatarsal.

Innervation. A branch of the deep peroneal nerve with fibers from the fourth and fifth lumbar and first sacral nerves.

Action. Prime mover for dorsiflexion and eversion of the foot.

EXTENSOR HALLUCIS LONGUS

A smaller muscle lying beneath the tibialis anterior and the peroneus tertius (Fig. 17–7).

Origin. The anterior surface of the fibula and of the interosseous membrane, at the middle half of the leg.

Insertion. The base of the distal phalanx of the great toe.

Innervation. A branch of the deep peroneal nerve. The fibers are from the fourth and fifth lumbar and first sacral nerves.

Structure. Like the preceding.

Action. Prime mover for extension of the great toe. Assists with dorsiflexion and inversion.

The four muscles just described, usually called the flexors of the foot, are brought into action in walking, running, and all similar movements to raise the toes and front of the foot and prevent their striking or scraping on the ground. The tibialis and the extensor digitorum longus are both needed to give even elevation of the foot; the extensor of the great toe is included in the coordination. People who have lost the use of this group of muscles scrape the foot on the ground at each step in walking.

GASTROCNEMIUS

The large muscle that gives the rounded form to the calf of the leg (Fig. 17–8).

Origin. By two tendons from the posterior aspect of the condyles of the femur.

Insertion. The posterior surface of the calcaneus (Fig. A–17).

Innervation. Branches of the tibial nerve which contain fibers from the first and second sacral nerves.

Structure. The upper tendons are flattened; the lower, the tendo-calcaneus (or tendon of Achilles), is very large and has a cross-section like a letter T, with the upright part between the right and left halves of the muscle and the crossbar on its posterior surface; the fibers from the two upper tendons pass diagonally downward to join the sides of the tendon of Achilles at various levels.

Action. A prime mover for plantar flexion; assists with knee flexion.

PLANTARIS

In most mammals it is larger than the gastrocnemius and flexes the toes. It is vestigial in man and absent in about 6 to 8 per of individuals.[6]

Origin. Linea aspera and oblique popliteal ligament of the knee joint.

Insertion. Posterior part of the calcaneus.

Innervation. Branch of the tibial nerve, containing fibers from the fourth and fifth lumbar and first sacral nerves.

Structure. At the proximal end a fusiform belly 7 to 10 cm. long is found between the heads of the gastrocnemius. Its very long tendon lies between the gastrocnemius and soleus muscles.

Action. Very weak assistant for knee flexion and plantar flexion.

SOLEUS

An associate of the gastrocnemius, lying immediately anterior to it (Fig. 17–8).

Origin. The upper part of the posterior surfaces of the tibia, fibula, and interosseous membrane (Fig. A–16).

Insertion. By the tendon of Achilles into the calcaneus.

Innervation. A branch of the tibial nerve which contains fibers from the first and second sacral nerves.

Structure. Penniform sheets.

Action. Prime mover for plantar flexion. The soleus and gastrocnemius together form a functional unit sometimes termed the *triceps surae*. Studies made by several investigators agree fairly well that the maximum force the gastrocnemius and soleus can exert in voluntary effort is about 450 kg.; that is, the muscles of each calf can exert on the ball of the foot a force of about 225 kg. They calculate the pull on the Achilles tendon is about three times as much.[7] However, a recent investigation has obtained a maximum muscle force in the tendo calcaneus of about 438 kg., or 3.9 kg. per sq. cm. of cross-section.[8] When the knee is flexed to 90 degrees or more the gastrocnemius seems to be left out of the coordination, leaving the work of extending the foot to the soleus, as in this position the heads of the gastrocnemius are so low that it cannot pull effectively.

PERONEUS LONGUS

This muscle is remarkable for its great power in proportion to its size and for the long and tortuous course of its tendon of insertion. It is situated along the fibula on the lateral side of the leg, just beneath the skin (Fig. 17–8).

Origin. The lateral condyle of the tibia and the upper two-thirds of the lateral aspect of the fibula (Fig. A–15).

Insertion. The lateral side of the first cuneiform bone and the lateral side of the proximal end of the first metatarsal (Fig. A–18).

Innervation. The superficial peroneal nerve with fibers from the fourth and fifth lumbar and first sacral nerves.

Structure. The fibers are short and arise directly from the fibula, one of the best examples of simple penniform arrangement; the tendon of insertion passes down behind the lateral malleolus, turns forward around its lower end at an angle of about 60 degrees, passes forward along the outer margin of the foot to the groove in the cuboid bone, where it makes another turn of about 100 degrees, then diagonally forward and across the sole of the foot to the place of insertion at the base of the great toe. A sesamoid fibrocartilage (occasionally a bone) is usually developed where it changes direction at the cuboid bone.

Action.   Prime mover for eversion; assists with plantar flexion.

FLEXOR DIGITORUM LONGUS

Situated on the medial aspect of the tibia (Fig. 17–9).

Origin.   The posterior surface of the body of the tibia from just below the popliteal line and from the fascia covering the tibialis posterior.

Insertion.   The bases of the distal phalanges of the four small toes. Each tendon passes through an opening in the corresponding tendon of the flexor digitorum brevis (Fig. 17–11).

Innervation.   Branch of the tibial nerve with fibers from the fifth lumbar and first sacral nerves.

Action.   Prime mover for flexion of the second through fifth toes; assists with plantar flexion and inversion.

The importance of hypertrophying the toe flexors for "drive" in sports has been stressed by Loewendahl.[9] Running in sand calls for powerful toe curling action and is an excellent conditioning exercise for these flexors, but may result in soreness of these muscles if the individual is unaccustomed to it.

FLEXOR HALLUCIS LONGUS

Situated on lateral aspect of fibula (Fig. 17–9).

Origin.   Inferior two-thirds of the posterior surface of the fibula and from the lowest part of the interosseous membrane.

Insertion.   Under surface of the base of the last phalanx of the great toe (Fig. 17–11).

Innervation.   A branch of the tibial nerve with fibers from the first lumbar and first and second sacral nerves.

Structure.   The tendon occupies nearly the whole length of muscle, passes around the medial malleolus, and runs forward along the medial side of the plantar aspect of the foot to its insertion.

Action.   Prime mover for flexion of the great toe; assists with plantar flexion and inversion. If this muscle is injured, it is difficult to maintain the equilibrium when standing on the toes.

TIBIALIS POSTERIOR

Situated deep beneath the triceps surae on the posterior aspect of the tibia (Fig. 17–9).

Origin.   The upper half of the posterior surface of the interosseous membrane and the adjacent parts of the tibia and fibula.

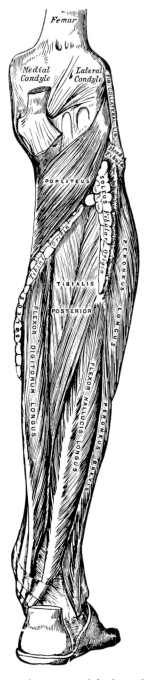

FIG. 17–9. Muscles of the posterior aspect of the leg—deep layer. (*Gray's Anatomy.*)

Insertion. The tuberosity on the inferior surface of the navicular, with offshoots to adjacent bones (Fig. A–18).

Innervation. A branch of the tibial nerve with fibers from the fifth lumbar and first sacral nerves.

Structure. Simple penniform; the tendon turns through 90 degrees around the medial malleolus.

Action. Prime mover for inversion; assists with plantar flexion. Loewendahl[9] has emphasized the need for resistive exercise of this muscle in strengthening the ankle joints for sports, commenting that it is the anchor of the foot and ankle. If it is weak the foot assumes a pronated position and the body is thrown out of alignment. Knee and low back pains may result. Resistive exercises for this muscle are essential for ice skating, hockey, skiing, and other sports in which ankle control is of importance. Such exercises should be performed in the standing position, with the foot inverted. One slip inserts on the third cuneiform. The flexor hallucis brevis arises in part from this tendon. It inserts on the sides of the base of the first phalanx of the great toe. This interconnection is uniquely human and serves to project the pull of the tibialis posterior to the metatarsophalangeal joint of the great toe, where it is a major factor in bringing about arch-raising. The continuity of the two muscles contributes to the elevation of the arch during walking and adds spring to the step.

PERONEUS BREVIS

A small associate of the longus (Fig. 17–9).

Origin. The lower two-thirds of the lateral surface of the fibula.

Insertion. The tuberosity at the proximal end of the fifth metatarsal.

Innervation. A branch of the superficial peroneal nerve which contains fibers from the fourth and fifth lumbar and first sacral nerves.

Structure. Fibers arranged like the longus. The muscle makes a similar turn around the outer malleolus, forward and downward to the insertion.

Action. Prime mover for eversion; assists with plantar flexion.

INTRINSIC MUSCLES OF THE FOOT
THE FIRST PLANTAR LAYER
ABDUCTOR HALLUCIS

Origin. Primarily from the medial process of the tuberosity of the calcaneus (Fig. 17–10).

Insertion. The medial side of the base of the proximal phalanx of the great toe.

Innervation. Medial plantar nerve, with fibers from the fourth and fifth lumbar nerves.

Action. Spreads the great toe away from the second toe.

FLEXOR DIGITORUM BREVIS

Occupies the central portion of the posterior surface of the foot (Fig. 17–10).

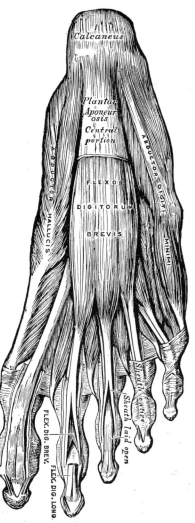

FIG. 17–10.   Muscles of the sole of the foot.   First layer.   (*Gray's Anatomy.*)

Origin. The medial process of the tuberosity of the calcaneus and the plantar aponeurosis.

Insertion. The tendons divide and are inserted into the sides of the middle phalanges of the second through fifth toes.

Innervation. A branch of the medial plantar nerve with fibers from the fourth and fifth lumbar nerves.

Action. Flexes the second through fifth toes.

ABDUCTOR DIGITI MINIMI

Origin. Primarily from the lateral process of the tuberosity of the calcaneus (Fig. 17–10).

Insertion. Lateral side of the base of the proximal phalanx of the fifth toe.

Innervation. Lateral plantar nerve, containing fibers from the first and second sacral nerves.

Action. Spreads the fifth toe away from the fourth toe.

THE SECOND LAYER

QUADRATUS PLANTAE

Origin. Two heads, the medial surface and the lateral border of the inferior surface of the calcaneus (Fig. 17–11).

Insertion. Fuses with the tendon of the flexor digitorum longus.

Innervation. Lateral plantar nerve, containing fibers from the first and second sacral nerves.

Action. Flexes the second through fifth toes.

THE LUMBRICALES

Four small bipennate muscles numbered from the medial side (Fig. 17–11).

Origin. The tendons of the flexor digitorum longus.

Insertion. Medial sides of the bases of the proximal phalanges of the second through fifth toes, and into the extensor expansions.

Innervation. The first by a branch of the medial plantar nerve, containing fibers from the fourth and fifth lumbar nerves; the remaining three by the lateral plantar nerve, containing fibers from the first and second sacral nerves.

Action. Flex the proximal and extend the distal phalanges of the second through fifth toes.

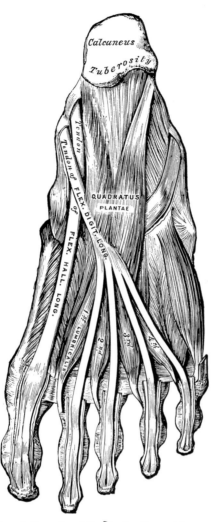

Fig. 17–11.   Muscles of the sole of the foot.   Second layer.   (*Gray's Anatomy*.)

THE THIRD LAYER
FLEXOR HALLUCIS BREVIS

Origin.   Medial part of the inferior surface of the cuboid bone (Fig. 17–12).

Insertion.   The tendon divides, being inserted on each side of the base of the proximal phalanx of the big toe.

Innervation.   Medial plantar nerve, containing fibers from the fourth and fifth lumbar and first sacral nerves.

Action.   Flexes the proximal phalanx of the big toe.

ADDUCTOR HALLUCIS

Origin. Two heads. The oblique head arises from the proximal ends of the second, third, and fourth metatarsals. The transverse head arises from the metatarsophalangeal ligaments of the third, fourth, and fifth toes (Fig. 17–12).

Insertion. Lateral side of proximal phalanx of the big toe.

Innervation. Lateral plantar nerve, containing fibers from the first and second sacral nerves.

Action. Draws the great toe towards the second toe.

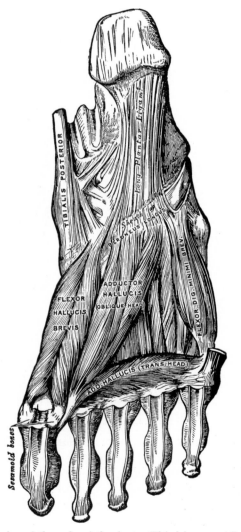

FIG. 17–12. Muscles of the sole of the foot. Third layer. (*Gray's Anatomy.*)

FLEXOR DIGITI MINIMI

Origin.   Proximal end of the fifth metatarsal bone (Fig. 17–12).

Insertion.   Lateral side of the proximal end of the proximal phalanx of the little toe.

Innervation.   Lateral plantar nerve, containing fibers from the first and second sacral nerves.

Action.   Flexes the proximal phalanx of the fifth toe.

THE FOURTH LAYER

DORSAL INTEROSSEI

Four bipenniform muscles between the metatarsal bones.

Origin.   Each muscle arises by two heads from the sides of the adjacent metatarsal bones (Fig. 17–13).

Innervation.   Lateral plantar nerve, containing fibers from the first and second sacral nerves.

Action.   First interosseus draws the second toe toward the great toe.   The second, third, and fourth draw the second, third, and fourth toes away from the great toe.   Flex the proximal and extend the distal phalanges of the second, third, and fourth toes.

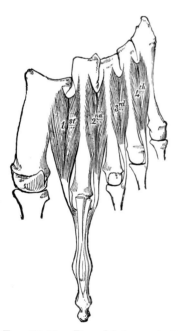

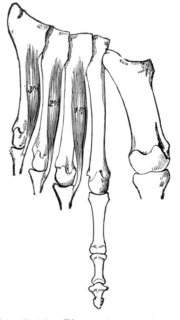

Fig. 17–13.   Dorsal interossei of left
foot.   (*Gray's Anatomy.*)

Fig. 17–14.   Plantar interossei of
left foot.   (*Gray's Anatomy.*)

PLANTAR INTEROSSEI

Three unipennate muscles, each of which lies under the metatarsal bones to which it is attached.

Origin. The medial sides of the bodies of the third, fourth, and fifth metatarsal bones (Fig. 17–14).

Insertion. The medial sides of the proximal phalanges of the same toes and the tendons of the extensor digitorum longus.

Innervation. Lateral plantar nerve, containing fibers from the first and second sacral nerves.

Action. Draw the third, fourth, and fifth toes toward the second toe. Flex the proximal and extend the distal phalanges of the third, fourth, and fifth toes.

THE DORSAL ASPECT

EXTENSOR DIGITORUM BREVIS

A broad, thin muscle.

Origin. Upper and lateral surface of the calcaneus (Fig. 17–15).

Insertion. Ends in four tendons. The most medial inserts into the dorsal surface of the proximal end of the first phalanx of the great toe; the other three insert into the tendons of the extensor digitorum longus of the second, third, and fourth toes.

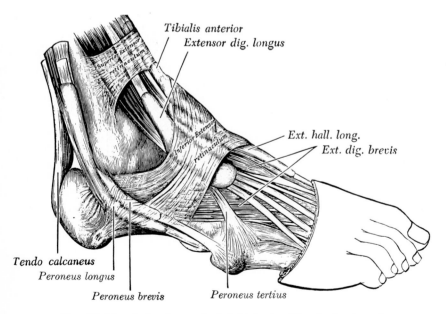

FIG. 17–15.   Lateral aspect of right foot.   (*Gray's Anatomy*.)

Innervation. Deep peroneal nerve, containing fibers from the fifth lumbar and first sacral nerve.

Action. Extends the proximal phalanges of the first through fourth toes.

KINESIOLOGY OF FOOT DEFECTS

The evolution of the foot from a flexible grasping organ characterized by powerful intrinsic muscles into a comparatively rigid mechanism designed for locomotion has been only partially successful. The functional grasping muscles are still present, but are reduced in size and subordinated to the structural demands required in providing propulsive leverage. Most babies are flat footed when they begin to walk. The short plantar muscles gradually tighten up, the anterior and posterior tibials lift the inner border, and the longitudinal arch forms. No one type of arch can be considered normal, and its height and shape are of no value in estimating the strength or usefulness of the foot.

There is, however, a lack of general agreement in regard to when a foot is "normal" either in its morphology or its function. It has been reported[4,10] that the feet of primitive peoples who do not wear shoes are extremely mobile. They appear almost flat when weight bearing in the relaxed state, but become highly arched in action. Such feet may tire easily under prolonged standing, but their functional capabilities are indicated by the fact that they are said to be frequently seen in runners and ballet dancers. The feet of most civilized men, however, are characterized by a pronounced logitudinal arch which is not depressed during weight bearing nor raised during action. The static condition is attributed to the fact that modern shoes in effect place the foot in a splint. The ligaments shorten, the joint capsules contract, adhesions form, and the arch becomes relatively rigid.

The relative roles of the ligaments and the muscles in supporting the arch of the foot has long been a matter of dispute. However, recent electromyographic studies indicate rather clearly that the intrinsic muscles of the foot do not react when placed under loads which surpass the stresses experienced during standing, but become active in the take-off phase of the gait, when rising on the toes, and during similar activities.[11,12] The evidence confirms Smith's[13] suggestion that the mechanism supporting the feet during static standing is osteoligamentous, but becomes primarily muscular during movement.

The weight during walking is transmitted to the heads of all the metatarsal bones. Hence there is no such thing as a transverse arch in the loaded foot.[14,15]

The most common deformities of the foot are the following:

1. Talipes calcaneus.   Paralysis of the triceps surae, or of the peroneus longus, or of both, permits the anterior muscles to elevate the forefoot so that the weight is carried on the heel.

2. Talipes equinus.   Paralysis of the tibialis anterior, the extensor digitorum longus, or of other dorsiflexors, permits the triceps surae to go into contracture, so that the heel is raised and the weight is carried on the toes.   Mild grades of talipes equinus are common in women who commonly wear high heeled shoes.   In such cases there is an overstretching of the tibialis anterior and the dorsal flexors, with an adaptive shortening of the tendo Achillis.   Callosities and hammer toes are a common after-effect.

3. Talipes varus.   Paralysis of the peroneus longus and/or peroneus brevis may allow the anterior and posterior tibials to pull the foot into a position in which the sole is turned inward.

4. Talipes valgus.   Loss of the posterior tibials and/or the intrinsic plantar muscles or contracture of the peroneus longus may cause the sole of the foot to turn outward.

5. Pes cavus occurs when loss of the triceps surae permits the flexors to draw the calcaneus forward, the talus dorsiflexes, and the plantar fascia contracts.   A very high arch is formed, tightening the long extensors of the toes.   The toes are cocked up and the condition known as "clawfoot" occurs.

6. Pes planus.   The ankles deviate inward, throwing an abnormally high percentage of the body weight on the plantar ligaments. The anterior and posterior tibials and the intrinsic plantar muscles are stretched, allowing the foot to sag, an action which may continue until its medial portion contacts the ground.   Pes planus may be recorded as 1st, 2nd, or 3rd degree, depending upon the extent of the sagging.   Weak foot, pronated foot, and flat foot may be successive stages of the same defect.

The propelling force of locomotion is provided chiefly by the gastrocnemius and the soleus.   It was perhaps Gottlieb[16] who first called attention to the antagonism in relation and function existing between the triceps surae, whose action tends to flatten the longitudinal arch, and the short plantar muscles, whose actions contribute to its retention, but his theories have been considerably elaborated by Jones.[17]   Briefly, it is their contention that stress on the longitudinal arch is directly proportional to the pressure borne by the ball of the foot.   For a person to raise himself on the ball of one foot, as in walking, requires a pull on the Achilles tendon equal to twice the body weight.   By far the greater portion of this force is exerted by the triceps surae.   The posterior tibials, flexor hallucis longus, flexor digitorum longus, and peroneus longus are considered relatively insignificant as plantar flexors; their mechanical advantage and absolute strength are such that they account for not over 5 per cent of the pressure in the ball of the foot in plantar flexion.

Not more than 15 to 20 per cent of the tension stresses in the arch is borne by the long leg muscles; the major support for the arch is furnished by the plantar ligaments, the plantar aponeurosis, and the short plantar muscles. If the powerful triceps surae shorten, they tend to displace the front part of the calcaneus downward. The superimposed weight of the body causes the adjoining navicular and talus to sink, the plantar muscles and ligaments are overstretched, and the foot is flattened.

Pressure of arch supports between the ball of the foot and the heel cannot reduce the stress on the arch incident to the pull of the triceps surae.

Certain physical conditions may predispose a weak foot to develop pes planus. Among them are:

1. An inactive life in childhood and adolescence may fail to develop the strength of muscles and ligaments needed to support the body weight.

2. A laying on of adipose tissue in later life may increase the load on the arches beyond the point which the muscles and ligaments can tolerate.

3. Constant walking on hard, even surfaces, such as cement sidewalks, gives too hard an impact with each step, and fails to provide the muscular development resulting from walking in open fields, where the uneven but softer surface causes the foot to take different positions and thus distribute the work load among the various muscles.

4. Structural defects may predispose to clinical disorders. Morton has stressed the role of a short first metatarsal as a definite morphological feature inducing a major disturbance in the function of the entire foot.[15]

5. Pes planus can sometimes be traced to a toxic condition brought about by infection, with a resulting weakening of the supporting tissues.

6. Badly fitting shoes have a large place in the cause of foot ills. Ober[18] has given the following as the requirements for a satisfactory shoe for the normal foot:

a. Sufficient length so that the end of the great toe is not against the end of the shoe, but not so long that the foot slides forward from the heel upper.

b. The front must be wide enough not to cramp the toes, but snug enough so that the forefoot will not slide about. The heel must be held snugly both at the sides and behind.

c. Sufficient height over the instep so that the instep is not pushed downward.

d. The lines of the shoe must correspond to the lines of the sole of the foot.

e. The shank fit is most important. If the whole sole of the foot is utilized as the weight bearing surface, it will be mechanically easier to carry the distributed load. This requires selection of a shoe whose shank fits the individual arch.

High heels are almost unanimously condemned by the medical profession. They have been termed "essentially a prosthesis for a deformity," and "from the physiological standpoint . . . are the most destructive factor in foot physiology."[19] It is contended that they:

1. Cause a decrease in the tone of the postural muscles and an increase in tension on the plantar fascia.

2. Shorten the leverage of the foot for propulsion and increase the muscular effort required in the pushoff.

3. Decrease the postural power of the erectors of the tibia. A structural shortening of the tendo Achillis results and the relaxation of the hamstrings upsets the whole postural mechanism.

4. Keep the toes in more or less complete dorsiflexion.

5. Increase the weight thrown on the articular surface of the metatarsal heads, especially of the slender middle metatarsals, which are essentially non-weight bearing structures.

6. Cause an increase in the energy cost of walking.[20]

Once a longitudinal arch has flattened it cannot be elevated by exercise of the muscles of the foot, as it is impossible for them to exert a tension great enough to raise a fallen arch. The most important role of corrective exercises would seem to lie in strengthening a weak foot before it collapses. Foot exercises have three main objectives:

1. To improve the local circulation.

2. To stabilize the foot in the correct position in relation to the leg.

3. To act as self-manipulative forces which will improve the range of movement of the individual joints.[10]

If it is decided to utilize corrective exercises, it is usually considered good policy to employ non-weight bearing movements in the early states of treatment. Suitable movements are described in texts on corrective exercise and need not be elaborated upon here. After some progress has been made and the strength of the muscles restored to some extent, weight bearing exercises in the standing position are ordinarily prescribed. In general these exercises are designed to strengthen the tibials and throw the body weight on the lateral borders of the feet.

Foot disabilities of a different type may result from long continued crossing of the legs, crouching, squatting, or kneeling. In some instances this may result in the compression of the peroneal nerve against the femur or fibula, or in a stretching of the nerve, especially in the case of tall, slender long-legged persons. The superficial peroneal nerve innervates the peroneus longus and brevis, which evert the foot; the deep peroneal nerve innervates the dorsiflexors of the foot and the extensors of the toes. If its function is interrupted, foot drop results. When the common peroneal nerve is injured, the affected foot cannot be dorsiflexed at the ankle, the toes cannot be extended, and inversion of the foot occurs. A hazard of weight reduction is that the disappearance of the fat may deprive the peroneal nerve of a certain amount of protection against the occurrence of injuries resulting from pressure.[21]

IMPLICATIONS FOR ATHLETIC TRAINING

The ankle joint is poorly stabilized by muscles and ligaments, but in the erect position must support the entire weight of the body. In feats such as the one shown in Figure 6–6, nearly every muscle in the leg must contract to stabilize the intertarsal and talocrural joints, and to prevent inversion, eversion, or dorsiflexion of the foot. The gastrocnemius appears to play the major role in adjusting the femur on the tibia and the plantar flexors control the relationship of the tibia to the foot.[22] The ankle joint is frequently injured in such sports as football, basketball, baseball, judo, and skiing. Some trainers believe that "shin splints" and certain knee troubles result from the dropping of the longitudinal arch of the foot. Preseason exercises designed to strengthen the musculature surrounding the joints and the use of protective wrappings during practice and competition may aid in the prevention of such disabilities, but cannot be expected to eliminate them entirely. Some experienced team physicians believe that reinforcing the ankle results in an increased number of knee injuries.[23] One investigator[24] concluded that there was a three-to-one chance that an ankle injury would be a sprain rather than a fracture, and that four out of five sprains would be to the anterior talofibular ligament.

Eighty-five per cent of all injuries to the ankle are *inversion injuries*, in which the foot is forced inward in relation to the leg. Since the medial malleolus is short, the talus may rotate over it when suffering an inversion injury. The result is that such injuries tend to be primarily a tearing of the lateral ligaments. In *eversion injuries* the foot is forced outward in relation to the leg. Since the talus cannot rotate over the longer lateral malleolus it may break it off, or even more severe damage to the bones and ligaments of the ankle and leg may result. Such considerations make it important to analyze the forces applied to an injured ankle in order to determine the mechanics of the injury and thus obtain a better diagnosis.

If a severe injury of this type does occur and the patient is in bed for some time, the pull of the calf muscles will almost certainly result in plantar flexion (foot drop). Tight bed covers will accentuate this tendency. A footboard is a useful aid in preventing this deformity and the patient should be taught a few simple exercises, such as those with a towel, designed to stretch the tendo Achillis.

TABLE 17-1.　Ankle and Foot Muscles and Their Actions

EXTRINSIC MUSCLES	*ANKLE AND FOOT*				*TOES*	
	Dorsi-flexion	*Plantar flexion*	*Inver-sion*	*Ever-sion*	*Flexion*	*Exten-sion*
Tibialis anterior	P.M.		P.M.			
Extensor digitorum longus	P.M.			P.M.		P.M.*
Peroneus tertius	P.M.			P.M.		
Extensor hallucis longus	Asst.		Asst.			P.M.†
Gastrocnemius		P.M.				
Plantaris		Asst.				
Soleus		P.M.				
Peroneus longus		Asst.		P.M.		
Flexor digitorum longus		Asst.	Asst.		P.M.*	
Flexor hallucis longus		Asst.	Asst.		P.M.†	
Tibialis posterior		Asst.	P.M.			
Peroneus brevis		Asst.		P.M.		

INTRINSIC MUSCLES

Abductor hallucis	Spreads great toe away from 2nd toe.
Flexor digitorum brevis	Flexes the 2nd through 5th toes.
Abductor digiti minimi	Spreads 5th toe away from 4th toe.
Quadratus plantae	Flexes the 2nd through 5th toes.
Lumbricales	Flex proximal phalanx and extend distal phalanx of 2nd through 5th toes.
Flexor hallucis brevis	Flexes proximal phalanx of the great toe.
Adductor hallucis	Draws the great toe toward 2nd toe.
Flexor digiti minimi brevis	Flexes proximal phalanx of 5th toe.
1st dorsal interosseous	Draws 2nd toe toward the great toe. ⎫ ⎡Also flex
2nd, 3rd, & 4th dorsal interossei	Draw 2nd, 3rd, & 4th toes away from the great toe. ⎬ proximal phalanx and extend distal phalanx of 2nd
Plantar interossei	Draw 3rd, 4th, & 5th toes away from 2nd toe. ⎭ through 4th toes.
Extensor digitorum brevis	Extends proximal phalanx of 1st through 4th toes.

* 2nd through 5th toes only.
† Great toe only.

References

1. Jones, Frederic Wood: *Structure and Function as Seen in the Foot*. London: Bailliere, Tindall & Cox, 1944, p. 2.

2. Shephard, Edmund: Tarsal Movements. J. Bone Joint Surg., *33-B*, 258–263, 1951.

3. Steindler, Arthur: *Kinesiology of the Human Body*. Springfield: Charles C Thomas, 1955, p. 379.

4. Drew, J. F.: The Painful Foot. Med. J. Aust., *1*, 239–244, 1957.

5. Basmajian, John V.: *Muscles Alive. Their Functions Revealed by Electromyography*, 2d Ed. Baltimore: The Williams & Wilkins Co., 1967, p. 237.

6. Acton, Rush K.: Surgical Anatomy of the Foot. J. Bone Joint Surg., *49-A*, 555–567, 1967.

7. Barcroft, H. and Millen, J. L. E.: The Blood Flow Through Muscle During Sustained Contraction. J. Physiol., *97*, 17–31, 1939.

8. Haxton, H. A.: Absolute Muscle Force in the Ankle Flexors of Man. J. Physiol., *103*, 267–273, 1944.

9. Loewendahl, Evelyn: Muscle Development in Athletic Training. J. Am. Ass. Health Phys. Ed. Rec., *21*, 331–332, 1950.

10. Morton, Dudley J.: *The Human Foot*. New York: Columbia University Press, 1935.

11. Basmajian, J. V.: *Op. cit.*, pp. 229–236.

12. Mann, Roger and Inman, Verne T.: Phasic Activity of Intrinsic Muscles of the Foot. J. Bone Joint Surg., *46-A*, 469–481, 1964.

13. Smith, J. W.: Muscular Control of the Arches of the Foot in Standing: An Electromyographic Assessment. J. Anat., *88*, 152–162, 1954.

14. Apshtein, Z. V. and Potikhanova, G. C.: Study of the Supportive Function of the Anterior Part of the Foot During Walking. Abstracted in Excerpta Med. (XIX), *8*, 266 (926), 1965.

15. Morton, Dudley: *Human Locomotion and Body Form*. Baltimore: The Williams & Wilkins Co., 1952.

16. Gottlieb, A.: Flatfoot and Its Relation to the Triceps Surae Muscle. Am. J. Phys. Ther., *8*, 321–323, 1932.

17. Jones, Russell L.: The Human Foot. An Experimental Study of its Mechanics and the Role of its Muscles and Ligaments in the Support of the Arch. Amer. J. Anat., *68*, 1–41, 1941.

18. Ober, Frank R.: Shoes and Feet. J.A.M.A., *114*, 1553–1557, 1940.

19. Stewart, S. F.: Physiology of the Unshod and Shod Foot with an Evolutionary History of Footgear. Amer. J. Surg., *58*, 127–138, 1945.

20. Mathews, Donald K. and Wooten, Edna P.: Analysis of Oxygen Consumption of Women While Walking in Different Styles of Shoes. Arch. Phys. Med., *44*, 569–571, 1963.

21. Sprofkin, Bertram: Peroneal Paralysis—A Hazard of Weight Reduction. A.M.A. Arch. Intern. Med., *102*, 82–87, 1958.

22. Houtz, S. J. and Walsh, Frank P.: Electromyographic Analysis of the Function of the Muscles Acting on the Ankle During Weight-Bearing with Special Reference to the Triceps Surae. J. Bone Joint Surg., *41-A*, 1469–1481, 1959.

23. Reid, Stephen E., *et al.*: Knee and Ankle Injuries in Football . Quart. Bull. Northw. Univ. Med. Sch., *33*, 250–253, 1959.

24. Lettin, Alan W. F.: Diagnosis and Treatment of the Sprained Ankle. Brit. Med. J., *1*, 1056–1060, 1963.

Laboratory Exercises

1. What relationship might be found between success in swimming and the size of the feet?

2. What relationship might be found between the length of the foot and success in jumping or running?

3. What relationship might be found between the length of the calcaneus and the girth of the gastrocnemius?

4. Why do girls accustomed to the use of high heeled shoes experience discomfort in the calves when wearing low heeled shoes?

5. An old parlor trick consists of having a person stand with his nose and abdomen touching the edge of an open door. He is then challenged to rise on tiptoe. Why does he find this impossible?

6. With the toes held upward, try to raise the heels off the floor. Why is this difficult?

7. What position should the foot be in when it is taped to reinforce an injured ankle?

8. Study Figure 22–12. If the runner's cleats "hang up" in the turf, the forced internal rotation of the lower leg on the fixed foot may result in what kind of an injury of the ankle joint?

9. Discuss the common practice of having individuals with flat feet exercise by rising on the toes in the light of the Gottlieb-Jones theories. What type of exercise might they recommend for the triceps surae of those exhibiting this condition?

10. It is said that the most common type of fall in skiing is with the knee and ankle abducted and externally rotated. Analyze the kinesiology involved in injuries of this type.

11. In the Army position of attention, the heels are together and the feet are turned out at an angle of 45 degrees. Analyze this position from the standpoint of foot hygiene.

12. "Tennis leg" is a partial tear of the medial gastrocnemius. It occurs when a middle-aged tennis player reaches for the ball with the knee fully extended and the ankle fully dorsiflexed. Explain the mechanisms involved. (Suggestion: see Avrum I. Fromison: Tennis Leg. J.A.M.A., *209*, 415–416, 1969.)

Chapter 18

Human Performance Analysis

THE USES OF MOVEMENT ANALYSIS

Analysis and evaluation of human performance is the central operation of kinesiology. It enables the scholar to develop and test new theories, and the professional practitioner to select or design effective movements and related environmental conditions in order to meet specific performance criteria. Professional kinesiologists—physicians, physical educators, therapists, human factors engineers, and researchers—need extensive factual knowledge and facility with analytical techniques as a basis for making specific professional decisions.

Deductive and Inductive Analysis. Kinesiological analysis can be employed either deductively or inductively. Deductive kinesiological analysis starts with a specific human movement or performance situation, identifies its characteristics, and finally evaluates it with respect to chosen criteria. For example, an orthopedic surgeon, therapist, or physical educator may analyze a sports skill or physical exercise, and evaluate it with respect to orthopedic rehabilitation, posture correction, strength development, physical fitness development, or possibility of injury. In similar manner, a body position, a simple joint movement, an entire occupational regimen, or a patented "magic" exercise device can be evaluated. Deductive analysis in structural-functional kinesiology answers the question, "Exactly how is this movement performed, and what are the effects on the organism?" A deductive analysis in mechanical kinesiology answers the question, "Exactly how is this movement performed mechanically (by experts, by beginners, etc.)?"

Inductive kinesiological analysis starts with a desired performance outcome, such as good posture, increased strength, conservation of energy expenditure, ability to use a prosthetic device, or some other performance criterion as its goal. Then the analyst postulates some exercise, sport, training device, or environmental circumstances as a means of achieving the performance criterion. Finally, he analyzes and evaluates the proposed means of achieving the outcome for its efficacy in satisfying the criterion. The inductive kinesiological analysis is designed to answer the question, "How can specific outcomes be realized?" In medicine and therapy, the question often is, specifically, "What is possible for this patient?" In aviation and space engineering, the specific question might be, "Can a human operator see, reach, and manipulate all cockpit instruments and controls?" Not necessarily less complex is the coach's question, "How can the blocker reach a certain point before the ball carrier arrives?" Inductive kinesiological analyses are more often resolved by changing the environment or the task than by changing the performance qualities of the performer, as is the case in deductive kinesiological analysis.

Both deductive and inductive kinesiological analysis require (1) extensive knowledge of kinesiological facts and principles, (2) consideration of individual human subjects and circumstances, and (3) a creative professional or theoretical approach.

FORMATS FOR KINESIOLOGICAL ANALYSIS

There can never be one universally-appropriate format for analytic procedure. Many researchers will utilize a format much more advanced and detailed than anything presented here. Highly experienced practitioners will be able to dispense largely with detailed written forms. Few working professionals would find time enough in a day to make all of the routinely required analyses in precise written form.

This chapter presents sample analytical methods in detail in order to expound a process which may be modified, condensed, or conceptualized by experienced kinesiologists. It centers attention on analytical problems in structural-functional kinesiology, since problems in mechanical kinesiology, except for the most cursory explorations, constitute a special challenge that requires separate treatment. The emphasis is almost exclusively on deductive analysis, since inductive analysis follows a similar pattern but with the introduction of creative and imaginative postulates.

Steps in Deductive Analysis for Structural-Functional Kinesiology. Deductive analysis involves three major procedural steps: (1) The movement to be analyzed must be described and (where necessary) divided into parts or phases; (2) each phase of the movement must be subjected to joint and muscle action analysis; (3) the movement must be evaluated by subjecting the analytical facts to the selected criteria. Each of these major steps involves subsidiary procedures, not all of which will be pertinent to every problem. Subsidiary procedures are outlined below and in the analysis forms of Tables 18–1 through 18–6.

Step I.   Description and Subdivision of the Movement.   First, it is convenient to give the selected movement a descriptive name, although names alone may be ambiguous. Second, the movement may be described by sequence photographs, or at least by a drawing. Third, an elgon (electrogoniometer) record, if available, makes a precise description of joint actions. Lacking this, a more casual notation of ranges of motion may be estimated or measured. Fourth, an electromyographic recording, or some other estimate of muscle activity (such as palpation), is valuable. Fifth, the movement sequence should be subdivided into two or more parts or phases, usually including a designation of the starting position. Each phase should be capable of unitary description in terms of muscle and joint actions. Subsequently, each phase of a compound movement should be analyzed as if it were a separate exercise. Perhaps not all of the phases will require detailed analysis. Sixth, each phase of the exercise may be described verbally, using anatomical terminology as much as possible. Some of these six descriptive devices may not be available, but in research laboratories additional objective descriptions may be possible. These procedures have no rigid sequence; for example, it may be best to write the verbal description before making the photographic record. Accuracy and clarity are criteria for exercise descriptions.

Step II.   Joint and Muscle Action Analysis.   This step is the most literally analytical one. For each phase of the movement, the action of each joint is identified, together with much subsidiary data. Tables 18–3 through 18–6 illustrate both long and short forms for analyzing joint and muscle action. In order to bring a large amount of related information together concisely, and to save time spent in writing, abbreviations are almost essential (see Table 18–1).

Step III.   Summary and Evaluation of the Movement.   The summary and evaluation should distil the meaning and implications of the analysis. The exact content will vary according to the specific criteria against which the movement is being evaluated, and with the peculiarities of the subject and the situation. As a professional judgment, it will not always be beyond argument, and its validity will depend upon the accuracy of the data of Step II. Accordingly, some detailed comments on the components of the joint and muscle analysis form are offered in the following section.

ITEMS IN THE JOINT AND MUSCLE ACTION ANALYSIS
(SEE TABLE 18-3)

Preliminary Information. Presumably the movement under analysis has been precisely described and resolved into parts or phases in Step I. In effect, a separate analysis chart must be devoted to each relevant phase of the movement. Some phases (such as preliminary and terminal ones) may be irrelevant to the central problem, and so can be omitted. Too, some joints of the body may be irrelevant (for example, when the interest is in the effects of swimming strokes on the posture of the spine and shoulder girdle, analysis of ankle joint action can be omitted).

Terminology for Joint Actions. Standard kinesiological nomenclature should always be used. "Raising the arm" has different connotations depending on the position of the total body, but "flexing the shoulder joint" has a precise meaning no matter what the body position.

The anatomical position, in which all joint angles are considered to be zero degrees, is the reference position. Any other position, or any joint movement, is described in terms of angular deviation from anatomical position with respect to the three perpendicular planes centered at the joint. The direction of the deviation or movement is designated by arbitrary terminology, such as flexion, extension, abduction, etc. (see pages 36–38 for general definitions, and the beginning pages of Chapters 9 through 17 for definitions of movements at specific joints). Thus, in erect sitting position, the ankle is in a position of 0°, and both knee and hip are in a position of 90° flexion. Upon standing, the knee is extended through 90° (90° to 0°), as is the hip joint.

Observed Joint Action. On the analytical chart, the entry under the heading "Observed Joint Actions" should be determined by precise inspection of the movement. It does not indicate what muscle group is active, if any. When outside forces, such as gravity, cause joint actions, the movement may be augmented by concentric contraction of the movers for that joint action, or may be braked by eccentric contraction of antagonists, or may consist of pure falling, with no muscular contraction at all. Determination of the entries in the columns for "Muscle Group Active" and "Kind of Contraction" depend upon comparing the "Observed Joint Action" with the "Joint Action Tendency of Outside Forces" (including gravity), and by simultaneously noting the "Kind of Body Movement." Ordinarily, enough of these entries are known so that the remaining ones can be deduced.

Joint Action Tendency of Outside Forces. The entry in this column is determined by noting the existence and direction of outside forces. The weight of a body segment, together with the weight of any superincumbent or suspended external object, will initiate a gravitational torque directed toward the center of the earth. The magnitude and direction of other external forces, such as those caused by catching a baseball or those resulting from an opponent's holds in wrestling, are also considered. When the performer's body moves and collides with an external object, as at footfall in walking or in landing from a jump, it must be remembered that the object encountered transmits a force equal in magnitude and opposite in direction to the force applied by the impinging body of the performer.

Consider the fallacious "abdominal exercise" described on page 63. Its originator neglected the force of gravity, an outside force. The upper body tends to "fall" forward in toe-touching from standing position. Clearly, the Observed Joint Action is flexion at the intervertebral joints. What is the Muscle Group Active? There are three possibilities. *First*, if the Kind of Body Movement is purely gravitational (GRAV), the trunk simply falls forward, and the Muscle Group Active is *None*. Such an uncontrolled fall might result in disaster. *Second*, if the Kind of Body Movement is vigorously forceful, it will be labeled as ballistic (BAL), and the Muscle Group Active is, successively, *flexors*, then *none*, and finally *extensors*, and the corresponding Kinds of Muscle Contraction are *concentric*, *relaxation*, and *eccentric*, respectively. Such a fall, first augmented and then arrested by muscle contraction, is difficult and inefficient, and would seldom be employed. *Third*, if the fall is continuously dampened by muscular control, the Muscle Group Active is the intervertebral *extensors*, and the Kind of Contraction is *eccentric*. The Kind of Body Movement is designated as sustained force (SF–). The exercise is ordinarily performed in this manner.

Muscle Group Active. By "muscle group" is meant the muscles, collectively, which are prime movers and assistant movers for a given joint action. Thus, one may refer to the "elbow flexors" as a group, without specifying individual muscles.

Electromyography is the most objective means of determining which muscle groups, and which specific muscles, are active. Lacking such evidence, the entry in the Muscle Group Active column can be determined logically from noting the entries in the columns on Observed Joint Action, Joint Action Tendency of Outside Forces, and Kind of Body Movement (see below). Additional clues are given by palpation and by subjective sensations while performing the movement.

Kinds of Contraction. The possibilities here are eccentric contraction (E), concentric contraction (C), static contraction (S), or relaxation (R). The logical determination is made simultaneously or in conjunction with the determination of the Muscle Group Active, and by the same process of comparison.

Kinds of Body Movement. (See pages 63–65.) The determination is made by observation, by subjective sensation during performance, by comparison of the entries in other columns, or by electromyography.

Specific Muscles Active. This column is used to specify individually the working members of the Muscle Group Active. In some physical education applications, only the prime movers need to be specified, but medical applications normally need to be more precise.

In a particular movement, perhaps not all of the members of a muscle group will be active. Assistant movers frequently are not activated unless the resistance is considerable, and some movers may not participate because they are also movers for undesired side actions that cannot be conveniently neutralized in a particular exercise situation. Whereas such details are ignored when determining the Muscle Group Active, they become pertinent when the column on Specific Muscles Active is considered.

If the prime and assistant movers have not been memorized, the muscle charts at the end of Chapters 9 through 17 may be consulted. Such material should be memorized in great detail by the orthopedic surgeon and the physical therapist. Every physical educator should know the most important members of muscle groups, especially the large and/or superficial ones, together with certain key postural muscles, such as the abdominals and the iliopsoas. But few physical educators need to memorize permanently the actions of small muscles of the shoulder joint, wrist, hand, hip joint, and foot; and the posterior spinal muscles can be memorized collectively as groups (for example, "semispinales" and "erector spinae" and "deep posterior spinals"). It is assumed, of course, that a reference book is close at hand, and that it will be used frequently during training in first aid evaluation of injuries and the formulation of exercise programs and fitness regimens.

Undesired Side Actions. Nearly every muscle has more than one joint action, and when it contracts it tends to perform all of these. It will be necessary, especially in heavily resisted contractions, to list some muscles with undesired side actions in the column on Specific Muscles Active. A comprehensive analysis requires that these side actions be noted. If two movers have opposite side actions, then their tendency to perform these side actions will be mutually neutralized (helping synergy). If not, logic requires that a separate muscle (but not an antagonist to the muscle group active) be activated for the sole purpose of neutralization (true

TABLE 18–1. Abbreviations for Use in Kinesiological Analysis Notations

NAMES OF JOINTS

SH.G. —Shoulder girdle joints
SH.J. —Shoulder joint
E&RU —Elbow & radio-ulnar joints
WRIST—Wrist joints
I–C —Intercarpal joint
C–M —Carpo-metacarpal joint
M–P —Metacarpo-phalangeal joint
CERV —Cervical intervertebral joints
THOR —Thoracic intervertebral joints
LUMB —Lumbar intervertebral joints
SPINE —Intervertebral joints
HIP —Hip joint
KNEE —Knee joint
A&F —Ankle and foot joints
I–T —Intertarsal joints
T–M —Tarso-metatarsal joints
ANK —Ankle joint

KINDS OF GROSS BODY MOVEMENT

SF —Sustained force movement
SF+ —SF with eccentric contraction
SFO —SF with static contraction
SF– —SF with concentric contrac-
      tion
PAS —Passive movement
MAN —Manipulation by outside force
INER —Inertial coasting movement
GRAV —Gravitational falling move-
       ment
BAL —Ballistic movement
GUI —Guided movement ("track-
      ing")
DB —Dynamic balance movement
OSC —Oscillating movements

MISCELLANEOUS TERMS

Syn —Synergic; synergy; synergist
HSyn —Helping synergy or synergist
TSyn —True synergy or synergist
Neu —Neutralization or neutralizer
PM —Prime mover
AM —Assistant mover
(?) —Questionable, or in doubt
Rep —Repetition; replication

Index gives page references for definitions and explanation of terms.

NAMES OF JOINT ACTIONS
(AND MUSCLE GROUPS)

Flex —Flexion (Flexors)
Ext —Extension (Extensors)
Abd —Abduction (Abductors)
Add —Adduction (Adductors)
Sup —Supination (-ors)
Pron —Pronation (-ors)
InRot —Inward rotation (-ors)
OutRot —Outward rotation (-ors)
RtRot —Right rotation (-ors)
LtRot —Left rotation (-ors)
UpwRot —Upward rotation (-ors)
DownRot—Downward rotation (-ors)
Elev —Elevation (-ors)
Depr —Depression (-ors)
Opp —Opposition (Opposers)
Rep —Reposition (Repositioners)
Ser —Seraption (Seraptors)
Der —Deraption (Deraptors)
DFlex —Dorsiflexion (-ors)
PFlex —Plantar flexion (-ors)
RFlex —Radial flexion (-ors)
UFlex —Ulnar flexion (-ors)
HorFlex —Horizontal flexion (-ors)
HorExt —Horizontal extension (-ors)
Hyp —Prefix for "hyper-"
HypExt —Hyper-extension (-ors)
LatFlex —Lateral flexion (-ors)
LatExt —Lateral extension (-ors)
Rt —Prefix for "right"
Lt —Prefix for "left"

KINDS OF MUSCULAR CONTRACTION

Con —Concentric contraction
Ecc —Eccentric contraction
Stat —Static contraction
Rel —Relaxation (no contraction)
CoC —Co-contraction

RELATIVE FORCE OF CONTRACTION

0 —None; no contraction
Sl —Slight force
Mod– —Moderate force or less
Mod —Moderate force
Mod+ —Moderate force or greater
Max —Great or maximum force

synergy). Synergies can be identified precisely, if desired, in the column devoted to Comments.

EXAMPLE NO. 1

ANALYSIS OF FLOOR PUSH-UPS

Floor push-ups will serve as a simple movement with which to introduce the process of kinesiological analysis. Table 18–1 provides a key to the abbreviations employed in this and other examples. Table 18–2 reports the first step in analysis—the description of the exact movement to be analyzed. Even a simple exercise like push-ups can be performed in many different ways. It is important to understand that the present analysis pertains only to push-ups as described here. It is specified that hands be placed directly under the shoulder joints in the starting position, that the body be held straight and rigid from head to heels, and that the arms and forearms be kept in a plane parallel to the trunk during the movement.

TABLE 18–2. Format for the Formal Description of a Movement (Description of Push-Up Exercise—Example No. 1)

A. NAME OF THE MOVEMENT: Floor push-up, a formal exercise.

B. IDENTIFICATION OF PARTS OR PHASES OF THE MOVEMENT:

Phase 1—Starting position, front-leaning support.
Phase 2—Downward movement.
Phase 3—Momentary prone position on floor.
Phase 4—Upward movement (the push-up proper).

C. GENERAL VERBAL DESCRIPTION:

Phase 1—*Starting position.* Front leaning support. Palms on floor directly beneath shoulder joints, shoulder width apart, fingers pointing "forward"; elbows completely extended; arms and forearms vertical; shoulder girdle markedly abducted, in "active support" position; spinal column extended in a straight line from heels to head; feet at right angle to lower leg (anatomical position); toes hyperextended, sharing the weight-bearing with the distal ends of the metatarsals.

Phase 2—*Downward movement.* Keeping trunk and legs stiff and straight, flex elbows in the anteroposterior plane, and lower the body until anterior surface of trunk and legs come to rest on the floor.

Phase 3—*Prone position on floor.* Upper arms and forearms remain in a vertical anteroposterior plane, with elbows completely flexed; chin and nose one-half inch off the floor.

Phase 4—*Upward movement.* Return to starting position by pushing up, while maintaining rigid extension in spine, hips, and knees.

Table 18–2. (continued)

D. Photo or Drawing:

Phase 1

Phase 2

Phase 3

Phase 4

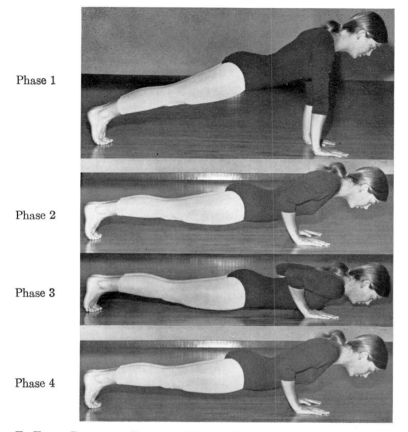

E. Elgon Record or Range of Motion Records: (Not included in this example).

F. Electromyographic Record: (Not included in this example).

Table 18–3 shows a complete, or long-form, analysis of joint and muscle action. For convenience, only Phase 2 (the "down-phase") is included. This long form provides a written record of the Joint Action Tendencies of Outside Forces, a column for listing in detail the Undesired Side Actions of the Active Muscles, and a place for Comments about synergies, reflexes, and other notations pertinent to the analysis. None of these three items is included in Table 18–4, a sample of the short form for analysis of joint and muscle action. The short form is more suitable for a user who has passed the begin-

TABLE 18–3. Joint and Muscle Analysis—Long Form

MOVEMENT ANALYZED:—Floor Pushups   PHASE:—No. 2 (Down-phase)

Name of Joint	Observed Joint Action	Joint Action Tendency of Outside Forces	Active Muscle Group	Specific Active Muscles (Prime movers) (capitalized)	Kind of Contraction	Kind of Body Movement	Force of Contraction	Muscle Groups Stretched	Undesired Side Actions of Active Muscles	Comments
SHOULDER GIRDLE	Add	Add	Abd	SERRATUS ANTERIOR PECTORALIS MINOR	Ecc Ecc	SF− SF−	Mod+ Mod+	Add	UpwRot DownRot	Side actions are neutralized
SHOULDER JOINT	Ext	Ext	Flex HorFlex?	ANTERIOR DELTOID PECT.MAJ.,CLAVICULAR Coracobrachialis Pect. Maj., Sternal	Ecc Ecc Ecc Ecc	SF− SF− SF− SF−	Mod+ Mod+ Mod Mod+	None	Abd; InwRot InwRot None? Ext;Add;InwRot	Fixation of hands on floor helps to prevent unwanted side actions
ELBOW & R–U JOINTS	Flex	Flex	Ext	TRICEPS BRACHII Anconeus	Ecc Ecc	SF− SF−	Mod+ Mod	Ext;Flex	Sh.Jt.Ext? Pron	Fixation prevents pronation
CERVICAL SPINE	None	Flex	Ext	SPLENIUS ERECTOR SPINAE SEMISPINALIS DEEP POSTERIOR GROUP	Stat Stat Stat Stat	SFO SFO SFO SFO	SI SI SI SI	None	RtLatFlex; LtLatFlex; RtRot; LtRot	Bilateral pairs prevent each other's unwanted side actions

Region				Muscles					{ Rt.Lat.Flex Lt.Lat.Flex Rt&Lt.Rot	Comments
THORACIC & LUMBAR SPINE	None	HypExt	Flex	RECTUS ABDOMINIS EXTERNAL OBLIQUE INTERNAL OBLIQUE	Stat Stat Stat	SFO SFO SFO	SI SI SI	None	None	Bilateral pairs prevent unwanted side actions
HIP	None	HypExt	Flex	ILIO-PSOAS RECTUS FEMORIS PECTINEUS	Stat Stat Stat	SFO SFO SFO	SI SI SI	None	None Abd Add;OutRot	Foot fixation prevents side actions
KNEE	None	Flex	Ext	RECTUS FEMORIS VASTUS LATERALIS VASTUS INTERMEDIUS VASTUS MEDIALIS	Stat Stat Stat Stat	SFO SFO SFO SFO	SI SI SI SI	Flex	None None None None	
ANKLE & FOOT	None	DFlex	PFlex	SOLEUS	Stat	SFO	SI	None	None	Gastrocnemius not active; would tend to flex knee

TABLE 18–4. Joint and Muscle Action Analysis—Short Form

Name of Joint	Observed Joint Action	Muscle Group Active	Kind of Contraction	Kind of Body Movement	Force of Contraction	Muscle Groups Stretched
MOVEMENT ANALYZED:—Floor Pushups			**PHASE:—No. 2 (Down-phase)**			
SHOULDER GIRDLE	Adduction	Abductors	Ecc	SF−	Mod+	Adductors
SHOULDER JOINT	Extension	Flexors	Ecc	SF−	Mod+	None
		Horizontal Flexors?	Ecc	SF−	Mod	None
ELBOW & R-U	Flexion	Extensors	Ecc	SF−	Mod+	Flexors & Extensors
CERVICAL SPINE	None	Extensors	Stat	SFO	Sl	None
THORACIC & LUMBAR SPINE	None	Flexors	Stat	SFO	Sl	None
HIP	None	Flexors	Stat	SFO	Sl	None
KNEE	None	Extensors	Stat	SFO	Sl	Flexors
ANKLE & FOOT	None	Plantar Flexors	Stat	SFO	Sl	None
MOVEMENT ANALYZED:—Floor Pushups			**PHASE:—No. 4 (Up-phase)**			
SHOULDER GIRDLE	Abduction	Abductors	Con	SF+	Mod+	Adductors
SHOULDER JOINT	Flexion	Flexors	Con	SF+	Mod+	None
		Horizontal Flexors?	Con	SF+	Mod	None
ELBOW & R-U	Extension	Extensors	Con	SF+	Mod+	Flexors & Extensors
OTHERS:—Same as for	Phase No. 2	as noted above.				

EVALUATION: The same muscle groups are active in Phases 1, 2, and 4 of floor pushups. Shoulder girdle abductors, shoulder joint flexors and horizontal flexors, and elbow extensors contract statically in the starting position (Phase 1), eccentrically during the down-phase (Phase 2), and concentrically in the up-phase (Phase 4). Muscle groups are relaxed in Phase 3 if performer rests on the floor between the down- and up-phases. *For strength development* of the active groups, the value of the exercise depends upon body weight, previous strength development, and number of repetitions performed. Exercise can be too easy for strong performers, and too difficult for weak ones. *For flexibility,* the exercise is valuable only for the shoulder girdle adductors, and elbow flexors and extensors. *For postural development,* pushups encourage abducted shoulders, a postural defect. Contraction of abdominals and cervical spine extensors is perhaps beneficial, but likely to be insignificant because of slight resistance and lack of range of movement. The unbalanced strengthening of shoulder girdle abductors, along with the stretching of the adductors, limits residual flexibility, unless other compensatory exercise is undertaken to strengthen shoulder girdle adductors and stretch shoulder girdle abductors. Administratively, pushups are convenient, requiring no special apparatus, costume, or surface. But for this reason, they are likely to be over-used, without providing compensatory exercises.

ning stage, and who can keep more of the details "in his head." It has the advantage of being much more concise; therefore, the opportunity has been taken to analyze two phases of push-ups, the downward movement (Phase 2) and the upward movement (Phase 4). Phases 1 and 3, the preliminary and intermediate static positions, do not seem significant enough to warrant precise analysis, although they might provide good examples of static contraction and relaxation for elementary practice.

Table 18–4 also shows the third major step in analysis—a summary and evaluation of floor push-ups with reference to several common criteria. If different criteria were assumed, the evaluation might be quite different. For instance, using push-ups as a warm-up exercise for college football players is entirely different from using them as a developmental exercise in a seventh grade class in adapted physical education. In the example, a somewhat "general" viewpoint has been taken.

This example illustrates the following concepts: (1) Kinesiological evaluation is a specific professional judgment, and its conclusions depend on one's viewpoint. Charles L. Lowman, M.D., a noted orthopedic surgeon, has listed floor push-ups as a contra-indicated exercise for routine developmental prescription for young people,* a viewpoint with which the authors concur. This does not mean that no human being should ever perform a push-up! (2) Even seemingly simple exercise involves complex muscular movements. Problems of influence of outside forces (gravity), of concentric and eccentric and static contraction, of neutralization and synergy, of stabilization (by musculature of the spine, hips, knees, and ankle), of reciprocal inhibition, and of flexibility all are illustrated. (3) The methodology of kinesiological analysis is deliberate and precise, although it may be carried out quickly and informally in the mind of the practicing professional during his daily work.

EXAMPLE NO. 2

ANALYSIS OF THREE RELATED HORIZONTAL SHOULDER JOINT MOVEMENTS

This example, consisting of three related sub-examples, illustrates the difference in muscle action occurring when the same Observed

* Personal communication to one of the authors. Other exercises on Lowman's contra-indicated list are straight-leg sit-ups with the feet held down, deep knee bends, and straight-knee double-leg-lifts from a supine position. An analysis of these exercises by the reader will be enlightening. Yet some obstetricians prescribe double-leg-lifting as a post-partum exercise for sedentary patients—even patients with lordosis. Such misunderstanding of kinesiology is common among physicians and physical educators.

Joint Action is performed in different general body positions, against outside forces having different directions.   An uncomplicated movement has been chosen, and the extent of the analysis has been abbreviated in order to center attention only on the principles being illustrated.   The entire analysis—description of the movements, the joint and muscle action analysis, and the evaluation—is presented in Table 18–5.

Still further variations of this movement (shoulder joint horizontal extension with shoulder girdle adduction) can be formulated. Analyzing them can provide good practice for the beginner, especially if the long format for joint and muscle action is used.   Suppose that the subject performs the movement while *facing* a set of wall pulley weights, holding the handles in his hands.   The ropes pass from the handles forward horizontally and over two pulleys at shoulder height, and then attach to weights that move up and down in a vertical track.   Both the weight of the arms, acting downward, and the force in the ropes, acting horizontally forward, affect the analysis.   Another variation occurs when the subject stands with his *back* to the wall pulleys.

EXAMPLE NO. 3
PRACTICE IN IDENTIFYING JOINT ACTIONS

In complex movements—and even in some seemingly simple movements—it is not always easy to identify joint actions.   But if an error is made in filling out the Observed Joint Actions column of an exercise analysis, the remainder of the work is also likely to be fallacious.   For this reason, it is worthwhile to consider some movements that have proven to be tricky for inexperienced analysts.

Sub-example 3A—Straight-leg twisting sit-up. *Starting position:* Supine lying; legs separated with extended knees; fingers interlaced lightly behind neck. *Movement:*   Curl-up forward, starting with the head, then shoulders, etc., until head approaches knees; then twist trunk so that the right elbow touches the lateral surface of the left knee.

What are the joint actions at the spine and the hip?   How shall this exercise be divided into phases?   Cervical, thoracic, and lumbar spine flexion obviously take place.   Left spine rotation also is apparent at the end of the movement.   Less obvious is the right lateral flexion of the spine, which must accompany the flexion and left rotation.   Hip flexion is another joint action sometimes neglected by the observer.

In dividing the exercise into phases for analysis, a mistake may be made by assuming that all of the actions listed above take place

TABLE 18–5. Example No. 2:
Analysis of Three Related Horizontal Shoulder Joint Movements

DESCRIPTION OF THE MOVEMENT

Phase 1—Starting Position. Spine, hips, and knees extended. Shoulder joints in a position of 90° flexion and 90° inward rotation, so that the palms are facing each other. Shoulder girdle in a position of complete abduction.

    Sub-example 2A—Body in erect standing position.
    Sub-example 2B—Supine on a high narrow bench.
    Sub-example 2C—Prone on a high narrow bench.

Phase 2—Movement. Move arms "sideward-backward" through the transverse plane as far as possible (shoulder joint horizontal extension and shoulder girdle adduction through a complete range of motion). No other joint actions occur. Movement is the same for all three sub-examples. For each, only Phase 2 will be analyzed.

JOINT AND MUSCLE ACTION ANALYSIS

Name of Joint	Observed Joint Action	Muscle Group Active	Kind of Contraction	Kind of Body Movement	Muscle Groups Stretched

Movement Analyzed:—Sub-example A (Standing)   *Phase No. 2*

Name of Joint	Observed Joint Action	Muscle Group Active	Kind of Contraction	Kind of Body Movement	Muscle Groups Stretched
SHOULDER GIRDLE	Adduction	Adductors Upward rotators	Con Stat	SF+ SFO	Abductors None
SHOULDER JOINT	Horiz.Extension	Horiz.Extensors Abductors	Con Stat	SF+ SFO	Horiz.Flexors None

Movement Analyzed:—Sub-example B (Supine) Phase No. 2

Name of Joint	Observed Joint Action	Muscle Group Active	Kind of Contraction	Kind of Body Movement	Muscle Groups Stretched
SHOULDER GIRDLE	Adduction	Abductors	Ecc	SF−	None (?)
SHOULDER JOINT	Horiz.Extension	Horiz.Flexors	Ecc	SF−	None (?)

Movement Analyzed:—Sub-example C (Prone)   *Phase No. 2*

Name of Joint	Observed Joint Action	Muscle Group Active	Kind of Contraction	Kind of Body Movement	Muscle Groups Stretched
SHOULDER GIRDLE	Adduction	Adductors	Con	SF+	Abductors
SHOULDER JOINT	Horiz.Extension	Horiz.Extensors	Con	SF+	Horiz.Flexors

EVALUATION:—*In 2A (Standing)*, gravity continually tends to cause shoulder joint extension or adduction, and shoulder girdle downward rotation, requiring static contraction of antagonists to these movements. *In 2B (Supine)*, gravity tends to cause the observed joint actions, which are performed under control of eccentric contraction of antagonists to the observed movement. *In 2C (Prone)*, gravity opposes the observed joint actions, which are performed by concentric contraction of the movers for those actions. *Stretching* occurs at the final stages of 2A and 2C, the stretched muscles being relaxed through reciprocal relaxation reflexes. In 2B, the eccentrically-contracting muscles will not be stretched at the end of the movement unless the hands carry weights, or unless an additional Phase 3 occurs, with concentric contraction of shoulder girdle adductors and shoulder joint horizontal extensors.

simultaneously. Neglecting the twist for the moment, careful inspection shows that if the sit-up is considered to involve almost 180° of total flexion, approximately the first third is characterized by spine flexion, approximately the middle third is predominantly if not entirely hip flexion, and the final third (or a little less) invokes slight spine flexion again, without appreciable hip flexion. With respect to spine flexion, then, it would be convenient to divide the sit-up into thirds, of which the first of the three phases produces practically all of the spine flexion, with its accompanying development of abdominal strength. The middle third, being predominantly hip flexion performed by the ilio-psoas muscles, can be subjected to severe criticism as a developmental exercise for postural improvement (see pages 292–294). The final phase, if performed vigorously, again stresses abdominal muscle contraction, more because of the twisting action than from the remaining amount of flexion.

If the influence of outside forces (gravity) is emphasized, perhaps the movement should be divided into a first half, a second 40 per cent, and a final 10 per cent. Gravity opposes flexion in the first half; but after the upright sitting position has been reached, gravity *causes* the continuing hip flexion and spine flexion until such time as the spine and hip extensors are elongated and put on stretch. Presumably this phase of the exercise is performed by eccentric contraction of hip *extensor* muscles rather than by concentric contraction of flexors. Gravity still assists with the final 10 per cent of the movement, but the resistance of taut spine and hip flexors has now become dominant, so that extremely forceful concentric contraction of flexors will be required in addition to gravity.

In order to bring these differing viewpoints precisely into the form of an analysis chart, some awkward footnoting will have to be included, introducing complexities which will tax the patience and intelligence of most readers. But it can be done.

Suppose the description of the exercise were changed to include only the first third of the curl-up, with the twist tacked on at that point. Then virtually all of the beneficial qualities of the complete exercise would emerge, and the possibly undesirable postural results of the ilio-psoas development would be obviated.

Sub-example 3B—Standing twist. *Starting position:* Erect standing, in anatomical position. *Movement:* Turn head and shoulders to the right as far as possible, keeping the hips in the original forward-facing position. What is the joint action in the spine? Clearly, it is right rotation, and the movement is cited here only to set the stage for the next two sub-examples.

Sub-example 3C—Hanging twist. *Starting position:* Hanging by the hands from a rigid high horizontal bar. *Movement:* Turn hips and legs to the right as far as possible, keeping shoulders in the original forward-facing position. What is the joint action in the spine? It is *left* spine rotation, because spine rotation is named right or left according to the change in orientation of the upper portion of the spine with respect to the lower portion, no matter which end appears to be the moving part.

Sub-example 3D—Supine bent-hip leg lowering sideways. *Starting position:* Supine; hips flexed to 90 degrees; knees extended; arms abducted to 90° (that is, reaching out sideways from the shoulders) with palms flat on the floor to prevent the body from rolling sideways. *Movement:* Keeping hands, arms, and shoulders flat on the floor, roll hips sideways right, lowering the legs sideways right until the right leg rests on the floor. What is the joint action? It is *left* spine rotation. (No hip joint action was called for.) What muscle group and what specific muscles are active? Do they contract concentrically or eccentrically? The answer is left to the reader, with the caution that this excellent postural exercise may be difficult to analyze. (Hint: any exercise that can be characterized as a *lowering* is likely to be performed with eccentric contraction.)

Sub-example 3E—Arm lowering from a standing upward reach. *Starting position:* Erect standing, with arms abducted to 180° and palms facing each other. *Movement:* Lower arms sideward-downward smoothly and gradually until *palms* are in contact with the lateral surfaces of the thighs. What are the joint actions, the muscle groups active, and the kinds of contraction?

The major action is shoulder joint adduction, with eccentric contraction of the shoulder joint abductors. Some inexperienced analysts do not notice the accompanying shoulder joint rotation needed to turn the palms in to the thighs. Is it inward or outward rotation? In answering, keep in mind the facts that shoulder joint rotation is named inward or outward according to specifications stated on page 37, and that reference is always made back to anatomical position when naming a joint action. Because this exercise starts with the arms moved 180 degrees away from the anatomical position, it is easy to name the direction of rotation exactly opposite from its true direction.

The shoulder joint adduction is performed with eccentric contraction, but since gravity has no influence on the shoulder joint rotation, presumably the rotation is performed by concentric contraction of rotators. In naming the specific muscles involved in these two simultaneous actions, it may be noted that the anterior deltoid and (above horizontal) the clavicular portion of the pectoralis major are assistant movers for *both* actions. Therefore, they should be listed.

But could a muscle contract eccentrically and concentrically at the same time? Obviously not, and perhaps only an electromyographer could fill in the muscle chart with precision.

Thus, one apparently simple exercise is shown to contain a number of pitfalls for the would-be analyst. A thorough study of this sub-example will be valuable to any person who wishes to master the intricacies of precise kinesiological analysis.

EXAMPLE NO. 4
THE SERAPE EFFECT

Many sports movements are, for all practical purposes, bilaterally symmetrical and also have joint actions that take place purely in one of the three standard perpendicular reference planes—antero-posterior, lateral, and transverse (see Figures 5–14; 7–1; 9–8; 10–7; and 16–13). Many more movements are non-symmetrical, primarily because limbs are used in alternation, or because spinal rotation takes place. But even in these movements the joint actions can be described as taking place essentially in one of the standard reference planes (see Figures 7–7; 21–3, 5, 6, 7, 8; 22–6, 7, 8, 9, 10, 12, 13, 16, 20, 21; and 23–4). This leaves perhaps the largest group of all—sports movements which not only involve spinal rotation, but which also are predominantly diagonal in direction (see Figures 8–7; 22–1, 2, 3, 4, 5, 11, 14, 15, 18, 19). In these movements, the diagonal motion of individual joints can of course be described as movements in two or more of the standard planes simultaneously, but when several body segments move together through virtually the same diagonal plane, it is useful to generalize by giving them a simple name. Logan[1] has done this by identifying *The Serape Effect*. [A serape (pronounced seh-rah'-peh) is a Mexican shawl hanging around the back of the neck and crossing in front of the body from each shoulder to the opposite hip.] The so-called serape effect is achieved by simultaneous concentric contraction of the "serape muscles," the diagonal chain formed by the left internal oblique abdominal, the right external oblique abdominal, the right serratus anterior, the right rhomboids, and continuing with the opposite members of these pairs in reverse order.

When half of the serape muscles (say, the chain from the right shoulder across the front of the body to the left hip) contract concentrically and vigorously, the result is a diagonal movement consisting of spinal flexion, right lateral flexion, and left rotation, together with shoulder girdle abduction, depression, and downward rotation. This is the serape effect; in this textbook, it will be given the name *seraption* to make it consistent with the terminology for

TABLE 18–6. Kinesiological Analysis of Baseball Pitching (Illustrating Seraption—Example No. 4)

DESCRIPTION OF THE MOVEMENT
A. NAME OF THE MOVEMENT: Baseball pitch (right-handed diagonal overarm-sidearm pitch, a ballistic movement).
B. PHOTOGRAPHIC DESCRIPTION: See Figures 20–4 and 20–5.
C. IDENTIFICATION OF PARTS OR PHASES:
Phase 1—Preliminary movement (deraption).
Phase 2—Acceleration phase of the ballistic motion (concentric contraction of movers; antagonists relaxed).
Phase 3—Coasting phase of the ballistic movement (relaxation of both movers and antagonists).
Phase 4—Deceleration or follow-through phase of the ballistic motion (original movers relaxed; eccentric contraction of antagonists).
Only Phase 2 will be analyzed below.
MUSCLE AND JOINT ACTION ANALYSIS OF PHASE 2

Name of Joint	Observed Joint Action	Joint Action Tendency of Outside Forces	Specific Muscles Active (Prime movers capitalized)	Kind of Contraction	Kind of Body Movement	Force of Contraction	Muscle Groups Stretched	Undesired Side Actions of Active Muscles	Comments
RIGHT SHOULDER GIRDLE	Seraption OR Abduction DownRot Depr	Not significant	PECTORALIS MINOR	Con	Bal	Max	Add	None	
			Subclavius	Con	Bal	Max	UpRot	None	
			PECT.MAJOR, STERNAL PART (indirectly)	Con?	Bal	Max	Elev	None	
			SERRATUS ANT. (?)	Con?	Bal?	?		UpRot	may not act at all
			Rhomboids (?)	Stat?	?	?		Add	may not act at all
RIGHT SHOULDER JOINT	Seraption OR Adduction Extension HorFlex	Not significant	PECTORALIS MAJOR, STERNAL PART	Con	Bal	Max	None	InRot	InRot may be desired, or neutralized by Infraspinatus & Teres minor
THORACIC & LUMBAR SPINE	Right seraption OR Flexion RtLatFlex LtRot	Not significant	Lt.INT.OBLIQUE	Con	Bal	Max	RtRot	LtLatFlex	
			Rt.EXT.OBLIQUE	Con	Bal	Max	Ext	None	
			Rt.Rectus Abdominis	Con	Bal	Max?		None	
			Rt.Quadratus Lumborum	Con	Bal	Mod?		None	

419

other joint actions.   The group of serape muscles will be called, then, *seraptors*.

Because seraption involves downward rotation of the shoulder girdle, the pectoralis minor muscle should replace the serratus anterior in the list of seraptors, for the serratus anterior is a powerful upward rotator tending to disrupt the unity of the diagonal movement.   When seraption includes an arm movement, as it frequently does, the sternal portion of the pectoralis major appears as a shoulder joint seraptor.   The pattern can be completed with forearm pronation, using the pronator teres as a seraptor, but of course not all seraptions will include so many joints—thoracic and lumbar spine, shoulder girdle, shoulder joint, and elbow joint.

Traditionally named joint actions have an opposite motion in the same plane, and seraption is no exception.   The opposite of seraption could be called *deraption*, and likened to a shawl hanging around the front of the neck, continuing to cross over from one shoulder to the opposite hip on the posterior surface of the body.   The chain of deraptor muscles are the right posterior deltoid, right infraspinatus and teres minor, right trapezius IV, right erector spinae, left semispinalis, left rotatores and multifidus of the deep posterior spinal group, and their opposite paired members, not to mention the supinator muscle of the radio-ulnar joints.   Deraption occurs in the preliminary "wind-up" movement preceding seraption.

Deraption and seraption are clearly illustrated by diagonal overarm-sidearm movements in throwing and serving (Figures 22–4, 5, 15, 19).   Deraption is the preliminary stretch, and seraption is the pitch or serve.   Table 18–6 shows how the baseball pitch of Figures 22–4 and 22–5 might be presented on a joint and muscle action analysis form, noting the joint action both as seraption and as a combination of traditional terms.

Diagonal movements other than seraption might be identified, but they are not sufficiently important to justify indiscriminate additions to the technical vocabulary.   From an engineering standpoint, three perpendicular reference planes are sufficient to describe all possible positions and movements in tri-dimensional space.   Roebuck[2] has proposed an expanded method for doing this with mathematical precision, in a manner ideally suited to computer-programmed mechanical analysis of human movement.

References

1. Logan, Gene A., and McKinney, Wayne C.: *Kinesiology*. Dubuque, Iowa: Wm. C. Brown Co., 1970, pp. 154–161.

2. Roebuck, J. A., Jr.: Kinesiology in Engineering. *Kinesiology Review, 1968*, pp. 5–11.

Chapter 19

Principles of Training and Development

The foregoing pages have presented a great many facts about how the human body moves and how movements can be analyzed. Facts and analytical data are sterile, however, unless they provide understanding. In this chapter, we shall use the information presented previously to derive a number of principles to show how the kinesiologist confronted with the problem of setting up an exercise program for some specific purpose can use general facts to derive specific training principles. No attempt has been made to make this summary exhaustive; it is not meant as a check-off list which frees the reader from the responsibility for creative thinking about his problem. Neither is it meant to provide a training program for any specific activity. Its purpose is to indicate the way in which the physical educator who understands his specialty might derive principles by which he could make a rational evaluation of training programs advocated by others and insure that his own are predicated on sound bases.

Master principles are listed first. These are the ones that apply pervasively to more than one of the identifiable performance factors —strength, circulatory-respiratory endurance, flexibility, speed of movement, and bone growth and development. Because some principles are relatively specific to individual performance factors, they are listed in a separate section following the master principles, but this does not imply that they are less important. It should be noted that there are, of course, more performance factors than the major ones considered here.[1-3]

MASTER PRINCIPLES

1. The Overload Principle. Beneficial human performance adaptations occur in response to stress applied at levels beyond a certain threshold value but within the limits of tolerance and safety. Low levels of stress, to which the body has already adapted, are not sufficient to induce a further training adaptation. In the useful range, an adequate training stimulus normally causes some disruption of tissues or of biochemical balance. During the interval between training bouts, repair and restoration occur, accompanied by some overcompensation that raises the person's capability to a new level. The *nature* of the training stimulus varies for each specific factor or quality of performance, and the exact *threshold value* varies with the immediate state of training and with other individual characteristics.

For *strength,* overload is provided by an amount of resistance that taxes the ability of a contracting muscle. Extremely light resistances do not stimulate appreciable gains in strength, no matter how many times the contraction is repeated. But if the resistance is greater than that to which the muscle is accustomed, even a single daily contraction ordinarily stimulates a significant strength increase. The threshold value, determining whether a contraction will or will not be an adequate training stimulus, cannot be precisely specified, for it occurs along a gradient. In practice, any exercise that can be repeated consecutively more than about 12 times involves a resistance that is too light to be efficient for strength development. Against resistances so heavy that only 1 to 12 consecutive repetitions are possible, the total amount of work performed during a given training period determines the amount of strength development, regardless of how the number of repetitions and the amount of resistance are combined in the program. A serious weight lifter may train effectively by using so heavy a resistance that he can perform only one repetition before taking a rest pause, after which he may perform another repetition, and so on. Another individual may choose a lighter weight and do more repetitions before his rest pause, especially if he wishes to train simultaneously for speed of movement or skillful coordination. Some skills that can *utilize* strength for optimal performance are poor *developers* of strength. Thus, although strength is helpful in batting a softball, the skill can be repeated consecutively an almost unlimited number of times, indicating that the amount of resistance is inadequate for efficient development of strength. With weight training equipment, the amount of resistance, the number of repetitions, and the number of sets of exercise can be regulated precisely to bring an efficient strength adaptation.

For circulatory-respiratory endurance, overload stress can be evaluated by measuring heart rate or, with laboratory equipment, O_2 uptake in milliliters per kilogram of body weight per minute. The maximum achievable human heart rate depends upon age, sex, and individual variables. For sedentary individuals pulse rates as low as 120 beats per minute may possess some training value.[4] For persons in better physical condition pulse rates above 140 to 150 beats per minute are necessary to produce a training effect.[5] Experienced athletes in serious training should approach their maximum heart rates in training bouts. However, at rates in excess of 200 beats per minute the action of the heart becomes inefficient, as it does not have time to fill with blood between beats.

For *flexibility*, training stress is provided by moving a body part past the point at which tissues surrounding the joint offer resistance. In clinical therapy, the maxim is, "Go to the point of pain, and just a little bit beyond."[6] Care is taken not to sever any tissues; usually this is impossible when the stretch is under voluntary control.

For *bone growth and development*, forces of compression, tension, shear, and bend stimulate an adaptation.

2. The Intensity Principle. Technically, overload refers only to the *amount* of work or stress. In determining the elements of an adequate training stimulus, not only its amount (overload) but also its *intensity* must be considered. The word "intensity" is defined here as it is in physics: an amount of force or energy per unit of area, volume, electrical charge, time, etc. With respect to the development of *strength* and of *circulatory-respiratory endurance*, the intensity of the training stimulus depends upon the energy expended in a unit of time. Thus, walking at 3 m.p.h. for 5 hours (a total distance of 15 miles) may be an overload for an unconditioned person, since the unaccustomed effort will certainly be fatiguing, but the work is not sufficiently intense to provide an adequate training stimulus for circulatory-respiratory endurance; whereas a lesser amount of overload (say, running only 3 miles in 18 minutes) gives an adequate training stimulus because of the combination of overload (3 miles) with intensity (10 m.p.h.). But even the most intense running will not provide an adequate training stimulus if the overload is insufficient, as in the case of running only 10 yards at maximum speed.

The fundamental consideration in formulating training schedules for the development of *strength* or *circulatory-respiratory endurance* is to provide for progressively more work to be performed in an inelastic time frame, or for the same amount of work to be performed in a progressively shorter time duration, or both (progressively more work performed in a progressively shorter time duration). If intensity is viewed as the ratio of work done to time duration, a good training progression provides for increasing the numerator, or decreasing the denominator, or both.

Work done at high levels of intensity induces acute fatigue, and requires temporary cessation of activity. In this situation, the most effective training procedure is to take a rest pause and then resume the activity at approximately the same high level of intensity. The other alternative—reducing intensity by decreasing the overload and increasing the time duration—soon tends to lower the training stimulus to a point below its threshold value. This second alternative is better suited to occupational and recreational activities, where the purpose is to work efficiently, or to practice skills, or to enjoy a game, rather than to induce a training stimulus.

In developing *circulatory-respiratory endurance*, the Intensity Principle is applied very effectively in *interval training*, involving repetition of high-intensity work bouts interspersed with brief rest pauses.

In *strength* development, high intensity of work is provided automatically by using relatively heavy resistances. Individual lifts need not be hurried, for even slow movements require a high intensity of energy expenditure if resistance is nearly maximal. Conversely, it is almost impossible to achieve great intensity of contraction with absurdly light weights, no matter how fast they are moved, because the combination of overload and intensity is below threshold value.

For *bone growth and development*, intensity of stress is expressed in terms of force per unit of cross-sectional area of compact bone. Although traumatic intensity must be avoided, relatively great intensity is essential to bone development. The normal rather great bony stresses incurred in vigorous running, jumping, stunts, dancing, and swimming are required for desirable skeletal growth in children. The deterioration of bones in aged adults or in bedridden patients is partly associated with inactivity (although increasing porosity and decalcification of bones seem currently to be an inevitable symptom of aging). Similarly, it is expected to be a serious problem in prolonged space flights.

3. The Frequency Principle. Training workouts should be sufficiently spaced to allow tissue growth, nutritional replenishment, and biochemical resynthesis to take place, and sufficiently frequent to provide for physiological development.

For the heaviest *strength* development programs, empirical evidence suggests that progressive resistance exercise on alternate days will bring maximal returns. Daily workouts may be detrimental unless resistance is reduced or alternate muscle groups are engaged. On the other hand, two days a week might be considered the minimal number of workouts from which to expect a noticeable development. For maintenance only, one day a week might be sufficient.

For *circulatory-respiratory endurance, flexibility,* and *bone growth and development,* five exercise periods each week are desirable, and daily workouts are feasible if interest can be maintained.

For *bone growth and development,* constantly-maintained stresses (as from habitual postural sagging) may be harmful even if they are low in intensity, but frequent and markedly intermittent stresses cause beneficial adaptation.

The optimal frequency characteristics of *speed* training have not been determined, but presumably they resemble those required for circulatory-respiratory endurance training.

4. The Transfer Principle. The factors (strength, endurance, etc.) of human performance are basically independent. Training for the development of one factor will improve performance only to the extent that previous performance ability was limited by that factor. Desired performance should be analyzed for its requirements with respect to each factor; capabilities of the performer should be assessed to determine his existing status in the light of the performance requirements; and training exercises should be selected in a proper mix to bring performance capabilities up to the requirements. An individual can train for more than one performance to the extent that the performances require the same mix of factors.

5. The Specificity Principle. No two performances require exactly the same mix of performance factors; beyond this bald statement, there are probably other (perhaps psychological) elements that make each performance skill, and even each repetition of it, unique. A person may exhibit "graceful coordination," for example, on the basketball court but not in the dance studio, and vice versa. As much as possible, training exercises should duplicate the exact conditions under which the results of training are to be utilized in performance skills. Although not all performances *develop* individual factors to the same extent that they *require* them, the required final performance would be the best single training exercise, if a person is thus limited in choices. But in sports, dance, special occupational tasks, and unexpected emergencies, it may not be feasible to duplicate the desired final performance in practice sessions.

Strength development is known to be highly specific. Strength may be divided into three discrete subfactors. *Dynamic strength* is the ability to move or support the weight of the body repeatedly over a given period of time. *Static strength* is the ability to exert a maximum force continuously for a brief period of time. *Explosive strength* is the ability to exert maximum energy in one short burst of effort. Furthermore, strength development is known to be specific, at least roughly, with respect to the practice conditions of speed, joint angles at which resistance is encountered, synergic and stabilizing action of other muscles, general body position, and probably also the degree of motivational effort involved. Training exercises should replicate the same mix of factors required in the desired final performance. For this reason, isometric strength exercises are questionable for basketball players, whereas gymnasts might practice with various kinds of exercise in proportion to their need to use dynamic, static, and explosive strength in their competitive routines.

Flexibility is often assumed to be a general (non-specific) factor, but experimental studies reveal that it is highly specific. Each performance activity requires its own unique set of flexibility characteristics, and flexibility developed in one kind of exercise may not be capable of utilization in another. Non-required flexibility sometimes is detrimental to performance.

Speed of movement generally resembles flexibility in its characteristics of specificity and transfer. Speed, however, may be more subject to neural and other innate individual characteristics; some people appear naturally to be faster movers than others.

It seems logical that *circulatory-respiratory endurance* might be a general factor in all performances limited by amount of oxygen delivery and capacity for incurring oxygen debt, but studies show that endurance gained from one activity cannot always be expressed in another, possibly because of extraneous and related conditions that contaminate the utilization of endurance capability.

Specificity in *bone growth and development* shows itself with respect to the exact nature of the stresses to which the skeleton is subjected. But here "stress" must be interpreted as "impulse" (force multiplied by the time it acts) rather than as force alone. Furthermore, bone stress must be resolved into its components of direction, magnitude, and kind (tensile, compressive, shearing, and bending).

6. The Trainability Principle. The more extensively the body is trained with respect to a given factor, the less its remaining trainability. The Trainability Principle is an expression of the concepts of limits, and of diminishing returns. It applies to all performance factors.

7. The Voluntary Stimulation Principle. In keeping with the Principles of Transfer and of Specificity, development of all performance factors proceeds best when training results from normal, voluntary neural stimulation.

For *strength,* development is optimal when achieved through voluntary neural stimulation. Direct electrical stimulation of muscles by artificial means is suitable only in pathology, under medical supervision. Passive exercise, massage, manipulation, and application of external forces affect contraction only through the possible activation of natural reflexes, without otherwise causing strength development in normal subjects. Methods and devices claiming effortless development of strength are fraudulent. Much evidence suggests that strength development is primarily neural (and perhaps even motivational) in its genesis, and that peripheral biochemical and morphological changes in muscle are important secondary derivatives.

For *endurance,* similar principles operate. There is no magic energy-producing food or procedure. While all energy is derived from foodstuffs, the concept of "quick energy" has been discarded by knowledgeable kinesiologists.

Flexibility may be gained by any exercise that forces the joint beyond the range of motion to which it has been adapted, whether this exercise be passive, assistive, or resistive. But even here, there are advantages to stretching by voluntary neural stimulation. A passive or ballistic stretch may initiate a stretch reflex within the very muscles being stretched. Minor injury is then likely to occur, since the muscles stretched are simultaneously contracting. If, however, the stretch is powered by slow concentric contraction of the antagonists, the stretched muscles presumably will be relaxed through the mechanism of reciprocal innervation, and the contractile fibers themselves are less susceptible to trauma. At the same time, strength and tonus are developed in the antagonists, tending more or less permanently to counterbalance the residual tension in the muscles which need to be stretched. The generalization is that slow, controlled stretch is preferable to passive or violent ballistic stretching.

For developing *speed,* motion caused by voluntary stimulation seems quite obviously preferable to any form of speed training by passive movement.

For *bone growth and development*, impinging forces that cannot be borne or effectively dissipated by an individual's musculature are likely to be traumatic. Forces generated entirely by one's own musculature, as in jumping from a level surface, seldom will exceed the existing capability of the bones. Outside forces can easily exceed safe limits.

8. The Progression Principle. Since the absolute value of a minimal training stimulus, with respect to any of the factors, tends to change regularly as progress is made, the amount of stress or overload should be increased gradually but persistently over a long period of training. If this is not done, the training stimulus (although it remains the same in absolute value) soon becomes subminimal; while if increments are made in very large steps the exercise becomes either impossible or dangerous.

For *strength* and *circulatory-respiratory endurance*, the statement of the Progression Principle may be extended by noting that the trainee must, progressively, either do more work in the same time or the same work in a shorter time. Progression here is made by increasing the amount or intensity of the overload, or both. This is a fundamental concept in designing training programs.

For *flexibility*, it is the extent of stretching, rather than the intensity, that is subjected to gradual and progressive enlargement.

9. The Efficiency Principle. When efficiency in work is desired, exercise should be conducted slowly, at a steady rate, and with frequent short rest pauses before fatigue accumulates. This applies particularly to *strength* and *endurance*. However, efficiency (the ratio of energy output to energy input) is more frequently a desired characteristic of final performance than of training efforts. Acceleration, especially, is costly in terms of energy; therefore at least some practice should be devoted to the pacing of performance if efficiency is a required factor in the application of training benefits. Involved here also—and perhaps worthy of statement as a separate principle—is the concept of optimum speed of performance. Any activity is inefficient if performed too slowly, and again if performed too rapidly. Usable energy is conserved if the optimum rate is determined, perhaps by subjective sensations, and practiced. Again, this concept is not applicable to every desired final performance. The prize in a sprint race goes to the swiftest competitor, not to the most efficient.

10. The Valsalva Principle. (See p. 313.) While training, and also as much as possible during final performance, the glottis should be kept open, and intrathoracic pressure should not be allowed to build up as a result of making an expiratory effort with the glottis closed. Ultimate straining efforts tend to be accompanied by the undesirable Valsalva maneuver. It is possible that this facilitates all-out contractile effort, especially in lifting, by stabilizing the rib cage against maximal contraction by muscles attaching thereto. But it also generates undesirable thoracic and cranial blood pressures, and if continued may subvert the return of venous blood to the heart, whereupon blood pressure falls drastically, and the athlete may "gray out" or "black out." If breathing movements are continued during great exertion, a side benefit occurs in the development of the musculature of the rib cage.

11. The Overtraining Principle. Overtraining, which can occur with respect to both *strength* and *endurance* development, is a state of chronic fatigue leading to undesirable morphological, systemic, and psychological changes. The cure for overtraining is temporary cessation of training, or changing the training regimen, together with recreational relaxation. Overtraining may be more hazardous than undertraining.

12. The Motivation Principle. The motivational acceptance of fatigue, effort expenditure, discomfort, and boredom of training is an important factor in the development of *strength, endurance,* and sometimes other factors. Some commercial advertisements to the contrary, there is no easy way to train seriously with fun and enjoyment. Most normal humans find unique rewards in the pure psycho-physiological euphoria that follows a session of training or vigorous performance. In fact, an antidote to the fatigue of prolonged sedentary work is an exercise bout that reaches well into the realm of physiological fatigue, followed by a shower, a meal, and a period of relaxation. In proper dosage under selected conditions, vigorous exercise and the creative challenges of dance and sport are transcendent agents of self-expansion and self-realization. Drugs and inactivity, on the other hand, are deadening. Quite obviously, those who depend on alcohol, anodynes, tranquilizers, or hallucinogens exhibit in their lives none of the qualities they often claim to derive.

PRINCIPLES PERTAINING TO INDIVIDUAL PERFORMANCE FACTORS

Strength.

1. The Range of Motion Principle. Ideally, a strength exercise should begin from a position in which the muscle is fully stretched, and end in a position in which it is fully shortened, if flexibility, maximum tension and strength throughout the range are desired as outcomes.

2. The Recovery Principle. Moving or massaging an exercised muscle during rest pauses will increase its speed of recovery; general body position also may influence circulation and prevent stagnation of metabolites in a muscle.

Endurance.

1. Muscular endurance and circulatory-respiratory endurance are separate factors in human performance; development of one does not necessarily accompany development of the other.

2. Increased strength and skill contribute significantly to muscular endurance, primarily by increasing the efficiency and reducing the energy cost and fatigue decrement associated with a given task.

3. The development of endurance depends largely upon training the oxygen up-take and transport mechanisms. The ability of the heart to pump blood is the most common limiting factor in circulatory-respiratory endurance, but not the only important one.

4. Circulatory-respiratory endurance requires both high aerobic ("pay-as-you-go") capacity and high anaerobic (oxygen debt) capacity. Although aerobic capacity is partly an innate factor, training programs must stress both aerobic and anaerobic capacities.

Flexibility.

1. Flexibility is related to body type, sex, bone and joint structure, and other factors beyond the individual's control.

2. Flexibility is predominantly a function of habits of movement, activity, and inactivity.

3. Work or exercise which constrains a joint within a restricted range of motion tends to reduce flexibility.

4. Lack of normal flexibility constrains the extent and quality of performance, and may be responsible for specific ailments.

5. The decrease in flexibility normally accompanying aging is caused by failure to maintain movement through a complete range of motion.

Speed of Movement.

1. Maximal speed of movement is partly an innate individual characteristic.

2. Speed of movement is influenced by reaction and response times, which are partly innate individual characteristics, but which can be minimized by training in attention, mental set, and skills.

3. Speed of movement is reduced by failure of antagonistic muscles to relax quickly and completely; to some extent this is a skill and is subject to training influences.

Bone Growth and Development.

1. The ability of bone to adapt healthfully to imposed stresses depends not so much on the absolute magnitude of externally applied force as upon (a) the torque, or force multiplied by the length of lever arm, (b) the bony area through which the force is transmitted, and (c) the magnitude of tensile, compressive, shearing, and bending components of that force.

2. Optimal growth and development of the skeleton depends critically upon the consistent, uninterrupted operation of the general factors in a healthful life regimen—freedom from debilitating disease, freedom from noxious drugs and chemicals, adequate intermittent periods of sleep and relaxation, and balanced nutrition. These conditions are particularly important in the period between conception and maturity.

References

1. Faulkner, John A.: New Perspectives in Training for Maximum Performance. J.A.M.A., *205*, 741–746, 1968.

2. Mollet, Raoul: Current Tendencies of Modern Training. Amer. Correct. Ther. J., *22*, 103–111, 1968.

3. Rasch, Philip J.: Principles of Human Performance. A.C.I.S.M. Technical Brochure No. 8, 39–50, 1969.

4. Shephard, R. J.: Commentary on Roskamm, H.: Optimum Patterns of Exercise for Healthy Adults. Canad. Med. Ass. J., *96*, 899, 1967.

5. Karvonen, M. J., *et al.*: The Effects of Training on Heart Rate. Ann. Med. Exp. Fenn., *35*, 307–315, 1957.

6. Billig, Harvey E. and Loewendahl, Evelyn: *Mobilization of the Human Body.* Stanford: Stanford University Press, 1949, pp. 20–22.

Laboratory Exercises

1. Select any two unitary individual skills. For each, determine the approximate demands in terms of various performance factors (strength, endurance, etc.). Suggest, and then compare, training programs designed to enhance an individual's performance of these skills.

2. Do the same for any two selected sports, or for two different playing positions in one sport.

3. Translate the principles of training and conditioning into simple statements of guiding rules for presentation to junior high school students.

4. Refer to an advertisement, literature, or actual experience with a commercial exercise device or fitness program. Examine its claims or implied effects, using kinesiological principles and facts as criteria for evaluation.

5. Write a speech or article, directed to professionally non-trained parents, entitled "How to Promote the Healthful Development of Your Child's Growth and Fitness." Document your advice with references to kinesiological principles.

6. Evaluate yoga exercises in terms of the principles set forth in this chapter.

Chapter 20

Kinesiology of Posture

EVOLUTION AND DEVELOPMENT OF ERECT POSTURE

Evolution of Erect Posture. The upright posture which distinguishes man from all other animals is the product of perhaps 350,000,000 years of evolution. In the evolutionary process the paired fins of certain tetrapods, whose nearest living relatives are the coelacanths, developed into limbs and provided for terrestrial locomotion. In the course of time—possibly 150,000,000 years ago—the first mammals came into existence. By 70,000,000 years ago quadruped primates about the size of rats and probably resembling the modern tree-shrews were in existence. Over the millennia certain changes in body form adapted them to life as brachiating animals whose weight was *suspended* from their arms. The lower limbs were extended in line with the body, which assumed a vertical position. Brachiation required great mobility in the shoulder girdle and joints, lengthened and strengthened upper limbs, increased powers of supination and pronation, and the development of the prehensile hand. The thorax became flattened anteroposteriorly, displacing the center of gravity backwards and simplifying the problem of standing erect. The scapula moved posteriorly. The pectoralis minor insertion shifted from the humerus to the coracoid process. The function of the serratus anterior was altered to produce elevation of the arm above the right angle.

Some 30,000,000 years ago the forests began to recede, forcing man's predecessors to become ground dwellers. It has been suggested that bipedalism arose as a solution to the problem of food carrying.[1] Further structural changes were necessary for effectively bearing the stresses of body weight, which was now *supported* by the lower limbs. The leg lengthened and straightened. The foot

FIG. 20–1. Posture, from horizontal to vertical. *Left to right:* Generalized Amphibian, Primitive Reptile, Pro-Mammal, Archaic Mammal, Very Ancient Primate, Gorilla, Man. (Courtesy Wallace Laboratories.) Man's remote ancestors seem to have originated during the early Pliocene (some 12,000,000 years ago) and he himself appears to have been largely developed by the early Pleistocene (about 1,000,000 years ago). Note that lumbar lordosis is distinctively human and seems to be associated with erect posture on extended legs.

lost most of its grasping abilities and became specialized for bipedalism. The large size of the gluteus maximus—an extensor of the hip joint—is peculiar to man. It is offset by a corresponding enlargement of the quadriceps femoris, which tends to prevent the knee from buckling as a result of the forward momentum of the center of gravity as the foot strikes the ground. The plantaris, which acts on the toes in most mammals, faded to a vestigial muscle, while the soleus, which acts on the ankle joint alone and is small in most mammals, became relatively very large. The extensor digitorum longus, which is attached to the femur in most mammals, lost this attachment and has no direct action on the knee of man.[1,2] The upper extremities, freed from the burden of supporting the body, evolved into instruments of great delicacy of movement (Fig. 20–1).

Not all these structural modifications have been equally successful. The lower extremities have been profoundly modified, but the pelvis, by which they are attached to the vertebral column, has remained essentially that of a quadruped. Mechanically considered, the spine represents a column. Under pressure a column becomes deformed and a curve develops. In the vertebral column itself there has been comparatively little adaptation to the demands of upright posture other than the development of a forward cervical convexity, a thoracic concavity, and a lumbar convexity. Too, the internal mesenteries are arranged for quadrupedal, rather than bipedal, position.

Posture of the Infant. The S-shaped spinal curve of the adult develops from the C-shaped curve seen in the infant and in anthropoids. In the brief interval between creeping and walking the baby recapitulates millions of years of evolutionary change. As Keith has observed:

> Indeed, it is not too much to say that the spine of the human baby, as regards the proportion of its parts and its curvatures, is in an anthropoid or troglodytian phase of evolution. We have only to watch an infant trying to support its body erect when learning to walk, to see reproduced the orthograde posture of a great anthropoid ape. The lower limbs are seen to be imperfectly extended, the body plainly inclines forward, and the arms stretch out to clutch at neighboring objects for support. In the second year of life, growth changes in the lumbar vertebrae make further extension of the body a permanent possibility; it is then that the loins elongate and the lumbar curve, seen only in the human species, makes its appearance.[3]

Effects of Erect Posture. Several results follow whenever a child or a species changes from a quadruped posture to an erect one: (1) changes in muscular development, (2) changes in coordination, (3) changes in the work of breathing, (4) changes in the mechanics of the circulation, and (5) increased tendency to displacement of the internal organs.

Muscular Development. Erect posture, with the weight borne by the lower limbs, must result in vastly greater size and strength of the extensor muscles of those limbs and of the lower portions of the trunk; greater strength in bones is also a necessity. The flexors of the trunk, relieved of much of the strain they have to bear in the quadruped position, have a tendency to deteriorate, sometimes allowing abdominal organs to sag forward (see p. 453).

Coordination. Greatly increased difficulty in poise and balance in the erect posture leads to a corresponding development of nervous reflexes to maintain exact balance under all conditions. The release of the forelimbs from support and locomotion permits them to be employed in skilled occupation under the guidance of the eyes.

Breathing. In the quadrupedal position the ribs hang down below the spinal column and swing back and forth like a pendulum in breathing, requiring very little muscular expenditure; when this mechanism is shifted to the upright position the entire weight of the chest wall must be lifted with each inspiration and must be held up to proper level continuously. So great is the pull of gravity on the chest, neck and spine that the ribs gradually sink as age increases, and the internal organs sink along with them.

Circulation. In the horizontal position the blood returning to the heart flows easily and evenly from the anterior and posterior portions of the body, but erect posture creates a column of blood which greatly increases the problem of returning blood to the heart against hydrostatic pressure. The inferior vena cava and its tributaries are distended, and in the absence of repeated muscular contractions fluids tend to accumulate in the intracellular spaces and in the cavities of the abdominal vessels and organs. Circulatory mechanisms are thus subjected to orthostatic stress.

Position of Internal Organs. In the horizontal position the abdominal organs are suspended from the arched spine by their mesenteries and are supported from below by the contracting abdominal muscles. When the erect position is assumed, these organs sag downward into the pelvic basin, creating pressure and congestion. This may alter the location of segmental centers of gravity, resulting in accentuation of spinal curves.

CRITERIA FOR GOOD POSTURE

Evaluation of Posture. The term "good posture" often conveys the thought of a standing position fulfilling certain esthetic and mechanical specifications. Sometimes the postures of school children are graded by such arbitrary standards (Fig. 20–2). Whatever the values of a prescribed posture, expecting everyone to meet any given standard is to ignore the fact that posture is largely an individual matter. Only the muscular type represents the posture generally considered ideal. Other types apparently cannot assume this stance and should not be expected to do so.

After a study of the posture of college women, Wells[4] concluded that their spinal structure could be divided into two classes: humanoid, with a long posterior concavity extending well up into the thoracic region, and anthropoid, with a posterior convexity extend-

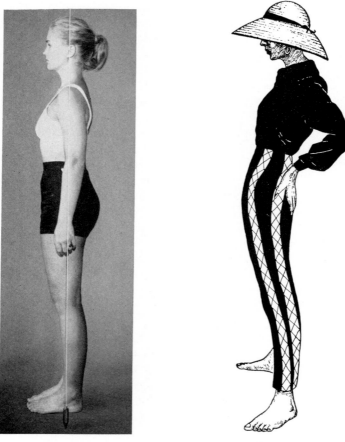

Fig. 20–2.   Fig. 20–3.

Fig. 20–2.   Excellent static posture. The subject was a winner in a Los Angeles City Schools posture contest. (Houston, courtesy Los Angeles City Board of Education.)

Fig. 20–3.   Typical fashion model's stance.

ing well down into the lumbar region. The latter she believes represents "inherited types of structures reflecting evolutionary tendencies." In her experience these types do not generally respond to corrective exercise.

An erect posture is not necessarily the most efficient one. The rigid military posture requires about 20 per cent more energy than an easy standing position, and an extremely relaxed standing position requires about 10 per cent less energy than an easy standing position.[5] Many famous athletes have attributed their success in part to the fact that they were almost completely relaxed between movements, thus conserving their energy for purposeful expenditure. There is no evidence of physiological benefit from the correction of common functional postural defects. The scientific basis for many of the current concepts of posture and statements about posture is unsatisfactory. It is plain that upright stance imposes hydrostatic handicaps which increase man's liability to peripheral circulatory collapse, but assumptions that attitudinal anomalies must be positively correlated with functional disturbances are based on very scanty experimental evidence. Fortunately, the body has a remarkable ability to compensate for deviations from the norm, and such compensating mechanisms are seldom considered by those who stress the malign functional effects of poor posture. After a detailed study of 2200 "relatively normal" men and boys Schwartz, et al. reported, "a record of physical impairments was obtained and checked against the posture measurements. A complete absence of relationship was found. (Except possibly in the case of myopia.)"[6]

The esthetic appeal of erect posture and poise, balance, and ease of motion are not to be denied (Fig. 20–4). Physique and beauty contest winners are almost invariably characterized by pleasing posture. Strangely enough, however, the typical fashion model's stance is apt to be characterized by pronated feet, hyperextended knees, exaggerated lumbar lordosis, protruding abdomen, round shoulders, and a forward head! (Fig. 20–3). The difficulties of satisfactorily defining good posture are evident. Wells[7] has rejected all static concepts, such as the one holding that the lobe of the ear, tip of the acromion process, middle of the trochanter, and head of the fibula should be aligned vertically, and has suggested that a vertical zone within a centrally located limited area might provide a satisfactory reference plane from which to measure anatomical landmarks.

Over forty years ago Schwartz, et al. complained that "there have as yet been devised no objective methods of judging posture sufficiently practical for use on a general scale."[6] In the intervening period conformateurs, comparagraphs, schematographs, silhouetto-

Fig. 20–4.   Perfect dynamic balance illustrated by dancers of the Ballet Russe de Monte Carlo.   Note the extreme range of motion demonstrated in the joints of the lower limbs of the feminine dancers and the precise adjustment of the center of gravity over the very small base.   The position of the feet shown in the mirror image of the leading dancer will repay careful study.   When a ballet dancer is on points the metatarsophalangeal joints are plantar flexed and the interphalangeal joints are dorsiflexed.   (Wolff, courtesy Pittsburgh Plate Glass Company.)

graphs and various other scientific-sounding devices have been introduced for the graphic measurement of posture.   The difficulty with apparatus of this type is that while they do provide data about the alignment of the parts of the body, the *significance* of this information rests upon subjective and arbitrary assumptions implicit in the judgment of the measurer.

Esthetic and culturally-determined standards cannot be entirely ignored in establishing criteria for posture.   The wasp-waist of the Gibson-girl of the 1890's or the breast-minimizing slouch of the flapper of the 1920's cannot be approved kinesiologically, but attempts by the kinesiologist to insist that his pupils adopt postures which are not culturally sanctioned will certainly encounter resistance.

Basketball players, boxers, and shot putters often develop short, strong pectoral muscles and weak shoulder girdle adductors.   Many sports, such as tennis, archery, baseball pitching and discus and javelin throwing, are likely to lead to asymmetrical development. With modern training methods, including supplemental weight training, undesirable adaptations can be minimized.   Minor postural divergencies in vigorous, healthy, active youngsters are not nearly so serious as the same degree of deviation in those who are convalescent, weak, inactive, undernourished, or obese.   It would hardly be wise to ignore postural deviations in athletes, but the practice of making indiscriminate assignments to corrective classes for minor asymmetries has sometimes been carried to the point of absurdity. Any occupation or sports specialty may lead to postural adaptations, but these are not necessarily pathological just because they depart from the traditional arbitrary plumbline standards. A careful professional judgment is required in each individual instance.

Posture must be considered from the standpoint of the individual's body and the use which he makes of that body. Perhaps the wisest words yet written on this subject are those of Metheny:

> There is no single best posture for all individuals. Each person must take the body he has and make the best of it. For each person the best posture is that in which the body segments are balanced in the position of least strain and maximum support. This is an individual matter.*

It has been suggested that the adaptability of a mechanism to make useful adjustments has in large part been determined by the factors of organic evolution, but that the agencies employed for this purpose exist primarily for physiological uses and have no special fitness for pathological adaptations.[8] The implications of such statements as the foregoing are that the corrective physical educator, the corrective therapist, the physical therapist or similar individuals should not attempt to "correct" an individual's posture unless they clearly understand precisely what steps should be taken and the rationale therefor. Ordinarily such information can be obtained only by medical examination, and experience indicates that physicians assign only a very small percentage of college students to corrective classes because of postural deviations. With younger groups the percentage may be somewhat higher.

Maintenance of Posture. The "righting reflexes" by which the animal maintains his posture have been studied in great detail by Magnus.[9] They appear to consist of five separate groups of reflexes: (1) labyrinthine righting reflexes; (2) body righting reflexes acting on the head; (3) neck righting reflexes; (4) body righting reflexes acting upon the body; (5) optical righting reflexes. The centers of these righting reflexes lie in the ventral part of the mid-brain behind a section just in front of the third nerves. Little is known about the way in which these reflexes cooperate to provide erect posture in the human. Presumably stimuli received from any of these sources and from stretch reflexes initiated by proprioceptive mechanisms in the striated muscles reflexly bring appropriate muscles into action to correct displacements from the desired position (Fig. 20–5).

---

* Quoted by permission from *Body Dynamics*, by Eleanor Metheny. Copyright, 1952, McGraw-Hill Book Co.

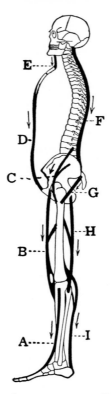

Fig. 20–5.   Antagonistic muscle groups responsible for erect posture. A, Tibialis anterior; B, Quadriceps femoris; C, Iliopsoas; D, Abdominals; E, Neck flexors; F, Spinal extensors; G, Gluteus maximus; H, Hamstrings; I, Triceps surae.

Righting Reflexes.   Although all of these righting reflexes may work simultaneously in some situations, not all of the appropriate stimuli may be available in special situations.   Thus, a somersaulting diver or tumbler will not be able to employ (3) or (4) above.   He must depend upon (1), (2), and (5).   If he has not conditioned his visual reflexes, or if he closes his eyes during performance, (5) is eliminated, and only (1) and (2) remain.   A person who both closes his eyes and, because of inexperience or fear, cannot utilize the labyrinthine reflexes of (1) and (2), must depend on more haphazard mechanisms.   Thus, some beginners in somersaulting report that they just "jump, tuck into a ball, wait a fraction of a second, and then open into the erect position."   Probably they depend upon an estimation of their speed of rotation, together with a guess at the time interval necessary for completion of their somersault; but there is always a strong element of luck in this kind of performance. Usually, experience and confidence will gradually lead to a more finished performance, in which a small amount of voluntary control is superimposed upon the workings of uninhibited reflexes.

Attitudinal Reflexes. Attitudinal reflexes are initiated by movements of the head and result in an adjusted static position. The stimuli act upon the receptor organs of the labyrinth; the change in posture is brought about by alterations in the tonus of trunk and limb muscles. For example, tilting the head back in order to look at an object overhead results in shortening of the trunk extensor muscles, relaxation of the abdominal muscles, adduction of the shoulder girdle, a tendency toward extension of the upper limbs, and a tendency toward flexion at the knees. Conversely, lowering the head in order to peer under an object results in flexion tendencies in the trunk and upper limbs. Rotation of the head to one side results in an increase in limb extensor tone on that side and in a decrease in limb extensor tone on the opposite side; lateral flexion of the neck (inclination of the head to one side) has a similar effect. In sports, a side-stepping motion is usually initiated by rotating and inclining the head to the side of the step; this reflexly increases extensor tone on that side and instantly prepares the leg on the same side to receive the body weight.

The muscles moving the eyeballs are also affected by labyrinthine stimuli resulting from head-tilting. A forward head movement reflexly tends to move the eyeballs upward; a backward head movement tends to move them downward. The tendency is always to preserve the original field of vision. These reflex tendencies may, of course, be inhibited when they do not serve the purpose of the organism. In the example of deliberately looking at an object overhead, the reflex tendency to lower the eyeballs, as the head is tilted back, is superseded by voluntary raising of the eyeballs.

Positive Supporting Reflexes. In all of the positive supporting reflexes, the result is to increase extensor tone or flexor and extensor tone in order to make the body rigid against the force of gravitational pulls. The following are examples: (1) The stretching of toe flexors, foot flexors, and ankle plantar flexors as a result of pressure on the ground causes reflex contraction of the extensors (or flexors and extensors) of the knee. (2) Any tendency toward overextension (stretching) of distal limb muscles causes a myotatic contraction of these muscles and their synergists, tending to correct the balance of the body and counteract gravitational forces. (3) Stepping on a surface stimulates the pressure receptors in the soles of the feet, causing a reflex contraction of limb extensors. This is known as the *extensor thrust* reflex; its utility in locomotion and standing is obvious.

The positive supporting reflexes are usually considered to be static reflexes—that is, useful in the maintenance of stationary erect posture. During locomotion, however, these same reflexes assume equal importance. For example, in the last phase of weight-bearing by a limb (the push-off phase), the toe and foot plantar flexors are stretched, resulting in a myotatic contraction of these same muscles, thus reflexly giving additional force to the push-off.

Negative Supporting Reflexes. The characteristic of negative supporting reflexes is a limb flexion followed by a placing and extension of the limb for support purposes. It is best demonstrated in blindfolded animal or human subjects (animals may also be labyrinthectomized). For example, a cat in such a state may be held by the body in mid-air. Then if a board is touched lightly to the top of one of its paws, that paw is reflexly withdrawn slightly, replaced on top of the board, and extended. Or, if the standing animal is pushed sharply to one side, there is a hopping reflex which involves sudden pushoff, flexion-withdrawal, and replacement of the paw under the new location of the center of gravity of the animal. The object of these and numerous allied reflexes is replacement of the foot (or hand) in a supporting position, with terminal contraction of the extensor muscles.

Developing Reflex Actions. All such reflexes as the foregoing, and many more, are learned or conditioned reflexes, probably. Very few are present in the newborn child, and maturation of the nervous system is inadequate to provide a complete explanation of their development. Many individuals depend upon visual reflexes for balance and dynamic movement. In sports and emergency situations, such strong dependency upon visual reactions and the consequent lack of development of the non-visual mechanisms may be a distinct disadvantage, because the vision may be temporarily impaired or obscured by numerous situational factors, and the visual field may not be sufficiently broad or steady to perceive all of the available visual cues. Normal people, like those who become permanently blinded, can develop labyrinthine, proprioceptive and other mechanisms far beyond so-called normal levels. Sports like tennis and baseball, which emphasize visual perception, may not be as suitable as aquatics, tumbling, and balancing for the sharpening of a broad repertoire of labyrinthine and proprioceptive reflexes, although these mechanisms, once developed, can be used in such sports. Conversely, hand-eye and other eye-to-muscle reflexes may be most easily trained in ball sports. A child's experience in motor activity should involve a great variety of activities. Specialization at too early an age may limit the ultimate extent of ability in that specialty. At the higher levels of performance in a given specialty, the better performers are likely to be those whose perceptual and motor learnings are most versatile. Some basketball players, for instance, can effectively initiate pivot-style shots while their backs are toward the basket. They rely upon a visual memory of the location of the basket with regard to themselves, upon initial movements guided by proprioceptive reflexes, and only at the last moment upon visual perceptions to make final adjustments to the motor act of shooting for the basket.

It has been calculated that the force which must be exerted by the calf muscles to maintain the upright position is equal to about one-quarter of the body weight. In subjects standing at ease, electrical potentials were recorded from the soleus muscles of all subjects and from the gastrocnemius muscles of the majority of the group. Potentials were occasionally obtained from the tibialis anterior and peroneus longus. Most subjects were found to stand at ease without detectable activity in the quadriceps and hamstrings. This was explained on the basis that since in this position the line of body weight usually falls in front of the center of the knee joints, the weight of the body above the knees is supported by the ligaments of the knee joints. Shifting of the line of body weight posteriorly or anteriorly to this point results in contractions of the quadriceps or hamstrings to preserve the stance. In the erect posture there is continuous contraction of the internal oblique fibers, possibly to protect the inguinal region from hernia. As the subject sways back and forth the rectus abdominis and sacrospinalis contract alternately to correct the resulting displacement.[10-13]

The basic response of individual muscle fibers to a stimulation is probably a twitch rather than tetanus. The immediate result is the production of essentially oscillatory forces. Tremor at the rate of about 10 cycles per second appears to accompany muscular contraction in mammals. With an increased load on the musculature a progressive increase in the amplitude of this tremor becomes evident. The approximate metabolic cost of various types of posture is shown in Table 20–1. These figures may be altered by the individual's body weight, degree of sway, and other factors.

TABLE 20–1.   Metabolic Cost of Various Types of Posture[14]

	Calories per Minute	Per cent greater than Lying
Lying	1.14	—
Sitting	1.19	4.4
Standing relaxed	1.26	10.5
Standing at attention	1.30	14.0

The natural position of the feet is one in which the heels are together and the foreparts of the feet are toed out sufficiently to give stability to the lateral balance of the foot. The line of the body's center of gravity is perpendicular to a point midway between the heels and the heads of the first metatarsal bones. In standing the weight should be about equally distributed between the ball of the foot and the heel. Under the stress of weight-bearing the foot both lengthens and broadens slightly. There is a reflex postural contraction of the abductors hallucis, the minimi digiti, and the adductor hallucis and the other plantar muscles in response to proprioceptive reflexes, but the greater portion of the tension stress is borne by the plantar ligaments. Structural or functional foot abnormalities must be corrected or compensated before good posture can be achieved.

The Legs and Knees. During the act of standing up, the ankle is controlled primarily by strong contractions of the tibialis anterior and extensor digitorum longus. The proper position of the legs, with regard to inward or outward rotation at the hip joints, is best explained by imagining that the patellae are eyes, and specifying that they should be "looking" in exactly the direction of a line drawn longitudinally from the heel through the center of the foot. If in any weight-bearing activity the feet are "toed out" or "toed in," there should be an accompanying outward or inward rotation of the thigh at the hip joint. Otherwise, there will be undesirable strain at the knee and ankle joints. This principle assumes more importance during body movement, and is often stressed by dance teachers, whose medium often requires foot position or progression in a diagonal direction. The military position of attention, with feet at a 45-degree angle, is disadvantageous to the entire lower extremity and especially to the foot. It tends to pronate the foot and stress the supporting structures of the arch.

The energy expenditure of stationary standing is less if the knee and hip joints are slightly hyperextended, since ligaments then bear the weight and allow extensor muscles to relax. However, this results in a pooling of venous blood in the lower extremities. So does standing with the knees slightly flexed, which has the additional disadvantage of hastening fatigue. If continued stationary standing cannot be avoided (as during a military review), venous stagnation can be allayed and fainting prevented by deliberate intermittent contraction of leg muscles.

The Pelvis. The importance of the function of the pelvis in maintaining the ideal erect posture and its role in good body mechanics cannot be overemphasized. It is one of the most important structural units of the body. It supports the body weight from above and conveys it to the legs. Because it joins the immovable portion of the spine to the flexible, mobile portion, deviations from its normal position are reflected the full length of the spinal column. The pelvis also acts as a sort of shallow cup which supports and partly contains the pelvic viscera.

Normally the anterior superior iliac spines and the front of the pubic crest lie in the same frontal plane. Any pronounced deviation from this position materially hinders the functioning of the pelvic viscera. An upward tilt of the pubis straightens the lumbar section while a downward position causes a lumbar curve, which, if prominent, is a hollow back. When the downward tilt is exaggerated, the pelvic contents are thrown forward and tend to spill over the anterior lip of the pelvic cup, the pubic arch. This throws an additional strain on the abdominal muscles.

In addition to the pelvis being tilted from its optimum position in the anterior-posterior plane it sometimes happens that one side of the pelvis is higher than the other. This may be caused by inequality in the length of the legs, a flat foot, or by muscular atrophy of one of the legs. The fixed portion of the spine is tilted to one side. The mobile portion of the spine therefore rests on an inclined surface, resulting in further deviations from the ideal erect posture.

It is extremely difficult to measure the pelvic angle in living subjects. An anterior-posterior tilt of 50 to 60 degrees in the male and 54 to 60 degrees in the female is generally accepted as normal.

An exaggerated pelvic tilt causes the buttocks to protrude, and gives rise to an awkward gait. Hyperextension of the knee tilts the pelvis forward, while flexion tips it backward.

The oblique position of the pelvis brings the pelvic organs far to the rear, where they are beneath the sacrum and protected somewhat by it from the weight of the organs above; it also brings the lower lumbar vertebrae far enough forward to be practically over the hip joints, so that little force is required to maintain poise.

The Vertebral Column. Viewed laterally, the vertical column exhibits three curves: a forward cervical convexity, a thoracic concavity, and a lumbar convexity. The lumbar region is not well buttressed by muscle, and the rectus abdominis is the only longitudinal anterior muscle directly controlling the amount of lumbar curvature. A common analogy is that it acts like a bowstring, the lumbar curve being the bow. Some assistance is afforded by the compression of the abdominal contents by the oblique abdominals, these compressional pressures being transmitted as forces tending to straighten out the lumbar curve.

The Abdominal Wall. The four pairs of muscles in the abdominal wall—recti, internal and external obliques, and transversali—are involved in two important reflexes: those of posture and breathing.

A third function of this group of muscles is to maintain suitable support for the internal organs.

The Shoulder Girdle and Chest. The best functioning of the internal organs calls for an erect position of the chest and neck, and a moderate adduction of the shoulder girdle. The tidal movements of the ribs should take place in a range midway between full inspiration and full expiration. This semi-elevated position of the ribs and sternum takes up the slack in the abdominal muscles and provides a good base for their action.

The Head. The head should be kept in a well-balanced position. When it is allowed to droop forward habitually, undue strain is placed on the ligaments and extensor muscles of the neck and back. People who frequently carry moderately heavy loads on their heads develop an excellent position for the head, neck, and back. If they did not keep the body, head and load in perfect balance, they would either drop the load or be subjected to so great a strain that they could not maintain their erect position.

Implications for Good Posture. What are the postural implications to be derived from knowledge of man's evolutionary past, and from biological, mechanical, and physiological data? The evidence does not lead to clear-cut answers, but the following generalizations might be suggested: *First,* static erect postures should be deliberately avoided, except for short periods. *Second,* in sitting or recumbent positions, properly placed environmental supports (such as firm mattresses or chair backs) should be available to replace the function of muscle groups which are relaxing. *Third,* in stationary postures, the center of gravity of each body segment should be vertically above the area of the supporting base, preferably near its center. If persistent gravitational torques are being borne by ligaments, or if excessive muscular contraction is required to maintain balance, this principle is being violated. Thus, it is permissible to bear weight on the knee or hip ligaments by slight hyperextension of these joints, but excessive weight-bearing by the spinal ligaments over a period of time will prove damaging. *Fourth,* rhythmic reciprocating movements (such as walking) are beneficial, because they facilitate return of venous blood toward the heart and because the intermittent relaxations tend to postpone fatigue. *Fifth,* the bones, tendons, and muscles should be strengthened and toughened through gradual progressive stresses and resistances, so that they may cope adequately with the common forces encountered in daily living. Ligaments apparently are but little affected by either exercise or stretching.[15] *Sixth,* in forceful dynamic movements (such as sprint starting or a football lineman's charge), the forces should be directed as much as possible in a straight line which intersects the major joints: metatarsophalangeal, knee, hip, and shoulder. At the same time, spinal curves should be minimized, so that they will be ready to bend in a spring-like fashion as they absorb impact forces. Impact forces may injure locked joints, but joints which are able to move in either direction are mechanically ready to absorb them (Goldthwait's factor-of-safety[16]). *Seventh*, the guiding principle in maintaining postures and in moving should be *efficient energy expenditure*. This concept of optimal (not minimal) energy expenditure has been extensively developed by Metheny.[17]

CAUSES AND CORRECTION OF POOR POSTURE

Causes of Poor Posture. Defects of posture may result from (1) injury, (2) disease, (3) habit, (4) muscular or nervous weakness, (5) mental attitude, (6) heredity, or (7) improper clothing.

Injury. When a bone, ligament or muscle is injured, it is apt to weaken the support at that point and throw the framework out of balance. As long as this condition is present, perfect posture is impossible; after the injury has been fully repaired a habit set up may persist and the faulty posture continue for a long time. Since minor injuries, like a sprained ankle, often occur, and since there is seldom any effort made to re-educate the reflexes of the wrong habit, we frequently see defects of posture that arose in this way.

Disease. Diseases that weaken bones or muscles or cause joints to lose their strength or their freedom of action upset the control of posture as badly as injuries. Rickets, due to faulty nutrition of bone, and tubercular disease of joints or vertebrae are examples of this kind. Infantile paralysis, by weakening or destroying the motor nerve cells in the spinal cord, causes partial or complete loss of function in certain muscle groups. This loss of power in the muscles upsets the control as in the former instances and also causes another kind of defect; the uninjured group that is the natural antagonist of the paralyzed one, not having its normal opposition, becomes gradually shortened and holds the joint out of normal position. For example, one with a paralyzed gastrocnemius gradually develops a flexed ankle which he cannot extend.

The treatment of cases involving severe injury or disease often requires surgical measures, such as cutting a muscle or tendon, removing or grafting bone, transplanting of tendons to make good muscles do the work of absent ones, and the making of braces to support the weight when the natural support is lacking.

Habit. Habits of posture, whether good or bad, are acquired in the same way as habits of speech or habits of walking, namely, by practicing a certain coordination so many times that the act finally becomes habitual and unconscious and is performed whenever the appropriate situation presents itself. In a very large percentage of the cases of faulty posture found among school children and college students, the bones, joints, ligaments and muscles are in normal condition; the fault is a wrong habit of coordination. Segments of the body have been held out of line so long, with some parts bearing too much weight and others too little, some muscles elongated and their antagonists shortened, that the wrong posture feels natural and a correct position seems strange.

Wrong habits of posture are caused by injury and disease and by occupation and environment as well. A boy who sprains his left ankle may learn to stand on his right foot during the period of lameness. This may develop into a habit which remains with him for years. A boy who has carried a heavy sack of papers on one shoulder every day for a year or two is apt to hold that shoulder low for the rest of his life. Bookkeepers are known by their peculiar habit of holding the head and cowboys by their bowlegged gait. Seats, shoes, and clothing produce similar effects when they have the wrong size or shape, so that they hold one in a faulty position; defects of vision and hearing, and resting positions on rocking chair, lounge, hammock or bed may induce such habits also.

On the other hand, those who are strongly impressed with the advantages of good posture, so that they study their own postures and try to improve them, just as thoroughly as they study to improve their complexions and the appearance of their clothes, are apt to have correct habits of posture, in spite of occupation and environment.

Weakness. The erect posture cannot be maintained without the expenditure of energy, and therefore requires some strength and endurance. Posture is a sensitive indicator, showing to one who can read it not only our habits but also the level of our store of energy. It has been demonstrated that a slouched position can be maintained at less metabolic cost than the erect alert position, largely because the subject is supported by the ligaments of hyperextended joints, which provide the necessary support, rather than by the action of muscles. Muscular weakness and the lack of vitality then necessarily predispose one to assume such a slouched posture as a matter of energy conservation. Because general muscular weakness is one of the common causes of poor posture, an active childhood involving vigorous exercise obtained by engaging in games and sports is perhaps the best preventive measure that can be undertaken. The type of activity or game selected is important. Interest of the pupil in the game should be one of the most potent guiding factors because strong interest results in continued participation. The correction of general muscular weakness may take a long time, therefore sustained interest is necessary. The activities should be sufficiently vigorous to provide for organic strength. If possible, the activities should also provide for a balanced bilateral development.

Mental Attitude. Posture frequently reflects the mental attitude. Feelings of elation, confidence and satisfaction help in the maintenance of erect posture; humility and depression hinder it. A good mental attitude is likewise reflected in an erect, alert posture; a poor mental attitude is reflected in poor posture.

Heredity. Kyphosis may be hereditary, and it is possible that other postural defects may have a genetic basis.

Improper Clothing. Electromyographic studies have shown that when high heels are worn a marked increase of activity in the gastrocnemius, soleus and peroneus longus muscles results, whereas the tibialis anterior is not affected to any great extent. This appears to result from the fact that with high heels the center of gravity is shifted forward and the dorsal muscles must contract in order to prevent the body from falling forward.[10,11]

Removing the Causes. Whenever faulty posture is due to disease, the disease must be treated before anything else is attempted; if it is due to an injury, the injury must be healed. In general, the cause must be removed before any measures for improvement are apt to be effective; a posture due to wearing high heels will not be much improved as long as the high heels are worn; an hour in the gymnasium will not cure bad postures when many hours are spent in the environment that caused them. Some cases of faulty posture are due to fatigue, mental strain, improper digestion and assimilation of food, malnutrition, or similar causes. Here rest and proper nutrition are fully as important as a program of corrective activities.

Special Posture Classes. Many pupils are not strong enough and skillful enough to assume and maintain correct posture. These require more personal attention than can be given the average pupil. Special classes of small size should be conducted for them. More complete study of each case and of its causes is then possible.

When poor posture is due to general muscular weakness, such students can be placed in the same class and given developmental exercises and games to suit their individual needs. Due regard must be taken for the cause of each individual's shortcomings, and corrective procedures in line with the best educational and orthopedic practice instituted. This demands individual attention. The placing of *all* students with postural defects in a single class and giving them the same treatment is as unwise as it would be for a physician to prescribe the same therapy for all patients exhibiting a skin rash.

Referral Cases. Posture defects which cannot be voluntarily corrected by the subject's own volitional movements are known as *resistant or structural defects.* All such cases should be referred to a physician, preferably an orthopedist. Expert diagnosis, including x-ray films and other medical techniques, is necessary before any treatment is given. Not all such cases yield to exercise therapy, but the physician may make an exercise prescription and direct the patient to a physical, corrective, or occupational therapist or to a physical educator for supervised exercise. Coaches and physical education teachers make a valuable professional contribution when they recognize the possibility of severe problems and make referrals to a physician, but they act unethically and perhaps illegally when they treat cases without the permission or prescription of a licensed doctor.

SPECIFIC DEFECTS AND THEIR CORRECTION

Foot Defects. The nature of the arches and the structures supporting them has been explained in pages 393 to 397. The term *flat feet,* or "fallen arches," may refer to several different defects. *Flexible flat foot* exhibits loss of the arches only during weight-bearing, and is not regarded as pathological unless accompanied by discomfort or interference with function. True flat foot, or *pes planus,* is a structural anomaly, sometimes hereditary or congenital, which may or may not be accompanied by discomfort and interference with function. *False flat foot* is not a defect, but a condition resulting from the presence of a pad of fat on the plantar surface, under the arch. None of the foregoing are likely to be affected beneficially by exercise. There remains the very common *functional flat foot* caused by weakened and stretched muscles, ligaments, and plantar fascia. This type ordinarily responds to exercise, and should be corrected even when no discomfort results, because it may distort the mechanical relationships in other joints, causing symptoms to appear at the ankle, knee, hip, and lumbar spine.

Such defects as *pes cavus* (a rigid and greatly accentuated longitudinal arch), *pes equinus* (permanent plantar flexion and raised heel), and the various club-foot conditions require surgical treatment.

Habitual pronation of the foot is a common defect which usually responds to exercise therapy and habit training, provided that the existence of structural and orthopedic lesions have been ruled out. The symptoms include a curved or slanted tendon of Achilles, protruding internal malleolus, toeing out, and a pseudo-flat foot caused by the rolling inward of the ankle. Flat foot may or may not be an accompaniment (Figs. 20–6 and 20–7).

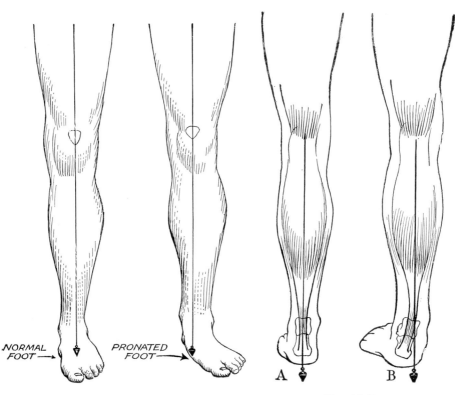

Fig. 20–6   Fig. 20–7

Fig. 20–6. Showing the position of a plumb line dropped from the middle of the patella in the normal and pronated foot. (Lewin, courtesy Am. J. Dis. Child.)

Fig. 20–7. The position of a plumb line dropped from the middle of the popliteal space in the normal A, and the pronated B. (Lewin, courtesy Am. J. Dis. Child.)

Stationary standing, although it demands much energy expenditure, does not provide good correction for any of the foot defects. Instead, it renders the individual susceptible to them, and may even be a primary causative factor in a sedentary person.

Exercise for the correction of habitual and functional defects should be general and involve the foot as a whole. Stronger individuals may benefit from rising on the toes, with the weight shifted toward the lateral borders of the feet, but usually non-weight-bearing exercises are preferred. The foot should be put through the extreme range of all of its motions by voluntary contraction, to stretch the shortened soft structures. The emphasis should be upon exercises involving toe flexion, foot and ankle plantar flexion, and supination.

Functional defects of the foot can be caused or intensified by a shortened tendon of Achilles, and this is very common among women and young girls who wear high heeled shoes constantly. To stretch the tendon and its muscles, assume the long sitting position (with knees extended in order to take up the slack in the gastrocnemius) and use muscular contraction to move the foot forcibly into a position of dorsiflexion and supination. An often recommended but questionable exercise is standing with the balls of the feet on the edge of a platform, with heels protruding over the edge. Any bouncing on the tendon of Achilles would tend to initiate a stretch reflex in the soleus and gastrocnemius muscles, and would tend to break down the longitudinal arch by reason of the rotational torque exerted on the calcaneus. Further, this exercise has no tendency to strengthen the supinators and plantar intrinsic muscles, which are usually weak and stretched in individuals having a shortened heel cord.

Leg and Knee Defects. *Genu valgum* ("knock-knees"), *genu varum* ("bowlegs"), *genu recurvatum* (hyperextended knee), and *tibial torsion* (twisting of the tibia on its long axis, so that its proximal end appears to be inward or outward rotated) are complicated deformities which require orthopedic attention. Exercise correction should not be undertaken without the permission or prescription of a physician. The defects may appear to be in the knee joint, but usually the entire length of the femur and tibia is involved, with abnormalities of growth occurring at the epiphyseal plates if the bones are immature.

The term *tibial torsion* is also frequently used to designate a functional inward rotation occurring at the hip and foot joints. The appearance of the defect is indicated by its nickname of "cross-eyed knees." It is often a functional result of habitual flat feet and pronated ankles, and (if severe structural conditions are ruled out by an orthopedist) exercise treatment may be undertaken, with emphasis on correcting the basic foot defects (Fig. 20–8).

Abdominal Wall Defects. The abdominal defects discussed here are intimately related to the spine defects considered in the following section, and vice versa. The division is made for convenience only.

The stomach, liver, small intestine, colon and other organs completely fill the abdominal cavity, and each is attached to the posterior body wall. As long as the trunk is horizontal, the organs lie normally in place, even when the abdominal wall is fully relaxed, but as soon as the erect position is assumed their weight pulls them downward, lengthwise of the cavity; the mesenteries by which they are attached are not composed of strong fibrous tissues, like true ligaments, but are mere folds of the soft peritoneum, in which the

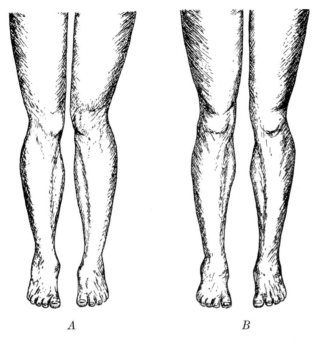

A   *B*

Fig. 20–8.   *A*, Tibial torsion.   *B*, Correction of tibial torsion resulting from contraction of the outward rotators of the femur.   (After Hawley.)

arteries, veins and nerves going to the organs are enfolded.   When
the right amount of pressure is maintained by a coordinated action
of the four pairs of abdominal muscles, the organs are held in proper
position in upright postures, even when subjected to the jar of running and horseback riding.

Visceral ptosis is the medical term for the sagging of the organs and
their downward drag upon their mesenteries that takes place when
there is not sufficient tension of the abdominal wall to hold them up
in place.   The pull on vessels and nerves causes nervous irritation
whose cause is not easy to find; if continued for a long time the organ
sags to a lower place in the cavity, stretching the connecting vessels
and crowding the organs below.   A sagging abdominal wall may permit displacement of the internal organs and contribute to their mal-
function (Fig. 20–9).

The lack of suitable muscular tension in the abdominal wall has
another effect; it leads to dilation of blood vessels in the digestive
organs, favoring inflammatory conditions.   This pooling and stagnation of venous blood is sometimes called *circulatory ptosis*.   The
presence of fat adds to the weight and hence to the tendency to sag
and to the distention of the wall.

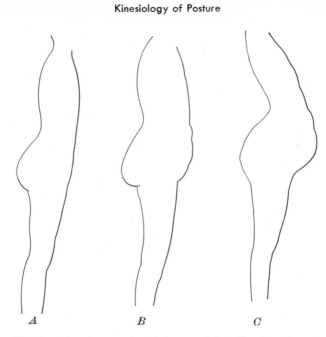

FIG. 20–9.   Tracings showing sagging abdomen with indication of ptosis; *A*, normal
outline; *B* and *C*, weak abdominal walls with apparent sagging of the viscera.

Hernia or rupture is a protrusion of some abdominal structure
through an opening in the abdominal wall.   The weakest point in the
abdominal wall in the male is usually the inguinal canal, just above
the groin and near the crest of the pubes; in the female it is usually
the femoral canal, where the femoral artery crosses the rim of the
pelvis; this is slightly lateral to the inguinal canal.   The immediate
cause of a hernia is usually some sudden and violent contraction of
the abdominal muscles, due to a fall or other accident or to a violent
fit of coughing, forcing a portion of the intestine through the weakened spot.   Sometimes no definite immediate cause can be assigned.

When a hernia has occurred once it is liable to occur again, since
the protrusion stretches the ring of tissue and makes the opening
larger.   The cure is accomplished by a simple operation.

Prevention of visceral ptosis and hernia depends upon maintaining
the strength and thickness of the abdominal wall.   Sedentary life
predisposes to these troubles by lack of bodily activity that is the
natural means of its development.   It also encourages a deposit of
fat in the mesenteries, the weight of which tends to increase the sagging.   Quiet breathing scarcely employs the abdominal muscles at
all; sitting, either when bending forward or leaning against a support, makes it unnecessary to use them in maintaining the posture.

Walking, running, and active games and sports bring them into action in the natural way, and so these activities are the best means of development and the best preventive measures. Special exercises in bending, twisting, raising, and lowering the trunk and moving the lower limbs can help if carefully used, but they are apt to be used too violently and for too short a time.

Round Shoulders (Abducted Scapulae). The most common defect in the position of the shoulder girdle is abducted scapulae. This is objectionable because it weakens the support which the coracoid should give to the pectoralis minor and thus reduces the tension that muscle should exert on the ribs. If the scapula is stabilized by the rhomboids and the trapezius, the pectoralis minor exerts a direct lifting force upon the third, fourth and fifth ribs, and an indirect force upon the others. In the absence of good scapular stabilization this muscle may tend to shorten and a pull downward upon the coracoid.

Abduction of the scapula, as a fault of posture, most often results from continuous occupation with the arms held in front of the trunk. In writing, sewing, holding a book in position to read, and numberless other occupations, the arms and shoulders are held forward by continuous contraction of the serratus, pectoralis major and minor, while the trapezius, rhomboid and levator are relaxed to permit the scapulae to move forward. This gradually tends to make the anterior muscles permanently shorter, while lengthening the posterior muscles. After a time the scapulae can be brought to the normal position only with difficulty, and this difficulty gradually becomes greater until the normal position becomes impossible.

Faulty shoulder posture of this nature can be prevented by frequent participation in sports or exercises which will develop, shorten and increase the tone of the trapezius, levator scapulae, and rhomboid, and at the same time stretch the muscles that have become shortened. The prevention of postural defects is a recognized aim of the physical educator and the corrective therapist. Because the nature of classroom work is such that it tends to cause round shoulders, the physical educator should include in the program exercises or sports which are calculated to prevent this condition. Among the best exercises for daily use is the one shown in Figure 20–10. The arms are raised sideward until slightly above the level of the shoulders and then the elbows are bent and the fingertips placed against the back of the neck, which is held vigorously erect; the elbows are held back strongly. The position is held long enough to insure an accurate position and complete contraction of the muscles, then the arms are returned to the sides through the same path and the movement repeated several times. A second efficient

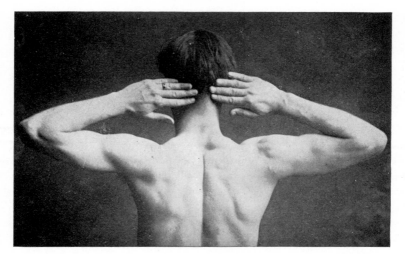

FIG. 20–10. An exercise for correction of habitual abduction of the scapulae.

corrective for abducted scapulae is pictured in Figure 20–11. The elbows are completely flexed, the entire arm is held horizontal, and the elbows are drawn strongly backward. Trapezius and deltoid hold up the arm and draw it back while the lower serratus rotates the scapula, tending to shorten and increase the tone of these muscles while stretching the pectorals. Another good exercise consists in strong adduction of the scapulae and outward rotation of the arms.

A crucial factor in obtaining value from these exercises is the forcefulness of the scapular adduction. Only in the final phase of the movement do the adductors contract sufficiently to stretch the abductors. An example of insufficient contraction is seen in Figure 20–12.

Some instructors advocate stretching the abductors by such exercises as "skinning the cat" and the "corner exercise." In the latter the subject faces a corner of the room, reaches forward and upward and places the palms against the wall and proceeds to stretch by letting gravity and force from the feet push the chest toward the corner. It should be noted that the adductors do not contract during this process; further, this passive stretch of the abductors may initiate a myotatic or stretch reflex in the abductors, resulting in their reflex contraction. Such an exercise may not be effective as a method of strengthening the adductors or stretching the abductors and may also strain the abductors.

Another common error is to exercise with pulley-weights ("chest-weights") while standing with the back toward the pulley apparatus. In this position forward and backward movements of the arms and

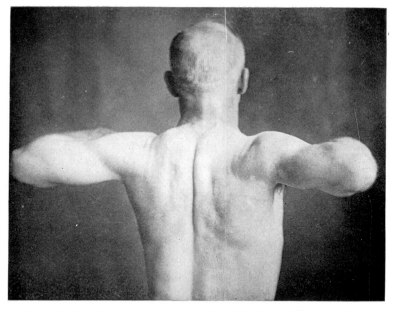

Fig. 20–11.   A corrective exercise for abduction of the scapulae.

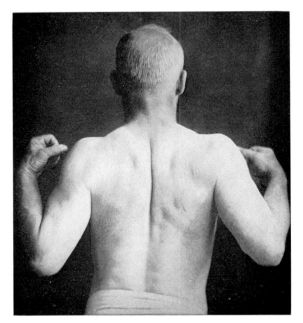

Fig. 20–12.   The Swedish exercise "shoulders firm," or "arms bend."   The position of the right arm illustrates a common fault; the hand is not held back far enough to give complete adduction of the scapula.

scapulae are the result of concentric contraction and eccentric contraction, respectively, of the shoulder girdle abductors, while the adductors remain relaxed. This type of exercise tends to accentuate the defect, not to correct it.

Habitually abducted scapulae are often associated with "forward head" and kyphosis in the thoracic or cervical spine. In corrective exercise, therefore, attention should be given to the total postural condition as well as to the specific musculature involved in the abduction of the scapulae.

A marked projection and upward tilt of the lower angle of the scapula, often known as "winged scapula," is usually due, as has already been observed, to a deficiency in the action of the rhomboid and serratus anterior and to a shortening of the pectoralis minor. In mild cases the exercise of Figure 20–12 is a good corrective, the effort to hold the elbows down giving vigorous but not straining work for the rhomboid, while a forceful effort to hold the hands back will stretch the pectoralis minor. As a general principle it is well to remember that exercises involving elevation of the humerus give work for the trapezius rather than for the rhomboid, while the reverse is true of exercises involving depression of the humerus.

Unequal height of the shoulders may be the result of unequal development of the shoulder girdle musculature on the right and left sides, or of unilateral paralysis (partial or complete) of shoulder girdle muscles. Most often another cause will be discovered: a lateral curvature of the spine, which, in turn, may be caused by unilateral short leg, unilateral flat foot, and other defects at a lower level. Obviously, it is essential to determine whether the unequal shoulder height is caused by a local or by a remote condition.

As in all correction of posture, it is of course not enough to stretch the short tissues and make it possible to assume an erect posture; the habit of correct posture must be fixed by the subject himself, through education of his nervous reflexes by persistent practice.

Kyphosis. Analytically, kyphosis and round shoulders are distinctly different, the former being an increased posterior convexity of the thoracic spine and the latter being a forward deviation of the shoulder girdle. However, one begets the other, and the two commonly appear together as an integrated defect.

Resistant or structural kyphosis, or any such defect accompanied by acute pain, indicates probable disease or hereditary defect of a more serious nature. Except on prescription of a physician, corrective exercises should never be given in such cases.

Lordosis. Lordosis is an increased posterior concavity of the normal lumbar or cervical curve, accompanied by a forward tilt of the pelvis (Fig. 20–13).

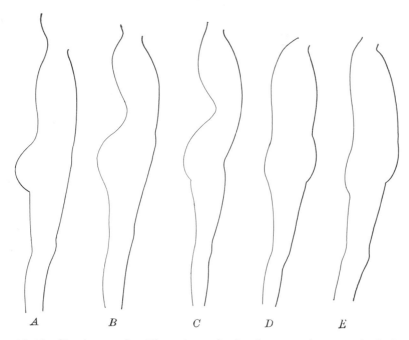

A   B   C   D   E

FIG. 20–13. Tracings made with pantograph, showing normal posture, lordosis and flat back; A, normal; B and C, lordosis; D and E, flat back.

The simpler type of hollow back is illustrated in Figure 20–13B. It is assumed temporarily whenever one carries a weight in the arms held in front of him, as when a waiter carries a heavy tray of dishes. The muscles of the lower back are shortened and the abdominal muscles are elongated. When this position is assumed habitually, too much weight is thrown on the posterior edges of the bodies of the lumbar vertebrae, and there is a marked tendency to assume a position of round shoulders to compensate for the backward shifting of the body weight. In flexible cases the subject has only to acquire the ability to assume the right position of the spine and then to practice it until the habit is established. In cases that are slightly resistant there are two kinds of exercises that will help to elongate the back muscles and to shorten the abdominal group.

Sitting on a bench against a wall and pushing the trunk backward so as to make it touch the wall in the lumbar region is good; it is a little stronger if taken while sitting on the floor, with the knees straight, as this tilts the pelvis backward and so helps to straighten the lumbar spine.

An exercise suitable for vigorous subjects is taken while lying on the back on the floor with the hips flexed until the feet are vertically over the face and 12 to 18 inches away from it; the hands or a pillow may be used to hold the hips off the floor. From this position move the feet in a circle as large as can be made conveniently. The back muscles are kept in a stretched position and the abdominal muscles used moderately in a shortened position. The so-called bicycle exercise is easier; here the hips are against the wall and the lower limbs extended upward along the wall; from this position one limb is flexed and extended in alternation with the other, as in bicycling.

When the pelvis is tilted too far forward, we have not only a wrong coordination of the flexors and extensors of the trunk, but also a wrong coordination of the flexors and extensors of the hips at the same time. In this case the back muscles and flexors of the hips are shortened, while the abdominal muscles and hamstrings are elongated. It will do no good to correct the imbalance of trunk muscles alone or of hip muscles alone; both groups must be adjusted and controlled to keep the pelvis in its proper degree of inclination.

The exercises that have been described to correct lordosis will not be of any use when the pelvis is inclined too far forward. None of these exercises will help to elongate the flexors of the hips, and the leg circling exercise described above will stretch the hamstrings still more. If the iliofemoral ligaments are short, they will tilt the pelvis forward in spite of all the muscles can do to prevent it. When the flexors of the hips and iliofemoral ligaments are just a little short it may be possible to stretch them in the following manner: lie supine, knees extended, and try to press the lumbar part of the back close to the floor. Possibly putting one hand there and trying to press the back against it will help. The work has to be done by the hamstrings, glutei, and abdominal muscles, against the resistance of the extensors of the lumbar spine, flexors of the hips, and iliofemoral ligaments. A variation that will sometimes help is to flex the knees a few degrees, sliding the feet along the floor toward the hips; then press the back down against the floor and hold it there while slowly extending the knees. This uses the extensors of the knees, along with the hamstrings and abdominal muscles, to stretch the flexors of the hips and the iliofemoral ligaments.

Making an intelligent decision as to when a lordotic back needs correction is a matter of some difficulty. Those who have seen the marvelous Danish gymnasts are aware that they exhibit marked lordotic curves. Scandinavian authors appear convinced that backs with greater than average lordotic curves are stronger and, vice versa, that stronger backs are more lordotic, than the average. They call into question the value of the Harvard standards.[18]

Flat Back (Lumbar Kyphosis) involves an abnormal decrease in the normal lumbar curve. The angle of obliquity of the pelvis is reduced, as the hamstrings are too short and the flexors of the hip and the iliofemoral ligaments are too long. It is commonly associated with the round shoulders, flat chest, and protruding abdomen characteristic of the clinical picture of fatigue. The condition is difficult to correct, but attention to increasing the strength and tone of the abdominal and erector spinae muscles may prove rewarding.

Lateral Curvature. Lateral curvature of the spine, which in pro-

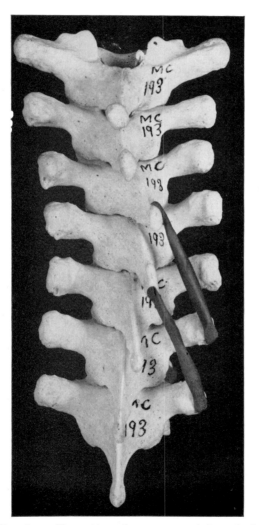

Fig. 20–14. The above illustration of a segment of the spinal column demonstrates the manner in which the unopposed action of the deeper muscles of the spine (semispinalis, multifidus, and rotatores) causes the vertebrae to rotate into a scoliotic position when the muscles of the opposite side are paretic. (Allbrook.)

nounced stages is called *scoliosis*, is a sideward deviation. It represents a combination of lateral deviation and longitudinal rotation.
One might expect that the muscles on the concave side of the curve
would be stronger than those on the convex side, and this is what
would be observed if the curve were due to unopposed action of the
longitudinal muscles. However, electromyographic studies have
shown that in the majority of cases the muscles on the concave side
are weaker than normal. This is attributed to the fact that imbalance of the deeper muscles (semispinalis, multifidus, and rotatores)
is the main factor in producing the deformity. These deep muscles
are important rotators. When those of one side are paretic, the
unopposed action of the muscles of the opposite side rotate the vertebrae into a scoliotic position[19,20] (Fig. 20–14). In some cases,
however, the muscles on the convex side are atrophied and those on
the concave side are contracted. Whether the changes that then
take place can be explained on the basis of muscle imbalance alone
is controversial.[20,21] Roaf[22] believes that lordosis is a lengthening of
the anterior longitudinal ligaments and a shortening of the posterior
components. Under the influence of the abdominal muscles, gravity, respiration, and other factors, a rotation of the vertebrae
develops and a lateral curvature appears. The complexities involved
in scoliotic defects should make it obvious that physical educators
and therapists should not attempt to "correct" them without the
advice and guidance of a qualified physician.

Lateral curvature lessens the ability of the spine to support the
body weight, distorts the body cavities and crowds the organs out
of place, and in advanced cases causes pressure on the spinal nerves
where they pass out of the vertebral canal. Scoliosis usually begins
with a single C-curve. This may be to either side, but since most
people are right handed, the muscles on the right side of the body
are generally stronger and the convexity tends to develop to the left.
The condition tends to be more prevalent in girls and among ecto-
morphic types, but is not confined to either. The curvature may
extend the whole length of the spine or it may be localized. A
C-curve may tilt the head sideways, in which case there is a reflex
tendency to right it until the eyes are again level. Over a period of
time this righting reflex creates a reversal of the C-curve at the upper
spinal levels, producing an S-curve. Further attempts at compensa-
tions may appear, creating additional undulations in the curve
(Fig. 20–15).

In the early stages scoliosis may be *functional*, or *postural*. These
terms indicate that the curve can be obliterated by voluntary effort
or by hanging from the hands. In the later stages the condition
becomes *resistant*, or *structural*, and the curve can no longer be so

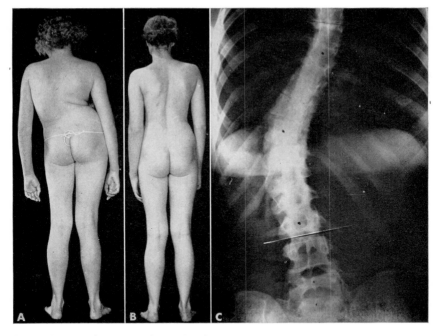

FIG. 20–15. *A*, severe thoracolumbar curve after poliomyelitis in a fourteen-year-old girl. *B*, the same girl two years later, following correction by turnbuckle cast and spinal fusion from the seventh thoracic to the third lumbar vertebra. *C*, X-ray of spine of this patient at age eighteen. (Reprinted with permission from Risser, J. C., Scoliosis, Past and Present. J. Bone Joint Surg., *46-A*, 167–199, 1964.)

obliterated. Many physicians classify all S-curves as structural, regardless of the degree of flexibility which they present. Therapists and corrective physical educators should refer all cases of scoliosis to a physician before any attempt at correction is made. Once a structural curve is established, corrective exercises may produce a compensatory curve rather than an abolition of the primary curve.

Scoliosis may be caused by numerous unilateral conditions, including the following:

Hereditary defects in structure.
Deterioration of vertebrae, ligaments, or muscles as the result of infections or diseases.
Unilateral paralysis of spinal muscles.
Unilateral short leg.
Unilateral flat foot or pronation.
Imbalance of muscular development as the result of occupation or habit.

16

After ruling out the necessity for surgical or medical treatments
the physician may refer scoliosis patients to a therapist or corrective
physical educator for special exercises. Correction of unilateral foot
defects often eradicates functional curves, and elimination of such
habits as that of standing on one foot may be of value. In schools,
physical educators should screen all scoliotic pupils for unilateral
vision and hearing defects, which may cause scoliosis and which require referral to medical specialists. Seat and desk adjustments
should also be checked.

Key-note Positions.   Cases of lateral curvature are so varied and
the complications are so many that correction is largely an individual
matter. "Key-note positions" have been much used for the correct-
tion of flexible cases. The key-note position is a device to help the
subject in assuming the correct position. When he tries to stand
straight and shows a thoracic curve convex to left, raising the right
arm to a certain height may bring muscles into action that will pull
the spine straight; in some cases it may require raising both arms,
but to different positions; when the curve is low it may require a
sideward or diagonal position of one foot. When a position is found
that brings the spine to a vertical and straight position, that is the
key-note position for that case. The subject practices this position
many times, and he takes pains in returning to the fundamental position to hold his spine in the erect position if possible; in this way he

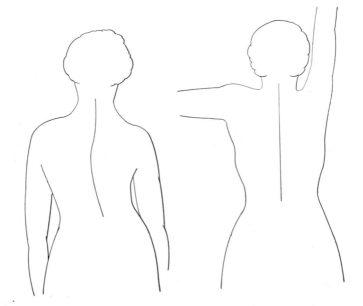

Fɪɢ. 20–16.   Straightening a lateral curve by use of a key-note position.

gradually acquires ability to assume the erect position at will (Fig. 20–16).

Seated Posture. Statements about posture usually refer to the individual in the erect position. In our sedendary culture it is probable that people actually spend more time sitting than they do standing. As in standing, seated posture is maintained by irregular volleys of action potentials, but the furniture itself may force the body to assume one position or another. Long continued poor seating habits may result in degenerative tissue changes and pain. It is only within recent years that the study of anatomical and physiological principles and anthropometric data has provided a basis for the scientific design of furniture. Among these data are the following:

1. Frequent changes of position are important in preventing fatigue. A chair should permit the sitter to move about, rather than restrain him in a given position.

2. The sitter should be supported over a large area to afford the smallest unit pressure on the flesh. Compression of the soft tissues affects the muscles, blood vessels, and nerves, with consequent discomfort and possible numbness, tingling or anesthesia. A number of cases of thrombosis of the deep leg veins due to continued sitting during long automobile rides or while watching TV programs have been reported in medical literature.

3. The height of the seat should be designed to prevent undue pressure on the soft tissue of the posterior aspect of the thigh. It is generally recommended that the height of the seat be slightly less than the length of the lower leg when the foot is flat on the floor and the knee bent at a right angle. Marked discomfort is caused by seats which are so high the sitter's feet do not reach the floor. The depth of the seat should be such that the edge of the seat does not exert pressure against the back of the knee.

4. Chairs should have a back rest providing support to the lumbar region of the sitter's spine in order that the lumbar erector spinae may be relaxed without full flexion of the trunk and undue ligamentous strain.

5. Axiomatically, the sitting worker's elbows should bear the same relation to his work table as they would if he were standing. This height varies according to the work to be done and the amount of pressure it is necessary to exert. For clerical work the forearms should be approximately horizontal.[23]

The push and pull forces which can be exerted in seated positions have been carefully studied at the University of Michigan.[24,25] It has been shown that in addition to muscular forces such factors as bracing of the body, inertia of body dead weight, position of the body mass relative to its support, and friction between the body and the seat must be considered in any analysis of the principles of body mechanics. The failure of earlier investigators to consider these points has resulted in considerable uncertainty regarding the application of their experimental findings to practical situations.

Low Back Problem. One of the most common failures of the adaptation of the human organism to environmental stress results in the so-called "low back problem." Of all the mammals only man shows evidence of lumbar breakdown, but in him it occurs with distressing frequency. A tilted pelvis places the lower lumbar vertebrae in such a position that compression forces tend to cause a superior vertebra to slip anteriorly over an inferior one. The powerful erector spinae, the rectus femoris, the tensor fasciae latae, and the iliotibial bands act to bring the spine into hyperextension. The principal muscles counterbalancing this effect are the abdominals, which are usually weak from disuse. With weak abdominals poor posture may result, the lordotic curve is augmented, the center of gravity of the body falls posterior to the bodies of the lower lumbar vertebrae, and the tendency for the lumbar vertebrae to slip is correspondingly increased. Injuries of this type almost always occur in the lumbo-sacral area. While the layman often speaks of sacroiliac strains, the vertebrae of this area are so strongly held together that injuries of this type seldom occur to them. Progressive resistance exercises designed to strengthen the back and abdominal musculature and to reduce the strength imbalance between the back extensors and the trunk flexors appear to provide relief from chronic, painful low back symptoms in a high percentage of cases.[26]

Interrelationships of Posture Defects. Although the subject matter of this chapter has been organized on a segment-by-segment basis, for clarity of presentation, the student of posture must integrate his thinking on a total-body basis. Muscles and ligaments are arranged so that they cross joints. Any tension in them will cause an equal pull at both of their ends. This arrangement may be likened to the links of a chain which forms an endless belt. Under ideal conditions, the various segmental tensions of this endless belt will be mutually neutralizing, so that the parts of the body are held precisely in equilibrium. The main force which can upset this equilibrium is gravity, which pulls constantly downward. Normally, the downward gravitational pull on any body part is borne on the segment or structure immediately below it, but if any body part deviates significantly from vertical alignment, its weight must be counterbalanced by the deviation of another body part in the opposite direction. Thus, postural defects are seen as total-body phenomena, tending to occur simultaneously at several levels.

Posture is a dynamic, not a static, concept. The body is seldom stationary for more than a few moments; often, it is engaged in movements of greatly varying extent and direction. The academic emphasis on static positions serves to simplify and clarify the explanation of postural mechanisms. The understandings derived from a study of statics can be applied to the limitless number of dynamic situations of the body, and the student should never be misled into forming a static concept of postural relationships.

References

1. Hockett, Charles and Archer, Robert: The Human Revolution. Amer. Sci., *52*, 70–92, 1964.

2. Hamilton, W. J., editor: *Textbook of Human Anatomy.* New York: St. Martin's Press, 1956, pp. 25–33.

3. Keith, Arthur: Man's Posture: Its Evolution and Disorders. II. The Evolution of the Orthograde Spine. Brit. Med. J., *3247*, 500, 1923.

4. Wells, Katharine F.: An Investigation of Certain Evolutionary Tendencies in the Female Human Structure. Res. Quart., *18*, 260–270, 1947.

5. Morehouse, Laurence E. and Cooper, John M.: *Kinesiology.* St. Louis: The C. V. Mosby Co., 1950, p. 140.

6. Schwartz, Louis, *et al.*: *Studies in Physical Development and Posture.* IV. Postural Relations as Noted in Twenty-two Hundred Boys and Men. Public Health Bulletin No. 199. Washington, D. C.: Government Printing Office, 1931.

7. Wells, Katharine F.: What We Don't Know About Posture. J. Health, Phys. Educ., & Rec., *29*, 31–32, 1958.

8. Welch, William H.: *Adaptation in Pathological Processes.* Baltimore: The Johns Hopkins Press, 1937, pp. 57–58.

9. Magnus, Rudolph: Some Results of Studies in the Physiology of Posture. Lancet, *5375*, 531–536, and *5377*, 585–588, 1926.

10. Joseph, J.: *Man's Posture: Electromyographic Studies.* Springfield: Charles C Thomas, 1960.

11. Basmajian, John V.: *Muscles Alive. Their Functions Revealed by Electromyography,* 2nd Ed. Baltimore: The Williams & Wilkins Co., 1967, pp. 145–160.

12. Floyd, W. F. and Silver, P. H. S.: Electromyographic Study of Patterns of Activity of the Anterior Abdominal Wall Muscles in Man. J. Anat., *84*, 132–145, 1950.

13. Portnoy, Harold and Morin, F.: Electromyographic Study of Postural Muscles in Various Positions and Movements. Amer. J. Physiol., *186*, 122–126, 1958.

14. Benedict, F. G. and Murschhauser, H.: *Energy Transformations During Horizontal Walking.* Carnegie Institute of Washington, Publication No. 231, 1915.

15. Rasch Philip J., *et al.*: Effects of Exercise Immobilization and Intermittent Stretching on Strength of Knee Ligaments of Albino Rats. J. Appl. Physiol., *15*, 289–290, 1960.

16. Goldthwait, Joel E., *et al.*: *Essentials of Body Mechanics in Health and Disease,* 5th Ed. Philadelphia: J. B. Lippincott Co., 1952, pp. 33–37.

17. Metheny, Eleanor: *Body Dynamics.* New York: McGraw-Hill Book Co., 1952.

18. Asmussen, Erling and Heebøl-Nielsen, K.: Posture, Mobility and Strength of the Back in Boys, 7 to 16 Years Old. Acta Orthop. Scand., *XXVIII*, 174–189, 1959.

19. Riddle, H. F. V. and Roaf, Robert: Muscle Imbalance in the Causation of Scoliosis. Lancet, *6877*, 1245–1247, 1955.

20. Allbrook, D. E.: Muscle Imbalance in Scoliosis. Lancet, *6882*, 196, 1955.

21. Zuk, Tomasz: The Role of Spinal and Abdominal Muscles in the Pathogenesis of Scoliosis. J. Bone Joint Surg., *44-B*, 102–105, 1962.

22. Roaf, Robert: The Basic Anatomy of Scoliosis. J. Bone Joint Surg., *48-B*, 786–792, 1966.

23. Floyd, W. F. and Roberts, D. F.: Anatomical and Physiological Principles in Chair and Table Design. Ergonomics, *2*, 1–16, 1958.

24. Gaughran, George R. L. and Dempster, Wilfrid Taylor: Force Analyses of Horizontal Two-Handed Pushes and Pulls in Sagittal Plane. Human Biol., *26*, 67–92, 1956.

25. Dempster, Wilfrid T.: Analysis of Two-Handed Pulls Using Free Body Diagrams. J. Appl. Physiol., *13*, 469–480, 1958.

26. Flint, M. Marilyn: Effect of Increasing Back and Abdominal Muscle Strength on Low Back Pain. Res. Quart., *29*, 160–171, 1958.

Recommended Reading

27. Hellebrandt, F. A., *et al.*: Methods of Evoking the Tonic Neck Reflexes in Normal Human Subjects. Amer. J. Phys. Med., *41*, 90–139, 1962.

28. Basmajian, J. V.: Man's Posture. Arch. Phys. Med., *46*, 26–36, 1965.

29. Editorial: Rudolf Magnus (1873–1927). Physiology of Posture. J.A.M.A., *205*, 789–790, 1968.

30. Sigmon, B. A.: Bipedal Behavior and the Emergence of Erect Posture in Man. Am. J. Phys. Anthrop., *34*, 55–60, 1971.

Chapter 21

Walking, Running and Jumping

WALKING

Individual differences in walking appear as soon as a baby takes its first steps. In part, at least, these differences are due to inherent structural features which are not under voluntary control and which limit the possible types of movement. Elftman[1] lists three such features:

1. Dimensions and configurations of the bones.
2. Restriction of movement in the joints.
3. Distribution of mass in the members.

Locomotion is an individual matter, each person tending to assume a type and speed which is the most efficient for his particular structure. A neuromotor theory based on the assumption that efferent neural control of gait represents different levels of functional neural organization in relation to posture, body transport, and manipulative movements has been advanced. This holds that since temporal characteristics are relatively fixed, duration of stride and contact time remain consistent through marked changes in age, body size, body function, body weight, and relative changes of length of limbs and torso.[2] Other investigators[3] contend that the ideal gait changes with body weight and length of leg, but can be calculated by kinesiological analysis if the body parameters are known.

In ordinary walking six distinct features require special attention: (1) the contact of the foot with the ground, (2) the position of the feet, (3) the movements of the center of gravity, (4) the transmission of weight stresses, (5) the energy expenditure, and (6) the muscular functions.

The heel usually strikes the ground first. The body weight is then transmitted forward along the lateral periphery of the entire foot, and finally passes to the metatarsal heads as the step is completed.

The supporting phase of one leg largely coincides with the swinging phase of the other, but there is usually a transitional period during which both feet are in contact with the ground. The mechanical shock of the transfer of body weight from foot to foot is cushioned by a flexion of the knee.

The majority of individuals toe out a little less than 7 degrees. This angle is believed to represent an adaptation of the body to the problems of support resulting from assumption of the vertical stance and the consequent elevation of the center of gravity. It is produced by lateral or medial rotation of the thighs and may be different in each foot. In those over sixty years of age the toeing-out angle may be almost 10 degrees. This is believed to constitute a means of providing additional lateral stability to compensate for the decline in neuromuscular function.[4]

Progression is best measured by the movement in space of the center of gravity, since from it the velocity and acceleration of the body as a whole can be computed. In normal walking the center of gravity describes a sinusoidal curve in both the vertical and the horizontal planes. The amount of vertical displacement is about 4.5 cm.; the horizontal displacement is nearly the same. Since these two displacements are about equal, the movement of the center of gravity in the body forms a figure of eight occupying approximately a 5 cm. square.[5] The longer the stride, the greater the movement of the center of gravity with each step.

By translating the center of gravity through a smooth sinusoidal pattern of low amplitude the body succeeds in conserving energy. The pattern is flattened by means of five separate but coordinated mechanisms:

1. Pelvic rotation. In walking the pelvis alternately rotates right and left. This elevates the extremities of the successive arcs formed by the passage of the center of gravity.

2. Pelvic tilt. In normal walking the pelvis tilts downward about 5 degrees on the side of the non-weight-bearing limb. This depresses the amplitude of the summits of the successive arcs.

3. Knee flexion. The body weight passes over the supporting leg at a time when the knee is being flexed. The magnitude of this flexion is about 15 degrees. The flexion also lowers the amplitude of the successive arcs.

The total effect of this elevation of the extremities of the arcs by pelvic rotation and the depression of the summits of the arcs by pelvic tilt and knee flexion is to cause the sinusoidal curves to more nearly approach a straight line and thus materially reduce the range of flexion and extension which would otherwise be required at the hip joint.

4. Foot and knee mechanisms. As contact with the ground is made by the heel, the foot is dorsiflexed and the knee joint is fully extended, so that the center of gravity attains its maximum depression. As the weight passes on to the forefoot and the heel is raised, the knee flexes so that abrupt inflexions of the arc of travel of the center of gravity are smoothed into sinusoidal waves.

5. Lateral displacement of the pelvis. Horizontal deviations of the center of gravity also aid in replacing sharp inflexions with sinusoidal curves in the horizontal plane. This movement is greatly exaggerated in competitive walking in order to achieve a longer stride. In walking each foot is subjected to forces approximating 1.2 times the body weight. In running this rises to twice the body weight, and to five times in landing on the feet when jumping from a height.[6]

A person whose work requires him to be on his feet may take as many as 19,000 steps daily. If he weighs 150 pounds, he will beat into his shoes about 2,900,000 pounds per day.[7] In walking at the rate of 120 three-foot steps per minute, one advances at the rate of 4.1 m.p.h. Each foot is at rest on the ground for one-half second, then moves forward six feet, and comes to rest again in the next one-half second. The moving foot passes the stationary foot at a maximum speed of about 12.8 m.p.h. The maximum acceleration is approximately 3.7 g.[8] Oscillations of the extremities are independent of oscillations of the body's center of gravity, but are an important factor in the metabolic cost of progression.

The energy expenditure in calories per minute per kilogram of body weight may be accurately calculated by the equation:

$$E_w \text{ (cal/min/kg)} = 29 + 0.0053v^2$$

where v is the speed in meters per minute.[9] This relationship is shown in graph form in Figure 19–1. The energy expenditure in calories per meter walked per kilogram of body weight may be determined by another form of the same equation:

$$E_w \text{ (cal/meter/kg)} = \frac{29}{v} + 0.0053v.$$

There are rather large individual differences in energy cost, however, since leg and foot length, muscular training and efficiency, weight of clothing (particularly shoes), differences in posture, length of stride, frequency of stride, and rhythm of movement affect the energy expenditure.[10] Stride length is positively correlated with height. About age sixty-five walking appears to become more

ENERGY

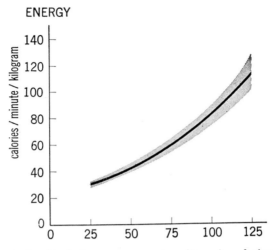

Fig. 21–1. Relationship between energy expenditure in calories per minute per kilogram of body weight and walking speed in meters per minute for normal adult subjects. The shaded area represents 1 standard deviation above and below the average curve. These are of the order of 10 per cent of the average value. (After Bard and Ralston,[9] courtesy Arch. Phys. Med.)

restrained, as if an effort is being made to obtain maximum stability. Walking speed becomes slower, stride length shortens, the time of the support phase is increased and that of the swing phase reduced, and the amplitude of the oscillations of nearly all parts of the body becomes less.[4] The energy cost of level walking is about 10 per cent less for women than for men.

The Kinesiology of Walking. As the individual advances the right leg in walking the dorsiflexors (extensor digitorum longus, tibialis anterior, and extensor hallucis longus) and the tibialis posterior of the right leg contract. The former provide a controlled approach of the plantar surface of the foot to the ground. The contraction of the latter is responsible for the customary wear on the lateral side of the shoe heel. Shortly after the heel strikes the ground the gluteus maximus begins to contract to prevent the pelvis from dropping forward. As the left foot enters the swing phase, it is held in dorsiflexion by the contraction of the muscles listed above in order to provide adequate clearance between the foot and the ground. The forward swing of the leg is carried out by the hip flexors. At the end of the swing the hamstrings act to halt the forward movement. The extent of the rotation of the pelvis is largely controlled by the abductors and adductors. As the weight on the right foot moves forward to the midtarsal region the tibialis anterior, peronei and triceps surae contract and the tibialis posterior relaxes. As the weight comes down upon the entire plantar surface of the foot, the peronei, triceps surae and extensor digitorum are in contraction, partially to prevent dorsiflexion of the foot. Further contraction of the gastrocnemius and soleus, assisted perhaps by the other plantar flexors, provides the force to elevate the heel and the weight shifts on to the forefoot. As the metatarsals strike, the abductor hallucis and flexor digitorum brevis begin to contract, although their action is not yet clear. The peronei and extensor digitorum place the foot into the valgus position as a preliminary to the transfer of the weight from the lateral to the medial side, while the extensor digitorum opposes the tendency for plantar flexion of the toes. The body weight is now transferred from the great toe of the right foot to the heel of the left foot and the cycle of muscular contraction and relaxation is resumed (Fig. 21–2).

Mechanics of Walking. Essentially, man propels himself forward by alternate and rhythmical drives from the legs. The body is inclined forward, immediately after which the driving or supporting

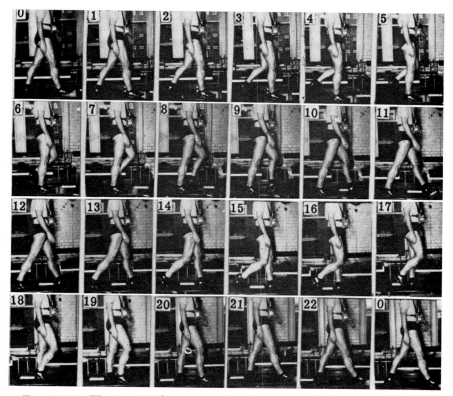

Fig. 21–2. The twenty-three successive stages constituting a complete step. Each frame represents about 0.05 sec. Men and women walk in a similar manner, but the energy cost of level walking is about 10 per cent less for women than for men.[11] (Courtesy C. K. Battye and J. Joseph and Medical and Biological Engineering.)

leg extends and pushes the trunk forward. When the forward motion of the trunk brings its center of gravity past the forward edge of its supporting base (the toes of the driving foot), the pull of gravity tends to cause the body to fall forward and downward. At this point, the other leg is swung forward and placed on the ground. This supplies a much wider base for support and saves the body from the fall. As the individual progresses, the lower extremities alternate in their function, each in turn driving and supporting, while the other swings forward.

The force resulting from the extension of the driving leg may be broken down into three components, a vertical component which acts against the pull of gravity and supports the body, and two horizontal components. One of these acts in the direction of progress, and the other, which is relatively insignificant, acts at a right angle to the preceding component. When one foot is on the ground, it supplies a small force in the medial direction. This component will not be included in our discussion.

These are the simple mechanical features characteristic of our forward progression. Needless to say this brief analysis is inadequate. It is necessary to study each individual movement made by the body, when walking or running, in order to understand its contribution to the entire activity.

Forward Inclination of the Body. Immediately before stepping forward, the trunk is inclined toward the direction of progress. The purpose of this forward inclination of the trunk is to place its center of gravity more nearly in a direct line with the force exerted by the driving leg. In this way, man is better able to overcome air resistance and the inertia of the trunk. If he fails to incline the trunk forward, he finds that the leg drive will carry the lower portion of the trunk forward well enough. The center of gravity of the trunk, however, is above and behind the force exerted by the driving leg, therefore, the inertia of the body is not overcome directly, and in effect will exert a torque about the hips in the reverse direction. This will tend to cause a person to fall over backward.

The faster a person intends to walk or run, the greater should be the inclination of the trunk. This is because the major horizontal component of the force supplied by the driving leg is relatively greater as compared to the vertical component (Fig. 21–3). Similarly, it will be found necessary to bend well forward when walking into a strong wind. Here again the major horizontal component of the driving force must be increased in order to overcome the great increase in air resistance. In each case the increased forward inclination brings the center of gravity of the trunk more nearly in line with the driving force.

Fig. 21-3. Bob Hayes, former World and 1964 Olympic 100-meter champion, starting a race. *B*, Center of gravity as determined by the suspension method described on page 124 applied to a cut out of the subject. *D*, Supporting surface area. *AB*, Horizontal component of body action. *DA*, Vertical component of body action. *DB*, Resultant body action. *BC*, Line of action of body weight (gravity line). This line must be ahead of the supporting surface during acceleration and behind it during deceleration from rapid movement. To be complete the diagram should include an arrow on the *BA* line representing inertia as a component resisting forward movement by a force whose magnitude depends upon the body mass and the rate of acceleration. These three factors, inertia, body mass, and acceleration, determine the line of action. (Athletic Journal.)

The Supporting or Driving Leg. When the center of gravity of the trunk has moved forward to the optimum position, which in very slow walking is a little back of the line of force to be exerted by the driving leg, but advances as the speed of walking is increased, the leg is extended at the hip, knee and ankle (Fig. 21–4).

The vertical component of force serves to support the body against the pull of gravity and the horizontal component propels the body forward; the two acting together accelerate the trunk forward and upward. During forward progress the foot is fixed, the pelvis moves forward, and the angle the leg makes with the ground decreases. The force exerted by the leg changes as the leg approaches complete extension and the relative magnitudes of the horizontal and vertical components also change.

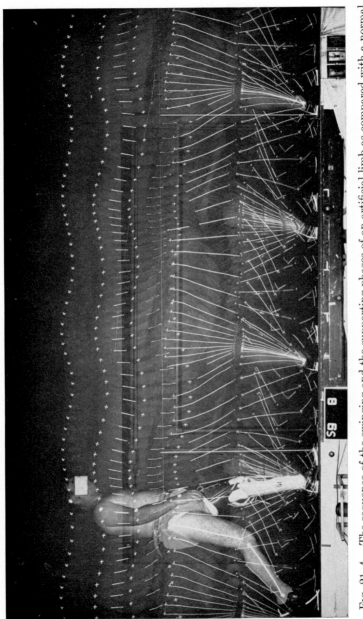

FIG. 21–4. The sequence of the swinging and the supporting phases of an artificial limb as compared with a normal limb are clearly shown in this static cyclogram of an amputee walking. The oscillating line of which Aristotle spoke (p. 129) is also made evident. According to Custance,[19] the rise per step is between $\frac{3}{4}''$ and $1\frac{1}{4}''$ for most subjects. (R. Drillis, courtesy Prosthetic Devices Studies, New York University.)

Once the body is in forward motion, the second and subsequent supporting phases differ only in that the supporting phase starts when the swinging leg strikes the ground. The force exerted by the leg at this point also may be resolved into two components. As before, the vertical component supports the body as soon as contact is made with the ground, but the horizontal component acts as a slight restraint to forward progress and slightly reduces the efficiency of the operation. With the forward movement of the body, this restraining force becomes progressively smaller and finally disappears when the center of gravity of the trunk is directly over the point of support. The point of support, however, is indefinite, shifting from the heel to the ball of the foot as the trunk moves forward. This restraining force may assume great magnitude when one wishes to come to a sudden stop.

When the supporting leg first makes contact with the ground, it is in almost complete extension, but flexes slowly until the center of gravity of the trunk is directly over the point of support. At this point extension begins and continues until the supporting phase is terminated.

Extension occurs at the hip, knee and ankle. Ankle extension is delayed somewhat, but persists longer than at the knee. When the heel lifts from the ground the knee is usually completely extended, but the foot and ankle continue to act. Extreme extension (plantar flexion) of the ankle acts to lengthen the supporting leg, and by transferring the supporting area from the heel to the ball of the foot, permits the time the force is exerted by the leg to be longer than otherwise.

Action of the Swinging Leg. Upon completion of the supporting phase the leg is lifted and swung forward in order to initiate a new supporting phase. The Weber brothers taught that the swinging leg acted as a pendulum in its forward motion. The fact that the knee flexes in the forward swing is sufficient to invalidate the pendulum concept. Studies on the acceleration of the limb, by Braune and Fischer, and later by Fenn[13-15] and by Elftman,[1,16-18] definitely show that the leg does not act as a pendulum. In the case of running, the torques exerted by the hip flexors during the first third of the forward swing are large. The forward swing of the leg starts with hip and knee flexion. As the speed of walking or running is increased so is the torque at the hip increased, because the speed of the forward swing is largely dependent upon the magnitude and duration of the torque exerted by the hip flexors. From the point when the thigh is vertical until near the end of the forward swing, the thigh swings freely at the hip except for the impetus provided by the momentum of the leg associated with extension of the knee.

Just before contact with the ground, torque may be exerted by the hip extensors to slow down the forward swing.

At the start of the foward swing the hip, knee and ankle are all in complete extension. As the leg swings forward, flexion of all the joints increases, especially at the knee and ankle. This flexion at the knee and ankle is in order that the foot will not scrape on the ground. When the foot has passed under the body, the hip, of course, continues to flex, but the knee extends. This is not necessarily an active muscular extension; the momentum of the leg, coupled with the slight restraint exerted at the end of the swing by the extensors of the hip, acts to extend the knee. When walking rapidly or running, the swinging phase requires less time and the extensors of the knee function in order that the knee be extended when the heel strikes the ground. The ankle extends slightly after passing under the center of gravity and is near its normal position when the heel strikes the ground.

Combining the Swinging and Supporting Phases. While the leg supports the body and propels it forward, the other leg swings forward to make contact with the ground. When walking, the time required for the swinging phase never exceeds that needed for the supporting phase. When walking slowly, there will be an overlapping of the two phases, and both feet may be on the ground as much as 30 per cent of the time. As the speed is increased, the supporting phase is shortened far more than the swinging phase, and the period of overlapping or double support decreases or vanishes completely. When the time required for the supporting phase becomes less than that required for the swinging phase, the swinging phases overlap and there will be a period when both feet are off the ground. At this point the individual has ceased to walk and has commenced to run.

Vertical Movements of the Pelvis. Because the legs alternate rhythmically with periods of support and non-support, so the pelvis finds itself supported alternately first on one side, and then on the other. If progress is slow, there will be periods when it is supported on both sides. Because the extent of support depends upon speed of progress, it is difficult to provide an accurate description of the vertical movements of the pelvis when walking. The pelvis is at its highest point on the supporting side, when the center of gravity is directly over the point of support. The lowest point is found in the forward swinging phase of the leg just before the foot strikes the ground. Intermediate conditions are dependent upon the length of the period of double support.

Rotation of the Pelvis and Legs. When the swinging leg advances, the pelvis on the same side is carried forward to a greater degree than it is on the opposite side. When the other leg swings ahead the situation is repeated, but the opposite side is involved. The amount of rotation produced in this manner will vary greatly, but the width of the pelvis and the speed of walking or running are major factors.

When the leg swings forward and that side of the pelvis moves forward and rotates, the foot would rotate inward if the thigh did not simultaneously rotate outward, as in normal walking. Likewise, after the foot contacts the ground, there is an equal amount of inward rotation during the supporting phase to compensate for the opposite rotation of the pelvis.

Pelvic rotation has been emphasized by coaches of competitive walking and running, and is commonly referred to as "hip roll." An optimal amount of hip roll improves running efficiency by increasing the length of stride and the duration of application of force by the driving leg.

Movements of the Shoulders, Arms, and Head. When one side of the pelvis moves forward during the swinging phase, the shoulders on that side drop back to compensate for pelvic rotation. The arms also swing in opposition to movements of the leg. The action of the arm in the anterior-posterior plane serves to reduce the rotation of the shoulders. This can be demonstrated by holding the hands against the thighs while walking and noticing the increased swing of the shoulders. By reducing the swing of the shoulders, the arms indirectly aid in keeping the head facing forward, otherwise the rotators of the head and neck would do an enormous amount of work. During normal walking the forward swing of the arms is about 20 degrees and the backward swing is about 9 degrees. The former is brought about by some of the inward rotators (teres major, upper part of the latissimus dorsi and subscapularis) rather than by the flexors; the latter by some of the extensors and outward rotators.[20]

The arm swing tends to be across the body to a slight degree. This is exaggerated if the individual is short and broad shouldered. The sideways movement of the arms helps to compensate for the sideways movement of the body caused by the swinging legs, and by the fact that the body is supported first on one side and then on the other. When walking slowly, the arms swing loosely at the sides and only a little muscular effort is employed. As speed is increased, so is the frequency of the arm swing, and the action becomes much more vigorous and complex. With increasing speed, there is an increasing tendency to drive the arms with greater violence and the elbow is bent in order to shorten the arm and make possible the faster alternating movement which is required.

Arm action, like leg action, is sometimes modified in special forms of marching. Soldiers of the English army are taught to use an exaggerated arm swing, and those of the German army are taught an exaggerated leg movement, the so-called "goose step." These movements are mechanically inefficient but are employed when show or ceremony are more important than efficiency. Extensive movements of this type form a direct contrast to the contracted arm muscles and restricted arm movements seen in a runner who is "tieing up" as a result of fatigue, but both decrease efficiency by interfering with the normal balance and respiratory mechanisms, as well as by requiring energy to contract the muscles.

The head does not move forward at the same velocity as the trunk, its velocity being slightly less than the trunk when the body is driven forward by the leg, and slightly greater when no propulsive force is being exerted. These fluctuations in head velocity are negligible when walking, but increase to a marked degree when running.

PATHOLOGICAL GAITS

Paralysis or other causes of deficiency in tone in certain muscles often result in characteristic types of pathological gaits. This can be touched upon only briefly here; students desiring more detailed information on such disabilities are referred to the text by Steindler.[21]

Paralysis of the Gluteus Maximus. Shortly after the heel touches the ground, a backward thrust of the trunk begins. This is completed at the end of the stance period. Its object is to move the center of gravity behind the hip joint and thus prevent jackknifing of the joint.

Paralysis of the Gluteus Medius. When the affected leg swings forward, the trunk is swayed to the sound side so that the swinging leg may clear the ground. During the supporting phase the pelvis drops to the sound side. To offset this the trunk is swayed to the affected side.

Spastic Gait. Contracture of the muscles hinders the rhythmic shortening and lengthening of the legs and the forward and backward swing of the limbs. The hips beome locked and stability is further disturbed by adduction and inward rotation at the joint. The patient may walk primarily on his toes (spastic equinus gait) or on his heels (spastic calcaneus gait).

RUNNING

Both pace frequency and step length increase with the square root of the speed of advance.[22]

When the speed of locomotion exceeds 4 m.p.h., a running gait becomes less fatiguing than the forced rate of walking, although the energy consumption is increased. This results largely from the fact that a greater part of energy expended in raising the body is utilized in propelling the runner forward than is true in the case of the walker. There is an additional saving in the reduction of arm and shoulder movements. The data in Table 21–1 make it clear why unloaded soldiers usually march at approximately 3.5 m.p.h. With a load of 50 to 60 pounds, however, the optimal speed drops to about $2\frac{1}{2}$ to $2\frac{3}{4}$ m.p.h. At these velocities the maximum rate of caloric expenditure is under 4 working kilocalories per minute, and the soldier should be able to keep up the pace for an eight-hour day over an indefinite period.[23]

In running, of course, there is no optimal speed. By the very act of breaking into a run the subject has exceeded the most economical rate of horizontal locomotion, and the energy expenditure increases as the speed increases. Studies by Fenn[13-15] and Elftman[16-18] determined that in running at maximum speed the legs work at the rate of approximately 2.95 h.p. Fenn's calculations are summarized in Table 21–2. Somewhat similar data for walking are available in a study by Dean.[24]

TABLE 21–1.   Energy Cost of Walking and Running[25]

Method and Speed	Cal./Hr.	O_2 Used Liter/Hr.
Walking		
2.3 m.p.h.	210	43
2.9	250	51
3.2	270	55
3.5	290	59
4.0	350	71
4.6	470	96
Running		
5.7	720	147
6.9	870	178
11.4	1300	265
13.2	2330	477
14.6	2680	547
14.8	2880	588
Sprinting		
15.8	3910	798
17.2	4740	967
18.6	7790	1590
18.9	9480	1935

TABLE 21–2.   Energy Consumption in Running
(Figures in Horsepower)

Chemical Energy from Oxygen Consumed			13.00
Energy of Anaerobic Phase of Muscle Contraction . . . (40% of Total Energy)		5.20	
Waste in Recovery		7.80	
Total		13.00	13.00
Energy of Anaerobic Phase of Muscle Contraction.			5.20
Total Useful Work in Propulsion . . . . (22.7% of Total Energy Expenditure; this figure may be 10–15% too high)		2.95	
Acceleration of Limbs . . . . (12.9% of Total Energy Consumption; figure may be 10% too low)	1.68		
Deceleration of Limbs . . . . (40% of Acceleration; figure may be 9% too high)	0.67		
Maintenance of Velocity	0.50		
Overcoming Gravity	0.10		
Total	2.95	2.95	
Fixation Energy, Waste Heat, Frictional Loss, Vertical Movements of the Body, Changes in Horizontal Velocity, Wind Resistance, Sidewise Movement, Movement of the Shoulders, etc.		2.25	
Total		5.20	5.20

In spite of these impressive figures and in spite of the fact that man is characterized by a comparatively low crural index (ratio of the length of the lower leg to that of the thigh) which theoretically better fits him for running than for jumping, as a running animal man falls into the slower group. Just how important variations of the crural index are to runners is yet to be determined.

The essential difference between walking and running is the absence of a period of double support, and the presence of a period of non-support, when neither foot is in contact with the ground (Fig. 21–5). As a result running is sometimes described as a series of jumps in which the body is alternately supported first on one foot and then on the other.[26] In order to achieve the increased speed characteristic of running, far more force must be exerted in the horizontal direction. The vertical force is also increased but not to as great an extent. In order to accomplish this, the angle which the leg makes with the ground during extension is smaller and the pelvis is necessarily carried lower.

The additional force supplied by the extensors of the driving leg at this new angle both requires and produces several changes in the mechanics of running when compared with walking. Then too, it must be recognized that running speed may vary from the slow jog to the extreme effort of the sprinter, and that the mechanical patterns will not be alike.

The lower position of the pelvis necessitates greater flexion of the knee of the supporting leg when the center of gravity of the trunk passes over the point of support. This increased flexion of the knee makes possible a more powerful extension of the driving leg. The greater drive of the leg increases the length of the stride. The increased speed coupled with the period of non-support should result in a greater impact when the foot of the swinging leg strikes the ground. To minimize the shock, the swinging foot does not meet

Fig. 21–5. Gale Sayers, the National Football League's 1965 Player-of-the-Year, at the start of a 61-yard touchdown run in the Chicago Bear-Baltimore Colt game. Note that both of Sayers' feet are off the ground. This period of non-support is the primary distinction between running and walking. (Wide World Photos.) See also Figure 22–12.

the ground with the heel as in walking. The leg reaches full extension and appears to have started back before contact is made with the ground. This change of the angle of impact permits the first contact with the ground to be made by the ball of the foot. This, of course, cushions the shock, and to some extent reduces the restraining force, because the center of gravity is more nearly over the foot at the instant of contact than would otherwise be the case. The greater the speed of running the less the amount of restraint caused by the contact of the foot of the swinging leg.

As the center of gravity of the body passes over the supporting leg, the heel of the foot may or may not be pressed to the ground. Slow running usually finds the heel on the ground whereas, in the case of a sprint, the heel may not touch the ground at any time.

When the supporting leg reaches complete extension, and the foot is lifted from the ground, the knee is flexed far more than when walking and the foot is brought up quite high in the rear. This, in effect, serves to shorten the swinging leg and reduces the amount of force needed to bring the leg forward. As a result, the runner exerting his maximum effort can swing the leg forward much faster and greatly increase his speed. This is important because the duration of the forward swing of the leg may be a limiting factor on total speed. Increased flexion of the knee is also necessary to provide for clearance for the swinging leg needed because of the lower position of the pelvis.

The arm action serves the same purpose as in walking but it must be done with far greater speed in order to keep in phase with the faster movement of the legs. This is accomplished by a great increase in muscular effort and by bending the arm at the elbow. Like flexing the knee in the swing phase of the leg, flexing serves to shorten the arm and permit greater speed. The tendency to draw the arm across the body increases with the speed.

The mechanical features of running, like walking, may undergo considerable change with changing speed. That there will be differences in the form used by marathon runners and sprinters is obvious. Endurance being a major factor for successful performance, the distance runner is greatly concerned about economy and must adjust his style and pace to provide for the greatest efficiency. Sprinters, on the other hand, do not exhaust themselves after 100 yards. They give little thought to the matter of efficiency from the standpoint of energy utilized and may make great sacrifices in economy to gain a little added speed.

Sprinting. It is important to get away to a fast start under racing conditions. A yard lost at the outset of a race, because of a slow start, must be made up; an unlikely event in a short race if the contestants are evenly matched. A short reaction time and great driving power are the chief natural prerequisites for a quick start. Good technique enables the athlete to capitalize on these advantages. Two artificial aids are employed, the spiked shoe and the starting block. The spiked shoe provides a firm base for the driving leg so that the magnitude of the horizontal component of force will not suffer because of inadequate traction. The starting block, or holes dug in the track, serve the same purpose for the initial drive.

In the crouch start the low position of the body makes it possible for the horizontal component of the driving force to be greatly increased because the body is more nearly directly in line. The legs can also provide a stronger drive upon extension from this position because the gluteus maximus is brought into play. This is the result of hip flexion. This muscle does not act to extend the hip when the body is more nearly erect.

When the sprinter is on his mark, his weight is largely supported on his feet and one knee. His hands are on the starting line and a little weight is supported by the thumb and fingers. The position of the feet is not exactly prescribed. Considerable latitude is permitted in their distance from the starting line. Selection should be governed by ascertaining which stance produces the fastest start for a given individual. This is determined by the energy supplied by the combined efforts of the legs. The force exerted against the ground and the length of time it is applied are the determining factors. The front leg seems to exert about the same amount of force for the same amount of time regardless of position. As the position of the rear foot is moved back the force it can exert is increased, but its duration will be reduced. Optimal conditions for the individual are a matter of trial and practice. The proper balancing of these factors against each other makes it possible to achieve the fastest start. Investigations by Henry[27] indicate that for most individuals optimum results are achieved when the spacing between the sprinter's feet at the start lies between 16 and 21 inches. Laterally, the feet should be spaced about 7 or 8 inches apart to avoid loss of balance and to insure a direct drive from the feet to the pelvis.

One kinesiologist[28] has suggested that when starting a sprint the stronger leg should be placed on the front block. Observe that in Figure 21–6 one team has been coached to start with the right foot and the other with the left foot forward, apparently without regard to which is the stronger.

The *get set* position elevates the hips to the optimum position where the legs can exert their most effective drive. The height will vary, depending upon the position of the feet, but will always be higher than the shoulders. Upon starting, the sudden extension of

Fig. 21–6. The start of a sprint race. Extension of the driving leg is not complete. Observe that one team has been coached to start with the right foot on the rear block, while the coach of the other team preferred the left foot.

the hips will elevate the shoulders, throw the center of gravity ahead of the feet, and drive the body horizontally rather than vertically. The experienced sprinter should concentrate on the movement which he is about to initiate and respond automatically to the sound of the starting gun. A number of studies have shown that a quicker reaction results when both the muscular and neural systems are in a state of activity when the stimulus is received.[29]

When the race starts, the sprinter drives as hard as possible with both legs. It is essential that the first few strides be relatively short and made with all the force possible in order to provide the needed acceleration to reach top speed quickly. The body gradually rises until full speed has been reached, at which time most sprinters lean forward about 20 to 25 degrees. This keeps the center of gravity ahead of the feet and simultaneously reduces the air resistance.

The remainder of the sprint has already been described except that a few features of running are exaggerated in order to gain top speed. Flexion of the knee in the swinging phase is increased in order to increase the speed of the forward swing. The swinging leg is often well on its way back when the foot strikes the ground, contact being made when it is directly under the center of gravity. This eliminates the restraining force present in the walk or slow run. When the toe of the swinging foot touches the track, the ankle flexes and the heel nears the ground. Force comes from extension of the knee and especially the ankle. This is applied as soon as the foot strikes the ground and is continued until the foot is lifted. Speed is increased by increasing the length of the stride, rather than the speed of leg movement alone, but after the optimal length of stride is achieved, any further extension will result in a reduction of speed.

The leg functions as a third class lever, with the fulcrum at the hip joint. The leg is pulled forward by the thigh flexors and backward by the glutei and hamstrings. The quadriceps and the triceps surae act to extend the knee and ankle respectively. The complex workings of the two-joint muscles, as exemplified in Lombard's Paradox (p. 357), increase the efficiency of these movements. If the toe flexor muscles are sufficiently developed, they can contribute significantly to the final phase of the propelling force. If they are flaccid, the result is, in effect, like reducing the length of the stride by an amount equal to the length of the toes.

Middle Distance Running. From the standpoint of the kinesiologist, middle distance running does not differ greatly from sprinting. The need for a fast start is almost as great when running 440 yards as it is when running 220 yards. The same principles apply in each case. The middle distance runner breathes during the race, which is not necessarily true of the sprinter in the 100 yard dash. This results in less fixation of the respiratory muscles.

The cadence of the middle distance runner is slower, consequently there may be less heel lift in the swinging phase of the leg and the knees are not lifted as high. The arms are not so tense and need not be flexed as much. The slightly slower speed permits the body to be carried more nearly erect, say at an angle of about 15 degrees, which also aids respiration. The drive from the legs being less, all the factors which contribute to the sprinter's great speed are given slightly less emphasis, but attention is devoted to keeping vertical movements of the center of gravity as small as possible while striding.

Newton's First Law of Motion indicates that changing the speed, regardless of whether it is increased or decreased, requires an expenditure of energy. It would thus appear that the middle distance or distance runner should immediately establish his optimal pace and maintain it unchanged throughout the race. Theoretically at least, a strong "finishing kick" would seem to be an expensive use of energy which might have been more effectively applied another way. However, Bannister[30] has pointed out that in middle distance racing runners seem to achieve their best times by running the first part of the race considerably faster than the latter part. On the other hand, certain physiological data suggest that precisely the opposite may be true in longer races.[31] Other factors may be the motivational or psychological state of the runner at various times in the race. Ideal pacing patterns must also be modified for strategic purposes, such as jockeying for position on a turn.

Distance Running. In track events such as the 2-mile run, endurance and muscular efficiency are of major importance. The energy-consuming start of the sprinter is not necessarily desirable, since a yard or two lost at this stage of the race may be regained later without too much expenditure of energy. Relaxation, rhythm, and adequate respiration are essential for effective distance running.

Because the leg drive is less, the trunk is carried more nearly erect than in the shorter runs. When the leg swings forward, the heel is not lifted quite as high as when running the shorter distances. The foot is often brought into contact with the track with the weight almost evenly distributed between the ball of the foot and the heel.

The distance runner endeavors to conserve his energy in every possible way. The arms are flexed less and swing loosely. There is little if any fixation of the shoulder muscles. The runner does not ordinarily consciously endeavor to greatly increase his stride, but moves as easily as possible.

JUMPING

The Long Jump. The goal of the long jumper is to propel his center of gravity horizontally through the air as far as possible. Since the distance of the jump is directly proportional to the energy of projection, maximum speed at the take-off would be desirable, but the necessity for changing the direction of movement demands a momentary stabilization of the body at the point of the change and this can be accomplished only by a reduction of speed. The forceful "beat" on the take-off board required to implement Newton's third law may further reduce his speed—and may also result in a tendency to incur heel bruises. Most jumpers take off at an angle of about 25 to 30 degrees and there are some students who feel that the body cannot develop sufficient power to attain a greater angle and still project itself forward to any distance. However, theoretical calculations support the theory that a higher angle than is customarily used would be advantageous.

As the jumper approaches the take-off board the knees are a little bent and he is in a slight crouch ("gather"). At the take-off the extensors of the hips, knees, and ankle are forcefully contracted. The amount of elevation and distance achieved may be increased by a forceful upward swing of the arms and the leading leg, since the mass of these limbs times their velocity produces a momentum which may be transferred to the body to assist in propelling it through the air. To increase this advantage the ancient Greek jumpers held weights (halteres) in their hands.

Once the runner has left the ground there is nothing he can do to increase his forward acceleration, but he can affect the distance achieved by changing the configuration of his body and the relative position of the partial masses. A "hitch-kick" will not increase momentum, and the legs cannot develop enough resistance against free air to enable the runner to increase his distance by continuing his running motions after the take-off. However, such movements may rotate the hips backward and give a greater forward reach with the legs.

While still in the air, the athlete must prepare to land (Fig. 21–7). The legs are brought forward and the arms down and back. This inclines the trunk forward so that the center of gravity is a little

FIG. 21–7. Long jumping technique of Ralph Boston, 1960 Olympic and World Champion. Boston is using the "stride-in-air" technique. The fact that he attains such height in his jump is important in providing time to execute the maneuver. It will be observed that the arms have been swung vigorously upward to assist in gaining altitude and there is a slight backward tilt of the torso to aid in knee extension. The right leg is being flexed to shorten the lever preparatory to swinging it forward. The "stride" will not add any distance to the jump, but will get the feet as far forward as possible while maintaining balance. As the jumper descends, both legs will be extended forward, the trunk will be inclined forward, and the arms will be forcefully swung downward and forward. The center of gravity will move forward and the jumper will fall forward on his hands and knees on landing. (Rich Roberts, San Pedro *News Pilot.*)

above the trajectory of the feet and there is less likelihood of the jumper falling backwards when he lands. When the actual landing takes place, the hips and knees are flexed to absorb the shock and the jumper rocks forward onto his hands and knees.

The High Jump. In contrast to the long jumper, the high jumper must propel his center of gravity vertically as far as possible. For this he need not have unusual horizontal speed, since his success will depend largely upon his height (his center of gravity is higher to begin with) and an unusual amount of leg spring. He needs only sufficient horizontal speed to carry him across the bar. The theoretical effects of distance of take-off, angle of take-off, velocity, time in the air, energy, and other factors for various heights of the bar have been calculated by Cureton.[32]

Four basic styles of high jumping may be observed: the scissors, the Eastern style, the Western roll, and the Fosbury flop. The following descriptions assume that the athlete takes off from his left foot, as is customary for right-handed men.

When executing a *scissors* jump, the approach to the bar is made from the right and at an angle of about 45 degrees. About 8 or 10 steps are all that are needed to insure sufficient horizontal speed. The take-off made by the left foot is at a point a little over 3 feet in front of the bar. The first 6 steps are made at moderate speed and the last 2 are slightly slower because it is here that the athlete adjusts for the final spring. The last stride may be a trifle longer and the body is carried somewhat lower in order to *gather* for the jump and to get a good swing with the right leg. When the center of gravity is directly over the left foot, which strikes the earth flat-footed and quite hard, the vertical drive is given and the right leg is thrown upward as far as possible. The flat-footed take-off and bent knee, due to the lowered body, permits powerful extension of the knee and ankle and projects the body vertically into the air. When the hips reach the height of the bar, the extended right leg is thrown over the bar and, as it descends, is followed by the now extended left leg. It is this scissors action of the legs which gives the style its name.

Before the mechanics of the high jump received much study, the scissors jump was executed with the trunk of the body nearly erect or leaning forward a few degrees. It is obvious that the center of gravity of the body need not be lifted so high above the bar. Too much energy is wasted in doing needless work, and this style is now seldom used in competitive jumping. The *Eastern* form gains greater height with the same amount of effort. As the athlete's foot leaves the ground, the hips are extended and the trunk dropped backward to permit the leading leg to be thrown upward and the hips lifted over the bar.   At the same time the opposite arm is swung forcefully upward to aid in lifting and rotating the body.   The knee of the jumping leg is tucked under to permit the body to rotate faster.   The athlete's body clears the bar almost as if he were lying on his back with his body nearly horizontal.   The center of gravity is only a little above the bar and no energy is wasted doing unproductive work.   By modifying the scissors style in this way greater height can be reached with the same force.

The jumper usually lands on his left side because the final scissors action of the legs tends to rotate the body on its longitudinal axis so that he faces the bar as he passes it in his descent.

Fig. 21–8.   Former world champion high jumper John Thomas approaching the bar.   Note that on the final long step the heel of the take-off foot strikes the ground first so that the jumper can rock up onto the toes and that the center of gravity has been markedly lowered so that the transition of the direction of movement from forward to upward can be made without loss of balance and so that the powerful extension of the leg and foot will provide a vigorous take-off. (Photo by Boston University Photo Service.)

The difficulty with the Eastern style is that the jumper must travel some distance horizontally in order to get his body over the bar. To overcome this the *Western roll* was introduced. In this style the bar is approached at an angle of approximately 45 degrees from the left. Again, only 8 to 10 strides are required. The speed is not great and the last two strides are used to make the necessary adjustments to get perfect coordination and spring. The position and initial portion of the take-off are about the same as for the scissors (Fig. 21–8). When the jump is made, the right leg and left arm are thrown high into the air. Their momentum is a great aid in getting added lift. During the ascent, the left leg is lifted and flexed, but the right remains extended. The upward swing of the right leg must be very vigorous because its momentum not only aids the lift, but also supplies the energy required to turn the body on its longitudinal axis as it passes over the bar. The arm, head, and shoulders rather than the leading foot pass over the bar first (Fig. 21–9). The right leg is in complete extension and the left leg is drawn up and flexed as the athlete rolls over the bar on his left side.

The body is flexed at the hips just before the bar is cleared, but straightens out when passing over the bar. When the jump is executed in good form, the body is as nearly horizontal as possible as it passes over the bar with slight and uniform clearance the entire

Fig. 21–9. John Thomas clearing the bar at 7 feet in straddle-roll style. This athlete weighs 185 pounds and is 6′ 5½″ tall. The length of his leg bones is an important factor in his success as a jumper, since the amount of work which a muscle can perform depends upon the number and size of its fibers and the distance through which they can contract. (Photo by Boston University Photo Service.)

length of the trunk. The left arm and the head and shoulders are dropped as soon as possible in order to provide a little lift for the hips as they clear the bar. This is the part of the body most likely to touch. In order to land safely, advocates of this style throw the flexed left leg forward, turn, and break their fall with the left leg and arm.

Fig. 21–10. Dick Fosbury, who revolutionized high jumping styles with his backwards "Fosbury Flop," is shown here clearing 7'0" at the Olympic Trials of 1968. The mechanics of this style are directed entirely to the problem of clearing the bar, and the problems of safe landing are relegated entirely to the special properties of the great thickness of a foam cushion. As the Fosbury Flop was widely copied by other jumpers, an alarming number of serious spinal injuries was reported. Perhaps these were related to skeletal immaturity, insufficient preliminary training and coaching, and inadequate materials for absorbing the impact of landing. (Photos by the Los Angeles *Times* News Bureau, reproduced by special permission.)

When clearing the bar, some jumpers rotate the body earlier than others and pass over the bar facing downward. During the descent the flexed right leg is thrown forward and the landing is ordinarily made face downward with the right leg and arm absorbing the shock.

The unusual "backwards" style of Dick Fosbury (Fig. 21–10) may make some of these statements appear dated, but it remains to be seen whether a great proportion of jumpers can utilize his style effectively.

References

1. Elftman, Herbert: The Basic Pattern of Human Locomotion. Ann. New York Acad. Sci., *51*, 1207–1212, 1951.

2. Smith, Karl U., *et al.*: Analysis of the Temporal Components of Motion in Human Gait. Amer. J. Phys. Med., *39*, 142–151, 1960.

3. Beckett, Royce and Chang, Kurng: An Evaluation of the Kinematics of Gait by Minimum Energy. J. Biomech., *1*, 147–159, 1968.

4. Murray, M. Patricia, *et al.*: Walking Patterns in Healthy Old Men. J. Geront., *24*, 169–178, 1969.

5. Saunders, J. B. DeC. M., *et al.*: The Major Determinants in Normal and Pathological Gait. J. Bone Joint Surg., *35-A*, 543–558, 1953.

6. Bowden, Ruth E. M.: The Functional Anatomy of the Foot. Physiotherapy, *53*, 120–126, 1967.

7. Kalbacher, Francis A.: American Foot Health Foundation, Personal Communication, October 21, 1964.

8. Sutton, Richard M.: Two Notes on the Physics of Walking. Amer. J. Physics, *32*, 490–491, 1955.

9. Bard, Gregory and Ralston, H. J.: Measurement of Energy Expenditure During Ambulation, with Special Reference to Evaluation of Assistive Devices. Arch. Phys. Med., *40*, 415–420, 1959.

10. Cotes, J. E. and Meade, F.: The Energy Expenditure and Mechanical Energy Demand in Walking. Ergonomics, *3*, 97–119, 1960.

11. McDonald, Ian: Statistical Studies of Recorded Energy Expenditure of Man. Nutr. Abstr. Rev., *31*, 739–761, 1961.

12. Battye, C. K. and Joseph, J.: An Investigation by Telemetering of the Activity of Some Muscles in Walking. Mech. and Biol. Engr., *4*, 125–135, 1966.

13. Fenn, Wallace O.: Mechanical Energy Expenditure in Sprint Running as Measured by Moving Pictures. Amer. J. Physiol., *90*, 343–344, 1929.

14.————: Fractional and Kinetic Factors in the Work of Sprint Running. Amer. J. Physiol., *92*, 583–611, 1930.

15. ————: Work Against Gravity and Work Due to Velocity Changes in Running. Amer. J. Physiol., *93*, 433–462, 1930.

16. Elftman, Herbert: Forces and Energy Changes in the Leg During Walking. Amer. J. Physiol., *125*, 339–356, 1939.

17. ————: The Function of Muscles in Locomotion. Amer. J. Physiol., *125*, 357–366, 1939.

18. ————: The Work Done by Muscles in Running. Amer. J. Physiol., *129*, 672–684, 1940.

19. Custance, Arthur C.: Differences in Energy Cost Between Road and Treadmill Walking. Defence Research Establishment Ottawa Report No. 603, February, 1970, p. 1.

20. Ballesteros, Maria L. Fernandez, *et al.*: The Pattern of Muscular Activity During the Arm Swing of Natural Walking. Acta Physiol. Scand., *63*, 296–310, 1965.

21. Steindler, Arthur: *Kinesiology of the Human Body Under Normal and Pathological Conditions.* Springfield: Charles C Thomas, 1955.

22. Milner, Morris and Quanbery, A. A.: Facets of Control in Human Walking. Nature, *227*, 734–735, 1970.

23. Redfearn, J. W. T., *et al.*: *The Metabolic Cost of Load-Carrying. A Discussion of Experimental Findings.* (British) Army Operational Research Group Report No. 4/56, 1956, pp. 8–9.

24. Dean, G. A.: An Analysis of the Energy Expenditure in Level and Grade Walking. Ergonomics, *8*, 31–47, 1965.

25. Morton, Dudley J. and Fuller, Dudley Dean: *Human Locomotion and Body Form.* Baltimore: The Williams & Wilkins Co., 1952, p. 171. Quoted by permission.

26. Slocum, Donald B. and James, Stanley H.: The Biomechanics of Running. J.A.M.A., *205*, 721–728, 1968.

27. Henry, Franklin M.: Force-Time Characteristics of the Sprint Start. Res. Quart., *23*, 301–318, 1952.

28. Mortensen, Jesse P. and Cooper, John M.: *Track and Field for Coach and Athlete.* Englewood Cliffs, N. J.: Prentice-Hall, Inc., 1959, p. 18.

29. Ford, A.: *Foundations of Electronics for Human Engineering.* San Diego: U. S. Navy Electronics Laboratory, 1957, pp. 58–59.

30. Bannister, R. G.: Muscular Effort. Brit. Med. Bull., *12*, 222–225, 1956.

31. Rasch, Philip J.: Endurance Training for Athletes. J. Ass. Phys. Men. Rehabil., *13*, 182–185, 1959.

32. Cureton, Thomas Kirk: Mechanics of the High Jump. Scholastic Coach, *4*, 9 *et seq.*, 1935.

Recommended Reading

33. Lloyd, B. B.: The Energetics of Running: An Analysis of World Records. Advancement of Science, January, 1966, pp. 515–550.

34. Craig, Albert B., Jr.: Limitations of the Human Organism. J.A.M.A., *205*, 734–740, 1968.

35. Napier, John: Antiquity of Human Walking. Sci. Amer., *219*, 56–66, 1967.

36. Inman, Verne T.: Human Locomotion. Canad. Med. Ass. J., *94*, 1047–1054, 1966.

37. Givoni, Baruch and Goldman, Ralph F.: Predicting metabolic energy cost. J. Appl. Physiol., *30*, 429–433, 1971.

Chapter 22

Kinesiological Principles in Sports and Games

Kinesiology finds its greatest practical applications in the fields of athletics, time and motion study, and the various services in physical medicine and rehabilitation. While the problems confronting the coach and the therapist are basically the same—that is, teaching the individual to make the most effective use of his bodily machinery—the methods of solving them may be very different. It is doubtful whether a corrective therapist, a physical therapist, or an occupational therapist is likely to hinder a patient's recovery by too much emphasis on kinesiology, whereas many a coach has completely disorganized an athlete's performance by injudicious emphasis on specific muscle actions.

LIMITATIONS OF KINESIOLOGY IN COACHING

As both Jackson and Beevor emphasized, it is movements, not muscles, which are represented in the higher nerve centers. The high jumper, for example, must concentrate only on propelling his body over the bar. The minute he begins to think of contracting the gastrocnemius-soleus of the take-off leg to lift himself by their action on the ankle lever, he is no longer thinking of his prime objective (Fig. 22–1). The result will probably be confusion and failure. It is an important kinesiological principle that the coach should seldom, if ever, emphasize the contraction of specific muscles when guiding athletes, although his teaching is more effective when his advice is based on such specific knowledge.

Neither should the coach err in the opposite direction and be too general in his admonitions. For example, the tennis teacher's order to "hit the ball harder" may be quite ambiguous to a novice who is already stroking as hard as he can. It becomes meaningful to the learner when the coach is precise in his instructions, calling attention

FIG. 22–1.   John Thomas at the take-off. Note that the jumper has rocked up on to the toes of the take-off foot, the take-off leg has been explosively extended (Newton's third law), the lead arm is swung vigorously upward, and the lead leg is fully extended and reaches above the cross bar, thus giving the jumper's segments a great momentum upward. (Newton's second law.) The advantage of height and leg length in this event is clearly illustrated by this photograph. (Photo by Boston University Photo Service.)

to the need for a longer preliminary backswing, a more definite "step into the ball," and an attempt to "stroke *through* the ball instead of chopping at it." The instructions then become specific and meaningful from the learner's point of view, although the coach may have derived his advice from a formal study of anatomy, kinesiology, and body mechanics.

If a knowledge of academic kinesiology were necessary for the learning of motor skills, no baby would be able to learn to walk. Motor skills can be acquired at highly effective levels by performers who are uninformed of the subject matter of kinesiology. Often great athletes have stopped to analyze their performance only after winning championships. In many cases they have given false and even absurd explanations of what they do and how they do it. For instance, champion tennis players have taught that in the forehand drive the axis through the shoulders should be at right angles to the net at the moment when the ball is contacted, although motion pictures reveal that they themselves rotate the shoulder axis back to a position parallel to the net and that at the moment of contact they

Fig. 22–2. William T. Tilden, forehand drive. (Courtesy of American Lawn Tennis, Inc. From *Mechanics of the Game of Lawn Tennis*, Vol. II, by J. Parmly Paret.)

are already beginning to return to centercourt position (Fig. 22–2). Such examples illustrate both the ease of making errors in kinesiological explanations and the fact that effective functioning may occur without a formal knowledge of such principles, if the other conditions of learning are adequate.

APPLICATION OF KINESIOLOGY TO COACHING

Even though kinesiological analysis is not essential to effective functioning, it does not follow that kinesiology has no contribution to make. Knowledge and application of kinesiological principles can make important and crucial differences in learning. The problem is to determine what kinesiological knowledge to select and how to apply it in a given teaching situation.

Much of the information in this text consists of formal background knowledge, some of which is not directly applicable in the form presented. At the practical level kinesiological knowledge is a professional tool which can be utilized effectively only by a skillful, artful practitioner who is the master of the basic subject matter. In the following paragraphs, specific ways of applying kinesiological principles to the teaching of sports and games are presented.

Describing the Movement to be Performed. It is an axiom of educational psychology that a learner must have a clear knowledge of what he is trying to learn, if orderly progress is to be made. This is especially important in learning motor skills. At the first attempt, a hook pass or a high jump or a kip on the horizontal bar is likely to be a mysterious and frustrating complexity. An important task of the teacher is to instruct the learner in exactly what to do.

Kinesiology helps the coach to view performances analytically. First, he must analyze expert performance (through the neuromuscular memory of his own past performance, or through observation of other experts, or through the study of pictures and descriptions), so that he may demonstrate, point out, or explain the desired performance to the learner. Second, he must analyze the learner's performance, so that he may call attention to the factors responsible for errors and successes, and thus provide a basis for subsequent and more successful attempts by the learner.

Descriptions of motor skills must take into account some or all of the following factors:

1. The posture or position at the start and the finish.
2. The direction of each action at each joint. (Hip flexion, spine rotation to the right, etc.)
3. The kind of motion at each joint. (Fixation, moving fixation, ballistic motion, etc.)

4. The sequence of joint actions.
5. The speed and acceleration of joint actions.
6. The force of joint actions.
7. The source of motive power for each joint action. (Concentric contraction, eccentric contraction, static contraction, or some external force such as gravity.)
8. The timing, coordination, and rhythm of joint actions.
9. The integrated pattern of the joint actions.
10. The muscular or skeletal or external stabilization necessary.

It is not implied that all of these factors should or could be brought to the conscious attention of the learner, nor that technical language should be used in communicating the ideas. In addition to the factors listed, there may be other important factors, such as clothing, implements, equipment, and other external masses, each with force, speed, direction, momentum, and so forth. Also, there may be non-kinesiological considerations, such as game strategy, fear, motivation, and so forth.

Analyzing the External Mechanics of the Performance. External mechanics refers to the movements of the gross body segments and their externally applied leverages, forces, and other physical factors. Since mechanics, as a branch of classical physics, is rather completely worked out and its validity firmly established, a person with a knowledge of mechanics can make logical applications to sports performance with relatively great confidence. Mechanical analysis thus becomes one of the most potent phases of applied kinesiology.

A knowledge of mechanics is particularly important to physical educators. A good physical education program includes such a tremendous variety of activities that no one teacher is likely to be able to obtain personal performance experiences in all the activities he will be called upon to teach. Mechanical analysis gives him a sound basis for intelligent coaching in the less-familiar activities.

Analyzing the Internal Mechanics of the Performance. Internal mechanics refers to the bone-muscle leverages, stress-resistances of the various body tissues, internal friction, range of movement, and numerous other intraorganismic workings. The significance of internal mechanics is equal to that of external mechanics, but the body, acting on information fed back through the proprioceptive and kinesthetic mechanisms, tends to make "automatic" or sub-rational adjustments in internal mechanics. Therefore, coaching attention is more often devoted to external mechanics than to internal mechanics.

Assessing the Kinesiological Requirements of the Activity. For successful performance each separate motor skill demands its own combination of kinesiological abilities and characteristics. Considerable body mass, for example, is a necessity for inside line play in football, but it is a hindrance in gymnastics. Both activities require great strength, but this should be predominantly in the legs for football and in the arms for gymnastics.

There is a need for studies of the intercorrelations between anatomical and psychological traits. A fuller understanding of the properties of bone and muscle, and the manner in which they are put together, might go far to explain psychomotor abilities. Neurological parts and properties might also account for many of the observed distinctions. Known psychomotor factors appear to include two general factors, strength and impulsion (rate at which movements are initiated from a stationary position), and several specific factors, among which are speed (rate of movements after they have started), static precision, dynamic precision, coordination, and flexibility. These may represent a simultaneous involvement of two or more regions. Muscular endurance, circulatory-respiratory endurance, agility, and power appear to be primary psychomotor abilities, but it is possible they are syndromes of physiological characteristics.

Assessing the Kinesiological Aptitude of the Performer. Just as each activity has its own demands, so each performer or each team has his or its own abilities and potentialities. Kinesiology helps the coach and teacher to match the performer to the activity and the activity to the performer. A short, stocky boy would be much more apt to be a successful gymnast than he would be to achieve fame as a high jumper. A basketball coach with a team of predominantly tall, heavy, slow-moving men might select the zone as his defensive system, although in theory he might prefer the man-to-man defense and would utilize it if he had personnel adapted to it.

Preventing Athletic Injuries. Although athletic injuries are usually associated with intense competitive activities at the interscholastic level, they refer as well to minor abrasions and sore muscles which might occur in a hop-scotch game in the elementary school. Their prevention depends in part upon intimate knowledge of the somatic materials and arrangements of the human body, of the quality and character of environmental objects and sports implements, of the nature of forces and other potential hazards in various activities, and of many other factors which constitute the subject matter of kinesiology. Typical applications of such knowledge are those which have led kinesiologists to recommend that full squats, full deep knee bends, and the duck walk be banned from the training program because of the role they may play in the production of knee ligament instability.[1] An instructive account of how fatigue in a wrestler forced him to violate sound kinesiological principles, resulting in a serious injury to the pectoralis major has been given by Marmor *et al.*[2]

Making First-Aid Diagnosis and Deciding upon First-Aid Care. Although the extent of first-aid care by the physical educator is limited, he needs an understanding of the nature of trauma. While he does not make diagnoses, he must be alert to the possibility of involvements which are not immediately apparent in the symptoms displayed at the time of injury. Kinesiological knowledge helps him to conduct first-aid care until the victim can be brought to a physician for definite diagnosis and treatment. When a doctor releases a patient from treatment, he often imposes some temporary restriction upon the nature of subsequent activity. He may, for example, indicate following an operation that the individual should engage in general exercise of moderate intensity, but should avoid activities which might put excessive strain upon the abdominal wall. Such a decision is the responsibility of the doctor alone, but he frequently leaves it to the judgment of the physical educator or therapist to determine what comprises "exercise of moderate intensity" or what activities might "strain the abdominal wall." In either event, an advanced knowledge of the nature of activities and the nature of the human body is essential if the physical educator or therapist is to be adequately qualified to undertake such responsibilities.

Adjusting Equipment, Clothing, Apparatus, Implements, Grounds, and Other Factors. Kinesiological knowledge determines, to a great extent, answers to such questions as the following: How long a bat should a baseball player use, and how much should he "choke his grip" on it? What is the optimal shape and length of football cleats for use on a turf of a certain quality? How close to the basketball court boundaries, at the side of the gym, can the parallel bars be safely stored? Are long trousers a hindrance to performance or a safety hazard for a boy engaged in tumbling? Is it safe to play soccer on a field which has small impressions left from the shot-put practice of the day before?

Evaluating the Effect and Worth of Activities. In the hey-day of the Swedish System of Gymnastics, it was argued that each movement should cause a definite and predetermined effect upon the physiology or development of the body, and that exercise dosages could be prescribed accurately by specifying a certain number of counts or repetitions. It is now known that such precision and predetermination of purpose is impossible. In the historic process of abandoning such precise systems, physical education has probably tended to give too little attention to evaluating the effect and worth of each activity.

A physical educator should constantly be asking, "What are the purposes of this activity, and to what extent does the activity help to achieve these purposes?" In most cases the answers require a broad knowledge of the biological sciences. When they deal with physical development or motor skills, an understanding of kinesiological principles becomes essential.

WARM-UP

Laboratory studies have shown that cooling intact muscle increases its reaction time 2 or 3 times as much as it does its contraction time, reduces the excitability of the muscle, increases the duration of the action potentials (indicating a decrease in the propagation velocity of the impulse over the muscle fiber), and decreases the amplitude of the action potential. Theoretically, at least, warming the muscle should reverse these effects. Although very small alterations in environmental temperature may cause subjective feelings of discomfort, it is not easy to change the deep temperatures of the body, because of the highly effective temperature control system of the organism. In order to raise deep temperatures, one must perform work of high intensity and long duration or must take rather extreme measures to subvert the natural heat-loss mechanisms. However, Buskirk and Beetham[3] report observations of rectal temperatures as high as 106° F. after a long distance race, which they believe approached limiting heat capacities. Diathermy and hot showers have also been found to increase deep muscle temperatures, whereas massage did not.

Athletes and coaches are almost universally convinced that warm-up must precede performance if optimal results are to accrue. However, the term "warm-up" is exceptionally ambiguous, and when the amount and kind is specified, the seeming unanimity of opinion evaporates. To one athlete, warm-up means a few bending and stretching exercises; to another, it denotes an hour or more of intense specific practice of the task to be performed subsequently; to a third, it consists of passively warming the body by hot showers or other external heat source. The traditional warm-up procedures in one sport differ radically from those in another. Furthermore, in spite of claims of the absolute necessity of warming-up, in emergencies (such as unexpected substitution into a football game on a cold day) athletes frequently enter competition cold and unprepared, and demonstrate spectacular ability to rise to the occasion.

The experimental studies of warm-up are conflicting and confusing. Reviews of the literature have been reported by Pacheco[4] and by Massey, et al.[5] It is difficult to draw general conclusions from the research literature, for researchers, like athletes, have used the term "warm-up" to cover a tremendous variety of different operational procedures. Warm-up may be active or passive, general (unrelated to the subsequent performance) or specific (preliminary practice of the subsequent performance), long or short in duration, and heavy or light in intensity. The elapsed time between warm-up and performance is undoubtedly an important variable, but this factor has not been investigated and is sometimes not even specified by experimenters.

A tabulation of results of the published investigations indicates statistically significant benefits from active and passive warm-up techniques in about half of the cases, whereas only about 5 per cent of such experiments would be expected to reach significance by chance alone if there were in fact no benefit from warming-up. If only the most carefully done experiments, such as those by Asmussen and Bøje,[6] Pacheco, and Massey et al., are evaluated, the proportion favoring warm-up remains about the same. These positive results cannot be ignored. The following general conclusions seem to emerge from a study of the literature:

1. Specific warm-up is almost invariably beneficial. Activities involving coordination and other educable factors, as distinguished from activities consisting primarily of pure physiological functions, are especially susceptible to preliminary practice. The beneficial results may be explained in terms of (a) learning, (b) neural facilitation, or the tendency for synaptic thresholds to be reduced after the passage of the first few adequate stimuli, and (c) the opportunity to review sensory cues immediately before performing complex coordinations. It seems clear that athletes should utilize the kind of warm-up which not only activates the established mechanisms enumerated above, but, if properly graded, elicits any purely physiological benefits which may accrue from general or non-specific warm-up.

2. In cool environments one purpose of warm-up is to bring the body temperature up to at least normal levels. Performance is inferior when deep temperatures are below normal.

3. Apparently general or non-specific preliminary exercise enhances subsequent performance under certain conditions, but these conditions cannot be accurately inferred from existing research. Some suggestions, bordering on speculation, appear dimly in the research reports:

a. Non-specific warm-up must be sufficiently intense to cause a rise of from 1 to 4° F. in deep body temperature, if it is to be effective.[6] However, warm-up becomes fatiguing if carried on too long or too intensely. Optimum intensity may be related to the available interval between warm-up and performance.

b. Non-specific warm-up probably does not enhance subsequent performance which depends strongly upon coordination, except when the body temperature has previously been below normal.

c. Non-specific warm-up probably enhances subsequent performance which depends strongly upon powerful acceleration of body parts, but not upon speed-of-movement *per se* or upon muscular or cardio-respiratory endurance alone.

4. Benefits from non-specific warm-up, where they have been shown at all, are fairly small in magnitude. Practice effects, by comparison, are easily demonstrated, even in experienced and trained performers. While the possible effects of warm-up upon championship-level performance are not to be ignored, it would probably be more profitable in general to devote attention to motivation, motor learning, preliminary practice, and the perception of sensory cues rather than to unrelated warm-up.

It is the empirical experience of coaches and athletes that warming-up appears to result in a decrease in injuries, and many localities now have laws requiring that high school football players be warmed-up before being sent into a game. This opinion does not enjoy the support of research findings,[7] but the experiences of hundreds of years are not to be lightly discarded. Until the matter has been definitely settled it might be suggested that specific warm-ups be utilized rather than general ones, since the practice effect is in itself of value regardless of whether it is accompanied by physiological benefits.

STARTING POSITIONS

Kinds of Positions. The starting positions in sports may be classified into three kinds, according to whether their purpose is (1) to provide stability and resistance to external forces, (2) to allow an optimal application of muscular force, or (3) to prepare generally for any one of several possible movements. Since these three purposes require the application of radically different principles of body mechanics, the athlete and the coach must give considerable attention to the determination of the requirements of the sport and to the analysis of the positions to be assumed by the athlete.

Stable Positions. A position will be stable, and will best resist the onslaught of various external forces, to the extent that the following conditions are fulfilled:

1. An imaginary line dropped vertically from the center of gravity should fall well within the area of the base of support. This area is defined by straight lines connecting the most peripheral points of the body parts contacting the supporting surface. Thus, in decreasing

order of stability, we find the effective area of the base of a wrestler in the referee's position on the mat is a four-point rectangle; that of a person performing a headstand is approximately a three-point triangle, with the head and each hand at its angle; a handstand has a stance composed of two-points on a single line; smallest and least stable of all is the one-point stance of the ballet dancer on the toes of one foot (Fig. 20–4) or an ice skater on the tip of one skate (Fig. 6–6).

2. Stability against a force from a given direction is proportional to the distance, in that direction, from the point at which the line of

Fig. 22–3. Amari Egadze, Russia, pinning Jorge Mendoza, Guatemala, in the first round of the Greco-Roman World Amateur Wrestling Championships at Toledo, Ohio, June 25, 1962. The position of Egadze's feet are of particular interest. Attempts by the student to describe their changes of position in terms of muscular actions will clearly illustrate the difficulties inherent in undertaking to make precise kinesiological analyses of the movements of athletes during the game situation. (Courtesy World Wide Photos.)

gravity falls to the edge of the base. If the direction of the upsetting force could be known in advance, the body position could be adjusted so that the distance from the point where the line of gravity falls to the edge of the base in the direction of the on-coming force is maximal. Thus, if a wrestler knew in advance that he was to be pushed forward, he could move his hips backwards and extend and brace his arms in a forward position. In practice he does not know whether he will be pushed, pulled, lifted, or turned (Fig. 22-3). In such ambiguous circumstances, the strategy of stability is to keep the center of gravity approximately over the center of the base.

3. If stability is the primary consideration, the center of gravity should be kept as low as possible. In most sports a semi-crouch stance is assumed when stability is threatened. This is usually a compromise between stability and mobility, but a few sports situations (such as a purely defensive attempt of a prone wrestler to avoid being turned over and pinned or a submarining lineman in football) require an extremely low center of gravity. A high center of gravity has two disadvantages—first, the body may be upset by a force of smaller magnitude; and, second, an upsetting force applied low may more easily undercut the supporting members of the body. In judo the lowering of the center of gravity to obtain greater stability is recognized as a tacit admission of the superiority of the opponent; in baseball, a catcher awaiting an oncoming runner crouches low so that there will be less chance of his being knocked down.

4. For a given stance, stability is proportional to the mass, or weight, of the body. A heavy object of the same size and shape is harder to upset than a lighter one. Therefore, body weight *per se* becomes a tremendously important factor in physical contact sports. Superiority in skill, quickness, strength, and other factors may modify this advantage to a greater or lesser extent.

Positions Designed for Optimal Force Production. In the racing starts of the runner and swimmer, in the waiting position of the baseball batter, and in many other sports situations the starting position is adjusted primarily to enhance the application of muscular force on an external object. The center of gravity tends to be at the edge of the area of the base opposite the edge next to which the force is to be exerted. The baseball batter or pitcher (Figs. 22-4 and 22-5), for example, carries his weight to the rear, so that he may step forward with sufficient momentum; the sprinter carries his weight forward, opposite the back edge of the base from whence he will be driving with his legs.

In these positions the joints through which the driving muscles act tend to be held in an intermediate phase—that is, about halfway between flexion and extension. Positions of extreme flexion or ex-

FIG. 22–4.   FIG. 22–5.

FIG. 22–4.   Larry Sherry starting a pitch. Note the backward lean of the body preparatory to the throw in order to attain the maximum summation of force.

FIG. 22–5.   Larry Sherry just after releasing the ball. Observe especially the extreme inward rotation at the shoulder joint and the pronation of the arm. The leverage of the swiftly moving limb creates a terrific strain on the elbow and shoulder and may produce epicondylitis, sore shoulder, or other trauma. (Los Angeles Dodgers.)

treme extension would either reduce the mechanical advantage of the muscle-bone levers by decreasing the angles of insertion of the tendons, or prevent effective movement because the shortening power would be all used up in attaining the extreme position. In the sprinter's starting position, 90-degree angles tend to predominate in the joints through which driving power will be exerted. Actually, it is not the angles of the joints but the angles of insertion of muscle tendons which must be arranged optimally.

"Ready positions" or "get-set positions" are not relaxed positions. The muscles which will exert propulsive force are contracting statically, while being held in check by co-contraction in their antagonists. When the "go" signal is given, contraction in the propulsive muscles intensifies and changes from static to concentric. The antagonists are relaxed and reaction time is decreased because the propulsive muscles have already contracted sufficiently to take up any slack in themselves (Figs. 22–6 and 22–7).

Relaxed starting positions are deleterious to performance. In sports language, the relaxed performer is said to be "caught flat-footed." This is the opposite of "being on your toes" (Fig. 22–8). No doubt there are central "alert mechanisms" as well as peripheral

FIG. 22–6. Rod Franz, former All-American guard, demonstrates a typical "ready position." (Photograph by Thomas McDonald.)

FIG. 22–7. The charge. The relative positions of the trunk and leg denote the application of maximum power. The position of the arms is characteristic of line play. (Photograph by Thomas McDonald.)

FIG. 22–8. A typical "on guard" position used by boxers.
(Photograph by Thomas McDonald.)

ones, and there is evidence that these are located in the hypo-
thalamus.[8]

When the initial propulsive movement is complete, the joints tend
to form a straight line, as evidenced in the position of a sprinter at
the end of the leg drive, the boxer as his left jab or straight right hits
its mark (Figs. 22–9 and 22–10), the swimmer as he leaves the
starting platform, and the shotputter as the shot leaves his hand
(Fig. 22–11). The extending forces have reached their maxima at
this terminal position of drive, and the extended joints are in the
best position to bear the reactive weight of the drive. If the joints
were still in a position of flexion at this moment, the forces could not
be borne efficiently.

By the same token the body is best able to maintain loads when
the joints are fully extended, so that the pull of gravity is offset by

FIG. 22–9.   The left jab. Notice fixation of the scapula. Stabilization of all of the joints of the upper extremity is important to deliver the momentum accumulated by the body. (Photograph by Thomas McDonald.)

the bones rather than by muscular contraction. A weight lifter can ordinarily sustain the bar overhead if he can get his arms straightened, but will find it impossible to support the same weight aloft with his arms only partially straightened out. In lifting the weight overhead, he keeps it as close to the body as possible in order to reduce the distance from the edge of his base to the point at which the line of gravity through the combined mass of his body and the weight falls. Similtaneously he lowers the center of gravity by "splitting" or "squatting," thereby reducing the distance through which he must move the weight in order to get it to the chest or overhead.

Positions of Readiness for Variable Movement. Somewhat different from the foregoing is the position of a baserunner taking a lead-off from first base, or a defensive basketball player waiting for

FIG. 22–10. A straight right. Power comes from ankle, knee and hip extension, body rotation and arm extension. The forward shift of the body weight accompanying a hard punch is evident. (Photograph by Thomas McDonald.)

his opponent to "declare himself" by making an offensive movement. Here the problem is not maintenance of stability, nor preparation to make a predetermined application of face. Instead the problem is to be ready to move quickly in any direction with maximum speed. The center of gravity must be kept over the area of the base until the decision to move is made, but the area of the base is ordinarily reduced so that a small displacement of the center of gravity results in an unbalanced position. Usually the weight must be shifted from both feet to one foot, and if the feet are placed widely apart, the weight-shift requires a longer time. Similarly, too low a center of gravity will slow the motion.

The joints are held in positions intermediate between flexion and extension so that quick movement in any direction is possible, and because of factors described above.

Fig. 22–11. Dallas Long, former World and Olympic shot-put champion, demonstrates modern shot-put technique.

A, By starting facing toward the back of the circle, and crouching, Long is able to move his arm through a larger arc and to apply force to the shot over a longer time than would otherwise be possible.

B, The kick of the left leg helps the putter to achieve speed and to maintain his equilibrium.

C, D, E, Progress of the summation of force, achieved by leg extension, hip rotation, shoulder rotation, arm extension, and finger extension, with a shifting of the weight from the back foot to the forward foot to move the mass of the body in the direction of the put. Observe that in D the center of gravity is lower than it was in C, due to the flexion of the left leg. This aids in maintaining balance. How close is the angle of projection to the theoretically optimal?

F, The position of the feet has now been reversed to achieve follow-through and maintain balance without stepping outside of the ring. Long is 6′ 4″ tall and weighs 260 lbs.

It is evident that there is incompatibility between the positional requirements for stability and those for quick movement in any direction (Fig. 22–12). When the two purposes come into direct conflict, the skilled performer adjusts his starting stance to effect a compromise. In sports which involve maneuvering between opponents, the stance of one player may provide information to his opponent regarding his intended actions at the "go" signal. The football guard must not take a stance when he is going to "pull-out" and run interference which is different than he assumes when he is going to charge forward, even though adjustments in stance would be mechanically more efficient (Fig. 22–6). Scouts closely observe the position of backfield players' feet, since many players tend to turn one foot in the direction in which they are to run. The resulting gain in mechanical efficiency is more than offset by the information given to the opponents. Therefore, the football player, unlike the sprinter on his starting blocks, is forced to assume virtually the same stance on every play and may face in a direction directly opposed to the one in which he is to run. This versatile compromise stance

Fig. 22–12. The ball carrier changing direction. Note the position of the right leg which is about to be planted to enable the runner to cut to his left. A defensive halfback may watch a "breakaway" runner's feet for the telltale "plant step" before committing himself on his tackle. (Photograph courtesy of Associated Students of the University of California.)

must be very carefully planned and practiced if it is to serve the performer well in all of the various maneuvers he must execute in the course of a game.

On the other hand, a performer may use variations of stance in order to deliberately mislead the opponent. He may also use movements of the eyes, head, shoulders, or hands in order to feint the opponent out of position. Ideally, such a feint is obvious enough to mislead an opponent, but subtle enough to avoid interfering with the movement which is actually contemplated. Primarily this means that it must be strong enough to cause the opponent to react to his disadvantage, but must not be so strong that it displaces the feinter's center of gravity in an undesirable direction, and thereby places him at the disadvantage. Every athlete and coach should study the kinesiology of effective feinting. Observation of skilled performers in action is essential; textbook descriptions cannot adequately describe feinting techniques in a practical manner, although many of the kinesiological principles mentioned above will be helpful.

TERMINAL POSITIONS

Terminal positions may be categorized as follows:

1. Those which are irrelevant to the performance. The high-jump and pole vault provide examples. While the performer has a need to avoid injury, which is usually met by providing a deep bed of soft shavings, the judges ignore terminal positions.

2. Those which are arbitrarily specified and which reflect the quality of the preceding performance. Instances are found in ski-jumping, diving, and gymnastics, as well as in events such as shot-putting (Fig. 22–11), discus (Fig. 22–14), and javelin (Fig. 22–15), in which a restraining line must be observed (Fig. 22–11). The gymnast is strongly judged on the steadiness of control of his landings and dismount because of the quality of the terminal position directly reflects the precision with which the body was controlled prior to the landing. A half knee-bend is employed in gymnastic landings not only to absorb impact force, but also to lower the center of gravity and thus increase stability. The arms may be extended outward to act as balancing poles (Fig. 22–13).

3. Those which are integrally related to the strategy or objective measurement of the performance. For example, the long jumper who lands and falls backward instead of forward reduces the measurement of his jump. The tennis player who reaches to make a beautiful backhand shot, but who then stumbles to the ground finds himself effectively penalized because he cannot return to center court in readiness for his opponent's return shot.

Fig. 22–13. Use of the arms as balancing poles to aid in maintaining equilibrium. The long poles, often weighted at the ends, utilized by high wire walkers and similar athletes, are an extension of this technique. (Nissen Corporation.)

Sport skills often employ the terminal position or terminal movements of one movement to contribute to the execution of the next one. The forward momentum of the tennis serve may be employed to carry the server forward into a strategic position on the court. Properly done, bunting a baseball is an integral part of the start of the run toward first base. A long fly ball may be caught high on an outfielder's throwing side, so that the subsequent throw to the infield can be commenced without wasted movement.

STRENGTH

Muscular strength is perhaps the most important of all factors in athletic performance. In certain cases, at least, strength measurements give the best index of ability to learn an unfamiliar or new activity.[9] This may also apply to activities which are not commonly thought of as strength-activated. The rationale for this statement is partly explained by a common physical formula expressing kinetic energy.

FIG. 22-14. Al Oerter, four times Olympic champion in the discus throw, demonstrates the ore and three-quarters turns style of throwing.

A, The athlete's back is toward the direction of the throw. This increases the arc through which the missile moves and consequently its velocity.

B, The first turn. The thrower turns as fast as he can and still maintain his equilibrium. The arm is kept extended at the elbow to give the maximum leverage. Note the path of the center of gravity of the athlete's body through the five pictures.

C, The extraordinary amount of rotation of the hips in advance of the shoulders is evident. Note the rotation of the shoulders in accordance with the principle of summation of force. The farther the discus is behind the thrower, the longer the period through which the force can be applied.

D, The final throwing position. The body is starting to "unwind." The relatively high angle of departure of the discus is evident. The legs have been forcefully extended and the rotators of the trunk are powerfully engaged. The spiral path followed by the discus is evident.

E, The finish. The general body position illustrates the principle that the mass of the body should move in the direction of the throw. Observe the complete extension of the body segments. (Photographs by Gene Mozee.) Oerter is 6' 3¾" tall and weighs 257 lbs.

FIG. 22-15.   Javelin throwing technique with which Lieutenant Al Cantello, U.S.M.C., set a new world's record in 1959.   This is probably the most extreme example of "follow-through" known to sports.   Note particularly that Cantello has "his eye on the ball" continuously, even while diving through the air and striking the ground.   (Official U. S. Marine Corps photo, courtesy *Leatherneck Magazine*.)

Most sports skills require the development of kinetic energy, which may be defined as $\frac{1}{2}mv^2$, in which m = the mass of the object and v = the velocity of the object. The object may be the body itself, as in the case of running and jumping, or a projectile, as in the case of a baseball or javelin, or a sports implement, such as a baseball bat or tennis racket. The greater the kinetic energy developed, the faster will be the run, the farther the throw, or the more powerful the striking of the ball. An elementary formula of physics states that $Fd = \frac{1}{2}mv^2$, in which F = force, d = the distance over which the force is applied, and $\frac{1}{2}mv^2$ = kinetic energy. The magnitude of kinetic energy, then, is directly proportional to both the force exerted and the distance over which it is applied. In sports, force is usually derived mostly or entirely from muscular strength.

In sports applications, the mass (m) in the kinetic energy formula is ordinarily constant. If we assume that the distance (d) through which the force is applied is also constant, it follows that velocity increases with an increase in force. In this situation, however, $F = v^2$, or $v = \sqrt{F}$. For each fourfold increase in force, there is only a doubling of velocity. This relationship points out the fact that there is a diminishing return for progressive increase in muscular strength, as follows:

Force	Velocity $(=\sqrt{F})$
1	1.0
2	1.4+
4	2.0
8	2.8+
16	4.0
32	5.7—
64	8.0
128	11.3+

Overload Principle. The overload principle states that increases in muscular strength, hypertrophy, and endurance result from an increase in the intensity of the work performed in the given time unit.[10] The work may be intensified by raising the cadence or by increasing the resistance against which the muscles contract. Examples of the use of these devices may be found in "interval training" in track, in the use of progressive resistance exercises in the gymnasium, and elsewhere. If an individual desires to increase his muscular strength, hypertrophy, and endurance he must be willing regularly to subject his body to the stress of repeated all-out efforts. In the case of a patient in a physical medicine and rehabilitation clinic this may be at a relatively low level of accomplishment on any absolute scale, but the important thing is that it represents a maximal volitional performance for the individual.   This is achieved only when the person concerned is motivated by some powerful psychological drive.   The physiological mechanisms underlying these responses have been discussed at length elsewhere,[11-15] but it is clear that responses to physical activity are neuromuscular not simply muscular.   The development of skill, the more effective utilization of the central nervous system, and the overcoming of psychological barriers are integral aspects of the overload principle.

As a corollary to this principle, the total amount of work done without any increase in the intensity thereof is without significance for the development of the kinesiological factors under consideration.   Once the body has become accustomed to and able to sustain the strain placed upon it by routine work, it will not automatically make additional gains in strength to make the work easier to perform.   For this reason the average manual worker or housewife does not display the well-developed body or physical ability of the athlete, even though the demands of their particular occupations may have developed certain abilities which the athlete might find it difficult or impossible to equal until he or she had had an opportunity to become proficient in the worker's specialty.

Athletes may attempt to intensify their training by practicing with a shot which is heavier than the one which they will put in competition, running distances greater than that of their event, swinging three bats while awaiting their turn at the plate, or by similar means.   While procedures of this sort do invoke the overload principle, they clash with the principle of specificity of training.   This again illustrates the need for professional training in kinesiology if the coach is to make wise use of its principles.

The Principle of Rest Pauses.   When the exercise is heavy, a greater amount of muscular work can be accomplished if it is interspersed with rest periods.   In general, short, frequent rest pauses seem to make for greater efficiency in muscular work than do long, infrequent rests.   The physiological principles underlying rest pauses have been considered by Mueller.[16]   Weight trainers have found from experience that it is advisable to take a short pause between each set of exercises; the studies of Clarke, et al.[17] suggest that about 2.5 minutes comprises the optimal time.   At track meets the program should be arranged in such a way as to provide a rest period between the 100-yard dash and the 220-yard dash, and between the half-mile and the mile runs, so that a competitor in either of these pairs may enter both of the events without too great a handicap being imposed upon him in the second one.   On physiological grounds, a rest of 40 minutes between sprints and 75 minutes between middle distance runs has been advocated.[18]

FOLLOW-THROUGH

The principle of follow-through is an important element in all sports skills involving powerful propulsion of an object. Such skills include stroking a tennis ball, batting, shot-putting, discus throwing, javelin throwing, punching (as in boxing), and blocking and tackling (as in football). In the popular mind, follow-through is often thought of as a continuation of motion after the contact with the propelled object has terminated (Fig. 7–9). However, it is obvious that after the contact has terminated, no action of the body can have any effect upon the path of the propelled object. The "body English" exhibited, for example, by a bowler as the ball rolls down the alley is a useless kind of motion, except as it may satisfy some little-understood psychological need of the performer.

Follow-through is more properly defined as a continuation of a propulsive force so as to increase the duration of its application on the propelled object as long as possible. Under this definition, the importance of follow-through can be explained by the physical law expressed by the formula

$$V = at$$

in which V is the final velocity of the propelled object, a is the acceleration (assumed here to be constant), and t is the duration of application of the accelerating force. For a given constant rate of acceleration, the terminal velocity is directly proportional to the time of application (Fig. 22–16). The time factor applies only to the duration of a *propulsive* force (that is, an accelerating force). A force which only follows along with the propelled object, without acting upon it so as to increase its velocity, has no effect on the object.

As a technique in communicating with a performer, a teacher may choose to emphasize a continuation of motion after the contact period, but this exaggerated coaching advice does not accurately reflect the physical principles involved.

STABILIZATION

Newton's third law of motion states that for every action there is an equal and opposite reaction. When a baseball pitcher throws a ball, he applies force about equally to the ball and to the pitching rubber. The earth, because of its great mass, is stable and does not

Fig. 22–16. *See opposite page for legend.*

move detectably. The pitching rubber is stable because of its anchoring pins attaching it to the earth. The pitcher's body moves forward by rotating at the ankle joint. Muscles stabilize the knee, hip, and spine joints to a great extent. The arm, forearm, hand, and baseball exhibit the greatest motion. The propelling force is largely applied to the baseball because the other parts were effectively stabilized (Figs. 22–4, 22–5).

A jump pass, in football or basketball, is poorly stabilized (Fig. 22–17). The product of the mass and velocity forward of the ball is equal to the product of the mass and velocity backward of the passer's body. Some of the energy generated by the muscles has been "wasted" in propelling the passer's body backward. Thus, the jump pass is inefficient mechanically, and is a skill employed only as a compromise with non-mechanical strategic aspects of the situation. Performance is often improved by attention to proper stabilization of the joints, through muscular contraction, and of the body against external objects, through the use of spikes, cleats, surfaces with a high coefficient of friction, and equipment such as track starting blocks or a pitcher's rubber. One of the advantages of the semicrouch stance employed in football, wrestling, boxing, track and swimming starts is its efficiency in directing forces of reaction into the earth, so as to secure adequate stabilization.

SUMMATION OF FORCES

From a mechanical point of view, the main problem in many elemental sports skills is that of creating maximal acceleration in an object or a body segment. If a given time period is available for the

---

FIG. 22–16. *A*, Jack Jensen, former All-American backfield star, demonstrates punting.

B, The first stride, taken just before the ball is dropped, starts the body in motion in the direction of the desired flight of the ball.

C, Bending the knee shortens the lever and gives greater angular velocity. As the foot comes forward to meet the ball, the swinging leg will come into full extension at the instant of impact to give the longest possible lever and impart the greatest force to the ball.

D, The follow-through. The kicking leg is swung toward the cardinal sagittal line in order to impart the spin necessary to stabilize the ball in its flight. Since the opposite hip is locked by the iliofemoral ligament, the force generated by the moving leg tends to carry the kicker into the air. Increasing the distances decreases the amount of energy necessary to halt the limb and reduces the chance of injury. Under game conditions the center must get the ball to the punter in not over .7 sec. The ball must be kicked within 1.75 sec. from the time received. It takes off at a speed in excess of 71 f.p.s. and remains in the air about 4 secs.[19,20] (Photographs by Thomas McDonald.)

FIG. 22–17. A jump pass executed with the left hand. (Photograph courtesy of the Associated Students of the University of California.)

application of force to an object, its acceleration will be directly proportional to the amount of force applied (F = ma, where F is the average force applied, m is the mass of the object, and a is the resulting acceleration). The basic problem, therefore, is to recruit all forces available, so that the total is maximal. A knowledge of the principle of summation of forces is helpful in analyzing such skills and in formulating coaching advice.

Assuming that all of the forces come from the contraction of muscles, there are two fundamental ways in which the forces from different muscles may be summed: first, by simultaneous contraction, and second, by sequential contraction.

In a given action of a single joint, the various muscles which perform that motion ordinarily contract simultaneously. Sometimes, however, one muscle, by virtue of its position and structure, acts mainly in the first part of a joint action, while another muscle acts mainly in the latter part of the joint action. Detailed knowledge of such facts may be important to the physician or the therapist in dealing with problems of surgery or rehabilitation, but the performer and the coach can safely ignore them, since the sequence of contraction of individual muscles is controlled automatically and subcon-

FIG. 22–18. Pete Gogolak demonstrates the soccer method of kicking, with Daryle Lamonica, American Football League 1969 Player of the Year, holding. (Courtesy Buffalo Bills.) It will be found instructive to analyze this technique in a manner similar to that done for the Jensen technique. Suggestion: Particular attention should be given to the movement of the pelvis. Under game conditions a field goal attempt should be gotten off within 1.3 sec.[19]

sciously in the normal individual. The performer, therefore, should concentrate only on what movement to make and on making it with maximal force (Fig. 22–18). However, the performer can often profit by making a deliberate attempt to adjust his body mechanics so that the muscular forces are applied to the object for the longest possible time (see, for example, the preceding section on "Follow-through").

Almost all sports skills involve combinations of actions in more than one joint, and the muscular forces at each joint are added together and applied to the object. For many reasons, some theoretical and some kinesiological or practical, it is ordinarily not possible or desirable to have all of these various forces act simultaneously. Instead, there is a definite sequence of joint actions and of the muscular forces powering them. With proper timing and body mechanics, the force of each subsequent joint action may be added, in effect, to that of the preceding one. This is somewhat analogous to the firing of a multi-stage rocket, and also, in a way, to the cracking of a whip.

The shot-put provides an example of summation of forces of various joint actions (Fig. 22–11). Although there is some overlapping in the application of the joint actions, they tend to take place sequentially, starting with those most distant from the shot and ending with those nearest the shot. The joints tend to be flexed at the beginning of the motion. Various joint actions set the body in motion across the ring, imparting an acceleration to the body as a whole. Then a series of extensions and twistings occurs, starting with the ankle, then the knee, the hip, the trunk (rotation), the shoulder, the elbow, and finally the hand. The force of each joint action accelerates all body parts above it, and the wrist and hand action applies a final force to the shot which is already moving and has considerable velocity.

For the summation of forces to be effective, there are two important conditions. First, for each successive joint action to make its maximal contribution, the joints below it must be firmly stabilized so that no back-sliding results from the reaction component of the force (Newton's third law). Thus, each joint action tends to end with a static contraction phase. Second, the forces of each successive joint action must be precisely timed. If any time intervenes between the application of the successive forces, the shot merely coasts along at its existing velocity. Better timing could have utilized this distance and time period for the imparting of additional force, thus providing additional acceleration.

The principle of summation of forces, together with its elements of adequate stabilization and optimal timing, can be observed in putting the shot (Fig. 22–11), throwing the discus (Fig. 22–14),

Fig. 22–19. Smash by Gerald Patterson. Note that Patterson is obviously not "keeping his eye on the ball." (Courtesy of American Lawn Tennis, Inc. From *Mechanics of the Game of Lawn Tennis*, Vol. II, by J. Parmly Paret.)

executing a left jab (Fig. 22–9), smashing a tennis ball (Fig. 22–19), kicking a football (Fig. 22–16) and many other skills. In some activities, the sequence of joint actions begins in the upper body and terminates at the ankle and foot. Various jumping styles, execution of a back somersault in tumbling, and performing the racing start in swimming are cases in point.

CONSERVATION OF ANGULAR MOMENTUM

Angular momentum is the product of the rotational inertia* and the angular velocity. This always remains constant unless the object is acted upon by an outside force (Newton's first law). If one of the two components (for example, the rotational inertia) is

---

* The rotational inertia is obtained by multiplying the mass of each particle of the body by the square of its perpendicular distance to the center of rotation, and summing products for the whole body.

18

decreased, the other (angular velocity) must be correspondingly increased, and vice versa, so that the product of the two factors remains unaltered. Applications of the law of conservation of angular momentum appear frequently in sports activities, being apparent whenever there is a spin, pivot, twist, somersault, or pendulum swing involved in a sports skill. The principle may be explained, non-technically, by describing two skills whose performance depends crucially upon its operation.

A figure skater, with arms stretched out sideways, swings into a series of spins or pirouettes while balanced on the point of one skate. The angular momentum was achieved originally by pushing off with the other skate, and by swinging the arms in a horizontal circle against this resistance. The original momentum continues to spin the skater, if he holds his outward-reaching arm position, until friction gradually decelerates him to the point of loss of balance. However, if the arms are drawn in and folded on the chest during the spins, the speed of rotation (angular velocity) is markedly increased, so that the pirouetting skater appears as a blur to the spectator. When the skater wishes to discontinue this rapid spinning, he thrusts his arms outward again, whereupon his angular velocity is greatly decreased.

A diver performing a one-and-one-half front somersault in tuck position gains his initial rotation by leaning forward on the take-off from the board. The speed of this original rotation is moderate, but as soon as the diver is in the air, he draws his arms and legs in toward the center of the body (tuck position), and the speed of his forward spin increases greatly. After about one full somersault, the diver emerges from the tuck position, and extends his arms, legs, and trunk into layout position, whereupon his angular velocity decreases markedly. The diver seems to float slowly through his last half-somersault before making his head-first entry into the water. The same principle holds when a gymnast executes a front somersault (Fig. 7–1).

Conservation of angular momentum may be further explained by returning to the example of the spinning skater. For simplicity, one arm only may be considered, and the mass of that arm may be assumed to be accumulated at its center of gravity, just above the elbow. The original momentum was sufficient to impart a certain angular velocity; and the center of gravity will traverse a certain circular distance, at elbow's distance from the center of rotation, in a given time period. Now when the arm's center of gravity is drawn in toward the center of rotation, it follows a circular path of smaller radius and shorter circumference. If the body continued to rotate at the same angular velocity, the distance traversed by the arm's center of gravity would be much smaller in the given time period. This, however, is not possible under the law of conservation of angular momentum. Instead, the angular velocity is increased sufficiently so that the arm's center of gravity traverses, in the given time period, a distance equal to that which would have been traversed along the circle of greater circumference at the slower original angular velocity. Neglecting outside forces, such as air resistance and friction between skate and ice, angular momentum must remain constant. When one of its components (the distance from the center of rotation to the center of gravity of the body part) is decreased, there must be a corresponding increase in another component (angular velocity), and vice versa.

The principle of angular momentum is so commonly involved in sports skills that a teacher who understands and can recognize it will be able to give effective coaching advice in many activities with which he has had little experience as a performer. In gymnastics and diving, the law has almost constant application. Mechanically speaking, the pole vault differs from the high jump largely in the fact that it involves the movement of a pendulum on a pendulum, *i.e.*, linear motion is converted to angular motion at the ground level, when the pole pivots within the box, and again at the other end of the pole, when the vaulter's body pivots around his hand grip. At the take-off the center of gravity is directly below the point of support. The take-off leg is flexed and then snapped down hard to implement Newton's third law (often giving rise to heel bruises). As the body leaves the ground the knees are flexed up toward the chest and the body rolled backward to conserve angular momentum. The center of gravity pivots around the center of rotation (hand grip) and the leverage of the pole flings the vaulter into the air. Once off the ground the vaulter keeps his center of gravity as close to the pole as possible, since any weight at an angle to the pole will slow the movement of the pole (Fig. 22–20).

As a football quarterback pivots to hand off the ball, he decreases the radius of his pivot by pulling one leg, his arms, and the ball closer to his vertical axis of rotation, thus increasing his speed. A basketball or football player, starting from a spread-out position with a relatively large radius measured from his pivot foot, can pivot or feint more rapidly if he draws his arms and free foot back toward a vertical axis of rotation over his pivot foot.

The tumbler, diver, or trampoline man who performs a twisting somersault employs the principle of conservation of angular momentum around two different axes of rotation simultaneously. First, his somersault may involve some shortening of radius around the axis through his hips, similar to that previously described for diving.

Second, his twist, which is a rotation around a head-to-toe axis, involves an initial arm swing like that of the figure skater, followed by a pulling-in of the arms toward the chest, which increases the speed of the twist. At the termination of the twisting somersault, both radii are lengthened again, slowing both of the rotations so that a controlled landing or entry into the water may be achieved.

Fig. 22–20. John Pennel, former holder of the world record in the pole vault. The kinetic energy of the vaulter's approach and take-off is converted largely into energy for bending the pole, swinging the pole as an inverted pendulum, and swinging the body as a pendulum around the hand grip. The increased speed of the body pendulum, achieved by shortening the distance from the hand grip to the body's center of gravity, demonstrates the principle of conservation of angular momentum. After take-off, the vaulter's maneuvers should be designed to regain the energy stored in the pole and to put his body in such a position that this regained energy will be applied to the raising of his center of gravity. (Stroboscopic photo by Dr. Harold E. Edgerton, of M.I.T., reproduced by permission from *Mechanics of the Pole Vault*, by Dr. Richard V. Ganslen. 6th Edition. St. Louis, Mo.: John Swift and Co., 1965.)

A baseball pitcher starts his throw with an extended arm, rotating around the shoulder axis with a large radius. As the arm is brought forward, elbow and shoulder joint motions draw the ball closer to the shoulder, effectively increasing the speed of the ball just before its release (Fig. 22–4). The football passer does not use this technique because (1) baseball pitching speeds, which approach 100 miles per hour, would be impractical in the football situation, (2) he cannot afford the time or risk the unbalanced position, and (3) the shape of the football and the choice of moving targets require a sacrifice of speed in favor of accuracy.

FALLING

The dangers of falling result largely from impact, or the reception of forces; therefore, some of the related kinesiological principles will also apply to the problem of receiving the impact of objects in sports, such as occur in catching a hard-driven ball. The following discussion, however, assumes for the most part that the body is falling under the influence of gravity. The factors to be considered are (1) the velocity at the moment of impact, (2) the mass of the falling body, (3) the distance through which the deceleration takes place, (4) the surface area through which the impact is absorbed, (5) the part of the anatomy subjected to the impact, and (6) the properties of the surface on which the body lands.

An equation derived from the formula for kinetic energy is helpful in understanding several of the problems of falling.

$$\text{Work} = \text{Fd} = \tfrac{1}{2}\text{mv}^2 = \text{kinetic energy.}$$

The problem is to do work so as to absorb the kinetic energy of the fall, and to do this work safely.

The kinetic energy of the fall is proportional to the square of the velocity. Anything which can be done to reduce the velocity will "pay off" with geometrically-accruing benefits. Usually, the velocity of the fall is the result of the acceleration of gravity. This gravitational acceleration constantly increases during the fall, and the speed increases geometrically. The time of falling can be decreased if there is some warning. A fainting person, for example, can sometimes start to sit or lie down before becoming completely unconscious, at which time falling becomes free and uncontrolled. A ladder or other tipping object starts to fall slowly, and although it may be impossible for the person on it to recover balance, there may be a moment in which he can climb, slide, or step down part way, and thus reduce the time and height of the fall. Sometimes grasping or contacting stationary objects on the way down may decrease the acceleration of the fall; people have fallen amazing distances through tree limbs or through an awning without sustaining serious injury.

The impact of landing is proportional to the mass of the falling body. Heavy masses do not fall any faster, however, and it is sometimes wise to retain a grasp on an object. For example, falling onto a large pasteboard carton held in one's arms may be preferable to falling directly onto a floor. But if the object in one's arms is heavy and will be on top at the moment of landing, it would be better to push it aside. Obese persons, because of their greater mass without equivalent agility or strength, are injured more seriously by falls.

The longer the distance through which deceleration takes place, the less the danger of trauma. The equation cited above demonstrates that the greater the distance through which force is applied, the less the decelerating force will have to be, since the product of the two must equal the kinetic energy of the fall. In the same manner that a fast ball is caught with "giving" of the arms, the arms or legs may sometimes be used as shock absorbers powered by the muscles. When the limbs are so used, they should be nearly but not quite extended at the moment of contact. Joints which are locked in complete extension must absorb the impact almost instantaneously; with the shock-absorbing distance element reduced to a minimum, the magnitude of the force required is likely to tear ligaments and shatter bones. Falling with the arm elevated over the shoulder may force the humerus out of the joint through the triangular opening formed by the muscles beneath the armpit. In such activities as football and trampolining, performers are coached to avoid extending the arms in order to break falls. Boxers are taught to "roll with the punch" in order to reduce the force of the impact.

If the impact of a fall is spread over a large surface area, the magnitude of the force at any one place on the body is reduced. It is obvious that landing on both feet is safer than landing on one (Fig. 22–21). In some cases, landing flat on one's back is preferable to landing on the small surface areas of one to four hands and feet. Circus acrobats falling from great heights are said to prefer to land flat on their backs rather than on their feet. The standard "breakfalls" of the sport of judo represent effective devices for spreading the impact of falls over large arm and body areas. The judoka is taught to land on the well-padded side of the thigh if possible and to take up as much of the shock as he can with the hands and feet. In many falls in which there is lateral as well as vertical momentum, part of the fall may be taken on the feet and the rest absorbed by doing a forward, sideward, or backward roll. The sideward roll is often known as the "football roll" because some coaches teach it during warm-up periods as a method of avoiding contact on the point of the shoulder after being tripped, blocked, or tackled.

The deformability and compressibility of the landing surface

FIG. 22–21.   John Rudometkin, of the University of Southern California, making a one-hand hook shot.   As the position of the player's body indicates, this shot is usually made on the run.   The man takes off from one foot and lands on one foot. Some experienced team physicians blame the increased popularity of one-hand shots for the greater incidence of "pounded heels" seen among basketball players during the last few years.   The injury is usually at the fibro-osseous junction of the plantar muscles and the calcaneus.   (Photograph courtesy Department of Intercollegiate Athletics, University of Southern California.)

makes a tremendous difference in the seriousness of falls. People who fall out of hotel windows are sometimes uninjured if they land on the roof of a parked car, which is surprisingly deformable and which increases the distance element in the work of absorbing the kinetic energy. Asphalt or "black top" is noticeably safer than cement as a landing surface, and may compare favorably with sand or compressed earth. Heavy turf, especially if the underlying earth is moist, is markedly superior to dry compacted bare earth.

The seriousness of trauma resulting from a blow depends largely upon the part of the anatomy receiving the impact. Damage to the head is probably most to be avoided; vertical and whip-lash forces on the spinal column, especially the upper parts, are probably next in seriousness. Injuries to the viscera are fairly common, but this area does possess certain means of self-protection. The sight of an approaching blow results in a reflex contraction of the abdominal muscles. When the blow is received, the intestines tend to slide out of the line of force. Most of the internal organs have a certain amount of mobility and are able to swing aside when their area is struck. The vertebral column against which they might be crushed arches backwards to reduce the impact, and is itself cushioned by the "hydraulic buffer" action of the aorta and inferior vena cava.[21]

References

1. Klein, Karl K. and Allman, Fred L., Jr.: *The Knee in Sports*. Austin: Pemberton Press, 1969.

2. Marmor, Leonard, *et al.*: Pectoralis Major Muscle. J. Bone Joint Surg., *43-A*, 81–87, 1961.

3. Buskirk, E. R. and Beetham, W. P., Jr.: Dehydration and Body Temperature as a Result of Marathon Running. Med. Sport., *XIV*, 493–506, 1960.

4. Pacheco, Betty A.: Improvement in Jumping Performance Due to Preliminary Exercise. Res. Quart., *28*, 55–63, 1957.

5. Massey, Benjamin H., *et al.*: Effect of Warm-Up Exercise Upon Muscular Performance Using Hypnosis to Control the Psychological Variable. Res. Quart., *32*, 63–71, 1961.

6. Asmussen, Erling, and Bøje, Ove: Body Temperature and Capacity for Work. Acta Physiol. Scand., *10*, 1–22, 1945.

7. Start, K. B. and Hines, Janer: The Effect of Warm-up on the Incidence of Muscle Injury during Activities Involving Maximum Strength, Speed and Endurance. J. Sports Med., *3*, 208–217, 1963.

8. Gelhorn, E.: The Physiological Basis of Neuromuscular Relaxation. AMA Arch. Int. Med., *103*, 392–399, 1958.

9. Rasch, Philip J. and Kroll, Walter: *What Research Tells the Coach About Wrestling*. Washington, D.C.: American Association for Health-Physical Education-Recreation, 1964, pp. 31–32.

10. Walters, C. Etta: Scientific Foundations of the Overload Principle. Scholastic Coach, *27*, 20 *et seq.*, 1958.

11. Rasch, Philip J., and Freeman, Richard V.: The Physiology of Progressive Resistance Exercise. J. Ass. Phys. Men. Rehabil., *8*, 35–41, 1954.

12. ————: Weight Training in a Neuro-psychiatric Hospital. J. Ass. Phys. Men. Rehabil., *8*, 146–151, 1954.

13. Rasch, Philip J.: The Problem of Muscle Hypertrophy. J. Amer. Osteopath. Ass., *54*, 525–528, 1955.

14. ————: Studies in Progressive Resistance Exercise. J. Ass. Phys. Men. Rehabil., *12*, 125–130, 1958.

15. ————: Progressive Resistance Exercise: Isotonic and Isometric. A Review. J. Ass. Phys. Men. Rehabil., *15*, 46 *et seq.*, 1961.

16. Mueller, E. A.: The Physiological Basis of Rest Pauses in Heavy Work. Quart. J. Exp. Physiol., *38*, 205–215, 1952.

17. Clarke, H. Harrison, *et al.*: Strength Decrements of Elbow Flexor Muscles Following Exhaustive Exercise. Arch. Phys. Med., *35*, 560–561, 1954.

18. Anderson, K. Lange, *et al.*: The Blood Lactate During Recovery from Sprint Runs. Acta Physiol. Scand., *48*, 231–237, 1960.

19. Kahler, Robert W.: Punt with a Purpose. Ath. J., XLX, 12 *et seq.*, 1969.

20. Roberts, Elizabeth M.: Unpublished data.

21. Sekhon, G. S.: Defensive Mechanism of the Body Against Blunt Abdominal Injuries. Indian J. Med. Res., *46*, 613–616, 1958.

Recommended Reading

22. Dyson, Geoffrey H. G.: *The Mechanics of Athletics*, 5th Ed. London: University of London Press Ltd., 1970.

23. Shatel, Art: Scientific Principles of Wrestling Skills. Scholastic Coach, *32*, 72–75, 1961.

24. Watanabe, Jiichi and Avakian, Lindy: *The Secrets of Judo.* Rutland: Charles E. Tuttle Co., 1960.

25. Crossman, E. R. F. W.: Information Process in Human Skill. Brit. Med. Bull., *20*, 32–37, 1964.

26. Edwards, William E.: *Factors in the Superiority of Chimpanzee over Human Strength.* 6571st Aeromedical Research Laboratory Report AMRL-TR-65-10, July, 1965.

27. Dillman, Charles J. and Nelson, Richard E.: The Mechanical Energy Transformations of Pole Vaulting with a Fiberglass Pole. J. Biomech., *1*, 175–183, 1968.

28. Mueller, Erich A.: Influence of Training and of Inactivity of Muscle Strength. Arch. Phys. Med., *51*, 449–462, 1970.

29. Kroemer, K. H. Eberhard: *Human Strength: Terminology, Measurement, and Interpretation of Data.* Aerospace Medical Research Report AMRL-TR-69-9, 1970.

30. Jacoby, Edward G.: *Physiological Implications of Interval Training.* West Point: United States Military Academy, n. d.

Chapter 23

Kinesiology in Daily Living

Lifting. Since the levers of the human body are adapted for range, speed and precision of movement, rather than for weight handling, it is not surprising that the incidence of back injuries attributed to lifting is extremely high. Such traumata may be due to acute injury, such as is sustained by the industrial worker, or to a continual mild overstretching of the muscles and ligaments, such as is experienced by the housewife. They may result from the "nutcracker" effect of compression forces or from lesions of the soft tissues. These conditions are especially apt to occur in the elderly, whose intervertebral discs and muscles have lost their strength and elasticity.

To offset the mechanical disadvantages inherent in the human machine requires the use of the most efficient techniques of body mechanics. General rules are difficult to apply, since the way in which burdens are lifted depends upon their size, shape, position in space, and the habits of the person lifting them. Davis[1] estimates that the theoretical maximum lift in the erect position is about 500 pounds, a figure which is achieved by weight lifters. A study[2] of the methods employed by them to raise these enormous poundages revealed that six cardinal principles were observed:

1. The feet are kept flat on the floor. The lifter does not balance himself on his toes, as is sometimes shown in shop posters depicting the techniques of lifting.

2. The legs are spread a comfortable distance (about 12 inches) apart to increase the stability of the body. If the stance is exceptionally wide the muscles of the groin are more easily strained.

3. The weight is kept as close to the lifter as is convenient.

4. The spine is kept as straight as possible.

5. The actual lifting is done by the largest and strongest muscles which can be utilized for the purpose—usually the extensors of the

FIG. 23–1. Incorrect technique of lifting. Note that in this position the principal stresses will come on the muscles of the spinal column, which, in this position, is literally "hanging from its ligaments." Those concerned with industrial accidents frequently term this the "cantilever" position and hold it responsible for many back strains. (Photo by Pierson.)

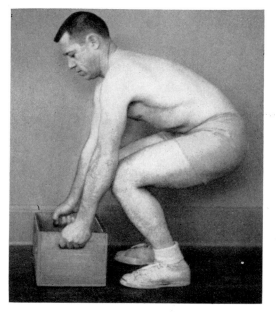

FIG. 23–2. Proper technique of lifting. Note that in this position the principal stresses will come on the quadriceps femoris, the largest and strongest muscles in the body. (Photo by Pierson.)

knees. In most cases the knees are bent, the object grasped in the hands, and then lifted by forcefully contracting the extensors of the knee and straightening the legs, not by pulling upward with the arms and back (Figs. 23–1 and 23–2).

6. The lifter faces in the direction in which he intends to move, so that he does not have to turn while holding the weight and thus set up centrifugal forces which may result in injury. In many cases, however, advantage may be taken of the counterbalancing of the body and "follow through" to perform in one smooth motion what might otherwise be accomplished in a series of inefficient discrete movements.

Upon careful analysis it will be found that almost all forms of work are performed most efficiently when these principles are kept in mind. In using the wringer on a mop bucket, for example, the cleaning woman will profit by facing in the direction in which the wringer handle moves so that the weight of her body may be applied on the down stroke and the strength of her legs employed on the up stroke. At the other extreme, one acute witness[3] of the hard rock drilling contests of the early Southwestern miners, has noted that the man swinging the hammer bent forward as much at the hip and knee as at the elbow and shoulder, caught the elbow of the lower arm on the forward thigh, and threw it back up into the air by the upward jerk of the leg. The two types of work are very different, but the principles involved are exactly the same.

Moving Weights. When possible, heavy objects should be pushed rather than pulled and slid rather than carried. In theory the force required to lift a weight is approximately 34 times that required to slide it, although in actual practice this difference is reduced by the amount of energy necessary to overcome the friction involved.[4] The principles for the most efficient method of pushing are very similar to those for lifting.

1. The feet are placed a comfortable distance apart, with one foot near to the object to be pushed and the other extended to the rear.

2. The spine is kept straight and the hips are kept low.

3. The hands are placed at the level of the object's center of weight. If they are placed above it, the object will tend to tip forward rather than to slide forward.

4. The object is moved by contracting the extensors of the hip, knee, and ankle and straightening the legs, not by extending the arms.

Variations on the utilization of the principle of pushing may be found in the use of the shovel, in which the advanced hand, or hand and thigh, may be used as a fulcrum and the weight lifted by pushing down on the shovel, and in canoeing, in which the principal effort is made by a push of the arm whose hand and fingers grasp the top of the paddle. It should be noted that in both cases first class leverage is involved and force is gained by the fact that the force arm is longer than the resistance arm.

Handling an Object Overhead. The problem of handling an object overhead, as in removing a box from a closet shelf, is rendered more severe by the fact that the moving of the object builds up a horizontal momentum and its position raises the center of gravity of the mover, thus decreasing his stability and rendering him more likely to be tipped in the direction in which the object is moving or to suffer a strain in trying to prevent undesired movement. A solution is to place one foot in advance of the other. The object is first moved with the body's center of gravity supported by the advanced foot. As the object comes forward, the body weight is shifted to the support of the back foot, which can be moved still further backward if necessary. In effect, this sacrifices space to gain a reduction of momentum. The inability to make this sacrifice and the dangers attendant upon loss of stability make lifting an object overhead while standing on a kitchen stool or similar support a potentially hazardous occupation. In all overhead lifting an effort should be made to avoid thrusting the hips forward or increasing the lordotic curve of the back.

Carrying Weights. If the weight must be carried, the normal erect posture is modified so that the center of gravity of the man plus the load approximates the center of gravity of the man alone. The trunk apparently functions as a counterbalance, altering its inclination so that the projection of the center of gravity at the feet remains in a relatively constant position.[5] The most common cause of accidents in carrying loads is loss of balance resulting in insupportable muscular strains being placed on the body. Observation of the following principles will assist in carrying loads in a safe and efficient manner:

1. If possible the load is divided into two equal parcels and one is carried in each hand, so that the spine is kept straight.

2. If the load is a single bundle, the free arm may be raised sideward to assist in keeping the spine erect.

3. The weight is carried close to the body. This reduces unbalancing leverage to a minimum and lessens the moments required to turn the body.

4. The most efficient handle to use on a bundle is the one which exerts the least concentrated pressure on the hands. Carrying pails, for example, is less fatiguing if the wire bale is covered with a handle.

5. When carrying packages in the hands, the elbows are kept slightly bent to take some of the strain off the elbow joint. Normally

only the ligamentous structure of the elbow prevents distraction of the loaded joint unless the muscles are voluntarily contracted.[6]

A study sponsored by the U. S. Air Force[7] recommended the following weight limits be placed on equipment that must be lifted by short (5′ 6″ and under) men:

To knee level (18″) . . . . 61.66 lbs.
To waist level (42″) . . . . 37.91 lbs.
To shoulder level (62.5″) . . . . . 27.19 lbs.

Taller men are normally heavier, and may lift somewhat greater amounts.

For women the most economical load appears to be about 35 per cent of the body weight. A load of about 45 pounds would appear to be the optimum for continuous carriage, although the average woman should be able to handle 50 pounds without strain. A possible 20 per cent additional load might be allowed when the burden is compact and easily handled. The optimal load for men is also about 35 per cent of body weight and the optimal rate of carry about 85 to 95 yd./min. Faster rates of carrying increase the energy consumption to a greater degree than does a 20 per cent increase in the weight.[8] When a worker must carry sacks, the weight of the sack should not exceed 60 kg. on the level and 50 kg. on stairs.[9] The recommended maximum load for men is 130 pounds, although the amount of weight that can be safely handled is so affected by constitutional type, strength, age, experience, compactness of load, and other factors that wide variations from this figure may be acceptable. In practice these concepts are often violated. It is almost universally agreed that an infantryman should not carry in excess of 40 pounds; the American soldier actually carries about 73 pounds.[10]

Bedale[11] measured the oxygen consumption per minute in various methods of carrying to determine the energy expenditure each required. As summarized in Table 23–1, it will be noted that the order of efficiency differs somewhat for different carrying methods.

Sitting and Rising. In Western cultures it is tacitly assumed that an individual accepting an invitation to be seated will sit on a chair or davenport, but this is not necessarily true elsewhere. Sitting on the floor with the legs stretched straight ahead or crossed at the ankles or knees is a characteristic feminine seated posture in many other parts of the world, perhaps because it enables the woman to nurse a baby and at the same time carry on the weaving, basket-making, and other tasks which usually engage her attention. Sitting on the heels with the knees resting on the floor and sitting with legs folded to one side are also common postures among women in other

TABLE 23–1.   Oxygen Consumption in cc. Per Min.
in Various Methods of Carrying

Weight in Pounds	20	30	40	50	60
	Oxygen Consumption Per Minute				
Methods of Carrying					
1. Tray carried in front of the body . .	464	522	613	675	
2. Tray carried in front, strap around shoulders	473	522	604	656	
3. Weight carried in equal bundles in each hand	455	492	534	667	
4. Weight distributed on board on left shoulder	428	547	609	608	778
5. Tray on left hip	574	657	694	725	
6. Rucksack on back	561	573	698	700	
7. Weight in two pails, supported by shoulder yoke	400	440	486	516	531
8. Tray on head	527	575	626	692	

societies. Body position reflects anatomical, psychological, cultural, kinesiological, and environmental factors. The relative advantages and disadvantages of different positions in general use in various parts of the world have never been studied and offer the kinesiologist a fascinating field of exploration.[12]

In sitting down and rising one is confronted with the problem of supporting the body while the center of gravity moves backward and downward or forward and upward, as the case may be. In sitting down on a chair the individual stands with his back to the chair, places one foot slightly to the rear, inclines the body forward from the hips to keep the center of gravity over the base of support, and lowers the body by relaxing the knee extensors and permitting the joint to bend. In arising from a chair one foot is placed slightly under the chair, the individual bends forward from the hips, and rises by contracting the knee extensors, transferring the center of gravity forward so that it is supported by the forward foot.

In sitting on or arising from a straight-backed chair, the aid of the hands is not normally required. In some deep chairs the center of gravity is thrown so far backward that it is difficult to sit down or rise, and in such cases the arms are often used to assist in the movement. Schools for fashion models and actors usually teach that it is ungraceful to employ the arms in rising.

Older persons may find it difficult to sit in comfort or to arise after being seated for long periods. Poorly designed chairs cause an excessive decrease in the pull of the thigh-trunk muscles. This permits the lumbar curve to flatten and the hydraulic pressure resulting from anterior wedging within the fourth or fifth intervertebral disc may force a degenerated piece to protrude, causing a painful stretching of the sensitive posterior longitudinal ligament of the disc.

When the "vasti" are paralyzed or weakened, the weight of the body may be too great to be withstood by the knee extensors and the individual may be able to stabilize his body in the erect position only by hyperextending the knees so as to throw the center of gravity forward of the normal line of body weight. A person so afflicted may sometimes be seen to place his hands on his knees and assist himself to rise by pushing the knees backwards as he leans forward.

When the seated individual is required to operate foot pedals of some kind, the thrust which can be exerted by the legs may be a matter of some importance. The thrust exerted by the legs is at a maximum when the knees are bent at an angle of approximately 165 degrees. At this point the mean thrust is about 227 kg. If the knees are bent at a smaller angle, there is a tendency for the upper part of the body to be pushed backward; if they are bent at a greater angle, there is a tendency for the body to be tilted forward.[13]

Squatting. Squatting is the normal resting position in large areas of the world. In the Western culture it is considered undignified and its use is largely restricted to athletes, who have traditionally included squats, duck walks, and similar exercises in their training programs. As has been stated previously, it is now generally agreed that this position predisposes the knee to injury from trauma. While this does not normally occur to gardeners and others who may work in this position, they should be careful to avoid twists of the joint when the knee is flexed, as the medial cartilage may be torn or detached.[14]

Kneeling. Certain types of work, such as that of charwomen, require frequent and prolonged kneeling. In the opinion of some surgeons this may result in a wearing thin of the quadriceps fibers, with a resultant tendency to rupture.

Stair Climbing. Stair climbing is a special case of locomotion, and an extremely fatiguing one. It has been estimated that a person expends the same amount of energy in climbing one average flight of stairs that he does in walking on the level fifteen times the distance represented by the vertical height of such a staircase.[15]

Placing the ball of the foot on the tread of the stair and then lifting the body by contraction of the gastrocnemius (plantar flexion) is considerably more fatiguing than is placing the entire sole of the foot on the tread and raising the body by extension of the knee joint. By keeping the center of gravity forward, the effect of the resistance arm of the thigh lever is reduced and energy is conserved. The most efficient rate of stair climbing has been determined to be about 1.3 seconds per step.[16] Elderly people may be observed to grasp the hand rail for support and to lean well forward. The increased flexion of the hip thus obtained enables them to employ the gluteus maximus to better advantage in extending the hip joint.

When descending stairs, the body is kept more erect in order to prevent the center of gravity from getting too far forward. The hip of the swinging leg is slightly flexed, the amount depending upon the width of the tread, and the knee and ankle are extended. The ex-

Fig. 23–3. "Nude Descending a Staircase," by Duchamp. This is the most famous attempt in modern art to depict kinesiological action in an essentially static medium. By the repetition of form Duchamp endeavored to indicate time and thus add a fourth dimension to art. Compare with Figure 22–20, page 530. (Philadelphia Museum of Art, Louise and Walter Arensberg Collection.)

tensors of the hip, knee, and ankle of the supporting leg gradually reduce the force which they are exerting and permit a slow flexion. This is a typical "lengthening contraction," or "negative work" where gravity does work and the extensors resist it. The body is lowered until the ball of the foot of the swinging leg makes contact with the step. The weight is then transferred to this leg, the knee of the other leg is flexed, the foot lifted and swung forward, and when the knee is extended, the cycle is repeated. The ratio of oxygen costs for ascending and descending stairs at 160 steps per minute is about 4.7:1 for males and 5.7:1 for females.[17] Even descending stairs requires a greater energy expenditure than does horizontal walking. Much of this appears to be expended in maintaining the body posture while moving from one step to another.

In walking down-hill the quadriceps femoris must contract to keep the knee joint extended against the gravitational forces working on the body. This continued stress is one of the reasons for the ache often experienced in that muscle after hiking. Rather interestingly, one of the most original and controversial works of art in our time arose from an attempt to depict this form of movement (Fig. 23–3).

Sex Factors. Where possible, duties involving heavy lifting should be done by male workers, since the strength of women as measured by dynamometer tests is about half of that of men. The fact that women's thighs incline in toward the knees makes it more difficult for them to maintain their balance; hence work which requires standing on a stool or at the top of a ladder is more safely assigned to men. The inward inclination of the female arm accounts for women's difficulty in handling screwdrivers and other equipment requiring a rotary motion.[18] In work requiring dexterity rather than strength, however, women are equal or superior to men.

The female also suffers certain mechanical disadvantages in running. Due to the relatively greater average width of her pelvis, her acetabula are further apart. Consequently a greater lateral shift of the center of gravity is necessary to bring the body weight over the hip joint at each stride and she is likely to show a marked lateral sway of the pelvis during running. Her legs are relatively short, reducing the distance she can cover at a stride, and her speed of muscle contraction is somewhat slower than in the male. This does not mean that a girl has to be masculine to be a good athlete; she can be a champion and still be as beautiful and graceful as any dancer (Fig. 23–4).

Working Space Arrangements. Regardless of sex, no worker can hope to function efficiently unless the arrangement of the equipment which he is required to use has been designed with a full considera-

Fig. 23–4. Wilma Rudolph, winner of three gold medals in the 1960 Olympics, illustrates that beauty and grace in a feminine athlete are compatible with championship performance. Miss Rudolph is 5′ 11″ tall, weighs about 120 pounds in hard training, has a starting stride of 1′ 9″, and a mid-race stride of 7′ 4″. What kinesiological factors may contribute to her success? (Photo courtesy John A. Harvey-Tennessee Agricultural and Industrial State University.)

tion of anatomical and kinesiological principles. Each job has its own peculiarities and may involve such details as determining the optimal load for a miner's shovel or the optimal length of a tuna fisherman's pole. The goals of human factors engineering are (1) to make it possible for any man to operate any machine, and (2) to avoid limiting the performance of the machine by human failure. Here only the barest and most general outline can be given.

1. Work benches and tables should be at the elbow height of the user whether he is sitting or standing.

2. The height of work chairs should be adjustable. They are in proper position when the operator's feet rest on the floor or on a support. For the average male American the distance from the floor to the top of the chair seat should be about 18 inches.

3. Levers to which maximum force must be applied should be at shoulder level for standing operators; at elbow level for seated operators.

4. Controls which must be used often should be between elbow and shoulder height.

5. Convenient arm reach is about 28 inches; controls more distant will probably require the average operator to bend his body.

6. For a side to side movement, the strength of pushing is greater than that of pulling; in forward and back movements, pulling strength is greater than pushing strength.

7. Horizontal movements of the hand are faster than are vertical movements.

8. Flexion movements of the arm are faster than extension movements.[19,20]

Rest Pauses. When Taylor made his classical study of the application of kinesiological principles to the carrying of billets of pig iron, he nearly quadrupled work output by the utilization of three basic techniques: (1) motivation (promising the worker an increased wage), (2) selection of the physical type best suited to the work, and (3) the introduction of rest pauses. The question of rest-pauses has received insufficient attention from the kinesiologists. Unlike its mechanical counterparts, the human machine cannot work continuously without a decided loss in efficiency. During World War I the British found that the weekly output for a $55\frac{1}{2}$ hour week was 13 per cent greater than that for a $74\frac{1}{2}$ hour week. During World War II American students determined that hours beyond 48 to 50 a week resulted in higher absenteeism, high injury rates, and lower output per man-hour.[21]

Numerous studies of the energy costs of various industrial, sports and domestic activities have been made. The energy output required is generally expressed in terms of calories used per minute. The British Ministry of Labour[22] has developed the so-called "Slough Scales" to classify different occupations in terms of energy expenditure required (Table 23–2).

TABLE 23–2. Classification of Occupational Levels by Energy Expenditure

Work Level	Gross kcal/m²/hr.	Gross kcal/min.	Pulmonary Ventilation l/kg/min.
Sedentary	40–70	1.1–2.0	<0.12
Light	70–110	2.0–3.0	0.12–0.20
Moderate	110–180	3.0–5.0	0.20–0.30
Heavy	180–300	5.0–8.0	0.30–0.50
Very heavy	300+	8.0+	0.50+

Apparently easy work may be strenuous if it is done by relatively weak muscles, is of a predominantly static character, is performed in an awkward position, or is carried out under extreme environmental conditions. For jobs requiring a large amount of fairly continuous effort, the maximal daily energy expenditure on the job should not exceed 2000 kilocalories for men and 1500 kilocalories for women.[23]

If left to himself, the worker will take voluntary rest pauses, perhaps as an unconscious means of self-protection. The frequency and duration of these will vary with the severity of the work being done, but for manual labor appears to approximate ten minutes out of every hour. It is not clear whether the figures optimal for men are necessarily so for women. Mead[24] has pointed out that women seem to possess a capacity for continuous monotonous work, whereas men are characterized by sudden spurts of energy, followed by a period of recuperation. These differences appear related to the endocrine systems of the two sexes; whether they have significance for kinesiology is yet to be determined.

Rhythm. Rhythm may be an important factor affecting the efficiency with which movements are made. Each individual has his own preferred speed of movement. The ease and efficiency of movement may be increased if it is done to a distinct rhythm. Perhaps one of the factors making for success in a famous backfield, such as the Four Horsemen of Notre Dame, or a dancing group, is the combination of individuals whose preferred movement speed is identical. On the other hand, an assembly line worker whose preferred speed of movement clashes with that imposed upon him by his work may find that he is subjected to stresses which render him both inefficient and unhappy.

Avoidance of Industrial Fatigue. Perrott[25] has suggested five practical ways in which a worker may avoid unnecessary fatigue and trauma:

1. Eliminate unnecessary movements. Repetition of even minute movements can be damaging.

2. Use gravity to accomplish work, as by leaning on a handle to depress it rather than by moving it by arm strength.

3. Position the body so that the prime movers, synergists, fixators, and antagonists may each play their proper roles. In general work at or above the facial level, below the knees, or within an inadequate space is to be avoided.

4. Properly balance the body, as in employing it as a counter weight in lifting a heavy object; in flexing the knees and lifting with the legs rather than with the back (Figs. 23–1 and 23–2), and in employing the strength of the legs rather than of the arms in pushing.

5. Minimize shearing stresses. In pronation of the forearm, for example, the radius rotates across the ulna, whereas in supination they lie side by side. By making a given movement in supination rather than in pronation, much torsion of the soft tissue around the joint may be avoided.

The industrial physician must give careful consideration to the possibility of improper body mechanics as an etiological factor if he hopes to be successful in the diagnosis and treatment of such trauma, but careful attention to the kinesiological aspects of work can do much to prevent the development of such conditions in the first place. In this and similar ways the student will find that the study of kinesiology will enrich his life by giving fresh insights into his daily experiences, and may lead him to make new discoveries in a field in which scientific investigation has only begun.

References

1. Davis, Peter R.: Posture of the Trunk During the Lifting of Weights. Brit. Med. J., *5114*, 87–89, 1959.

2. Rasch, Philip J.: Practical Body Mechanics for Hospital Workers. J. Ass. Phys. Men. Rehabil., *5*, 8–13, 1952.

3. Chisholm, Joe: *Brewery Gulch*. San Antonio: Naylor Company, 1949, pp. 113–114.

4. Fash, Bernice: *Body Mechanics in the Nursing Arts*. New York: McGraw-Hill Book Company, Inc., 1946, p. 29.

5. Thomas, D. P.: The Effect of Load Carriage on Normal Standing in Man. J. Anat., *93*, 75–86, 1959.

6. Basmajian, J. V.: *Muscles Alive. Their Function Revealed by Electromyography*, 2nd Ed. Baltimore: The Williams & Wilkins Co., 1967, pp. 131–139.

7. Switzer, S. A.: *Weight-Lifting Capabilities of a Selected Sample of Human Males*. Aerospace Medical Laboratories Report, MRL-TDR-62-67, June, 1962.

8. Teeple, John B.: Work of Carrying Loads. Percept. Mot. Skills., *7*, 60, 1957.

9. Glasow, W. and Miller, E. A.: Carrying Heavy Sacks on the Level and on Stairs. Arbeits., *14*, 322–327, 1951. Abstracted in *Index & Abstracts of Foreign Physical Education Literature*. Indianapolis: Phi Epsilon Kappa Fraternity, 1955, *1*, 56–57.

10. United States Army Combat Developments Command: *A Study to Conserve the Energy of the Combat Infantryman*. Alexandria: Defense Documentation Center, 5 February, 1964.

11. Medical Research Council, Sixth Annual Report of the *Industrial Fatigue Research Board*. London: His Majesty's Stationery Office, 1926, p. 19.

12. Hewes, Gordon W.: The Anthropology of Posture. Scient. Amer., *196*, 122–123, 1957.

13. Clark, W. E. LeGros: The Contribution of Anatomy to War. Brit. Med. J., *4436*, 39–43, 1946.

14. Helfet, Arthur J.: Mechanism of Derangements of the Medial Semilunar Cartilage and Their Management. J. Bone Joint Surg., *41-B*, 319–336, 1959.

15. Benedict, Francis G. and Parmenter, Hazeltine Sedman: The Energy Metabolism of Women While Ascending or Descending Stairs. Amer. J. Physiol., *84*, 675–698, 1928.

16. Lupton, Hartley: An Analysis of the Effects of Speed on the Mechanical Efficiency of Human Muscular Movement. J. Physiol., *LVII*, 337–353, 1923.

17. Hesser, C. M.: Energy Cost of Alternating Positive and Negative Work. Acta Physiol. Scand., *63*, 84–93, 1965.

18. Tuttle, W. Gerard: Women Who Work for Victory. Mechanical Engineering, *65*, 657–660, 1943.

19. Woodson, Wesley E. and Conover, Donald W.: *Human Engineering Guide, for Equipment Designers*, 2nd Ed., (Revised.) Berkeley: University of California, 1964.

20. *Handbook of Human Engineering Data*, 2nd Ed. (Revised.) Medford: Tufts College Institute of Applied Experimental Psychology, 1951. Part VI, Chapter IV, Section II.

21. Kossoris, Max D.: The Facts About Hours of Work vs. Output. Reprinted from Fac. Manag., 1951.

22. Brown, J. R. and Crowden, G. P.: Energy Expenditure Ranges and Muscular Work Grades. Brit. J. Industr. Med., *23*, 277–283, 1963.

23. Floyd, W. F. and Slade, I. M.: Fitting the Job to the Worker. Ergonomics, *2*, 305–309, 1959.

24. Mead, Margaret: *Male and Female*. New York: William Morrow & Co., 1949, pp. 163–182.

25. Perrott, J. W.: Anatomical Factors in Occupational Trauma. Med. J. Aust., *1*, 73–82, 1961.

Appendix A

AREAS OF MUSCULAR ATTACHMENT

In Figures A–1 to A–18, all of which are taken from *Gray's Anatomy*, the bony origins of the muscles are shown in red and the insertions in blue. The lines of attachment of articular capsules are indicated by a heavy blue line.

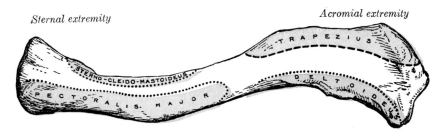

Fig. A–1. Left clavicle. Superior surface.

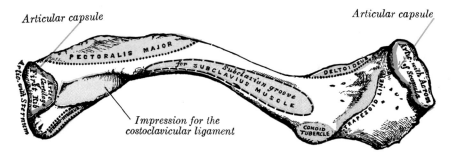

Fig. A–2. Left clavicle. Inferior surface.

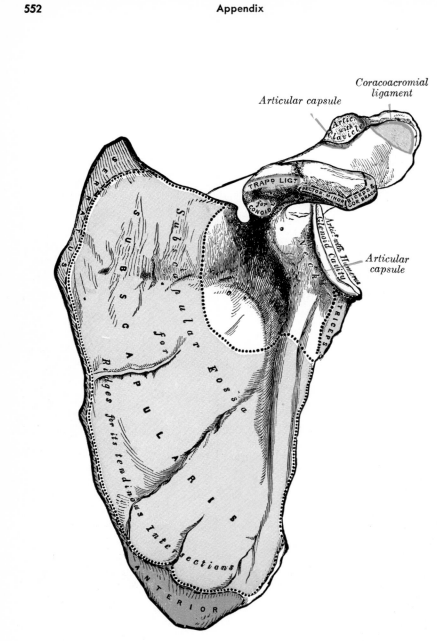

Fig. A–3.   Left scapula.   Costal surface.

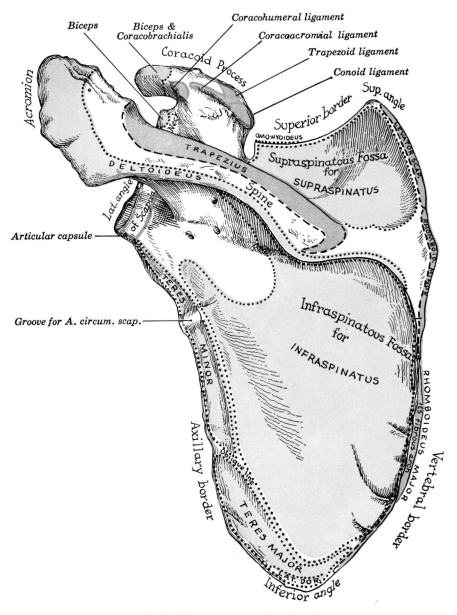

Fig. A–4. Left scapula. Dorsal surface.

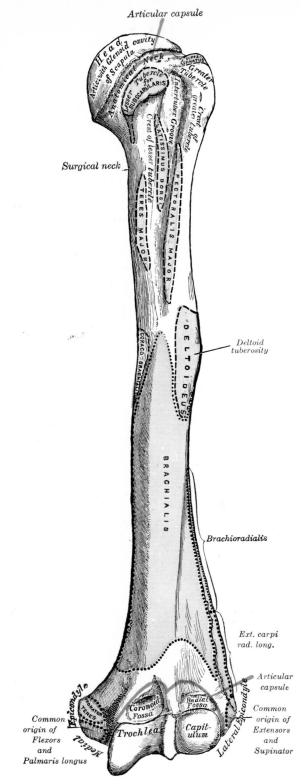

FIG. A-5.   Left humerus.   Anterior view.

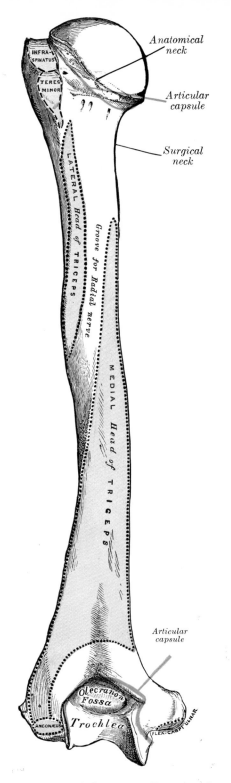

FIG. A-6. Left humerus. Posterior view.

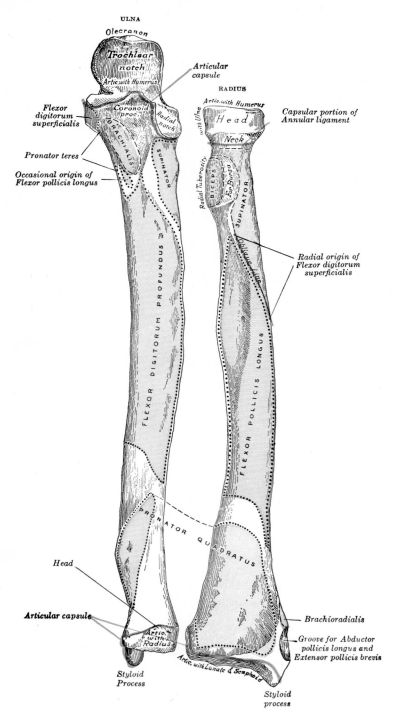

FIG. A-7. Left ulna and radius. Anterior aspect.

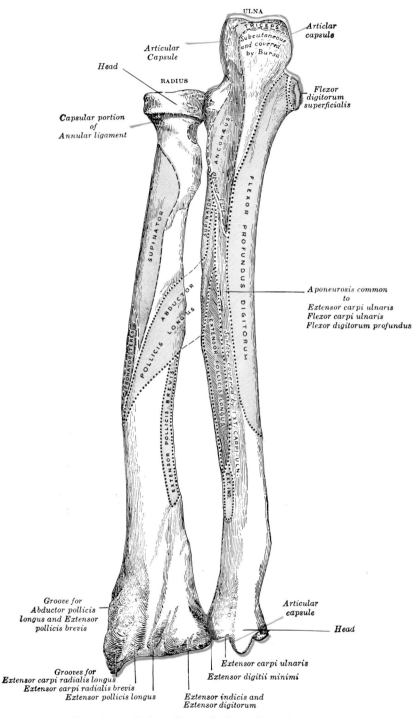

ULNA

TRICEPS

Subcutaneous and covered by Bursa

Articlar capsule

Articular Capsule

Head

RADIUS

Flexor digitorum superficialis

Capsular portion of Annular ligament

SUPINATOR

SUPINATOR

ANCONEUS

FLEXOR PROFUNDUS DIGITORUM

PRONATOR TERES

ABDUCTOR POLLICIS LONGUS

EXTENSOR POLLICIS BREVIS

EXTENSOR POLLICIS LONGUS

Surface covered by EXT. CARPI ULN.

EXT. IND.

Aponeurosis common to Extensor carpi ulnaris Flexor carpi ulnaris Flexor digitorum profundus

Groove for Abductor pollicis longus and Extensor pollicis brevis

Articular capsule

Head

Grooves for Extensor carpi radialis longus Extensor carpi radialis brevis Extensor pollicis longus

Extensor indicis and Extensor digitorum

Extensor carpi ulnaris Extensor digitii minimi

FIG. A–8. Left radius and ulna. Posterior aspect.

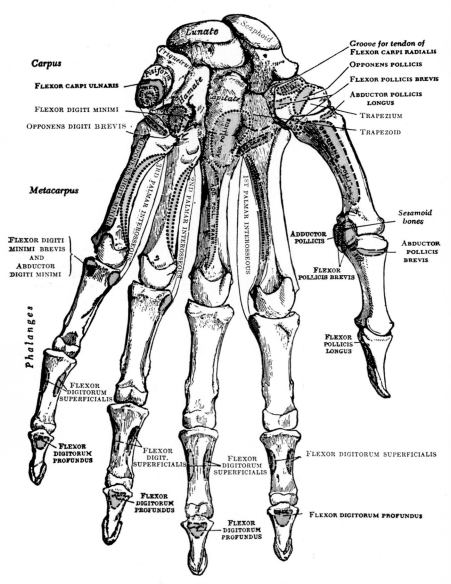

Fig. A–9.   Bones of left hand.   Palmar surface.

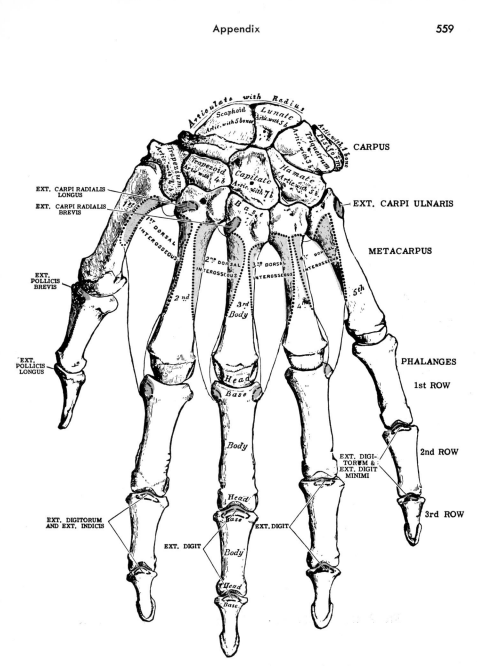

FIG. A–10. Bones of left hand. Dorsal surface.

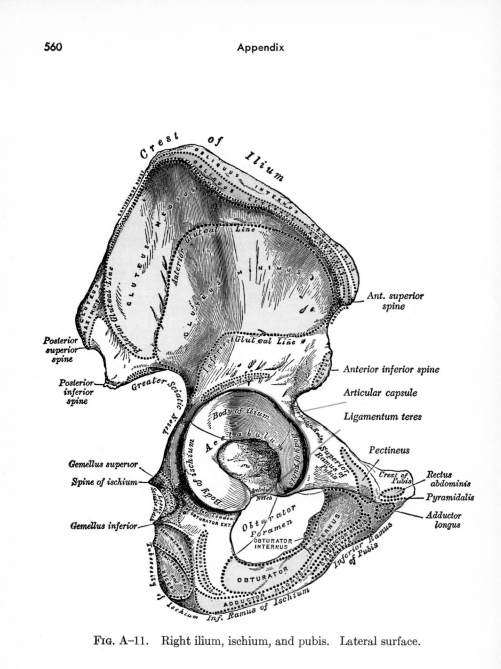

Fig. A–11. Right ilium, ischium, and pubis. Lateral surface.

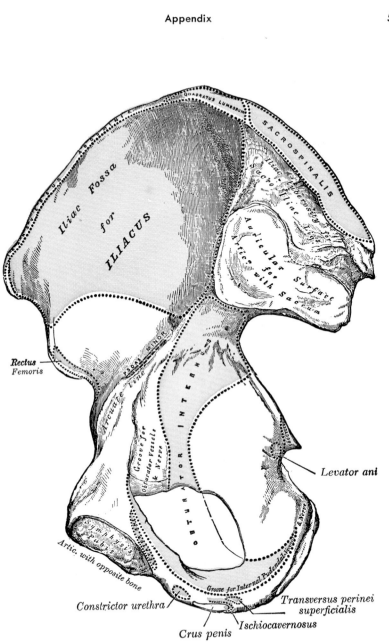

Fig. A–12.   Right ilium, ischium, and pubis.   Medial surface.

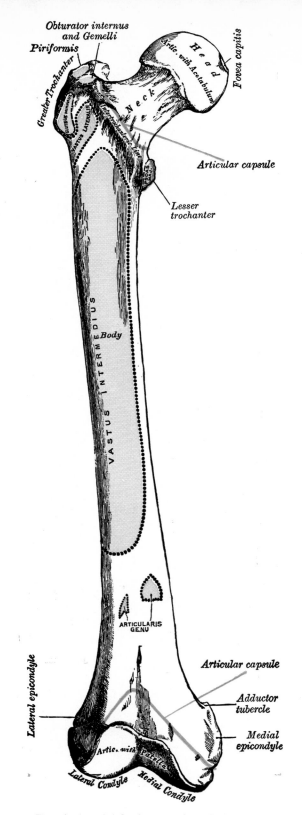

FIG. A–13.   Right femur.   Anterior surface.

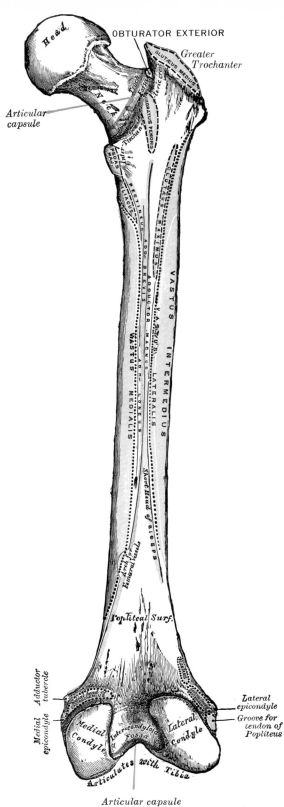

FIG. A–14.   Right femur.   Posterior surface.

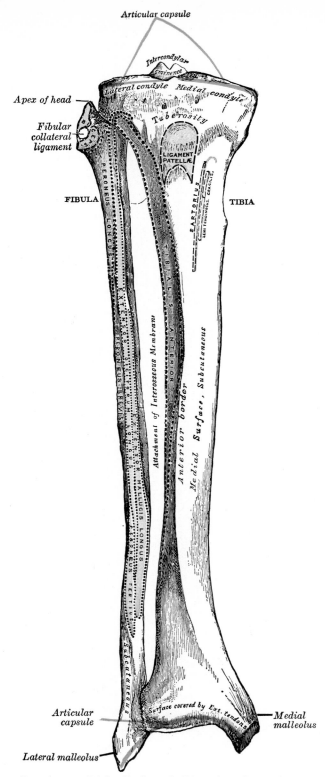

FIG. A–15.   Right fibula and tibia.   Anterior surface.

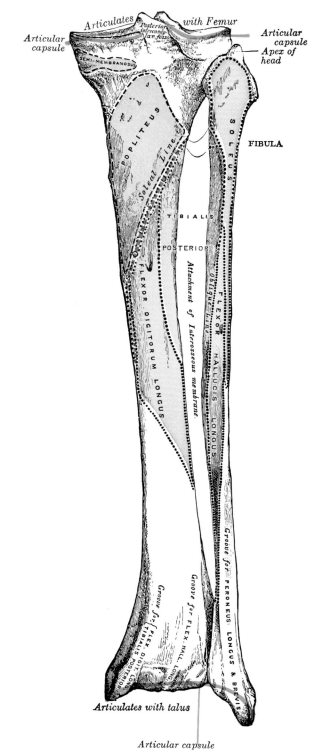

FIG. A–16.   Right tibia and fibula.   Posterior surface.

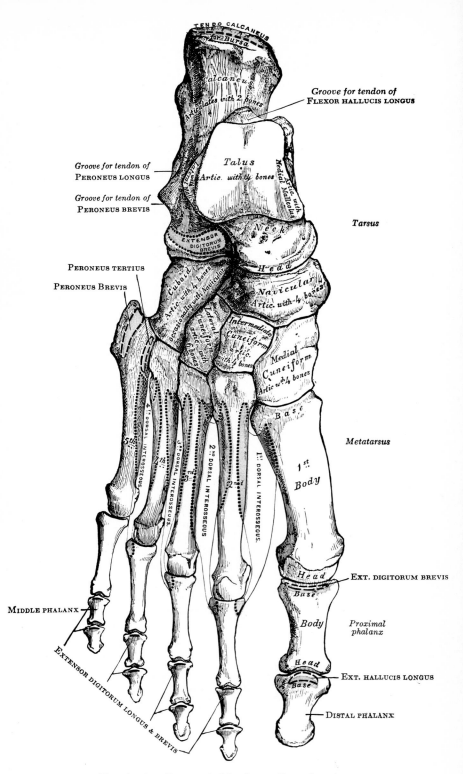

FIG. A–17. Bones of right foot. Dorsal surface.

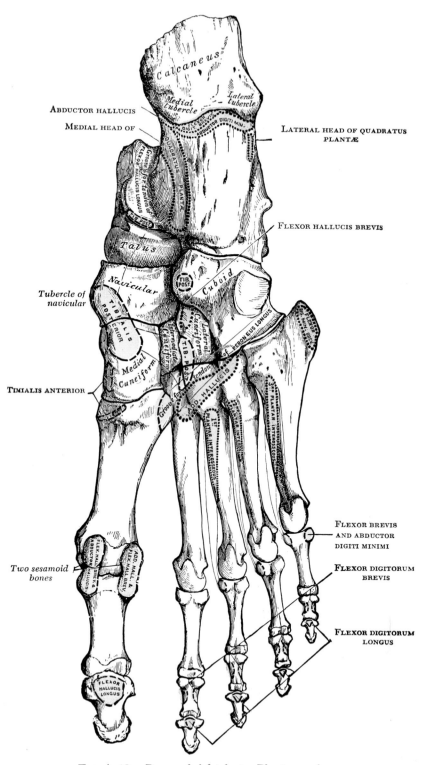

FIG. A–18.   Bones of right foot.   Plantar surface.

Appendix B

THE PLEXUSES

The following diagrams of the major plexuses are included for the convenience of those engaged in medical and therapeutic work.

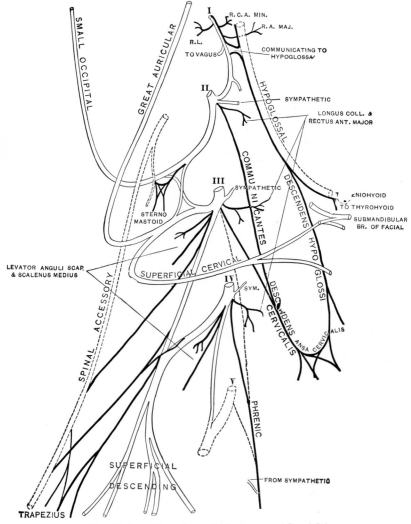

FIG. B-1.   Plan of cervical plexus.   (*Gerrish.*)

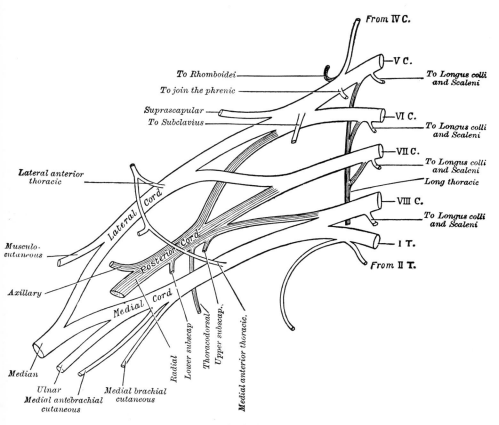

FIG. B–2. Plan of brachial plexus. (*Gray's Anatomy*.)

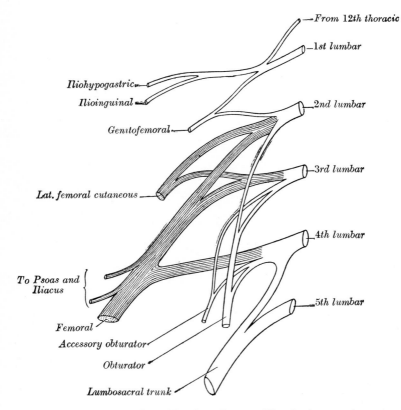

From 12th thoracic

1st lumbar

Iliohypogastric

Ilioinguinal

2nd lumbar

Genitofemoral

3rd lumbar

Lat. femoral cutaneous

4th lumbar

To Psoas and
Iliacus

5th lumbar

Femoral

Accessory obturator

Obturator

Lumbosacral trunk

Fig. B–3.   Plan of lumbar plexus.   (*Gray's Anatomy.*)

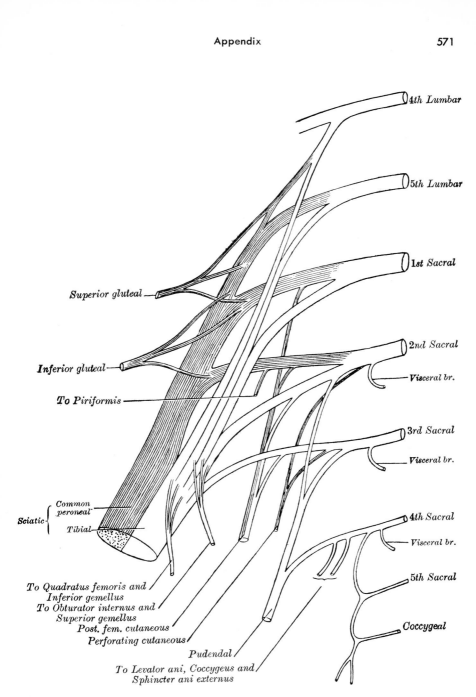

FIG. B–4.   Plan of sacral and coccygeal plexuses.   (*Gray's Anatomy.*)

Appendix C

TRIGONOMETRIC RELATIONSHIPS FOR RIGHT ANGLES

For the convenience of students in dealing with problems of bone-muscle leverage, some of the elementary trigonometric relationships for right triangles are summarized below.

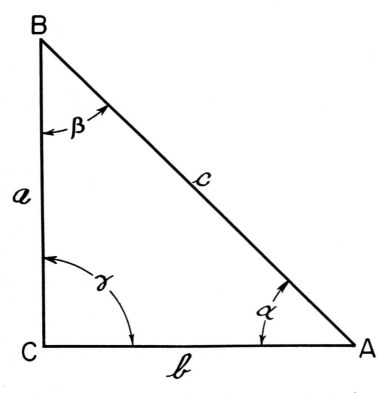

FIG. C-1. Relationships of sides and angles in a right triangle.

A, B, and C are the points of a triangle; a and b are the sides oppo-site angles α and β, respectively; c is the hypotenuse, opposite angle γ, the right angle (Fig. C–1).

1. The sum of the angles of any triangle is equal to 180°.

$$\alpha + \beta + \gamma = 180°$$

2. Two angles are called complementary when their sum is equal to 90°. In a right triangle the two angles between the hypotenuse and the adjacent sides are complementary.

$$\alpha + \beta = 90°$$

3. The sum of the squares of the sides of a right triangle is equal to the square of the hypotenuse (Pythagorean Theorem).

$$a^2 + b^2 = c^2 \qquad\qquad a^2 = c^2 - b^2$$

$$\sqrt{a^2 + b^2} = c \qquad\qquad a = \sqrt{c^2 - b^2}$$

4. The sine of an angle of a right triangle is equal to the side opposite divided by the hypotenuse, and is equal to the cosine of the complementary angle.

$$\sin \alpha = \frac{a}{c} = \cos\beta = \cos (90° - \alpha)$$

5. The cosine of an angle of a right triangle is equal to the side adjacent divided by the hypotenuse, and is equal to the sine of the complementary angle.

$$\cos \alpha = \frac{b}{c} = \sin\beta = \sin (90° - \alpha)$$

Following is a table of sines of the whole angles from 0° to 180°. The cosines of the angles may be found by taking the sine of the complementary angle, according to 5, above.

Degrees	Sines	Degrees	Sines	Degrees	Sines	Degrees	Sines
0 or 180	.00000	23 or 157	.39073	46 or 134	.71934	69 or 111	.93358
1 or 179	.01745	24 or 156	.40674	47 or 133	.73135	70 or 110	.93969
2 or 178	.03490	25 or 155	.42262	48 or 132	.74314	71 or 109	.94552
3 or 177	.05234	26 or 154	.43837	49 or 131	.75471	72 or 108	.95106
4 or 176	.06976	27 or 153	.45399	50 or 130	.76604	73 or 107	.95630
5 or 175	.08716	28 or 152	.46947	51 or 129	.77715	74 or 106	.96126
6 or 174	.10453	29 or 151	.48481	52 or 128	.78801	75 or 105	.96593
7 or 173	.12187	30 or 150	.50000	53 or 127	.79864	76 or 104	.97030
8 or 172	.13917	31 or 149	.51504	54 or 126	.80902	77 or 103	.97437
9 or 171	.15643	32 or 148	.52992	55 or 125	.81915	78 or 102	.97815
10 or 170	.17365	33 or 147	.54464	56 or 124	.82904	79 or 101	.98163
11 or 169	.19081	34 or 146	.55919	57 or 123	.83867	80 or 100	.98481
12 or 168	.20791	35 or 145	.57358	58 or 122	.84805	81 or 99	.98769
13 or 167	.22495	36 or 144	.58779	59 or 121	.85817	82 or 98	.99027
14 or 166	.24192	37 or 143	.60182	60 or 120	.86603	83 or 97	.99255
15 or 165	.25882	38 or 142	.61566	61 or 119	.87462	84 or 96	.99452
16 or 164	.27564	39 or 141	.62932	62 or 118	.88295	85 or 95	.99619
17 or 163	.29237	40 or 140	.64279	63 or 117	.89101	86 or 94	.99756
18 or 162	.30902	41 or 139	.65606	64 or 116	.89879	87 or 93	.99863
19 or 161	.32557	42 or 138	.66913	65 or 115	.90631	88 or 92	.99939
20 or 160	.34202	43 or 137	.68200	66 or 114	.91355	89 or 91	.99985
21 or 159	.35837	44 or 136	.69466	67 or 113	.92050	90	1.00000
22 or 158	.37461	45 or 135	.70711	68 or 112	.92718		

Index